WORD

BIBLICAL

COMMENTARY

VOLUME 38ᴮ

Romans 9-16

JAMES D. G. DUNN

WORD BOOKS, PUBLISHER • DALLAS, TEXAS

Word Biblical Commentary
ROMANS 9–16
Copyright © 1988 by Word, Incorporated

Library of Congress Cataloging-in-Publication Data
Main entry under title:

Word biblical commentary.

   Includes bibliographies.
   1. Bible—Commentaries—Collected Works.
BS491.2.W67   220.7′7   81–71768
ISBN 0–8499–0252–5 (vol. 38B)   AACR2

Printed in the United States of America

The author's own translation of the Scripture text appears in italic type under the heading *Translation*.

89801239 AGF 987654321

EDITOR'S NOTE

For the convenience of the reader, page numbers are included for both volumes of this commentary on Romans (38A and 38B) in the Contents. Page numbers for the volume in hand are printed in boldface type, while those for the other volume are in lightface.

In addition, all of the front matter from vol. 38A but the *Introduction* has been repeated in vol. 38B so that the reader may have abbreviations, bibliography, and other pertinent information readily at hand.

Contents

Editorial Preface

The launching of the *Word Biblical Commentary* brings to fulfillment an enterprise of several years' planning. The publishers and the members of the editorial board met in 1977 to explore the possibility of a new commentary on the books of the Bible that would incorporate several distinctive features. Prospective readers of these volumes are entitled to know what such features were intended to be; whether the aims of the commentary have been fully achieved time alone will tell.

First, we have tried to cast a wide net to include as contributors a number of scholars from around the world who not only share our aims, but are in the main engaged in the ministry of teaching in university, college, and seminary. They represent a rich diversity of denominational allegiance. The broad stance of our contributors can rightly be called evangelical, and this term is to be understood in its positive, historic sense of a commitment to Scripture as divine revelation, and to the truth and power of the Christian gospel.

Then, the commentaries in our series are all commissioned and written for the purpose of inclusion in the *Word Biblical Commentary*. Unlike several of our distinguished counterparts in the field of commentary writing, there are no translated works, originally written in a non-English language. Also, our commentators were asked to prepare their own rendering of the original biblical text and to use those languages as the basis of their own comments and exegesis. What may be claimed as distinctive with this series is that it is based on the biblical languages, yet it seeks to make the technical and scholarly approach to a theological understanding of Scripture understandable by— and useful to—the fledgling student, the working minister, and colleagues in the guild of professional scholars and teachers as well.

Finally, a word must be said about the format of the series. The layout, in clearly defined sections, has been consciously devised to assist readers at different levels. Those wishing to learn about the textual witnesses on which the translation is offered are invited to consult the section headed *Notes*. If the readers' concern is with the state of modern scholarship on any given portion of Scripture, they should turn to the sections on *Bibliography* and *Form and Structure*. For a clear exposition of the passage's meaning and its relevance to the ongoing biblical revelation, the *Comment* and concluding *Explanation* are designed expressly to meet that need. There is therefore something for everyone who may pick up and use these volumes.

If these aims come anywhere near realization, the intention of the editors will have been met, and the labor of our team of contributors rewarded.

General Editors: *David A. Hubbard*
Glenn Barker †
Old Testament: *John D. W. Watts*
New Testament: *Ralph P. Martin*

Author's Preface

To write a commentary on the apostle Paul's letter to the Christians in Rome is a daunting undertaking. Paul's letters are such a dominant element in the New Testament, and so form a central part of the Christian scriptures, the constitutional documents of the Christian faith, which have exercised an influence quite literally beyond measure on Christian faith and life and on Western culture for more than nineteen centuries. And of all Paul's letters the one to Rome is the fullest and most carefully constructed statement of the Christian gospel and of the faith it called for during the foundation period of Christianity. To grapple with Romans is to engage in dialogue with one of the most creative theological minds of all time from the most creative period of Christian thought. Its influence on seminal theologians like Augustine, Luther and Barth has often been noted. And certainly it seems to have attracted more commentaries of note than any other NT or biblical writing. On not a few occasions during the writing of this commentary I have felt that even to attempt to follow in the train of commentators of the stature of Calvin, Godet, Sanday & Headlam, Lagrange, Michel, Kuss, Käsemann, Cranfield, Schlier and Wilckens is an act of foolhardiness at times bordering on impiety.

When the possibility of contributing Romans to the Word Biblical Commentary was put to me ten years ago I almost declined the invitation. I had of course worked with Romans frequently in the past, had indeed learnt the AV/KJV translation by heart as a young Christian, and relished the possibility of a sustained inquiry into this most systematic contribution of one whom I personally regard as the greatest theologian of all time. But with so many commentaries of high merit already on the shelves, why inflict another on fellow students of the NT? "Not another commentary on Romans!" was a frequent response when I described my research project in the early '80s. A sentiment that echoed my own first reaction. After such a wealth of scholarship has been expended on Romans over the years, is there anything fresh or original to be said? Would I not simply fall into one of the worst errors of the commentary genre—that of simply repeating the thoughts (in a different "mix") of those who had gone before?

On further reflection, however, I came to the conclusion that there were probably two areas where a further contribution would be possible and indeed desirable, two deficiencies which affected most previous work on Romans in greater or less degree. One was that in many large commentaries readers were frequently prevented from seeing the wood for the trees. With the commentator immersed in meticulously detailed word study, or complex debate regarding alternative renderings, or lengthy analyses of previous interpretations, the movement of Paul's thought was often lost sight of, and readers could find themselves very easily lost in a maze of detail. A letter written to be read out as a live exposition, and to be heard (and understood) at one or two sittings, had too often become as it were an antique corpse to be dissected over and over again in the mortuary of Christian curiosities so that its individual parts and limbs could be held up to mawkish display. Of course there had been several attempts to provide brief overview commentaries, some of them singularly successful on the whole, but mostly they had either skimmed the surface without penetrating into the depth of the argument, or they had succumbed to the second deficiency. This second weakness was the failure of most commentators to penetrate more fully into the historical context within which the letter was written and to which the letter was addressed, the life-setting in which it was first heard to speak as the word of God. The blinkers which for centuries have narrowed and distorted Christian appreciation of first-century Judaism also affected the view of Paul in relation to his ancestral faith, a relationship so very much at the heart of this letter in particular. But with the perspective-shifting work of E. P. Sanders fresh in mind it quickly became clear to me that a major attempt to set Paul's letter to Rome within "the new perspective on Paul" could and should be undertaken.

My first objective therefore was to grasp the movement of Paul's thought, the logic which led him from verse to verse and chapter to chapter. The format of the Word Commentary series lent itself to the endeavor in that I decided to use the final part of each section (*Explanation*) to write a running commentary on the letter as a whole. The first part of the commentary to be written therefore was the *Explanation* of chaps. 1–11, written over a period of two years with the aim of grasping the inner coherence of the text, the flow of Paul's argument and its theological logic within its historical context. I deliberately restricted my use of technical aids to concordances, lexica and the Kittel-Friedrich *Wörterbuch* (ET: *TDNT*), following up all cross-references and possible parallels of language and thought in other sources of the period, but allowing only a minimal reference to one or two recent commentaries, in the hope that the resultant exposition would be determined more by the questions arising from the text itself than by the history of its interpretation and the debates which have marked that history. All the while I tried to remember that the letter was written to be heard as it was read out in a congregation in Rome in the mid-first century A.D. All the while I was asking, What would this have meant to them? What understanding could Paul expect his readers to have of what he wrote? One of the immediate corollaries was an increased readiness to let ambiguities in the language stand as ambiguities, recognizing that Paul may have intended to be deliberately ambiguous, or at least that occasionally he so formulated his thought as to allow his readers/ hearers some freedom to hear it with different nuances. I hope that by such frequent reminders of original context I may enable the modern reader to experience again something of what the first readers experienced and to recover something at least of the freshness of the original text, or at least to share something of the excitement I experienced as the text became alive for me and I became aware of hidden currents and interconnections in arguments which had previously seemed obscure or confused.

A further corollary is that the *Explanation* section can be read through as a continuous, nontechnical, indeed almost independent commentary. The nearest parallels would be the excellent commentaries of Schlatter and Barrett; and if I have achieved only part of the insight they have derived from the

text I will be well pleased. It also means that the more extensive, detailed
and technical treatments in the *Comment* sections may be regarded as equivalent to footnotes to the *Explanation*. It was a matter of some encouragement
(and relief) to find that when I came to engage in the detailed interaction
with other commentaries for the *Comment* sections it was only occasionally
necessary to make a major revision of the *Explanation* section (3:9 in particular). For the most part the "feel" I had gained for the argument in that
initial "running commentary" exercise I found to be sustained or sustainable
in the face of other interpretations.

In consequence readers of this commentary who want to do more than
consult specific verses or issues are advised to read first the *Explanation,* and
only then to consult the *Comment.* The *Explanation* is not a mere summary
of the main line of exposition, or of the findings of the *Comment* section. It
is a full exposition of the argument in which I have attempted so far as
possible to get inside the thought, to fill out the allusions and sentiments
which Paul's words would have prompted in the minds of those who heard
the letter first being read to them in Rome. Where the argument is tightly
packed or the logic less clear to modern ears I have not hesitated to develop
and explain it. Anyone reading lengthy sections of the commentary at a
single sitting will inevitably find a degree of repetition—something which
cannot be avoided since the more normal episodic use of a commentary
requires that each section be sufficiently self-contained to be meaningful for
such usage. Repetition of key points of Paul's argument, not always appreciated in their historical context and force, may be no bad thing anyway. But
I am not sure that the balance between exposition in the *Explanation* and
detailed analyses in the *Comment* has always been successful, though I have
at least attempted to maintain a full cross-referencing in the *Comment* section,
so that consultation of any verse in which a word or theme occurs should
find a clear reference to where that word or theme is more fully treated.
For briefer treatments and overviews the *Introductions* to lengthier passages
and *Form and Structure* sections will usually be sufficient. I hope readers will
find the format valuable and will welcome comments on the success or otherwise of my endeavors at this point.

With regard to my second objective, it should already be clear that for
me the first task of exegesis is to penetrate as far as possible inside the historical
context(s) of the author and of those for whom he wrote. So much of this
involves the taken-for-granteds of both author and addressees. Where a modern reader is unaware of (or unsympathetic to) these shared assumptions
and concerns it will be impossible to hear the text as the author intended it
to be heard (and assumed it would be heard). In this case, a major part of
that context is the self-understanding of Jews and Judaism in the first century
and of Gentiles sympathetic to Judaism. Since most of Christian history and
scholarship, regrettably, has been unsympathetic to that self-understanding,
if not often downright hostile to it, a proper appreciation of Paul in his
interaction with that self-understanding has been virtually impossible. But
with the new perspective on Paul it has become possible to gain a more
sensitively historical and theological appreciation of Paul's interaction with
his own past, with his ancestral faith and with his fellow Jewish believers in

Messiah Jesus. It has been my second major objective to understand Romans within this new perspective. What this means in terms of the principal themes of Romans I begin to spell out in more detail in §5 of the *Introduction*. But perhaps I can convey here something of the excitement that the resulting insight brought to me as I began to work with the text both in its continuity of thought and in its detail, an excitement frequently renewed as fresh overtones and undertones came again and again from long-familiar passages.

The conviction began to grow in me that the reasons why Romans is such a powerful piece of writing, and why it has been so influential in Christian history, are one and the same. Because in it we see the emergence of Christianity from Judaism actually taking place; we see Paul the Pharisee, Paul the apostle, caught in the tension between his Jewishness and the impact of the risen Christ, between his inability to escape from the Jewish conviction of God's special choice of and revelation to Israel and the impact of a gospel that came to him independently of his Jewishness and despite his Pharisaic zeal for the law. We see Paul the Jew wrestling with the implications of his own and his converts' experience of grace and Paul the Christian wrestling with the implications of his Jewish heritage. We see in Romans Paul operating at the interface between Pharisaic Judaism and Christianity, and the transition from the one to the other in process of being worked out.

That, I would suggest, is why the letter has always struck a chord in those of subsequent generations conscious of a similar tension, caught at a similar point in time when long established traditions came under question from their own insight and experience, when well entrenched institutions and ideologies ceased to provide an answer to the sharpest of the new questions. That is probably why it exerted such a powerful influence on such as Augustine, Luther and Barth. Not for its literary or aesthetic appeal; not because they saw it as some dogmatic treatise; but because they too were at similar transition points in history (the disintegration of the western Roman Empire, the breakdown of medieval Christendom, the profound shock of the 1914–18 war on the old European empires and on the hitherto dominant liberal optimism). And in the Paul of Romans they recognized a kindred spirit whose wrestling with the tensions between his tradition and his experience spoke with word-of-God power to their own situation.

This also points up the importance of maintaining the right hermeneutical balance, why the attempt to get back into the historical context of the letter is so important. Because it is when Paul is most clearly seen within his own times and context, when the function of Romans is most clearly understood as Paul's thinking out the questions which deeply disturbed and profoundly affected him as a Jew who believed in Messiah Jesus as Lord, it is then that we come closest to Paul. And it is as we learn to hear him speaking to the reality of his own situation (not compiling an abstract treatise) that we begin to recognize that such periods of transition and tension are not new within the purposes of God, we begin to hear him speaking to our own situations of transition and of confusion in personal and national identity.

One of the most challenging lessons about Romans then is this: the more we see it as a dogmatic treatise which speaks the same message to every age, the less able are we to hear it in the way it was intended to be heard;

whereas when we hear it in all its historical relativity, then we may begin to appreciate the full power of its message to the great moments of crisis in world and ecclesiastical (as well as personal) history. To rediscover Romans as a statement sketched out on the interface between diverse traditions and visions and cultures is to liberate it to speak with fresh force to those concerned at the interface between Christianity and modern cultures, at the interface not least between Judaism and Christianity. To appreciate something of its power as word of God to the Christians in first-century Rome may be a vital first step to hearing it as God's word to equivalent situations today.

If there is anything in this, another volume would be required to work it out. I had envisaged a brief *Conclusion* at the end of the volume to develop these ideas, but that I fear would be inadequate since the temptation to read it without reference to the commentary itself would be unavoidable; and a lengthier treatment would extend still further an already too long manuscript. On reflection it seemed better to send forth the commentary as it is, as the indispensable exegetical foundation for such a theological endeavor. As part of an ongoing dialogue (I would never presume that anything I wrote was the last word on a subject) it would be better to let the commentary draw out the necessary and desired response of comment and criticism. If the foundation proves solid enough in the light of inspection by others, then would be the time to see what could be built on it; and if not, better to refrain from building on unsure foundations. It would be my hope, then, God willing, to return to the subject in a few years time, to attempt, in the light of any comment and criticism received in the interval, a fuller and integrated description of Paul's theology at the time he wrote Romans, and if possible to reflect on its continuing significance for today.

It should now be clear that, for all its length, the objectives of this commentary are limited. I have not attempted, for example, to provide a full-scale text critical analysis in the *Notes*. That is a task for others more proficient than I in the art, though of course I have not hesitated to make decisions regarding various disputed readings when that was necessary. Nor have I given full lists of witnesses for variants: the textual apparatus of Aland[26] and UBS will provide sufficient detail for almost all readers. In the *Notes* I have been content to provide brief explanations for the choice of readings where it is important, and sometimes to point out the significance of the fact that there are particular variants.

Nor have I attempted to provide a history of interpretation of the letter or of particular passages and themes. Here too I have had to leave that to others more proficient than I in the Fathers or medieval and reformation periods. The resulting deficiencies will be obvious to many, and I cannot but envy the depth of familiarity with the scholarship of previous centuries shown by commentators like Lagrange and Cranfield and acknowledge my indebtedness to the history of interpretation excurses particularly of Kuss and Wilckens. Many of the hermeneutical issues have remained little changed over the centuries, of course, but the issues thrown up by modern scholarship are complex and demanding enough, and to extend the hermeneutical dialogue back to earlier centuries would have lengthened to unmanageable proportions the commentary itself and the time needed to write it.

I cannot even claim to have engaged fully in dialogue with all the more recent scholarship on Romans. In fact my main discussion partners have come from the last hundred years, and I have sought out particularly those who have illuminated the historical context through their familiarity particularly with Jewish and Greco-Roman life and thought. But no doubt I have missed not a few contributions even from this more limited period which would have given me further insight into the text and its thought. And such is the flood of publications now on Romans itself that it has been almost impossible to keep up with everything which has been written. I do not therefore pretend to have scoured all periodicals and symposia, particularly of the more popular type, to ensure that the bibliographies are comprehensive. With the explosion of publishing made possible by modern techniques, scholarship will simply have to become more selective anyway or else drown in a flood of words. So too on disputed issues in the text I have attempted simply to be illustrative in the bibliographical references; anything more would merely have produced wearisome strings of names. No doubt here too there are many individual hypotheses and arguments to which I have done insufficient justice. And for that I can only beg indulgence in view of an already-too-well-packed manuscript.

May an author hope therefore that the value of his commentary will be judged in relation to the objectives he set in writing it, and not in terms of what he refrained from attempting.

Finally it is my pleasure and privilege to say thank you to all who have contributed to these volumes in various ways. First of all, there are those who have responded to lectures and papers which emerged as offshoots or "firstfruits," or who sent me offprints of their own contributions. The sequence of seminars on Paul at the annual meeting of the Society for New Testament Studies was particularly valuable. And my most helpful critics include the members of the postgraduate NT seminar here in Durham. I am particularly grateful to my own postgraduates, many of whose own work has overlapped or interacted with my own most fruitfully. The theses of Don Garlington and Paul Trebilco appear in the *Bibliography*. Others *in via* who have given me valuable help with bibliography (especially in periods when I was under great pressure from other university responsibilities) are David Goh, Dennis Stamps, Lung Kwong Lo, Ellen Christiansen, John Chow and Bruce Longenecker. The Inter-Library Loan service was indispensable and I am grateful to the Libraries of Cambridge and Tübingen, and particularly of Durham, of course, for their ready and efficient help. Above all, my wife Meta has had to bear an increasing burden of backup and support, particularly during the last year when the completion of the commentary seemed to consume more and more of my time. How can I thank her enough?

Two years after starting work on the commentary I had the honor of being appointed to the Chair of Divinity at Durham. The appropriateness of my project quickly became apparent to me. My predecessor, Kingsley Barrett, was appointed to his chair in 1957, the year in which his Black commentary on Romans was published. And his colleague, Charles Cranfield, was awarded his chair in between the publication of the two volumes of his International Critical Commentary on Romans. Clearly then a commentary on Romans is a kind of initiation test for Professors of New Testament at Durham. It is no little relief to have completed the task at last—only five years late! But have I passed?

January, 1988   JAMES D. G. DUNN
University of Durham

Note on bibliographical references and cross-references within the text:

(a) Commentaries as such have usually been cited by name alone and without page reference, the location of the reference being given by the verse commented on. Full details of the commentaries can be found in the *Commentary Bibliography* (p. xxxviii).

(b) In the case of other references, full details will be found either in the *Bibliography* section at the beginning of the passage; in the *General Bibliography*; or, in the case of chaps. 9–11, in the *Bibliography* at the beginning of chaps. 9–11.

(c) Cross-references usually take the form *see on 7:8, see on 14:2,* etc. Unless otherwise stated the reference is to the *Comment* on the passage indicated.

Abbreviations

A. General Abbreviations

Apoc.	Apocrypha	MT	Masoretic text (of the Old Testament)
c.	*circa*, about		
cent.	century	n.d.	no date
cf.	*confer*, compare	N.F.	*Neue Folge,* new series
chap(s).	chapter(s)	NS	New Series
DSS	Dead Sea Scrolls	NT	New Testament
ed.	edited by, editor(s)	OT	Old Testament
e.g	*exempli gratia,* for example	p., pp.	page, pages
et al.	*et alii,* and others	*pace*	with due respect to, but differing from
ET	English translation		
EV	English Versions of the Bible	par(s).	parallel(s)
		passim	elsewhere
f., ff.	following (verse or verses, pages, etc.)	q.v.	*quod vide,* which see
		sic	an unusual form exactly reproduced from the original
frag.	fragments		
FS	Festschrift, volume written in honor of		
		t.t.	technical term
hap. leg.	*hapax legomenon,* sole occurrence	*v.l.*	*varia lectio,* alternative reading
ibid.	*ibidem,* in the same place	viz.	*videlicet,* namely
i.e.	*id est,* that is	vol.	volume
LXX	Septuagint	v, vv	verse, verses
MS(S)	manuscript(s)		

For abbreviations of Greek MSS used in *Notes,* see Aland[26].

B. Abbreviations for Translations and Paraphrases

AV	Authorized Version = KJV	NIV	New International Version (1978)
GNB	Good News Bible = Today's English Version	NJB	New Jerusalem Bible (1985)
KJV	King James Version (1611) = AV	RSV	Revised Standard Version (NT 1946, OT 1952, Apoc. 1957)
Moffatt	*A New Translation of the Bible* (NT 1913)		
		RV	Revised Version (1881)
NEB	New English Bible (NT 1961; OT and Apoc. 1970)		

C. Abbreviations of Commonly Used Periodicals, Reference Works, and Serials

AB	Anchor Bible	AnBib	Analecta Biblica
ABR	*Australian Biblical Review*	Aquila	Aquila's Greek translation of the Old Testament
Aland[26]	Nestle-Aland 26th ed. of NT Greek text (see under C.)		
		ANRW	*Aufstieg und Niedergang des römische Welt*
ALBO	Analecta lovaniensia biblica et orientalia	ATANT	Abhandlungen zur Theologie des Alten und Neuen Testaments
ALW	*Archiv für Liturgiewissenschaft*		

BASOR	*Bulletin of the American Schools of Oriental Research*	ConB	Coniectanea biblica
BDB	E. Brown, S. R. Driver, and C. A. Briggs, *Hebrew and English Lexicon of the Old Testament* (Oxford: Clarendon, 1907)	ConNT	*Coniectanea neotestamentica*
		DBSup	*Dictionnaire de la Bible, Supplément*
		Dit., Syll.	W. Dittenberger, *Sylloge Inscriptionum Graecarum, 4 vols. (1915–24)*
BDF	F. Blass, A. Debrunner, and R. W. Funk, *A Greek Grammar of the New Testament* (University of Chicago/University of Cambridge, 1961)	DJD	Discoveries in the Judean Desert
BETL	Bibliotheca ephemeridum theologicarum lovaniensium	EB	Études bibliques
		EGT	The Expositor's Greek Testament
BEvT	Beiträge zur evangelischen Theologie	EKK	Evangelisch-katholischer Kommentar zum Neuen Testament
BGD	W. Bauer, *A Greek-English Lexicon of the New Testament and Other Early Christian Literature*, ET, ed. W. F. Arndt and F. W. Gingrich; 2d ed. rev. F. W. Gingrich and F. W. Danker (University of Chicago, 1979)	ER	*Epworth Review*
		ETL	*Ephemerides theologicae lovanienses*
		ETR	*Études théologiques et religieuses*
		EvQ	*Evangelical Quarterly*
		EvT	*Evangelische Theologie*
		EWNT	*Exegetisches Wörterbuch zum Neuen Testament*, ed. H. Balz and G. Schneider, 3 vols. (Stuttgart: Kohlhammer, 1980–83)
Bib	*Biblica*		
BJRL	*Bulletin of the John Rylands University Library of Manchester*		
		ExpT	*The Expository Times*
BJS	Brown Judaic Studies	FBBS	Facet Books, Biblical Series
BR	*Biblical Research*	FRLANT	Forschungen zur Religion und Literatur des Alten und Neuen Testaments
BTB	*Biblical Theology Bulletin*		
BWANT	Beiträge zur Wissenschaft vom Alten und Neuen Testament		
BZ	*Biblische Zeitschrift*	GLAJJ	M. Stern, *Greek and Latin Authors on Jews and Judaism*, 3 vols. (Jerusalem: Israel Academy of Sciences and Humanities, 1976, 1980, 1984)
BZNW	Beihefte zur ZNW		
CB	Clarendon Bible		
CBQ	*Catholic Biblical Quarterly*		
CBQMS	CBQ Monograph Series	HBT	*Horizons in Biblical Theology*
CIG	*Corpus inscriptionum graecarum (1828–77)*	HeyJ	*Heythrop Journal*
		HKNT	Handkommentar zum Neuen Testament
CH	*Corpus inscriptionum iudaicarum* (I, 1936; II, 1952)	HNT	Handbuch zum Neuen Testament
CIL	*Corpus inscriptionum latinarum (1863–1909)*	HR	E. Hatch and H. A. Redpath, *A Concordance to the Septuagint* 2 vols. (Oxford: Clarendon, 1897)
CJT	*Canadian Journal of Theology*		
CNT	Commentaire du Nouveau Testament		

HTKNT	Herders theologischer Kommentar zum Neuen Testament	LCL	Loeb Classical Library
		LD	Lectio divina
HTR	*Harvard Theological Review*	LPGL	G. W. H. Lampe, *Patristic Greek-Lexicon* (Oxford: Clarendon, 1961)
HUCA	*Hebrew Union College Annual*		
		LR	*Lutheranische Rundschau*
IB	*Interpreter's Bible*	LSJ	H. G. Liddell and R. Scott, *A Greek-English Lexicon*, rev. H. S. Jones (Oxford: Clarendon, ^{9}1940; with supplement, 1968)
ICC	International Critical Commentary		
IDB	G. A. Buttrick, ed., *Interpreter's Dictionary of the Bible* 4 vols. (Nashville: Abingdon, 1962)		
		LTK	*Lexikon für Theologie und Kirche*
IDBSup	Supplementary volume to IDB	LumVie	*Lumière et Vie*
IKZ	*Internationale Kirchliche Zeitschrift*	MAMA	*Monumenta Asiae Minoris Antiqua, 6 vols. (1928–39)*
Int	*Interpretation*	MM	J. H. Moulton and G. Milligan, *The Vocabulary of the Greek Testament* (London: Hodder, 1930)
ITQ	*Irish Theological Quarterly*		
JAAR	*Journal of the American Academy of Religion*		
		MNTC	Moffatt NT Commentary
JAC	Jahrbuch für Antike und Christentum	MThS	Münchener Theologische Studien
JBC	R. E. Brown, et al. eds., *The Jerome Biblical Commentary*	MTZ	*Münchener theologische Zeitschrift*
JBL	*Journal of Biblical Literature*		
JBR	*Journal of Bible and Religion*	NCB	New Century Bible (new ed.)
JES	*Journal of Ecumenical Studies*		
JETS	*Journal of the Evangelical Theological Society*	NDIEC	G. H. R. Horsley, *New Documents Illustrating Early Christianity* (North Ryde, Australia, 1981–)
JJS	*Journal of Jewish Studies*		
JLW	*Jahrbuch für Liturgiewissenschaft*		
		Neot	*Neotestamentica*
JR	*Journal of Religion*	NICNT	New International Commentary on the New Testament
JSJ	*Journal for the Study of Judaism in the Persian, Hellenistic and Roman Period*		
		NIDNTT	C. Brown, ed., *The New International Dictionary of New Testament Theology*, 3 vols. (Exeter: Paternoster, 1975–78)
JSNT	*Journal for the Study of the New Testament*		
JSNTSup	*JSNT Supplement Series*		
JSOT	*Journal for the Study of the Old Testament*	NovT	*Novum Testamentum*
		NovTSup	Supplement to *NovT*
JSS	*Journal of Semitic Studies*	NRT	*La nouvelle revue théologique*
JTC	*Journal for Theology and the Church*	NTAbh	Neutestamentliche Abhandlungen
JTS	*Journal of Theological Studies*	NTD	Das Neue Testament Deutsch
Jud	*Judaica*		
		NTF	Neutestamentliche Forschungen
KD	*Kerygma und Dogma*	NTS	*New Testament Studies*
KEK	H. A. W. Meyer, *Kritisch-exegetischer Kommentar über das Neue Testament*	NTTS	New Testament Tools and Studies

OBO	Orbis Bilicus et Orientalis	SBLTT	SBL Texts and Translations
OCD	N. G. L. Hammond and H.	SBM	Stuttgarter biblische
	H. Scullard, *Oxford Classical*		Monographien
	Dictionary (Oxford:	SBS	Stuttgarter Bibelstudien
	Clarendon, 1970)	SBT	Studies in Biblical Theology
OGI	W. Dittenberger, ed.,	*ScEc*	*Sciences Ecclesiastiques*
	Orientis Graeci Inscriptiones	SE	*Studia Evangelica I, II, III*
	Selectae (Leipzig, 1903–5)		(= TU 73 [1959], 87 [1964],
			88 [1964], etc.)
PCB	M. Black and H. H. Rowley,	*SEÅ*	*Svensk exegetisk årsbok*
	eds., *Peake's Commentary on*	SH	W. Sanday and A. C.
	the Bible (London: Nelson,		Headlam, *Romans*, ICC
	1962)		(1895; ⁵1902)
PGM	K. Preisendanz, ed., *Papyri*	*SJT*	*Scottish Journal of Theology*
	graecae magicae, 2 vols.	SJTOP	*SJT* Occasional Papers
	(Leipzig/Berlin, 1928, 1931)	SNT	Studien zum Neuen
PIBA	*Proceedings of the Irish*		Testament
	Biblical Association	SNTSMS	Society for New Testament
P. Oxy.	Oxyrhynchus Papyri		Studies Monograph Series
		SPCIC	*Studiorum Paulinorum*
RAC	*Reallexikon für Antike und*		*Congressus Internationalis*
	Christentum		*Catholicus 1961.* AnBib 17–
RB	*Revue biblique*		18 (Rome: Pontifical
RBén	*Revue bénédictine*		Institute, 1963)
RelSRev	*Religious Studies Review*	Spicq	C. Spicq, *Notes de*
RevScRel	*Revue des sciences religeuses*		*Lexicographie Néo-*
RGG	*Religion in Geschichte und*		*testamentaire,* OBO 22,
	Gegenwart		Editions Universitaires
RHPR	*Revue d'histoire et de*		Fribourg Suisse (1978)
	philosophie religieuses	*SR*	*Studies in Religion/Sciences*
RHR	Revue de l'histoire des		*religieuses*
	religions	*ST*	*Studia theologica*
RNT	Regensburger Neues	Str-B	H. Strack and P. Billerbeck,
	Testament		*Kommentar zum Neuen*
RQ	*Revue de Qumrân*		*Testament,* 4 vols. (Munich:
RSPT	*Revue des sciences*		Beck'sche, 1926–28)
	philosophiques et théologiques	SUNT	Studien zur Umwelt des
RSR	*Recherches de science religieuse*		Neuen Testaments
RTL	*Revue théologique de Louvain*	SVM	E. Schürer, *The History of the*
RTR	*The Reformed Theological*		*Jewish People in the Age of*
	Review		*Jesus Christ,* rev. and ed. G.
			Vermes and F. Millar, vol. 1
SANT	Studien zum Alten und		(Edinburgh: T. & T. Clark,
	Neuen Testament		1973)
SBL	Society of Biblical Literature	SVMB	Vol. 2 of the same, with M.
SBLASP	SBL Abstracts and Seminar		Black (1979)
	Papers	SVMG	Vol. 3 of the same, with M.
SBLDS	SBL Dissertation Series		Goodman (1986, 1987)
SBLMS	SBL Monograph Series	SymBU	Symbolae Biblicae
SBLSBS	SBL Sources for Biblical		Upsalienses
	Study	Symm.	Symmachus' Greek
SBLSCS	SBL Septuagint and		translation of the Old
	Cognate Studies		Testament

TDNT	G. Kittel and G. Friedrich, eds., *Theological Dictionary of the New Testament,* 10 vols., ET (Grand Rapids: Eerdmans, 1964–76)	*UBS*	The United Bible Societies Greek Text (1966)
		UNT	Untersuchungen zum Neuen Testament
TDOT	G. J. Botterweck and H. Ringgren, eds., *Theological Dictionary of the Old Testament,* ET (Grand Rapids: Eerdmans, 1974–)	*USQR*	*Union Seminary Quarterly Review*
		VC	*Vigiliae christianae*
		VD	*Verbum domini*
Th	*Theology*	*VF*	*Verkündigung und Forschung*
ThBeit	*Theologische Beiträge*	*VT*	*Vetus Testamentum*
ThBl	*Theologische Blätter*		
Theod.	Theodotion's Greek translation of the Old Testament	WBC	Word Biblical Commentary
		WH	Westcott and Hort, *The New Testament in the Original Greek* (1881)
THKNT	Theologischer Handkommentar zum Neuen Testament	✓ WMANT	Wissenschaftliche Monographien zum Alten und Neuen Testament
ThViat	*Theologia Viatorum*	*WTJ*	*Westminster Theological Journal*
TJT	*Toronto Journal of Theology*		
TLZ	*Theologische Literaturzeitung*	WUNT	Wissenschaftliche Untersuchungen zum Neuen Testament
TNTC	Tyndale New Testament Commentary		
TP	*Theologie und Philosophie*	*ZAW*	*Zeitschrift für die alttestamentliche Wissenschaft*
TQ	*Theologische Quartalschrift*		
TR	Textus Receptus (Oxford, 1873)	*ZKT*	*Zeitschrift für katholische Theologie*
TR	*Theologische Rundschau*	*ZNW*	*Zeitschrift für die neutestamentliche Wissenschaft*
TS	*Theological Studies*		
TSK	*Theologische Studien und Kritiken*	*ZRGG*	*Zeitschrift für Religions- und Geistesgeschichte*
TTZ	*Trierer theologische Zeitschrift*	*ZTK*	*Zeitschrift für Theologie und Kirche*
TU	Texte und Untersuchungen		
TynB	*Tyndale Bulletin*		
TZ	*Theologische Zeitschrift*		

D. Abbreviations for Books of the Bible with Apocrypha

OLD TESTAMENT

Gen	2 Chron	Dan
Exod	Ezra	Hos
Lev	Neh	Joel
Num	Esth	Amos
Deut	Job	Obad
Josh	Ps (Pss)	Jonah
Judg	Prov	Mic
Ruth	Eccl	Nah
*1 Sam	Cant	Hab
*2 Sam	Isa	Zeph
*1 Kgs	Jer	Hag
*2 Kgs	Lam	Zech
1 Chron	Ezek	Mal

NEW TESTAMENT

Matt	1 Tim
Mark	2 Tim
Luke	Titus
John	Philem
Acts	Heb
Rom	James
1 Cor	1 Pet
2 Cor	2 Pet
Gal	1 John
Eph	2 John
Phil	3 John
Col	Jude
1 Thess	Rev
2 Thess	

APOCRYPHA

Add Esth	Additions to Esther	2 Macc	2 Maccabees
Bar	Baruch	Pr Man	Prayer of Manasseh
Bel	Bel and the Dragon	Sir	Ecclesiasticus (Wisdom of
Ep Jer	Epistle of Jeremy		Jesus the son of Sirach)
1 Esdr	1 Esdras	S Th Ch	Song of the Three Children
2 Esdr	2 Esdras	Sus	Susanna
Jud	Judith	Tob	Tobit
1 Macc	1 Maccabees	Wisd Sol	Wisdom of Solomon

Texts used:

Biblica Hebraica Stuttgartensia. Ed. K. Elliger and W. Rudolph. Stuttgart: Deutsche Bibelgesellschaft, 1967/77, 1984.

Septuaginta. Ed. A. Rahlfs. 2 vols. Stuttgart: Württembergische Bibelanstalt, [7]1962.

Novum Testamentum Graece. Ed. E. Nestle, K. Aland et al. Stuttgart: Deutsche Bibelgesellschaft, [26]1979 = Aland[26]

*Note: to avoid unnecessary repetition and possible confusion I have almost always cited 1 Sam, 2 Sam, 1 Kgs and 2 Kgs as above, rather than using the LXX titles, 1–4 Kingdoms, when referring to the Greek text.

E. Abbreviations of Other Early Jewish Literature (usually called OT Pseudepigrapha)

Adam and Eve	Life of Adam and Eve	*4Ezra*	4 Ezra (late 1st cent. A.D.)
Apoc. Abr.	Apocalypse of Abraham (1st to 2nd cent. A.D.)	*Gk Ap. Ezra*	Greek Apocalypse of Ezra (2nd to 9th cent. A.D.)
Apoc. Adam	Apocalypse of Adam (1st to 4th cent. A.D.)	*Jos. As.*	Joseph and Asenath
2 Apoc. Bar.	Syriac Apocalypse of Baruch (early 2nd cent. A.D.)	*Jub.*	Jubilees
		LAB	*Liber Antiquitatum Biblicarum* = Ps. Philo
3 Apoc. Bar.	Greek Apocalypse of Baruch (1st to 3rd cent. A.D.)	*3 Macc.*	3 Maccabees
		4 Macc.	4 Maccabees
		Mart. Isa.	Martyrdom of Isaiah
Apoc. Mos.	Apocalypse of Moses	*Odes Sol.*	Odes of Solomon
Apoc. Elij.	Apocalypse of Elijah (1st to 4th cent. A.D.)	*Pr. Jos.*	Prayer of Joseph
		Ps. Philo	Pseudo-Philo = *LAB*
Asc. Isa.	Ascension of Isaiah	Ps. Phoc.	Pseudo-Phocylides
As. Mos.	*Assumption of Moses* (see *T. Mos.*)	*Pss. Sol.*	Psalms of Solomon
		Sib. Or.	Sibylline Oracles
1 Enoch	Ethiopic Enoch (2nd cent. B.C. to 1st cent. A.D.)	*Sim. Enoch*	Similitudes of Enoch (= *1 Enoch* 37–71)
		T. Abr.	Testament of Abraham (1st to 2nd cent. A.D.)
2 Enoch	Slavonic Enoch (late 1st cent. A.D.)	*T. Adam*	Testament of Adam (2nd to 5th cent. A.D.)
3 Enoch	Hebrew Enoch (5th to 6th cent. A.D.)	*T. Ash.*	Testament of Asher (in *T. 12 Patr.*)
Ep. Arist.	Epistle of Aristeas		

T. Ben.	Testament of Benjamin (in *T. 12 Patr.*)	*T. Levi*	Testament of Levi (in *T. 12 Patr.*)
T. Dan	Testament of Dan (in *T. 12 Patr.*)	*T. Mos.*	Testament of Moses (1st cent. A.D.) (= As. Mos.)
T. Gad	Testament of Gad (in *T. 12 Patr.*)	*T. Naph.*	Testament of Naphtali (in *T. 12 Patr.*)
T. Isaac	Testament of Isaac (2nd cent. A.D.)	*T. Reub.*	Testament of Reuben (in *T. 12 Patr.*)
T. Iss.	Testament of Issachar (in *T. 12 Patr.*)	*T. Sol.*	Testament of Solomon (1st to 3rd cent. A.D.)
T. Job	Testament of Job (1st cent. B.C. to 1st cent. A.D.)	*T. 12 Patr.*	Testaments of the Twelve Patriarchs
T. Jos.	Testament of Joseph (in *T. 12 Patr.*)	*T. Zeb.*	Testament of Zebulun (in *T. 12 Patr.*)
T. Jud.	Testament of Judah (in *T. 12 Patr.*)		

Texts used:

Apocalypsis Henochi Graece. Ed. M. Black. Leiden: Brill, 1970.

Fragmenta Pseudepigraphorum Quae Supersunt Graeca. Ed. A.-M. Denis. Leiden: Brill, 1970.

Septuaginta. Ed. A. Rahlfs (as APOCRYPHA). For *Pss. Sol.* and *3–4 Macc.*

The Testaments of the Twelve Patriarchs. Ed. M. de Jonge. Leiden: Brill, 1978.

The Apocrypha and Pseudepigrapha of the Old Testament. Ed. R. H. Charles. 2 vols. Oxford: Clarendon, 1913.

The Apocryphal Old Testament. Ed. H. F. D. Sparks. Oxford: Clarendon, 1984.

The Old Testament Pseudepigrapha. Ed. J. H. Charlesworth. 2 vols. London: Darton, 1983, 1985.

F. Abbreviations of Dead Sea Scrolls, Philo, and Josephus

DEAD SEA SCROLLS

CD	Cairo (Genizeh text of the) Damascus (Document)	1QIsa[a,b]	First, second copy of Isaiah from Qumran Cave 1
p	Pesher = interpretation, commentary	1QpHab	*Pesher on Habakkuk* from Qumran Cave 1
Q	Qumran	1QM	*Milḥāmāh* (*War Scroll*) from Qumran Cave 1
1Q, 2Q, 3Q, etc.	Numbered caves of Qumran yielding written material; followed by abbreviation of the book	1QS	*Serek hayyaḥad* (*Community Rule, Manual of Discipline*) from Qumran Cave 1
1QapGen	*Genesis Apocryphon* from Qumran cave 1	1QSa	Appendix A (*Rule of the Congregation*) to 1QS
1QH	*Hôdayôt* (*Thanksgiving Hymns*) from Qumran Cave 1	1QSb	Appendix B (*Blessings*) to 1QS

4QFlor	*Florilegium* (or *Eschatological Midrashim*) from Qumran Cave 4	4QPrNab	Prayer of Nabonidus from Qumran Cave 4
4QMess^{ar}	Aramaic "Messianic" text from Qumran Cave 4	4QTestim	*Testimonia* text from Qumran Cave 4
4QPat	*Patriarchal Blessings* from Qumran Cave 4	11QMelch	*Melchizedek* text from Qumran Cave 11
4QpNah	*Pesher on Nahum* from Qumran Cave 4	11QTemple	*Temple Scroll*, probably from Qumran Cave 11
4QpPs37	*Pesher on Psalm 37* from Qumran Cave 4	11QtgJob	*Targum of Job* from Qumran Cave 11

PHILO

Abr.	*De Abrahamo*	*Mos.*	*De Vita Mosis*
Agr.	*De Agricultura*	*Mut.*	*De Mutatione Nominum*
Cher.	*De Cherubim*	*Opif.*	*De Opificio Mundi*
Conf.	*De Confusione Linguarum*	*Plant.*	*De Plantatione*
Cong.	*De Congressu quaerendae Eruditionis gratia*	*Post.*	*De Posteritate Caini*
Decal.	*De Decalogo*	*Praem.*	*De Praemiis et Poenis*
Det.	*Quod Deterius Potiori Insidiari Soleat*	*Prob.*	*Quod Omnis Probus Liber sit*
Ebr.	*De Ebrietate*	*Qu. Ex.*	*Quaestiones et Solutiones in Exodum*
Fuga	*De Fuga et Inventione*	*Qu. Gen.*	*Quaestiones et Solutiones in Genesin*
Gig.	*De Gigantibus*		
Heres	*Quis Rerum Divinarum Heres sit*	*Sac.*	*De Sacrificiis Abelis et Caini*
Immut.	*Quod Deus Immutabilis sit*	*Sobr.*	*De Sobrietate*
Jos.	*De Josepho*	*Som.*	*De Somniis*
Leg. All.	*Legum Allegoriae*	*Spec. Leg.*	*De Specialibus Legibus*
Legat.	*De Legatione ad Gaium*	*Virt.*	*De Virtutibus*
Migr.	*De Migratione Abrahami*	*Vit. Cont.*	*De Vita Contemplativa*

JOSEPHUS

Ant.	*Jewish Antiquities*	*Life*	*Life*
Ap.	*Contra Apionem*	*War*	*The Jewish War*

Texts used:
Die Texte aus Qumran. Ed. E. Lohse. Darmstadt: Wissenschaftliche Buchgesellschaft, 1964, 1971.
The Temple Scroll. J. Maier. JSOTSupp 34. Sheffield: JSOT, 1985.
The Dead Sea Scrolls in English. Tr. G. Vermes. Harmondsworth: Penguin, ²1975.
The Essene Writings from Qumran. A. Dupont-Sommer. Oxford: Blackwell, 1961.
Josephus. Ed. H. St.J. Thackeray et al. LCL. 9 vols. London: Heinemann, 1926–65.
Philo. Ed. F. H. Colson et al. LCL. 12 vols. London: Heinemann, 1929–53.

G. Abbreviations of Early Christian Writings

Ap. Const.	Apostolic Constitutions	Ign. Philad.	Ignatius, Letter to the Philadelphians
Barn.	Barnabas		
1–2 Clem.	1–2 Clement	Ign. Pol.	Ignatius, Letter to Polycarp
Clement, Strom.	Clement of Alexandria, Stromata		
Did.	Didache	Ign. Rom.	Ignatius, Letter to the Romans
Diogn.	Diognetus	Ign. Smyrn.	Ignatius, Letter to the Smyrneans
Epiphanius,			
Haer.	Epiphanius, Panarion seu adversus LXXX haereses	Ign. Trall.	Ignatius, Letter to the Trallians
		Justin, Apol.	Justin Martyr, Apology
Eusebius, HE	Eusebius, Historia Ecclesiastica	Justin, Dial.	Justin Martyr, Dialogue with Trypho
Eusebius, Praep.		Mart. Pol.	Martyrdom of Polycarp
Evang.	Eusebius, Praeparatio Evangelica	Origen, Cont. Cels.	Origen, Contra Celsum
Herm. Man.	Hermas, Mandates	Origen, In	
Herm. Sim.	Hermas, Similitudes	Matth.	Origen, Commentary on Matthew
Herm. Vis.	Hermas, Visions		
Ign. Eph.	Ignatius, Letter to the Ephesians	Pol. Phil.	Polycarp, Letter to the Philippians
Ign. Magn.	Ignatius, Letter to the Magnesians		

Texts used:

The Apostolic Fathers. K. Lake. LCL. 2 vols. London: Heinemann, 1912–13.
Patristic Evidence for Jewish-Christian Sects. NovTSupp 36. Leiden: Brill, 1973.
Eusebius: Ecclesiastical History. K. Lake and J. E. L. Oulton. LCL. 2 vols. London: Heinemann, 1926, 1932.
The Apocryphal New Testament. M. R. James. Oxford University, 1924.
New Testament Apocrypha. E. Hennecke. Ed. W. Schneemelcher. ET ed. R. M. Wilson. 2 vols. London: Lutterworth, 1963, 1965
For Gnostic and Nag Hammadi texts:
Gnosis. W. Foerster. ET ed. R. M. Wilson. 2 vols. Oxford: Clarendon, 1972, 1974.
The Nag Hammadi Library. Ed. J. M. Robinson. San Francisco: Harper and Row, 1977.

H. Rabbinic writings

b.	before a tractate indicates Babylonian Talmud	Sipra	Sipra
		Sipre	Sipre
Frg. Tg.	Fragmentary Targum	Tg. Isa.	Targum of Isaiah
m.	before a tractate indicates Mishnah	Tg. Neof.	Targum Neofiti
		Tg. Onq.	Targum Onqelos
Rab.	Rabbah, as in Gen. Rab. = Genesis Rabbah	Tg. Ps.-J.	Targum Pseudo-Jonathan
		Tg. Yer.	Targum Yerusalmi

Tractates

ʾAbot	Pirqe ʾAbot	Nazir	Nazir
ʿArak.	ʿArakin	Ned.	Nedarim
ʿAbod. Zar.	ʿAboda Zara	Neg.	Negaʿim
B. Bat.	Baba Batra	Nez.	Neziqin
Bek.	Bekorot	Nid.	Niddah
Ber.	Berakot	Ohol.	Oholot
Beṣa	Beṣa (= Yom Ṭob)	ʿOr.	ʿOrla
Bik.	Bikkurim	Para	Para
B. Meṣ.	Baba Meṣʿia	Peʾa	Peʾa
B. Qam.	Baba Qamma	Pesaḥ.	Pesahim
Dem.	Demai	Qinnim	Qinnim
ʿEd.	ʿEduyyot	Qidd.	Qiddušin
ʿErub.	ʿErubin	Qod.	Qodašin
Giṭ	Giṭṭin	Roš Haš.	Roš Haššana
Ḥag.	Ḥagiga	Sanh.	Sanhedrin
Ḥal.	Ḥalla	Šabb.	Šabbat
Hor.	Horayot	Šeb.	Šebiʿit
Ḥul.	Ḥullin	Šebu.	Šebuʿot
Kelim	Kelim	Šeqal.	Šeqalim
Ker.	Keritot	Soṭa	Soṭa
Ketub.	Ketubot	Sukk.	Sukka
Kil.	Kilʾayim	Taʿan.	Taʿanit
Maʿaś.	Maʿaśerot	Tamid	Tamid
Mak.	Makkot	Tem.	Temura
Makš.	Makširin (= Mašqin)	Ter.	Terumot
Maʿas Š.	Maʿaser Šeni	Ṭohar	Ṭoharot
Meg.	Megilla	T. Yom.	Tebul Yom
Meʿil.	Meʿila	ʿUq.	ʿUqṢin
Menaḥ.	Menahot	Yad.	Yadayim
Mid.	Middot	Yebam.	Yebamot
Miqw.	Miqwaʾot	Yoma	Yoma (= Kippurim)
Moʿed	Moʿed	Zabim	Zabim
Moʿed Qa.	Moʿed Qa	Zebaḥ	Zebahim
Našim	Našim	Zer.	Zeraʿim

Texts used:

The Mishnah. H. Danby. Oxford: Clarendon, 1933.
The Babylonian Talmud. I. Epstein. 34 vols. Soncino, 1935–52.
Midrash Rabbah. H. Freedman and M. Simon. 10 vols. Soncino, [2]1951.
The Targums of Onkelos and Jonathan ben Uzziel on the Pentateuch with the Fragments of the Jerusalem Targums I–II. J. W. Etheridge. London: Longmans, 1862–65.
Neophyti I: Targum Palestinense MS de la Bibliotheca Vaticana. A. Diez Macho. 5 vols. Madrid, 1968–78.

For other ancient classical texts such as Epictetus, Juvenal, Seneca, LCL was used; *GLAJJ* also includes many relevant excerpts.

General Bibliography

Alexander, P. S. "Rabbinic Judaism and the New Testament." *ZNW* 74 (1983) 237–46. **Allison, D. C.** "The Pauline Epistles and the Synoptic Gospels: The Pattern of the Parallels." *NTS* 28 (1982) 1–32. **Amir, Y.** "The Term Ἰουδαϊσμός: A Study in Jewish-Hellenistic Self-Identification." *Immanuel* 14 (1982) 34–41. **Aune, D.** *The New Testament in Its Literary Environment.* Philadelphia: Westminster, 1987. Chap. 6. **Aus, R. D.** "Paul's Travel Plans to Spain and the 'Full Number of the Gentiles' of Rom 11:25." *NovT* 21 (1979) 232–62. **Baeck, L.** "The Faith of Paul." *Judaism and Christianity.* New York: Harper, 1966. 139–68. **Baird, W.** "On Reading Romans Today." *Int* 34 (1980) 45–58. **Banks, R.** *Paul's Idea of Community.* Exeter: Paternoster, 1980. **Barrett, C. K.** *From First Adam to Last.* London: Black, 1962. **Barth, M.** "Was Paul an Anti-Semite?" *JES* 5 (1968) 78–104. ———. *Justification: Pauline Texts Interpreted in the Light of the Old and New Testaments.* Grand Rapids: Eerdmans, 1971. **Bartsch, H.-W.** "Die antisemitischen Gegner des Paulus im Römerbrief." In *Antijudaismus im Neuen Testament.* Ed. W. Eckert, et al. Munich: Kaiser, 1967. 27–43. ———. "The Concept of Faith in Paul's Letter to the Romans." *BR* 13 (1968) 41–53. ———. "Die Empfänger des Römerbriefes." *ST* 25 (1971) 81–89. **Bassler, J. M.** *Divine Impartiality: Paul and a Theological Axiom.* SBLDS 59. Chico: Scholars Press, 1982. **Baumgarten, J.** *Paulus und die Apokalyptik.* WMANT 44. Neukirchen: Neukirchener Verlag, 1975. **Baur, F. C.** *Paul.* 2 vols. London: Williams & Norgate, 1873, 1875. **Beare, F. W.** *St Paul and His Letters.* Nashville: Abingdon, 1962. **Beker, J. C.** *Paul the Apostle.* Philadelphia: Fortress, 1980. ———. "The Faithfulness of God and the Priority of Israel in Paul's Letter to the Romans." *HTR* 79 (1986) = *Christians Among Jews and Greeks.* FS K. Stendahl, ed. G. W. E. Nickelsburg and G. W. MacRae. Philadelphia: Fortress, 1986. 10–16. **Benoit, P.** *Jesus and the Gospel.* Vol. 2. London: Darton, 1974. **Berger, K.** "Zum traditionsgeschichtlichen Hintergrund christologischer Hoheitstitel." *NTS* 17 (1970–71) 391–425. **Betz, H. D.**, ed. *Plutarch's Theological Writings and Early Christian Literature.* Leiden: Brill, 1975. ———. , ed. *Plutarch's Ethical Writings and Early Christian Literature.* Leiden: Brill, 1978. ———. *Galatians.* Hermeneia. Philadelphia: Fortress, 1979. **Bindemann, W.** *Die Hoffnung der Schöpfung: Römer 8:18–27 und die Frage einer Theologie der Befreiung von Mensch und Natur.* Neukirchen: Neukirchener Verlag, 1983. **Bjerkelund, C. J.** ΠΑΡΑΚΑΛΟ: *Form, Funktion und Sinn der parakalo-Sätze in den paulinischen Briefen.* Oslo: Universitetsforlaget, 1967. **Blank, J.** *Paulus: Von Jesus zum Urchristentum.* Munich: Kösel, 1982. **Bloch, R.** "Midrash." In *Approaches to Ancient Judaism: Theory and Practice,* ed. W. S. Green. BJS 1. Missoula: Scholars Press, 1978. 29–50. **Boers, H.** "The Problem of Jews and Gentiles in the Macro-structure of Romans." *Neot* 15 (1981) 1–11. **Bornkamm, G.** *Early Christian Experience.* London: SCM, 1969. ———. *Paul.* London: Hodder & Stoughton, 1971. ———. "Paulinische Anakoluthe." *Das Ende des Gesetzes.* Munich: Kaiser, 1952. 76–92. ———. "The Revelation of God's Wrath (Romans 1–3)." *Experience,* 47–70. ———. "The Letter to the Romans as Paul's Last Will and Testament." In Donfried, *Debate.* 17–31. **Bousset, W.** and **Gressmann, H.** *Die Religion des Judentums im späthellenistischen Zeitalter.* Tübingen: Mohr, ⁴1966. **Brown, R. E.** and **Meier, J. P.** *Antioch and Rome.* London: Chapman, 1983. **Bruce, F. F.** *Paul: Apostle of the Free Spirit.* Exeter: Paternoster, 1977. **Bultmann, R.** *Der Stil der paulinischen Predigt und die kynisch-stoische Diatribe.* Göttingen: Vandenhoeck & Ruprecht, 1910, 1984. ———. *Theology of the New Testament.* 2 vols. London: SCM, 1952, 1955. ———. "Glossen im Römerbrief." *Exegetica.* Tübingen: Mohr, 1967. 278–84. **Buren, P. M. van.** *A Theology of the Jewish Christian Reality.* 2 vols. New York: Harper & Row, 1980, 1983. **Byrne,**

B. *"Sons of God"—"Seed of Abraham."* AnBib 83. Rome: Biblical Institute, 1979. **Cambier, J.** "Romans." In *Introduction to the New Testament,* ed. A. Robert, et al. New York: Desclee, 1965. 447–470. ———. *L'Évangile de Dieu selon l'épître aux Romains.* Bruges: Brouwer, 1967. **Campbell, W. S.** "The Romans Debate." *JSNT* 10 (1981) 19–28. ———. "Romans 3 as a Key to the Structure and Thought of the Letter." *NovT* 23 (1981) 22–40. ———. "The Freedom and Faithfulness of God in Relation to Israel." *JSNT* 13 (1981) 27–45. **Carcopino, J.** *Daily Life in Ancient Rome.* Yale University, 1940. **Cerfaux, L.** *Christ in the Theology of St Paul.* Freiburg: Herder, 1959. ———. *The Church in the Theology of St Paul.* Freiburg: Herder, 1959. ———. *The Christian in the Theology of St Paul.* London: Chapman, 1967. **Childs, B. S.** *The New Testament as Canon: An Introduction.* Philadelphia: Fortress, 1985. 243–63. **Collins, J. J.** *Between Athens and Jerusalem: Jewish Identity in the Hellenistic Diaspora.* New York: Crossroad, 1983. ———. "A Symbol of Otherness: Circumcision and Salvation in the First Century." In *"To See Ourselves As Others See Us": Christians, Jews, "Others" in Late Antiquity,* ed. J. Neusner and E. S. Frerichs. Chico: Scholars Press, 1985. 163–86. **Conzelmann, H.** *An Outline of the Theology of the New Testament.* London: SCM, 1969. ———. "Die Rechtfertigungslehre des Paulus: Theologie oder Anthropologie?" *Theologie als Schriftauslegung.* Munich: Kaiser, 1974. 191–206. **Cranfield, C. E. B.** *A Commentary on Romans 12–13.* SJTOP 12. Edinburgh: Oliver & Boyd, 1965. ———. *The Bible and Christian Life.* Edinburgh: T. & T. Clark, 1985. ———. "Some Comments on Professor J. D. G. Dunn's *Christology in the Making* with Special Reference to the Evidence of the Epistle to the Romans." In *The Glory of Christ in the New Testament: Studies in Memory of G. B. Caird,* ed. L. D. Hurst and N. T. Wright. Oxford: Clarendon, 1987. 267–80. **Cullmann, O.** *Christ and Time.* London: SCM, [3]1962. ———. *The Christology of the New Testament.* London: SCM, 1959. **Cunningham, P. A.** *Jewish Apostle to the Gentiles: Paul As He Saw Himself.* Mystic: Twenty-third, 1986. **Dabelstein, R.** *Die Beurteilung der "Heiden" bei Paulus.* Frankfurt/Bern: Lang, 1981. **Dahl, N. A.** "The Missionary Theology in the Epistle to the Romans." *Studies.* 70–94. ———. "The Doctrine of Justification: Its Social Function and Implications." *Studies.* 95–120. ———. *Studies in Paul.* Minneapolis: Augsburg, 1977. **Dalman, G.** *The Words of Jesus.* Edinburgh: T. & T. Clark, 1902. **Daube, D.** *Paul and Rabbinic Judaism.* London: Athlone, 1956. **Davies, W. D.** *Paul and Rabbinic Judaism.* London: SPCK/Philadelphia: Fortress, 1948; [2]1955, [4]1981. ———. "Paul and the People of Israel." *NTS* 16 (1969–70) 4–39. ———. *The Gospel and the Land: Early Christianity and Jewish Territorial Doctrine.* Los Angeles: University of California, 1974. ———. *Jewish and Pauline Studies.* London: SPCK; Philadelphia: Fortress, 1984. **Daxer, H.** *Römer 1.18–2.10 im Verhältnis zu spätjüdischen Lehrauffasung.* Naumburg: Pätz'sche, 1914. **Deidun, T. J.** *New Covenant Morality in Paul.* AnBib 89. Rome: Biblical Institute, 1981. **Deichgräber, R.** *Gotteshymnus und Christushymnus in der frühen Christenheit.* SUNT 5. Göttingen: Vandenhoeck & Ruprecht, 1967. 61–64. **Deissmann, A.** *Bible Studies.* Edinburgh: T. & T. Clark, 1901. ———. *Light from the Ancient East.* Grand Rapids: Baker, 1965. **Delling, G.** "Partizipiale Gottesprädikationen in den Briefen des Neuen Testaments." *ST* 17 (1963) 1–59. **Dibelius, M.** *From Tradition to Gospel.* London: Ivor Nicholson & Watson, 1934. ———. "Vier Worte des Römerbriefs, 5:5, 5:12, 8:10 and 11:30f." *SymBU* 3 (1944) 3–17. **Dodd, C. H.** *The Bible and the Greeks.* London: Hodder & Stoughton, 1935. ———. "The Law." *Bible.* 25–41. ———. *According to the Scriptures.* London: Nisbet, 1952. **Donfried, K. P.** "Justification and Last Judgment in Paul." *ZNW* 67 (1976) 90–110. ———, ed. *The Romans Debate.* Minneapolis: Augsburg, 1977. **Doty, W. G.** *Letters in Primitive Christianity.* Philadelphia: Fortress, 1973. **Dülmen, A. van.** *Die Theologie des Gesetzes bei Paulus.* SBM 5. Stuttgart: KBW, 1968. **Dunn, J. D. G.** "Paul's Understanding of the Death of Jesus." In *Reconciliation and Hope,* FS L. L. Morris, ed. R. J. Banks. Exeter: Paternoster, 1974. 125–41. Rev. as "Paul's Understanding of the Death of Jesus as Sacrifice." In *Sacrifice and Redemption: Durham Essays in Theology,* ed. S. W.

Sykes. Cambridge University, 1989. ———. *Jesus and the Spirit*. London: SCM, 1975. ———. *Unity and Diversity in the New Testament*. London: SCM, 1977. ———. *Christology in the Making*. London: SCM, 1980. ———. "The Incident at Antioch." *JSNT* 18 (1983) 3–57. ———. "The New Perspective on Paul." *BJRL* 65 (1983) 95–122. ———. "Works of the Law and the Curse of the Law (Galatians 3:10–14)." *NTS* 31 (1985) 523–42. ———. "Pharisees, Sinners and Jesus." In *The Social World of Formative Christianity and Judaism*. FS H. C. Kee, ed. P. Borgen, J. Neusner, et al. Philadelphia: Fortress, 1988. **Dupont, J.** *Gnosis: La connaissance religieuse dans les épîtres de Saint Paul*. Louvain: Nauwelaerts/Paris: Gabalda, 1949. ———. "Le problème de la structure littéraire de l'Épître aux Romains." *RB* 62 (1955) 365-97. **Eckstein, H.-J.** *Der Begriff Syneidesis bei Paulus*. WUNT 2.10. Tübingen: Mohr, 1983. **Eichholz, G.** *Die Theologie des Paulus im Umriss*. Neukirchen: Neukirchener Verlag, 1972. **Ellis, E. E.** *Paul's Use of the Old Testament*. Grand Rapids: Eerdmans, 1957. ———. "Exegetical Patterns in 1 Corinthians and Romans." *Prophecy and Hermeneutic in Early Christianity*. WUNT 18. Tübingen: Mohr/Grand Rapids: Eerdmans, 1978. 213–20. **Feuillet, A.** "Le plan salvifique de Dieu d'après l'Épître aux Romains." *RB* 57 (1950) 336–87, 489–529. **Fitzmyer, J. A.** "The Use of Explicit Old Testament Quotations in Qumran Literature and in the New Testament." *Essays on the Semitic Background of the New Testament*. London: Chapman, 1971. 3–58. ———. "'4Q Testimonia' and the New Testament." *Essays*. 59–89. **Friedrich, G.** *Die Verkündigung des Todes Jesu im Neuen Testament*. Neukirchen: Neukirchener Verlag, 1982. **Funk, R. W.** "The Apostolic Parousia: Form and Significance." In *Christian History and Interpretation*. FS. J. Knox Ed. W. R. Farmer et al. Cambridge University, 1967. 249–68. **Furnish, V. P.** *Theology and Ethics in Paul*. Nashville: Abingdon, 1968. ———. *The Love Command in the New Testament*. Nashville: Abingdon/London: SCM, 1973. ———. *The Moral Teaching of Paul*. Nashville: Abingdon, 1979. **Gager, J. G.** *The Origins of Anti-Semitism*. Oxford University, 1985. **Gale, H. M.** *The Use of Analogy in the Letters of Paul*. Philadelphia: Westminster, 1964. **Garlington, D.** *"The Obedience of Faith": A Pauline Phrase in Historical Context*. Ph.D. Diss., Durham University, 1987. **Gaston, L.** "Paul and the Torah." In *Antisemitism and the Foundations of Christianity*, ed. A. T. Davies. New York: Paulist Press, 1979. 48–71. = *Paul*. 15–34. ———. "Paul and the Law in Galatians 2–3." In *Anti-Judaism in Early Christianity*. Vol 1, *Paul and the Gospels*, ed. P. Richardson and D. Granskou. Wilfrid Laurier University, 1986. 37–57. = *Paul*. 64–79. ———. *Paul and the Torah*. Vancouver: University of British Columbia, 1987. ———. "For *All* the Believers: The Inclusion of Gentiles as the Ultimate Goal of Torah in Romans." *Paul*. 116–34. **Georgi, D.** *Die Geschichte der Kollekte des Paulus für Jerusalem*. Hamburg: Herbert Reich, 1965. **Goppelt, L.** *Jesus, Paul and Judaism*. New York: Harper, 1964. ———. *Theology of the New Testament*. Vol. 2. Grand Rapids: Eerdmans, 1982. **Grayston, K.** "'I Am Not Ashamed of the Gospel': Romans 1.16a and the Structure of the Epistle." *SE* 2:569–73. **Gundry, R. H.** *Sōma in Biblical Theology*. SNTSMS 29. Cambridge University, 1976. **Haacker, K.** "Exegetische Probleme des Römerbriefs." *NovT* 20 (1978) 1–21. **Haenchen, E.** *The Acts of the Apostles*. Oxford: Blackwell, 1971. **Hahn, F.** *Mission in the New Testament*. London: SCM, 1965. ———. *The Titles of Jesus in Christology* (1963). London: Lutterworth, 1969. ———. "Das Gesetzesverständnis im Römer- und Galaterbrief." *ZNW* 67 (1976) 29–63. ———. "The Confession of the One God in the New Testament." *HBT* 2 (1980) 69–84. **Hainz, J.** *Ekklesia, Strukturen paulinischer Gemeinde-Theologie und Gemeinde-Ordnung*. Regensburg: Pustet, 1972. **Halter, H.** *Taufe und Ethos: Paulinische Kriterien für das Proprium christlicher Moral*. Freiburg: Herder, 1977. **Hanson, A. T.** *The Wrath of the Lamb*. London: SPCK, 1957. ———. *Studies in Paul's Technique and Theology*. London: SPCK, 1974. ———. *The New Testament Interpretation of Scripture*. London: SPCK, 1980. ———. *The Image of the Invisible God*. London: SCM, 1982. **Hebert, G.** "'Faithfulness' and 'Faith.'" *Th* 58 (1955) 373–79. **Heilegenthal, R.** *Werke als Zeichen*. WUNT 2.9. Tübingen: Mohr, 1983. **Hengel, M.** *Die Zeloten*. Leiden: Brill,

1961. ———. *Judaism and Hellenism.* Lon don: SCM, 1974. ———. *The Son of God.* London: SCM, 1976. **Herold, G.** *Zorn und Gerechtigkeit bei Paulus: Eine Untersuchung zu Röm 1:16–18.* Frankfurt/Bern: Lang, 1973. **Hill, D.** *Greek Words and Hebrew Meanings.* SNTSMS 5. Cambridge University, 1967. **Hock, R. F.** *The Social Context of Paul's Ministry: Tentmaking and Apostleship.* Philadelphia: Fortress, 1980. **Hofius, O.** "Das Gesetz des Mose und das Gesetz Christi." *ZTK* 80 (1983) 262–86. **Hort, F. J. A.** *Prolegomena to St Paul's Epistles to the Romans and the Ephesians.* London: Macmillan, 1895. **Hübner, H.** "Existentiale Interpretation der paulinischen 'Gerechtigkeit Gottes.'" *NTS* 21 (1974–75) 462–88. ———. *Law in Paul's Thought.* Edinburgh: T. & T. Clark, 1984. ———. "Paulusforschung seit 1945: Ein kritischer Literaturbericht." *ANRW* II. 25.4 (1987) 2699–2840. **Hultgren, A. J.** *Paul's Gospel and Mission.* Philadelphia: Fortress, 1985. **Jeremias, J.** *The Central Message of the New Testament.* London: SCM, 1965. ———. "Zur Gedankenführung in den paulinischen Briefen." *Abba.* Göttingen: Vandenhoeck & Ruprecht, 1966. 269–72. ———. "Chiasmus in den Paulusbriefen." *Abba.* 276–90. ———. *Jerusalem in the Time of Jesus.* London: SCM, 1969. ———. *New Testament Theology. I. The Proclamation of Jesus.* London: SCM, 1971. **Jewett, R.** *Paul's Anthropological Terms.* Leiden: Brill, 1971. ———. *Dating Paul's Life.* London: SCM, 1979. ———. "Major Impulses in the Theological Interpretation of Romans since Barth." *Int* 34 (1980) 17–31. ———. "Romans as an Ambassadorial Letter." *Int* 36 (1982) 5–20. ———. *Christian Tolerance: Paul's Message to the Modern Church.* Philadelphia: Westminster, 1982. ———. "The Law and the Coexistence of Jews and Gentiles in Romans." *Int* 39 (1985) 341–56. **Jones, F. S.** *"Freiheit" in den Briefen des Apostels Paulus.* Göttingen: Vandenhoeck & Ruprecht, 1987. **Judge, E. A.** "St Paul and Classical Society." *JAC* 15 (1972) 19–36. **Jüngel, R.** *Paulus und Jesus.* Tübingen: Mohr, [3]1967. **Käsemann, E.** "'The Righteousness of God' in Paul." *New Testament Questions of Today.* London: SCM, 1969. 168–82. ———. "Paul and Israel." *New Testament Questions.* 183–87. ———. *Perspectives on Paul.* London: SCM, 1971. **Karris, R. J.** "Romans 14:1–15:13 and the Occasion of Romans." *CBQ* 25 (1973). Repr. in Donfried, *Romans Debate,* 75–99. **Kaye, B. N.** *The Thought Structure of Romans with Special Reference to Chapter 6.* Austen: Schola, 1979. **Keck, L. E.** *Paul and His Letters.* Phildelphia: Fortress, 1979. **Kennedy, G. A.** *New Testament Interpretation through Rhetorical Criticism.* University of North Carolina, 1984. **Kertelge, K.** *"Rechtfertigung" bei Paulus.* Münster: Aschendorff, 1967; [2]1971. **Kettunen, M.** *Der Abfassungszweck des Römerbriefes.* Helsinki, 1979. **Kim, S.** *The Origin of Paul's Gospel.* WUNT 2.4. Tübingen: Mohr, 1981. **Klaiber, W.** *Rechtfertigung und Gemeinde: Eine Untersuchung zum paulinische Kirchenverständnis.* FRLANT 127. Göttingen: Vandenhoeck & Ruprecht, 1982. **Klein, G.** "Paul's Purpose in Writing the Epistle to the Romans" (1969). ET in Donfried, *Romans Debate,* 32–49. ———. "Romans, Letter to the." *IDBS,* 752–54. **Kleinknecht, K. T.** *Der leidende Gerechtfertigte.* WUNT 2.13. Tübingen: Mohr, 1984. **Knox, J.** *Chapters in a Life of Paul.* London: Black, 1954. **Knox, W. L.** *St Paul and the Church of Jerusalem.* Cambridge University, 1925. ———. *St Paul and the Church of the Gentiles.* Cambridge University, 1939. **Koester, H.** *Introduction to the New Testament.* Vol. 2. Philadelphia: Fortress, 1982. 138–42. **Kramer, W.** *Christ, Lord, Son of God* (1963). ET. London: SCM, 1966. **Kümmel, W. G.** *The Theology of the New Testament.* London: SCM, 1974. ———. *Introduction to the New Testament.* Rev. ed. London: SCM, 1975. 305–20. ———. "Die Botschaft des Römerbriefes." *TLZ* 99 (1974) 481–88. **Kuss, O.** *Auslegung und Verkündigung* 1. Regensburg: Pustet, 1963. ———. *Paulus: Die Rolle des Apostels in der theologischen Entwicklung der Urkirche.* Regensburg: Pustet, 1971. **Ladd, G. E.** "Paul and the Law." In *Soli Deo Gloria,* FS W. C. Robinson, ed. J. M. Richards. Richmond: John Knox, 1968. 50–67. = chap. 35 of Ladd, *A Theology of the New Testament.* London: Lutterworth, 1975. **Lampe, P.** *Die stadtrömischen Christen in den ersten beiden Jahrhunderten.* WUNT 2.18. Tübingen: Mohr, 1987. **Lapide P.** and **Stuhlmacher, P.** *Paul: Rabbi and Apostle.* Minneapolis: Augsburg, 1984. **Leon, H. J.** *The Jews of Ancient Rome.* Philadelphia:

Jewish Publication Society of America, 1960. **Leon-Dufour, X.** "Situation littéraire de Rom 5." *RSR* 51 (1963) 83–95. **Lightfoot, J. B.** "The Structure and Destination of the Epistle to the Romans." In *Biblical Essays*. London: Macmillan, 1893. 285–374. **Lindars, B.** *New Testament Apologetic*. London: SCM, 1961. **Ljungman, H.** *Pistis: A Study of Its Presuppositions and Its Meaning in Pauline Use*. Lund: Gleerup, 1964. **Lohmeyer, E.** *Probleme paulinischer Theologie*. Stuttgart, n.d. 33–74. **Lohse, E.** *Die Einheit des Neuen Testaments*. Göttingen: Vandenhoeck & Ruprecht, 1973. ———. *Die Vielfalt des Neuen Testaments*. Göttingen: Vandenhoeck & Ruprecht, 1982. **Longenecker, R. N.** *Paul: Apostle of Liberty*. New York: Harper & Row, 1964. **Lorenzi, L. de,** ed. *Battesimo e giustizia in Rom 6 e 8*. Rome: Abbayia S. Paolo, 1974. ———, ed. *The Law of the Spirit in Rom 7 and 8*. Rome: St Paul's Abbey, 1976. ———, ed. *Dimensions de la vie chrétienne*. Rome: Abbaye de S. Paul, 1979. **Luedemann, G.** *Paul, Apostle to the Gentiles: Studies in Chronology*. Philadelphia: Fortress, 1984. **Lührmann, D.** *Das Offenbarungsverständnis bei Paulus und in paulinischen Gemeinden*. WMANT 16. Neukirchen: Neukirchener Verlag, 1965. ———. *Glaube im frühen Christentum*. Gütersloh: Gütersloher Verlag, 1976. **Lütgert, W.** *Der Römerbrief als historisches Problem*. Gütersloh: Bertelsmann, 1913. **Luz, U.** *Das Geschichtsverständnis des Paulus*. Munich: Kaiser Verlag, 1968. ———. "Zum Aufbau von Röm 1–8." *TZ* 25 (1969) 161–81. ———, with **Smend, R.** *Gesetz*. Stuttgart: Kohlhammer, 1981. **Lyonnet, S.** "Note sur le plan de l'Épître aux Romains." *RSR* 39 (1951/52) 301–316. ———. *Quaestiones in Epistulam ad Romanos*. 2 vols. Roma: Pontificio Instituto Biblico, 1962, 1975. **Maccoby, H.** *The Mythmaker: Paul and the Invention of Christianity*. London: Weidenfeld & Nicolson, 1986. **MacMullen, R.** *Roman Social Relations 50 B.C. to A.D. 284*. Yale University, 1974. ———. *Paganism in the Roman Empire*. Yale University, 1981. **Manson, T. W.** "St Paul's Letter to the Romans—and Others." *Studies in the Gospels and Epistles*. Manchester University, 1962. Repr. in Donfried, *Romans Debate*, 1–16. **Manson, W.** "Notes on the Argument of Romans (chapters 1–8)." In *New Testament Essays in Memory of T. W. Manson*, ed. A. J. B. Higgins. Manchester University, 1959. 150–64. **Marquardt, F.-W.** *Die Juden im Römerbrief*. Theologische Studien 107. Zürich: TVZ, 1971. **Marxsen, W.** *Introduction to the New Testament*. Oxford: Blackwell, 1968. 92–109. **Mattern, L.** *Das Verständnis des Gerichtes bei Paulus*. Zürich/Stuttgart: Zwingli, 1966. **Meeks, W. A.** "Towards a Social Description of Pauline Christianity." In *Approaches to Ancient Judaism*, vol. 2, ed. W. S. Green. BJS 9. Chico: Scholars Press, 1980. 27–41. ———. *The First Urban Christians: The Social World of the Apostle Paul*. Yale University, 1983. ———. "Breaking Away: Three New Testament Pictures of Christianity's Separation from the Jewish Communities." In *"To See Ourselves As Others See Us": Christians, Jews, "Others" in Late Antiquity*, ed. J. Neusner and E. S. Frerichs. Chico: Scholars Press, 1985. 93–115. **Merk, O.** *Handeln aus Glauben: Die Motivierungen der paulinischen Ethik*. Marburg: Elwert, 1968. **Minde, H.-J. van der.** *Schrift und Tradition bei Paulus*. Munich/Paderborn/Wien: Schöningh, 1976. **Minear, P. S.** *The Obedience of Faith: The Purpose of Paul in the Epistle to the Romans*. London: SCM, 1971. **Mohrlang, R.** *Matthew and Paul: A Comparison of Ethical Perspectives*. SNTSMS 48. Cambridge University, 1984. **Montefiore, C.-G.** "The Genesis of the Religion of St. Paul." *Judaism and St Paul* (1914). Repr. New York: Arno, 1973. 1–129. **Moore, G. F.** *Judaism in the First Centuries of the Christian Era*. 3 vols. Harvard, 1927–30. **Morris, L.** "The Theme of Romans." In *Apostolic History and the Gospel*, FS F. F. Bruce, ed. W. W. Gasque et al. Exeter: Paternoster, 1970. 249–63. **Moule, C. F. D.** *An Idiom–Book of New Testament Greek*. Cambridge University, [2]1959. ———. *The Origin of Christology*. Cambridge University, 1977. **Moulton, J. H.** *Grammar of New Testament Greek*, vols. 1, 2. Edinburgh: T. & T. Clark, 1906, 1929. **Moxnes, H.** "Honour and Righteousness in Romans." *JSNT* 32 (1988) 61–77. **Müller, C.** *Gottes Gerechtigkeit und Gottes Volk: Eine Untersuchung zu Römer 9–11*. FRLANT 86. Göttingen: Vandenhoeck & Ruprecht, 1964. **Müller, K.** *Anstoss und Gericht: Eine Studie zum jüdischen Hintergrund des paulinischen Skandalon-Begriffs*.

SANT 19. Munich: Kösel, 1969. **Müller, U. B.** *Prophetie und Predigt im Neuen Testament.* SNT 10. Gütersloh: Gütersloher, 1975. **Munck, J.** *Paul and the Salvation of Mankind.* London: SCM, 1959. 196–209. **Mundle, W.** *Der Glaubensbegriff des Paulus.* Leipzig: Heinsius, 1932. **Murphy-O'Connor, J.,** ed. *Paul and Qumran.* London: Chapman, 1968. **Mussies, G.** *Dio Chrysostom and the New Testament.* London: Brill, 1972. **Mussner, F.** "Heil für Alle: Der Grundgedanke des Römerbriefes." *Kairos* 23 (1981) 207–214. ———. *Tractate on the Jews: The Significance of Judaism for Christian Faith.* London: SPCK; Philadelphia: Fortress, 1984. **Neirynck, F.** "Paul and the Sayings of Jesus." *L'Apôtre Paul: Personnalité, style et conception du ministère.* Ed. A. Vanhoye. Leuven University, 1986. 265–321. **Neusner, J.** *From Politics to Piety.* Englewood Cliffs, NJ: Prentice-Hall, 1973. ———. *Judaism: The Evidence of the Mishnah.* University of Chicago, 1981. **Newton, M.** *The Concept of Purity at Qumran and in the Letters of Paul.* SNTSMS 53. Cambridge University, 1985. **Nilsson, M. P.** *Geschichte der griechischen Religion.* Munich, 1950. **Noack, B.** "Current and Backwater in the Epistle to the Romans." *ST* 19 (1965) 155–66. **Norden, E.** *Agnostos Theos* (1913). Darmstadt, [4] 1956. **O'Brien, P. T.** *Introductory Thanksgivings in the Letters of Paul.* NovTSup 49. Leiden: Brill, 1977. **Ortkemper, F. J.** *Leben aus dem Glauben: Christliche Grundhaltungen nach Römer 12–13.* Münster: Aschendorff, 1980. **Osten-Sacken, P. von der.** *Römer 8 als Beispiel paulinischer Soteriologie.* FRLANT 112. Göttingen: Vandenhoeck & Ruprecht, 1975. **Patte, D.** *Paul's Faith and the Power of the Gospel: A Structural Introduction to the Pauline Letters.* Philadelphia: Fortress, 1983. 232–96. **Paulsen, H.** *Überlieferung und Auslegung in Röm 8.* WMANT 43. Neukirchen: Neukirchener Verlag, 1974. **Penna, R.** "L'évolution de l'attitude de Paul envers les Juifs." *L'Apôtre Paul: Personnalité, style et conception du ministère.* Ed. A. Vanhoye. Leuven University, 1986. 390–421. **Perkins, P.** *Love Commands in the New Testament.* New York: Paulist Press, 1982. **Perrin, N.** *The New Testament: An Introduction.* New York: Harcourt, 1974. 106–114. **Piper, J.** *The Justification of God: An Exegetical and Theological Study of Romans 9:1–23.* Grand Rapids: Baker, 1983. **Pohlenz, M.** "Paulus und die Stoa." *ZNW* 42 (1949) 69–104. Repr. in *Das Paulusbild in der neueren deutschen Forschung,* ed. K. H. Rengstorf. Darmstadt: Wissenschaftliche Buchgesellschaft, 1969. 522–64. **Poland, F.** *Geschichte des griechischen Vereinswesens* (1909). Repr. Leipzig, 1967. **Porter, C. L.** "A New Paradigm for Reading Romans: Dialogue Between Christians and Jews." *Encounter* 39 (1978) 257–72. **Prat, F.** *The Theology of Saint Paul.* 2 vols. London: Burns & Oates, 1927. **Prümm, K.** "Zur Struktur des Römerbriefes." *ZKT* 72 (1950) 333-49. **Räisänen, H.** *Paul and the Law.* WUNT 29. Tübingen: Mohr, 1983. ———. *The Torah and Christ.* Helsinki: Finnish Exegetical Society, 1986. **Reicke, B.** "Paulus über das Gesetz." *TZ* 41 (1985) 237–57. **Reitzenstein, R.** *Hellenistic Mystery-Religions* (1910; [3] 1927). Pittsburgh: Pickwick, 1978. **Rengstorf, K. H.** "Paulus und die älteste römische Christenheit." *SE* 2 (1964) 447–64. **Reumann, J.,** et al. *Righteousness in the New Testament.* Philadelphia: Fortress/New York: Paulist Press, 1982. **Reynolds, J.,** and **Tannenbaum, R.** *Jews and Godfearers at Aphrodisias.* Cambridge Philological Society Supp. 12. Cambridge, 1987. **Rhyne, C. T.** *Faith Establishes the Law.* SBLDS 55. Chico: Scholars Press, 1981. **Richardson, P.** *Israel in the Apostolic Church.* SNTSMS 10. Cambridge University, 1969. **Ridderbos, H.** *Paul: An Outline of his Theology.* Grand Rapids: Eerdmans, 1975. **Robinson, D. W. B.** "The Priesthood of Paul in the Gospel of Hope." In *Reconciliation and Hope,* FS L. L. Morris, ed. R. J. Banks. Exeter: Paternoster, 1974. 231–45. **Robinson, H. W.** *The Christian Doctrine of Man.* Edinburgh: T. & T. Clark, [3] 1926. 104–136. **Robinson, J. A. T.** *The Body.* London: SCM, 1952. **Roller, O.** *Das Formular der paulinischen Briefe.* Stuttgart, 1933. **Rowland, C.** *The Open Heaven.* London: SPCK, 1982. **Russell, D. S.** *The Method and Message of Jewish Apocalyptic.* London: SCM, 1964. **Sahlin, H.** "Einige Textemendationen zum Römerbrief." *TZ* 9 (1953) 92–100. **Sanders, E. P.** *Paul and Palestinian Judaism.* London: SCM, 1977. ———. "On the Question of Fulfilling the Law in Paul and Rabbinic Judaism." In *Donum Gentilicium,* FS D. Daube, ed. C. K. Barrett et al. Oxford: Clarendon, 1978.

103–126. ⸺. "Paul's Attitude toward the Jewish People." *USQR* 33 (1978) 175–87. (With "A Response" by K. Stendahl, 189–91.) ⸺. "Jesus, Paul, and Judaism." *ANRW* II.25.1 (1982) 390–450. ⸺. *Paul, the Law, and the Jewish People.* Philadelphia: Fortress, 1983. ⸺. *Jesus and Judaism.* London: SCM, 1985. **Sandmel, S.** *The Genius of Paul* (1958). Philadelphia: Fortress, 1979. **Schechter, S.** *Aspects of Rabbinic Theology* (1909). New York: Schocken, 1961. **Schelkle, K. H.** *Paulus.* Darmstadt: Wissenschaftliche Buchgesellschaft, 1981. **Schenke, H. M.** "Aporien im Römerbrief." *TLZ* 92 (1967) 882–88. **Schlier, H.** *Die Zeit der Kirche.* Freiburg: Herder, 1955, [5]1972. ⸺. "Von den Juden. Röm 2:1–29." *Zeit.* 38–47. ⸺. *Grundzüge einer paulinischen Theologie.* Freiburg: Herder, 1978. **Schmithals, W.** *Der Römerbrief als historisches Problem.* Gütersloh: Güterlsoher, 1975. ⸺. *Die theologische Anthropologie des Paulus: Auslegung von Röm 7.17–8.39.* Stuttgart: Kohlhammer, 1980. **Schnabel, E. J.** *Law and Wisdom from Ben Sira to Paul.* WUNT 2.16. Tübingen: Mohr, 1985. **Schoeps, H. J.** *Paul: The Theology of the Apostle in the Light of Jewish Religious History.* London: Lutterworth, 1961. **Schrage, W.** *Die konkreten Einzelgebote in der paulinischen Paränese.* Güterlsoh: Gütersloher, 1961. **Schweitzer, A.** *The Mysticism of Paul the Apostle.* London: Black, [2]1953. **Scroggs, R.** *The Last Adam: A Study in Pauline Anthropology.* Oxford: Blackwell, 1966. ⸺. "Paul as Rhetorician: Two Homilies in Romans 1–11." In *Jews, Greeks and Christians,* FS W. D. Davies, ed. R. Hamerton-Kelly et al. Leiden: Brill, 1976. 271–98. **Segundo, J. L.** *The Humanist Christology of Paul.* New York: Orbis; London: Sheed & Ward, 1986. **Selwyn, E. G.** *The First Epistle of St Peter.* London: Macmillan, 1947. 365–466. **Snodgrass, K.** "Spheres of Influence: A Possible Solution to the Problem of Paul and the Law." *JSNT* 32 (1988) 93–113. **Stanley, D. M.** *Christ's Resurrection in Pauline Soteriology.* AnBib 13. Rome: Pontifical Biblical Institute, 1961. 160–99. **Stendahl, K.** "The Apostle Paul and the Introspective Conscience of the West." *HTR* 56 (1963) 199–215. Repr. in *Paul,* 78–96. ⸺. *Paul among Jews and Gentiles.* London: SCM, 1977. **Stowers, S. K.** *The Diatribe and Paul's Letter to the Romans.* SBLDS 57. Chico: Scholars Press, 1981. **Strecker, G.** "Befreiung und Rechtfertigung: Zur Stellung der Rechtfertigungslehre in der Theologie des Paulus." *Eschaton und Historie.* Göttingen: Vandenhoeck & Ruprecht, 1979. 229–59. **Stuhlmacher, P.** *Gerechtigkeit Gottes bei Paulus.* FRLANT 87. Göttingen: Vandenhoeck & Ruprecht, 1966. ⸺. *Das paulinische Evangelium.* FRLANT 95. Göttingen: Vandenhoeck & Ruprecht, 1968. ⸺. *Versöhnung, Gesetz und Gerechtigkeit: Aufsätze zur biblischen Theologie.* Göttingen: Vandenhoeck & Ruprecht, 1981. ⸺. "Das Gesetz als Thema biblischer Theologie." *Versöhnung.* 136–65. ⸺. "Sühne oder Versöhnung?" In *Die Mitte des Neuen Testaments,* FS E. Schweizer, ed. U. Luz and H. Weder. Göttingen: Vandenhoeck & Ruprecht, 1983. 291–316. ⸺. "Jesustradition im Römerbrief?" *ThBeit* 14 (1983) 240–50. ⸺. "Paul's Understanding of the Law in the Letter to the Romans." *SEÅ* 50 (1985) 87–104. **Suhl, A.** *Paulus und seine Briefe.* SNT 11. Gütersloh: Gütersloher, 1975. **Synofzik, E.** *Die Gerichts- und Vergeltungsaussagen bei Paulus.* Göttingen: Vandenhoeck & Ruprecht, 1977. **Theissen, G.** *The Social Setting of Pauline Christianity.* Edinburgh: T. & T. Clark, 1982. **Theobald, M.** *Die überströmende Gnade: Studien zu einem paulinischen Motivfeld.* Würzburg: Echter, 1982. **Thüsing, W.** *Per Christum in Deum: Das Verhältnis der Christozentrik zur Theozentrik.* Münster: Aschendorff, 1965; [3]1986. **Thyen, H.** *Studien zur Sündenvergebung im Neuen Testament und seinem alttestamentlichen und jüdischen Voraussetzungen.* FRLANT 96. Göttingen: Vandenhoeck & Ruprecht, 1970. **Travis, S. H.** *Christ and the Judgment of God: Divine Retribution in the New Testament.* Basingstoke: Marshall, 1986. **Trebilco, P.** *Studies on Jewish Communities in Asia Minor.* Ph.D. Diss., Durham University, 1987. **Trench, R. C.** *Synonyms of the New Testament* ([9]1880). Repr. Grand Rapids: Eerdmans, 1953. **Trocmé, E.** "The Jews As Seen by Paul and Luke." In *"To See Ourselves As Others See Us": Christians, Jews, "Others" in Late Antiquity,* ed. J. Neusner and E. S. Frerichs. Chico: Scholars Press, 1985. 145–61. **Vielhauer, P.** *Geschichte der urchristlichen Literatur.* Berlin: de Gruyter, 1975. 174–

190. ———. "Paulus und das Alte Testament." *Oikodome: Aufsätze zum Neuen Testament* 2. Munich: Kaiser, 1979. 196–228. **Watson, F.** *Paul, Judaism and the Gentiles.* SNTSMS 56. Cambridge University, 1986. **Watson, N. M.** "Simplifying the Righteousness of God: A Critique of J. C. O'Neill's *Romans.*" *SJT* 30 (1977) 453–69. **Wegenast, K.** *Das Verständnis der Tradition bei Paulus und in den Deuteropaulinen.* WMANT 8. Neukirchen: Neukirchener Verlag, 1962. **Wengst, K.** *Christlogische Formeln und Lieder des Urchristentums.* Gütersloh: Gütersloher, 1972. **White, J. L.** *Studies in Ancient Letter Writing.* Semeia 22. Chico: Scholars Press, 1981. ———. "Saint Paul and the Apostolic Letter Tradition." *CBQ* 45 (1983) 433–44. **Whiteley, D. E. H.** *The Theology of St Paul.* Oxford: Blackwell, 1964. **Wiefel, W.** "The Jewish Community in Ancient Rome and the Origins of Roman Christianity." *Judaica* 26 (1970). ET in Donfried, *Romans Debate,* 100–119. **Wikenhauser, A.** *New Testament Introduction.* Freiburg: Herder, 1958. 398–411. **Wilckens, U.** *Rechtfertigung als Freiheit.* Paulusstudien. Neukirchen: Neukirchener Verlag, 1974. ———. "Über Abfassungszweck und Aufbau des Römerbriefes." *Rechtfertigung.* 110–70. ———. "Christologie und Anthropologie im Zusammenhang der paulinischen Rechtfertigungslehre." *ZNW* 67 (1976) 64–82. **Williams, S. K.** "The 'Righteousness of God' in Romans." *JBL* 99 (1980) 241–90. **Wright, N. T.** *The Messiah and the People of God.* D.Phil. Diss., Oxford University, 1980. **Wuellner, W.** "Paul's Rhetoric of Argumentation in Romans." *CBQ* 38 (1976). Repr. in Donfried, *Romans Debate,* 152–74. **Zahn, T.** *Introduction to the New Testament.* Edinburgh: T. & T. Clark, 1909. 1:352–438. **Zeller, D.** *Juden und Heiden in der Mission des Paulus: Studien zum Römerbrief.* Stuttgart: KBW, 1973. ———. "Der Zusammenhang von Gesetz und Sünde in Römerbrief: Kritischer Nachvollzug der Auslegung von Ulrich Wilckens." *TZ* 38 (1982) 193–212. **Ziesler, J. A.** *The Meaning of Righteousness in Paul.* SNTSMS 20. Cambridge University, 1972. ———. "Some Recent Works on the Letter to the Romans." *ER* 12 (1985) 96–101.

Commentary Bibliography

M. Luther. Lectures (1515–16). ET, ed. W. Pauck. London: SCM, 1961. **J. Calvin** (1540). ET Edinburgh: Oliver & Boyd, 1961. **J. A. Bengel** (1742). ET Edinburgh: T. & T. Clark, 1866. **J. J. Wettstein.** Ἡ Καινὴ Διαθήκη. Amsterdam, 1752. **F. Godet.** (1879). ET 2 vols. Edinburgh: T. & T. Clark, 1880–81. **E. H. Gifford.** London: Murray, 1886. **J. B. Lightfoot.** *Notes on the Epistles of St Paul.* London: Macmillan, 1895. **W. Sanday** and **A. C. Headlam.** ICC. Edinburgh: T. & T. Clark, 1895; [5]1902. **J. Denney.** EGT. Vol. 2. London: Hodder & Stoughton, 1900. **H. Lietzmann.** HNT. Tübingen: Mohr, 1906; [4]1933. **A. Jülicher.** In *Die Schriften des Neuen Testaments,* vol. 2. Göttingen: Vandenhoeck & Ruprecht, 1910; [3]1917. **T. Zahn.** Leipzig, 1910; [3]1925. **E. Kühl.** Leipzig: Quelle & Meyer, 1913. **K. Barth.** (1919; [6]1929). ET Oxford University, 1933. **M.-J. Lagrange.** EB. Paris: Gabalda, [2]1922; [6]1950. **C. H. Dodd.** Moffatt. London: Hodder & Stoughton, 1932. **P. Althaus.** NTD 6. Göttingen: Vandenhoeck & Ruprecht, 1932; [10]1966. **A. Schlatter.** *Gottes Gerechtigkeit.* Stuttgart: Calwer, 1935. **K. E. Kirk.** CB. Oxford: Clarendon, 1937. **E. Brunner.** (1938, 1956). ET London: Lutterworth, 1959. **E. Gaugler.** 2 vols. Zürich: Zwingli, 1945, [2]1958; 1952. **E. F. Scott.** London: SCM, 1947. **A. Nygren.** (1951). ET London: SCM, 1952. **J. Knox.** IB 9 (1954). **W. Barclay.** Edinburgh: St Andrew, 1955. **V. Taylor.** London: Epworth, 1956. **K. Barth.** *A Shorter Commentary on Romans* (1956). ET London: SCM, 1959. **C. K. Barrett.** London: Black, 1957. **F. J. Leenhardt.** CNT (1957). ET London: Lutterworth, 1961. **O. Michel.** KEK. Göttingen: Vandenhoeck & Ruprecht, [11]1957; [14]1978. **O. Kuss.** 3 vols. Regensburg: Pustet, 1957, 1959, 1978. **J. Murray.** NICNT. 2 vols. Grand Rapids: Eerdmans, 1959, 1965. **T. W. Manson.** In *PCB* (1962) 940–53. **F. F. Bruce.** TNTC. London: Tyndale, 1963. **H. W. Schmidt.** THKNT. Berlin: Evangelische, 1963. **J. A. Fitzmyer.** In *JBC* (1968) 291–331. **B. M. Metzger.** *A Textual Commentary on the Greek New Testament.* London: UBS, 1971; corr. 1975. **M. Black.** NCB. London: Oliphants, 1973. **E. Käsemann.** HNT (1973). ET London: SCM, 1980. **J. C. O'Neill.** Harmondsworth: Penguin, 1975. **C. E. B. Cranfield.** ICC. 2 vols. Edinburgh: T. & T. Clark, 1975, 1979. **H. Schlier.** HTKNT. Freiburg: Herder, 1977. **U. Wilckens.** EKK. 3 vols. Zürich: Benziger/Neukirchen: Neukirchener Verlag, 1978, 1980, 1982. **J. A. T. Robinson.** *Wrestling with Romans.* London: SCM, 1979. **R. A. Harrisville.** Minneapolis: Augsburg, 1980. **W. Hendriksen.** 2 vols. Edinburgh: Banner of Truth, 1980, 1981. **R. Pesch.** Würzburg: Echter, 1983. **A. Maillot.** Paris: Le Centurion, 1984. **P. Achtemeier.** *Interpretation.* Atlanta: John Knox, 1985. **D. Zeller.** RNT. Regensburg: Pustet, 1985. **B. Byrne.** *Reckoning with Romans.* Wilmington: Glazier, 1986. **J. P. Heil.** *Romans—Paul's Letter of Hope.* AnBib 112. Rome: Biblical Institute Press, 1987. ———. *Paul's Letter to the Romans: A Reader-Response Commentary.* New York: Paulist Press, 1987.

WORD
BIBLICAL
COMMENTARY

Romans 9-16

V. The Righteousness of God—From God's Faithfulness: The Outworking of the Gospel in Relation to Israel (9:1–11:36)

Bibliography

Aageson, J. W. "Scripture and Structure in the Development of the Argument in Romans 9–11." *CBQ* 48 (1986) 265–89. ———. "Typology, Correspondence, and the Application of Scripture in Romans 9–11." *JSNT* 31 (1987) 51–72. **Barth, M.** *The People of God.* JSNTSupp 5. Sheffield: JSOT, 1983. 29–49. **Beck, N. A.** *Mature Christianity.* 66–71. **Beker, J. C.** *Paul.* 328–47. **Betz, O.** "Die heilsgeschichtliche Rolle Israels bei Paulus." *ThBeit* 9 (1978) 1–21. **Blackman, E. C.** "Divine Sovereignty and Missionary Strategy in Romans 9–11." *CJT* 11 (1965) 124–34. **Caird, G. B.** "Predestination—Romans 9–11." *ExpT* 68 (1957) 324–27. **Campbell, W. S.** "Freedom." **Cerfaux, L.** "Le privilège d'Israel selon S. Paul." *ETL* 17 (1940) 5–26. **Dahl, N. A.** "The Future of Israel." In *Studies.* 137–58. **Davies, W. D.** "Paul and the People of Israel." *NTS* 24 (1977–78) 4–39. Reprinted in *Studies.* 123–52. **Dinkler, E.** "The Historical and Eschatological Israel in Romans Chapters 9–11: A Contribution to the Problem of Predestination and Individual Responsibility." *JR* 36 (1956) 109–27. **Dinter, P. E.** *The Remnant of Israel and the Stone of Stumbling in Zion according to Paul (Romans 9–11).* Ph.D. diss., Union Theological Seminary, 1979. **Eckert, J.** "Paulus und Israel." *TTZ* 87 (1978) 1–13. **Eichholz, G.** *Theologie.* 284–301. **Evans, C. A.** "Paul and the Hermeneutics of 'True Prophecy': A Study of Rom 9–11." *Bib* 65 (1984) 560–70. **Evans, D. D.** "The Mystery of Israel." *CJT* 4 (1958) 30–36. **Flesseman-van Leer, E.** "The Significance of the Mystery of Israel for the Church." *CJT* 3 (1957) 5–14. **Gager, J. G.** *Origins.* 223–25. **Getty, M. A.** "Paul on the Covenants and the Future of Israel." *BTB* 17 (1987) 92–99. **Goppelt, L.** *Jesus.* 151–54. **Gorday, P.** *Principles of Patristic Exegesis: Romans 9–11 in Origen, John Chrysostom, and Augustine.* New York/Toronto: Mellen, 1983. **Grässer, E.** "Zwei Heilswege? Zum theologischen Verhältnis von Israel und Kirche" (1981). *Der Alte Bund im Neuen. Exegetische Studien zur Israelfrage im Neuen Testament.* Tübingen: Mohr, 1985. 212–30. ———. "Christen und Juden. Neutestamentliche Erwägungen zu einem aktuellen Thema" (1982). In *Bund.* 271–89. **Güttgemanns, E.** "Heilsgeschichte bei Paulus oder Dynamik des Evangeliums. Zur strukturellen Relevanz von Röm 9–11 für die Theologie des Römerbriefes." In *Studia linguistica Neotestamentica.* Munich, 1971. 34–58. **Haacker, K.** "Paulus und das Judentum." *Judaica* 33 (1977) 161–77. ———. "Das Evangelium Gottes und die Erwählung Israels." *ThBeit* 13 (1982) 59–72. **Hofius, O.** "Das Evangelium und Israel. Erwägungen zu Römer 9–11." *ZTK* 83 (1986) 297–324. **Hübner, H.** *Gottes Ich und Israel. Zum Schriftgebrauch des Paulus in Römer 9–11.* Göttingen: Vandenhoeck & Ruprecht, 1984. **Klappert, B.** "Traktat für Israel (Römer 9–11)." In *Jüdische Existenz und die Erneuerung der christlichen Theologie,* ed. M. Stöhr. Munich, 1981. 58–137. **Klein, G.** "Präliminarien zum Thema 'Paulus und die Juden.'" In *Rechtfertigung,* FS E. Käsemann, ed. J. Friedrich et al. Tübingen: Mohr, 1976. 229–43. **Kümmel, W. G.** "Die Probleme von Römer 9–11 in der gegenwärtigen Forschungslage." In *Israelfrage,* ed. Lorenzi. 13–33. **Lindars, B.** "The Old Testament and Universalism in Paul." *BJRL* 69 (1987) 511–27. **Lorenzi, L. de,** ed. *Die Israelfrage nach Römer 9–11.* Rome: Abtei von St Paul, 1977. **Lübking, H.-M.** *Paulus und Israel im Römerbrief. Eine Untersuchung zu Römer 9–11.* Frankfurt: Lang, 1986. **Luedemann, G.** *Paulus und das Judentum.* Munich: Kaiser, 1983. **Maier, F. W.** *Israel in der Heilsgeschichte nach Röm 9–11.* Münster: Aschendorff, 1929. **Maillot,**

A. "Essai sur les citations vétérotestamentaires contenues dans Romains 9 à 11, ou comment se servir de la torah pour montrer que le 'Christ est la fin de la Torah.'" *ETR* 57 (1982) 55–73. **Mayer, B.** *Unter Gottes Heilsratschluss. Prädestinationsaussagen bei Paulus.* Würzburg: Echter, 1974. Esp. 167–313. **Müller, C.** *Gerechtigkeit.* **Munck, J.** *Christ and Israel: An Interpretation of Romans 9–11.* Philadelphia: Fortress, 1967. **Mussner, F.** "Gesetz-Abraham-Israel." *Kairos* 25 (1983) 200–222. ———. *Tractate.* Esp. 208–12. **Österreicher, J. M.** "Israel's Misstep and Her Rise. The Dialectic of God's Saving Design in Rom 9–11." *SPCIC* 1:317–27. **Peterson, E.** *Die Kirche aus Juden und Heiden.* Salzburg: Pustet, 1933. **Plag, C.** *Israels Wege zum Heil. Eine Untersuchung zu Römer 9 bis 11.* Stuttgart: Calwer, 1969. **Radermakers, J.** and **Sonnet, J.-P.** "Israel et l'Eglise." *NRT* 107 (1985) 675–97. **Räisänen, H.** "Römer 9–11: Analyse eines geistigen Ringens." *ANRW* 2.25.4 (1987) 2891–939. **Refoulé, F.** "Unité de l'Epître aux Romains et histoire du salut." *RSPT* 71 (1987) 219–42. **Reichrath, H.** "Römer 9–11. Ein Stiefkind christlicher Theologie und Verkündigung." *Judaica* 23 (1967) 160–81. **Rese, M.** "Die Rettung der Juden nach Römer 11." In *L'Apôtre Paul,* ed. A. Vanhoye. BETL 73. Leuven University (1986) 422–30. ———. "Israel und Kirche in Römer 9." *NTS* 34 (1988) 208–17. **Richardson, P.** *Israel.* 126–36. **Robinson, D. W. B.** "The Salvation of Israel in Romans 9–11." *RTR* 26 (1967) 81–96. **Ruether, R. R.** *Faith and Fratricide: The Theological Roots of Anti-Semitism.* New York: Seabury, 1974. 95–107. **Schmitt, R.** *Gottesgerechtigkeit-Heilsgeschichte. Israel in der Theologie des Paulus.* Frankfurt: Lang, 1984. **Schoeps, H. J.** *Paul.* 235–45. **Senft, C.** "L'élection d'Israel et la justification (Romains 9 à 11)." In *L'Évangile, hier et aujourd'hui,* FS F.-J. Leenhardt. Geneva, 1968 131–42. **Siegert, F.** *Argumentation bei Paulus, gezeigt an Röm 9–11.* Tübingen: Mohr, 1985. **Theobald, M.** *Gnade.* 129–66. **Villers, J. L. de.** "Kirche und Israel nach Röm 9–11." *Kairos* 29 (1987) 1–22. ———. "The Salvation of Israel according to Romans 9–11." *Neot* 15 (1981) 119–221. **Vischer, W.** "Das Geheimnis Israels. Eine Erklärung der Kapitel 9–11 des Römerbriefs." *Judaica* 6 (1950) 81–132. **Walter, N.** "Zur Interpretation von Römer 9–11." *ZTK* 81 (1984) 172–95. **Watson, F.** *Paul.* 160–73. **Zeller, D.** *Juden.* 108–37.

Introduction

Chaps. 9–11 are a carefully composed and rounded unit with a clear begin-ning (9:1–5) and end (11:33–36), and with 9:6a giving the text or thesis to be expounded (see on 9:6). It both poses the challenge—has God's word failed?; and determines the style of the response—an exposition which draws heavily on scripture and which may legitimately be entitled a midrash. The exposition is developed step by step with each claim regarding God's saving purpose as revealed in his word having a *two-sided* character which builds up to the solution of the problem.

The problem is that God's word of call and promise to Abraham has evi-dently not been fulfilled (as Paul counts fulfillment) in his own people the Jews. But this is not brought to the surface immediately. (1) Initially the focus is on the two-sided nature of God's choice: of only some of Abraham's offspring to bear the promise and election (9:6–13) and experience of his mercy (9:15–18, 23), but also of others as expressions of his wrath (9:13–23). (2) The outworking of this in the first instance is a fulfillment of the promise in Gentiles as well as Jews, in a Jewish remnant as well as Gentiles (9:24–29). This leads into (3) a comparison of the twofold response to God's word—an Israel which has missed the way (9:30–10:5, 18–21), and Gentiles who have responded in faith (9:30; 10:6–17). (4) In a brief recapitulation the conclusions of the preceding paragraphs in relation to Israel are recalled: only a remnant chosen (11:1–6), and the rest hardened (11:7–10). (5) Israel's fall has had a positive result in salvation for the Gentiles (11:11–16), but also serves as a standing warning to Gentiles lest they make a similar mistake (11:17–24). (6) The climax is the unveiling of the overall purpose of God: to use Israel's failure as an opening of the gospel to Gentiles with a view to bringing Israel into still greater blessing in the end (11:25–32), in which the recall of key words from earlier in the discussion (ἐκλογή, κλῆσις, and ἐλεέω/ ἔλεος) provides a fitting rounding off of the whole argument.

The sequence and structure of the discussion thus reflects the two-sided nature of God's purpose:

(1) Election of mercy // purpose of wrath;
(2) Gentiles called too // only a remnant of Israel;
(3) Righteousness from the law // righteousness from faith;
(4) A remnant according to grace // the rest hardened;
(5) Jewish failure—the reason // Gentile failure—a warning;
(6) Israel hardening—Gentile incoming // Gentile fullness—Israel salvation.

Other characteristic features include the use of larger conclusions than the preceding discussion warrants to provide a transition to the next phase of the argument (particularly 9:13, 18 and 11:7–10, 16), early hints of what is to come (particularly 9:15, 23 → 11:30–32; 9:18, 22–23 → 11:7–10, 25; 9:33 → 11:11–12; and 10:19 → 11:13–14), the thematic link provided by the hope of "salvation" (9:27; 10:1, 9, 10, 13; 11:11, 14, 26), and the resumption of the diatribe style (9:14, 19–24, 30–32; 11:1–4, 11, as well as 11:17–24). Also striking is Paul's personal involvement, both in the problem he poses and in its solution (9:1–3; 10:1; 11:13–14), and the more epistolary character of this section (Dahl, "Israel," 139–41); "the inner unity of Paul's mission and theology is nowhere more obvious than in Rom 9–11" (Dahl, "Missionary Theology," 86).

It is important to realize that these chapters are not an excursus, or an appendix to an argument already complete in itself (e.g., Goppelt, *Jesus,* 153; Stendahl, *Paul,* 4; Kümmel, "Probleme," 15–17; Wilckens; Beker, *Paul,* 87; against SH; Barth, *Shorter*; Beare, *Paul,* 97; Refoulé, "Unité"; but Noack's (164) description of chaps. 5–8 as "backwater" is too strong). The problem posed in 9:6 and 11:1 is in fact the problem raised by the indictment of 1:18–2:29 and expressed in 3:1, 3 (note not least the continuity of concern in 1:4, 3:2, 21, and 9:6; Robinson, *Wrestling,* 109, suggests that chaps. 9–11 can be set in parallel to the whole of chap. 3). Its initial resolution in more general terms (3:21–5:11) is the basis for its resolution in relation to Israel in particular (9:30–10:13). In effect 3:21–8:39 is the first part of Paul's response to 1:18–2:29 and only serves to pose the same problem more sharply: for how could God be trusted to be so faithful to his own (8:31–39) if he had been unfaithful to Israel? (see on 8:31). "Romans 1–8 create the problem to which 9–11 is the solution . . . 1–8 is ultimately incomprehensible without 9–11, and vice versa" (Wright, *Messiah,* 220). The discussion, we might say, still revolves round the central motif enunciated in 1:16—salvation "to Jew first, but also to Gentile." The problem was that in the transition of the ages, Israel by not accepting Christ had put themselves behind the Gentiles (9:30–31; 11:7), had in effect been siding with Adam rather than with Christ (5:12–21; see on 11:30). How to square this with God's call and promise to Abraham was the issue to which the whole of the preceding exposition had been building up. Particularly noticeable is the deliberate recall of key motifs from 1:18–3:20 and 5:12–21 in the climactic summary of 11:30–32 (see on 11:25–32 *Form and Structure*). See also Lübking, 21–51.

The degree to which these chapters depend on the preceding argument for their coherence lessens the likelihood that Paul here uses a completely preformed unit, a diatribe or missionary sermon (as suggested by Dodd; cf. Kirk). On the other hand, Paul had probably rehearsed the arguments in so many discussions and expositions that it was more a matter of shaping familiar material than of *de novo* composition. In the same way the recognition of the coherence and climactic character of these chapters in relation to the argument of Romans as a whole strongly reinforces the now widespread objection against the older attempts to interpret chaps. 9–11 primarily as the exposition of a dogma of predestination in relation to the individual (e.g., SH, Munck; "one of the most confused sections of the Epistle"—W. L. Knox, *Jerusalem*, 352 n.17; the criticism applies only partially to Dinkler, but more so to G. Maier, *Mensch;* see 9:6–29 *Bibliography*). The theme is Israel's destiny, not the doctrine of justification illustrated by Israel (Schlier). So too we should hesitate to entitle this section "The Church and Israel" (as Eichholz, *Theologie* 10. Kap.; Rese, "Röm 9:4 f." and "Israel"; Radermakers and Sonnet) or "church and synagogue" (as effectively Peterson), since that is precisely to misrepresent Paul's point; the church is not a separate entity from Israel, but, if anything, a subset of Israel (branches grafted into the tree of Israel). The true theme of chaps. 9–11 is God and Israel (cf. Althaus, 101; Gaugler, 2:23–27; Davies, "Israel"; Beker, *Paul,* 77; Hübner, *Israel*). Even so it is a fair deduction (despite the misgivings of Kümmel, "Probleme," 26) that the issues discussed were of considerable moment for the Roman readership (see particularly Eichholz, *Theologie*, 290–91; Campbell, "God and Israel," 38–41; and further *Introduction* §2).

Particularly striking is the midrashic interweaving into the three chapters of OT quotations, which comprise more than 30 percent of the whole (cf. Ellis, "Exegetical Patterns," 218; Stegner; Aageson, "Scripture," 286–87). More than half the OT quotations in Romans come in chaps. 9–11, and about 40 percent of these are from Isaiah (see the analysis in Maillot, "Essai"). "The Old Testament becomes not only a support for the Pauline train of thought, but is itself the basis from which Paul argues" (Michel, 306). Not least in importance is the fact that scripture itself attests the two-sided character of God's dealings with his people, acting both as witness for Israel and accuser of Israel (Michel, 289; see also Evans, "True Prophecy"). Especially notable as regards structure is the use of scripture to sum up and underpin the first two main sections (9:6–29; 9:30–10:21) and the key role played by scripture in 11:1–10 and 11:26–27, as indeed also in the final hymn (11:33–36). The attempt to draw from more than one section of the scriptures (law, prophets, writings) is also evident in 9:12–13, 14–20, 10:5–13, 18–21, and 11:8–10. Lyonnet's suggestion ("Note") that chaps. 9–11 function as scripture proof for chaps. 5–8 (as chap. 4 does also for chaps. 1–3) does not, however, make much sense. On the originality of Paul's use of the OT here see Lindars, "Universalism."

A. What Then of Israel? Paul's Concern for His Kinspeople (9:1–5)

Bibliography

See also 9:1–11:36 *Bibliography*.

Bartsch, H. W. "Röm 9:5 und 1 Clem 32:4. Eine notwendige Konjektur im Römerbrief." *TZ* 21 (1965) 401–9. **Byrne, B.** *Sons*. 79–84. **Cullmann, O.** *Christology*. 306–14. **Dreyfus, F.** "Le passé et le présent d'Israel (Rom 9:1–5; 11:1–24)." In *Israelfrage*, ed. Lorenzi. 131–39. **Epp. E. J.** "Jewish-Gentile Continuity in Paul: Torah and/or Faith? (Romans 9:1–5)." *HTR* 79 (1986) = *Christians among Jews and Gentiles*, FS K. Stendahl, ed. G. W. E. Nickelsburg and G. W. MacRae. Philadelphia: Fortress, 1986. 80–90. **Grässer, E.** *Der Alte Bund im Neuen*. Tübingen: Mohr, 1985. 17–20. **Kuss, O.** "Zu Römer 9:5." In *Rechtfertigung*, FS E. Käsemann, ed. J. Friedrich et al. Tübingen: Mohr, 1976. 291–303. **Lorimer, W. L.** "Rom 9:3–5." *NTS* 13 (1966–67) 385–86. **Luz, U.** *Geschichtsverständnis*. 26–28, 269–74. **Metzger, B. M.** "The Punctuation of Rom 9:5." In *Christ and Spirit in the New Testament*, FS C. F. D. Moule, ed. B. Lindars and S. S. Smalley. London: Cambridge UP, 1973. 95–112. **Osten-Sacken, P. von der.** *Christian-Jewish Dialogue: Theological Foundations*. Philadelphia: Fortress, 1986. 19–40. **Piper, J.** *Justification*. 3–30. **Rese, M.** "Die Vorzüge Israels in Röm 9:4 f. und Eph 2:12." *TZ* 31 (1975) 211–22. **Roetzel, C.** "*Diathekai* in Romans 9:4." *Bib* 51 (1970) 377–90. **Stählin, G.** "Zum Gebrauch von Beteuerungsformeln im NT." *NovT* 5 (1962) 115–43. **Thüsing, W.** *Per Christum*. 147–50.

Translation

[1] *I speak the truth in Christ,*[a] *I do not lie, my conscience bearing me witness in the Holy Spirit,* [2] *that my grief is great and the anguish of my heart unceasing.* [3] *For I could pray that I myself be anathema from*[b] *the Christ for the sake of my brothers, my kinsmen in terms of the flesh,* [4] *inasmuch as they are Israelites: theirs is the adoption, the glory and the covenants,*[c] *the law, the service and the promises;*[d] [5] *theirs are the fathers and from them came the Christ insofar as the flesh is concerned.* [e]*God who is over all, may he be blessed for ever. Amen.*

Notes

[a] A natural expansion was to read Χριστῷ Ἰησοῦ, as some witnesses attest.

[b] Paul's language obviously caused some problems, prompting emendations like ὑπό or ὑπέρ for the ἀπό.

[c] The singular is strongly supported (by P46 and B among others), but the plural is the more likely as being the more unusual (see Metzger, *Textual Commentary*).

[d] The singular here is not so strongly attested (but also by P46), but in most cases was probably

the consequence of having already changed the more difficult διαθῆκαι to the singular, to give a consistent line of feminine singulars.

ᵉThere is no ground for the textual emendation ὧν ὁ (argued still by Lorimer and Bartsch, but see Black and Cranfield). For the discussion regarding punctuation see *Comment.*

Form and Structure

The care with which this opening paragraph is constructed is very clear. (1) The absence of any conjunction suggests that the reader of the letter was intended to pause at the end of 8:39 before beginning chap. 9 (see further on 9:1). (2) Vv 1–3 are set out in a sequence of doubled expressions that would increase the pathos and solemnity:

ἀλήθειαν λέγω	οὐ ψεύδομαι
τῆς συνειδήσεώς μου	ἐν πνεύματι ἁγίῳ
λύπη μεγάλη	ἀδιάλειπτος ὀδύνη
ἀνάθεμα	ἀπὸ τοῦ Χριστοῦ
τῶν ἀδελφῶν μου	τῶν συγγενῶν μου

Paul wants his audience to be in no doubt of the depth of his identity with and concern for his own people. (3) The enumeration of Israel's blessings in vv 4–5 is also carefully formulated, with Ἰσραηλῖται as the principal category to which the rest are subordinated in a ὧν . . . ὧν . . . ἐξ ὧν . . . sequence. The elegant double sequence of feminine nouns ending in -θεσια, -α, -αι would be pleasing to the ear:

υἱοθεσία	νομοθεσία
δόξα	λατρεία
διαθῆκαι	ἐπαγγελίαι

The small degree of artifice to achieve this effect is sufficient explanation for the somewhat unexpected appearance of the more elaborate forms, υἱοθεσία and ὀνομοθεσία, and quite possibly also for the plural διαθῆκαι (rather than διαθήκη, which would spoil the effect). More important, the words are evidently deliberately chosen to remind the predominantly gentile audience that the blessings they share are Israel's blessings; particularly υἱοθεσία (8:15, 23), δόξα (8:18, 21), and ἐπαγγελία (4:13–14, 16) (Luz, *Geschichtsverständnis,* 273; Lübking, 53–57). Significant also is the fact that Paul counts the law (νομοθεσία) as one of Israel's blessings. These structural considerations strongly suggest that Paul intended the final doxology as a benediction to God. A devout Jew would naturally end a recollection of God's goodness to Israel with such a benediction to Israel's God, and a Jewish Christian would naturally think of "the Christ/Messiah" as one of the most important examples of that goodness. On the possibility that Paul was using a traditional Jewish list see Michel, 295 and n.18, but see also Luz, *Geschichtsverständnis,* 270 n.13, and Piper, *Justification,* 6–7.

Comment

1 ἀλήθειαν λέγω ἐν Χριστῷ, οὐ ψεύδομαι, "I speak the truth in Christ, I do not lie." The absence of any conjunction possibly indicates that a pause was intended between 8:39 and 9:1 (but "a sharp, almost brutal break at 8:39" [Minear, 72] is too strong). When we add the absence of a joining particle with οὐ ψεύδομαι, the impression becomes overwhelming that Paul intended these words to be read slowly, with solemn emphasis. This is borne out by the double form of the protestation: "I am speaking honestly, I am not lying" (cf. particularly John 1:20); 1 Tim 2:7 may be a deliberate echo of this Pauline oath (Michel). On ἀλήθειαν λέγω cf. also 2 Cor 12:6.

For ἐν Χριστῷ see on 6:11. Here the implication is strong that Paul is speaking primarily in terms of religious experience (cf. v 2), not as a believer who is determined by the saving work of Christ, or "as a Christian" (NEB), or as a member of the body of Christ (as the phrase might elsewhere imply), but as one who is conscious of his dependence on the living Christ and on his authorization and approval (Dunn, *Jesus*, 324; cf. Käsemann). Paul elsewhere uses the denial form, οὐ ψεύδομαι, when speaking with feeling and some vehemence (2 Cor 11:31 and Gal 1:20), and as in these cases may be responding to actual criticisms leveled against him (so, e.g., Althaus, Knox); Minear (73) attempts to reconstruct the criticisms to which Paul responds.

συμμαρτυρούσης μοι τῆς συνειδήσεώς μου ἐν πνεύματι ἁγίῳ, "my conscience bearing me witness in the Holy Spirit." The phrase is in effect a combination of 2:15 and 8:16 (cf. also 1:9). The dative here (μοί) is more likely to be the recipient of the testimony (in contrast to 8:16; otherwise Cranfield)—conscience being perceived or rather experienced as a semi-autonomous faculty (not wholly autonomous—"my conscience") whose independence of testimony can be trusted (Jewett, *Anthropological Terms*, 445–46; see further on 2:15). This confidence is underlined by the ἐν πνεύματι ἁγίῳ, which is essentially charismatic in force, expressing a sense of basic inspiration informing and determining his conscience and the whole process of its witness bearing (cf. 2:29; 7:6; 8:9; 14:17; 15:16; 1 Cor 6:11; 12:3, 9, 13; 14:16; 2 Cor 6:6; Gal 6:1; Eph 2:18, 22; 3:5; 5:18; 6:18; Phil 1:27; 1 Thess 1:5; outside the Pauline writings, Mark 12:36 par.; Luke 2:27; 4:1; John 4:23–24; Acts 15:29; 19:21; Jude 20; Rev 1:10; 4:2; 17:3; 21:10). For πνεῦμα ἅγιον see on 1:4 and 5:5. In the ἐν phrases the ἐν does not have quite the same force, the former being more local (Adam Christology), the latter more instrumental ("inspired by"). An equivalence of "Christ" and "Spirit" should therefore not be derived from this verse (cf. Lietzmann), though, of course, the two phrases are two aspects of the basic condition of the believer for Paul—the being *in* Christ, sustained *by* the Spirit (cf. Schlatter; and see also on 8:9 and 10).

2 ὅτι λύπη μοί ἐστιν μεγάλη καὶ ἀδιάλειπτος ὀδύνη τῇ καρδίᾳ μου, "that my grief is great and the anguish of my heart unceasing." The doubling of λύπη ("grief, sorrow, pain of mind or spirit") and ὀδύνη ("mental pain") (see BGD) intensifies the already strong emotive force of the affidavit. It will be no accident that the only places in biblical Greek where the two words are associated are Isa 35:10 and 51:11:

> The ransomed of the Lord shall return,
> and come to Zion with singing;
> they shall obtain joy and gladness,
> and sorrow and sighing shall flee away.

In both verses LXX renders "sorrow" (יָגוֹן) by the double expression, ὀδύνη
καὶ λύπη. Paul probably has these passages in mind, with the implication
intended that this is the "sorrow" which will be banished when the ransomed
of the Lord return to the Lord and experience God's saving righteousness
(Isa 51:1–11). ἀδιαλείπτως, "constantly, unceasingly," increases the emotional
intensity still further (see also on 1:9). Likewise the use of καρδία reinforces
the depth of sincerity Paul seeks to convey (cf. 10:1; and see further on
1:21, 2:15, and 8:27). Such lament over Israel is a quite well-established
motif in Jewish and apocalyptic literature, particularly in reference to the
destruction of Jerusalem (Jer 4:19; 14:17; Lam; Dan 9:3; *T. Jud.* 23.1; *4
Ezra* 8.16; 10.24, 39; *2 Apoc. Bar.* 10.5; 35.1–3; 81.2; *Par. Jer.* 4.10; 6.17
[Schlier, Zeller]).

3 ηὐχόμην γὰρ ἀνάθεμα εἶναι αὐτὸς ἐγὼ ἀπὸ τοῦ Χριστοῦ, "for I could pray
that I myself be anathema from the Christ." For the construction see BDF
§405.1. ηὐχόμην . . . is difficult to render into English in a way which satisfacto-
rily represents the force and range of the Greek. εὔχομαι normally means
"pray" but can have the less directive sense "wish," which the absence of
the prefix προσ- allows (προσεύχομαι always means "pray"). This ambiguity is
evident elsewhere in NT usage (Acts 26:29—"would to God" renders it nicely;
27:29; 2 Cor 13:9; 3 John 2); see also BGD. The imperfect indicates a genuine
desire, but is not specific as to whether Paul thought of it is a realizable or
unrealizable desire (cf. Acts 25:22; Gal 4:20; BDF §359.2). The ambiguity is
not resolved by the ἀνάθεμα, since Paul could envisage being excluded from
Christ (cf. 8:13; 11:20–22; 1 Cor 9:27; 10:12; 2 Cor 13:5; Col 1:22–23; see
further on 11:21), but not that his sacrifice would avail on Israel's behalf
when Christ's had been inadequate (see below on ὑπέρ). See the full discussion
in Cranfield, who probably argues for greater precision than the Greek allows:
"I would pray (were it permissible for me so to pray and if the fulfilment of
such a prayer could benefit them). . . ." In cases like this it is always wise
to ask not simply, What did the author intend to say? but also, What could
the author have expected his readers to understand by this language? At
the very least we have an expression of passionate concern for and intensely
felt commitment to the future good of his fellow Jews. As Kuss wisely notes,
"One cannot measure the speech of the heart with the rules of logic"; this
is all the more obvious since the assertion follows so closely on the exultation
of 8:31–39, similarly emotive but differently directed. See also Michel.

ἀνάθεμα can mean something dedicated to God, literally "set up" in the
temple (as in Judg 16:19; 2 Macc 2:13; Luke 21:5 *v.l.;* see also BGD, and
TDNT 1:354). But in LXX it is used to translate חֵרֶם, devoted to God to be
destroyed, so that the sense "accursed" becomes dominant (Lev 27:28; Deut
7:26; 13:17 [LXX 18] ; Zech 14:11; the episode of Achan obviously making
a lasting impression [Josh 6:17–18; 7:1, 11–13; 22:20; 1 Chron 2:7]), and it
is this sense, also attested more widely (see MM) which Paul clearly has in
mind each time he uses the word (1 Cor 12:3; 16:22; Gal 1:8–9). That something more is in view than an ecclesiastical act of excommunication, or sacramental exclusion equivalent to the initiatory significance of baptism, is fairly
self-evident (cf. Leenhardt; against Käsemann), though חֵרֶם did come to be
used for excommunication in later Rabbinic Judaism (*TDNT* 7:849). See further below (ὑπέρ). Whether Paul intended his readers to understand that

Israel was ἀνάθεμα (Räisänen, "Römer 9–11," 2896–97) is more than open to question; the thrust of Paul's assertions here is in a different direction, and the failure of Israel to believe is brought to the fore much more slowly in these chapters and with much greater care.

The αὐτὸς ἐγώ increases the pathos, especially coming so soon after the glowing assurance of 8:38–39; Paul expresses a willingness to be personally isolated from the security of the community of God's love for the sake of his brothers. The ἀπὸ τοῦ Χριστοῦ also sharpens the contrast with 8:38–39, since it is precisely "in Christ" that this love of God is experienced (8:39). The definite article will be deliberate here—"the Messiah" (so v 5; see further on 7:4); Paul's anguish, its reason not yet specified, is that God's people have failed to recognize their Messiah.

ὑπὲρ τῶν ἀδελφῶν μου, "on behalf of my brothers." Paul echoes, not in language but in theme, the martyr aspiration that by sacrifice of oneself others, or indeed, as here, the nation as a whole, might be saved from God's wrath (so, classically, Moses [Exod 32:32], but also the mysterious Servant [Isa 53:5–6, 11; 4 *Macc.* 17.22; Josephus, *War* 5.419; see also on 5:6–7, and Str-B, 3:261]; cf. Black). Paul could certainly see his own ministry in terms of sharing in Christ's sufferings (see on 8:17) and as some sort of fulfillment of the Servant's role (see on 15:21), but that is somewhat different from what Paul has in mind here, and certainly any suggestion that Paul could conceive of such a martyrlike death as having the same effect or being more effective than Christ's has to be read in here (see particularly Michel, against Windisch). More to the fore, if anything, is the consciousness of playing a role of decisive salvation-history significance, like Moses (Munck, *Christ*, 29–30).

Elsewhere Paul always uses ἀδελφός for his fellow Christians (see on 1:13). So the reference here to his fellow Jews, though in accord with traditional Jewish usage (see again on 1:13), is distinctive. We may assume that Paul would not regard the two uses as antithetical; his becoming a member of the family of Christ (8:29) did not make him any the less a Jew (cf. Cranfield— "unbelieving Israel is within the elect community, not outside of it"); but see also below. In view of the double reference to "the Christ" of Jewish expectation in the context (vv 3, 5), it is possible that Deut 18:15, 18 was in the back of Paul's mind.

τῶν συγγενῶν μου κατὰ σάρκα, "my kinsmen in terms of the flesh." The unusualness of the reference of ἀδελφός (see above) is acknowledged and clarified by this addition. For συγγενής in this sense ("fellow countryman") see also 16:7, 11, 21, 2 Macc 5:6, Josephus, *War* 7.262 and *Ant.* 12.338; further Spicq, 838). κατὰ σάρκα here should not be regarded as neutral in meaning (as, e.g., Davies, *Paul*, 19; Cranfield; the modern translations as usual go out of their way to avoid the straightforward translation [e.g., NIV, "those of my own race"; Maillot, "of the same human race as me"] and thus lose the overtones in Paul's talk of "flesh"). On the contrary it contains its usual negative overtone for Paul in the sense that here it denotes a too restricted understanding of the family who are God's people ("perhaps a note of resignation: 'only in terms of the flesh'" [Schmidt]). The lopsided narrowing of the grace of God thereby implied expresses a κατὰ σάρκα mind-set as much as "the desires of the flesh" (cf. 2:28; 7:5; 8:5–6, 12–13); see also on 1:3 and 4:1.

4 οἵτινές εἰσιν Ἰσραηλῖται, "inasmuch as they are Israelites." For ὅστις see Moule, *Idiom Book*, 123–24; BGD, ὅστις 2—"Paul's anguish arises precisely from the fact that his people are Israelites . . . . If any name characterized Jewish self-understanding it was 'Israel.'" As the covenant name given to the one from whom the twelve tribes sprang (Gen 32:28; 35:10–12) it was their favorite self-designation, particularly the fuller phrase "children of Israel," as the regular recurrence throughout the OT indicates (e.g., Piper, 15, gives as examples Pss 25:22; 53:6; 130:7–8; Isa 49:3; 56:8; 66:20; Joel 2:27; 4:16 MT; Obad 20). K. G. Kuhn notes a significant distinction between Ἰσραήλ and Ἰουδαῖος in the postbiblical (intertestamental) period; "Israel" being the people's preferred name for itself (cf., e.g., Sir 17:17; *Jub.* 33.20; *Pss. Sol.* 14.5), while "Jew" was the name by which they were known to others (*TDNT* 3:359–65; borne out by the almost exclusive use of Ἰουδαῖος by Philo in *Flacc.* and *Legat.*; see also *TDNT* 3:369–72). Paul observes this distinction, having used Ἰουδαῖος exclusively in the opening chapters where "the Jews'" sense of distinctiveness over against others was in question (see *Introduction* §5.3.1, and on 2:17). But now he turns to speak of his people's own view of themselves, as himself an insider rather than as one looking in from outside (9:6, 27, 31; 10:19, 21; 11:1, 2, 7, 25, 26; 12 of the 19 occurrences of Ἰσραηλ [ίτης] in the Pauline corpus are found in chaps. 9–11); whereas Ἰουδαῖος (9 times in chaps. 1–3) occurs here only twice (9:24 and 10:12) (see also Goppelt, *Jesus,* 135–36). Ἰσραηλίτης is therefore deliberately chosen by Paul to evoke his people's sense of being God's elect, the covenant people of the one God. Whatever is made of Paul's talk of "Israel" in v 6, it should not be forgotten that he prefaces the whole discussion with the firm statement "the Jews are *Israelites*" (Vischer, 86); "they *are* Israelites" (Osten-Sacken, *Dialogue,* 20).

ὧν ἡ υἱοθεσία, "whose are the adoption." The use of υἱοθεσία is surprising, since it occurs nowhere in the LXX or in other Jewish writings of the period (also the rabbis—Str-B, 3:261). The choice, however, may have been determined by stylistic reasons (see *Form and Structure*), and the allusion to his people's national sense of having been chosen to be God's son(s) (e.g., Deut 14:1; Isa 43:6; Jer 31:9; Hos 1:10; Wisd Sol 9:7; *Jub.* 1.24–25) would be plain enough (see further on 1:3). Indeed the form, denoting adoptive rather than natural sonship, helps bring out the sense of election more clearly; see also on 8:15, same word, same privilege (see especially Byrne, *Sons,* 128; Piper, *Justification,* 16–18).

καὶ ἡ δόξα, "and the glory." The reference is clearly to "the glory of the Lord," particularly, no doubt, to the theophanies which had been Israel's special privilege as God's people (Exod 16:10; 24:15–17; 40:34–35; Lev 9:23; Num 14:10; etc.; see also on 1:21). Paul would no doubt be mindful of the eschatological promise that the divine glory would be more fully and more widely revealed through Israel to the nations (particularly Isa—35:2, 40:5, 59:19, 60:1–3, 66:18–19). The use of "the glory" as an absolute form (rather than "the glory of the Lord") is very unusual, but Paul may again have been motivated by stylistic concerns (see *Form and Structure*), though usages such as מֶלֶךְ הַכָּבוֹד (Ps 24:7–10) may also have been in mind. It could also be that the absolute form is a natural expression of his monotheism (he does not need to be more specific, "the glory of . . ."); cf. his summary indictment in 1:21 and Acts 7:2 (ὁ θεὸς τῆς δόξης). Not least, Paul would no doubt have had in mind the fact that his readers entertained a hope of sharing this glory (5:2; 8:18, 21). See also on 1:21, 3:23, and 6:4.

καὶ αἱ διαθῆκαι, "and the covenants." The plural is usually taken to denote the various covenants made at different points in Israel's history, on analogy with the use of the plural in Sir 44:12, 18; Wisd Sol 18:22; 2 Macc 8:15; *4 Ezra* 3.22, 5.29; Str-B 3:262—the covenants with Abraham (Gen 15, 17), with Israel at Mount Sinai (Exod 19:5–6), in the plains of Moab (Deut 29–31), and at Mounts Ebal and Gerizim (Josh 8:30–35); possibly also the covenant with David (2 Sam 23:5) (Cranfield); also with Noah (Gen 9:8–17) (Michel); possibly also with Phinehas (Num 25:12–13; see also on 10:2). But the covenant with Noah was not given to Israel alone, so is hardly likely to be in view here, or in Eph 2:12 (also plural). More likely the thought is not of different covenants but of the covenant given to Abraham and renewed to Isaac and Jacob (cf. particularly Lev 26:42–45)—that is, the covenant(s) with the fathers (Deut 4:31; 7:12; Wisd Sol 18:22; 2 Macc 8:15; *Pss. Sol.* 9.10; CD 6.2; 8.18; 1QM 13.7; 14.8; *T. Mos.* 4.5; Ps. Philo 10.2; 13.10; 19.2; Roetzel's attempt to argue for the sense "commandments," "decrees," or possibly "oaths" is both unnecessary and unjustified). This use of the plural to denote what could otherwise be regarded as a single covenant is attested both in Sir 44:18 (covenant with Noah) and in secular Greek (*Diogenes Laertius* 4.44; 5.16, 51, 57). A Jewish reader would naturally think preeminently of the covenant made at Sinai, since that is the covenant *par excellence* in the OT (BDB, בְּרִית II.2c), but in view of the argument of Gal 3 Paul would probably prefer to think in terms of the initial statements of God's covenant to the patriarchs (hence vv 6–13), in which statements the opening to the Gentiles is more clearly in view. Alternatively, since he elsewhere speaks in terms only of two covenants, old and new (1 Cor 11:25; 2 Cor 3:6, 14; Gal 4:24), and since he would regard the promise of the *new* covenant as given to Israel, as well as the old (Jer 31:31–34; note also Rom 11:26–27), he may have intended to refer to these covenants (Epp, 83; cf. Maillot; Grässer, 15, 18). On the implications of διαθήκη (= last will and testament in Hellenistic literature) being used to translate בְּרִית see BGD.

καὶ ἡ νομοθεσία, "and the giving of the law." νομοθεσία occurs only here in biblical Greek, apart from 2 Macc 6:23; also *4 Macc.* 5.35 and 17.16; other references in BGD and Cranfield. The sense can be either active (lawgiving) or passive (the law given); Luz, *Geschichtsverständnis*, 272, and Epp, 89, argue for the former against the latter, but it is doubtful if the distinction would have been seen to make any difference. In fact the form is again most probably determined by stylistic considerations (see *Form and Structure*). That the Mosaic law is in view hardly needs saying; no Jew would dispute that the law was one of Israel's greatest blessings (see *Introduction* §5.3; also on 2:14 and 6:14); to have failed to mention it here would in effect have opened up an unbridgeable chasm between Judaism and Paul's gospel.

καὶ ἡ λατρεία, "and the service." The worship of the temple cult is specifically in view (cf. Josh 22:27; 1 Chron 28:13; 1 Macc 2:22; Philo, *Decal.* 158; *Spec. Leg.* 2.167; Josephus, *War* 2.409; Heb 9:1, 6). Paul spiritualizes or secularizes the concept in 12:1 (see on 12:1; also on 15:16), and that broader usage presumably lies below the surface here (cf. his use of λατρεύειν in 1:9 and

Phil 3:3), though there is no evidence that non-Christian Jews yet gave it a wider reference prior to the destruction of the temple (Str-B, 3:262).

It is worth pausing to note that in the last four words Paul has summed up the four most distinctive features of first-century Judaism, as perceived and noted both by Jews themselves and by non-Jews: monotheism ("the glory," that is of "the God"; Deut 6:4, etc.); Israel as God's covenant people; the law of Moses as the charter for the covenant people; the temple with its cult ensuring atonement and forgiveness. On the last two cf. the frequently quoted *m. 'Abot* 1.2.

καὶ αἱ ἐπαγγελίαι, "and the promises." For ἐπαγγελία see on 4:13; Davies, *Land*, 167–68, thinks the absence of specific mention of the land is deliberate. It would accord most with the train of thought if we assume Paul had in mind primarily "the promises of the fathers" (15:8; see on διαθῆκαι above; and note the next phrase [οἱ πατέρες] and the subsequent argument, vv 7–9; cf. 4:13–20, Gal 3:14–29 and 4:23, 28). The promises in view would include not only the inheritance of the land (see on 4:13), but also the blessing of the nations (Gen 12:2–3; 18:18; 22:18; 26:4; 28:14; Sir 44:21; Acts 3:25). A broader reference (Cranfield) cannot be excluded, but would distract from the primary thrust of Paul's argument.

5 ὧν οἱ πατέρες, "whose are the fathers." The plural form is regularly used in the OT and other Jewish literature to denote particularly the patriarchs, but also the wilderness generation and outstanding figures of generations prior to the speaker; e.g., "the God of your fathers" (Exod 3:15, etc.), "the covenant with your fathers" (see on 9:4), "the commandments . . . which he commanded our fathers" (1 Kgs 8:58), "famous men . . . our fathers" (Sir 44–49), "the tradition of the fathers" (Josephus, *Ant.* 13.297); see further *TDOT* 1:10–12 and *TDNT* 5:976–77. In the NT cf. particularly 11:28; 15:8; 1 Cor 10:1; also Luke 1:55; John 6:31; Acts 3:13, 25; Heb 1:1; 8:9. As with all the preceding privileges, this one is shared by Jew and Christian (cf. v 10); see also on 4:1.

καὶ ἐξ ὧν ὁ Χριστὸς τὸ κατὰ σάρκα, "and from whom is the Christ insofar as the flesh is concerned." For ἐξ ὧν rather than ὧν, see Piper, *Justification*, 27: "the climactic character of Christ's coming." More clearly here than anywhere else in Paul, Χριστός retains its full titular force—the Messiah/ Christ (I find astonishing Gaston's claim [*Paul*, 7] that "Jesus is for Paul not the Messiah"; see further on 7:4). The addition of τό "strongly emphasizes the limitation" implied in the following two words (BDF §266.2). For κατὰ σάρκα see on 9:3, where it has the same restrictive sense as denoting a seriously inadequate understanding of the term or relation so qualified.

ὁ ὢν ἐπὶ πάντων θεὸς εὐλογητὸς εἰς τοὺς αἰῶνας, ἀμήν, "God who is over all, may he be blessed for ever, Amen." The arguments on how to punctuate this much disputed line have been well rehearsed on both sides and need not be labored here. There are two main options.

(1) The first is to read it as a relative clause, whose antecedent is Χριστός; that is, as a reference to Christ. The key considerations here are: (a) this is stylistically the most natural reading. (b) It accords with Paul's style elsewhere (1:25; 2 Cor 11:31; Gal 1:5; 2 Tim 4:18); though 2 Cor 11:31, the closest parallel in form, could perhaps point the other way, since the relative clause is so poorly articulated to its context—"he who is blessed for ever." (c) In an

independent doxology we would expect εὐλογητός to come first (as in Luke 1:68; 2 Cor 1:3; Eph 1:3; 1 Pet 1:3); though Pss 67:19 LXX [= 68:18 with added doxology] and 71:17 LXX [= 72:17] do provide something of an alternative precedent. See further particularly SH; Murray, 2:245–48; Cranfield (also "Comments," 272–73); and Metzger, "Rom 9:5"; preferred by NIV and NJB.

(2) The second option is to read it as an independent doxology. (a) This is the more natural reading in terms of the flow of thought: (i) a Jew thinking of God's blessings to Israel would naturally end with such a benediction to the God of Israel; (ii) "God *over all*" is precisely what we would expect Paul to say, since he enumerates Israel's blessings not as theirs alone but as God's blessings for all (cf. 3:29–30; 4:13–17; and the converse argument of 3:1–6); (iii) the titular reference to Christ, "the Messiah," ranks him as one of Israel's privileges, indeed, in Paul's perspective, the greatest (the climactic point in the list), whereas a jump to describe the Messiah as "God over all" would be unexpected, to say the least; (iv) and if some kind of contrast is intended between Christ's earthly and heavenly state (Cranfield, Schlier) we would have expected that to be more clearly marked, either by some kind of antithetic parallelism (1:3–4) or by some adversative. (b) The Christology implied in (1) is without parallel in Paul. Where Paul elsewhere ascribes universal lordship to Christ there is a clear note of theological reserve: the exalted Christ as fulfilling Adam's intended role (see, e.g., on 8:29); Christ as "Lord" as a way of distinguishing him from the one God (see on 10:9)—hence 10:12 is not such a close parallel. To render the text as (1) would imply that Paul had abandoned all his inhibitions and theological circumspection so carefully maintained elsewhere (even in Col 1:15–20, note both halves of the hymn; in Phil 2:6–11 note the final phrase; and in Titus 2:13 Christ is identified more precisely as "the glory of the great God"). It is more likely that an unqualified reference to "God over all" would be naturally intended and taken as a reference to the one God (cf. Eph 4:6; against Michel). (c) The implication of the *lack* of Christological focus in the matching doxological conclusion to this whole section (11:33–36) strongly suggests that Paul wanted to retain his categories within the recognized limits of current Jewish theology (cf. Berger, "Abraham," 79; and see particularly on 11:36). See also Kuss, 678–96, particularly 678 and 695–96, and "Römer 9:5," especially 302–3. Among recent commentators, so also Kümmel, *Theology*, 164; Käsemann; Robinson, *Wrestling*, 111–12 (but with fresh doubts); Wilckens; Harrisville; Maillot; Zeller; preferred by RSV and NEB.

On πάντα = "all things, everything," see BGD, πᾶς 2aδ, 2bβ, though Barrett's imaginative rendering (". . . God, who stands over the whole process") is attractive. For possible use of θεός in reference to Christ see BGD, 2, bearing in mind that θεός could have a broader reference in the ancient world (see Dunn, *Christology*, 16–17; cf. Leenhardt, also Schlatter). For the rest of the formula see on 1:25.

Explanation

It would be quite possible to read the transition from chap. 8 to chap. 9 as though 8:31–39 was the climax of the complete exposition, as though

Paul, having uttered this paean of praise and triumphant assurance, had
stopped dictating before turning, after a break, to a new subject, an afterthought to the main argument. And it is certainly hardly to be doubted that
the thought of such love extended to the nations at large would provoke by
contrast the doleful thought of what his own nation was failing to appreciate
by its large-scale rejection of that more widely extended love. But to hear
the transition from chap. 8 to chap. 9 in this way would be to miss the
underlying movement of thought which has determined the major thrust of
the argument so far: that it is precisely the righteousness of God testified to
by the law and the prophets (3:21), the promise of God to and through
Abraham (chap. 4) into which the nations have entered; that it is the business
of the law (2:15), the circumcision of the heart (2:29), the law of the Spirit
of life (8:2) which has been realized and come to fulfilled expression in the
nations' obedience to the gospel. The nations have begun to experience the
grace and faithfulness of God which was once Israel's special privilege.

The difficulty which Paul's exposition would cause for the faithful Jew is
not that his gospel is so different from the understanding most Jews had
come to take for granted, rather that his gospel is so much *the same*. It is
precisely the faithfulness of God proclaimed by Paul in his gospel of free
grace which lies at the heart of Israel's assurance of election and divine favor.
Hence the problem: how is it that Gentiles are entering into the promises
to Abraham so readily while most of his own people to whom the promises
were given seem to be missing out? If God is not faithful to Israel, how can
Paul proclaim his faithfulness to the Gentiles? The problem had been clearly
exposed by the line of argument in chap. 2. The logic of that argument
seemed to be that God's initial choice of Israel no longer counted for anything,
that the Jews at large had so badly abused their privileges that God should
have abandoned them and started afresh with the devout Gentile. But at
the beginning of chap. 3 Paul had resolutely refused to draw that conclusion.
The faithfulness of God to his covenant bond with Israel was axiomatic for
the Jew, and *remained so* for Paul. At that stage in his argument Paul had
been unable to develop that basic claim. First it had been necessary to explain
how in the new stage of God's dealings with humankind his righteousness is
offered to all, Jew first but also Gentile. That done, and having lingered
over the exposition to resolve misunderstandings, explore tensions, and exult
in the sweet foretaste of the not-yet consummation, Paul can now at last
return to the questions he had left hanging in such unsatisfactory fashion
at the beginning of chap. 3: given such righteousness extended to all, given
such faithfulness to faith, what of his covenant righteousness to Israel, how
stands his faithfulness in face of Israel's unfaithfulness?

1 The reader can hardly help being moved at this sudden and sharp
transition—from the heights of triumphant assurance to the depths of an
unfulfilled longing—the pathos made all the more touching by the solemnity
of the opening words and the depth of feeling expressed. The double form
of the oath ("I speak the truth . . . I do not lie") is particularly striking.
Paul evidently felt himself under attack here (somewhat as at the beginning
of chap. 6, but whereas there he had responded with indignation, here he
responds with gravity). Almost certainly there were those who considered

that the apostle to the Gentiles had turned his back on his own people, was too little concerned for them, their prerogatives, their susceptibilities. It is not simply Protestant exegetes of later centuries who misinterpreted Paul's gospel as having an anti-Semitic flavor; Paul himself was conscious that his position was open to misunderstanding.

The extra phrases add further weight. "In Christ": Paul takes his stand as one for whom everything focuses in Christ—his gospel, his relation to his people, his day-by-day responsibility as believer and apostle—the implication being that any kind of deliberate falsification is not possible for one so conscious of his dependence on Christ. The effect for the Christian listeners would be to underscore the reliability of the oath. Likewise the appeal to the accord of conscience would carry weight with his Gentile listeners; to make such a solemn assertion without a twinge from the moral monitor within would confirm that what was about to follow was being said with all the honesty and seriousness Paul could muster. And lest there be any quibble as to the value of conscience for the believer, Paul adds "in the Holy Spirit"; the conscience to which he appeals is conscience informed and inspired by the Spirit of God.

The echoing of the "truth-lie" antithesis of 3:4, 7 and of the phrase "conscience bearing witness" in 2:15, may be unconscious, or it may be deliberate. Either way the language confirms that Paul's thought here returns to the problem posed so sharply in 2:1–3:8.

2 The depth of feeling expressed here would be almost melodramatic were it not for the strength of the oath introducing it. Paul evidently felt the strain imposed upon his Jewishness by his vocation as a sharp pain within himself. Those who think Paul has reneged on his heritage, Paul would insist, have misunderstood both the heritage and Paul. Paul's claim is precisely that he is being *true* to his heritage in taking the gospel to the Gentiles. And it is precisely the misunderstanding of that claim which causes him such continuous and painful anguish, for it means that most of his fellow Jews are failing to enter into their own heritage.

3 With v 3 Paul's anguish becomes even more intense. He even contemplates the extreme solution of forgoing his own life and salvation if that would ensure his fellow kinsmen's participation in the fullness of God's salvation now made possible by Christ. With the curse he called upon those who perverted his gospel in Galatia ("if anyone preaches a gospel contrary to what we preached, let him be set aside for destruction") he now expresses a willingness to suffer himself, if it would accomplish his heart's desire for Israel's salvation. Presumably he was thinking of a precedent like Achan (Josh 6–7), whose failure to devote all of Jericho's booty to destruction brought Yahweh's wrath on Israel and who himself had to suffer destruction in order to avert Yahweh's anger from Israel. So Paul expresses his willingness to suffer such a fate if it might avert that wrath which was preventing Israel from hearing and believing the word of faith (cf. 9:22; 11:7–8).

A striking feature is the way in which Paul supplements the idea of being "accursed" with the phrase "(cut off) from Christ." He cannot contemplate a worse fate than to be separated from Christ. Moreover, where the non-Christian Jew would probably see the worst fate as being cut off from his people (as in Gen 17:14; Acts 3:23), Paul sees it as being cut off from Christ. Whether deliberate or unconscious on Paul's part, the linking of the two phrases ("accursed, from Christ") reinforces the point that for Paul Christ is nothing if he is not the Messiah of his people (cf. v 5), the one in whom Israel's promises find their fulfillment (cf. v 4), the one in whom indeed Israel is summed up and brought to precise focus (cf. Gal 3:16, 29). Paul is already suffering anguish because his faith in Christ has caused many of his fellow Jews to disown him, to treat him as one who has cut himself off from his own people. But he is ready to suffer the further exclusion, from Christ, if it means that thereby they come to recognize their Messiah. He himself would still be cut off from his race, but otherwise the roles would be reversed: *he* would be outside Christ, while *they* were one in their Messiah.

Whether it is a real prayer which he offers here ("I would like myself to be accursed . . .") or an eventuality he regards as impossible in fact ("I could wish myself to be accursed . . .") is a question which we do not need to settle; Paul himself may not have known the answer! The point is that he can only contemplate such an extreme course because the situation is so intolerable. It is not that the eventuality of his own being cut off from Christ is impossible (cf. 8:13; 1 Cor 9:27), so much as the situation which confronts him—the intolerableness of Israel rejecting its own Messiah, the impossibility of God's faithfulness to Israel finally failing of its object. Why it is so agonizing for Paul is that if Israel does not finally embrace the Christ, then *his own* gospel is flawed at its heart—the gospel of God's righteousness, his free grace and faithfulness to the undeserving and ungodly; if it does not continue to Israel despite Israel's unfaithfulness then it is not the gospel which he proclaims to all. That is why he can even contemplate such an extreme solution to this intolerable situation. He is so convinced of the truth of his gospel, that is, of God's faithfulness to Israel, to Jew first as well as Gentile, that he can rest assured that there will be no need to resort to that extreme solution. And if it is indeed to be the case that Israel will finally fail to recognize Jesus as Messiah then his gospel is so wrong that complete abandonment by Christ and his people is all that remains for him. This is the offer of a man so sure of his gospel that he is willing to stake everything, his own life included, on it; the offer will not be taken up, because Israel will be saved (chap 11).

Despite the lack of any verbal parallel it is more than likely that Paul has in mind the similar offer of Moses in Exod 32:32. As Moses recoiled in horror at the possibility of the Lord's people being rejected so soon after the covenant had been ratified (Exod 24:3–8), so Paul recoils in anguish at the equivalent insensitivity and perverseness of his own generation in failing to recognize God's fulfillment of the covenant in Jesus the Messiah. As Moses was willing to stake all on God's faithfulness to the covenant so recently given by God's grace, so Paul stakes his all on God's continued faithfulness to his covenanted people.

The tension Paul feels between his own identity as a Jew and his conviction that God is offering a restored righteousness to all of Adam's fallen race comes to equally poignant expression in the brief catalog he runs through in vv 3b–5a. Each word and phrase gives a new agonizing twist to his basic axiom, "to Jew first and also to Gentile," for each element of God's covenanted goodness to his own people he wants to claim for every believer in Christ but without denying it to his own people. That which his own people had understood only in *kata sarka* (according to the flesh) terms, Paul now understands in *kata pneuma* (according to the Spirit) terms (cf. 8:4–13). Not that the latter has disqualified the former, despite his own kinsmen's rejection of the gospel; rather it has transposed them to a different level. The blessings are those of Israel first and foremost, but to understand and claim them only on the level and in terms of the flesh is to misunderstand them and to fail to enter into their fullness.

He introduces the catalog of privileges by speaking of his "brothers" and "kinsmen according to the flesh." The first is a unique use of "brothers" in the Pauline letters; elsewhere it is one of his favorite ways of addressing or describing his fellow believers. In rejoicing to belong to the wider family made possible by Christ's resurrection (8:29) he will not deny his national family, primarily because so far as he is concerned, in the purpose of God, the two families are one. In the same spirit he calls his fellow Jews who thus far reject the gospel, "my kinsmen on the human level." In rejoicing to participate in the wider kinship on the level of the Spirit he cannot and will not forget his natural blood relationships.

4 "Who are Israelites." The choice of title is obviously deliberate, "Israelite" being preferred to "Jew" (contrast 2:17, 28–29; 3:29). "Israel" was clearly established in scriptural thought as the name equally of the covenant people and of the covenanted land. So when Paul uses it he is not thinking of his fellow countrymen and blood relations as such, but of them as the people of the covenant, first made with Abraham and renewed with Jacob (Gen 35:10–12). "Israelite" then is the larger title, able to embrace all who inherit the promise to Abraham, Isaac, and Jacob. Paul uses it even when speaking of the Israel which has not responded to the gospel, for his thought is primarily of the covenant people to whom God will remain faithful (even as he remained faithful to deceitful Jacob).

"Adoption" is as distinctive for its complete absence from the OT as "Israel-(ite)" is by its frequency. Yet, of course, the thought is clearly present in the Hebrew scriptures, the singular noun here probably evoking the folk memory of that initial great act of redemption whereby God took the children of Israel as his own (Exod 4:22; Hos 11:1). The attentive reader could not help being struck by Paul's diversity of usage for the same metaphor (8:15, 23; 9:4), the point being underlined thereby that his gospel to Jew and Gentile is all of a piece with, wholly continuous from, that first divine act of sheer grace. Gentile believers should not think that their adoption has nullified the original adoption of Israel. Unbelieving Israel should recognize that in and through Paul's gospel God is exercising the same gratuitous mercy which first established the covenant with Israel.

Gentile readers might again raise their eyebrows at Paul's attribution of "the glory" to his kinsmen without qualification. He had after all indicted all as lacking the glory of God (3:23), and characterized the Christian hope in terms of glory (5:2; 8:18, 21); only through Christ will the glory lost by man/Adam be finally restored to man. It could be that Paul is thinking of the theophanies which Israel or particular Israelites had been privileged to witness; historically speaking Israel had been given unique glimpses of the glory of God. But to speak of the glory of God per se simply as "the glory" would be most unusual. And set between "adoption" and "covenants" it must surely denote something in which man shares. More likely therefore Paul intended the reference here to be part of the leitmotif which forms a consistent thread through the main section of the letter: the glory of God as something man was made to share in, which he "exchanged" and lost (1:23; 3:23), but which will always be the goal of the good man (2:7, 10), a goal made into a realistic hope by Christ's resurrection (5:2; 6:4). The point once again therefore seems to be the priority of Israel in God's purpose of salvation—the gospel of glory to Jew first as well as Gentile, the Gentile convert as entering into Israel's promised blessings.

"The covenants." The plural is somewhat surprising: Paul elsewhere normally speaks simply of two covenants, old and new (Gal 4:24). It could be that he is referring to the different covenants made with Israel in the past (with Abraham, at Sinai, with David), or simply to the covenant made with and renewed to the patriarchs. But quite likely he intended his readers to think just of the usual two, old and new. If so, the tension between his natural loyalty as an Israelite and his convictions regarding the gospel is maintained. Israel has first "claim" on the new covenant as well as the old. However much more widely the new has been extended, it was still primarily Israel and Judah who were in view when it was first announced (Jer 31:31–34).

Less surprising in a list of benefits composed by an Israelite is "the giving of the law." But with the impression now clearly established that he is talking of the blessings brought to all believers, Jew and Gentile, through the gospel, it is less likely that the Roman readership would give the word the kind of negative connotation implied in Gal 3:19. Rather the implication is that the law was one of the blessings given to Israel in which Gentile believers can now share—the law understood as the law of the mind, the law of the Spirit of life, of course (7:23; 8:2), but no less the law of God given to Israel at Sinai. Once again there is a positive attitude to the law clearly implied which should not be ignored.

"The worship" is another peculiarly Jewish prerogative which Paul considers to have been widened beyond Israel according to the flesh by being spiritualized (1:9; 12:1). The worship of the one God which Israel preserved through all these centuries in the cult is now being offered where the God and Father of our Lord Jesus Christ is being worshiped and served in the Spirit.

As striking as any of the other elements in the catalog is the listing of "the promises" shortly after "the law-giving." In his letter to the Galatians the central section was dominated by the antithesis of law versus promise (Gal 3–4)—the former linked with the present Jerusalem and slavery, the latter with the heavenly Jerusalem and freedom. The same contrast had been posed less sharply in Rom 4:13–22. But here Paul sets them side by side as all belonging to Israel's special privileges. Both are Jewish privileges which Gentile believers now share. The Gentile believer can no more claim a monopoly on the promises of God so as to exclude the Jew, no more than he can regard the law as an exclusively Jewish, old-covenant possession. The promises are still there for unbelieving Israel to claim, just as the requirements of the law are still there for all believers to fulfill as they walk according to the Spirit (8:4).

5 "The fathers" might again seem to be the exclusive property of the Jewish people: it was the promise given first to Abraham and repeated particularly to Isaac and Jacob which was the basis of the children of Israel's claim to the land of Israel (Gen 17:8; 26:3; 28:13–14). But Paul has already argued that Abraham is "our father," "father of all who believe," uncircumcised as well as circumcised (4:11–12, 16–17). And he is about to point out that a line of promise through Isaac ("our father") and Jacob is not simply a natural line of descent (9:6–13). So once again Paul has in mind a peculiarly Jewish relationship which can no longer be regarded as theirs alone: the fathers are the fathers of his own people, and so they remain, but their paternal blessing now extends to a much wider circle; the nations who believe can call them "father" too.

"The Christ." Even when he is already well accustomed to saying "Christ" more or less as a proper name, Paul does not forget that "the Christ" is first and foremost the Messiah of Israel. But once again he adds the qualifying phrase "according to the flesh." The bracketing of the catalog with the two *kata sarka* ("according to the flesh") phrases will hardly have been accidental on Paul's part (vv 3 and 5). Here as there the implication is that the Christ belongs also to another relationship. Perhaps he has in mind once again the contrast with which he opened his letter: Jesus Christ who was both "born of the seed of David according to the flesh" and "appointed Son of God in power according to the Spirit of holiness" (1:3–4). But he may simply imply that he who came as Messiah of his own people is now also the Lord Christ on whom all can call (cf. 10:9–13). As with all the previous items listed in the catalog, so with Christ above all, he belongs by birth and divine purpose to the Jews, and they always have first claim to him, but the offer of redemption and salvation through him is now open to all.

In this list of Israel's blessings then, and more clearly than anything he has said so far in the letter, Paul makes plain his fundamental conviction as to the continuity between Israel of old and the believer now, Jew first but also Gentile. His gospel is the good news of Israel's heritage and Israel's covenanted blessings. To break the link between old and new covenant is not to liberate his gospel but to destroy it, for his gospel is nothing if it is not the continuation and fulfillment of all that God intended for and through his chosen people.

The thought so moves Paul that he cannot refrain from uttering a doxology: "God who is over all be blessed for ever, Amen." As the syntax stands, the line could very readily be punctuated to read the doxology as referring to "the Christ according to the flesh who is God. . . ." On the other hand, Paul's syntax is notably irregular and readers who would be conscious of the need to phrase the unpunctuated text would not necessarily read on without a break. The recognition of a doxology in the text would invite a pause as much as the opening relative clause would invite an unbroken phrasing. Again, while Paul was already well used to associating Christ with God and attributing divine functions to Christ (1:7; 1 Cor 8:6), it is less likely that he would have intended Christ to be hailed as "God *over all*" (contrast

1 Cor 15:24–28). Just as unlikely is it that the juxtaposition of references to the Messiah of Israel and "God over all" would be read as an identity; the more conscious his readers were of the continuity between Israel's faith and Paul's gospel the less likely they would be to read the ambiguous phrasing as the abrupt departure from Israel's monotheism which the more straightforward syntax would imply. In fact it is probably Paul's desire to stress the universality of God's embrace, Gentile as well as Jew, which results in the unusual phrasing. Just as in 3:29–30 he used Jewish monotheism to make the same basic point, so here rather than the more regular form of doxology to the one God ("Blessed be God . . .") he chooses to stress that the God he adores is God *over all*: "he who is God over all, may he be blessed for ever, Amen."

B. The Call of God (9:6–29)

Bibliography

See also 9:1–11:36 *Bibliography*.

Berger, K. "Abraham in den paulinischen Hauptbriefen." *MTZ* 17 (1966) 77–83. **Bornkamm, G.** "Anakoluthe." 90–92. **Brandenburger, E.** "Paulinische Schriftauslegung in der Kontroverse um das Verheissungswort Gottes (Röm 9)." *ZTK* 82 (1985) 1–47. **Burchard, C.** "Römer 9:25 ἐν τῷ Ὡσηέ." *ZNW* 76 (1985) 131. **Byrne, B.** *Sons.* 130–40. **Derrett, J. D. M.** "'Running' in Paul: The Midrashic Potential of Hab 2:2." *Bib* 66 (1985) 560–67. **Dion, H. M.** "La notion paulinienne de richesse de Dieu." *ScEc* 18 (1966) 139–48. **Ellingworth, P.** "Translation and Exegesis: A Case Study (Rom 9:22 ff.)" *Bib* 59 (1978) 396–402. **Gale, H. M.** *Analogy.* 198–205. **Gaston, L.** "Israel's Enemies in Pauline Theology." *NTS* 28 (1982) 400–423, here 411–18 (= *Paul.* 80–99). **Hanson, A. T.** "Vessels of Wrath or Instruments of Wrath? Rom 9:22 f." *JTS* 32 (1981) 433–43. **Hübner, H.** *Law.* 57–60. **Luz, U.** *Geschichtsverständnis.* 28–30, 64–78, 235–50. **Maier, G.** *Mensch und freier Wille nach den jüdischen Religionsparteien zwischen Ben Sira und Paulus.* WUNT 12. Tübingen: Mohr, 1971. **Montagnini, F.** "Elezione e libertà, grazia e predestinazione a proposito di Rom 9:6–29." In *Israelfrage,* ed. Lorenzo. 57–86. **Mussner, F.** *Tractate.* 23–25. **Pfitzner, V. C.** *Paul and the Agon Motif.* NovTSup 16. Leiden: Brill, 1967. 135–36. **Piper, J.** *Justification.* 31–54, 131–99. **Schelkle, K. H.** *Paulus Lehrer der Väter. Die altkirchliche Auslegung von Römer 1–11.* Düsseldorf, 1956. **Stegner, W. R.** "Romans 9:6–29—A Midrash." *JSNT* 22 (1984) 37–52. **Wright, N. T.** *Messiah.* 189–97. **Zeller, D.** "Sühne und Langmut." *TP* 43 (1968) 51–75, here particularly 62–64. ———. *Juden.* 113–21, 203–8.

Form and Structure

Repeatedly throughout the letter Paul has taught, both implicitly and explicitly, that the gospel he proclaims to Gentiles is the fulfillment of God's covenant promise to Israel. Not yet explicit is the fact of Israel's own failure to respond to the gospel. The way in which Paul brings this failure to explicit expression in chaps. 9–10 is parallel, and not accidentally so, to Paul's technique in bringing the identity of the Jewish interlocutor step by step into focus in chap. 2 (Gaston, "Israel's Enemies," treats 9:6–29 too much in isolation from chaps. 10–11). Here Paul chooses to go directly to the theological problem which Israel's failure poses—as also his indictment of "the Jew" in chap. 2: viz., the faithfulness of God to his promises given to Israel (v 6; cf. 3:3). The more strongly expressed the assurance of faith in chap. 8 (vv 28–39), the more pressing the question: Was he not equally faithful to his word of promise to Israel (see particularly Luz, *Geschichtsverständnis*, 20–21; M. Barth, *People*, 29–31; Luedemann, *Judentum*, 31)? The problem is not simply of Israel's unfaithfulness, but of God's credibility (F. W. Maier, 12–13; Luz, *Geschichtsverständnis*, 28; Hübner, *Israel*, 16).

The heart of Paul's initial answer is that God's call has both a positive and a negative side. On the positive side Paul can effectively summarize his earlier argument in chaps. 2–4 that God's call comes to effect in terms of promise, not in terms of natural (national, ethnic, or racial) descent (vv 7–9), and as determined by God's own purpose of mercy, not by works which document covenant membership and Jewish particularity (vv 10–18). On the negative side the corollary of God's choosing some is that he rejects others. Here Paul moves beyond the terms of debate familiar from the earlier argument (seed, works) into more problematic territory. The resumption of the diatribe style in vv 19 ff. (addressed now to the presumption of the creature in questioning the purpose of the Creator) has a double function, as in 3:1 ff: to tide him over until he is ready to unveil the solution he has (11:25–32) and to cope with the hard issues posed by falling back on fundamental axioms regarding God (in 3:1–8, as Judge; here, as God of mercy). Significant for his argument as a whole is the broadening of perspective to set thought of election within that of creation and to prepare (vv 18–23 → 11:25–32) for the final climax (cf. Brandenburger, 32, 35–36, 39–43). The sharpness of this first confrontation posed between God's mercy and God's wrath is softened immediately by Paul running on to remind his readers that the recipients of mercy include Gentiles as well as Jews, even though the scriptures cited envisage only a remnant of Israel being saved (vv 24–29).

Indicative of the careful composition of the paragraph is its chiastic structure:

vv 6–9	λόγος, Ἰσραήλ, κληθήσεσθαι, σπέρμα, τέκνα (θεοῦ)
vv 10–13	καλεῖν, ἀγαπᾶν
vv 14–18	ἐλεεῖν, θέλων
vv 19–23	θέλων, ἔλεος
vv 24–25	καλεῖν, ἀγαπᾶν
vv 26–29	κληθήσεσθαι, υἱοὶ (θεοῦ), Ἰσραήλ, λόγος, σπέρμα.

The opening assertion that the word of God has not failed is documented by the series of OT quotations in the body of the paragraph (vv 7, 9, 12, 13, 15, 17, 20) and the concluding catena of four passages (vv 25–29). The interweaving of texts probably warrants the description of "midrash" for the passage (Stegner; though his suggestion of exegetical traditions depends too much on later material).

1. The Character of God's Free Choice (9:6–13)

Translation

⁶ *But it is not as though* ᵃ *the word of God has failed. For not all those descended from Israel are "Israel."* ᵇ ⁷ *Nor is it as though all his children are Abraham's "seed," but "in Isaac shall your seed be called."* ⁸ *That is, it is not the children of the flesh who are the children of God, but the children of the promise are reckoned as "seed."* ⁹ *For this word is one of* promise: *"at this time I will come and Sarah shall have a son."*

¹⁰ *Not only so, but also in the case of Rebekah who conceived by the one act of sexual intercourse with Isaac our father.* ¹¹ *For when they were not yet born nor had done anything good or evil,* ᶜ *in order that the purpose of God should stand in terms of election,* ¹² *not from works but from him who calls,* ᵈ *it was said to her, "The elder will serve the younger,"* ¹³ *as* ᵉ *it is written: "Jacob have I loved, but Esau have I hated."*

Notes

ᵃ p⁴⁶ it syrᴾ attest an early attempt to resolve the confusion of idiom by omitting the ὅτι.

ᵇ As might be expected, an attempt to ease the ambiguity of the text by reading Ἰσραηλῖται for the second Ἰσραήλ is found in the regular grouping of witnesses (D F G etc.).

ᶜ p⁴⁶ D F G etc. replace φαῦλον with the more regular antithesis κακόν.

ᵈ Some modern versions make the verse division at this point (see UBS text).

ᵉ B reads καθάπερ (see on 3:4 *Notes*).

Form and Structure

See also 9:6–29 *Form and Structure*.

In vv 6–13 the most striking stylistic features are the broken syntax of vv 10–13, with v 10 left incomplete while vv 11–12a are brought in as a kind of parenthesis, and with v 12b serving syntactically as the completion of both. As so often with Paul the conclusion to a section (v 13) serves also as introduction to the next section (see 5:20–21 *Form and Structure*).

Comment

6 οὐχ οἷον δὲ ὅτι, "not as though"—a mixture of οὐχ οἷον ("by no means") and οὐχ ὅτι ("not as if"); see BDF §§304, 480(5) and BGD, οἷος.

ἐκπέπτωκεν ὁ λόγος τοῦ θεοῦ, "the word of God has failed." ἐκπίπτω means literally "fall off or from"—so of flowers (as in Job 14:2; 15:30, 33; Isa 28:1, 4; 40:7; James 1:11; 1 Pet 1:24), but also of chains falling off (Acts 12:7) or a boat failing to hold its desired course or position (Acts 27:17, 26, 29). But the sense was sufficiently broad for the word to be used in a range of meanings (LSJ), and the derived sense "fail" is also well enough known (Sir 34:7; 1 Cor 13:8 *v.l.*; see BGD, 3b; MM).

ὁ λόγος τοῦ θεοῦ in the NT frequently denotes the Christian gospel, particularly in Luke-Acts (Luke 5:1; 8:11, 21; etc.; 1 Cor 14:36; 2 Cor 2:17; 4:2;

Phil 1:14 *v.l.;* Col 1:25; 1 Thess 2:13; BGD, λόγος 1bβ). But here it is God's word as Paul's fellow Jews would understand it, that is, not just God's word in principle (as in Num 23:19; Ps 119:89; Isa 31:2; 55:10–11), but God's specific word (= promise) to Israel (Gaugler; Munck, *Christ,* 34; Müller, *Gerechtigkeit,* 29; Zeller, *Juden,* 114; Käsemann; Kümmel, "Probleme," 20; Wilckens [so v 9]; against Güttgemanns, "Heilsgeschichte," 40 ff.), "the word of election" (Mayer, 170). The closest parallels, using different forms of πίπτω, are Josh 21:45, 23:14, Tob 14:4(S = א) and Jud 6:9 (see further Berger, "Abraham," 79–80 n.77). Of course Paul would regard "the word of God" (= promise to Israel) as fulfilled in "the word of God" (= the gospel of Christ); this is indeed the main thrust of the scriptures he will quote in abundance in the following argument (especially 9:25–29, 33; 10:6–10, 11, 13, 18–21; 11:26–27). The verse is therefore thematic not only for the next paragraph or two (Campbell, "God and Israel," 28; Aageson, "Scripture," 268; cf. Zeller, *Juden,* 114–16; Brandenburger, 10, 16–20) but for the whole section (chaps. 9–11), climaxing in 11:29 (Käsemann; Dahl, "Israel," 155; Cranfield; Wilckens; Schmitt, 72–77; Siegert, 124, 174; Rese, "Römer 11," 423); v 6a is the thematic statement more than v 6b (Lübking, 67–68). It responds to a question which arises naturally from a Jewish perspective on Paul's gospel; we need not envisage a specific question put to Paul by the Roman congregations (Kuss). That Paul is now about to develop the assertion made in 3:4 is clearly seen by Vischer (91, 97).

οὐ γὰρ πάντες οἱ ἐξ Ἰσραὴλ οὗτοι Ἰσραήλ, "for not all those descended from Israel are Israel"; or, more precisely, "For all those from Israel, these are not Israel" (Piper, 47–48). For the significance of Ἰσραήλ see on 9:4. There was a natural tendency, on the part of some at least, to regard descent from the patriarchs as guarantee of salvation (attested in Matt 3:9 // Luke 3:8; Justin, *Dial.* 140; *m. Sanh.* 10.1; see also SH, 249, and Str-B, 1:116–21). But there is more evidence in contemporary literature of a wrestling with the problem of Jewish unfaithfulness by those who saw themselves as "the righteous," "the devout," "the chosen of Israel," "the elect of righteousness" (as in *1 Enoch* 1; Wisd Sol 2–5; *Pss. Sol.* 3 and 13; CD 2.16–4.12; 5.15–6.11; 1QH 2.6–37; 4.5–27; see further *TDNT* 4:184; Sanders, *Paul,* 245, 361, 378, 408; Zeller, *Juden,* 116–18; Dunn, "Pharisees"), a wrestling which is quite closely parallel to Paul's (see also on 1:17 and 9:27–28). In Paul's case the issue can be summed up in terms of whether οἱ ἐξ Ἰσραὴλ are to be identified with οἱ ἐκ νόμου or with οἱ ἐκ πίστεως (4:14, 16), an alternative most of his Jewish contemporaries would not recognize (see also 3:27–28).

It is important to note that by the second Ἰσραήλ Paul does not mean believers over against national Israel (Robinson, "Salvation," 83–88; Käsemann; Hübner, *Israel,* 17; Zeller). Hence the inadequacy of any talk of a transfer of the name and blessings of "Israel" to "the church" (as Wright, *Messiah,* 193–97), as though Paul saw them as distinct entities. Nor will it be Paul's concern to argue that God always had in view "only an elect part of Israel" (Schoeps, *Paul,* 239), rather to explain *how* the election of Israel works. Even less justified is talk of "a decisive contradiction between 9:6–13 and 11:1–32" (Dinkler, 116; likewise Luedemann, *Judentum,* 32–35, followed by Walter, 173–76; Watson, *Paul,* 168–70; and Räisänen, *Torah,* 74; also "Römer

9–11," 2893, 2910–12, 1927–28, 2930–35; cf. Gal 6:16; on the unity of chaps.
9–11, however, see Lübking, 135–56). "The Israel of God" is still God's covenant people, the character of whose covenant some Israelites (οὐ πάντες) have
misunderstood and into whom believing Gentiles are being incorporated (see
also on 9:4 and 11:26). There are no grounds for (far less expression of)
anti-Semitism here. And to speak of Paul's "anti-Judaism" (as Ruether, 104–
7) is little better, since for Paul at least it is still a debate *within* Judaism
about the eschatological significance of their common heritage. Watson makes
the astonishing claim that "the point of 9:6ff. is to deny that the Jewish
people were *ever* elected for salvation" (*Paul*, 227 n.9), and Räisänen similarly
claims the clear implication of the passage to be that "the majority of Israel
has never been called" ("Römer 9–11," 2900), both quite missing the point
that Paul's argument concerns the character and mode rather than the fact
of election. Contrast Gager's thesis (*Origins*, chap. 15, developed from Gaston)
that for Paul the Torah remains the path of righteousness for Israel, while
Christ has become the way of righteousness for Gentiles—which makes no
sense either of Paul's anguish in 9:1–3, nor of the line of argument now to
be developed. More to the point is Theobald's recognition that the common
denominator throughout, which provides the key to the solution of "the question of Israel," is the grace of God, both as the basis of election and as lasting
through and reaching beyond human disobedience (*Gnade*, 132, 165–66).

7 οὐδ᾽ ὅτι εἰσὶν σπέρμα Ἀβραάμ πάντες τέκνα. Translation here is surprisingly
difficult and depends on whether the construction carries on from v 6 and
whether σπέρμα or τέκνα is regarded as the more restricted category—that
is, only Isaac, and not Ishmael (Gen 16:15; 17:15–21; 21:10, 12) or the other
sons whom Abraham is said to have fathered in later life (Gen 25:2). The
sentence can thus be rendered: "nor because they are seed of Abraham are
all his children" (so almost all—e.g., RSV, NEB, NIV, NJB). This regards τέκνα
as the more restricted category; NEB margin suggests the rendering ". . .
children of God," presumably in anticipation of v 8 (cf. 8:16–17, 21) and
reflecting v 4 (υἱοθεσία); so also Byrne, *Sons*, 130–31. But οὐδ᾽ ὅτι could be a
resumption of the οὐχ ὅτι of v 6; and in the immediately following quotation
σπέρμα is the more restricted category (v 7b; also v 8), whereas τέκνα embraces
both Abraham's "children of the flesh" and his "children of the promise" (v
8). Better therefore to render: "nor as if all his children are Abraham's seed"
(cf. Barrett). The argument is the converse of 4:13–18, where the point is
that Abraham's "seed" is much more *extensive* than his physical or "legal"
descendants (by the customs of the day, of course, Ishmael was a legitimate
son of Abraham; cf. Gen 30:3, 9). But in effect the central point is the same:
the true heirs of Abraham are to be reckoned in other than national (physical
or legal) terms (see also on 4:13). It is important to recognize that the antithesis
here describes the mode, not the objective, of the promise (Lübking, 62–64;
also 139, 148).

ἀλλ᾽ ἐν Ἰσαὰκ κληθήσεταί σοι σπέρμα, "but in Isaac shall your seed be called."
The quotation from the LXX of Gen 21:12 (itself a close rendering of the
Hebrew) is verbatim—as also in Heb 11:18. The ἐν is restrictive—only in
Isaac. Strictly speaking, in this instance, καλέω has the sense "be given a
name, be named" (cf. BGD, 1aγ); as the Genesis verse indicates, Hebrew

has the same idiom (BDB, קָרָא 6). But Paul would certainly expect his readers to be mindful of the thematic function of the verb in this section (see *Form and Structure*); so to preserve the overtones, "shall be called" is preferable (cf. NEB margin).

8 τοῦτ᾽ ἔστιν, "that is," usually introduces a brief explanatory or clarificatory note (Matt 27:46; Mark 7:2; Acts 1:19; 19:4; Rom 7:18; 10:6, 8; Philem 12; 1 Pet 3:20; and frequently in Hebrews [2:14; 7:5; 9:11; 10:20; 11:16; 13:15]), but here begins a new sentence and longer explanatory note (as in Ign. *Trall.* 7.2). See also on 10:6–8.

οὐ τὰ τέκνα τῆς σαρκὸς ταῦτα τέκνα τοῦ θεοῦ, "it is not the children of the flesh who are the children of God," or "the children of the flesh, these are not the children of God" (Piper, 49). The two contrasting genitive formulations (τέκνα τῆς σαρκός/ἐπαγγελίας) define in a more limiting way the broader category "children" (genitives of quality—BDF §165). σάρξ continues to have the same negative overtone as in vv 3 and 5—not strongly negative, as though constituting a *dis*qualifying factor in itself, but as *not* constituting a qualifying factor in itself; divine sonship can neither be defined (nor disqualified) in these terms, that is, by natural or ethnic criteria. See also on 1:3, 4:1, and 9:3. For the concept of "children of God" see on 1:3 and 8:14, and for the variation between υἱός (v 9) and τέκνον (vv 7–8) see on 8:16; similarly in the parallel argument in Gal 4: υἱοί (4:22, 30), τέκνα (4:25, 27, 28, 31).

τὰ τέκνα τῆς ἐπαγγελίας λογίζεται εἰς σπέρμα, "the children of promise are reckoned as seed." The strong echo of the argument in chap. 4 is no accident: ἐπαγγελία (4:13, 14, 16, 20; 9:4, 8, 9), λογίζεσθαι (4:3–6, 8–11, 22–24; 9:8), σπέρμα (4:13, 16, 18; 9:7–8). Käsemann's observation that "Paul's dualism of flesh and promise" has replaced "that of flesh and spirit" fails to appreciate the integrated salvation-history character of Paul's argument: "flesh" and "law" are twin aspects of his critique of what he regards as the typical Jewish misunderstanding of God's covenant and grace; "promise" and "Spirit" summary expressions of the alternative he now stands for. In his exposition each element implies the others, even when not explicitly mentioned; see particularly on 2:28–29, and, of course, 4:13–18, as well as Gal 4:22–31, particularly vv 28–29 (ἐπαγγελίας τέκνα = τέκνα κατὰ πνεῦμα). For ἐπαγγελία see on 4:13, λογίζεσθαι on 4:4–5 (also Barrett), and σπέρμα on 4:13.

9 ἐπαγγελίας γὰρ ὁ λόγος οὗτος, "for this word is one of *promise*." The ἐπαγγελία is given a position of emphasis. For λόγος see on 9:6.

κατὰ τὸν καιρὸν τοῦτον ἐλεύσομαι καὶ ἔσται τῇ Σάρρᾳ υἱός, "at this time I will come and Sarah shall have a son." The verse seems to be an amalgam of LXX Gen 18:10 (a somewhat free rendering of the Hebrew as we have it) and 18:14 (close to the Hebrew):

18:10   ἐπαναστρέφων ἥξω πρὸς σὲ κατὰ τὸν καιρὸν τοῦτον εἰς ὥρας, καὶ ἕξει υἱὸν Σαρρα . . .
18:14   εἰς τὸν καιρὸν τοῦτον ἀναστρέψω πρὸς σὲ εἰς ὥρας, καὶ ἔσται τῇ Σαρρα υἱός.

Paul omits the εἰς ὥρας ("in spring"), thus freeing the κατὰ καιρόν somewhat from its temporal restriction to resonate with eschatological overtones (see on 5:6). The choice of ἐλεύσομαι ("I will come"), rather than Genesis's "I will (surely) return to you," may also be deliberate for the same reason, allowing the same overtone: the fulfillment of the promise depends on a divine act or epiphany in the future (Byrne, *Sons*, 133, and Hübner, *Israel*, 24, 30–31, stress the first person singular both here and in the quotation used in v 13, though ἐγώ appears neither time). As in Gal 4:28, but without such a developed allegorical outworking, Isaac's birth and its circumstances are understood typologically (Aageson, "Typology," prefers the term "correspondence").

10 οὐ μόνον δέ, ἀλλὰ καί, "not only so, but also"—signifying both continuity and development of thought; see on 5:3. The sentence which follows is left incomplete (see *Form and Structure*) but can be rounded out by implication: ". . . a further but closely related point emerges when we consider . . ." (as the γάρ at the beginning of v 11 confirms).

Ῥεβέκκα ἐξ ἑνὸς κοίτην ἔχουσα, "Rebekah having conceived by the one act of sexual intercourse." The reference is to Gen 25:21. By a natural association κοίτη can mean "bed" (as in Luke 11:7), "marriage bed" (as in Heb 13:4), "sexual intercourse" (Wisd Sol 3:13, 16; see also on 13:13), and "seminal emission" (Num 5:20; κοίτη σπέρματος [Lev 15:16–17, 32; 18:20; 22:4]). The idiom is quite close to our own: "having sex with one man." The point, however, is not simply that Jacob and Esau had the same father (NEB, NIV)— that was true of Isaac *and* Ishmael; but rather they were conceived in the very same act of sexual intercourse—this is the further ("not only, but also") and more difficult case (cf. Wilckens, n.858 with bibliography).

Ἰσαὰκ τοῦ πατρὸς ἡμῶν, "Isaac our father." Isaac is rarely mentioned on his own in Jewish and Christian tradition, reinforcing the impression of the Genesis narratives themselves that he was thought of as a rather colorless figure (contrast Jacob!). He is remembered as one of the three patriarchs in a standard and often repeated formula ("the fathers, Abraham, Isaac, and Jacob"), but principally as being Abraham's promised offspring, father of Jacob, and particularly as Abraham's intended sacrifice (see, e.g., Charlesworth, vol. 2, index "Isaac"). For the significance of ἡμῶν see on 4:1.

11 μήπω γὰρ γεννηθέντων μηδὲ πραξάντων τι ἀγαθὸν ἢ φαῦλον, "for when they were not yet born nor having done anything good or evil." The γάρ indicates that Paul's train of thought is fuller than has so far been expressed (cf. Cranfield). This fuller thought immediately becomes apparent (vv 11–12), but he would presumably have expected the substantial echoes of the argument of chap. 4 (see particularly 9:8) to have signaled his train of thought clearly enough to his readers. Similarly the subject of γεννηθέντων (i.e., υἱῶν) does not need to be expressed; "Paul writes for readers who know the Bible" (Wilckens). For γεννάω, only here in Romans (but cf. again Gal 4:23–24, 29), see BGD, 1a. πράσσω may have a more general sense than ποιέω (see on 2:3), allowing the emphasis to rest more heavily on the τι; thus, not "having *done* anything good or evil," but "having done *anything* good or evil." Paul seems deliberately to depart from his usual contrast ἀγαθός/κακός (2:9–10; 3:8; 7:19; 12:21; 13:3–4; 16:19; also 1 Thess 5:15; see on 2:10) in favor of ἀγαθός/φαῦλος (as also 2 Cor 5:10), presumably because φαῦλος allows a deeper note of "good-for-nothingness" (Trench, *Synonyms*, 315–18); even if they (or Esau in particular) were to do deeds of the basest kind, that was *not* the ground of God's choosing Jacob.

ἵνα ἡ κατ᾽ ἐκλογὴν πρόθεσις τοῦ θεοῦ μένῃ, "in order that the purpose of

God should stand in terms of his free choice." The ἵνα is certainly one of intended purpose (Cranfield). ἐκλογή means "selection" (cf. particularly Polybius' use of the phrase, κατ᾽ ἐκλογήν, "by selection," denoting commissioning for service—*TDNT* 4:176), or "choice" (*Pss. Sol.* 9.4; 18.5; *Ep. Arist.* 33; Josephus, *War* 2.165; *Ant.* 8.24; *TDNT* 4:177–78; Michel, 302 n.15). Although it does not occur in the LXX (in Aquila, Isa 22:7; in Symm. and Theod., Isa 37:24), Paul obviously has in mind the idea of divine election, which is certainly present in the use of the near cognate ἐκλεκτός (*TDNT* 4:182–83), particularly οἱ ἐκλεκτοί (see on 8:33). So also in 11:5, 7, 28 (cf. 1 Thess 1:4). For πρόθεσις see on 8:28, where the thought moves on the same lines (Mayer, 184). On the conjunction of the two phrases (κατ᾽ ἐκλογήν and πρόθεσις—"God's selective purpose," NEB) see particularly G. Maier, *Mensch,* 359–62. The continuity of thought from v 6 is indicated by the μένειν which can serve as the antithesis to ἐκπίπτειν (as in Isa 40:8; cf. Ps 33 [LXX 32] :11; Prov 19:21; Isa 14:24; see also Cranfield); in the NT cf. John 6:27; 12:34; 1 Cor 13:13; 2 Cor 3:11; 9:9; Heb 7:3, 24; 12:27; 1 Pet 1:23, 25 (Isa 40:8); 1 John 2:17; 3:15 (Wilckens). Once again, it is important to realize that the election of Israel as a people is not at issue (against Murray, 15–19), as most realize (see, e.g., Munck, *Christ,* 42); rather the issue is how God's purpose of election comes into effect. "The Israel of *God* remains always the *Israel* of God" (Althaus on 9:9).

12 οὐκ ἐξ ἔργων ἀλλ᾽ ἐκ τοῦ καλοῦντος, "not from works but from him who calls." One of the key phrases of the whole letter (ἐξ ἔργων) here reemerges into prominence, and at crucial points in the rest of this section (9:32 and 11:6). To regard this as an unnecessary digression (SH, Dodd) misses the point: (1) Paul contests the contemporary dominant view among his fellow Jews that the election of Israel depends for its maintenance on Israel's faithfulness to the law (ἐξ ἔργων—see on 3:20; despite Hübner, *Israel,* 25, Paul certainly means, as always with the ἐξ ἔργων formulation, works of *the law*). This is the crux of the whole argument with his fellow kinsfolk (and with his own past): that the continuation (μένειν) of God's purpose (as in Jacob), not just its initial expression (as in Isaac), depends on nothing the elect can do, but only on God's continual call (see on 10:3). (2) In this connection it may be significant that Philo expounds Gen 25:23 by referring to God's knowledge beforehand of their works and experiences (τὰ ἔργα τούτων καὶ πάθη—*Leg. All.* 3.88), since it may reflect a contemporary Jewish understanding (in the diaspora?) which Paul here goes out of his way to counter (see also on 9:13). The early Greek and Latin commentators who argued that election is based on God's foreknowledge of good works completely turn Paul's argument on its head, as Schelkle has noted (*Paulus,* 337). (3) This fuller line of argument has been implicit from the first echo of chap. 4 (see on 9:11 γάρ). To say that "the problem of Israel . . . stands under the criteria of the doctrine of justification" (Käsemann, citing Luz, Bornkamm, and Eichholz), although true, is also not quite the point, since it implies a previously formulated doctrine by which Paul resolves "the problem of Israel." But the point here is that Paul's understanding of justification, or of God's calling, only achieves this particular expression (οὐκ ἐξ ἔργων) in the course of his wrestling with "the problem of Israel"; to that extent we should rather say that the doctrine emerges from the problem (cf. Stendahl; Dahl, "Israel," 156; Zeller, 112); whereas the doctrine of (Jacob's divine) election was one Paul shared with his contemporaries (cf., e.g., *Jub.* 15.30; *4 Ezra* 3.16).

For καλέω see on 1:1, 4:17, and 8:30, and for its prominence in this section see *Form and Structure*. Käsemann is right to see a continuity in Paul's thought between God's act of creation and his act of justification (against Wilckens), as this further echo of chap. 4 (4:17) is enough to confirm. Paul's point is precisely that God's dealings with man have the same character from start to finish; it is not a call to covenant keeping (ἔργα) on which the effectiveness of the call then depends. It is doubtful whether Paul intends a distinction here between "called" to a task and "called" to salvation, as suggested, e.g., by Leenhardt.

ἐρρέθη αὐτῇ ὅτι ὁ μείζων δουλεύσει τῷ ἐλάσσονι, "it was said to her, 'The elder will serve the younger.'" The "divine passive" (ἐρρέθη) is used in place of Genesis's εἶπεν κύριος. The quotation is verbatim Gen 25:23 LXX. The idiom (small/great = young/old) is well enough known in wider Greek usage (BGD, μέγας 2aα). The fuller oracle speaks of the two children as two nations (so Mal 1:3 in v 13), but Paul evidently does not have this dimension in view, so that the issue of whether Paul sees Esau and Jacob as two peoples (SH, Lietzmann, Michel) or two types (Käsemann) does not arise from the text (Wilckens). Paul is content to have a text from the account of the birth of Esau and Jacob which shows that from the first precedence did not depend on the natural order of birth, even if the text reinforces the argument of vv 7–9 more than that of vv 11–12. But strictly speaking this text is illustration more than proof; the proof text follows in v 13. At the same time, if implications are to be drawn they would certainly extend beyond the historical destinies of two nations and embrace all who belong to "Israel" and are "children of God" (vv 6, 8); see particularly Piper, 38–52. Gaston has some justification in protesting against a too straightforward interpretation of Esau as a type of the synagogue and Jacob as a type of the church (as, e.g., Peterson, 20–21) ("Israel's Enemies," 412), but fails to take sufficient account of the integrated character of chaps. 9–11.

13 καθὼς γέγραπται, "as it is written"; see on 1:17. The proof text as usual comes as the final clincher in the argument; we may note that by structuring his argument this way Paul in effect gives more weight to the text from the prophets than that from the Torah.

τὸν Ἰακὼβ ἠγάπησα, τὸν δὲ Ἠσαῦ ἐμίσησα, "Jacob have I loved, but Esau have I hated." Apart from slight modification of word order the text is verbatim from Mal 1:2–3 LXX. As in the case of Gen 25:23 (cf. Philo, *Leg. All.* 3.88; see on 9:12), so here, Paul may be combating a contemporary Jewish line of interpretation which (naturally) understood Mal 1:2–3 in the sense "God loved Jacob, but he hated Esau *because of his deeds*" (Ps. Philo 32.5, emphasis added). This would be enough to explain why Paul quotes the full text, with its double note of selection *and* deselection; in Mal 1:2–5 the initiative is entirely God's, without any reference to Esau's (or Edom's) deeds. At the same time, following his regular pattern, this larger conclusion to this section of the argument (vv 7–13) serves as a lead into the next section (see 5:20–21 *Form and Structure*). The force of μισέω should not be exaggerated (cf.

Murray); its meaning is determined by the fact that it stands as the antithesis of ἀγαπάω—a familiar antithesis in Jewish writing (Deut 21:15; 22:13; 24:3; Judg 14:16; and regularly implied in the wisdom literature—e.g., Prov 13:24; 15:32). "What is meant is not so much an emotion as a rejection in will and deed" (*TDNT* 4:687; cf. Leenhardt, Kuss); cf. the targums of Mal 1:2–3 in Str-B 3:267. See also Cranfield. In *Jub.* 37.24 and *1 Enoch* 89.12 Esau is depicted as a wild boar (cf. Ps 80:13) and in *4 Ezra* 6.9 "Esau is the end of this age, and Jacob is the beginning of the age that follows" (cf. *4 Ezra* 3.16); see further Munck, *Christ,* 39–41.

Some form of double predestination can of course be deduced from this Malachi passage, as Paul is aware (vv 18–23), but the thrust and context of the argument needs to be borne in mind. (1) The idea of divine rejection (Ἠσαῦ ἐμίσησα) arises only as a corollary to the principal claim (Ἰακὼβ ἠγάπησα); it is the assumed or logical converse of Israel's sense of election. However much the sentiment may grow to embrace (virulent) hatred of (often hostile) others, its starting and central point is the sense of grace freely extended in an unexpected way to one who was wholly undeserving (see R. Otto, *The Idea of the Holy,* 91, cited by Dodd, 141). If there is any certainty in the doctrine, or better in the experience of predestination, it is the sense of assurance of election. The converse can be drawn out at best (if at all) with hesitancy and many a question mark. Anything more definite would mean an abandoning of the sense of wonder and unworthiness which is the only religious attitude in which the idea of election can be embraced with safety. (2) Here in particular it should be remembered that Paul's aim is to prick the bubble of Israel's presumptuousness as the elect, not to affirm Esau's rejection. Paul's argument, in fact, is an attack on the only dogma of predestination then current, and constitutes a standing warning against any attempt to define or rationalize a doctrine of election (cf. Munck, *Christ,* 76). Indeed, somewhat surprisingly, since Esau (Edom) belongs to the outsiders to whom electing grace now stands open in Paul's gospel, Paul uses this text *against* Jacob (Israel). The principle enunciated here envisages an Israel not determined as such by ethnic identity, and so also an Esau who is not simply to be identified with another ethnic group. The mystery of God's "purpose in terms of election" (v 11) is not so easily defined—it is as wide (or as narrow) as "grace" and "faith"—and the warning is as much to the new "elect" as to the "old" (11:17–24). (3) So also the refusal to find a solution to the problem posed by the Malachi passage in the deeds done by the two parties, or the works performed by Jacob (and his heirs), as again Philo, *Leg. All.* 3.88, and Ps. Philo 32.5 (see on 9:12 and above), does not leave only one alternative— God as wholly arbitrary. The appeal to the imagery of the potter (vv 20–33) is in effect an appeal to a higher design in the mind of the Creator which the created cannot be expected to grasp. (4) Since the idea of election is a *hindsight* perspective which grows from the exposition of grace (1), properly used it can never be predictive, far less a tool for dividing prematurely into classes (elect and nonelect). Indeed, properly speaking, election is an *eschatological* doctrine. It can never be properly formulated until the final judgment! Only then can it be clear who are "vessels of wrath" and "vessels of mercy" (vv 22–23). Until then, while the outworking of God's electing purpose is

unclear in extent and content, any statement about it must be provisional
and tentative (cf. particularly Schmidt, 159). (5) Above all, it needs to be
remembered that Paul includes the idea of divine rejection in order to explain
what he regards as a temporary phenomenon—viz., God's rejection of *Israel*
in order to achieve a wider election, which will then *include* Israel (11:25–
32). The main thrust of the whole is not in terms of an even-handed, equal-
weighted selection and rejection, but of an overall purpose in which rejection
has a part only in order to achieve a final outcome of "mercy upon all"
(11:32). (6) In short, Paul's concern is not to expound a doctrine of predestination (for the history of interpretation of chaps. 9–11 where this issue stands
in the forefront see Kuss, 828–935), whatever corollaries in this connection
may legitimately be pressed from his argument, but to explain the situation
in which he finds himself where God's word of promise to Israel (9:6) seems
to have been called in question both by the Gentiles' acceptance of his own
gospel about the Jewish Messiah and particularly by Israel's large-scale rejection of it (cf. Wilckens, 2:209).

Explanation

6 The more Paul stresses the continuity between his brothers according
to the flesh and his brothers in Christ, between the privileges bestowed on
his own nation and the blessings of his gospel, the more difficult becomes
the problem of his countrymen's failure to accept the gospel. If the gospel
of God's righteousness is the gospel of God's faithfulness, does not what
appears to be God's passing over of Israel cast doubt on Paul's message as a
whole? It is not enough simply to assert that the word of God to the Jewish
people is carried forward in the proclamation to Gentile as well as Jew, that
the covenanted purpose of God for Israel is being fulfilled in the gospel of
Christ, as Paul has been doing explicitly and implicitly throughout, as clearly
in the catalog of vv 4–5 as anywhere else so far in the letter. The question
is whether the word given to Israel as such has failed. After all there can be
a continuity by transformation, where the caterpillar becomes a butterfly,
and the empty skin of the caterpillar is all that is left behind of the old
stage of existence. Is Paul arguing for that kind of continuity and fulfillment?
Has God's purpose for Israel as such failed because Israel as such is now
only the empty skin of the earlier stage of God's purpose? But there is also
continuity by development and extension, as when a tree grows substantial
new branches, or new branches are grafted in, where the new stage does
not require the abandonment of the old, but new and old are part of the
larger whole. Paul clearly thinks more in terms of the latter image, as chap.
11 will show. The problem is that Israel as such by its large-scale rejection
of the new stage of God's purpose seems to be denying the continuity. So
the question cannot be avoided: Has God's word to Israel faded and withered
away, no longer vital and productive? Has God's purpose failed to hold its
course and run aground in irreparable shipwreck?

Paul dismisses the thought completely: "Not so, by no means!" And by
way of justification he immediately states his bold thesis: "not all who are of
Israel are Israel, not all who are descended from Israel can actually claim

the name Israel." Here is explicitly stated what was already implicit in vv 3–5; the blessings and relationships of which his own people rightly boast cannot be claimed exclusively or completely on the natural level. Not all who can properly claim blood ties to Israel actually belong to the Israel of God (cf. Gal 6:16). Paul makes this apparently self-contradictory assertion in a matter-of-fact way as though it was an unexceptional statement. For him it was evidently an obvious conclusion to draw from the scriptural history of God's covenant relation with his people. Either he assumes that it was already sufficiently obvious to his Christian readers as well, or he is confident that Israel's own scriptures provide him with an irrefutable argument. It is this argument from scripture which he now takes up. That he is so confident of its force tells us not only of Paul's fundamental respect for the authority of the Jewish scriptures, but also that he is dealing with an audience who (he can assume) will share a similar depth of respect—both Jews and Gentile God-worshipers who have come to believe in "the good news of God promised beforehand in the holy scriptures" (1:1–2).

7 V 7 quickly makes it clear that Paul is embarking on an *ad hominem* argument: "It is not as if the descendants of Abraham are all children; rather, 'Through Isaac shall your descendants be called' (Gen 21:12)." Israelites should not need reminding that the line of covenant promise is not the same as the line of natural descent. They themselves would not claim that Ishmael (Abraham's son by Hagar) was within the covenant, despite his having been circumcised by Abraham (Gen 17:23–27). So, clearly, the beneficiaries of the covenanted blessings (vv 4–5), even on Jewish presuppositions, cannot be identified simply in terms of blood relationship and natural kinship. The quotation from the LXX of Gen 21:12 could be understood as giving the verb little weight—"in Isaac will you have your descendants." But in view of its repetition several times in this section (vv 7, 11, 24, 25, 26) it is more likely that Paul would have wanted the sense of "call" to be understood by his audience: "God's call shall come to your descendants only in the line of Isaac." Either way his point is clear enough: God had told Abraham that his promise of seed and land applied only to the line of descent through Isaac, that so far as his covenant with Abraham was concerned only Isaac and his offspring would be recognized as Abraham's seed.

8 Paul's own interpretation ("that is" = "this means") not only presses home the point but develops it significantly by clarifying the ambiguity of the word "children"; the distinction between "seed (descendants) of Abraham" and "children (of Abraham)" is at least potentially confusing since both Ishmael and Isaac were both "seed" and "children." So Paul makes a twofold distinction: first between "children of the flesh" and "children of God," that is, between children purely by natural descent and children who stand within this special covenant relation with God. The introduction of the latter phrase ("children of God") would cause no surprise. The idea of the chosen people as sons or children of God (as well as the nation as the son of God) was sufficiently familiar in the LXX (e.g., Deut 32:5–6, 19–20; Isa 63:8; Wisd Sol 16:21) and is implied in "the adoption" of v 4. But once again alert listeners would recall that Paul had given prominence to the phrase in his description of their own privileges and prospects as believers just a few paragraphs earlier

(8:16–17, 21). That which he describes as the covenanted status of the descendants of Abraham is their status before God. It is a status which the natural descendants of Abraham cannot assume for themselves by virtue of being the natural descendants of Abraham. The ground of filial relationship to God is not simply filial relationship to Abraham.

The second distinction is between "children of the flesh" and "children of the promise"—"children of God" = "children of the promise" = "descendants of Abraham." Almost certainly by drawing in once again the word "promise" (especially in conjunction with "reckoned") Paul intends to recall his readers to the argument of 4:13–21, and to the antithesis developed there between law and promise. Once again the *ad hominem* force of the point is clear: Paul's fellow countrymen assume a direct linkage and equation between their nationhood, the covenant, and the law, but their founding fathers *dis*prove rather than prove the equation. As scripture itself shows, God's covenanted blessings are to be reckoned in terms neither of blood relationship nor of law, but in terms of promise.

9 Paul rams the point home with a clinching text: "This word is a *promise*, 'At the appointed time I will come and Sarah shall have a son' (Gen 18:10, 14)." The explicit reference back to God's promise of a son to Abraham when he was yet childless would again recall the force of the last point made in the argument of chap. 4 (the midrash on Gen 15:6): the faith through which Abraham was justified was nothing more than simple trust in God's power and firm reliance on his promise (4:18–21). Although he has not mentioned either law or faith Paul's line of argument is clear: scripture confirms Paul's earlier exegesis; the founding fathers show that Israel's own election was not in terms of natural descent and law, but from the outset and thus characteristically in terms of promise and faith. Consequently, Paul implies, the Jews as a people cannot and should not object to Paul's gospel; to do so is to misunderstand their *own* gospel (of election).

10–12 What was implicit in the allusion back to the argument of chap. 4 becomes more explicit in vv 10–13. Paul's kinsmen understood their status as the chosen people in terms of nationhood and law—a membership of the covenant determined by birth and marked from earliest days by circumcision and the subsequent works of the law which distinguished them as God's chosen people. In vv 6–9 Paul has demonstrated the untenability of the first (membership determined by birth); in vv 10–13 he draws on what scripture says about the next generation of the founding fathers to disprove the second (membership distinguished by "works of the law"). Rebekah had borne two children by the same father, Isaac, the second of the founding fathers (v 10). God's choice of one of them, and the younger one at that, as scripture reminds us (Gen 25:23), to provide the line of covenant succession, was made before they were born, when they had not yet done anything good or evil. This was to prove, Paul asserts, that God's purpose not only begins but also *continues* in terms of election (v 11), that its continuation depends not on the obedience to the law which marks out the Jews (Israel according to the flesh) as the chosen people, but is a matter of God's call from start to finish (v 12).

Here once again the references to "doing good or evil" and to "works" are not to be construed as an accusation on Paul's part that his fellow Jews as a whole thought of their election or of their final acquittal at God's judgment as something to be *earned* by performing works of the law. (The Judaism contemporary with Jesus and Paul is not to be charged with the abuses of the pre-Reformation western church.) "Doing good" cannot be thought of as something disparaged by Paul; on the contrary he has already spoken of it more than once as something desirable (2:7, 10, 25; 7:18–19). "Doing good" is certainly not to be equated with "works of the law" with its much more negative connotation (in view of 4:4–5 Paul's choice of "do" rather than "work" as the verb may also be significant). Paul's point in v 11 therefore is not that God chose Jacob instead of Esau before either had opportunity to prove himself worthy of election or to disqualify himself from election. It is rather that God made his choice of Jacob and not Esau *without reference* to their subsequent conduct, whether it was conduct he approved or disapproved of. Since he made his choice before they were born, their subsequent conduct is unrelated to God's choice. Israel of all people must recognize that the selection of their eponymous forefather had nothing at all to do with the way he conducted his life—an appropriate point in the case of "supplanter" Jacob (contrast Deut 21:15–17). So too, by implication, the children of Israel should recognize that their own selection as God's people was solely a matter of God's free choice, and that his purpose continues to unfold solely in terms of what God determines.

12 In particular Paul is concerned to demonstrate that his fellow Jews should not attempt to understand Israel's election in terms of law keeping. Israel's selection took place before his birth and therefore neither depends on nor can be characterized by such distinctive Jewish "works of the law" as circumcision and observance of food laws, sabbath, and feast days. It depends only on God's call; it is the call of God which makes, maintains, and characterizes the covenant. Here too Paul probably wants his readers to direct their minds back to his careful dismissal of "works of the law" as a factor in justification (3:27–4:8) and calling (4:17), and his close association of God's "purpose" and "calling" (vv 11–12) may well be intended also as an echo of the similar juxtaposition in 8:28. All the while he is thinking of gospel and covenant choice and promise as a tightly bound package applicable equally to the Israel of God's purpose and to his fellow believers, Gentile as well as Jew. It is this continuity and indeed identity of God's call and purpose across the covenants which makes it so clear to Paul that Jews who insist on "works of the law" as the indispensable mark of God's chosen people are actually denying not simply the gospel but also their *own* election—an intolerable situation indeed for one who desperately wants to be loyal both to his Jewish heritage and to the revelation of Christ.

13 The final quotation of Mal 1:2–3 ("Jacob I loved, but Esau I hated") rounds off the first stage of the argument introduced by v 6—"the word of God has not failed." It has not failed, it has simply been misunderstood— misunderstood by the people whose scriptures they are! The word of God was always in terms of election, of God's purpose fulfilled through his free choice, never in terms of the natural kinship of blood ties, never in terms of a community characterized and bounded by particular ritual acts (works of the law). The word of God has not failed (as the success of the gospel shows); it is Israel according to the flesh who have failed. By emphasizing God's selection of Jacob afresh ("Jacob I loved") the Malachi proof text repeats and confirms the character of God's covenant through Jacob, as a relationship given and maintained by God's free choice. But it also introduces a further element: the choice of Jacob was also a choice against Esau. This negative corollary to the election of Isaac and Jacob was always implicit in vv 7–12, but now Paul deliberately brings it to the fore to introduce the transition to the next phase of the argument.

2. *Those Not Chosen Are Still within the Purpose of God* (9:14–23)

Bibliography

See 9:1–11:36 and 9:6–29 *Bibliography*.

Translation

[14] *What then shall we say? There is no injustice with God, is there? Certainly not!* [15] *For to Moses he says, "I will have mercy on whom I have mercy, and I will show compassion to whom I show compassion."* [16] *So then, it is not a matter of the one who wills or the one who runs, but of God who shows mercy.* [17] *For the scripture says to Pharaoh, "For this purpose I raised you up, in order that I might demonstrate in you my power and in order that my name might be proclaimed in all the earth."* [18] *So then, to whom he wills he shows mercy, but whom he wills he hardens.*

[19] *You will say to me then: "Why does he still find fault? For who has resisted his will?"* [20] *On the contrary, who are you, man, who answers back to God? "Does the thing made say to its maker, Why have you made me thus?"* [21] *Or does the potter not have the right over the clay to make from the same lump one vessel for honorable use and another for dishonorable use?* [22] *But what if God, willing to demonstrate his wrath and to make known his power, bore with much patience vessels of wrath made ready for destruction,* [23] *and*[a] *in order that he might make known the wealth of his glory*[b] *on vessels of mercy which he prepared beforehand for glory?*

Notes

[a] The omission of καί by B and some other witnesses is probably the result of an attempt to simplify the construction (Metzger).

[b] P reads χρηστότητος (instead of δόξης) presumably in unconscious or deliberate echo of 2:4.

Form and Structure

See also 9:6–13 *Form and Structure*.

The section forms a unity round the attempt to explicate the two sides of God's election of mercy, expressed in the transitional verse 13 and reiterated in v 18. The leading motif is God's mercy (ἐλεέω, ἔλεος—vv 15, 16, 18, 23). The old suggestion of Origen that vv 15–19 express the sentiments of Paul's opponents (SH, 269–70, Kuss, 717–18) misses the point.

Vv 15–18 are set in parallel:

15–16: τῷ Μωϋσεῖγ ἀρ λέγει . . . scripture . . . ἄρα οὖν οὐ τοῦ θέλοντος · · ·

17–18: λέγει γὰρ . . . τῷ Φαραὼ . . . scripture . . . ἄρα οὖν ὃν θέλει . . .

Vv 22–23 echo v 17:

17: . . . ἐνδείξωμαι . . . τὴν δύναμίν μου καὶ ὅπως διαγγελῇ τὸ ὄνομά μου

22–23 . . . ἐνδείξασθαι . . . τὸ δυνατὸν αὐτοῦ . . . καὶ ἵνα γνωρίσῃ τὸν πλοῦτον τῆς δόξης.

The two infinitive clauses in v 22 obviously stand in parallel dependence on θέλων and the two σκεύη phrases also provide a further contrasting pair (like those already in vv 13, 18, and 21), but what their mutual relation is, and the force of the parallelism, remains unclear from the structure itself and depends on how the θέλων is construed. For the most elaborate structural layout see F. W. Maier, 44 (followed by Zeller), and for the possibility of running the sense into v 24 see also RSV, *TDNT* 7:363, and Kuss (with review of older literature, 731–32); but Paul probably intended the εἰ δὲ θέλων to introduce a deliberately incomplete thought (see on 9:22).

Comment

14 τί οὖν ἐροῦμεν; "what then shall we say?" See on 3:5 and 6:1 (also Cranfield).

μὴ ἀδικία παρὰ τῷ θεῷ; "there is no injustice with God, is there?"—the μή indicating that a negative answer is expected. The question is one which derives from faith, not from skepticism or hostile unbelief. Whether we understand it simply as Paul's own rhetorical question (Cranfield) or as a "real discussion of considerable explosive effect" (Wilckens), the point is that it is an in-house discussion; it arises from the Jewish conception of Israel's election, and is a question posed by a Jew for Jews, all of whom would take it for granted that God is righteous (Deut 32:4—θεὸς πιστός, καὶ οὐκ ἔστιν ἀδικία, δίκαιος . . . ; cf. Rom 3:5). "The question of 9:14 does not mean 'Is election immoral?' . . . The question is—Is God *righteous*? i.e., has he been true to his covenanted word?" (Wright, *Messiah,* 211). The question is not to be disparaged therefore as though it necessarily involved man measuring God by some humanly conceived measure (e.g., Schlier, Zeller); it is rather an invitation to explore how the election and rejection of God (v 13) fit into another key (covenant) category derived from God, namely, righteousness and unrighteousness. Thus it may also be noted that ἀδικία is used by Paul in antithesis to ἀλήθεια (1:18; 2:8; 1 Cor 13:6; 2 Thess 2:10, 12; Piper, 71–73); it is God as he is known (τὸ γνωστὸν τοῦ θεοῦ), "the truth of God" (1:19, 25), the faithfulness of God (see on 3:3–5; cf. again Deut 32:4 above), with which the talk of election/rejection must be coordinated. παρὰ τῷ θεῷ is Semitic (Str-B, 3:79–80; Michel); see also 2:11.

μὴ γένοιτο, "not at all!"; see on 3:4.

15 τῷ Μωϋσεῖ γὰρ λέγει, "for to Moses he says." Moses is referred to here not as a way of identifying the citation, but as an example and representative of God's mercy—in contrast to Pharaoh in v 17 (Lagrange; Munck, *Christ,* 45, 47–49); that it is precisely *Moses* to whom God so speaks is important for Paul's *ad hominem* argument (SH; F. W. Maier, 34–35; Schmidt). The γάρ indicates that Paul intends to answer the question (v 14); that is, to show how election/rejection is to be understood in relation to the truth and righteousness of God (see on 9:14; see Piper, 74–75, against those who think Paul disallows the question, e.g., Nygren).

ἐλεήσω ὃν ἂν ἐλεῶ καὶ οἰκτιρήσω ὃν ἂν οἰκτίρω, "I will have mercy on whom I have mercy, and I will show compassion to whom I show compassion." The quotation agrees with the LXX of Exod 33:19 precisely, which in turn is a close rendering of the Hebrew. There are no grounds for the view (Schlier) that Paul ignores the context. On the contrary the specific mention of Moses surely indicates that Paul had in mind the particular character of the utterance as an exceptional unveiling of God, of his glory and his name (Exod 33:18–19). That is, God in his fullest self-disclosure prior to Christ, God in the fullest extent to which he could be known by man—his glory (cf. particularly 1:21–23; see on 1:21) and his name (see *TDNT* 5:253–58; the Fourth Gospel expresses well the link between God's δόξα and his ὄνομα [5:272])—is God as merciful and compassionate (in Exod 33:18–19, LXX uses δόξα to translate כָּבֹד, "glory," as usual, and טוּב, "goodness," exceptionally). That Paul would see, and intend, an association of language and emphasis between Exod 33:19 and Exod 3:14 is probable (Cranfield). But even more likely is an intended link with the repetition and development of Exod 33:19 in 34:6, since the latter is one of the most cited and echoed passages in the OT and postbiblical Jewish literature (Num 14:18; Neh 9:17; Pss 86 [LXX 85]:15; 103 [LXX 102]:8; 145 [LXX 144]:8; Joel 2:13; Jonah 4:2; Nah 1:3; cf. also Deut 7:9–10; 2 Kgs 13:23; 2 Chron 30:9; Neh 9:31; Pss 111 [LXX 110]:4; 112 [LXX 111]:4; Isa 30:18; Jer 32:18; Sir 2:11; Wisd Sol 3:9; 4:15; 15:1; Pr Man 7; *Pss. Sol.* 9.8–11; *T. Jud.* 19.3; *T. Zeb.* 9.7; *Jos. As.* 11.10; Ps. Philo 13.1; 35.3; *4 Ezra* 7.33; see also Bousset-Gressmann, 383; Trebilco, chap. 3, notes that the use of the "children's children" curse on Jewish tombs in Asia Minor, as a warning to potential grave violators, indicates that Exod 34:7 would have been well known); see also Piper, 55–68: "Paul saw in Exod 33:19 a paraphrase of God's 'name'" (*Justification,* 67); see further on 9:22 μακροθυμία. The double emphasis on the mercy/compassion of God which Exod 33:19 provides (rather than the more even-handed form of the extended statement of 34:6–7) is presumably the reason why Paul chose the former as the basic statement of the character of God's electing/rejecting purpose (see also Barth, *Shorter,* and Cranfield); see also on 10:20. ἐλεέω, introduced here from Exod 33:19, is the key word in this section (vv 15, 16, 18) and in the final resolution of the problem wrestled with in chaps. 9–11 (11:30–32); cf. ἔλεος (9:23; 11:31); hence the double inappropriateness of Beker's comment that "Paul avoids ἔλεος (in favor of χάρις) because in Judaism ἔλεος often complements what a person lacks in works, so that God's mercy becomes a supplementary gift" (*Paul,* 266)! οἰκτείρω occurs only here in the NT (but cf. οἰκτιρμός [12:1]).

16 ἄρα οὖν οὐ τοῦ θέλοντος οὐδὲ τοῦ τρέχοντος, "so then it is not a matter of the one who wills or the one who runs." The genitive formulation is not specific and should be left vague in translation. θέλω is involved in a double contrast between man's willing (v 16) and God's (vv 16, 18, 22), which alone is decisive, and between "willing" and "running," which is equivalent to the "willing" and "doing" of 7:15–21. The former is the controlling contrast (hence the reference to individuals—"the one who"—rather than to intentions and actions as such) and helps determine the force of the latter as complementary rather than antithetical. That is to say, Paul does not intend to play off "willing" as against "running," as though the point was that willing might be possible but not doing, analogous to 7:15–21; hence an allusion to Sir 15:14–15 and *Pss. Sol.* 9.4–5 is unlikely (argued by G. Maier, *Mensch,* 368–69, 373); rather "willing" and "running" together sum up the totality of man's capacity. Similarly the force of τρέχω can be distorted by emphasizing the idea of effort involved in it (BGD—"exert oneself to the limit of one's powers in an attempt to go forward, strive to advance"), as though Paul was warning against the very idea of moral effort as wrong-headed in itself (cf. Michel, Käsemann). Certainly the imagery of an athletic contest lies close to hand (1 Cor 9:24–26; Heb 12:1; cf. particularly Pfitzner, 135–36), but nowhere else in Paul has τρέχω a negative overtone (Gal 2:2; 5:7; Phil 2:16). Rather, τρέχω should be taken as a more intense form of περιπατέω ("walk") in the sense of "conduct oneself" (see on 6:4), and so be understood as a reference to the lifestyle of the devout Jew in the intensity of his devotion (see particularly Ps 119:32; cf. Rom 9:31; cf. also *TDNT* 8:229–31; Gaugler; Piper, 132; NJB; Derrett, "Running," thinks it is derived from Hab 2:2–4). In short, Paul does not disparage "willing" and "running"; willing and running are, of course, part of the human response to God (see also on 9:17 γάρ). But they are not factors in election, neither in the initial choice nor in its maintenance. Paul's concern is *not* to debate the issues of predestination and free will with Pharisee and Essene (against G. Maier, *Mensch,* 363–65, 368–70, 373; "the Essene character of his train of thought in this chapter" [385]) but to clarify what the covenant means for Israel. See also on 9:17.

ἀλλὰ τοῦ ἐλεῶντος θεοῦ, "but of God who shows mercy." God as essentially merciful is a fixed point in Jewish theology; in addition to the references under 9:15 see Isa 49:10; Sir 50:19; *T. Mos.* 12.7; 1QH 4.32, 36–37; 6.9; 7.27; 9.8, etc. (Str-B, 3:268; Michel, n.8; Wilckens); so also Paul (1 Cor 7:25; 2 Cor 4:1; Phil 2:27; as also 1 Tim 1:13, 16; 1 Pet 2:10).

17 λέγει γὰρ ἡ γραφὴ τῷ Φαραὼ ὅτι, "for scripture says to Pharaoh." The γάρ may introduce a second explanation of v 14 (Cranfield, Wilckens), though in that case we might have expected something like the οὐ μόνον δέ, ἀλλὰ καί of v 10 (which introduces the second explanation of v 6). The use of γάρ suggests rather that Paul feels able to treat vv 17–18 as a development of v 16 (cf. Piper, 138–39). If so, it confirms that Paul used θέλω and τρέχω in v 16 as morally neutral terms, describing human motivation and action (see on 9:16), and able to embrace the attitude and conduct of Pharaoh as well as the piety of his fellow Jews. More important it underlines the degree to which *God's* mercy is the central motif (see also below). That γραφή forms the subject is a graphic illustration that Paul thinks of scripture as the word of God (cf. Gal 3:8; 4:30); the variation certainly does not imply that he wanted to avoid any idea of God speaking directly to a gentile king (so, rightly, Cranfield and Schlier), though it does weaken the stress Hübner again wants to put on the first person of the text (*Israel*, 44–45), cloaked as it is also in the "divine passive" of v 12 (see also on 9:9).

The following quotation is from Exod 9:16 with a number of variations:

Exod:	ἕνεκεν	τούτου διετηρήθης ἵνα	ἐνδείξωμαι	ἐν σοὶ τὴν ἰσχύν
Rom:	εἰς αὐτὸ	τοῦτο ἐξήγειρά σε ὅπως	ἐνδείξωμαι	ἐν σοὶ τὴν δύναμίν.
Exod and Rom:		μου καὶ ὅπως διαγγελῇ	τὸ ὄνομά μου	ἐν πάσῃ τῇ γῇ

For the significance of the variations, which all serve to bring out more sharply the sovereignty of God's purpose, see Cranfield's and Piper's (146–48) detailed discussions. For εἰς αὐτὸ τοῦτο cf. 13:6; 2 Cor 5:5; Eph 6:22; Col 4:8. For ἐξεγείρω in the sense "cause to appear, bring into being" see SH; BGD, 4; and cf. Jer 50 [LXX 27] :14; Hab 1:6; and Zech 11:16. For ἐνδείκνυμι see on 2:15.

δύναμις is usually taken as a reference to God's power as creator (Michel, referring to Sir 16:15–16, an insertion to the text; Käsemann); but Cranfield is probably right in seeing here a reference primarily to God's saving power (1:16; 1 Cor 1:18, 24; 2:5; 6:14; 2 Cor 4:7; 6:7; 13:4; etc.). For one thing the thought is not so much of judgment directed against Pharaoh but of God's covenant mercy to Israel (hence again the connection of thought between vv 16 and 17 [γάρ]; see above); the thought of divine hardening comes in as a corollary (v 18), as did the thought of Esau's rejection (v 13), not as the principal line of thought. And for another, δύναμις and ὄνομα are here parallel and indeed overlapping concepts (cf. Ps 54:1; Acts 4:7; *TDNT* 5:277), so that the clear implication of the quotation of Exod 33:19 (God reveals his name as the merciful one; see on 9:15) carries over here. What is to be "proclaimed in all the earth" is the Lord's championing and powerful defense of his people in situations where they are under threat from strong adversaries (Pss 2:7; 59:13; 106:8; 2 Macc 3:34; 1QH 2.24). Here again it must be observed that the whole argument is mounted from a Jewish perspective: it is as a Jew that Paul makes a point in relation to his fellow Jews; Pharaoh serves as a foil to the central point held in common—that is, God's choice of Israel as an expression of his sovereign mercy (cf. F. W. Maier, 37–38). All the more commendable is it, therefore, that Paul should not stick on this point, but attempt to face squarely the harsh corollary.

18 ἄρα οὖν ὃν θέλει ἐλεεῖ, "so then to whom he wills he shows mercy." The opening is parallel to v 16, indicating that the conclusions are coordinate and underscoring the point of contrast (not as man "wills" [v 16] but as God wills). For ἐλεέω see on 9:15 and 16.

ὃν δὲ θέλει σκληρύνει, "but whom he wills he hardens"—"harden" in the obvious sense of "make unresponsive, unyielding" (see also on 11:7), "make stubborn" (NEB). In drawing this conclusion from Exod 9:16 Paul shows very clearly that he is conscious of its context, since that word ("harden") is particularly prominent in that section of the Exodus narrative (Exod 4:21; 7:3, 22; 8:15 [LXX 11] ; 9:12, 35; 10:1, 20, 27; 11:10; 13:15; 14:4, 8, 17). Whether or not a case can be made for a distinction in the Exodus narrative between a *self*-hardening on the part of Pharaoh (Exod 7:22; 8:15; 9:35; 13:15) and a hardening inflicted by God (the latter is obviously the dominant thought), Paul for his part clearly has in view the divine initiative (Kuss, 723–24; Piper,

139–52). So to look for reasons for God's hardening in Pharaoh's "evil disposition" or previous self-hardening (Lagrange, Murray, Leenhardt) is a rationalizing expediency (equivalent to the old rationalist treatments of the miracle stories in the Gospels which D. F. Strauss so effectively torpedoed). Such a thought clearly has no place in Paul's exposition and in fact contradicts what Paul has been so careful to stress in vv 11 and 16 (Michel; Schmidt; Blackman, 130; Luz, *Geschichtsverständnis*, 78 n.211; Käsemann; Piper, 154–56). It is to his credit that Paul himself does not resort to such expedients, or interpose a demonic intermediary (as in *Jub.* 48.17; *T. Sol.* 25.3), but faces up to the clear indications of the Exodus narrative without flinching. Dodd thinks that Paul here (vv 17–18) takes "a false step"; however, for a monotheistic (rather than dualistic) system in which the Creator/creature distinction is fundamental (cf. Harrisville) some such assertion is an unavoidable corollary of v 16 (Mayer, 195, refers particularly to 1 Sam 2:25; Tob 4:19; Jud 8:14–15), whose moral questionableness from the creature's perspective permits only of eschatological resolution (see further on 9:13).

At the same time it is again important to bear in mind the chief focus and thrust of Paul's argument. It is an in-house Jewish argument. In responding to those who make great play of Israel's covenant responsibility as an integral part of God's electing purpose, Paul naturally puts all the emphasis on the divine initiative. He is not at this point attempting a fuller and more rounded exposition. If we now wish to develop such a fully rounded treatment of predestination we do it best *not* by reading in qualifications here but by referring to other parts of Paul's writings where human responsibility is clearly drawn out (just as the unqualified statements at the beginnings of chaps. 6–8 have to be taken together with the exhortations which follow later in each chapter; see chaps. 6–8 *Introduction*); here human responsibility is drawn in from 9:30 onwards. The fact that Paul's focus is thus limited at this point also makes it more doubtful that Paul has in view here "eternal reprobation" than Piper thinks (156–60, citing also Michel, Luz, G. Maier, Käsemann, and Kuss), since the talk of Pharaoh's hardening evidently prepares for the later talk of Israel's hardening (πωρόω/πώρωσις—11:7, 25) which Paul sees as a partial and temporary phase of God's purpose (11:26–31). Moreover we should not forget that Paul intends this discussion of hardening to be contained and understood within an argument bounded by 9:15 and 11:32; cf. SH, Barrett, and Cranfield.

19 ἐρεῖς μοι οὖν, "you will say to me, therefore." The diatribe style comes clearly to the fore (cf. 11:19). A specific objection need not be in view, but since the argument is so in-house Jewish, and since there is some indication that Jewish thinkers did wrestle with the theological problems posed by the scriptural talk of the divine hardening of Pharaoh (*Jub.* 48.17), it is, if anything, more probable that Paul sees this as an expression of Jewish theological sensitivity over the harsher-sounding corollaries to their own doctrine of election.

τί ἔτι μέμφεται; "why does he still find fault?" or "what fault can he still find?" (BGD, μέμφομαι, with parallels); cf. 3:7. Yet if *God's* act is the *effective* cause of human hardness, what room is left for *human* responsibility? The question is a legitimate one, and Paul's response indicates that he does not dispute its logic: the objector has not misunderstood the thrust of vv 17–18 (cf. Murray, 2:31–32; Piper, 170–73), and Paul does not attempt to deny its force by offering some sort of double causality explanation (God and Pharaoh, or God and Mastema).

τῷ γὰρ βουλήματι αὐτοῦ τίς ἀνθέστηκεν; "for who has resisted his will?" βούλημα is comparatively rare (only three times in the LXX; elsewhere in the NT only Acts 27:43 and 1 Pet 4:3). The idea of "purpose" is strong (TDNT 1:636–37), and the -μα formation strengthens the implication of enacted purpose. ἀνθίστημι has the middle sense of "set oneself against, resist" (BGD). The question is not about the impossibility of resisting ("Who can resist . . . ?" NEB) but looks back on God's completed will (βούλημα) to ask, "Who (in the event) has resisted [perfect tense] God's will?" (cf. particularly Cranfield). Paul may well have had in mind the similarly formulated thought in Job 9:19 LXX (τίς οὖν κρίματι αὐτοῦ ἀντιστήσεται) taken up also in Wisd Sol 12:12. See also on 13:2.

20 ὦ ἄνθρωπε, μενοῦνγε σὺ τίς εἶ ὁ ἀνταποκρινόμενος τῷ θεῷ; "on the contrary, who are you, man, who answers back to God?" The address (ἄνθρωπε) is not merely rhetorical (as in 2:1, 3; so Barrett, NEB). An antithesis between man and God is intended (Schlatter, Lagrange, Althaus, Gaugler, Michel, Schlier, RSV, NJB), as the setting of the words at the places of emphasis in the sentence (beginning and end) makes clear (Cranfield). μενοῦνγε is used especially in answers to emphasize or correct (BDF §450.4; BGD). It could thus emphasize the ridiculousness of mere man so speaking to God: "who do you think you are in answering back to God" (so in effect Schmidt, Kuss, Schlier); cf. Phil 3:8. But probably the force is one of correction—"on the contrary"—as in 10:18 (SH, Cranfield, Wilckens). ἀνταποκρίνομαι occurs infrequently (in the LXX only Judg 5:29[A]; Job 16:8; 32:12; in the NT elsewhere only Luke 14:6), but Paul obviously chooses the double compound form to strengthen the implication that the reply is unwarranted, improperly contentious. "Paul has been misunderstood and unfairly criticized through failure to recognize that it is the God-defying rebel and not the bewildered seeker after God whose mouth he so peremptorily shuts" (Bruce, 190).

μὴ ἐρεῖ τὸ πλάσμα τῷ πλάσαντι· τί με ἐποίησας οὕτως; "does the thing made say to its maker, Why have you made me thus?" The first six words are drawn verbatim from the LXX of Isa 29:16, but the actual question adapts the following straight denial in Isaiah (οὐ σύ με ἔπλασας) to a protest more appropriate to the train of argument here, perhaps with conscious allusion to the τί ποιεῖς; of Isa 45:9 (the correlation of themes, including that of the potter in both passages, would naturally bring them to close association in Paul's mind); cf. the τί ἐποίησας; of Job 9:12 and Wisd Sol 12:12, though the context of thought in these cases is more distant. The use of πλάσσειν in Gen 2:7–8, 15 was quite often taken up in Jewish thought in talk of God's creative activity (e.g., Job 10:8–9; Ps 33 [LXX 32]:15; 2 Macc 7:23; Sib. Or. 3.24–25; Josephus, Ant. 1.32, 34; 1QS 11.22; in Philo πλάσσειν is used exclusively of God; see further TDNT 6:256–60); it is true that the potter does not create the clay, but that hardly lessens an allusion to Gen 2:7 (against Leenhardt: "it is not here a question of God the Creator but of God as Providence"). The idea of a creator is also present in wider Greek thought (TDNT 6:254–55), but the idea here is characteristically Jewish, particularly the thought of God as creator having a continuing oversight and responsibility for his creation such that the possibility of the creature answering back is even conceivable (contrast the Greek idea of "fate"—OCD 430–32; see also Luz, *Geschichtsverständnis,* 238–41). By stressing God's sovereign rights as Creator (*TDNT* 6:257, 260; Müller, *Gerechtigkeit,* 30 and passim; Michel; Siegert, 134–35) Paul does not have any thought of pushing him back to some remote mythological period in the past. It is not without significance that πλάσσειν is used also of God's election of Israel (Deut 32:6 R; Isa 43:1, 7; 44:2, 21, 24; cf. 49:5, 8; 53:11), since it is the role of Israel within God's purpose in creation and election which is the main thread of chaps. 9–11. πλάσσειν and ποιεῖν are used as near synonyms (*TDNT* 6:257, 260). See further on 9:21. Dodd's much quoted protest ("the weakest point in the whole epistle") is honest (as ever) but does an injustice both to Paul's integrity and to the deeper current of Paul's argument.

21 ἢ οὐκ ἔχει ἐξουσίαν ὁ κεραμεὺς τοῦ πηλοῦ ἐκ τοῦ αὐτοῦ φυράματος ποιῆσαι; "or does the potter not have the right over the clay to make from the same lump?" The potter with his clay (πηλός) was a popular image for God as Creator in Jewish thought (Ps 2:9; Isa 29:16; 41:25; 45:9; Jer 18:1–6; Sir 33:13; *T. Naph.* 2.2, 4; 1QS 11.22; 1QH in particular delights in the self-description יֵצֶר (ה)חֶמָר, "creature of clay" [1.21; 3.23–24; 4.29; 11.3; 12.26, 32; 18.12]; Str-B, 3:271). There is no quotation as such here, but the allusion is plain and no one familiar with Jewish understanding of God as creator would mistake it (Michel). ἔχειν ἐξουσίαν is a familiar phrase meaning "to have the right" (as also in 1 Cor 7:37; 9:4–6; 2 Thess 3:9; BGD, ἐξουσία 1). In itself it does not indicate the ground of the right asserted, but here of course it refers to the undisputed right of the one who makes something of his own volition over what he has made.

ἐκ τοῦ αὐτοῦ φυράματος, "from the same lump." Paul's point could be made without this emphasis, and though he may in part be influenced by the similar language in Wisd Sol 15:8, he no doubt intends a reminder that all humanity, Israel included, is made of the same common (lump of) clay; (cf. 9:10, ἐξ ἑνός). In 11:16 he uses the same word in a different image (lump of dough) to make a complementary point.

ὃ μὲν εἰς τιμὴν σκεῦος ὃ δὲ εἰς ἀτιμίαν, "one vessel for honorable use and another for dishonorable use." Paul's imagery is clear: one bowl may be highly decorated and grace a king's palace; another, made from the same clay, may serve as a chamber pot in a lowly household. That Paul intended a specific reference with the imagery (individuals and final judgment) is hardly as clear as Piper (173–86) argues: the imagery of creator and creation was used of Israel as well as of individuals, and it is Israel's sense of *national* distinctiveness which Paul seeks to counter; and though the idea of final judgment is not far away (τιμή as a close associate to δόξα—2:7, 10; and cf. 9:23, but note the δέ in 9:22), the more natural sense of the metaphor is of vessels put to differing uses within history (as v 17; so in the closest parallel, 2 Tim 2:20; cf. 1 Thess 4:14 and 1 Pet 3:7; and in the OT cf. particularly Jer 22:28 and Hos 8:8; cf. Lagrange, Leenhardt, Käsemann, Cranfield). Paul almost certainly had Wisd Sol 15:7 in mind (. . . κεραμεὺς . . . πλάσσει . . . ἐκ τοῦ αὐτοῦ πηλοῦ . . . σκεύη. . . .); in which case he must have intended a certain degree of irony, since in his development of the idea it is unbelieving Israel which parallels the role of the unclean, dishonorable vessels, which in Wisd Sol are identified as idols (for the parallels between Wisd Sol 11–15 and Rom 9:19–23, see SH, 267–69).

22 εἰ δὲ θέλων ὁ θεὸς ἐνδείξασθαι τὴν ὀργὴν καὶ γνωρίσαι τὸ δυνατὸν αὐτοῦ; "but what if God, willing to demonstrate his wrath and to make known his power?" The sentence running through vv 22–23 is incomplete, but such elliptical constructions, with the apodosis unstated, were as acceptable then (LSJ, εἰ B.VII.1, 2; cf. John 6:62, Acts 23:9, Luke 19:42; SH, Lietzmann) as now—"What if it were the case that . . . ?"—with the hearer left to complete the sense and draw his own conclusions (cf. Schlatter, Heil). The δέ is probably "lightly adversative" (Schlier, Cranfield), indicating that the thought is not simply an alternative formulation of vv 20–21, but a further and slightly different thought (cf. NEB; Robinson, *Wrestling*, 117). This would be sufficient to put in question a complete equation of the "vessels" in v 21 with those in vv 22–23. It is difficult to take the θέλων in any other sense than "wanting to," denoting desired purpose. In the much debated issue of whether θέλων is concessive (as in SH, Denney, Moffatt, Fitzmyer, Black, NJB) or causal (so most; brief review in Luz, *Geschichtsverständnis*, 242–44), the latter certainly is the more probable. But that may be a false antithesis since the participle is ambiguous and would probably be read simply as a relative (Schlier), describing what is always true of God, rather than a specific purpose as such (contrast v 17—ὅπως; v 23—ἵνα); see also *Form and Structure*. For ἐνδείκνυμαι see on 2:15. Paul echoes the language of Exod 9:16 (v 17; see *Form and Structure*). Cf. also 3:25–26 (ἔνδειξις; Dodd, Michel), Eph 2:7 and 1 Tim 1:16. For ὀργή see on 1:18; here, as there, the thought seems to be of a historical process—how God deals with recalcitrant humanity. γνωρίζω is a natural complement to ἐνδείκνυμαι (cf. 9:17 with 16:26). τὸ δυνατόν can serve as a synonym for ἡ δύναμις (BGD, δυνατός 2d), strengthening the parallel with v 17 (see *Form and Structure*); note the echo of 1:19–20—τὸ γνωστὸν τοῦ θεοῦ = ἡ αὐτοῦ δύναμις.

ἤνεγκεν ἐν πολλῇ μακροθυμίᾳ σκεύη ὀργῆς, "bore with much patience vessels of wrath." For φέρω in the sense "bear patiently, endure, put up with," see BGD, 1c. To appreciate the force of μακροθυμία here it must be recalled that God's patience with his chosen people was one of Israel's most common refrains (Exod 34:6; see on 9:15). Jonah 4:2 and Ps 145 [LXX 144]:8–9 represent a protest against a nationalist narrowing of the refrain, and Sir 18:13 a similar universalist variation (cf. Wisd Sol 15:1). But 2 Macc 6:14–16 thinks of God's patience with regard to other nations simply as an allowing them to reach the full measure of their sins, in contrast to his purpose of mercy in disciplining his own people; cf. Wisd Sol 15, *Pss. Sol.* 13, *4 Ezra* 7.74, and the fiercer language of 1QH 15.14–20 (though note the more tolerant version of Wisd Sol 12). It would be possible to read Paul here in a similar vein, as the protest of the small minority sect rationalizing the prosperity of their adversaries as God simply allowing them rope enough to hang themselves; see particularly *TDNT* 4:382–83; Lietzmann; Schmidt; Wilckens; Piper, 189–92. But Paul is surely not simply echoing the voice of Jewish particularism. The way in which he has constantly echoed (in order to counter) the note of Jewish national confidence in this section suggests rather that he intends a similar allusion here. God endures the "vessels of wrath" ἐν πολλῇ μακροθυμίᾳ, possibly a rejoinder to the μακρόθυμος καὶ πολυέλεος of Exod 34:6; God's μακροθυμία is not confined to the "vessels of mercy," and is therefore not necessarily a sign of his favor (Murray). Paul's treatment would also provoke a more devastating "double take" when his readers came to realize that Paul saw the bulk of Israel as the "vessels of wrath" (as they now filled the role of Ishmael, Esau, and Pharaoh!). This certainly allows a more positive sense for μακροθυμία, that is, patience with a view to repentance (as explicitly in 2:4, also with Jewish "hardness" in view) (so particularly Cranfield, Schlier), thus quite closely parallel to Wisd Sol 11:23, 12:2, 10, 16, 18, 20 (see also SH, 267–69; but note also Luz, *Geschichtsverständnis*, 246–48, and Zeller, "Sühne," 64), even though the thought remains undeveloped at this point.

The genitive construction of σκεύη ὀργῆς allows various senses—vessels made in anger or made to experience eschatological wrath. But since the following phrase has more clearly in view final destruction and its cause, σκεύη ὀργῆς here is probably intended in the sense "vessels which are objects of God's wrath now" (cf. *TDNT* 7:364, Käsemann; for ὀργή see on 1:18). Insofar as the image of the potter is still in mind Paul presumably is thinking of the potter breaking the flawed pot to reconstruct it (by no means a speedy process when man or Israel is in view). But the precise relation to v 21 is not clear; the δέ introducing v 22 indicates that Paul could intend a complementary application of the potter metaphor (see above); a straight identification between ὁ εἰς ἀτιμίαν σκεῦος and the plural σκεύη ὀργῆς is certainly not self-evident (cf. particularly Cranfield; against Piper, 181–82). The appearance of the phrase in the sense "weapons/instruments of wrath" in Isa 13:5 Symm. and Jer 50 [LXX 27]:25—ἐξήνεγκεν τὰ σκεύη ὀργῆς αὐτοῦ—is interesting but of doubtful relevance here (cf. *TDNT* 7:364; Michel, 315 n.23; Travis, 40–41); despite Munck, *Christ*, 67–68; Hanson, *Wrath*, 90–92; Dahl, "Future," 145; Harrisville.

κατηρτισμένα εἰς ἀπώλειαν, "made ready for destruction." The view is strongly held that κατηρτισμένα is intended by Paul as a direct parallel of προητοίμασεν (v 23) and so in a strongly predestinarian sense parallel to the double predestination expressed at Qumran (as in 1QS 3.15–16; 4.24–26; 1QH 15.12–22); cf. Sir 33:7–13, *Apoc. Abr.* 22.3–7 (Müller, *Gerechtigkeit*, 77; Luz, *Geschichtsverständnis*, 245; G. Maier, 381; Michel; Käsemann; Kuss; Piper, 193–96; Räisänen, "Römer 9–11," 2904). But several considerations weigh strongly against this view. (1) καταρτίζω seems to have the basic sense of "fit together" and thus "adjust, restore, make ready or complete" (LSJ, Lightfoot on 1 Thess 3:10; see also Spicq, 416–19). That is to say, the implication is of an action performed on something already to hand in order that it might be put in proper order. This is certainly how Paul uses it elsewhere (1 Cor 1:10; 2 Cor 13:11; Gal 6:1; 1 Thess 3:10; cf. 2 Cor 13:9; Eph 4:12; 1 Pet 5:10). The perfect passive therefore does not of itself indicate the *initial* act of creation, but more probably the effect of action in the period since then (the perspective of the perfect is from the time of "destruction"). Consequently it must be judged quite likely that Paul did not intend the κατηρτισμένα as equivalent to the active προητοίμασεν of v 23, and the choice of καταρτίζω rather than προκαταρτίζω (which he uses in 2 Cor 9:5) is probably deliberate (so SH, Leenhardt, Cranfield, Maillot). The agent in the ongoing "making ready" is not specified. The passive is presumably a "divine passive" and indicates the outworking of God's ὀργή, along the lines already envisaged in 1:18–32 (cf. Siegert, 138; and further Mayer, 204–9). (2) Here again the suggestion that Paul is simply echoing the sterner double predestination notes elsewhere in Judaism is not so likely. The primary focus of the argument is not predestination but Jewish particularism. If he echoes Jewish language which presupposes the predestined destruction of the nonelect, it is to question the terms of that presupposition and by transforming the categories in effect to allow the possibility and hope that the "vessels of wrath" (redefined to include unbelieving Israel) will become "vessels of mercy" (cf. Isa 54:16–17 LXX—ἐγὼ δὲ ἔκτισά σε οὐκ εἰς ἀπώλειαν φθεῖραι). See also on 11:22.

ἀπώλεια however almost certainly has the sense "final destruction," as in Phil 3:19 (BGD, Wilckens), the eschatological antithesis to δόξα (εἰς ἀπώλειαν, εἰς δόξαν = εἰς σωτηρίαν, 1:16; cf. the contrast of 1 Cor 1:18 and 2 Cor 2:15). Paul does not dispute the reality of a final destruction (= annihilation?), but the thrust of the sentence focuses on the ἤνεγκεν ἐν πολλῇ μακροθυμίᾳ.

23 καὶ ἵνα γνωρίσῃ τὸν πλοῦτον τῆς δόξης αὐτοῦ ἐπὶ σκεύη ἐλέους, "and in order that he might make known the wealth of his glory on vessels of mercy." Unless this is taken as a new thought, whether completed (v 24) or not (see *Form and Structure*), the ἵνα clause has to be read as a purpose clause following on from the main clause of v 22 (against Wilckens), with the two preceding infinitives (ἐνδείξασθαι and γνωρίσαι) functioning more as descriptions of what God wants than as alternative or subordinate purposes (see on 9:22, θέλων). The καί then indicates that the main clause of v 22 could stand on its own, as a possibility to be weighed in its own terms, but that Paul went on to elaborate the further possibility that such divine patience might have a very definite and positive purpose in view (cf. NIV). It is at this point that a clear parallel becomes evident with the strong sense of divine purpose in the reformulated Exod 9:16 cited in v 17 (see on 9:17 and *Form and Structure*).

The πλοῦτος τῆς δόξης αὐτοῦ may be a liturgical formula (Phil 4:19; Col 1:27; Eph 1:18, 3:16; Käsemann); cf. 2:4, Eph 1:7 and 2:7; see also Dion and on 11:12. For δόξα see on 1:21 and 9:4, and as eschatological hope see on 8:17 and below. Paul probably intended an allusion back to Exod 33:18–19, with its double use of δόξα in describing the self-disclosure of God as merciful and compassionate (see on 9:15 and *Form and Structure*).

As with σκεύη ὀργῆς, the force of the genitive in σκεύη ἐλέους is to indicate those in and through whom God displays his mercy (see on 9:22). As expressed here the two phrases of course denote two different groups (Wilckens), but the end point toward which Paul is driving (11:32) can never be left out of the reckoning in any overall assessment of Paul's argument. God's mercy is the fundamental category in this whole discussion (vv 15, 16, 18), with the clear implication that Paul is calling on and reworking one of Israel's most fundamental categories (see again on 9:15); cf. F. W. Maier, 50–51.

ἃ προητοίμασεν εἰς δόξαν, "which he prepared beforehand for glory." The note of divine predetermination is clear here (as in its only other NT usage [Eph 2:10]; cf. Wisd Sol 9:8—ἀπ᾿ ἀρχῆς); the προ- is evidently intended to distinguish the verb from its equivalent (κατηρτισμένα) in the parallel phrase in v 22 (he could have used ἐτοιμάζω here, just as he could have used προκαταρτίζω there); see on 9:22. Paul does not express the same weight of confidence and clarity of insight regarding the divine purpose for the two different groups. For εἰς δόξαν see on 8:17 and 9:22 (ἀπώλεια). The thought brings us back to the same end point as 2:10; 5:2; and 8:17, 30.

Explanation

Thus far Paul has argued in effect that his kinsmen's large-scale failure to respond to the gospel is rooted in a misunderstanding of the word of God about their own election as the people of God. He has more to say about the word of God to Israel and its continuity or fulfillment in the gospel which he preaches (9:28; 10:5–13). But at this point he evidently has decided to examine further the corollary of nonelection, to explore the dark side of the moon of God's purpose in election using whatever light he can find in scripture. His first readers might think that in so doing he has taken an unnecessary sidetrack; it was enough surely to have shown that Israel had misunderstood the gospel. But Paul's anguish at his own people's failure is not so easily assuaged, and his more sensitive readers would probably realize that he is still grappling with the problem of Israel's unbelief, that in posing the problem of those passed over by God he is still thinking primarily of Israel, that in achieving some sort of theological rationale concerning the nonelect Paul could hope to find a theological rationale for Israel's de facto denial of their election.

14 "What then shall we say? Is God unjust? By no means!" By ending the last phase of the argument with Mal 1:2–3 and introducing the thought of a deliberate choice against Esau (when his central argument already had sufficient scriptural support) Paul clearly intended to set up this question as one which an attentive audience would naturally ask. The doctrine of God's free choice thus defined sounds very arbitrary. If God chooses some and rejects others without reference to anything they do, surely that is unjust? The echo of 3:5 may again be deliberate. But there the question was directed to the thought of God's role in the final judgment. If God's faithfulness disregards Israel's unfaithfulness and God's righteousness disregards their unrighteousness, is God not unjust if he condemns that same unrighteousness? Here the question is posed from the other end of the time scale, from the perspective of election rather than that of judgment. The implication could well be that while it is appropriate to ask about justice when talking of the final judgment, it is less appropriate when talking of election. After all, election does not exclude judgment, as Paul himself had shown (chap. 2). From the different perspective of election the primary question is to do with God's choice (and rejection), not with man's merits (or demerits); the central issue focuses on God's purpose and intention, not on man's deserving of praise or blame.

15 That Paul is thinking along those lines seems to be confirmed by v 15. He grounds his denial that God is unjust in Exod 33:19: "I will have mercy on whom I have mercy, and I will have compassion on whom I have compassion." Paul almost certainly intends that that verse be taken in context (an intention probably signaled by his introductory phrase—a word specifically directed to Moses, rather than the less specific "it is written"), in which case the point of significance is that Exod 33:18–23 comes closer than anywhere else in the Jewish scriptures to revealing the innermost nature of God. No man can see God and live. But Moses was evidently permitted to see something of his glory and given a deeper insight into the meaning of his name. And the revelation was summed up in those very words quoted by Paul. The God of Israel is first and foremost a God of mercy and compassion. The covenant name (Yahweh) signifies that his choice of Israel was motivated solely by pity and compassion.

16 So Paul draws out the obvious conclusion: "it is not a matter of someone wanting or of someone being energetic, but of God exercising mercy." In effect he has reworked the earlier assertion of v 11. There he spoke in terms of God's purpose and election; here of his showing mercy. But for Paul the two thoughts are synonymous. The central motivation in election is God's compassion; his purpose has the primary object of showing mercy. There too he spoke of doing good or bad; here of wanting and running. And as there he was not disparaging "doing good," so here he is not disparaging "wanting and running." "Works of the law" he does consistently disparage, but he speaks approvingly of inner resolve (7:15–21), and elsewhere he encourages his converts to show the disciplined exertion of the athlete (1 Cor 9:24–26). The point being underlined again then is that God's purpose is not conditioned on Israel's good will and effort, that God's faithfulness is predicated on God's election and does not depend on what anyone desires or does. The additional assurance afforded by God's word to Moses is that that purpose is one of compassion, that that election is God demonstrating his character of mercy.

Modern commentators should beware of generalizing too quickly from this passage. The line of argument has a specific and limited purpose and continues to be essentially *ad hominem*. Paul is thinking solely in terms of salvation-history, of God's purpose for Israel. Having established that Israel's election rests entirely in the will of God without reference to what Israel would do thereafter, and that it has been effected simply by the call of God without regard for any works of the law (vv 11–12), Paul takes one further step forward: his people should never forget that God's selection of Israel is essentially an act of mercy and compassion—a point to which Paul clings as firmly as any of his fellow countrymen. Whatever is the matter with Israel now, God's faithfulness is not a whit modified by it, and his purpose of mercy for Israel remains unchanged. A more extensive doctrine of election is not to be found here. Nor should the antithesis of v 16 be overdrawn, as though Paul was advocating an ethical attitude of total passivity. He has already emphasized the believer's obedience and moral responsibility far too much for such a corollary to be possible (e.g., 1:5; 6:12–23; 8:13). The contrast too is limited to the point at hand and the alternatives posed are God's election on the one hand and Israel's widespread belief that their obedience to the law (whether in intention or in fact) was a factor in sustaining their covenant status before God. It is the latter which Paul disputes on the basis of Israel's own scriptures dealing with their election. Beyond that we should not push Paul's argument at this stage.

17 In the preceding section of the argument Paul had not turned a blind eye to the corollary of the election of Jacob—namely, the rejection of Esau. So now having brought the discussion further on to the period of the Exodus and of Sinai he does not ignore the corollary here too: God's redemption of Israel from Egypt meant that Pharaoh had filled the same sort of antithetical role. His quotation from Exod 9:16 is significantly different from the LXX, and it is difficult to think that just these divergences can be explained solely by a variant text with which Paul was familiar. At the very least Paul has gone out of his way to translate the more ambiguous Hebrew in order to emphasize that Pharaoh's role in the drama of the Exodus was wholly in accord with God's will: "for this very purpose I raised you up in order that I might demonstrate my power in you and in order that my name might be proclaimed in all the world." His name, Paul may well imply, is still his name as the merciful one (v 15 = Exod 33:19). For Paul the Jew could, of course, claim that the result of the Exodus had been to make known the redemptive power of God throughout the world; the centrality of the Exodus in Jewish thought, and their own dispersion throughout the world, meant that God's saving act in calling his people out of Egypt was celebrated wherever Jews of the Diaspora came together for prayer. And it was within that context that Pharaoh was remembered too, within the proclamation of God's electing grace, as part of the demonstration of God's purpose of mercy. Within that purpose, Pharaoh's obduracy served as the foil to set off God's redemptive power, the darker melody in a minor key which played counterpoint to the major key of God's powerful call of Israel. The sensitive reader might already recognize the implication that Israel's rejection of the gospel was to be explained in a similar way. The antithetical role filled by Esau and Pharaoh in relation to Israel's election and redemption is now being filled by the bulk of Israel in relation to God's calling of Gentile as well as Jew through the gospel. But the full development of that theme is yet to come.

18 In the meantime Paul does not balk at bringing out the full awkwardness of the corollary. If Israel's election and redemption was an act of God's free choice, without reference to Israel's intention and conduct, then the antithetical role of Pharaoh within that purpose must have been similarly without reference to Pharaoh's intention and conduct. It must have been something brought about by God himself. Paul does not hesitate to draw this severe conclusion: "So then he has mercy on whomever he wills, and he hardens the heart of whomever he wills." Paul does not quote any passage in particular, but clearly he has in mind the repeated emphasis throughout the Exodus account (Exod 4–14) that God "hardened" Pharaoh's heart. Pharaoh's obduracy was not simply his choice or doing, as though any man could thwart God's saving purpose for others. Nor was it that God had to adapt and modify his purpose to take account of Pharaoh's attitude and actions as though they were something unexpected. Pharaoh's opposition was willed by God, was brought about by God, as the scriptures clearly relate; it was part of God's same merciful purpose, an essential element in the demonstration of God's saving power. We should be careful to note that Paul does not make this point simply out of a desire for a rigorously logical theology. His line of argument is determined by scripture; it is because this emphasis is part of God's word that he cannot avoid it. He pursues it partly because he wants his own theology to be shaped in accord with scripture, and partly (we may already guess) because he sees in this biblical emphasis on divine hardening an explanation for Israel's present hardness (2:5; cf. 11:7–12).

However, in making the point Paul has also deliberately broadened it out beyond the particular case of Israel and Pharaoh—"whom(ever) he wills"— presumably precisely because he sees in this key incident within salvation-history an important principle of wider application. All honor to Paul that he does so, that he does not retreat into a narrow election-conscious position of superiority over the nonelect, careless for the salvation of all but the elect. But then this is what we should expect from the apostle to the Gentiles who has clearly shown so far in this letter that it is just such pride in national identity and election which is at the root of Israel's misunderstanding of the covenant, and which largely explains Israel's failure to recognize that God's purpose of mercy extends beyond Israel "according to the flesh." By liberating the clear scriptural principle from its narrower salvation-history context he can explain God's wider purpose of mercy and throw light on the puzzle of why the bulk of Israel has (so far) rejected the gospel.

19 The trouble with such a strong view of election and rejection without reference to subsequent deeds and misdeeds is that it makes God's judgment on these deeds and misdeeds seem so unfair. "If he hardens whom he will, why then does he find fault? For who has resisted his will?" The two perspectives on human life from opposite ends of the time scale (election and judgment) seem to conflict. How can one retain a belief in a judgment that is just when the deeds on which that judgment falls were not the acts of free agents? How can God blame others for what he himself brought about? Does scripture not in fact present Pharaoh simply as a puppet? Anyone knows that if blame attaches to a puppet's actions it is the puppeteer who should be blamed, not the puppet!

Paul might have replied by pointing to the other passages in the Exodus narratives which speak of Pharaoh hardening his own heart (Exod 8:15, 32; 9:34). From the perspective of Israel's election Pharaoh's obduracy was part of God's purpose, but for Pharaoh himself it was his own act of free choice, and as such deserving of blame. But Paul does not take that path. Those in close touch with his train of thought would have remembered that he had in fact already shown that election and judgment can be reconciled, in 2:1– 3:20—that being outside the elect people of God is no guarantee of final condemnation, just as being inside the elect people of God is no guarantee of final justification—that, as we might say, God's firm purpose in the broad sweep of salvation-history through the centuries does not exclude or excuse any individual within that purpose from answering for his or her own deeds. So it may well be that Paul thought he need say no more on the subject of judgment.

20–21 Instead he continues to look at the issue in terms of God's purpose, from the perspective of God the Creator rather than of God the Judge. What does man the creature think he is when he questions God the Creator?

Paul has already shown that it is man's rebellion against his creaturely status which lies at the root of all his failings (1:18–32). Here he insists with unyielding firmness that the starting point in any attempt to come to terms with the two faces of God's purpose is the humble spirit of the creature before the Creator. And once again it is scripture which prompts his response—particularly the image of the potter and his clay. A truly humble spirit would think it inconceivable to protest against what it was, what God had made it, as inconceivable as the pot questioning the purpose of the potter, "Why did you make me like this?" (Isa 29:16; 45:9). A truly humble spirit would acknowledge that God the divine potter can and does make people different, out of the same human clay very different characters and personalities, that there is a givenness in peoples' make-up which fits them for different roles, differences in temperament, differences in capacities and capabilities. There are some of whom one can truly say, "That one is made for greatness," while others seem to be fit only for menial and disreputable roles (cf. Wisd Sol 15:7).

It is important to grasp the wider context of Paul's argument here and the force of what he is saying within that context. His first readers would be well aware of the widespread preoccupation in the ancient world with the problem of fate and destiny, the sense of the inevitability of what transpires, the often oppressive awareness that one could never escape one's appointed portion in life, and above all one's lot in death. Hence the popularity of the art of astrology, not least in Rome itself. Paul's readers would probably be aware also that this wider speculation was no stranger to the kind of problems Paul poses here: the recognition that a person's fate might be as much the outworking of his or her own nature as the outcome of divine action, and the unresolved issue of whether Zeus was master of fate or ultimately subject to it like the other gods. So Paul is not dealing with a question which would be foreign to his readers, nor would the element of determinism in his treatment be at all surprising or offensive. The significance of his treatment would be seen rather to lie in his insistence on treating the question in Hebraic rather than Hellenistic terms, in terms of God the Creator rather than of implacable and remorseless fate.

For Paul there is no higher power than God; the ultimate shaper of human destiny is none other than the purpose of God. The imagery of the potter and his clay artifacts serves this end well, for it was both characteristically and distinctively Jewish in its emphasis that the divine potter's authority over his products was the authority of a powerful creator (cf. particularly Sir 33:10–13). Moreover the probably deliberate echo of the most famous of the scripture's potter passages (Jer 18:1–11) would be an invitation to his Roman readers to recognize that the divine purpose could be tempered and changed, that the pot made for a disreputable use could be remade into a work to be treasured. However much or little background knowledge he could assume on the part of his readers, the effect of his rhetorical questioning here is to highlight the futility of protesting against one's "make-up," of trying to fulfill a role for which one is not "cut out." The only sensible course for each one, whether menial pot or treasured bowl, is to submit in creaturely humility before the divine potter, and perhaps by implication, to submit thereby also to his power to remake.

22–23 That, however, is not a corollary Paul stops to draw out, as well he might; just as he might have limited the harshness of his unqualified assertion that God hardens whom he will by noting that according to scripture Pharaoh hardened his own heart. But that is not his concern here; he does not intend to be sidetracked into the problems of reconciling an undeserved divine election/rejection and a deserved divine judgment. His focus remains fixed primarily on the problems caused for the former by Israel's rejection of the gospel which seems to fly in the face of (Paul's understanding of) the gospel. And it is becoming increasingly evident that he has raised the problem of divine rejection and hardening simply because, as a corollary to Israel's own doctrine of election, it can actually serve to explain Israel's own apparent rejection. It is the recognition that Paul refuses to be drawn into a discussion of the fairness or unfairness of God's judgment, and that he is intent on using Israel's history to illuminate God's purpose in salvation-history, which provides the key to the difficult verses 22–23/24.

22 The best way of understanding the opening words (literally, "but if . . . ?") is as the question "What if . . . ?"; that is, "What if it is the case that . . . ?" The preceding sequence of three rhetorical questions amounts to the rebuke, Do you think the creature knows better than the Creator? Now Paul also asks his readers to consider one possible way of understanding the divine purpose. It is the understanding which he himself has come to, as v 24 will make clear. But he does not at this stage put it forward as a dogmatic thesis (that will come later, in chap. 11). Instead he offers it for consideration. It will not answer all the problems which have been posed in the preceding verses, but it will give sufficient hint of possible answers, and more important, will provide the answer to the problem of Israel's intransigence in the face of a divine election which no longer focuses on Israel so exclusively.

"What if it is the case that God, wishing to demonstrate his wrath and to make known his power . . . ?" Paul simply recalls what he said in 1:18–32, and probably it was his intention to recall his readers to that earlier exposition. Here, as there, "wrath" denotes divine judgment. God displays his power as creator as much in rejecting what he has made as in making it. Paul does not escape the sharpness of the question in v 19 ("Why does he still find fault?") by denying that God does find fault. On the contrary it is God's express purpose to eradicate all such faults in his handiwork (whether by destruction and remaking, or simply by destruction, Paul does not say). Nor, on the other hand, does he exclude the clear implication of the earlier exposition (1:18–32) that God's wrath includes the self-destructive consequences of man's rebellion. His point simply is that God will not settle for a flawed creation: his will expressed both in the outworking of man's own sin and in the day of judgment is the destruction of that flawedness.

Given that, "what if it is the case that God has borne with much patience the objects of wrath made ready for destruction . . . ?" This is the principal clause of the sentence and thus bears the main weight of the argument. Paul invites his readers to consider the possibility that the creator God who as creator passes judgment on his creation, nevertheless has withheld that judgment out of concern for his creation, flawed as it is. It is not as though

Paul is embarrassed at the thought of God's judgment, and wants to maintain as a generalization that God's mercy will always triumph over his judgment. They are still "objects of wrath," "ready for destruction." It is simply that he wants to draw his readers' attention to a possibility which strengthens still further the contrast between Greek belief in fate and Hebraic belief in the purposeful Creator: viz., that even God's purpose of judgment is tempered by patience, even with earthenware fit only for the scrap heap we can hardly think of a pitiless end that brooks no delay, but must recognize a divine readiness to delay the final rejection (cf. Luke 13:6–9).

There may be a similar element of softening of the more rigorous statement of God as the hardener of hearts (v 18) in the phrase "made ready for destruction." For the verb has the sense of "fully prepared, completely ready," and in contrast to the parallel phrase in v 23 Paul seems deliberately to refrain from saying "which he (God) made ready . . ." or "made ready beforehand." So the implication may be intended by Paul that the "being prepared" for destruction was not entirely or solely the action of the divine potter. As he had argued so clearly in 1:18–32, God's wrath comes upon man's *rebellion,* his rebellion precisely against his creaturely role; man cannot escape responsibility for his fitness for destruction; on the contrary, in striking free from God he assumed the primary responsibility for what he became. In all this Paul and his readers would no doubt be aware of the inadequacy of the metaphor of an inanimate pot to describe human beings. He retains it because it highlights so powerfully the purpose of the Creator as the moving force in history. But in speaking of the Creator's patience toward the "objects of wrath" he signals his awareness that he has in mind human beings who provoke the wrath which God brings to bear on them (cf. 3:5–6).

However here again we must avoid being sidetracked. Paul has no intention of engaging in a debate about election and judgment (far less about predestination and free will). The appeal of his questions is to those who already recognize that the determining force is God the creator, God in his creative and forbearing purpose. In particular he has in view still his own people's theological determinism, in terms of the covenant election of Israel and its corollary rejection of Esau and hardening of Pharaoh. He put the issue in more general terms in v 18, not least because he wants to turn Israel's own doctrine of election and rejection into an explanation for Israel's current failure to respond to the gospel. It is this twist in the *ad hominem* argument which his readers would begin to become aware of beginning in v 22 and coming to clear expression in v 24. The point is that in the context of the preceding argument "objects of wrath" would most naturally be understood with reference to Esau and Pharaoh, those who suffer the negative corollary of Israel's election. But Paul is about to make it clear that the "objects of wrath" are the covenant people themselves, or more precisely, the bulk of the covenant people who have rejected the continuity/fulfillment of the covenant in the gospel. Likewise no Jew could speak of the patience of God without immediately thinking of the oft-repeated formula in his scriptures, first promulgated in Exod 34:6: "The Lord . . . forbearing and very merciful. . . ." And though psalmist and prophet recognized that what was true of God in his covenant relationship with Israel would be no less true of God as creator as well (Ps 145:8–9;

Jonah 4:2), it would be his patient forbearance to Israel in particular which would most naturally spring to mind. Here indeed Paul may well be making another deliberate allusion to Wisd Sol 15, where we find just such an expression of Israel's confidence in God's patience (15:1–3) followed immediately by use of the potter metaphor to disparage Gentile idolatry (15:4–17; v 7 already echoed in Rom 9:21). The alert reader who had been aware of Paul's allusion to Wisd Sol 12–15 in Rom 1:18–32, and who recalled how Paul had turned the tables on his people's excessive self-confidence in 2:1–6 (2:4 also echoing Wisd Sol 15:1 ff.), might well therefore suspect that in 9:22 he is about to do precisely the same. The "objects of wrath" are not (just) pagan idolaters but (also) unbelieving Israelites! It follows also that the more clearly the turn around in the argument was recognized, the more likely would the reader be to recognize the double entendre intended by Paul: Israel has indeed to recognize that it has abused its covenant confidence ("made ready for destruction!"); nevertheless its confidence in God's forbearance *is* well founded. This "double-take" implication aimed first at puncturing Israel's excessive self-assurance, and then at reaffirming its basis, typifies the twin emphases of Paul's argument in the letter as a whole, and also prepares the reader for Paul's resolution of the tension between the two emphases in chap. 11.

23 "What if it is the case that God . . . has borne with much patience the objects of wrath made ready for destruction, so also as to make known the wealth of his glory to the objects of mercy which he prepared beforehand for glory?" The case Paul asks his readers to consider involves not only a purpose of wrath (however tempered by "much patience") but also a purpose of mercy. However we take the connection of clauses it is clear enough that Paul does not think of the two destinies ("objects of wrath," "objects of mercy") as independent of each other. The delay in bringing wrath to bear on those made ready for destruction has also in view those prepared beforehand for glory. There is a unity of purpose in what God wills: as his purpose of mercy to Israel involved also his rejection of Esau, and as his purpose of redemption for the children of Israel involved also his hardening of Pharaoh's heart, so his treatment of the objects of wrath is bound up with his purpose of mercy for the objects of mercy.

Here too a readership familiar with the measured tones of Israel's oft-repeated confidence in God's "forbearance and great mercy" would probably notice Paul's separation of the two terms, patience and mercy. The point is that just as Israel could still affirm confidence in God's patience, but now to Israel according to the flesh as "objects of wrath," so too the "objects of mercy" are no longer to be understood as Israel per se but, as v 24 is about to state explicitly, Gentiles as well as Jews. The double repetition of the word "glory," a leitmotif in Paul's exposition of the gospel, would also warn of the imminent transformation in v 24, since Paul's use of it so far in the letter has been consistently to underscore the universality of man's plight (1:23; 3:23) and the hope of everyone who is good (2:7, 10) as well as the believer's hope in particular (5:2; 8:18, 21). So too the emphasis that "he (God) chose the objects of mercy beforehand" (in contrast to the less specific "made ready" in v 22) would underline Paul's assertion of the continuity of the gospel with God's covenant election while again bringing the overconfident

Israelite up short. The broadening out of God's call beyond Israel as a national entity was *always* in view. It was not simply an afterthought, a change of plan in view of Israel's intransigence. God planned it so from the beginning! His choice of Israel as a covenant people, as the objects of his patience and mercy, always had this wider call in view, an objective of mercy which extended well beyond Israel as such. So too, the message is becoming steadily clearer, Israel's present intransigence is no less within the purpose of God, part of his purpose of mercy for all, Gentile and Jew alike.

3. *Those Called Include Both Jews and Gentiles, As Prophesied* *(9:24–29)*

Bibliography

See 9:1–11:36 and 9:6–29 *Bibliography*.

Translation

24*By which I mean us, whom also he called, not only from Jews but also from Gentiles,* 25*as he says in*a *Hosea;*

> *I will call the "not my people" my people*
> *and the "not loved" loved;*
> 26*and it shall be in the place where it was said to them,*
> *You are not my people,*
> *there they shall be called sons of the living God.*

27*Isaiah proclaims concerning Israel,*

> *Even if the number of the sons of Israel are as the sand of the*
> *sea, (only) the remnant*b *shall be saved,*
> 28*for the Lord will complete and cut short*c *and will perform*
> *his word on the earth.*

29*And as Isaiah said beforehand,*

> *Except the Lord of Sabaoth had left us seed*
> *we would have become like Sodom and we would have been the*
> *same as Gomorrah.*

Notes

ᵃp⁴⁶ (apparently) and B omit the ἐν (God says *to* Hosea), presumably in recognition of the unusualness of the formula.

ᵇThe reading κατάλειμμα has strong support (including p⁴⁶), but is almost certainly an alteration to accord with the LXX.

ᶜThere was a natural scribal tendency to introduce the words of Isa 10:23 omitted by Paul (see on 9:27–28; Metzger).

Form and Structure

See also 9:6–13 *Form and Structure.*

Most prefer to read the argument as continuing without a significant break from vv 19–23, and some prefer to treat v 24 as the completion of vv 22–23 (see 9:14–23 *Form and Structure*), but a pause for breath does seem to be indicated between vv 23 and 24 (see on 9:24), and a new paragraph in the translation seems to be the best way to signal that (as NEB, Käsemann).

Vv 25–29 form an effective string of scriptural citations. Such catenae were probably quite common in preaching and teaching (Michel; see also Fitzmyer, "4Q Testimonia," 65–70), but this one is too closely integrated to the argument for it to have been a preformed piece and was probably constructed by Paul when chaps. 9–11 were composed; though it would be possible to argue that there was a pre-Pauline Christian "florilegium" on the single theme of Israel's restoration which Paul adapted by changing the reference of the first two Hosea passages to the Gentiles (Wilckens, 2:198–99; Lindars, "Universalism," 516–17). At all events the catena here clearly functions to confirm the thematic claim of 9:6a.

Comment

24 οὓς καὶ ἐκάλεσεν ἡμᾶς, "whom also he called, us." The awkwardness of the phrasing is presumably deliberate and almost certainly meant that in being read aloud the words would have to be taken slowly and with emphasis, particularly on the awkward ἡμᾶς (cf. Black). We should envisage therefore that the careful reader (to the congregation) was intended to leave the incomplete vv 22–23 hanging, pause, catch fresh attention with the unexpected οὓς (following ἅ), and reinforce the impact with the identifying ἡμᾶς. Obviously encouraged thereby is the "double-take" corollary indicating the implied identity of the other "vessels" (of wrath). For alternative ways of taking the syntax see Cranfield (but the ἡμᾶς is hardly merely "slipped in"); see also *Form and Structure*. The καί does not belong with ἡμᾶς (as Lietzmann) as though the "us" were different from the "vessels of mercy" (v 23); rather, it picks up and builds on the προητοίμασεν (Käsemann, Kuss, Schlier), giving a sequence like that in 8:30 (οὓς δὲ προώρισεν, τούτους καὶ ἐκάλεσεν). After the predominant emphasis on "mercy" in vv 14–23, the principal thematic word reemerges in ἐκάλεσεν (vv 7, 12, 24–26; see on 1:1, 4:17, and 8:30; also Schlier and Wilckens). The predetermined election is enacted in the reality of the present calling (cf. Käsemann).

οὐ μόνον ἐξ Ἰουδαίων ἀλλὰ καὶ ἐξ ἐθνῶν, "not only from Jews but also from Gentiles." The contrast resumes an even earlier thematic emphasis (Jew/Greek—1:16; 2:9, 10; 3:9; see on 1:16), but this time as Jew/Gentile and recalling the "not only/but also" argument of 4:16 (cf. 3:29); for ἔθνος see on 1:5. The ἐκ indicates a calling "out of," with implication of separation, from a larger body (as also the use of Ἰουδαῖος again over against the predominant Ἰσραήλ; see on 9:4). There is a slight sectarian overtone (the smaller "us" over against the much larger bodies), but the sense of the "us" as a new and distinct body (cf. Eph 2:15), let alone a "third race," is still over the horizon (see also Richardson, *Israel*).

25 ὡς καὶ ἐν τῷ Ὡσηὲ λέγει, "as also he says in Hosea." The καί indicates that the following quotation not merely documents the claim of v 24 but develops it as well; that is, "furthermore, moreover" (cf. Schlier, Wilckens). The formula reference ("in Hosea") is unusual but occurs also in Mark 1:2, and either is simply a stylistic variation, or refers to the Hosea portion of the Book of the Twelve Prophets (Burchard). The most obvious subject of λέγει is the same as the previous verbs; the point is not emphasized, and a vaguer "it says" would be quite acceptable (NEB, Black) without reducing the force of the scriptural authority cited.

The rest of the verse is a quotation from Hos 2:25 LXX (MT 2:23), though with considerable variation from the OT (MT = LXX).

Hosea: ἐλεήσω τὴν οὐκ ἠλεημένην
                 καὶ ἐρῶ τῷ οὐ λαῷ μου λαός μου εἶ σύ
Romans: καλέσω τὸν οὐ λαόν μου λαόν μου
                 καὶ τὴν οὐκ ἠγαπημένην ἠγαπημένην·
Hosea: I will have pity on 'Not pitied'
                 and I will say to 'Not my people,' 'You are my people.'
Romans: I will call the 'Not my people' my people
                 and the 'Not loved' loved.

The καλέσω is almost certainly Paul's insertion: it sustains his main thematic emphasis and eases the awkwardness of the LXX Greek, without changing the sense. Why he abandons the previous line of the Hosea text is less clear; perhaps he wanted to retain ἐλεέω in a consistently positive sense throughout these chapters (the merciful purpose of God consistent throughout history). It is possible that the LXX read also καὶ ἀγαπήσω τὴν οὐκ ἠγαπημένην (B), but that is probably a later Christian insertion prompted by Paul's rendering here. In view of the prominence of ἀγαπᾶν in Hosea Paul presumably thought this an appropriate alternative rendering (cf. Rom 8:28, 37; 9:13), and he may even have intended it to sum up the whole message of Hosea—a suggestion strengthened by the fact that he runs the quotation straight on without a break to another verse from Hosea (v 26; cf. rabbinic practice—Str-B, 3:274). Whatever the reason, his freedom in quoting the text combined with respect for its sense should be noted; see also on 9:27–28 (cf. Schmidt, 169). Dodd thinks the prophecy "ill-chosen" (it would have fitted better in the exposition of chap. 11) but misses the point that Hosea's allegorical case study and the promise to the Northern Kingdom of Israel enshrine a principle (that those once rejected can be taken back again), which, coming as it does in the wake of 9:6–23, can be referred to rejected Ishmael, Esau, and Pharaoh as much as to hardened Israel, who of course may also be in mind (Barrett).

26 καὶ ἔσται ἐν τῷ τόπῳ οὗ ἐρρέθηαὐτοῖς, οὐ λαός μου ὑμεῖς,
               ἐκεῖ κληθήσονται υἱοὶ θεοῦ ζῶντος,
          "and it shall be in the place where it was said to them,
               'You are not my people,'
          there shall they be called sons of the living God."

The verse is a word for word citation of Hos 2:1 LXX (MT 1:10). In Hosea the phrase ἐν τῷ τόπῳ ("in the place") would most naturally be taken to refer to Palestine, where Hosea prophesied (Hos 1:8–9). If Paul had this implication in mind it could be, as Munck argues (12–13, 72–73), that he intended to evoke the idea of the eschatological pilgrimage of the Gentiles to Zion (as in Ps 22:27; Isa 2:2–3; 56:6–8; 60:2; Mic 4:2; Zeph 3:9; Zech 2:11; 14:16; Tob 13:11; 14:6–7; *Pss. Sol.* 17.34; *Sib. Or.* 3.710–20, 772–75; *T. Zeb.* 9.8; *T. Ben.* 9.2; cf. Mark 11:17 = Isa 56:7; 12:9 pars.; Matt 8:11 // Luke 13:29; see also on 10:20, 11:12, 25; and 15:25). But if he intended any force in the phrase at all his emphasis was more likely theological than geographical = "even there where . . ." (cf. Cranfield, Wilckens). It will have been the contrast "not my people"/"sons of the living God" which will have attracted Paul most of all, reinforcing as it does the contrast, which is so basic to his whole argument, between the national/ethnic perspective of his people and the potentially much more universal category "sons of God" (see on 1:3 and 8:14); though it should not be forgotten that the argument still stands under the rubric of 9:6a (Dahl, "Israel," 146). θεὸς ζῶν ("living God") is a formulation which characterizes the Jewish conception of God (in contrast to "dead idols" [F. W. Maier, 56]), and which as such was taken over by the first Christians (cf. particularly 2 Cor 6:16 and 1 Thess 1:9; see further BGD, ζάω 1aε).

The contrast between Paul's attitude to the Gentiles and that of his fellow Jews should not be exaggerated (as by Käsemann, who cites only *4 Ezra* 6.55, 59; 7.11). It is true that there are many statements in Jewish writings hostile to the other nations and often eager for their subjugation or destruction, but there are also many other positive ones which hope for the salvation of the nations (see the texts collected by Sanders, *Jesus,* 214), including those which envisage the eschatological pilgrimage of the nations (see above), and not least *Jos. As.* 19.8, which uses the same phrase "sons of the living God" as part of the book's appeal to potential proselytes. The difference lies not in the attitude to Gentiles as such, but in the terms on which their salvation may be envisaged—that is, by walking in the ways of the law (e.g., Isa 2:3; *Sib. Or.* 3.719), including not least the observance of such key covenant markers as the sabbath (Isa 56:6; *Jub.* 2.19)—whereas Paul thinks in terms of the unrestricted possibilities of faith (emphasized in the next section [9:30–10:13]).

As Käsemann notes, by citing the passages which can be said to envisage the Gentiles (the "not my people") first, Paul reverses the usual order (Jew first, but Greek/Gentile as well), thus making more effective the impact of his redefinition of the "vessels of mercy." On rejected Israel (the ten northern tribes addressed by Hosea) as the type of both Gentiles and unbelieving Israel, see Cranfield.

27a Ἠσαΐας δὲ κράζει ὑπὲρ τοῦ Ἰσραήλ, "Isaiah proclaims concerning Israel." κράζει is not merely stylistic (cf. Str-B, 3:275; *TDNT* 3:900), but probably indicates a degree of intensity or urgency (cf. BGD) which gives the following citation a more threatening color. ὑπέρ = περί, as elsewhere in Paul (BGD, ὑπέρ 1f). Ἰσραήλ is used again, not simply as given by the Isaiah passage about to be quoted, but because Paul is no longer speaking of two separate entities (Jew and Gentile, as in v 24) and is intent once again to redefine his people's favorite self-designation (see on 9:4).

27b–28 The quotation which follows is an amalgam (conscious or unconscious) of Hos 1:10 [LXX 2:1] and Isa 10:22–23.

Hosea: καὶ ἦν ὁ ἀριθμὸς τῶν υἱῶν Ἰσραὴλ ὡς ἡ ἄμμος τῆς θαλάσσης . . .
Isaiah: καὶ ἐὰν γένηται ὁ λαὸς   Ἰσραὴλ ὡς ἡ ἄμμος τῆς θαλάσσης
Romans: ἐὰν ᾖ ὁ ἀριθμὸς τῶν υἱῶν   Ἰσραὴλ ὡς ἡ ἄμμος τῆς θαλάσσης

Isaiah: τὸ κατάλειμμα αὐτῶν σωθήσεται· λόγον γὰρ συντελῶν καὶ
Romans: τὸ ὑπόλειμμα   σωθήσεται· ²⁸ λόγον γὰρ συντελῶν καὶ
Isaiah: συντέμνων ἐν δικαιοσύνῃ,   ²³ ὅτι λόγον συντετμημένον
Romans: συντέμνων
Isaiah: ποιήσει ὁ θεὸς ἐν τῇ οἰκουμένῃ ὅλῃ
Romans: ποιήσει κύριος ἐπὶ της γῆς.

Paul is obviously following the LXX: its reading σωθήσεται for בוּשָׁי—("return") would appeal to him (cf. 1:16; 5:9–10; 8:24; 10:1, 9–13; 11:26); and its rendering of the difficult Hebrew in the following lines could be understood more as a promise than the Hebrew (*TDNT* 8:64). Paul's abbreviation could be deliberate (though the omission of a δικαιοσύνη reference is somewhat surprising) or accidental (a kind of mental haplography, the mind running συντέμνων and συντετμημένον together). The variation in the final phrase could indicate that Paul's version was different at this point, or that he assimilated (again consciously or unconsciously) the similarly worded Isa 28:22.

The most difficult issue is to catch the precise sense of the συντελῶν καὶ συντέμνων phrase. συντελέω is familiar enough in the sense "complete, carry out, accomplish" (BGD). The much less frequent συντέμνω (only here in the NT) has the basic sense of "cut short, cut down, cut off" (LSJ). The combination is certainly threatening in Isa 28:22 and Dan 5:28, but much more hopeful in Dan 9:24 Theod. Some kind of threat does seem implicit, as in v 29b (Michel, Käsemann), and the rendering "complete and decisive" (Cranfield; so Zeller) seems to diminish the force of συντέμνω unwarrantably (NEB's "summary and final" is better). A temporal sense (cutting short the time, that is, the time available for Israel's coming to faith (cf. Zahn, Althaus, Schmidt, NJB) seems to read too much into the language at this point (see also BGD, συντέμνω). If we give more weight to the λόγον ποιεῶ (see Wilckens, n.931) it must also be considered unlikely that Paul intended the thought of God "cutting short" his word (in the light of 9:6). However the phrase is rendered, it must have in view God *accomplishing* his purpose in a (temporarily) *diminished* Israel (Schlier, Wilckens).

The "remnant" language (τὸ ὑπόλειμμα) could be used negatively and threateningly (2 Kgs 21:14; Isa 14:22, 30; Ezek 5:10), but Paul here obviously has the positive sense in mind (found also in Gen 45:7; 2 Kgs 19:31; Mic 4:7; 5:7–8; Sir 44:17; 47:22; 1 Macc 3:35). See further particularly *TDNT* 4:196–214, and on 11:5. Qumran knows the same double use—"a remnant" as a threatening concept (1QS 4.14; 5.13; CD 2.6; 1QM 1.6; 4.2; 14.5; 1QH 6.32; 7.22), but also themselves as the remnant of the covenant people (CD 1.4–5; 1QM 13.8; 14.8–9; 1QH 6.8). Paul's use of these texts written in the face of the particular historical circumstances of the Assyrian threat would have been regarded as quite acceptable in Jewish circles. Here again it needs to be recalled that Paul was not the only Jew who wrestled with the problem of relating the reality of the faithful few to the Israel of promise (see on 9:6).

29 καὶ καθὼς προείρηκεν Ἡσαΐας, "and as Isaiah said beforehand." The second explicit mention of Isaiah may reflect the special significance of this prophet for Paul (Schlier; cf. 1:1, 5; see chaps. 9–11 *Introduction*), as for earliest Christianity generally. For προείρηκεν cf. 1:2 and Gal 3:8.

> εἰ μὴ κύριος Σαβαὼθ ἐγκατέλιπεν ἡμῖν σπέρμα,
> ὡς Σόδομα ἂν ἐγενήθημεν
> καὶ ὡς Γόμορρα ἂν ὡμοιώθημεν,
> "except the Lord of Sabaoth had left us seed
> we would have become like Sodom
> and we would have been the same as Gormorrah."

The quotation is in verbatim agreement with Isa 1:9 LXX, including LXX's use of σπέρμα to translate שָׂרִיד כִּמְעָט ("a few survivors"); see Cranfield. But the ideas of "seed" and "remnant" can be treated as closely correlated concepts (cf. Isa. 6:13; 37:3–4; CD 2.11–12; *1 Enoch* 83.8 with 84.5; Zeller). Since so many of the themes in these closing verses pick up key motifs from the opening of the section (see 9:6–29 *Form and Structure*) it is most likely that Paul intends the σπέρμα to recall the σπέρμα of vv 7–8 (Barrett; against Cranfield). The language also points forward to 11:4–5 (κατέλιπον . . . λεῖμμα) (Michel). Sodom and Gomorrah (Gen 19) are used elsewhere as types of eschatological judgment (Deut 32:32–35; *Jub.* 16.5–6; Matt 10:15 par.; 11:23–24; Luke 17:28–30; 2 Pet 2:6; Jude 7; Rev 11:8; cf. Jer 23:14 and Ezek 16:46–49) (Wilckens). "The situation of Israel is such that Paul can mention Israel in the same breath as Sodom and Gomorrah" (Lübking, 76). Mayer (224) rightly notes that vv 27–29 speak not of the sovereign choice of God, but simply of the *fact* that at present only a remnant of Israel believe.

Explanation

24 Having put forward his suggested understanding of the Creator's purpose for both kinds of product as a hypothetical question, Paul now abruptly transposes the hypothesis into a statement of fact: "by which I mean ourselves, whom he called not only from among the Jews but also from among the Gentiles as well." The tables are turned indeed. It is now clear who the "objects of mercy" are, and the not-so-perceptive reader would suddenly realize by way of contrast who the "objects of wrath" are. The attitude which Paul neatly turns against itself may well be illustrated by 2 Macc 6:13–16, where the same contrast is made—God's "patience" with other nations delaying punishment "until they have reached the full measure of their sins," contrasted with his unfailing "mercy" toward his people, even when expressed as immediate punishment designed as discipline. It is just this contrast which Paul has turned on its head. It is Israel who now benefits from God's delay in punishment, and the call in which Israel rested (9:7, 11) is now extended to Gentiles as well as Jews, as God had always intended it should be.

25–29 Paul has now brought into the open what he had been building up to throughout chap. 9, both in demonstrating that Israel's call never had regard to race or conduct (including "works"), and in turning on its head Israel's belief that others were rejected in order that Israel might be chosen and redeemed. He now follows through by citing a catena of texts which confirm that God's purpose never had Israel as a people solely in view and never Israel as a whole or Israel the nation as such. The seemingly new range of God's call, embracing neither Jew alone nor Gentile alone, but all who respond to that call, whether Jew or Gentile, was foreseen and spoken of long before in scripture.

25–26 Paul sees in the words addressed to the Northern Kingdom (Israel), prior to its annihilation by the Assyrians, a foreshadowing of his point. By his call God can transform the covenant status of those outside the covenant, or rejected from the covenant. He can invite those with no standing whatsoever to become "sons of the living God" (Hos 1:10; 2:23). It is hardly likely that Paul means to imply that the Gentiles who have responded to God's call have shown themselves thereby to be the lost and dispersed ten northern tribes. It is simply that scripture proves that those who were not God's people can by God's gracious act become his people. Paul may also have it in mind that it was Israel who by its adultery lost its covenant status and so may also see in the words of Hosea a promise of Israel's restoration. But the main force of the quotation, achieved by altering Hos 2:23 to introduce the word "call," is to emphasize that being the people of God is something brought about solely by God's invitation, that his call can completely transform what had appeared to be a clear-cut case of divine rejection. And that in the first instance would be seen as a firm scriptural counter to Israel's presumption of a still sustained favored nation status. The privilege of sonship with which Israel had been favored (vv 4, 8) has been extended to all who respond to God's call now through the gospel.

27–28 The second scripture refers exclusively to Israel. For someone as familiar with the sacred writings of his people as Paul was, the association of Isa 10:22–23 with Hos 1:10 [2:1 LXX] was both verbally and thematically appropriate—both passages referring as they do to the Northern Kingdom in its decline and fall. The Isaiah passage is striking, for it echoes one of the central covenant promises to the patriarchs, of seed "like the sand of the sea" (particularly Gen 32:12), and implies therefore that even the foundation promises of the covenant could provide no guarantee that God would exercise an undiscriminating favor toward Israel. On the contrary, the promise could be fulfilled, and yet only a small proportion, a remnant, be saved. Here again then scripture gave clear warning against an exclusive presumption of final salvation based solely on God's original promises: the promises remain sound; the presumption would prove false. Paul certainly shows once more his awareness, his troubled consciousness (9:1–3), that so few of his people had (so far) responded to the gospel. But no doubt he saw Isaiah's words as divine confirmation that the relatively poor response of his people was part of God's overall purpose for the end time. And perhaps too he hoped that by seeing Isaiah's proclamation thus fulfilled his people would be provoked to swell the ranks of the remnant (cf. 11:13–16).

V 28 is an abbreviation of Isa 10:23. The idea of God enacting his word on the land is clear enough, but the two participles add a peremptory note, something about "completing" and "cutting short." Their meaning is unclear, and Paul makes no effort to clarify it; indeed his abbreviation makes it more ambiguous, as Paul may well have intended. He could mean his readers to refer the verbs to each of the preceding clauses: God will indeed fulfill his promise (Israel like the sand of the sea) and cut it short (only a remnant saved). Or he may simply have intended to preserve the warning and menace of the Isaiah passage, with the implication that further delay on the part of Israel could prove fatal. Alternatively he may have been uncomfortable with Isaiah's proposition: it was precisely because only a "remnant" had responded to the gospel that Paul was so upset (9:1–3). So possibly he wanted the ambiguity of Isa 10:23 to serve as some qualification or softening of the harsh outline of the preceding verse: just as God could complete and cut short his promise of seed like the sand of the sea, so he could complete and cut short his warning that only a remnant would be saved. Paul will not settle for only a remnant; his hope and prayer is that "all Israel will be saved" (11:26). At all events the talk of God enacting his word through or despite Israel's rejection of the gospel serves as further proof that God's word has not failed (9:6).

29 The idea of a remnant leads Paul to his final text—an earlier word of Isaiah on the same theme, which Paul again sees as a scripture that speaks directly to the case in point. What was a warning in Isa 10:22–23, in Isa 1:9 is more a gasp of gratitude that God had not allowed his people to be totally destroyed, as they richly deserved. The LXX, while retaining the idea of remnant, had, however, used the word "seed": "Except the Lord of Sabaoth had left us seed. . . ." Paul could fairly expect that his readers would see the link with his earlier argument in 4:16–18, already echoed a few verses previously (9:8). The "seed"/descendants which Isaiah gives thanks for, Paul sees as the seed of promise, the "many nations" promised to Abraham as descendants. This more positive emphasis struck by Isa 1:9 and the broader reference in the word "seed" enables Paul to round off this stage of his argument on a more hopeful note: a "remnant" sounds depressingly few; "seed" can embrace all the nations, Gentile as well as Jew.

C. The Word of Faith   (9:30–10:21)

Introduction

The reason that Gentiles have responded to God's call, while Israel for the most part seems to have lost the way, has already been indicated with sufficient clarity in chaps. 2–4. But now Paul addresses the issues posed by this surprising contrast more directly. Significantly he expresses his point in terms of the letter's primary theme—righteousness and faith—with the counterpoint theme of the law now fully integrated. The trouble with Israel is that they have confused the law and the righteousness it speaks of with works like circumcision which serve to make righteousness a function of Jewish identity rather than of God's gracious outreach to and through faith. This failure came to eschatological expression and climax in their refusal to recognize Christ as Messiah (vv 30–33). To reinforce the point Paul repeats the sequence of the indictment (cf. Refoulé, "Note"): they have confused zeal for God with the fervor for ethnic purity of a Phinehas; they have regarded righteousness as something peculiarly their own and not anyone else's; they have sought to establish the covenant like a Mattathias (1 Macc 2:27), forgetting that only God can do that. But Christ marks the end of that narrowing and superficializing of the law in reference to righteousness for all who believe (vv 1–4).

Paul's thesis then is of the law misunderstood and abused to give a concept of righteousness restricted to those living according to Jewish tradition and custom (the equivalent of the law abused and corrupted by sin in chap. 7). This view of the law is characterized by Lev 18:5 (note the linking γάρs in vv 2–5), whereas Deut 30:11–14 expresses a righteousness much more universal in character which makes an eschatological "fit" with the word of the gospel offered to faith and to all who believe in Christ (vv 5–13) (Dunn, "Romans 10:1–10"). Israel has heard this word, but not believed or obeyed it (vv 14–21). This final scriptural description of Israel's unbelief as disobedient corresponds to the characterization of Israel's failure to reach the law in 9:31 and to the indictment of 2:17–29, so justifying the earlier charge that Israel's focusing of the law too narrowly on works and ethnic identity amounts to law-breaking. Thus, while Munck is justified in his protest against putting the whole section under the heading of Israel's disobedience (*Christ*, 78), it remains nevertheless true that the most consistent theme is Israel's failure (though what that failure consists of has to be stated carefully).

Paul's recall of the key vocabulary and motifs of the central section of his earlier argument, and the fresh elaboration of them throughout this section, presumably indicates that he wants it to be held together and intends this section to be definitive in tying the problem of Israel's unbelief to his major theme:

	1:16–17	3:20–5:21	6–8	9:1–29	9:30–10:21	11	12–16
δικαιοσύνη	1	14	6	0	11	0	1
πίστις	3	20	0	0	5	1	7
πιστεύω	1	7	1	0	8	0	3
νόμος	0	17	30	0	4	0	2
ἔργα	0	5	0	1	1	1	1

Also to be observed is the way Paul rings the changes in his use of these key categories in a sequence of antithetical pairs:

(9:30)	δικαιοσύνη ἐκ πίστεως		
(9:31–32)	= νόμος δικαιοσύνης (ἐκ πίστεως)	/	νόμος δικαιοσύνης (ἐξ ἔργων)
(10:3)	= δικαιοσύνη θεοῦ	/	ἡ ἰδία δικαιοσύνη
(10:5–6)	= δικαιοσύνη ἐκ πίστεως	/	δικαιοσύνη ἐκ νόμου

Gaston, *Paul*, 126–30, suggests that Isa 51:1–8 lies behind this section.

1. Israel Has Misunderstood God's Righteousness   (9:30–10:4)

Bibliography

See also 9:1–11:36 *Bibliography*.

Badenas, R. *Christ the End of the Law: Romans 10:4 in Pauline Perspective.* JSNTSup 10. Sheffield: JSOT, 1985. **Barrett, C. K.** "Rom 9:30–10:21: Fall and Responsibility in Israel." In *Israelfrage*, ed. Lorenzi. 99–121. **Betz, O.** "Felsenmann und Felsenge-meinde." *ZNW* 48 (1957) 49–77. **Bring, R.** "Die Gerechtigkeit Gottes und das alttesta-mentliche Gesetz: Eine Untersuchung von Röm 10:4." In *Christus und das Gesetz.* Leiden: Brill, 1969. 35–72. ———. "Paul and the Old Testament: A Study of the Ideas of Election, Faith, and Law in Paul, with Special Reference to Rom 9:30–10:13." *ST* 25 (1971) 21–60. **Campbell, W. S.** "Christ the End of the Law: Romans 10:4." *Studia Biblica 1978.* Vol. 3. Ed. E. A. Livingstone. JSNTSup 3. Sheffield: JSOT, 1979. 73–81. **Cranfield, C. E. B.** "Some Notes on Romans 9:30–33." In *Jesus und Paulus,* FS W. G. Kümmel, ed. E. E. Ellis and E. Grässer. Göttingen: Vandenhoeck & Ruprecht, 1975. 35–43. **Dinter, P. E.** *Remnant.* **Dülmen, A. van.** *Theologie.* 123–27, 204–218. **Dunn, J. D. G.** "'Righteousness from the Law' and 'Righteousness from Faith': Paul's Interpretation of Scripture in Romans 10:1–10." In *Tradition and Interpretation in the New Testament,* FS E. E. Ellis, ed. G. F. Hawthorne. Grand Rapids: Eerdmans, 1987. 216–28. **Flückiger, F.** "Christus, des Gesetzes τέλος." *TZ* 11 (1955) 153–57. **Gaston, L.** "Torah." ———. *Paul.* 126–30. **Hofius, O.** "Gesetz." 276–78. **Howard, G. E.** "Christ the End of the Law: The Meaning of Romans 10:4." *JBL* 88 (1969) 331–37. **Jewett, R.** "Law." 349–54. **Kertelge, K.** *Rechtfertigung.* 95–99. **Lindars, B.** *Apologetic.* 169–86. **Ljungman, H.** *Pistis.* 80–84, 102–5. **Luz,** *Geschichtsverständnis.* 96–98, 139–45, 156–58. **Martin, B. L.** "Paul on Christ and the Law." *JETS* 26 (1983) 271–82. **Meyer, P. W.** "Romans 10:4 and the End of the Law." In *The Divine Helmsman,* FS L. H. Silberman, ed. J. L. Crenshaw and S. Sandmel. New York: Ktav, 1980. 59–78. **Müller, K.** *Anstoss.* 71–83. **Mussner, F.** "Christus (ist) des Gesetzes Ende zur Gerechtigkeit für jeden, der glaubt (Röm 10:4)." *Paulus—Apostat oder Apostel?* Regensburg: Pustet, 1977. 31–44. **Räisänen, H.** *Law.* 53–56, 174–75. **Refoulé, F.** "Romans 10:4: Encore une fois." *RB* 91 (1984) 321–50. ———. "Note sur Romains 9:30–33." *RB* 92 (1985) 161–86. **Rhyne, C. T.** *Faith.* 95–116. ———. "*Nomos dikaiosynes* and the Meaning of Romans 10:4." *CBQ* 47 (1985) 486–99. **Sanders, E. P.** *Law.* 36–43. **Sanders, J. A.** "Torah and Paul." In *God's Christ and His People,* FS N. A. Dahl, ed. J. Jervell and W. A. Meeks. Oslo: Universitetsforlaget, 1977. 132–40. **Schnabel, E. J.** *Law.* 290–99. **Schneider, E. E.** "Finis legis Christus, Rom 10:4." *TZ* 20 (1964) 410–22. **Selwyn, E. G.** *1 Peter.* 268–77. **Stuhlmacher, P.** *Gerechtigkeit.* 91–99. ———. "Das Ende des Gesetzes: Über Ursprung und Ansatz der paulinischen Theologie." *ZTK* 67 (1970) 14–39. Repr. in *Versöhnung, Gesetz und Gerechtigkeit.* Göttingen: Vandenhoeck & Ruprecht, 1981. 166–91. **Williams, S. K.** "Righteousness." 281–84. **Ziesler, J.** *Righteousness.* 205–7.

Translation

   [30] *What then shall we say? That Gentiles who do not pursue righteousness have attained righteousness, the righteousness which is from faith,* [31] *whereas Israel pursuing the law of righteousness has not reached the law.*[a] [32] *Why so? Because they did*

so not from faith but as if it was from works.[bc] *They have stumbled over the stone of stumbling—* [33] *as it is written,*

"*Behold, I place in Sion a stone of stumbling and a rock of offense;*
and he[d] *who believes in me shall not*[e] *be put to shame.*"

[10:1] *Brothers, the desire of my heart and prayer to God on their behalf is*[f] *for salvation.* [2] *For I bear witness regarding them that they have a zeal for God, but not in accordance with knowledge.* [3] *For, not knowing the righteousness of God and seeking to establish their own (righteousness),*[g] *they have not subjected themselves to the righteousness of God.* [4] *For Christ is the end of the law as a means to righteousness for all who believe.*

Notes

a Some early scribes made the natural expansion νόμον δικαιοσύνης to match the preceding phrase; but the emendation δικαιοσύνην for νόμον is wholly modern.

b A similar tendency to add νόμου is attested a little more widely, but the shorter text is certainly more likely to be original (Metzger).

c A lesser break could be intended here (". . . from works and stumbled . . ."), but it makes little material difference to the meaning.

d A similar tendency to assimilate the quotation here to 10:11 resulted in the insertion of πᾶς (Metzger).

e D F G assimilate the text to that of the LXX by reading οὐ μὴ καταισχυνθῇ.

f The same concern for tidying up the text is evidenced in the insertion of ἐστιν. The later substitution of τοῦ Ἰσραήλ ἐστιν for αὐτῶν may reflect a need for clarity occasioned by 10:1 becoming the beginning of a lesson read in church services (Metzger).

g Manuscript evidence for insertion or omission of δικαιοσύνην is equally divided.

Form and Structure

A matter of some dispute is the function of vv 30–33 and whether 10:1 constitutes a significant break in the argument. The impression that vv 30–33 are transitional is probably in large part due to the modern chapter division. (1) τί οὖν ἐροῦμεν; is a typical Pauline introduction to a new line of thought (4:1; 6:1; 7:7; 8:31; 9:14). (2) The scriptural reference in v 33 certainly builds on the catena of vv 25–29 (note also the association of Hos 2:23 [LXX 25] and Isa 28:16, 8:14 in 1 Pet 2:6–10); but it constitutes a development rather than just a summary of the thought there, and looks forward to the next section of the argument (10:11) and beyond. Indeed the repetition of Isa 28:16 in 9:33 and 10:11 serves to bind the section together. (3) The chief reason for treating 10:1 as the beginning of a new paragraph is the opening ἀδελφοί. But Paul's usage elsewhere hardly requires such a conclusion (1:13; 7:4; 8:12; 1 Cor 1:11; 7:24, 29; etc.). Certainly such an appeal raises the emotional intensity of the argument, but it does not necessarily indicate a new phase of argument. (4) Above all (as noted in the *Introduction* to 9:30–10:21) Paul's sudden recall of key vocabulary and motifs of the central section of his earlier argument and the fresh elaboration of them in a sequence of antithetical pairs throughout this section presumably indicate that he wants it to be held together.

Comment

9:30 τί οὖν ἐροῦμεν, "what then shall we say?" See on 3:5. The question is usually followed by another question (3:5; 6:1; 7:7; 8:31; 9:14), but in a more debating style. Here the following ὅτι and the content of the sentence it introduces (something Paul would want to affirm on his own part) suggests rather that he intended the sentence to be read as a statement, or, if with the suggestion of a question in the voice, at least as a question to which he would give an affirmative answer. The διὰ τί of v 32 also implies that the preceding sentence was intended primarily as an assertion (SH; Michel, 320 n.1). Schmidt suggests an easing of the translation problem by rendering the ὅτι, "since it is the case that. . . ."

ὅτι ἔθνη τὰ μὴ διώκοντα δικαιοσύνην κατέλαβεν δικαιοσύνην, "that Gentiles who do not pursue righteousness have attained righteousness." The significance of there being no definite article with ἔθνη is now generally recognized—not "the Gentiles" as a class, but (some) Gentiles, some ἐξ ἐθνῶν (v 24). διώκω/καταλαμβάνω is a familiar sequence denoting pursuit and catching up or overtaking (Gen 31:23; Exod 15:9; Deut 19:6; Josh 2:5; 1 Sam 30:8; 2 Kgs 25:5; Ps 7:5 [LXX 6]; Lam 1:3; Sir 11:10), but the imagery of the race may be closer to Paul's mind (as in Phil 3:12; cf. 1 Cor 9:24 and v 16 above; BGD, καταλαμβάνω). Whatever the imagery, it easily transferred to pursuing a goal like justice/righteousness (Deut 16:20; Prov 15:9; Isa 51:1; Sir 27:8); cf. 2 Esdr 9:4 LXX and Hos 6:3; in Paul, Rom 12:13; 14:19; and 1 Cor 14:1. Hübner, *Israel*, 64–65, thinks that Paul was particularly mindful of Isa 51:1 within its context. For δικαιοσύνη see on 1:17.

To say that "2:14 f. is long forgotten" (Zeller) misses the point. Paul is not speaking at all of Gentile morality (contrast 1:18–32), as Michel and Cranfield recognize. He is speaking of covenant righteousness, that is, of a righteousness defined by the covenant between God and Israel, of a righteousness which can be pursued only within the covenant and from which those outside the covenant, *ipso facto,* are excluded (of the closest OT parallels cf. particularly Deut 16:20 and Isa 51:1). This recognition enables us to give proper weight to the present tense of τὰ διώκοντα: Gentiles are by definition "the ones who do not pursue righteousness" (cf. Lietzmann).

δικαιοσύνην δὲ τὴν ἐκ πίστεως, "righteousness which is from faith." The triple repetition of δικαιοσύνη within the space of four words leaves no doubt that this is the key thematic word, recalling the argument to the central motif of the letter as a whole (see on 1:17 and 9:30–10:21 *Introduction*). Somewhat surprisingly this is the first time the phrase appears in just this form. But its closest predecessor is 1:17 itself, so that if there is a double reference there (from God's faithfulness as well as man's faith), that could be implicit here too—the inference being that Israel has misunderstood what God's faithfulness means (cf. 3:3–6; 9:6–13); cf. particularly Gaston, *Paul,* 58. Also being recalled is the whole argument of 3:21–5:1 (especially 3:26, 30; 4:16; 5:1). This becomes the definitive Christian slogan in 10:6. Here the force of the defining phrase is to redefine "righteousness," or better, to bring out or reclaim what Paul regards as its proper meaning in contrast to the implied nationalistic narrowness of the first reference. Paul, of course, is well aware that to redefine (covenant) righteousness is to redefine the covenant, or as Paul would prefer, to recall his readers to the original terms of the covenant (chap. 4; 9:6–13).

31 Ἰσραὴλ δὲ διώκων νόμον δικαιοσύνης, "whereas Israel pursuing the law of righteousness." The choice of Ἰσραὴλ rather than Ἰουδαῖοι (cf. v 24) is probably significant: Paul's charge is not against a whole sequence of individual Jews as such; it is against his people's self-understanding of what it means to be the covenant people (see on 9:4). διώκων like τὰ διώκοντα is descriptive, not causal (cf. θέλων—v 22). The implication is not that dedicated application is the mistake ("because they *pursued* the law . . ."); cf. particularly Barth, *Shorter*; NEB: "made great efforts after"). The verb simply describes, in terms his fellow Jews would approve (see on 9:30), the committed lifestyle of the devout covenant member (parallel τρέχω ; see on 9:16). It is not the "pursuing" which Paul criticizes but how that was understood (v 32; cf. on 10:2—ζῆλος θεοῦ).

This gives the key to the otherwise surprising νόμον δικαιοσύνης. Paul uses the phrase to evoke the typical Jewish understanding of the law, as a goal to be pursued (διώκω), as a standard which defines what God requires of his covenant people = righteousness (cf. the nearest parallel use in Jewish literature—Wisd Sol 2:11: might as the law which determines what can be done in relation to others = νόμος τῆς δικαιοσύνης). For his own part Paul regards this as a perfectly acceptable way of formulating what God demands, so long as it is understood in terms of faith and not of works (v 32; so rightly van Dülmen, 125; Cranfield; Rhyne, 99–100; Hübner, *Israel*, 61–63; against RSV's inadmissible reversal of the terms—"the righteousness which is based on law" (similarly Maillot; also NJB—"looking for a saving justice by law-keeping"). We may say therefore that Paul sees both terms in a double sense (Michel), since everything hangs on how νόμος δικαιοσύνης is understood in practice; for Paul also sees the law as defining righteousness (3:31; 8:4, 7), but is wholly opposed to its defining that as *Jewish* righteousness, as a possibility only for those within the boundary of ethnic Israel (3:28–30; 4:5). Consequently it is not necessary to read a negative sense into the phrase (as, e.g., Schmidt; Hofius, "Gesetz," 277), or to give it a fuller meaning, e.g., the law as promising righteousness (Lietzmann; Käsemann; Schlier; Rhyne, *Faith*, 100; also "Rom 10:4," 489; Hübner, *Israel*, 63, 65), or making possible righteousness (Wilckens). This seems to overload the sense too much, though Luz's cross-reference to the double function of the law in 7:7–13 is closer to Paul's thought (*Geschichtsverständnis*, 158; Lübking, 80, refers to 7:10); νόμος = "divine revelation in its widest sense" (Badenas, 103) is even more remote from the context. Barrett's suggestion that it is simply an adjectival genitive that is involved ("a righteous law"—"Fall," 108) goes too far the other way, however, and dissolves the tension which is fundamental to the point being argued. νόμος = "norm" (Mayer, 227–28) makes as good and as poor sense as in 3:27, q.v.

εἰς νόμον οὐκ ἔφθασεν, "has not reached the law." With φθάνω, the metaphor of pursuit (not necessarily of a race, but cf. particularly *Ap. Const.* 7.33.3, "a race course for righteousness") is retained (v 30; Phil 3:16; cf. Judg 20:42; 2 Sam 20:13; *T. Naph* 5.3, 7; see further BGD, 2; *TDNT* 9:88–90) RSV's and NJB's "did not succeed in fulfilling the law" moves too far away from the metaphor. νόμος is certainly the (Jewish) law, as usual (not "norm" or "rule," as SH, Murray; see Kuss), and the point should not be obscured by substituting a phrase like "the will of God" (as Käsemann); even the expansion "the fulfillment of the law" (Lietzmann, Althaus, Schmidt) dulls the point. The repetition of νόμον (and not the δικαιοσύνην, which too many commentators instinctively reach for—most recently Zeller) is obviously deliberate. Paul knows that the assertion would have been at best puzzling and probably offensive to many of his Jewish contemporaries. For many would have considered that they "reached the law," were up with the law in the continuing pursuit, that is, lived in terms of its (God's) demands (Lev 18:5; see on 10:5) and belonged to "the righteous" (see on 1:17 and 9:6)—not a claim, of course, to moral perfection, but to responsible covenant membership. Paul knew the attitude well (Phil 3:6). The apologetic tactic is neatly worked: having gained their assent by using a phrase (v 31a) which devout Jews would have accepted as a description of Israel's obligation under the covenant, Paul achieves maximum shock effect by his outright denial that Israel has in fact lived up to the law (cf. Wilckens); it is this apologetic tactic rather than "the desire for a balanced antithesis" (Sanders, Law, 42) that explains the formulation here. Paul of course has in mind the same criticism he made in 2:17–29: they have "reached" it at a too superficial, nationalistic level, which is a distortion of the deeper level. But in v 32 he will make clear what he means; it is quite important to realize that Paul's meaning in v 31 would not have been wholly clear (and deliberately so) without v 32a.

32 διὰ τί; "why so?" The abruptness of the interrogative indicates a strength of feeling (cf. 2 Cor 11:11). Paul would be conscious of the shock effect of his preceding assertion (see on 9:31).

ὅτι οὐκ ἐκ πίστεως ἀλλ' ὡς ἐξ ἔργων, "because they did so not from faith but as if it was from works." As most agree, the verb διώκειν must be understood, and if so the object must also be that of the last sentence—"the law of righteousness" = the law as defining righteousness (see on 9:31); see further Cranfield. Wilckens argues that ἔφθασεν should be understood, on the ground that the contrast is between pursuing (v 31) and not pursuing (v 30), with the implication that it is the very attempt to pursue which was the mistake. But Paul does not disparage the idea of "pursuit" (or of "doing" the law; see on 10:5); it was the way that pursuit was envisaged and practiced (so rightly Rhyne, 100–101, and Badenas, 105, with other bibliography). Here too "pursuit" does not in itself carry the overtones of frantic striving to achieve a claim on God—"an excess of ethical endeavor as the essence of guilt" (Gaugler, 2:79, quoted also by Schmitt, 92). Nor should the ἐκ πίστεως / ἐξ ἔργων antithesis be allowed to degenerate into the same sort of polemic against self-accomplishment or self-assertion (as, e.g., Bultmann, Theology 1:315–16; Schlier; see Wilckens's justified protest—2:215). Rather, Paul reverts once again to the contrast which has been fundamental to his own apologetic (3:20, 27–28; 4:2; 9:11): on the one hand, the law defining righteousness understood too narrowly in terms of the requirements of the law which mark off Jew from Gentile (cf. Watson, Paul, 165; NEB's "deeds" and NJB's "actions" for ἔργα are not focused sharply enough); on the other hand, the law defining righteousness understood in terms of the obedience of faith which a Gentile can offer *as Gentile* (see further on 3:20; 3:27; 9:12; and 11:6). Israel's mistake was to understand righteousness as something peculiarly theirs (see on 10:3). The ὡς indicates that this is Israel's own view of the matter (cf. 2 Cor 2:17 and 11:16; SH, Michel, Schlier), though it is not impossible that Paul intended the ὡς to be ambiguous, denoting also that Israel's view of the matter was an illusion (cf. Käsemann, Cranfield, Zeller). Sanders ignores the negative force of the antithesis by focusing exclusively on the οὐκ ἐκ πίστεως: "Israel's failure is not that they do not obey the law in the correct way, but that they do not have faith in Christ" (*Law,* 37; cf. Räisänen, *Law,* 175–76). It is true, of course, that the chief thrust of the passage is toward documenting Israel's failure to believe in Christ (vv 32–33; Wilckens; Räisänen, *Law,* 174); but the negative note against "works" *is* clearly struck and is clearly intended to evoke the indictment of Israel summed up in 3:20 (cf. Barrett, "Fall," 113).

προσέκοψαν τῷ λίθῳ τοῦ προσκόμματος, "they have stumbled over the stone of stumbling." The lack of a linking particle would indicate to readers that they should read these words with solemnity (Cranfield). προσκόπτειν means "to strike against"—as of a foot against a stone (Ps 91 [LXX 90]:12). Intransitively, and in the present context, "stumble" is the most natural rendering (cf. Prov 3:23; Jer 13:16; Tob 11:10); so also in its only other use in Paul (14:21). πρόσκομμα is the same image and denotes the "stumble" itself, or the cause of stumbling (as in Sir 31:7; 1 Pet 2:8), hence also "offense, obstacle, hindrance" (as in Exod 23:33; Rom 14:13, 20; 1 Cor 8:9); see also on 14:13.

33 καθὼς γέγραπται, "as it is written"; see on 1:17.

The quotation which follows is a mixture of Isa 28:16 and 8:14 such as we do not find in Jewish exegesis (Müller, *Anstoss,* 71), but which seems to have been acceptable in Christian circles (cf. 10:6 and 11:8, 26–27; see Ellis, *Paul's Use,* 186; and cf. further Matt 2:23; Luke 11:49; John 7:38; 1 Cor 2:9; James 4:5).

Isa 28:16	ἰδοὺ ἐγὼ ἐμβαλῶ εἰς τὰ θεμέλια Σιὼν λίθον . . .
Rom 9:33	ἰδοὺ τίθημι ἐν Σιὼν λίθον . . .
(Isa cont.)	καὶ ὁ πιστεύων ἐπ᾽ αὐτῷ οὐ μὴ καταισχυνθῇ.
(Rom cont.)	καὶ ὁ πιστεύων ἐπ᾽ αὐτῷ οὐ καταισχυνθήσεται.

In neither case does the first line exactly match the Hebrew, but each is sufficiently close to the sense. The major difference is in the final four or five words. The Hebrew reads, "He who believes will not be in haste." The ἐπ᾽ αὐτῷ is lacking in the B text of Isa 28:16, but since the targum gives the text an explicit reference to the royal messiah (Str-B, 3:276) it must be judged unlikely that a messianic interpretation first emerged in Christian circles (see further below) and quite likely that the ἐπ᾽ αὐτῷ belonged at least to the version of the Greek text which Paul knew and used (*TDNT* 4:272–73; Müller, *Anstoss,* 78–80); it is this LXX addition which enables Paul to give the unusual absolute usage of the Hebrew (*TDNT* 6:216) its reference to Christ. Paul's use of the verb καταισχύνω similarly shows dependence on the Greek, even though his future tense more closely reflects the Hebrew.

The use of Isa 8:14, while more problematic, seems to indicate a Greek rendering closer to the MT than the LXX, but reflected also in Aquila and Theodotion.

Hebrew:	(the Lord) will become . . .
	a stone of offense and a rock of stumbling
LXX:	ἐὰν ἐπ' αὐτῷ (the Lord) πεποιθὼς ᾖς, ἔσται σοι . . . οὐχ ὡς
	λίθου προσκόμματι . . . οὐδὲ ὡς πέτρας πτώματι
Theodotion:	εἰς λίθον προσκόμματος καὶ εἰς πέτραν πτώματος
Aquila:	καὶ εἰς λίθον προσκόμματος καὶ εἰς στερεὸν σκανδάλου
Romans:	λίθον προσκόμματος καὶ πέτραν σκανδάλου

The rationale for the combination is clear enough: the mention of λίθος and of trust ἐπ' αὐτῷ in each would be grounds enough; and of course by merging the texts at the point of the "stone" reference and thereby excluding the more positive description of the stone in Isa 28:16 Paul would hardly intend to deny it (cf. 1 Pet 2:6). The idea of a "stone" having a negative as well as a positive role in relation to Israel and as something intended by God himself is in line with the original meanings of both Isaiah texts (cf. Dinter; Hübner, *Israel*, 68–69, overstates the significance of the insertion of Isa 8:14 at this point).

The reason Paul is able to give the resulting mixed text a christological reference is also clear. As already noted, the Isaiah targum gives the text a messianic interpretation whose beginnings may be reflected already in the ἐπ' αὐτῷ of the LXX. Other "stone" references in the OT would almost certainly attract messianic interpretation in Jewish circles, particularly Dan 2:34 (*TDNT* 4:272–73; see further SH). And at Qumran Isa 28:16 was taken as referring to "the council of the community" (1QS 8.7; cf. 1QH 6.26–27; see also Betz, 50–54, 61–63). A christological reference is attested as well in 1 Pet 2:6. The fact that 1 Pet 2:6–8 also combines Isa 28:16 (in fuller form) with Isa 8:14 (with Ps 118:22 in between) is probably sufficient indication that a collection of "stone" testimonies was early made in Christian circles for apologetic use (cf. also the use of Ps 118:22 in Mark 12:10–11 pars. and Acts 4:11, and the combination of Isa 28:16 with Ps 118:22 in *Barn.* 6.2–4). In this case, Paul could be abbreviating a well-established (oral, Käsemann) proof-text collection (Luke 20:17–18 presupposes a similar combination; cf. again *Barn.* 6.2) which he would assume was well enough known among the Roman congregations (it is of relevance to note that both 1 Pet and Mark are most often linked to Rome as the place of their composition; see further Selwyn, *1 Peter*, 268–77, and Lindars, 177–79; but also K. Müller, *Anstoss*, 74–75.

τίθημι ἐν Σιών, "I lay in Zion." As Paul no doubt intended, the combination of the texts strengthens the note of divine purpose behind the "stone of stumbling." Israel's fall was intended by God. This note both catches up the predestinarian emphasis of vv 18–22 (despite Hübner's [*Israel*, 69–70] objections against C. Müller, *Gerechtigkeit*, 36) and prepares for the resolution of the problem in 11:7 ff. Paul would also be well aware that "Zion" was a highly evocative term for his fellow Jews (e.g., Isa 1:27; 2:3; 4:3–5; 24:23; 33:20; 35:10; 46:13; 51:3, 11; 52:8; 59:20; 62:11; see further *TDNT* 7:312–

19); though there is no indication that Paul made use of the idea of "the law going forth from Zion" (Isa 2:3; Mic 4:2) as an eschatological conception of the law, to be distinguished from the Sinai law (so Gese, "Law," 81–82; Stuhlmacher, "Gesetz"), which he could use to retain a positive function for the law (contrast 10:6–9).

For πρόσκομμα, see on 9:32. σκάνδαλον, "that which gives offense or causes revulsion, that which arouses opposition, an object of anger or disapproval" (BGD); in LXX usually "cause of ruin" (*TDNT* 7:342), but never used quite as here (the nearest is probably Wisd Sol 14:11). πρόσκομμα and σκάνδαλον are near synonyms (see 14:13), but the latter is the more important word in Christian apologetic (Matt 16:23; 1 Cor 1:23; Gal 5:11); see also on 14:13. The fact that the same image of a stone yields such different and even opposing metaphors (cornerstone, stone of stumbling) is precisely what Paul needs for his apologetic at this point (Ps 118:22 is less useful, since he needs the metaphor of a stone which continues to trip up Israel). Barrett and Meyer argue the implausible theory that what Israel stumbled over was the law ("Fall," 112–13; "Rom 10:4," 64; "the gospel contained in Torah"—Gaston, *Paul*, 129); but the ἐπ' αὐτῷ must certainly be referred to Christ, as 10:11 confirms (see also Badenas, 106). Wilckens drives the thought back as usual to the curse of the law and the death of Christ (2:216), but more likely it is the God-givenness of Christ as the climax of his purpose for Israel which is in view here (cf. Käsemann; and 10:6–7).

For πιστεύειν see on 1:16; for πιστεύειν ἐπί (used in only one other passage in the LXX) see on 4:24. (Black asks needlessly whether the ἐπ' αὐτῷ should be taken with καταισχυνθήσεται.) This key verb thus reintroduced through the Isaiah quotation (it occurs only four times in Isaiah) becomes the central thematic word in the next chapter (10:4, 9–11, 14, 16); NJB's "relies on" here obscures this continuity. For καταισχύνω, see on 5:5, though here the future certainly has the final judgment in view (Käsemann); cf. also on 1:16; BGD's "be disappointed" is not strong enough; that Paul still has in mind the metaphor of pursuit or race (Gaugler; Leenhardt; Badenas, 101, 107) is not at all certain.

10:1 ἀδελφοί, "brothers." See on 1:13. Used here, when his thoughts are on his natural brothers and kinsmen (9:3), the word has a particular poignancy, expressive of the tensions of the twin loyalties that word embraced.

ἡ μὲν εὐδοκία τῆς ἐμῆς καρδίας, "the desire of my heart." The omission of the δέ following μέν can be regarded as in accord with good classical usage: "so far as it depends on my desire" (BDF, §447.4). εὐδοκία is hardly known outside of biblical Greek. Its predominant sense and that of the underlying Hebrew (רָצוֹן) is "good pleasure," usually with reference to God. But in Sirach, where it occurs 23 times, the range of meaning includes the more active sense of a will which asserts itself (as the monarch who prefaces an action with the words, "It is our good pleasure to make . . ."); cf. Sir 11:17; 15:15; 33:13; 39:18; 41:4. And in Sir 18:31 it stands in close conjunction with (human) desire (ἐπιθυμία); cf. also 2 Chron 15:15 and Ps 145:9. So "good pleasure" in the sense of "wish" or "good will" or "desire" is quite acceptable here; cf. particularly Eph 1:5 (see further *TDNT* 2:742–46 and Lietzmann; otherwise SH). As elsewhere in Paul, καρδία denotes the inward person (see on 1:21; 2:15; and 8:27), and therefore the depth and sincerity of his claim,

a motivating force which engages the whole person, not just a "mere feeling."
καὶ ἡ δέησις πρὸς τὸν θεὸν ὑπὲρ αὐτῶν εἰς σωτηρίαν, "the prayer to God on
their behalf is for salvation." The prayer or entreaty is to God, in accord
with the normal OT/LXX pattern (contrast LSJ), a pattern from which Paul
does not depart (Phil 1:3–4 and 4:6; cf. 1 Tim 5:5 and 2 Tim 1:3; see also
on 1:8). The ὑπὲρ αὐτῶν goes with the δέησις (as in 2 Cor 1:11; 9:14; Phil
1:4). The εἰς σωτηρίαν probably echoes the thematic emphasis of 1:16 (since
the thought of this section [9:30–10:13] has so obviously returned to 1:16–
17); for the sense, see on 1:16. It is clearly important for Paul that his concern
for Israel is the same as the goal of his own life work (1:16): to bring about
salvation. The wholeness he works for and desires is a wholeness of the whole
people of God, Jew and Gentile together. In praying for his own people's
salvation, Paul would be conscious that he stood in a noble tradition (e.g.,
Exod 32:11–14; Num 21:6–9; 1 Sam 7:8–9; Ps 99:6; Jer 42:2–4, 19–22; Ezek
11:13; T. Mos. 11.17; Zeller). Leenhardt fairly notes that such a prayer runs
counter to a strong predestinarian (= determinist) interpretation of chap. 9.

2 μαρτυρῶ γὰρ αὐτοῖς ὅτι, "for I bear witness regarding them that." The
construction is typically Greek, with the dative of the persons about whom
the testimony is given, and ὅτι indicating the content of the testimony (LSJ,
μαρτυρέω 2; BGD, μαρτυρέω 1). The fact that the usage is rooted in legal
terminology (a testimony given in open court) adds weight to what follows.
But more important is the fact that the witness speaks out of his personal
experience (as in Gal 4:15 and Col 4:13). Paul can attest to the zeal of Israel
from his own experience as a zealous Jew (see further below). The phrase
itself does not indicate whether the testimony is one favorable or unfavorable
to those regarding whom the testimony is given.

ζῆλον θεοῦ ἔχουσιν, "they have a zeal for God." ζῆλος in itself is neither
good nor bad, and in the NT usage is almost equally divided between the
two (BGD); in Paul, positive—2 Cor 7:7, 11; 9:2; 11:2 (cf. 1 Cor 12:31; 14:1, 39;
Titus 2:14); negative—Rom 13:13; 1 Cor 3:3; 2 Cor 12:20; Gal 5:20 (cf. 1
Cor 13:4). But the usage here is one not found in secular Greek and is
characteristic of Jewish piety, passionate consuming zeal focused on God
(TDNT 2:878), as evidenced by an overwhelming concern to do his will, in
correspondence to God's own "zeal" (Exod 20:5; 34:14; Deut 4:24; 5:9; 6:15;
Josh 24:19; Nah 1:2 [Schmitt, 91]). The classic examples of such zeal (as
attested by the number of references to them) were those who were prepared
to use the sword to maintain Israel's set-apartness and purity as God's covenant
people—Simeon and Levi (Jud 9:4 and Jub. 30.5–20, referring to Gen 34),
Phinehas (Num 25:10–13; Sir 45:23–24; 1 Macc 2:54; 4 Macc 18.12), Elijah
(Sir 48:2; 1 Macc 2:58) and Mattathias (1 Macc 2:19–26; Josephus, Ant. 12.271).
This ideal is characterized in the Maccabean literature as "zeal for the law"
(1 Macc 2:26, 27, 50, 58; 2 Macc 4:2); cf. IDB 4:936–39; Hengel, Judaism
1:305–314. Note also 1QS 4.4; 9.23; and 1QH 14.14—"zeal for just ordinances," "zeal against evildoers and men of falsehood." In T. Ash. 4.5 "zeal
for God" (ζήλῳ θεοῦ) is defined precisely as "abstaining from what God also
hates and forbids through his commandments." It is this depth of Jewish
dedication to God's covenant with Israel that Paul clearly has in mind: (1)

Ps 106:30–31 and *Jub.* 30.17 (cf. 30.23) both use the language of Gen 15:6 in reference to Phinehas and Simeon and Levi as warranted by their zeal (*Jub.* 30.20 describes Levi's act of slaughter as his "righteousness"); in drawing in this language as he turns back to his main theme of "God's righteousness" (1:17; 10:3), Paul shows that he is moving in the same train of thought. (2) He would no doubt be aware of the increasingly serious Zealot activity in Palestine and be aware that Phinehas was one of the great Zealot heroes (Hengel, *Zeloten,* 175–81; SVM 2:598–606). (3) Acts confirms that such "zeal for the law" was characteristic of the Jerusalem Christian congregations (Acts 21:20). (4) Above all, Paul knew the depth of sentiment from inside: as such a "zealot" he too had taken the sword to protect Judaism's distinctive prerogatives (Gal 1:13–14; Phil 3:6—κατὰ ζῆλος διώκων τὴν ἐκκλησίαν; Acts 22:3–4—ζηλωτὴς τοῦ θεοῦ. In other words, he saw his own earlier zeal as characteristic for the Judaism of the time (Haacker, "Paulus," 167). And note the present tense (ἔχουσιν): this zeal continues to characterize the intensity of his kinsmen's devotion to God. See also on 4:3.

ἀλλ' οὐ κατ' ἐπίγνωσιν, "but not in accordance with knowledge." For ἐπίγνωσις see on 1:28. The implication of the context is that Paul now judges his fellow Jews' and his own former zeal as misdirected—that is, not based on a recognition of how God's righteousness is bestowed (the point he elaborates in v 3), nor issuing in commendable living (defending prerogative by killing, rather than fulfilling the law by loving one's neighbor—13:8).

3 ἀγνοοῦντες γὰρ τὴν τοῦ θεοῦ δικαιοσύνην, "for not knowing the righteousness of God." ἀγνοέω could be translated here "disregarding" (BGD, ἀγνοέω 2), and therefore imply some culpability (cf. 1 Cor 14:38) (contrast Munck, *Christ,* 81–84). The charge is clearly directed against what Paul regarded as a basic misunderstanding of how God deals with his people and what he requires of his people—that is, God's righteousness as God's gracious accepting and sustaining power to faith, therefore open to all and not the special prerogative of Israel to be defended by the sword (see on 10:2). See further on 2:4. For δικαιοσύνη θεοῦ see particularly on 1:17.

καὶ τὴν ἰδίαν (δικαιοσύνην) ζητοῦντες στῆσαι, "and seeking to establish their own (righteousness)." ζητέω has a fairly intensive meaning, "searching for," a deliberate and sustained (present tense) intention, reflecting also the use of ζῆλος in v 2 (see also on 2:7). ἴδιος is usually taken in the sense of "their own" as attained by them—"the righteousness which man exerts himself to achieve by fulfilling the 'works of the law' " (Bultmann, *Theology* 1:285); "a righteous status of their own earning" (Cranfield); a "self-willed" (Wilckens) and self-achieved righteousness (similarly, e.g., Knox; Gaugler; Leenhardt; Harrisville; Hübner, *Law,* 121, 128–29, and *Israel,* 71). But ἴδιος has more the sense of "mine" as belonging to me in contrast to what someone else can claim as belonging to him, "mine" as "peculiar to me" (BGD). That is, it expresses Israel's covenant-consciousness, righteousness as the appropriate expression of their covenant status, and so peculiarly theirs—"collective righteousness, to the exclusion of the gentiles" (Howard, "Romans 10:4," 336; similarly Gaston, "Torah," 66; Wright, *Messiah,* 98; Sanders, *Law,* 38; moving in the right direction, van Dülmen, 177–78). See further *Introduction* §5.3.3.

Still less has it been recognized that στῆσαι reflects the Hebrew הֵקִים (hiphil of קום) and in particular the characteristic use of the verb in connection with the covenant—usually of God's "establishing" his covenant (Gen 6:18; 9:11; 17:7, 19, 21; 26:3; Exod 6:4; Lev 26:9; Deut 8:18; 9:5; 29:13; Jer 11:5; Sir 17:12; 45:7, 24), but also of Israel's responsibility within the covenant (Jer 34 [LXX 41]:18; cf. 35 [LXX 42]:16; Sir 11:20). Particularly noticeable, in view of the allusions in ζῆλος θεοῦ (see on 10:2) and the context of Paul's argument, are the references in Sir 44:20—Abraham (or God?) "ἔστησεν διαθήκην in his flesh" (cf. 45:23—Phinehas stood firm [στῆναι] when the people turned away); and 1 Macc 2:27, Mattathias' summons to defend the covenant: πᾶς ὁ ζηλῶν τῷ νόμῳ καὶ ἱστῶν διαθήκην ἐξελθέτω ὀπίσω μου, "Let everyone who is zealous for the law and supports the covenant come out after me." Clearly it is this kind of loyalty to the covenant which Paul has in mind, the concern to maintain covenant righteousness as Israel's peculiar obligation. Here is a good expression of "covenantal nomism" (E. P. Sanders), the claim to a special relationship with God secure for all who remain loyal to the covenant (NEB's "try to set up their own" thus misperceives the sense). Paul's criticism in effect is that in seeking to "establish" covenant righteousness as "theirs" they failed to appreciate the full significance of the fact that only God's righteousness can "establish" the covenant (see on 10:6a). The thought and contrast in Phil 3:9 is effectively the same: "my own righteousness which comes from the law" (ἐμὴν δικαιοσύνην τὴν ἐκ νόμου), the righteousness of one who lives within the boundaries of (the people of) the law (οἱ ἐκ νόμου— Rom 4:14, 16), the righteousness of a covenant-keeper, as opposed to the righteousness from God (ἐκ θεοῦ). The distinction corresponds to that between γράμμα and πνεῦμα (Schmitt, 91). There is no inconsistency with the positive reference to the giving of the law in 9:4 (pace Räisänen, "Römer 9–11," 2908).

τῇ δικαιοσύνῃ τοῦ θεοῦ οὐχ ὑπετάγησαν, "they did not subject themselves to the righteousness of God." The force of Paul's negative assertion here is determined by the contrast he has posed, as also in 3:31. To seek to maintain righteousness as something peculiar to the Jews as the covenant-keeping people is, in Paul's view, to disobey God. Since righteousness is always something received from God (God's accepting and sustaining power), only the faith which receives that righteousness sustains the law (3:31). And since God's covenant promise always had the Gentiles in view from the first (4:13–18), the attempt to define that righteousness in terms of the works of the law which mark out Israel's distinctiveness is in fact a form of unrighteousness (2:17–24; 3:9–20), a withdrawing oneself from the complete dependence ("submission") on grace for which God looks (see also on 8:7). The synonymity of the different phrases used in 9:30–31 and 10:3 is very instructive here— "righteousness," "righteousness from faith," "law of righteousness," "righteousness of God" (see 9:30–10:21 Introduction). They show clearly the continuity Paul sees between God's covenant with Israel, the law, and the faith which he proclaimed; they confirm that for Paul obedience—obedience to the law (8:7), the "obedience of faith" (1:5; cf. 16:26)—is a fundamental aspect of covenant righteousness, as much for him as for his fellow Jews; what he objected to was Israel's attempt to maintain a claim of national monopoly to that covenant righteousness and the consequent misunderstanding of "the righteousness of God" which that entailed. Cranfield and Badenas (110) refer ὑπετάγησαν to the historical event of Paul's kinsmen's rejection of the Messiah, and Wilckens to the particular significance of the cross. That properly recognizes the decisive eschatological "now" of 3:21 and the force of 9:33 and 10:4. But the thought here is the broader corollary to these more specific claims which Paul draws also in 3:27–31 (cf. Hübner, *Israel,* 92–93).

4 τέλος γὰρ νόμου Χριστὸς εἰς δικαιοσύνην παντὶ τῷ πιστεύοντι, "for Christ is the end of the law as a means to righteousness for all who believe." Discussion of this crucial verse has been marred by two main flaws: (a) the attempt to push the meaning of τέλος into a strict either-or—either "end = termination" (NEB: "Christ ends the law"; see also those cited by Badenas, 156 n.49) or "end = goal" (NJB : "The law found its fulfillment in Christ"; see also those cited in Badenas, 156–57 n.50); (b) the failure to take the immediate context of the verse sufficiently into account.

(a) τέλος has a degree of ambiguity, as LSJ and BGD demonstrate. But it is difficult to avoid the conclusion that the most natural sense of it is most accurately given in the English word "end," with its similar degree of ambiguity. That is to say, even when the thought is of "end result" or "outcome" (as in 6:21–22; see on 6:21), it is not realistic to exclude the sense of termination (against especially Badenas, who treats the LXX data in particular somewhat tendentiously; contrast *TDNT* 8:52). Cf. the close formal parallels in Plutarch, *Mor.* 780E: δίκη . . . νόμου τέλος ἐστίν, "justice is the end/goal of law," which includes the sense that law has completed its task when justice is established; Amatorius, *Mor.* 750E: τέλος γὰρ ἐπιθυμίας ἡδονή, "pleasure is the end/object of desire," which includes the sense that desire finds consummation and completion in pleasure—when that which has been desired is attained, it is no longer desired, desire has ended in giving way to pleasure (cited by Badenas, 46–47); so also with 1 Tim 1:5, the only reference from the Pauline corpus which gives any real support for Badenas. The same implication holds if the imagery of a race is still in mind from 9:31 (as Badenas argues, 114–15; following Flückiger, 154; also Bring, "Paul," 47; but see on 9:31 ἔφθασεν and 9:33 καταισχυνθήσεται), for when the goal (= finishing line) is attained, the race has ended. So even if the idea of "goal" or "object" is in view here it is not possible to exclude the thought of "end" = "completion, conclusion, cessation" (as Black recognizes; cf. Michel; Gaugler; Leenhardt; Bruce; Fitzmyer; Ladd, "Law," 58; Kuss; Maillot; Achtemeier; Schnabel, 291–92; further bibliography in Badenas, 157–58 nn.51–52; Jewett, "Law," 353, following Badenas, is therefore unjustified in regarding this as "the least satisfactory" exegesis). The argument that Paul sees a continuing role for the law, which is certainly true (see, e.g., on 3:31 and 13:8–10), is therefore not apposite here, since the thought of completion and finality is present too (Käsemann in particular overstates the antithesis between "law" and "gospel" at this point; cf. Barrett, "Fall," 120). Whatever else Paul means, he intends his readers to understand that the law has come to an end in some sense, in accordance with his normal use elsewhere (1 Cor 1:8; 10:11; 15:24; 2 Cor 11:15; Phil 3:19; on 2 Cor 3:13 see below) (Murray).

(b) Even those who recognize the danger of taking v 4 out of context (including most recently Meyer, "Romans 10:4," 65; Rhyne, *Faith,* 103–4, 110–

12; Badenas, 112) have failed to appreciate its full force (in particular, Cranfield's lengthy discussion is completely undermined by this failure). The thought of v 4 follows on from the two preceding verses (as the repeated γάρ indicates). What Paul has in view therefore is the zeal for the law which fights to preserve Israel's distinctiveness (see on 10:2) and righteousness defined in terms of the law as Israel's (Israel's law, so Israel's righteousness; see on 10:3). This is a misunderstanding of God's purpose (v 2) and of God's righteousness (v 3), now clearly exposed by the coming of Christ (3:21–22). The inevitable conclusion is that "the end of the law" has just that misunderstanding in mind, the end of the law as so understood—ὡς ἐξ ἔργων (9:32); whereas the attempt to maintain a reference to Christ's death as ending the curse of the law (Stuhlmacher, Versöhnung, 195; Wilckens; Hofius, "Gesetz," 276; Martin, 279) is not supported by the context. Likewise v 5 carries forward the thought of v 4 (γάρ again), the most obvious implication being that ἡ δικαιοσύνη ἐκ νόμου takes up the preceding νόμος . . . εἰς δικαιοσύνην, and that νόμος and πίστις are being used antithetically in v 4 as in vv 5–6 (see 9:30–10:21 Introduction; and cf. 4:16). Paul therefore probably intended εἰς δικαιοσύνην to go with νόμος, as the repeated association of the two words in the context (9:31 and 10:5) suggests (so explicitly Longenecker, Paul, 146; Murray; Williams, "Righteousness," 284; Hübner, Israel, 94), rather than with Χριστός, which would be an unparalleled thought (against Gaugler, NEB; cf. O'Neill). The grammatical formation where a particular contrast is achieved (between Christ and the law) by inserting Χριστός into the phrase νόμος εἰς δικαιοσύνην is paralleled in 9:21 where the contrast between potter and clay is brought out by inserting ὁ κεραμεύς into the phrase ἐξουσίαν τοῦ πηλοῦ. Strictly speaking, it would make better grammatical sense to take εἰς δικαιοσύνην with the whole of the preceding phrase (e.g., Käsemann; Cranfield; Sanders, Law, 39–40, Badenas, 116), but Paul's flow of dictation often offends grammatical propriety, and the net result may be the same. Against Rhyne, Faith, 104, 113, and also "Rom 10:4," 494–95, 498–99, it should be noted that recognition of a negative sense for νόμος in v 5 makes it very difficult to give νόμος a positive sense in v 4, since the two are linked by γάρ; νόμος . . . εἰς δικαιοσύνην (parallel δικαιοσύνη ἐκ νόμου) is equivalent not to νόμος δικαιοσύνης (9:31) but to νόμος δικαιοσύνης ἐξ ἔργων (9:32).

Paul's point, then, is not so much that the law finds fulfillment in Christ, though he does no doubt have the eschatological significance of Christ's death and resurrection in mind, and that thought is not excluded. But it does not provide sufficient answer to the specific abuse of the law documented in the preceding verses (9:32; 10:2–3); the interpretation turns what is primarily a soteriological, or better, salvation-history, point into a primarily christological one—"Christ embodies that righteousness which the law promised" (Badenas, 118; cf. Schmidt; M. Barth, People, 39–40; Campbell, "Romans 10:4," 77; Gaston, Paul, 130); and despite a superficial parallel in the following exposition of Deut 30:12–14, it misses the point that the word (of the law) is fulfilled in salvation-history terms in the word of faith (see on 10:8). The closest parallel in Paul's own writing is 2 Cor 3:13–14, where it is the end (τέλος) of the old covenant which Paul clearly has in mind, and the failure of the disciples of Moses to recognize that it has been "done away with in Christ" (see, e.g., J. D. G. Dunn, "2 Corinthians 3:17—'The Lord is the Spirit,'" *JTS* 21 [1970] 311; Räisänen, *Law,* 56; Furnish, *2 Corinthians,* 207; contrast the strained exegesis of Badenas, 75). The suggestion that the recognition of Christ as the end of the law was given in and with the Damascus road epiphany (Stuhlmacher, "Ende," 179; and particularly Kim, *Origin*) also misses the specific sense which Paul intends here, a sense which probably came to coherent expression in Paul's debate with Jewish Christians regarding the necessity of covenantal nomism (see further *Introduction* §§1.2–3). So too the statement that Torah and Christ are "mutually exclusive categories" for Paul (as in Gaston, "Torah," 54, and Gager, *Origins,* 213) is much too sharply polarized and fails to do justice to the other thematic concerns of Paul expressed in such passages as 3:25–26, 31; 8:3–4; and 13:8–10.

As usual the absence of the definite article with νόμος is not significant; the Torah is clearly in view (against SH, as usual). And in view of the context, Paul will presumably intend Χριστός to have titular significance = Messiah, as in its previous usage (9:5; see particularly Badenas, 112–13). For εἰς δικαιοσύνην, see also on 6:16 and 10:10. As in the preceding occurrences of the phrase, πᾶς ὁ πιστεύων characterizes the eschatological universalism of the gospel (see on 1:16 and 10:11), in contrast to the national particularism of Israel now brought to an end by Christ (cf. particularly Refoulé, "Rom 10:4," 350). Attempts (as in Plag, 19–26) to find Paul's idea of the abrogation of the law foreshadowed in some Jewish traditions are not well grounded (see R. J. Banks, "The Eschatological Role of the Law in Pre- and Post-Christian Jewish Thought," in *Reconciliation and Hope,* FS L. L. Morris, ed. R. J. Banks [Exeter: Paternoster, 1974] 173–85; Wilckens).

Explanation

Paul has now developed two good reasons for his opening assertion that God's word has not failed, despite his kinsmen's large-scale refusal of the gospel (9:6). His confidence rests in the fact that scripture clearly shows God's purpose of mercy to work through election and rejection (judgment will have reference to behavior in this life, not so election), and that scripture had foreseen both God's call extending to the Gentiles and the covenant people reduced to a remnant. The tension between his equally firm confidence in God's faithfulness to Israel (3:3–4) and Israel's rejection and reduction is thereby only partially resolved, and he will return to the issue shortly (chap. 11). But he has been able to lay the foundation for the complete resolution and for the moment he is content.

Oddly enough, however, throughout the preceding section Paul has never stated explicitly the problem with which he is wrestling, viz., Israel's failure to believe in the gospel of the Messiah Jesus, the Son of God. It was clearly enough implied from the beginning (9:3, 6, 12, 27–29), but never expressed in so many words. Now at last Paul exposes the underlying theme and begins to bring it to the surface. More striking still is the way he does so by tying it in to the overall theme of the letter—"righteousness from faith to faith" (1:17). After a silence lasting almost unbroken from the beginning of chap. 5, the talk of faith and of "the righteousness of faith" reemerges with all the force which marked the critical expositions of 3:21–4:25. Following his sustained conclusion of that exposition in chap. 5, his exploration of what it meant for sin, death, and the law in chaps. 6–8, and the first stage of his attempt to make sense of Israel's unbelief in chap. 9, the two most important themes in his argument at last come together—"righteousness from faith to faith" and Israel's refusal to believe. Once he has used each to throw light on the other he will be able to confront with resolution the anguish of Israel's refusal of the word of faith.

9:30 As so often already, Paul introduces a new phase of his argument with the question "What shall we say then?" What follows is a half question, half statement. It summarizes what was expressed in other words in vv 24–26: "Gentiles who did not pursue righteousness have attained righteousness, the righteousness of faith. . . ." Clearly he has in mind not all Gentiles or Gentiles as a class, but the Gentiles who have responded to God's call in the gospel, the Gentiles who have come to faith in Christ. They did not pursue righteousness; that is to say, they did not strive after the relation with the one God given and sustained by his grace. Here, perhaps more clearly than anywhere else, Paul shows that he understands "righteousness" as a covenant word: it is not something which was possible to Gentiles through nature, or an ethical ideal which good men anywhere might attain to (hence its absence from chap. 2); it is always something which depends ultimately on God, the power of God sustaining man in his creaturely dependence on the creator and enabling him to live through that relation. It was this relation which God set forth in his covenant with Israel and of which Gentiles remained largely ignorant until the gospel made known the offer of God's righteousness to everyone. Paul characterizes it once again as "the righteousness from faith," drawing the whole discussion back to its starting point (1:17). Probably here as there he uses the phrase in the double sense: the righteousness which man must simply accept from start to finish and never presume upon (cf. v 32); the righteousness which God in his covenant faithfulness offers to Jew first but now also to Gentile (cf. 10:3).

31 The irony and tragedy is that while Gentiles who never sought that righteousness are now attaining it, Israel as a whole has failed to reach it despite earnest effort to that end. The sentence, however, is worded in a somewhat surprising way. Instead of the balanced antithesis, "whereas Israel pursuing righteousness did not reach it," Paul writes, "whereas Israel pursuing *the law of* righteousness did not reach that *law.*" But only those who had missed the point of such earlier assertions as 3:31 ("we confirm the law through faith") and 8:2 ("the law of the Spirit of life in Christ Jesus . . .") would find the fuller phrase ("law of righteousness") puzzling. It is clear enough from the train of thought that "the law of righteousness" is not being disparaged by Paul; it is a goal worthy of pursuit. Israel's failure is not that it misunderstood righteousness as a law, that it put the law in place of righteousness, that it reached as far as law but failed to reach righteousness, or anything like that. Any interpretation which poses law and righteousness as alternatives at this point has missed the train of Paul's thought altogether. On the contrary, the larger phrase, "the law of righteousness," is clearly intended by Paul as more or less *synonymous* with the one word of the previous verse, "righteousness." Paul describes the right relationship offered by God in terms of the law no doubt partly because no Jew could think of Israel's covenant relationship with God apart from the law. But he describes it *positively* in terms of the law primarily because for Paul, Paul the Christian as well as Paul the Jew, the law has a positive role in relation to righteousness: the law is indeed the definition and measure of righteousness (4:15; 5:13); righteousness is the fulfillment of "the just requirement of the law" (8:4).

We should therefore give Paul's positive affirmations about Israel and the law of righteousness full weight, while at the same time taking care not to press his metaphor of the racetrack (or of the chase) into an allegory. He is *not* thinking of righteousness as something that can be earned or merited by hard work. The contrast of vv 30–31 is simply that despite its tradition of law-keeping earnestness, stretching back through many generations, Israel has missed the way; while Gentiles, who had no such heritage or training, have in a trice closed the centuries-old gap, overtaken the bulk of Israel, and reached the goal Israel had for so long held before itself.

32 Why so? Why has Israel failed to reach (the law of) righteousness, despite its earnestness for the covenant and its law? Not because Israel had sought (and chased) a moral perfection which is impossible to man, but, says Paul, because it saw its obligation under the covenant as a matter of works and not a matter of faith. His nation had made the mistake of understanding righteousness in terms of works. And not just righteousness—they had misunderstood the law itself by understanding it in terms of works. Paul here reverts to the distinction made in 3:27, between "the law of works" and "the law of faith." And the point is precisely the same. Israel's mistake was not that they had understood righteousness as obedience to the law (for that is what righteousness shows itself to be), but that they had understood obedience to the law too much in terms of specific acts of obedience like circumcision, sabbath observance, and ritual purity. That is to say, they had treated the law and the righteousness it requires at too superficial and too nationalistic a level, as requirements which could be fulfilled at the level of the flesh and which were applicable only to the Jewish people (2:28–29). But the obedience God looked for was the obedience of faith, obedience from the heart (6:17), that is, from a commitment and a lifestyle which penetrated far below matters of race and of ritual and which could be sustained and maintained independently of either. This was the lesson Israel ought to have learned from its own scriptural record of God's choice of Isaac and Jacob (9:6–13) but evidently had failed to do so.

32b–33 Paul finds this failure once again predicted in Isaiah. In warning against the national policy at the time of the Assyrian crisis and calling for faith in Yahweh, Isaiah had likened that faith to "a stone, precious, selected as cornerstone and highly valued" (Isa 28:16). Earlier, and still in the same vein, he had warned that both houses of Israel would find Yahweh to be "a stone which causes stumbling, a rock which brings about a fall" (8:14). Paul, who draws heavily on Isaiah throughout this section (chaps. 9–11), was probably aware of the context, read both passages quite appropriately as part of Isaiah's hope for a faithful remnant, and saw the parallel between the situation confronting Isaiah and his own: the faithful remnant of which Isaiah had spoken is only now fully materializing in the minority of Jews who have accepted the gospel, whereas the bulk of Israel are stumbling over this stone as Isaiah had predicted. Isaiah's encouragement to faith (28:16—one of the very few references to faith in Isaiah) provides Paul with sufficient link with v 32a, especially since the LXX had added "in it/him"—"he who believes in him will not be put to shame." Israel's failure to understand the law as the law of faith is most clearly seen in their failure to respond to the call for faith in Christ, their failure to appreciate that obedience to the law means obedience to Christ (Rom 6:17). The stone of which Isaiah spoke in fact is Christ (an identification probably already familiar to Christian apologetic from the use elsewhere of Ps 118:22–23). Moreover, the earlier "stone" reference permits Paul, by the quite acceptable hermeneutical technique of his day, to link and indeed identify the two stones: the stone of Christ or of faith in Christ (Isa 28:16) is also the stone of stumbling (Isa 8:14). In the composite reference, therefore, Paul finds the full measure of his agonizing frustration foreshadowed: Israel's failure to heed Isaiah foreshadows Israel's failure to heed the gospel; the trust which Isaiah called for is wholly of a piece with the faith Paul calls for. Israel at large had found Isaiah's call for faith to be an offense; it is the same reliance on human contrivance which causes his own kinsmen to stumble at Paul's gospel. Just as Isaiah had to think in terms only of a remnant who would believe, so Paul finds some comfort for his sorrow that so few of his own people have come to faith in their Messiah; and as the remnant of Isaiah's day could be assured that their trust would not be disappointed, so too the Jews who had come to faith in Christ could be confident that, even though a minority, God would not fail them. If only Israel would heed the warnings and promises of their own scriptures!

10:1 The thought flows on without a break; Paul does not even need to specify who it is he is referring to. The thought of Israel missing the point of the law and repeating the same old mistake, with such distressing results, causes the anguish of Paul the Jew to break surface again (as in 9:1–3). His concern for Israel is deeply rooted and engages his whole person. He makes entreaty to God on their behalf—no doubt in regular prayer as such, but also in the very character of his mission and message itself: "to Jew first . . . ." His earnest desire for them is summed up in one word, "salvation"— the wholeness of a whole people in whom God's final purpose has been wholly realized, the very salvation his gospel proclaims and brings about for all who believe, Jew first as well as Gentile (1:16). Despite the scripture's testimony about the remnant and the downfall of the rest, he cannot remain content with only a remnant. Christian now he is, but Jew he has always been and will never cease to be.

2 With much of the same solemnity with which he began this section (9:1) Paul testifies to something he still finds to be truly admirable about his fellow countrymen—their zeal for God, their ardor in the practice of their religion. There is nothing cheap or dismissive in Paul's attitude here, nothing of the caricature or antagonism which a convert often uses against his former faith. As in 9:31, so here, Paul does honor to his fellow Jews for the fervor of their devotion to God and his law. In this he speaks for many in the ancient world who were impressed by the Jews and the extent of their dedication.

At the same time most of his readers would be aware that zeal can go to extreme, in this case particularly, to a nationalistic extreme. At this very time the tide of Zealot opposition to the Roman occupation of Palestine was rising rapidly, and several serious incidents had already taken place. The Zealots demonstrated their zeal for the law and for Israel's purity as God's people by taking up arms, following in the steps of such heroes of the faith as Phinehas (Num 25:10–13), Elijah (1 Kgs 18:40), and Mattathias (1 Macc 2:19–26, 54, 58). Paul knew the attitude well, since he had once embraced it himself in his persecution of the first Christians (Phil 3:6; Acts 22:3–4). All this would have been known about in greater or lesser degree among the Roman Christians. And it was presumably this to which Paul referred when he added the qualification "but not in accordance with knowledge." The trouble with Israel's zeal was that it was too nationalistically centered, too much concerned to defend national prerogative as the people of (the one) God.

3 Lest the implication be lost on his readers, Paul goes on to explain. "For they do not know the righteousness of God." Paul's reasoning might well have caused many of the first listeners in Rome to blink in surprise. The Jews as a whole, surely, more than any other people, could be said to know God's saving power. They celebrated the righteousness of God accounted to Abraham as much as Paul in particular (Gen 15:6); they rejoiced in the election of grace of Israel as God's chosen people (Gen 21:12; 25:23; Exod 33:19); they knew the same use of the concept in psalmist and in Isaiah ("righteousness of God"), which probably shaped Paul's understanding of it (1:17). Even the heathen at large knew something of the power and nature of God (1:18–21). So what on earth could Paul mean?

The answer already hinted at in v 2 is provided more explicitly in the next clause, which clearly serves as the obverse side of the same thought: "they seek to establish their own righteousness." The two words which illuminate the whole are "their own" and "establish." The former denotes something belonging to them or peculiar to them; and the implied contrast is "to them" rather than "to others." So the thought is not of "their own" as opposed to "God's," that is, "their righteousness" as something accomplished by them. Rather Paul is thinking of Israel's claim to a righteousness which was theirs exclusively, shared by no other people, possessed by them alone. The verb ("establish") likewise denotes not an act of creation, a bringing about of something which previously did not exist, but a setting or establishing or confirming of something which is already in existence. They did not seek to achieve or earn or bring about a positive relationship which they did not already enjoy; on the contrary, they sought to establish and confirm what God had already given them (cf. 9:4), as Mattathias had called on those "zealous for the law" to "establish the covenant" by taking arms to sustain Israel's distinctive identity as God's own people (1 Macc 2:27). So Paul's criticism of his people is that they sought to make firm and clear the notion that God's saving power was extended to them exclusively. In Paul's mind, this is clearly the same criticism as that already leveled in 9:32: they sought to establish righteousness as something peculiar to them, by observances of the law which set them apart from other peoples, by works of the law (circumcision, sabbath, etc.) which marked out a righteousness peculiarly their own.

Hence, what Paul thinks his people are ignorant of is not God's righteousness in general, but the *character* of that saving power, the terms on which it can be received and known. They knew God's electing grace well enough, but had failed to recognize the implications of their own original election, the implications of the facts already set out in 9:6–18—that God's righteousness is extended to humankind not in terms of race, nor as a relationship dependent on or made firm by particular acts of men. God's righteousness is from faith to faith; it always was (chap. 4) and always will be.

"They did not subject themselves to the righteousness of God." This last clause describes both the consequence of Israel's ignorance and a further expression of it. It was *not* that they had misunderstood righteousness by understanding it in terms of law, by understanding that the covenant relation with God required obedience. Not at all: God's righteousness can only be received in humble subjection, the creature recognizing its total dependence on the Creator. Israel had indeed recognized the need for obedience to the law, but unfortunately had so misunderstood what that obedience entailed that their zealous obedience had actually become disobedience, a zeal attested more by sword than by love of neighbor. By pursuing obedience at the level of the flesh (cf. 8:7), in terms of ethnic and particular rituals, they showed their misunderstanding of God's righteousness; and, irony of ironies, by seeking to establish righteousness as something peculiarly theirs they were actually putting themselves outside God's righteousness, resisting rather than receiving the saving grace of God.

4 V 4 gives a further reason explaining Israel's lack of knowledge and ignorance of God's righteousness, and provides a transition to the next phase of the argument. "For the end of the law is Christ, as a means to righteousness to all who believe." The phrasing is awkward, but the word "end" is put first obviously to give it the place of emphasis, and that is probably sufficient to explain the resulting awkwardness. The train of thought strongly suggests that "law" and "righteousness" should be taken together—not in the vaguer sense of "law of righteousness" or "law with reference to righteousness" (as in 9:31), but "law for righteousness, so that righteousness happens, as a means toward righteousness"—a suggestion surely confirmed by the exposition which immediately follows: "righteousness *out of* the law" (v 5) is obviously "law *into* righteousness" put the other way round. Paul then is probably thinking here of the law of Moses understood not as a definition of righteousness (9:31), but the law misunderstood in terms of "works" (9:32), the law misunderstood as a means of establishing and fixing firmly righteousness as Israel's special prerogative (10:3).

All that is now finished! Christ is the end of any such function of the law; since the coming and work of Christ that misunderstanding of the law has no more scope. The implication is that prior to Christ there was some ground for that understanding of the law. After all, prior to Christ, God's purpose had worked with particular reference to Israel (9:6–18), and the righteousness of God had been more or less confined to Israel—so that a closer correlation between God's righteousness and Israel's practice of the law could be readily assumed. But now with Christ a new stage in God's dealings with humankind has been reached (3:21). Christ is the end of the old epoch and of Israel's exclusive privileges with it.

The word "end" therefore is probably intended in the primary sense of "termination, cessation." What has been brought to an end by Christ's coming and work is that stage of God's saving purpose which focused principally on Israel, is the resulting ground of Israel's presumption that God's choice of Israel had Israel as such exclusively in view, is the consequently plausible assumption that God gave the law to Israel as a means for Israel to confirm its special place within God's favor. It is possible that Paul intended "end" here to have also the fuller or further sense of "fulfillment, goal." Israel had after all been specially chosen by God (hence the misunderstanding), but that choice had always been wholly in terms of grace (9:6–13) and always had the extension of that grace to all the nations wholly in view from the first (4:16–18), in which case Christ is the realization of God's final purpose in choosing Israel initially. But this reads a good deal more into Paul's argument at v 4 than the reader has thus far been given to expect. Nothing Paul has said so far would invite such an association of Christ and the law—faith as the fulfillment of the law perhaps (3:31), Christ as the fulfillment of righteousness even (3:26), but not Christ as the fulfillment or goal of the law, true though it may be to Paul's thought elsewhere (cf. Gal 3:24). Moreover, to press for such a fuller sense at this point probably involves too great a slackening of the connection between "law" and "righteousness" which engages Paul's attention throughout this section. The point is rather that whatever good reasons Israel had for its misunderstanding of the law and of righteousness, it is precisely these reasons that have been ended by Christ. This is what believers generally have found—that God's righteousness is now to be known apart from the law, is open to all simply on the grounds of faith, Jew and Gentile alike (3:21–22).

Since this has been such an important verse in the history of interpreting Paul's theology it is perhaps worth adding two further observations. The first is that Paul's thought here is to be understood chiefly in terms of his salvation-history perspective. "Christ is the end of the law . . ." refers to the once-for-all transition in God's saving purpose effected by the life, death, and resurrection of Christ. It does not denote a timeless sequence which subsequent generations may expect to find constantly repeated in their own lives—as though every one had to go through a "law" phase before coming to Christ. However true *that* may be of any number of particular individuals, it was not what Paul had in mind (cf. 5:20–21). And even if we find the note of "fulfillment" ringing more loudly in the word "end" than has been suggested above, the dominant note is still that of salvation-history—Christ as the end of one stage of God's dealings (with Israel as such) and the introduction of a new stage, the climax of his purpose from the beginning.

Second, in view of so much misunderstanding of Paul's theology of the law, we should stress that Paul neither says that the law as such has been brought to an end in Christ—how could he in the light of such assertions as 3:31; 8:4; and 9:31? Nor does he imply that the law was seen as a way of earning or meriting righteousness: that interpretation would not only give a picture of Judaism hard to square with what we know of Judaism contemporary with Paul from other sources, it would also fall foul of Paul's careful distinction between law and *works* of the law (expressed most clearly in 3:27 and 9:31–

32). As the context makes clear, it is not the law as such which ceased with the new epoch brought in by Christ, but the law seen as a way of proving righteousness, of documenting God's special regard for Israel, of marking Israel out from the other nations, the law understood in terms of works. The epoch of Israel's exclusive prerogative is ended; the role of the law as a badge of election is over and done. Christ has come, and with his coming the original purpose and promise of God can now be seen to extend to all nations, in accordance with its original terms, to Jew first still but to Gentile as well, and all alike solely in terms of the faith by which father Abraham was justified in the beginning.

2. The Righteousness from the Law and the Righteousness from Faith   (10:5–13)

Bibliography

See also 9:1–11:36 Bibliography.

Badenas, R. Christ the End of the Law. 118–35. **Black, M.** "The Christological Use of the Old Testament in the New Testament." NTS 18 (1971–72) 1–14. **Bring, R.** "Das Gesetz und die Gerechtigkeit Gottes: Eine Studie zur Frage nach der Bedeutung des Ausdruckes τέλος νόμου in Röm 10:4." ST 20 (1966) 1–36. **Campenhausen, H. von.** "Das Bekenntnis im Urchristentum." ZNW 63 (1972) 210–53. **Cullmann, O.** The Earliest Christian Confessions. London: Lutterworth, 1949. **Delling, G.** "'Nahe ist dir das Wort': Wort—Geist—Glaube bei Paulus." TLZ 99 (1974) 402–12. **Dunn, J. D. G.** "'Righteousness from the Law' and 'Righteousness from Faith': Paul's Interpretation of Scripture in Romans 10:1–10." In Tradition and Interpretation in the New Testament, FS E. E. Ellis, ed. G. F. Hawthorne. Grand Rapids: Eerdmans, 1987. 216–28. **Fitzmyer, J. A.** "The Semitic Background of the New Testament Kyrios-Title." A Wandering Aramean: Collected Aramaic Essays. Missoula: Scholars Press, 1979. 115–42. **Führer, W.** " 'Herr ist Jesus.' Die Rezeption der urchristlichen Kyrios-Akklamation durch Paulus Römer 10:9." KD 33 (1987) 137–49. **Goldberg, A. M.** "Torah aus der Unterwelt: Eine Bemerkung zu Röm 10:6–7." BZ 14 (1970) 127–31. **Hanson, A. T.** "Paul's Interpretation of Scripture." Studies. 136–68. **Heller, J.** "Himmel- und Höllenfahrt nach Römer 10:6–7." ET 32 (1972) 478–86. **Howard, G.** "The Tetragram and the New Testament." JBL 96 (1977) 63–83. **Kaiser, W. C.** "Leviticus 18:5 and Paul: Do This and You Shall Live (Eternally?)" JETS 14 (1971) 19–28. **Käsemann, E.** "The Spirit and the Letter." Perspectives. 138–66. **Lindemann, A.** "Die Gerechtigkeit aus dem Gesetz: Erwägungen zur Auslegung und zur Textgeschichte von Röm 10:5." ZNW 73 (1982) 231–50. **Ljungman, H.** Pistis. 84–91. **Lyonnet, S.** "Saint Paul et l'exégèse juive de son temps: A propos de Romains 10:6–8." In Mélanges Bibliques rédigés en l'honneur de André Robert. Paris: Bloud & Gay, 1957. 494–506. **McNamara, M.** The New Testament and the Palestinian Targum to the Pentateuch. AnBib 27A. Rome: Biblical Institute, 1978. 70–81. **Minde, H.-J. van der.** Schrift. 107–19. **Neufeld, V. H.** The Earliest Christian Confessions. Leiden: Brill, 1963. **Schweizer, E.** "Zur Herkunft der Präexistenzvorstellung bei Paulus." Neotestamentica. Zürich: Zwingli, 1963. 105–9. **Suggs, M. J.** "The Word Is Near You: Rom 10:6–10 within the Purpose of the Letter." In Christian History and Interpretation, FS J. Knox, ed. W. R. Farmer et al. Cambridge University, 1967. 289–312.

Translation

⁵ *For Moses writes with reference to*ᵃ *the righteousness which is from the law,*ᵃ *"The man who has done the same*ᵃ *shall live in them."* ⁶ *Whereas the righteousness from faith speaks thus:*
Do not say in your heart,
"Who will go up into heaven?"
that is, to bring Christ down; ⁷ *or*
"Who will go down into the abyss?"
that is, to bring Christ up from the dead. ⁸ *But what does it say?*
"The word is near you, in your mouth and in your heart,"
that is, the word of faith which we preach. ⁹ *Because if you confess*ᵇ *"with your mouth"*ᵇ *"Jesus is Lord," and believe "in your heart" that God raised him from the dead, you will be saved.* ¹⁰ *For with the "heart" belief is exercised for righteousness, and with the "mouth" confession is made for salvation.* ¹¹ *For the scripture says, "Everyone who believes in him shall not be put to shame."* ¹² *For there is no distinction between Jew and Greek, for the same one is Lord of all, rich to all who call upon him.* ¹³ *For "everyone whoever calls upon the name of the Lord shall be saved."*

Notes

ᵃ Several variations raise the possibility that Paul intended τὴν δικαιοσύνην to be the object of ὁ ποιήσας (with αὐτά omitted and αὐτῇ read for αὐτοῖς)—"he who does the righteousness which is from the law shall live in it" (so RSV; Käsemann; Cranfield; Wilckens; Rhyne, 104–5; Badenas, 118–19). But it is more likely that Paul followed the LXX (αὐτά and αὐτοῖς), as in Gal 3:12, without feeling it necessary to specify an antecedent for αὐτά (= P⁴⁶; so Aland²⁶ and NIV), and that the alternative readings arise from one or more early scribal attempts to improve the syntax, assuming that the ὅτι should follow the γράφει. The alternative must be judged less likely (that the awkward γράφει τὴν δικαιοσύνην and the unspecified αὐτά were the result of a scribal attempt to harmonize Paul's quotation with the LXX), precisely because scribal emendation is more likely to remove syntactical difficulty than to create it. Metzger also notes that the phrase ποιεῖν τὴν ἐκ νόμου δικαιοσύνην is not Pauline. See further particularly Lindemann. Hübner's preference for the sole attested B text (reading αὐτά and αὐτῇ; cf. NEB and NJB), taking αὐτῇ as "this legal righteousness" (*Israel*, 79–80) is consistent with his continued misunderstanding of this righteousness as something achieved rather than as a description of how life should be lived within the covenant (see further on 10:5).

ᵇ B witnesses to an attempt to express Paul's meaning more precisely by inserting τὸ ῥῆμα and ὅτι, so that it becomes clear that a confession is involved.

Form and Structure

The division between vv 4 and 5 is not substantial. Indeed we might say that vv 5–10 provide the climax of the sequence of points made in vv 1–4, each introduced as an explanation of the preceding one (γάρ . . . γάρ . . . γάρ . . . γάρ . . .). The γάρ of v 5 introduces the final reason in the sequence. But since what it introduces is the scriptural underpinning of the whole section, 9:30–10:4 (see also 9:30–10:21 *Introduction*), and is a more involved attempt at proof from scripture than usual, leading into a new line of thought (vv 11–13; though for Dahl to speak of 10:5–21 as a digression

["Israel," 148] is a considerable overstatement), it is convenient to treat vv
5–13 as a separate paragraph. It is important, however, to appreciate that
the two texts of vv 5 and 6–8 are structurally linked to the preceding argument
as documenting the sequence of contrasts drawn in vv 1–4:

v 2	zeal for God	but not in accordance with knowledge
v 3	sought to establish their own righteousness	did not submit to God's righteousness
v 4	law . . . to righteousness	Christ . . . to all who believe
v 5/	righteousness from the law	righteousness from faith
vv 6–9	Lev 18:5	Deut 30:12–14

Comment

10:5 Μωϋσῆς γὰρ γράφει τὴν δικαιοσύνην τὴν ἐκ (τοῦ) νόμου ὅτι, "For Moses
writes with reference to the righteousness which is from the law." Paul refers
explicitly to Moses on a number of occasions. It may simply be for stylistic
variation (cf. 9:15; 10:19; 1 Cor 9:9). But since at least some contrast between
Israel's concept of righteousness and that which Paul here promulgates is
certainly involved in the context (9:31–32; 10:3), it is more likely that Paul
intends Moses to characterize the old epoch now superseded by Christ (cf.
5:14; 1 Cor 10:2; 2 Cor 3:7–15). The γάρ clearly indicates that v 5 is an
explanation or further elaboration of the train of thought running from vv
2–4 (see further on 10:4).

Some have found in the two different verbs used to introduce the scriptural
references in v 5 (γράφει) and vv 6–8 (λέγει) a deliberate contrast (Schlatter,
Michel, Schlier), which Käsemann in particular has taken as signaling a sharp
antithesis between "letter" and "Spirit" in which he finds the key to interpreting
the whole passage ("Spirit," 155–66; cf. Stuhlmacher, *Gerechtigkeit*, 93–94;
Schmitt, 93–94). Käsemann certainly tries to press too much from the context
(criticized by Cranfield and Wilckens; see also Badenas, 252 n.285); but the
thought of 2:28–29 and 2 Cor 3 is related; and the fact that Paul avoids his
usual formula (καθὼς γέγραπται; see on 1:17), whereas the λέγει formula in
9:15 and 10:19 introduces a continuingly or eschatologically relevant scripture,
presumably indicates that Paul was attempting to bring out some contrast
by means of the different verbs. The present tense denotes the continuing
force of this word of Moses for Paul's own people.

τὴν δικαιοσύνην τὴν ἐκ νόμου, "the righteousness which is from the law," is
no doubt intended to characterize the understanding of righteousness which
Paul attributes to his fellow Jews (9:31–32; 10:3; cf. particularly 2 *Apoc. Bar.*
67.6). The semantic equivalent in 9:31–32 is not νόμος δικαιοσύνης but the
fuller and more restrictive phrase νόμος δικαιοσύνης ἐξ ἔργων. The restriction
is indicated in 10:3 by ἰδίαν and here by ἐκ νόμου = a righteousness delimited
by the law, restricted to those who observe the law, the covenant people (as
in 4:14, 16; Gal 3:18, 21). The phrase is the inverse of νόμος . . . εἰς δικαιοσύνην
(see on 10:4). For reading ὅτι at this point, see *Notes*.

The scripture quoted is Lev 18:5:

Leviticus: "You shall keep all my statutes and all my ordinances
and shall do the same, which by doing a man shall live in them"
καὶ ποι ήσετε αὐτά, ἃ ποιήσας ἄνθρωπος ζήσεται ἐν αὐτοῖς
Romans: ὁ ποιήσας αὐτὰ   ἄνθρωπος ζήσεται ἐν αὐτοῖς
"the man who does the same shall live in them."

For the text see *Notes*. Lev 18:5 can be regarded as a typical expression of what Israel saw as its obligation and promise under the covenant (e.g., Deut 4:1; 5:32–33; 8:1; 16:20; 22:7; 30:15–20; Neh 9:29; Ezek 18:9, 17, 19, 21; 20:11, 13, 21; 33:15–16, 19; *Pss. Sol.* 14.2–3; *4 Ezra* 7.21; see also on 2:13 and 7:10; Luke 10:28 should not be overlooked!). Hence one finds the phrase "the law of life" in Sir 17:11; 45:5 and *4 Ezra* 14.30 (cf. Bar 3:9). In most of these cases the covenant is explicitly in view (as also in *Tg. Ps.-J.* on Lev 18:5); and "life" means life within the covenant (as also in Philo's use of Lev 18:5—*Cong.* 86–87), not the life of the age to come as such (cf. Kaiser; the future tense is not eschatological, as NEB seems to assume), even in the Ezekiel passages, where the promise is that life will not be cut off, as failure to maintain the covenant would entail (in subsequent rabbinic usage, when national identity was no longer possible, an eschatological interpretation became more prominent without supplanting the other—Str-B, 3:278). Paul would certainly understand his text in the same way, that is, as an expression of how his fellow Jews understood righteousness—life within the covenant, "covenantal nomism," the pattern of religion and life which marked out the righteous, the people of the covenant (recognized, e.g., by Murray, 2:249; Lindars, *Apologetic*, 229; Ladd, "Law," 51; Lindemann, 241–42; but wholly missed by Bring, "Gesetz," 19, in his argument that ὁ ποιήσας ἄνθρωπος "is the man who seeks righteousness not ὡς ἐξ ἔργων, but by the way of faith"!). The line of argument is different from his other use of the same passage in Gal 3:12, but it characterizes the same attitude in both cases (see Dunn, "Works," 535–36; against Hübner and Badenas, 249 n.259, who oppose reference to Gal 3:12 here).

It needs to be said yet again that there is no thought of "achieving righteousness" here (against particularly Leenhardt). And the verb should *not* be emphasized, as though Paul was objecting to the idea of "doing" the law (contrast 2:13; so, rightly, Badenas, n.256, and Watson, *Paul*, 165; against Schlatter; Bultmann, *Theology* 1:264; van der Minde, 112; Beker, *Paul*, 246; Lübking, 85–86; and Käsemann, who speaks repeatedly of "the demand for achievement"). Nor does the thought enter here of the unfulfillability of Lev 18:5 (as is usually argued, particularly on the basis of Gal 3:10–12—see, e.g., Luz, *Gesetz*, 94–95; Hübner, *Israel*, 80–81; Hofius, "Gesetz," 272; and those cited in Dunn, "Works," 540–41 n.38); that quite mistakes the character of "covenantal nomism," also evident in Phil 3:6; as Sanders points out, "the righteous (in Jewish thought) are not the sinless, but those who confirm the covenant" ("Fulfilling the Law," 121). The suggestion that ὁ ποιήσας . . . is *Christ* (Barth, *Shorter*; M. Barth, *People*, 39; Campbell, "Romans 10:4," 77–78; Cranfield; Reicke, "Gesetz," 249–50) also completely misses the point; within the context of Jewish thought outlined above it would make Jesus an exemplar of Israel's nationalist righteousness—the very opposite of Paul's intention.

6a ἡ δὲ ἐκ πίστεως δικαιοσύνη οὕτως λέγει, "whereas the righteousness from faith speaks thus." The usual view that Paul intends a contrast here with v 5 has come under recent fire, by those who argue that Paul can hardly have intended to set two such closely related passages from the Pentateuch (cf. Lev 18:5 with Deut 30:15–20) against each other (most recently Campbell, "Romans 10:4," 78; Cranfield; Badenas, 118–33; others in Rhyne, 166 n.16). But the contrast is nevertheless plain, as Rhyne (105) recognizes. (1) Righteousness ἐκ πίστεως is a central motif in Romans (see on 1:17). That alone should be enough to indicate that the preceding reference is a foil to what is now said, and not another way of saying the same thing. (2) When Paul sets righteousness ἐκ πίστεως alongside righteousness ἐκ something else, with δέ as the linking word, he obviously intends his readers to understand a contrast between the two phrases (4:16; 9:30, 32; as well as Gal 2:16 and 3:21–22). (3) In the same way, it is hard to avoid the conclusion that δικαιοσύνη here is set in contrast to Moses (see on 10:5). (4) A very similar contrast involving a more polemical treatment of Lev 18:5 is clear in Gal 3:10–12 (see on 10:5); consequently the argument that Paul would not set scripture against scripture cannot stand. Rather we should say he follows good Jewish hermeneutical precedent in consulting different scriptures to see if he can resolve the difficulty he now perceives in the characteristic Jewish understanding of Lev 18:5.

In keeping with the dual thread of thought which Paul draws from his text (1:17a), the ἐκ πίστεως will refer primarily to man's response to divine grace (9:32), but quite likely also to God's faithfulness as that which establishes the covenant (see on 10:3) rather than Israel's covenant loyalty (see on 1:17). The "righteousness" of God can be personified (see also on 6:18 and 22), like other expressions of God's self-manifestation and outreach to his creation and his people (wisdom, name, word, glory), as in Ps 85:10–13 and Isa 45:8; the latter in particular may have been in the back of Paul's mind, since it is closely related to the image of the potter (45:9) which had been so important in 9:20–23; once again we notice the cosmic dimension of God's righteousness (cf. Stuhlmacher, *Gerechtigkeit*, 98). To identify "the righteous from faith" with Christ (Barth, *Shorter*) is less to the point, since Christ belongs with the content of the scripture quoted rather than as its author (vv 6–10). For the possibility that λέγει is set in deliberate contrast to the γράφει of v 5 see on 10:5.

μὴ εἴπῃς ἐν τῇ καρδίᾳ σου, "do not say in your heart." That Paul attaches this repeated phrase from Deut 8:17 and 9:4 is generally recognized. Michel, Cranfield, and Harrisville rightly note the importance of the context of these passages—both directed against self-complacency and presumptuous boasting—without recognizing the full force of the allusion. The point is that both passages are directed against the assumption that Israel's righteousness has been the ground of Israel's military triumph and prosperity. To "speak in the heart," then, is to forget that the success is *entirely* God's doing from start to finish, that it is *God* who confirms the covenant (ἵνα στήσῃ τὴν διαθήκην αὐτοῦ—Deut 8:18; 9:5). The echo of 10:3 will be deliberate: Paul attacks the same attitude in both cases (see on 10:3). For καρδία see on 10:1.

6–8 There is some dispute as to whether Paul intended to quote Deut 30:12–14 or was simply using some of its language and imagery to make his own point without dependence on Deut 30:12–14 as such (e.g., SH, Zahn, Denney, Barrett; see further Kuss and Badenas, 125–26, with bibliography). But Paul almost certainly does intend to cite Deut 30:12–14, or more precisely, to explain and expound it. (1) The text is too close to that of the Deut passage to be accidental:

Deuteronomy	Romans
. . . τίς ἀναβήσεται ἡμῖν	τίς ἀναβήσεται
εἰς τὸν οὐρανόν . . . ;	εἰς τὸν οὐρανόν; . . .
τίς διαπεράσει ἡμῖν εἰς	τίς καταβήσεται εἰς τὴν
τὸ πέραν τῆς θαλάσσης . . . ;	ἄβυσσον; . . .
ἔστιν σου ἐγγὺς τὸ ῥῆμα	ἐγγύς σου τὸ ῥῆμά ἐστιν
σφόδρα ἐν τῷ στόματί σου	ἐν τῷ στόματί σου
καὶ ἐν τῇ καρδίᾳ σου . . .	καὶ ἐν τῇ καρδίᾳ σου . . .

(On the second clause see below.)

(2) Particularly in the light of the DSS we can now recognize more clearly characteristic features of Jewish exposition of a scriptural text: specifically the partial citing of a passage followed by an explanation of it (as most clearly in 1QpHab 5.6–8; 6.2–8; 7.3–5; 10.2–4; 12.2–10); with the explanation introduced by an identifying formula—"it/he/this is . . ." (as in 1QS 8.14–15; 4QFlor 1.11; 4QpIsaᵇ 2.6–7), or "the interpretation is . . ." (repeatedly in the Qumran exegetical writings). See further M. P. Horgan, *Pesharim: Qumran Interpretation of Biblical Books*, CBQMS 8 (1979); W. H. Brownlee, *The Midrash Pesher of Habakkuk*, SBLMS 24 (1979). The closest parallel within the NT is Heb 10:5–10, and elsewhere in the Pauline corpus, Eph 4:8–11 (see further Dunn, *Unity*, chap. 5; *pace* Siegert, 162). For τοῦτ᾽ ἔστιν see further on 9:8. Of course, as an introductory formula, τοῦτ᾽ ἔστιν had a much wider currency throughout the Greek-speaking world (see BGD, εἰμί II.3). Paul's language and technique here are a nice blend of Jewish and Hellenistic style. Likewise the τί λέγει; of v 8 is clearly intended as an appeal to the authoritative text being expounded; cf. 4:3; 11:2, 4; and Gal 4:30 (Badenas, 126; see also BGD, λέγω I.7). This alone would serve to correct the inference which some draw from the absence of γέγραπται or a λέγει formula at the beginning of the reference to Deut 30:12–14 (cf. Hübner, *Israel*, 88–89); the reason for that omission is sufficiently explained by the contrast Paul is making between the two Mosaic texts (Lev 18:5 and Deut 30:12–14), only the latter of which points beyond Israel's covenantal nomism (see on 10:5 and 10:6a; cf. the lack of any introduction in a fair number of Paul's quotations—see on 10:18).

This appeal to Deut 30:12–14 would resonate with a diaspora Jewish audience. It is self evident that Deut 30:1–10 would be greatly cherished by the devout of the diaspora, with its promise explicitly to those scattered among the nations that conversion and obedience would result in restoration and a circumcision of the heart which would produce love of God from the heart. This *a priori* likelihood is confirmed by Philo, *Praem.* 163–72, and the clear allusion to Deut 30:7 in Jewish tomb inscriptions of Asia Minor, where the curse is evoked as something well enough known to protect the tombs from abuse and robbery (*MAMA* 6:335a, 6:335; *CIJ* 770; see Trebilco, chap. 3).

The implication is near to hand that Paul would see his ministry among the Gentiles as seeking just that conversion and obedience (of faith, 1:5), and as bringing about just that circumcision of the heart (see on 2:29, the "deep down Jew") and love from the heart (see on 5:5) of which Deut 30:1–10 spoke.

Paul's use of Deut 30:11–14 has striking parallels. In the following extracts the underlining indicates the lines of the text also taken up by Paul (the broken underlining indicating a less close parallel).

Deuteronomy 30:11–14 (LXX)

¹¹ For this commandment which I command you today is not too excessive, nor far from you. ¹² It is not up in heaven saying, "Who will go up for us into heaven, and get it for us; and having heard it we shall do it?" ¹³ Neither is it across the sea saying, "Who will go across to the other side of the sea for us, and get it for us; and he will make it audible to us and we shall do it?" ¹⁴ But the word is very near you, in your mouth and in your heart and in your hands, so that you can do it.

Baruch 3:29–30

²⁹ Who has gone up into heaven and got it and brought it down from the clouds? ³⁰ Who has gone across to the other side of the sea and found it, and will gain it with choice gold? (referring to divine Wisdom, subsequently identified with "the book of the commandments of God"—4:1).

Philo, *Post.* 84–85

What he describes as "close by" and "near" is the good. For it is not necessary, he says, "to fly up into heaven" or to go "to the other side of the sea" in search-ing for what is good. For it is "near" and "close by" for each... "For," he says, "it is in your mouth and in your heart and in your hands.

Targum Neofiti on Deuteronomy 30

¹¹ For this precept which I command you this day is not hidden from you, neither is it far away. ¹² The law is not in the heavens, that one should say: Would that we had one like Moses the prophet who would go up to heaven and fetch it for us, and make us hear the commandments that we might do them. ¹³ Nor is the law beyond the Great Sea, that one should say: Would that we had one like Jonah the prophet who would descend into the depths of the Great Sea and bring up the law for us and make us hear the commandments that we might do them. ¹⁴ For the word is very near you, in the word of your mouth and in your hearts, that you may do it.

(1) It is plain that Deut 30:11–14 was a subject of considerable reflection among Jews both in Palestine and in the diaspora. Philo indeed makes explicit use of the text no less than four times (*Post.* 84–85; *Mut.* 236–37; *Virt.* 183; *Praem.* 80), with several further allusions elsewhere (*Som.* 2.180; *Spec. Leg.* 1.301; *Prob.* 68). Paul's turning to this text would occasion no surprise to his hearers. (2) The text was very freely handled, certainly as freely handled as in Paul's treatment. For example, Philo repeatedly makes use of the LXX's addition of "in your hands" to the MT (v 14), and, like Paul, pays little

attention to the final clause ("so that you can do it"). *Neofiti* stays closer to the MT at this point, but, like Paul, replaces the idea of going across the sea with that of descending into the depths (see further on 10:7). The freedom Paul demonstrates in handling the text would likewise occasion little surprise among his Jewish contemporaries. (3) It is also evident that Deut 30:11–14 was widely understood to have a reference which transcended a simple one-to-one correlation with the Torah—with Wisdom (Baruch), with "the good" (Philo). Although Paul clearly does rechannel the thrust of the passage in accordance with his own theological insight, the possibility and propriety of his so doing would therefore not necessarily have been a subject of controversy, even if his conclusions would have been resisted by many of his fellow countrymen. Cf. on 10:18.

To describe Paul's use of Deut 30:12–14 as "purely fanciful" (Dodd), "drastic and unwarrantable allegorizing" (Kirk), "especially crass" (Gaugler) or "most arbitrary" (Byrne, *Reckoning*, 196) is therefore inappropriate and betrays a twentieth-century perspective insufficiently tutored by first-century parallels and techniques; cf. particularly Suggs and Hanson, "Interpretation," 145–49. On the other side, since the above parallels provide such a complete context for Paul's use of the Deut text, it seems unnecessary to follow Goldberg in detecting a reflection of rabbinic polemic against apocalyptic mysticism.

6b τίς ἀναβήσεται εἰς τὸν οὐρανόν; "who will go up into the heaven?" Cf. Prov 30:4. The question is an interesting precursor of the emphasis in John that *no one* can go up to heaven except the Son of Man who came down from heaven (particularly John 3:13 and 6:62), reflecting the same desire of the ancients to explore the heavens and learn its secrets (by vision or heavenly journey) which the Fourth Evangelist insists is impossible (see further Bühner and Dunn, cited on 8:3).

τοῦτ' ἔστιν, "this is"; see on 10:6–8.

Χριστὸν καταγαγεῖν, "to bring Christ down." Despite first impressions, the intention is probably not to identify Christ with "the commandment" of Deut 30:11, since "the word" (which in Deut 30:14 = the commandment) is subsequently identified as the word of faith = belief in Jesus' resurrection and confession of him as Lord (vv 8–10). Christ features here more in the role of Moses and Jonah in *Neofiti*, as one whose coming (again) from heaven (where he now reigns as Lord) or raising (again) from the dead would make "the word" easier to believe and confess; the objective is to tie the language of Deut 30 into the established kerygmatic confession of Christ's lordship and resurrection (cf. van der Minde, 112–15). As in 10:4 the thought is not so much Christological as soteriological, or salvation-historical. The reference therefore is not to Christ's incarnation, as is often assumed (e.g., Lagrange; Nygren; Barrett; Bruce; Schweizer, "Herkunft," 107; Cranfield, also "Comments," 273–74; contrast the greater caution of German scholarship, e.g., Lietzmann, Schmidt, Zeller). Paul rather contests the idea that because Jesus' exaltation and resurrection belong to the past they are harder to believe and confess—the order of clauses (ascent/exaltation, descent/resurrection) of course being determined by the order of clauses in Deut 30:12–13 (the point is ignored by Hanson, *Image*, 74; see further Dunn, *Christology*, 184–86).

7 *ἤ, τίς καταβήσεται εἰς τὴν ἄβυσσον;* "or, 'Who will descend into the abyss?'"
Is this a quotation from Deut 30:13? In view of the targumic tradition preserved
in the *Fragmentary Targum* (Lyonnet, "Rom 10:6–8," 502–5) and *Neofiti* (see
on 10:6–8), the possibility cannot be excluded that there was a text form of
Deut 30 in which the horizontal contrast (heaven/other side of the sea) had
been replaced by the vertical contrast (heaven/*sheol*; cf. particularly McNamara). It is more likely, however, that the two contrasts were recognized in
Jewish circles as equivalent, so that one could be used in place of or to supple-
ment the other without loss of or addition to the meaning. This is also implied
in *Neofiti* and in Ps 139:8–9, and the idea of the primeval waters of chaos
under the earth would facilitate the association (cf. Barrett). Of the two, the
heaven/underworld contrast is the more natural (cf. Ps 107 [LXX 106]:26,
which Paul may possibly echo, whether consciously or unconsciously—

ἀναβαίνουσιν ἕως τῶν οὐρανῶν
καὶ καταβαίνουσιν ἕως τῶν ἀβύσσων;

Isa 7:11; Amos 9:2; Sir 16:18; 24:5; *Jub.* 24.31; *4 Ezra* 4.8), and brings out
the impossibility (for man) of what is envisaged more effectively (cf. Str-B,
3:281).

τοῦτ᾽ ἔστιν, "that is"; see on 10:6–8.

Χριστὸν ἐκ νεκρῶν ἀναγαγεῖν, "to bring Christ up from the dead." The language echoes that of Ps 71 [LXX 70]:20—*ἐζωοποίησάς με καὶ ἐκ τῶν ἀβύσσων
τῆς γῆς πάλιν ἀνήγαγές με;* Wisd Sol 16:13—"you have power of life and
death, and you lead down to the gates of hell and back again (*ἀνάγεις*)."
This imagery, as distinct from that of resurrection—that is, of a descent into
the realm of the dead and return—presumably is the basis of the creedal
affirmation of Christ's descent into hell, already developed in 1 Pet 3:19
and 4:6 (cf. Kuss). See also on 14:9.

8 *ἀλλὰ τί λέγει;* "but what does it say?" See on 10:6–8.

ἐγγύς σου τὸ ῥῆμά ἐστιν, ἐν τῷ στόματί σου καὶ ἐν τῇ καρδίᾳ σου, "the word is
near you, in your mouth and in your heart." See on 10:6–8.

τοῦτ᾽ ἔστιν, "that is"; see on 10:6–8.

τὸ ῥῆμα τῆς πίστεως ὃ κηρύσσομεν, "the word of faith which we preach."
ῥῆμα is little used by Paul, but since it is given by the text Paul not only
explains it but uses it as a thematic link (vv 8–9, 17–18; elsewhere in Paul
only in 2 Cor 12:4 and 13:1; also Eph 5:26 and 6:17). As so often with
such genitive constructions, we need not press for an either-or meaning, as
though Paul could have in mind only the word "which calls for (the response
of) faith" (Cranfield), or only the word which proclaims the faith that is
believed (Käsemann, Schlier; alternatives reviewed by Kuss). In view of the
double emphasis of vv 9–10, in which the twofold theme of "in the mouth"
and "in the heart" is still further expanded, it is most likely that Paul intended
the ambiguity of the genitive to embrace both aspects (see also on 1:5). The
more developed idea of Christ being present in the word of preaching (Käsemann, Schlier), however, goes too far beyond the text. It is characteristic of
Paul that he uses *κηρύσσω* with first person plural (1 Cor 1:23; 15:11; 2 Cor
1:19; 4:5; 11:4; 1 Thess 2:19). He does not see his preaching as idiosyncratic,
but as an expression of the gospel held in common, which unites the new

movement round the one "word of faith"—an important expression of solidarity with the relatively unknown Roman church (so vv 14–15). In contrast, the unusual first-person language of Gal 2:2 and 5:11 probably betrays a sense of some isolation on Paul's part at that time. The characteristic objects of κηρύσσω in Paul are "the gospel" (Gal 2:2; Col 1:23; 1 Thess 2:9) and "Christ" (1 Cor 1:23; 15:12; 2 Cor 1:19; 4:5; 11:4; Phil 1:15); see further on 10:14. The whole phrase is broken down and recast in vv 9–10, with πίστις reexpressed by πιστεύειν (undermining Gaston's persistence in translating the former as "faithfulness"—*Paul*, 179).

9 ὅτι ἐὰν ὁμολογήσῃς ἐν τῷ στόματί σου, "for if you confess 'with your mouth.'" English translation is unable to reproduce the ambiguity present in both the ὅτι—"that" (Barrett) and "because" (Cranfield)—and the ἐν ("in," as in Deut 30:14, or "with," as makes better sense here). Once again "either-or exegesis" should be avoided—though it makes little difference to the sense in this case. The ἐν τῷ στόματί σου, like the subsequent ἐν τῇ καρδίᾳ σου, should be in quotation marks in translation, since Paul is clearly picking up and expounding phrases from the preceding quotation (Bruce). For the "midrash-pesher" technique as exemplified in the DSS, see on 10:6–8. The closest parallel is 1QpHab 11.17–12.10; cf. 12.14–13.4. Somewhat surprisingly, Paul uses ὁμολογέω only here (vv 9–10), though note also 1 Tim 6:12 and Titus 1:16, and the use of ὁμολογία in 2 Cor 9:13 (also 1 Tim 6:12–13), and ἐξομολογέω in Rom 14:11; 15:9; and Phil 2:11 (all given by the OT passages cited). What is in view is clearly a public confession of a solemn nature (the word has judicial overtones), though not necessarily confession in a judicial context (as Cullmann, *Confessions*, 27–28, and Munck, *Christ*, 89, suggest; see further Neufeld, 13–20). The confession which follows functions therefore as an (or the) equivalent of the Shema (Deut 6:4): as he who says the Shema identifies himself as belonging to Israel, so he who says κύριον Ἰησοῦν identifies himself as belonging to Jesus. As a "slogan of identification" it would no doubt be used at baptism, but also much more widely in worship (1 Cor 12:3), evangelism (2 Cor 4:5), and parenesis (Col 2:6) (cf. particularly Campenhausen, 231–32; Kuss, 765–66). See further BGD, ὁμολογέω; *TDNT* 5:207–12; and particularly Schlier.

κύριον Ἰησοῦν, "Jesus is Lord." For the double accusative cf. John 9:22; 1 John 4:2; and 2 John 7 (BDF §157.2); also 2 Cor 4:5. As is now generally agreed, Paul cites here a well-established creedal formula. Despite its lack of clear attestation outside Paul (Neufeld, 143), the formula may go back to the earliest days of the new movement, or at least is a very early expression of the earliest faith: Acts 2:36 and Phil 2:11 reflect the impact of the resurrection on Christology; in this connection Ps 110:1 was obviously much used as an early proof text (see on 8:34); and its established use in Aramaic is attested particularly by 1 Cor 16:22. The briefer form, "Jesus is Lord," rather than "Jesus Christ is Lord," is appropriate for such a distinguishing confession, as attributing lordship to the particular historical individual, Jesus (as in 4:24; 1 Cor 11:23; 12:3; cf. Rom 14:14; 1 Cor 5:4; 9:1; 2 Cor 4:14; Eph 1:15; 1 Thess 2:15; 2 Thess 1:8), and perhaps reflects its early fixation as a formula (before "Jesus Christ" became the standard referent for the central figure of the new movement; cf. particularly 2 Cor 4:5; Phil 2:11; Col 2:6).

The significance that this confession intended and would be heard to bear is also broadly agreed, but can be exaggerated. κύριος was widely used to denote an asserted or acknowledged dominance and right of disposal of superior over inferior (master—slave, king—subject, god—worshiper; see BGD; MM; Lietzmann; *TDNT* 3:1041–58; Hahn, *Titles,* 68–70). So to confess someone as "lord" denotes an attitude of subserviency and sense of belonging or devotion to the one so named. And if the confession here was used in baptism, as again is widely agreed to be very likely, it would also indicate a transfer of allegiance, a change in acknowledged ownership. How much more of Christological significance would be seen in the confession in Greco-Roman circles is less clear, since there were many "lords" (1 Cor 8:5), and since different lordships could be acknowledged in different spheres without necessarily involving conflict between them (*pace* Cullmann, a conflict between κύριος Καῖσαρ and κύριος Ἰησοῦς is not yet in evidence). To be sure, Paul does insist that in contrast to these "many lords" Jesus Christ is *the* Lord (1 Cor 8:5–6), whose lordship will eventually be acknowledged by all (1 Cor 15:24–27; Phil 2:9–11), but this is as much a consequence of his Jewish monotheism as of his belief in the uniqueness of the resurrected Christ: Jesus is the one Lord, because God is the one God (1 Cor 8:5–6; 15:28; Phil 2:11); see also on 8:34.

Within Jewish and Jewish-influenced circles the significance would correspondingly be greater. κύριος was recognized as at least an acceptable translation of יהוה in diaspora circles (see Fitzmyer, particularly 119–23), as Paul's own quotations of the scriptures (OT) also make clear; and even if the custom of transcribing יהוה in the Greek text of the OT was more common (Conzelmann, *Outline,* 83–84; Howard, "Tetragram"), κύριος would almost certainly have been used when the text was *read.* The reference of several such passages to *Jesus* as Lord is a striking feature in Paul's letters (v 13; 1 Cor 2:16; Phil 2:11—using the powerfully monotheistic Isa 45:23; 1 Thess 5:2 and 2 Thess 2:2—"the day of the Lord"). The clear implication is that Jesus as Lord shares in the one God's lordship. At the same time, however, it should again be noted that Paul saw Jesus' lordship as coordinate with the confession of God as one (1 Cor 8:5–6; 15:28), that he regularly spoke of God as "the God . . . of our Lord Jesus Christ" (see on 15:6; God is Christ's lord—1 Cor 3:23), and that Christ's lordship was also seen as the eschatological fulfillment of the Creator's purpose for man—Ps 8:6 (1 Cor 15:25–27; Eph 1:20–22; Phil 3:21; Heb 1:13–2:8; 1 Pet 3:22). See also on 1:4, 7, 8; 8:34; and 10:12. Where "appointment" to postresurrection status is concerned (1:4; Phil 2:9), and against the background of a Judaism which had already expressed the idea of human figures being exalted to share in divine functions (see on 1:8 and 2:16), it surely cannot still be maintained that "a necessary implication of this (Christ's lordship) is that Paul believed in Christ's preexistence and in the Incarnation," or that such a concept of exaltation would have been "nonsense" to a first-century Jew (against Cranfield, "Comments," 274–75).

καὶ πιστεύσῃς ἐν τῇ καρδίᾳ σου ὅτι, "and believe 'in your heart' that." For πιστεύειν see on 1:16; with ὅτι see on 6:8. But here, somewhat surprisingly, Paul uses it in the aorist tense of the act of Christian commitment for the first time (as also 10:14, 16; 13:11). The word καρδία is given by the text (Deut 30:14; see above), but also indicates clearly enough that an affective and deeply motivating belief (καρδία; see on 10:1) is in view and not merely a recitation of creedal form. Although the association of "mouth" and "heart" is given by the text, it is evident that Paul sees inward belief and outward expression in word as inextricably linked, the two sides of the one coin (cf. Michel); cf. the way Philo makes use of the triple division of the LXX text (see on 10:6–8). This propositional or creedal belief should not be set in antithesis to belief = trust, which comes to clear (and climactic) expression in v 13 (so rightly Robinson, *Wrestling*, 123–24).

ὁ θεὸς αὐτὸν ἤγειρεν ἐκ νεκρῶν, "God raised him from the dead," is a second familiar formula (see on 4:24). It is noticeable that belief in the resurrection of Jesus is here the corollary of the confession that Jesus is Lord.

σωθήσῃ, "shall be saved." The future is a genuine future—salvation as an eschatological good, the end product of the process. Note the three tenses involved here—*present* belief and confession, of the epochal *past* event of Christ's resurrection, resulting in *future* salvation. It is not by accident that the formulation here recalls the thematic statement in 1:16. See on 1:16 and 5:9.

10 καρδίᾳ γὰρ πιστεύεται εἰς δικαιοσύνην, στόματι δὲ ὁμολογεῖται εἰς σωτηρίαν, "for with the 'heart' belief is exercised for righteousness, and with the 'mouth' confession is made for salvation." Paul evidently thought it important to emphasize the double aspect of saving faith once again, this time in the more natural order (inward belief coming to expression in spoken word) (see also Gaugler). For the balancing words καρδία/στόμα, πιστεύειν/ὁμολογεῖν, see on 10:9. The allocation of the remaining element to each clause (εἰς δικαιοσύνην, εἰς σωτηρίαν) could be reversed without loss of meaning (cf. the equal association of believing with δικαιοσύνη and σωτηρία in 1:16–17); it is generally recognized that the distinction is determined by the Deut quotation rather than by any theological distinction (cf. also 4:25). The near equivalence of "righteousness" and "salvation" in this context is wholly Jewish in character, as their frequent use in parallel in the Psalms and Second Isaiah makes clear (see on 1:17). The evocation of the letter's thematic statement (1:16–17), as so often in this section, is obviously deliberate. And since the εἰς σωτηρίαν clearly looks to future eschatological fulfillment (see again on 1:16), it is a further reminder that δικαιοσύνη in the parallel formula will almost certainly have the same forward look (see also on 6:16)—God's righteousness not just as his initial acceptance of the believer, but also his ongoing sustaining power and final vindication.

11 λέγει γὰρ ἡ γραφή, "for the scripture says." The chain of scriptures linked by γάρ (see *Form and Structure*) serve to confirm the exposition of Deut 30:12–14. If the λέγει of v 6 is a significant variation on the γράφει of v 5 (see on 10:5), that may have determined the choice of formula here (though it is regularly used in Rom [4:3; 9:17; 11:2]). For the formula see on 4:3.

πᾶς ὁ πιστεύων ἐπ᾽ αὐτῷ οὐ καταισχυνθήσεται, "all who believe in him shall not be put to shame"—Isa 28:16 again (see on 9:33), but with πᾶς added, perhaps under the influence of Joel 3:5 [EV 2:32] in v 13 (Aageson, "Scripture," 276). This is a further example of interpretative quotation, where the interpretation is actually built into the citation itself (Ellis, *Paul's Use*, 140).

As with Deut 30:11–14, Paul evidently felt justified in giving the text a more universal scope because of the eschatological significance of Christ. NIV's "will not be disappointed" is too weak; NJB is better—"will (not) be brought to disgrace."

12 οὐ γάρ ἐστιν διαστολὴ Ἰουδαίου τε καὶ Ἕλληνος, "for there is no distinction between Jew and Greek." For the first half see on 3:22; for the second half see on 1:16. The repeated reappearance of themes from the first major section of the letter is no accident (see 9:30–10:21 *Introduction*). This is the positive equivalent of 3:22. Within the Adam phase of human history it is the universality of sin's power which diminishes differences between Jew and Greek to insignificance (3:22); in the eschatological time introduced by Christ it is the universal openness of God's grace to *all* who believe which leaves Jew without advantage over Greek, since Gentile can now share in what was previously a more exclusively Jewish covenant relationship. (Paul may indeed have had in mind the unique use of διαστολή in just this connection at Exod 8:23 [LXX 19].) "Where the word is taken up in faith and confession, there the salvation-historical distinction between Jews and Gentiles is removed" (Wilckens). Cf. 1 Cor 12:13; Gal 3:28; and Col 3:11 (also Acts 15:9), and the more fully worked-out statement of Eph 2:11–22.

ὁ γὰρ αὐτὸς κύριος πάντων, "for the same (Lord) is Lord of all" (cf. 1 Cor 12:5). Paul may be citing a more widely used Christian formula (cf. Acts 10:36), taken over from what was probably already established hellenistic Jewish usage in reference to God (Job 5:8 LXX; Esther LXX 13:11 = 4:17c; T. Mos. 4.2; Josephus, Ant. 20.90). The argument is again parallel to the earlier argument in 3:29–30: the universal lordship of Christ is the eschatological expression of the one God's sovereign purpose. The formula is not an exact equivalent to the disputed benediction in 9:5 (see on 9:5), since θεός is evidently not a *full* equivalent to κύριος in Paul's thinking. κύριος is a status given to the exalted Christ by God, and though it consists in a sharing in God's sovereign authority it is always derivative from God and therefore to be distinguished in the end from God; it can even be seen as the dominion over all other creation which God intended for man (see further on 10:9).

πλουτῶν εἰς πάντας τοὺς ἐπικαλουμένους αὐτόν, "rich to all who call on him." The metaphor of spiritual wealth is one used by Paul on a number of occasions—of God (2:4; 9:23; 11:33; also Eph 3:16), or of Christ (2 Cor 8:9; also Eph 3:8), or of God's giving to people in or through Christ (1 Cor 1:5; Phil 4:19; Col 1:27; also Eph 1:7; 2:7). The sense of *God's* riches in Christ is strongly present here in the following clauses. The prepositional formulation is unusual, but the meaning is clear: to call on him is to draw on the immensity of his spiritual resources.

ἐπικαλεῖν a god is a Greek usage (LSJ, BGD, 2b), but the language is much more typically Jewish—"to call upon the Lord" (Deut 4:7; 1 Sam 12:17–18; 2 Sam 22:4, 7; etc.; Pss 4:1; 14:4; 18:3, 6; etc.; Isa 55:6; Lam 3:57; Jud 6:21; 8:17; 9:4; 2 Macc 3:22, 31; 4:37; 7:37; 8:2; 12:6; etc.; Pss. Sol. 2.36; 9.6; T. Jud. 24.6; T. Dan. 5.11; 6.3) = "to call upon the name of the Lord" (Gen 4:26; 12:8; 13:4; 21:33; etc.; Isa 64:17; Jer 10:25; Lam 3:55; Joel 2:32 [LXX 3:5]; Zeph 3:9; Zech 13:9; Jud 16:2); see also TDNT 3:498–500 and BGD, 2b. A typical assumption in these passages is that this is an activity which marks off the devout of Israel—though Paul's eschatological perspective is shared by at least Zeph 3:9 and *T. Jud.* 24.6 (Christian?). Christians early on took over the language as their own self-designation (Acts 2:21; 9:14, 21; 22:16; 1 Cor 1:2; 2 Tim 2:22; 1 Pet 1:17). A clear implication is that in so doing they saw themselves in continuity with the people of Israel—belonging to the people who call on the one God and the one Lord; this is the privilege of the people of the covenant (cf. SH; Gaugler, 138). Such "calling on" can be described as prayer, but it has less the character of entreaty (δέησις— 10:1) and more the character of an appeal to the covenant partner to honor his (covenant) obligations. This too will have been in Paul's mind in his repeated "all" (vv 11–13).

13 πᾶς γὰρ ὃς ἂν ἐπικαλέσηται τὸ ὄνομα κυρίου σωθήσεται, "for everyone who calls upon the name of the Lord shall be saved." πᾶς appears for the fourth time in vv 11–13. Apart from the linking γάρ the verse is in exact agreement with the LXX, itself a fair translation of the Hebrew of Joel 3:5 [EV 2:32]. Since Paul has already made much play of the prophetic idea of a remnant (9:27–29), we may presume that he has the context of the Joel passage in mind, since it continues, "for in Mount Zion and in Jerusalem there shall be one who is rescued (ἀνασῳζόμενος) . . . and they who receive (or preach) good tidings (εὐαγγελιζόμενοι), whom the Lord has summoned (προσκέκληται)." The logic would be the same: the prophets clearly envisaged that those called by God in the last days would not be precisely equivalent to Israel as a whole (national Israel), whether smaller in number or involving other peoples (see on 9:26 and 27b–28). Here the use of πᾶς and the appearance of εὐαγγελίζεσθαι ("preach [good news]") in the immediate context would be sufficient justification for Paul's interpreting the passage as he does. In addition the same Joel passage was probably more widely used in early Christian self-understanding (Acts 2:17–21, with other echoes in Rom 5:5 and Titus 3:6; Mark 13:24 pars. and Rev 6:12; Acts 2:39), which would give the passage added credibility in Christian circles. For ἐπικαλέσηται see on 10:12; for ὄνομα see on 1:5; for the significance of κύριος and of employing a Kyrios Yahweh reference to Kyrios Jesus see on 10:9; for σωθήσεται see on 10:9.

Explanation

Having reintroduced the idea of two epochs—one characterized in terms of the law, the other in terms of faith, with Christ marking and effecting the transition—Paul proceeds to document and undergird it with scriptural justification. Just as he followed the intense theological argument of 9:22–24 with scriptural proof in 9:25–29, so now he looks to scripture to sustain the equally intense argument of 10:2–4. The scriptural proof he finds by juxtaposing two texts from the Torah—Lev 18:5 and Deut 30:11–14.

10:5 The righteousness which Israel sought (v 3) is now expressed as "the righteousness which comes from or arises out of the law." Since v 5 is introduced as a further explanation or justification for the line of argument developed over the preceding verses, Paul's readers would have no difficulty in reading off the equation, "law of righteousness in terms of works" (9:31–32) = "their own righteousness" (10:3) = "righteousness out of the law" (v

5). So too it can hardly be doubted that "righteousness from the law" would inevitably be seen as the inverse statement of the phrasing in the preceding verse, "the law for righteousness" (v 4). So the reader would be in no doubt as he began this section that Paul was referring to an attitude to the law and to righteousness which he saw to be both typical of his own people and to be now rendered out of date by Christ. "Righteousness out of the law" then is righteousness understood as sustained and dependent upon acts of law keeping, righteousness understood as marking out a relationship with God peculiar to the people of the law and documented and validated by their faithfulness to those ancestral customs in particular which gave them their distinctiveness among the nations.

This attitude, however obsolete now, at least had some justification in the old epoch, as Moses shows: "he who does these things shall live by them" (Lev 18:5). Paul seems to understand the passage in its most obvious sense— that keeping the statutes and ordinances of the law was the way of living appropriate to the covenant, which the covenant required. Moses did *not* say, and Paul does not understand him to say, that keeping the law was a means of earning or gaining life (in the future; cf. Gal 3:21; Rom 7:10). Rather the law prescribes the life which is to be lived by the covenant people (cf. Hab 2:4). The life sustained by God is life in accordance with the regulations and institutions of the law.

6 In contrast Paul puts forward another speaker—not Christ, but "the righteousness from faith." The contrast seems to be deliberate, since Paul would regard Moses as the author of the second quotation as well as of the first. Paul must mean therefore to identify the old epoch with Moses, not unnaturally since "the law" and "Moses" would be obvious correlates in his thought (cf. 2 Cor 3). It is less clear what motivates his personification of "righteousness" as the opposite side of the antithesis. Certainly he sees the new epoch introduced by Christ as characterized by "the righteousness from faith," but quite possibly also he has in mind the vigorous metaphorical use of "righteousness," even personification of "righteousness," precisely as one of scripture's ways of depicting the eschatological salvation of God (as in Isa 45:8). Whatever the reason, this righteousness is clearly the same righteousness which he has been referring to variously since 9:30 as "the righteousness from faith," "the law of righteousness" (9:31), and "the righteousness of God" (10:3). That is, it denotes God's giving and sustaining of that relationship with him without which man cannot know salvation, a relationship which on man's side depends first and foremost on his reliance on God, open to his power in trustful obedience.

The antithesis between law and faith at this point is of course not to be pressed too far: Paul neither confines the law to the old epoch (cf. 8:2; 9:31), nor believes that faith only becomes possible with the new epoch (cf. chap. 4). It is a *characterization* of the two epochs he is striving for, not a definition, far less a complete description. As a Jew he has no doubt that God's saving power prior to Christ centered on and worked through his people, and since the law is the obvious identity factor which characterizes his people most distinctively he can describe their relationship with God not unfairly or wholly negatively in terms of "righteousness from the law." But as a Christian he is also convinced that the eschatological effect of Christ has been to bring God's purpose to a new and final stage, where relationship with God can no longer be circumscribed by national and ritual boundaries but must be described in terms of "righteousness from faith."

6–8   The second quotation which the "righteousness from faith" introduces is from Deut 30:11–14. The initial reaction of the commentator, as it must have been of many when they first heard the passage, is that Paul is posing a *false* antithesis, that the two quotations from Leviticus and Deuteronomy are correlative rather than antithetical. For Deut 30 like Lev 18 is intended to encourage the *keeping* of the law: the point of Deut 30 is to emphasize that the commandment of God is not too hard; God does not require of his people something unattainable; they know what he wants, and they can do it if they have the mind to do so. For anyone familiar with Deut 30:11–14 the most striking feature of Paul's citation of the passage is that the last part stops short and misses out the most important phrase (v 8). Where Deut 30:14 says, "The word is very near you, in your mouth and in your heart *to do it*," Paul quotes only, "The word is near you, in your mouth and in your heart." But what is more surprising still is the way in which Paul's interpretation of the passage seems to change its sense completely: where Deuteronomy speaks of the *commandment* as being neither too far away nor too hard, Paul interprets it of Christ—"'Who will ascend to heaven' (that is, to bring Christ down), or 'Who will descend to the abyss?' (that is, to bring Christ up from the dead)"; and where Deuteronomy refers to the commandment when it speaks of "the word," Paul interprets it of the gospel—"'The word is near you, in your mouth and in your heart' (that is, the word of faith which we preach)."

However, the contrast between Deuteronomy's original meaning and Paul's interpretation of it is not so sharp as at first appears. We have already noted that the antithesis implied in vv 5–6 between the law and faith should not be pressed (v 6 above). This applies equally to Paul's use of Deut 30. The point is that for Paul the commandment of the law is not nullified or controverted by the word of faith; on the contrary the commandment is fulfilled in the word of faith (cf. 3:31), the word of faith we might say *is* the law of righteousness properly understood (9:31–32). What Paul is objecting to throughout this letter is *not* the law or the commandment as such, but the law and the commandment *understood in terms of works* (9:32), in terms of national righteousness (10:3). To put the same point another way. Deut 30 can be taken as referring to *both* epochs of God's saving purpose, to the epoch of Israel before Christ and the epoch of all the nations brought in by Christ. The contrast between Lev 18 and Deut 30 therefore is not that the former is to be wholly referred to the old epoch while the latter solely to the new. Rather it is that the Leviticus passage emphasizes the *dis*continuity between the epochs, whereas the Deuteronomy passage can bring out the *continuity* between the epochs, the continuity precisely between the law and the obedience of faith. In this sense too it can be seen that "the word of God" has not failed (9:6).

We can see the same point emerging from the way Paul focuses attention on the "heart" in this passage. He deliberately introduces Deut 30:12–14 by inserting the words from Deut 8:17 and 9:4, "Do not say in your heart" (v 6)—the Deuteronomist's repeated warning against presumption on the part of his people, of a forgetfulness that the covenant is sustained solely by God and not by their doing (10:3). And in his elaborated interpretation in vv 9–10, Paul underlines the fact that faith operates from the level of the heart. In view of his repeated emphasis earlier that the real business of the law is "in the heart" (2:15), that the circumcision God wants is "of the heart" (2:29), that the obedience God calls for is "from the heart" (6:17), the repeated reference to the heart here can hardly be accidental. The implication is that when Deut 30:14 speaks of the word in the heart Paul understands it to be speaking of the law written in the heart (Jer 31:33), understands the obedience called for to be the "obedience of faith" and not merely the obedience of works. The point of the contrast with Lev 18, then, is that Deut 30 emphasizes *both* levels of obedience, heart as well as mouth, inward as well as outward (cf. 2:28–29), whereas Lev 18 seems to emphasize only the "doing," only the one level which consequently can too easily become merely the level of works. So once again Deut 30 can be said to provide a deeper insight into what the law is about, whereas Lev 18 tends to encourage the shallower interpretation which in Paul's view characterized most of his kinsfolk's current understanding of the law.

But how was it possible for Paul to interpret the commandment of Deut 30:11 as a reference to Christ? The answer is probably given in the fact that Deut 30:11–14 seems to have provoked a considerable interest in Jewish thinking at about this time. Baruch had already used the passage in speaking of the hiddenness of divine Wisdom (Bar 3:29–30). Philo, closer to the time of Paul, refers it to "the good" (*Post.* 84–85; *Mut.* 236–37; *Praem.* 80). And *Targum Neofiti* also elaborates the same two verses (Deut 30:12–13) in reference to the law. The implication is that there was a widespread impression during this whole period that Deut 30:11–14 was referring not simply to the commandment of Moses, not merely to the law as such. Even to suggest that the commandment was "in heaven" or "beyond the sea" was enough to indicate that there was something bigger in view than the written commands of the law, something of cosmic or universal scope. Baruch and Philo both took up the hint and interpreted the passage in terms which would have appealed to a much wider audience—the heavenly wisdom which far more than Israel coveted, "the good" which was the goal of ethical discipline for so many in the ancient world. For both Baruch and Philo, of course, divine wisdom and what is good focused particularly and nowhere else so clearly as in the law. The point is, however, that they saw the law as the focus and embodiment of something more mysterious, more ultimate. Paul evidently shares the same intuition. But for him the something more, of cosmic scope and universal significance, can only be an allusion to Christ. So just as these others saw in Deut 30 a reference to a grander theme which nevertheless comes to clearest articulation in the law, so Paul sees in Deut 30 a reference to Christ who comes to clearest expression in the gospel, the word of faith which defines the deeper meaning of Deuteronomy's "commandment," at the level of the heart.

The reference to Christ is facilitated by the fact that the two questions of

Deut 30:12–13 match so neatly with two stages of the Christ event—his exaltation to heaven (v 6) and his resurrection from the dead (v 7). It is less than likely that Paul's readers would understand the first question as a reference to incarnation, since there is no evidence that Christian thought had so far evolved the idea of incarnation, or that the language of preexistence when referred to Christ (1 Cor 8:6) would as yet be taken to imply his personal preexistence, or that talk of his being "sent" (Rom 8:3) was as yet understood to imply a descent from heaven. The order of the two stages of the Christ event in vv 6–7 is fully explained by the order of the clauses in Deut 30:12–13. In the same way in v 9 the order of phrases in Deut 30:14 determines the fact that Paul puts confessing Christ as (exalted) Lord *before* believing that God raised him from the dead; Paul hardly means us to think that Christ's exaltation preceded his resurrection, or that confession should precede belief! In neither case is it likely that Paul intends the order of clauses to be understood as a chronological order.

Paul thus takes Deut 30:11–14 seriously. The commandment, properly understood as calling for the obedience of faith, from the heart, does not call for something impossible. Righteousness does not require earthbound man to scale the heights of heaven or to plumb the depths of the abyss; neither does its attainment depend on Christ's continued (or restored) bodily presence on earth. The word which expresses God's will is near; it is not unattainable, because as scripture says, it is "in your mouth and in your heart." That word is "the word of faith," a word characterized by faith from start to finish, that is, a word which in particular calls for faith from its hearers; though (in line with the ambiguity in his use of "the righteousness from faith") Paul may also have in mind that the word he preached proclaimed God's faithfulness. In contrast to the focus of Lev 18 on *doing,* the emphasis which emerges from Deut 30 for Paul is on *believing*—not because he wants to set faith and deeds in antithesis, but because whereas Lev 18 lends itself to being understood in terms of ethnic customs and ritual ordinances, Deut 30 points to that deeper level of obedience now called for in the gospel's call to faith.

In short, Paul's exegesis here is by no means so arbitrary and unjustified as at first might appear. He can take Lev 18:5 as characterizing "righteousness from the law," as characterizing righteousness understood in terms of nationalistic practices and rituals, precisely because that is the way the bulk of his own countrymen seem to understand "the law of righteousness" as a whole. And he can take Deut 30:11–14 as characterizing "righteousness from faith," not only because it speaks of a deeper level of obedience, of the level of obedience which the law properly understood really looked for, of the level of obedience which his gospel in continuity with the law of righteousness now proclaims; but also because its wording invites a reference to the cosmic lordship of Christ proclaimed by the same gospel.

9–10 Paul continues his exposition with a clarification of the two phrases, "in the mouth" and "in the heart." He has already identified "the word" of Deut 30 as "the word of faith which we preach," so he could have taken the two phrases as referring to the apostolic message and its proclamation. But, presumably because he remains mindful that Deut 30:11–14 was speaking of the "commandment," of a word calling for response, he naturally refers the two phrases to the response called for by the gospel—viz., confession of Jesus' lordship, and belief in his resurrection. This emphasis on belief and its expression in open confession marks out clearly the difference from a response characterized by "works." This presumably is the reason that the point is put as a conditional clause: the one essential condition of salvation is faith, the acceptance by heart and lip of what God has done in and through Christ. But the emphasis also highlights what Paul clearly regards as the central emphasis of his gospel: the fundamental and indispensable belief that "God raised him from the dead" (cf. 1 Cor 15:17), and the equally firm conviction that "Jesus is Lord" (cf. 1 Cor 8:6 and Phil 2:11). On both points it is almost certain that Paul cites formulae which would be familiar to his readers, formulae which would probably recall their own conversion and initiation into the new movement, formulae in fact which go back to the earliest days of the new movement. In posing the gospel as an alternative to what he sees as the typical Jewish presumption of a favored status before God demonstrated and affirmed by the identifying rituals of the law and ancestral customs, Paul is concerned to describe the gospel in terms which would command the fullest consent from other Jewish Christians as well as from Gentile believers too.

The point is repeated in a generalized assertion in v 10, where the clauses are distinct only for rhetorical effect, as determined by the wording of Deut 30:14. The generalization heightens still further the contrast with righteousness from the law. To talk of the "heart" is to talk of faith; faith operates at and from the level of the heart. To talk of the "mouth" is to talk of confession; confession is the primary and essential outward manifestation corresponding to faith, not a sequence of ritual "works." If righteousness is in view, faith which cannot hold back from public expression is the way into that gracious relationship with God. If salvation is in view, confession which springs from a wholehearted inner conviction is the means through which God's final purpose is achieved. This is what Deut 30:11–14 always looked for, as the resurrection and exaltation of Christ have now made clear. In understanding righteousness in terms simply of (Israel's) keeping the law the bulk of Israel had misunderstood how God's righteousness is received and had put their ultimate salvation in jeopardy (v 1).

11 That the thrust of Paul's thought is still directed toward exposing and explaining his fellow countrymen's misunderstanding of their own scripture is confirmed by the way he rounds off the present paragraph. Verse 11 picks up the quotation from Isa 28:16 cited in 9:33, reminding us that the argument from 9:30 is all of a piece. The faith which Deut 30 calls for with its talk of the word in the heart is the same faith of which Isa 28:16 spoke. The mutual applicability of both passages to Christ no doubt served for Paul as confirmation that he was interpreting both correctly. The one alteration Paul makes is significant. He adds "all" at the beginning. Thereby he universalizes what in its narrower context had primary reference to Israel—just as in v 10 he generalized the truth expressed by Deut 30:14. In neither case would Paul think the procedure illegitimate—simply because it is a firmly rooted conviction on Paul's part that the privileges initially given to the Israelites (9:4–5, including the giving of the law) always had the nations as whole in view. It is the new and climactic stage of God's purpose achieved in the resurrection and exaltation of Christ which has brought that wider purpose into focus and triggered off its universal implementation.

12–13 The implication of the added "all" in v 11 is spelled out in the sequence of three explanatory clauses. "There is no difference between Jew and Greek." The assertion so simply made would be astonishing to any members of the Roman congregations less familiar with this basic postulate of the Gentile mission (1 Cor 12:13; Gal 3:28). The distinction between Greek and barbarian had been rendered less widely applicable by the spread of Hellenism, but the distinction between Jew and Gentile was still basic to Jewish thought. And for all that Paul had emphasized "to Gentile as well as Jew" earlier in his letter, he had still emphasized the priority of the Jews (1:16; 2:9–10) and confirmed their special privileges under the covenant (3:1–2; 9:4–5). But here he states the other side of his dialectic, and with a sharpness unmatched even in 1 Cor 12:13 and Gal 3:28. For those, however, who have followed the line of his argument, the point is clear: he who first gave his covenant grace to Israel alone has now broadened it out to include *all*, and on the same terms—faith; what was always called for by the law, faith from the heart in the one who gave the covenant, can now be reexpressed as faith in the one through whose resurrection and exaltation God has broadened out the same covenant. In terms of historic privilege Israel is still distinctive. In terms of the righteousness of God open to all, there is now no difference between Jew and Greek.

The two following "for" clauses (vv 12b, 13) might also have caused some surprise, for Paul seems deliberately to merge the role of Jesus as Lord with that of God himself. In calling Christ "Lord of all" he echoes, no doubt deliberately, the argument used in 3:29–30: if Jews believe God is one, then he must be God of Gentiles as well as Jews; so if Christ is "Lord of all" he is Lord for both Jew and Greek. Moreover, he speaks of the Lord Christ as "rich to all who call upon him," where the most obvious connotation is of calling in prayer or entreaty on a divinity who might be expected to provide help from his abundant resources. Paul would hardly be unaware of how frequently the scriptures speak of "calling upon the name of the Lord," and the appropriateness of talking of God's richness toward humankind is hardly unfamiliar to him (2:4; 9:23). Most striking of all is the way in which he cites Joel 2:32 [LXX 3:5], evidently with the full intention of referring it to "the Lord Jesus"—"for all who call on the name of the Lord shall be saved." This hope and promise held out in Joel with reference to the God of Israel, Paul refers without any apparent qualm to the exalted Christ.

The point Paul is making is not, however, a Christological one; rather it is a salvation-history point. At its simplest he is stressing the complete continuity between God's purpose through his covenant with Israel and the climax of that purpose in Christ. The remnant of Judah, who according to Joel will be saved (cf. 9:27–29), are once again to be identified as those who call upon the name of the Lord Jesus. But there is more involved in Paul's thought than that, for it is precisely through the exaltation of Christ to his right hand that God can now be seen to exercise his own lordship as a lordship over all, Greek as well as Jew; for in fact it is through Christ's exaltation that God has extended his effective lordship and covenanted authority to all nations—a point Paul might easily draw from the combination of Ps 110:1 and Ps 8:6 which was already well established in primitive Christian apologetic (cf. particularly 1 Cor 15:25–27). So too as God's vice-regent and executive he is the one to whom and through whom requests for divine aid should be made; he is the one who can dispense God's own riches. Now that God has acted in and through Christ to bring in the final stage of his purpose for all humankind, the Jew can no longer claim special rights of access to God which are unavailable to the uncircumcised Greek, but must recognize that God has so disposed himself that access is now henceforth through Christ. Paul does not shrink from the boldness of his conclusions. It is not simply that the extension of God's grace to all has ended Israel's special covenant privileges as privileges enjoyed by Jews alone. It is also that the God who committed himself to Israel in covenant can no longer be thought of as simply or primarily the God of Israel. It is also that God, who showed himself to be concerned for all humankind in raising Christ from the dead and exalting him to his right hand, cannot now be understood or recognized other than in terms of this Christ. In committing himself to act so decisively in and through Christ, he obliged men and women to recognize God-in-Christ and to address themselves to God-through-Christ. Thus it is now through this Christ that all will be saved, share in the final wholeness of God's fulfilled purpose for the world—and that "all" includes Jew as well as Greek. This is the seriousness of Israel's plight so long as it continues to reject the gospel. To reject the word of faith is to reject its own covenant as now transposed into universal terms by Christ; to turn one's back on Christ is to refrain from making that appeal to God in and through Christ by which salvation comes, the salvation for which Paul prays (10:1).

3. Israel's Failure to Respond to the Gospel (10:14–21)

Bibliography

See also 9:1–11:36 *Bibliography*.

Howard, G. "The Tetragram and the New Testament." *JBL* 96 (1977) 63–83. Ljungman, H. *Pistis*. 91–102. Müller, F. "Zwei Marginalien im Brief des Paulus an die Römer." *ZNW* 40 (1941) 249–54. Rehkopf, F. "Grammatisches zum Griechischen des Neuen Testamentes." In *Der Ruf Jesu und die Antwort der Gemeinde*, FS J. Jeremias, ed. E. Lohse. Göttingen: Vandenhoeck & Ruprecht, 1970. 213–25.

Translation

[14] *How therefore shall they call on him in whom they have not believed? And how shall they believe in him whom they have not heard? And how shall they hear[a] without someone preaching?* [15] *And how shall they preach unless they have been sent? As[b] it is written, "How timely are the feet[c] of those who preach[d] good*

news." [16]But not all have obeyed the gospel. For Isaiah says: "Lord, who has
believed our report?" [17]So then, faith comes from hearing, and hearing through
the word of Christ.[e]

[18]But, I say, is it the case that they have not heard? On the contrary:

Their sound has gone out into all the earth
and their words to the ends of the inhabited world.

[19]But, I say, is it the case that Israel has not known? First,[f] Moses says:

I will provoke you to jealousy by a not nation;
By a senseless nation I will make you angry.

[20]And Isaiah is so bold as to say:

I have been found by those who do not seek me;
I have revealed myself to those who do not ask for me.

[21]But concerning Israel he says:

All the day I stretched out my hands
to a disobedient [g]and obstinate[g] people.

Notes

[a]The subjunctive should be read throughout, including ἀκούσωσιν here; see SH.

[b]For the variation καθάπερ see on 3:4.

[c]The expected tendency to assimilate the text to the LXX by inserting τῶν εὐαγγελιζομένων εἰρήνην is clearly attested and clearly secondary (Metzger).

[d]Whether τά should be read is uncertain; see Cranfield, 535 n.1.

[e]There was a similar tendency in the same text tradition (as *Note* c) to replace the unique ῥῆμα Χριστοῦ (only here in the NT) with the more familiar ῥῆμα θεοῦ (Luke 3:2; John 3:34; Eph 6:17; Heb 6:5; 11:3) (Metzger). Howard, 78–79, argues in favor of θεοῦ on the hypothesis that (1) κύριε of v 16 was probably initially (as in first-century LXX texts) a transcription of the Tetragram, and (2) its subsequent replacement by κύριε caused an ambiguity (God or Christ?) which resulted in θεοῦ being replaced by Χριστοῦ. But the willingness of NT writers to use the phrase ῥῆμα θεοῦ and the absence of any NT parallel to ῥῆμα Χριστοῦ undermine the logic of (2).

[f]πρῶτος should certainly be read with Μωϋσῆς rather than with the question, as Bentley and Zahn have suggested; see Kühl and Cranfield.

[g]F G Ambst omit this phrase, presumably in recognition that the MT has a shorter line.

Form and Structure

The chain effect of a developing line of argument linked at each step by
a quotation from scripture, begun in v 9, continues through to v 21, with
the scriptures themselves actually carrying the line of argument in the final
stages.

Statement	Scripture
9–10	11
12	13
14–15a	15b
16a	16b
conclusion 17	
18	
19	
20	
21	

As with the first stage of the discussion in chaps. 9–11, Paul rounds off the argument with a sequence of scriptural quotations closely linked together (9:24–29; 10:18–21).

Although other divisions of the text are possible (in view of the awkwardness of vv 16–17), particularly the suggestion that vv 14–15 go with the preceding context (Lietzmann, Moffatt), it is much more natural to link vv 14–15 with vv 16–17 (as, e.g., Lagrange, Michel, Käsemann), especially when the function of vv 16–17 is properly appreciated (see on 10:16). The unjustifiable nature of wholly speculative emendation is illustrated by the implausibility of Müller's thesis that the original order of the text was vv 13, 14, 15b, 15a, 17, 16, 18 (see Michel, 333 n.1; Kuss). Particularly notable is the sequence of rhetorical questions in vv 14–15a (cf. 5:4 and 8:29–30), and the verbal link effected by the use of ὑπακούω (v 16), ἀκοή (vv 16–17), and ἀκούω (v 18), which is impossible to reproduce in English, but which the original audiences would no doubt have appreciated. There is also something of an *abcdeedcba* sequence in vv 14–20 (Leenhardt, 276).

Comment

10:14 πῶς οὖν ἐπικαλέσωνται εἰς ὃν οὐκ ἐπίστευσαν; "how therefore shall they call on him in whom they have not believed?" For πῶς in rhetorical questions, which call an assumption into question or reject it altogether, inviting the response "It is impossible," cf. 3:6; 6:2; and 8:32, and see BGD, 1d. For ἐπικαλεῖν see on 10:12. Since ἐπικαλεῖν does not usually need a preposition, the εἰς certainly goes with ἐπίστευσαν. Paul uses πιστεύειν εἰς only occasionally (Gal 2:16; Phil 1:29; cf. Col 2:5), but it is used elsewhere in the NT (Matt 18:6; Acts 10:43; 14:23; 19:4; 1 Pet 1:8; and frequently in the Gospel and Epistles of John). In this letter Paul usually uses πιστεύειν in the present tense (see on 1:16). Here the aorist with the εἰς points to the act of commitment which expresses itself in ἐπικαλεῖν; the question clearly harks back to v 9. Paul leaves the subject ambiguous, so that a decision between "the Jews" (as Cranfield) and the πάντες of v 12 (Wilckens) is unnecessary. Paul formulates a gospel principle (Munck, *Christ*, 91–92), and the target of vv 14–18 is as much Jewish(-Christian) objection to the universal (gentile) mission of the gospel (Wright, *Messiah*, 178–79; Watson, *Paul*, 166–67; cf. Gaston, *Paul*, 132), with Israel itself coming to explicit reference only in v 19.

πῶς δὲ πιστεύσωσιν οὗ οὐκ ἤκουσαν; "and how will they believe on him whom they have not heard?" In accordance with normal grammatical usage the οὗ must mean the speaker rather than the message (SH, Lagrange; further Schlatter). So presumably Paul still has in mind the imagery of Deut 30:12–13 interpreted in vv 6–7, with Christ as the bearer of the message (cf. v 17— ῥῆμα Χριστοῦ). If weight was to be given to the point we would have to think of Christ as the authority behind the one sent (Barrett; cf. Murray; see on 10:15, ἀποσταλῶσιν). But the syntactical constructions of the parallel questions were probably the chief determinant rather than a theological point. See also on 10:18.

πῶς δὲ ἀκούσωσιν χωρὶς κηρύσσοντος; "and how will they hear without someone preaching?" κηρύσσειν ("proclaim aloud, publicly") is not much used in the LXX, but the surprisingly infrequent usage for the preaching of the prophets is nevertheless significant and no doubt influenced the Christian usage, particularly the messianic and eschatological references (Isa 61:1; Joel 2:1; Zeph 3:14; Zech 9:9; so elsewhere in the NT—Mark 1:4, 7, 14, 38–39; etc.; note, e.g., Luke 4:18–19; Acts 20:25; and 28:31), and not least in Paul's case those which envisaged a proclamation to the nations (Joel 3:9; Jonah 1:2; 3:2–7; cf. also *Sib. Or.* 1.128; with different emphasis, Josephus, *Ant.* 9.214; so in Paul, particularly Gal 2:2 and Col 1:23; cf. Mark 13:10 and 1 Tim 3:16). See further on 10:8. The question reflects a society where the chief means of mass communication was oral; communication of the gospel by written means is not yet envisaged.

15 πῶς δὲ κηρύξωσιν ἐὰν μὴ ἀποσταλῶσιν; "and how shall they preach unless they have been sent?" The image of the preacher/herald (κῆρυξ) is implicit; fundamental to Paul's conception is the preacher as spokesman for another, not as someone with his own message authorized by himself—hence the emphasis of 1 Cor 15:9–11; 2 Cor 4:5; 11:4; and Gal 2:2. The link with ἀποστέλλειν is therefore not accidental (as also in Isa 61:1; Mark 3:14; Luke 4:18, 43–44; 9:2; 1 Tim 2:7; 2 Tim 2:11; *TDNT* 3:712), since at this point the κῆρυξ and the ἀπόστολος are largely overlapping concepts (see on 1:1). Cranfield draws attention to Jer 14:14; 23:21; and 27:15. Paul would presumably think of the commission as coming from Christ (1:5; 1 Cor 1:17, the most closely related of Paul's surprisingly infrequent use of the verb; so, e.g., Michel and Zeller).

καθὼς γέγραπται, "as it is written"; see on 1:17. Lietzmann's comment that the following quotation is "merely ornamental" has not won support and contradicts the force of the introductory formula (see also Cranfield). For the function of the quotation in vv 14–15, see also on 10:16.

The quotation is from Isa 52:7, with possibly also an echo of Nah 2:1; the text may have been prompted by the connecting links with Joel 2:32 [LXX 3:5] used in v 13 ("Zion" and εὐαγγελίζομαι—but note that Paul had already used Isa 52:5 at 2:24).

Nahum:	ἰδοὺ ἐπὶ τὰ ὄρη	οἱ πόδες εὐαγγελιζομένου . . . εἰρήνην
Isaiah:	ὡς ὥρα ἐπὶ τῶν ὀρέων, ὡς πόδες εὐαγγελιζομένου ἀκοὴν εἰρήνης,
Romans:	ὡς ὡραῖοι	οἱ πόδες τῶν εὐαγγελιζομένων
(Isa)	ὡς εὐαγγελιζόμενος ἀγαθά . . .
(Rom)	(τὰ) ἀγαθά

Paul's rendering seems to show knowledge both of the Hebrew ("How beautiful upon the mountains are the feet of him who brings good tidings, who publishes peace, who brings good tidings of good, who publishes salvation, who says to Zion, 'Your God reigns'"—the underlining indicating the closeness of the translation with the obvious exception that Paul thinks of not just one but many preaching), but perhaps also of the Greek (Wilckens; and note the appearance of ἀκοή; see vv 16–17). For ὡς, see on 11:33. The basic meaning of ὡραῖος is "timely, produced at the right season," with the idea of "beautiful, graceful" a natural derivative. So although the other NT references have the latter sense (Matt 23:37; Acts 3:2, 10) and the nearest parallel in the LXX likewise (Sir 26:18), it is very likely that the sense "timely, coming at the right time" is intended here by Paul (BGD). NEB offers a useful compromise, "How welcome . . . ." For Paul's use of εὐαγγελίζεσθαι, see on 1:15, and also on 1:1; cf. *TDNT* 2:719–20; here it is more or less synonymous with κηρύσσειν (v 14). The omission of εἰρήνη is a little surprising, in view of its importance for Paul (see on 1:7 and 5:1), as perhaps also the omission of mention of Zion (which with 9:33 and 10:13 = Joel 2:32 [LXX 3:5] would have made a striking Zion catena); but Paul presumably felt it necessary to give only an abbreviated reference. That the verse lent itself to a messianic or eschatological sense is self-evident from the original context (the prospective return from exile to the promised land). That such an interpretation was already current in Jewish circles at this time is now confirmed by 11QMelch 15–19, where Isa 52:7 is explicitly interpreted of "the anointed by the Spirit" (for later rabbinic messianic interpretation see Str-B, 3:282–83; Stuhlmacher, *Evangelium*, 148–50). This is perhaps then another case where Paul consciously sees the apostolic mission as one of sharing and completing that of the Messiah (see also on 15:20–21).

16   ἀλλ᾽ οὐ πάντες ὑπήκουσαν τῷ εὐαγγελίῳ, "but not all have obeyed the gospel." The οὐ πάντες should perhaps be classified as an example of meiosis (SH) or litotes (Rehkopf, 224); cf. 3:3; 11:17, 25. But it is equally likely that it is formulated simply in antithesis to the πᾶς of v 13 (Michel)—not "all," without specification of how many. This link back to v 13 suggests that Paul intended vv 14–15 as a rounded statement of all that "calling on the name of the Lord" depended on, with Isa 52:7 intended as a scriptural confirmation of the necessary role of preaching rather than as an assertion that two of the preconditions had been met (sent, and preached) (as Cranfield suggests). V 16 therefore is best understood as a first response to the sequence of vv 14–15, *not* intended to pick on any particular link in the chain, but simply asserting the fact that it has not worked in the case of "all." The question *why*, or *how* has the breakdown occurred is not actually addressed until v 18. Paul's use of ὑπακούω here, then, will be deliberate: (1) he wants to sum up the breakdown of the chain of vv 14–15, rather than to focus on any particular broken link (otherwise he would have used πιστεύω; but see below); (2) the wordplay ἀκούειν/ὑπακούειν is irresistible: their ἀκούειν has not been ὑπακούειν (Schlatter); (3) perhaps more important, he sees the opportunity to reinforce the note of obedience which he also sees as fundamental to the gospel (1:5; 6:16–17; 15:18; 16:19, 26; see also 2 Cor 10:5 and 2 Thess 1:8; Käsemann exemplifies typical Lutheran nervousness on the point), and which could be in danger of being overlooked every time the contrast of law/faith is pressed (as in 10:5 ff.). See further on 1:5; and note also 10:3. For εὐαγγέλιον, suggested, of course, by the preceding quotation, see on 1:1.

Ἡσαΐας γὰρ λέγει, "for Isaiah says," is the third of four scriptural passages drawn from Isaiah with explicit acknowledgment (9:27, 29; 10:16, 20).

Κύριε, τίς ἐπίστευσεν τῇ ἀκοῇ ἡμῶν; "Lord, who has believed our report?" The quotation is verbatim from Isa 53:1 LXX, though the Hebrew lacks the vocative "Lord." The text is used in John 12:38 for the same purpose; presumably, as a corollary to Isa 53's being seen to have a Christological reference, Isa 53:1 offered itself as another indication that by and large Israel would not accept the gospel of Jesus Messiah—a conviction likely to emerge first in Hellenistic circles (hence the LXX form). For Paul, therefore, it probably serves as a statement documenting the fact of the breakdown of the chain of cause and effect (vv 14–15), not as pinpointing the link where the break actually occurred. And this will be true even though for Paul ὑπακούω and πιστεύω are closely related, as this verse shows (cf. also 1:5; 16:26), a factor which is the main reason for the confusion as to the role of this verse in the argument (vv 14–18). For ἀκοή, see on 10:17. That ἀκοή occurs also in Isa 52:7 LXX (see on 10:15) is not brought out, but the presence of the same word in two passages from the same part of Isaiah and in consecutive verses here suggests that Paul was conscious of the context of his quotations.

17 ἄρα ἡ πίστις ἐξ ἀκοῆς, "so then, faith comes from hearing." When the function of v 16 is appreciated—as a statement of the breakdown of the chain (vv 14–15) rather than an analysis of the breakdown itself (see on 10:16)—the ἄρα can be given its proper force as introducing a conclusion or summing up, "so then, consequently," as in 7:21 and 8:1. Hence there is absolutely no need to treat the verse as a gloss (as Bultmann, "Glossen," 280; Michel; Luz, *Geschichtsverständnis*, 32 n.76; Schmithals, *Römerbrief*, 207); cf. Cranfield, whose explanation, however, is too complex, and Wilckens.

ἀκοή can have the sense both of "(act of) hearing" and of "that which is heard" (LSJ, BGD). But whereas in v 16 ἀκοή is best taken in the latter sense, as almost all agree, in v 17 the former sense seems to be required (SH, Barrett, NIV, NJB; otherwise, RSV and NEB). (1) What seems unnatural to us because we have to use two different words ("report" and "hearing") would not seem so to the Greek hearer; the range of meaning of one and the same word is simply being exploited. (2) The distinction from ῥῆμα (= "the word we preach," v 8) in v 17b almost certainly necessitates the sense "hearing," otherwise v 17b becomes largely meaningless. (3) It is the sense of "hearing" which the ἤκουσαν of v 18 picks up. (4) In the nearest parallel passage in Paul (Gal 3:2, 5) the natural sense is again "hearing," since it is precisely faith as the responsive hearing/acceptance of the gospel/Spirit which Paul clearly has in mind.

διὰ ῥήματος Χριστοῦ, "through the word of Christ." For ῥῆμα, see on 10:8. In this summing-up verse, Paul deliberately recalls v 8 (Lagrange, Gaugler), with perhaps the same sort of ambiguity intended in the genitive (the word of which Christ is content and author), or possibly with the same implication intended as in v 14 (Christ as the bearer of the message; see on 10:14); see Kuss, also Käsemann. Munck, on the basis of the OT parallel ἐγένετο ῥῆμα κυρίου suggests "command" (*Christ*, 94 and 135n.). Fitzmyer offers as a possible translation "the message of the Messiah." Schlier's reference to the "word-event" of Christ is far too modern to serve as exegesis.

18 ἀλλὰ λέγω, μὴ οὐκ ἤκουσαν; μενοῦνγε, "but I say, is it the case that they have not heard? On the contrary." Paul uses this personal style of engagement in discussion (λέγω) several times in these chapters (10:18–19; 11:1, 11). A question introduced by μή expects a negative answer (as in 9:14), but where the main verb is itself negated (μή . . . οὐ) an affirmative answer is anticipated (BDF §427.2). The ἤκουσαν picks up the ἐξ ἀκοῆς of v 17 (Wilckens). It is regrettable that English cannot reproduce the cognate link between ὑπακούω ("obey"), ἀκοή ("hearing, report") and ἀκούω ("hear"), which is an obvious feature of vv 16–18 and which would of course be evident to the first hearers— all the more so where they were familiar with Hebrew usage, since all three were used in the LXX to represent שָׁמַע (see also on 1:5). For μενοῦνγε, see on 9:20.

εἰς πᾶσαν τὴν γῆν ἐξῆλθεν ὁ φθόγγος αὐτῶν, καὶ εἰς τὰ πέρατα τῆς οἰκουμένης τὰ ῥήματα αὐτῶν, "their sound has gone out into all the earth, and their words to the ends of the inhabited world." The quotation is drawn word for word from the LXX of Ps 19:4 [LXX 18:5]. The absence of an introductory formula need not be significant (cf. 9:7; 10:13; 11:34–35; 12:20; 1 Cor 2:16; 10:26; 15:27, 32; 2 Cor 10:17; 13:1; see Ellis, *Paul's Use*, 156–85); but it should not be assumed that Paul intends to cite the passage as prophetic, as most seem to (rightly, Lagrange, Bruce). Paul could simply be using the language of the psalmist as providing a hyperbolic vision of the full eschatological sweep of the gentile mission (cf. 1:8; 2 Cor 2:14; 3:2; Col 1:6, 23; 1 Thess 1:8; but hardly an assertion that the mission to the Jews had been completed—so Munck, *Christ*, 96–99, Black; cf. also on 15:19, 23). On the other hand, he could have been fully aware of the whole psalm, with its second half focused on the law, and intended to imply that the law is an expression of a more transcendent witness, as with Deut 30:11–14 (vv 6–8), and that it is the ῥήματα of the law in its transcendent form that is the ῥῆμα they preach (v 8; cf. also the στόμα/καρδία of Ps 19:14 [LXX 18:15] with vv 8–10). It is this message that has gone "into all the world" in the ῥῆμα(τα) of the apostolic preaching. By using such a scripture Paul reminds his readers that "the Gentile mission is not an action apart from Israel but is the act of Israel's God" (Wilckens). Käsemann reflects on "the rift between Paul's apocalyptic hope and earthly reality," and he points out that "the apostle's salvation-history is the most vulnerable part of his theology." Presumably he is recalling the critique of Reimarus on this point referring to this verse (cited by Kuss). But Paul would scarcely be conscious of such a rift as yet (cf. 11:15, 25–27; and see on 15:19); and in his use of a *theologia crucis* to control the triumphalism at Corinth (2 Cor 4:7–5:5; 12:6–10; 13:3–4) he had already provided a theological means of dealing with that rift. NJB translates ἐξῆλθεν oddly as "stands out." φθόγγος can denote the sound of an instrument (as in its only other NT reference, 1 Cor 14:7) or of the human voice. For τὰ πέρατα as "the ends, limits (of the earth)" see BGD, πέρας. Οἰκουμένη, "the inhabited earth, the world," occurs only here in Paul (8 of the 15 NT occurrences are in Luke-Acts); cf. particularly Matt 24:14.

19 ἀλλὰ λέγω, μὴ Ἰσραὴλ οὐκ ἔγνω; "but I say, is it the case that Israel has not known?" For μὴ . . . οὐ see on 10:18. For Ἰσραήλ see on 9:4. The charge is particularized following the less specific statements of vv 14–18. As in 9:31 the use of Ἰσραήλ (rather than οἱ Ἰουδαῖοι) will be deliberate; it is precisely the question of who constitute the covenant people that is at stake. The problem of correlating the use of γινώσκω here with ἀγνοέω in 10:3 (e.g., SH, Michel) is not substantial. The range of meaning possible in γινώσκω makes it much more than a simple antonym of the latter. So it could be intended as a near synonym of ἀκούω in v 18 (given the range of meaning possible likewise in עֵמָע; see on 10:18), and bear a sense like "acknowledge"; or it could be intended to take a step beyond ἀκούω, and thus mean "understand, comprehend" (so, e.g., Cranfield, Schlier, Wilckens; cf. BGD, γινώσκω 3).

πρῶτος Μωϋσῆς λέγει, "first Moses says." For πρῶτος, "first," where there is no following δεύτερος, see on 1:8; perhaps here in the sense, "Moses was the first to say," "even as early as Moses" (SH). Moses is explicitly cited here not because he characterizes the old epoch (cf. 10:5), but to give weight to the following passage, which will become the key that unlocks the mystery of Israel's rejection of the gospel in chap. 11.

ἐγὼ παραζηλώσω ὑμᾶς ἐπ᾿ οὐκ ἔθνει, ἐπ᾿ ἔθνει ἀσυνέτῳ παροργιῶ ὑμᾶς, "I will provoke you to jealousy by a not nation; by a senseless nation I will make you angry." The verse cited is verbatim from the LXX of Deut 32:21, except that Paul replaces the αὐτούς in both lines by ὑμᾶς. Quite why he should do so is not clear, since the change does not modify the sense of the original —the αὐτούς refers to "his sons and daughters" (Deut 32:19); but it may indicate that Paul is still thinking in terms of a diatribe, and, more important, that he sees himself, or rather God, as actually addressing his fellow countrymen. "Paul alters the citation so that this I of God directs itself to the Thou of Israel" (Hübner, *Israel,* 97). The future tenses were obviously thought to give the verse the force of a prophecy (NJB translates the first as a present tense—perhaps a slip). Various identifications of the "no people" were to be offered—Philistines and Samaritans (Sir 50:25–26), Babylonians (*Tg. Yer.*), and the north Africans (see Str-B, 3:284–85). Paul sees it as an eschatological prophecy and naturally thinks of his own mission to the Gentiles (11:13–14). The wording too would be particularly appealing to him: ὀργή and παροργίζω (32:19, 21), υἱοί (32:19, 20), in close conjunction with the only occurrence of πίστις in the Torah (32:20)—the implication being that Israel's present lack of "faith" is the eschatological equivalent of Israel's unfaith in its most idolatrous periods. παραζηλώσω also foreshadows 11:11, 14 (see on 11:11). The importance of the verse, not least for Paul, is that it begins to bring together the two strands so far treated separately in chaps. 9–10— God's purpose to call a "no-people" (9:25) and Israel's rejection of the gospel: the former will provide the solution to the latter within the purpose of God (ἐγώ emphatic). παροργίζω usually denotes Israel's provoking God to wrath in OT usage; cf. not least Isa 65:3 (see also *T. Lev.* 3.10; *T. Zeb.* 9.9; *T. Ash.* 2.6). Paul would probably be conscious of the uniqueness of Deut 32:21b as *God's* provoking Israel; the playoff of ideas with Ezek 32:9 and Bar 4:6 is particularly interesting. He would almost certainly be aware that in the two verbs he was taking language used of Israel (ζῆλος—10:2) and in a neat reversal was using it to explain Israel's present role within God's overall purpose. The influence (or usefulness) of the Song of Moses in early Christian apologetic and parenesis is indicated by 1 Cor 10:20, 22 (cf. Deut 32:16–17), Phil 2:15 (cf. Deut 32:5) and Heb 1:6 (= Deut 32:43 LXX) (Bruce).

20 Ἠσαΐας δὲ ἀποτολμᾷ καὶ λέγει, "Isaiah is so bold as to say" (BGD). In classic Jewish style, a citation from the prophets follows one from the law; for the importance of Isaiah's quotations for Paul in chaps. 9–11, see chaps.

9–11 *Introduction.* ἀποτολμάω occurs only here in the Greek Bible (cf. 15:15, 18) and probably indicates the boldness of Isaiah's prediction, rather than Isaiah's boldness (Cranfield).

The citation is from Isa 65:1 LXX, with different word order, which makes no difference to the sense:

Isaiah:	ἐμφανὴς ἐγενόμην	τοῖς ἐμὲ μὴ ζητοῦσιν
Romans:	εὑρέθην ἐν	τοῖς ἐμὲ μὴ ζητοῦσιν
Isaiah:	εὑρέθην	τοῖς ἐμὲ μὴ ἐπερωτῶσιν
Romans:	ἐμφανὴς ἐγενόμην	τοῖς ἐμὲ μὴ ἐπερωτῶσιν·

The inversion is what one would expect in a quotation from memory. At the same time it should be noted that the LXX had already inverted the Hebrew order ("I was ready to be inquired of by those who did not ask for me; I was ready to be found by those who did not seek me"), so that it is equally possible that Paul also had the Hebrew in mind. The most striking difference between the Hebrew and the Greek is the use of ἐμφανὴς ἐγενόμην for the niphal of שׁרֵד = "let oneself be inquired of, consulted." ἐμφανῆ γενέσθαι, "to become visible"—so ἐμφανὴς ἐγενόμην, "I have been revealed, that is, revealed myself" (BGD)—could of course refer to God's self-revelation to Israel and to Moses in particular (Exod 3:14; etc.); and thus Paul could have in mind the argument from Exod 33:19 already picked out at 9:15. In nonbiblical Greek, however, ἐμφανής was used especially of the gods appearing bodily among humans (LSJ)—a more questionable assertion in Jewish ears—though, of course, already for Paul it could be taken to refer to the embodiment of divine Wisdom in Christ (cf. 1 Cor 1:24, 30).

The original prophecy had Israel in mind, but the language lends itself to being interpreted of nonIsraelites (cf. 9:30); and for those who thought of themselves as seekers of God (cf. 9:31; 10:2) a reference to those outside the circle of covenant faithfulness would be very attractive or indeed called for. It would then be seen to belong with the stream of Jewish expectation which looked for the eschatological incoming of the Gentiles (see on 9:26). Such emphases need to be borne in mind in the face of the stereotype of Israel's hatred directed against the Gentiles (as in Dodd, 171). In later rabbinic thought it was in fact referred to Rahab and Ruth (Str-B, 3:285). Paul's use of the text to refer to the success of his own mission to the Gentiles falls within that tradition, even though it involves pulling Isa 65:1 and 2 (v 21) in different directions. The present tense of ζητοῦσιν and ἐπερωτῶσιν should not be lost in translation (as do most translations). Paul sees here, as in 9:30, definitions of the Gentiles—those who do not (by definition) seek and ask after (the) God (of Israel).

21 πρὸς δὲ τὸν Ἰσραὴλ λέγει, "but concerning Israel he says." For πρός = "with reference to," see BGD, III.5a. Paul specifies Israel as the target, thereby making still clearer the point that v 20 referred to Gentiles. There is no attempt, however, to hide the fact that the second scripture follows from the first in Isa 65 (v 20—Isa 65:1; v 21—Isa 65:2).

ὅλην τὴν ἡμέραν ἐξεπέτασα τὰς χεῖράς μου πρὸς λαὸν ἀπειθοῦντα καὶ ἀντιλέγοντα,

"all the day I stretched out my hands / to a disobedient and obstinate people."
The passage is verbatim from Isa 65:2, with the exception that Paul has
pulled the phrase ὅλην τὴν ἡμέραν, which comes at the end of the first line
in the LXX and MT, to the beginning of the line for emphasis (followed by
Barn. 12.4). It is unclear whether the LXX has expanded the too-short line
of the MT by adding καὶ ἀντιλέγοντα (cf. 1QIs^a, and the omission of the
phrase from some witnesses to the Pauline text; see *Notes*), or whether alternatively the LXX and Paul should be counted as witnesses to a longer Hebrew
text (but *difficilior lectio* would suggest otherwise).

The emphasis is on the divine initiative. It is no accident that all three of
the concluding OT quotations are in direct speech of God and indeed in
first-person language (Michel; Hübner, *Israel*, 98); hence also the ὅλην τὴν
ἡμέραν (cf. 8:36) in the place of emphasis—"daily" (Michel), "continually"
(Cranfield). The fact that ἐκπετάννυμι τὰς χεῖρας was more proper to man's
appeal to God (Exod 9:29, 33; Ezra 9:5; Sir 48:20; 51:19) would heighten
the poignancy of the text. Moreover, it should be recalled that this line of
argument leads into a further question regarding God's responsibility—"Has
God rejected his people?"—indicating clearly that it is not merely the guilt
of Israel which is in view (Schmidt). In this way Paul continues to elaborate
a fundamental aspect of his theme—*God's* faithfulness, not to Jew alone, and
not to Gentile in disregard of Jew. Both are in view, and it must have been
important for Paul that he could express both aspects of God's outreaching
concern by means of the same scripture (Isa 65:1–2), and with the Deuteronomy quotation as well (v 19), thereby tying the whole together in the first
anticipatory statement of the resolution of the whole. At the same time it is
not entirely accurate to say that "the statement of Israel's disobedience is
strictly incidental" (Cranfield; but see Barrett, "Fall," in *Israelfrage*, ed. Lorenzi,
102, criticizing Munck, *Christ*, 75–79; also 89–91, 104). ἀπειθεῖν has a key
role in Paul's analysis of Israel's failure (11:30–32; see also on 2:8) as the
opposite of ὑποτάσσεσθαι (10:3) and ὑπακούειν (10:16), and with ἀντιλέγειν it
stands in opposition to the πιστεύειν and ὁμολογεῖν which the word of faith
evokes (10:8–10, 14). That divine predestination works through disobedience
does not make it any less disobedience (cf. SH, Käsemann, Kuss). The unbelief
of an Israel which has heard and understood (vv 18–19) is proof that God's
saving power works through faith (cf. Schlatter).

Explanation

It is becoming steadily clearer that Paul's intention is to explain the rejection
of the gospel by Israel, as rooted in their failure to understand their own
law and their own scriptures. The bulk of his fellow Jews have misunderstood
the law of righteousness in terms of works; they have focused too much on
the level of outward actions and national customs and failed to appreciate
what obedience from the heart involves; and most of all they have failed to
see how scripture pointed to Messiah as one whose resurrection and exaltation
effects the end of the old epoch of Israel's exclusive privilege and the beginning
of the wider extension of God's saving purpose—an eschatological end that
God always had in view from the first promise to Abraham (indeed from

the disobedience of the first Adam). But *why* this misunderstanding and rejection by the majority of Israel of what seems so obvious to Paul himself? Why is Israel not calling on the Lord for salvation as encouraged to do so by Joel? Paul has already hinted at a deeper and more profound answer in 9:14–23. But evidently he is not yet ready to develop that hint into a fuller statement. However, there is an alternative explanation which demands at least a brief treatment. And to this he turns—almost as though he hesitates to plumb that deeper depth of God's purpose, or at least as though he wishes to clear the ground of alternative explanations, to make it all the more convincing that the explanation of Israel's failure must lie ultimately in and within the purpose of God.

14–15 Joel's encouragement to call upon the Lord invites the logical train of thought drawn out in a chain of rhetorical questions: such a calling upon comes from faith, faith from hearing, hearing from preaching, preaching from commissioning. To appeal to another is to put oneself in that other's power; and who would do that unless one believed in that other—believed that he could help, trusted oneself to him for that help? Salvation can only come to a person who believes in God like that, whose faith is not a merely verbal utterance, but who entrusts himself to God without holding anything back, and whose commitment is demonstrated and lived out in his unreserved appeal to God and surrender to God's mercy. As in vv 9–10, faith and utterance go together: there, faith and confession; here, in vv 14–15, faith and entreaty. In rejecting the outwardness of works, Paul does not make the mistake of opting for a mere inwardness; commitment without outward expression is not commitment, certainly not the commitment of the whole person for which Paul looks.

Such faith comes from hearing—a hearing which is not merely a registering of a sequence of words on the mind, but a hearing with an understanding of the significance of those words and a response appropriate to that significance. The reference to hearing is not simply a logical link in the chain between believing and preaching; it also reflects Paul's self-consciousness as a preacher, as one who thought in terms of communication by the spoken word and whose success depended on winning the sort of attentive hearing which so often resulted in commitment among his hearers. Paul was well aware of how critical that transaction was between speaker and hearer—when, mysteriously, not merely words are conveyed, but an understanding, a conviction, a life-changing commitment—and of how dependent as a preacher he was on the Spirit to make his word the word of God (1 Thess 2:13; 1 Cor 2:4).

"How shall they hear without a preacher?" The argument has moved far beyond questions of whether there are other sources for knowledge of God (such as might have been appropriate in chaps. 1 and 2). Nor is he thinking of his and others' missionary proclamation at large. The train of thought is now wholly directed to the question of Israel's failure to believe in the Lord Christ, and so moves wholly within the common assumption, shared by Paul and his fellow Jews, that God had revealed himself particularly and clearly to Israel. What is now at stake is the fulfillment and completion of that revelation in Christ. For Israel to hear of that climax to God's purpose in Christ, proclamation of Christ is necessary. All Jews, scattered as they were throughout the world, might not yet have heard the message of their Messiah. Reflected here too then is not only Paul's concept of spreading the news of Christ by preaching, but also his sense of urgency to get the news out and to ensure its widest possible broadcast as soon as possible, to Jew as well as Gentile.

15 The preacher must be sent; the proclamation presupposes a commission. Here it is even more clearly the case that Paul is not indulging in mere rhetoric or logical word spinning. Fundamental to Paul's own self-consciousness as an apostle was the conviction that he had been called and commissioned for the task of proclaiming the good news (1:1; 1 Cor 15:8–11; Gal 1:15–16). Without that divine authorization and compulsion his proclamation would not be the power of God to salvation (1:16). What was true for himself was no less true for all preachers. This is the start of the chain; here is the source of the power which leads (by means of preaching, hearing, believing, and appealing) to salvation.

The scripture Paul quotes by way of confirmation, Isa 52:7 slightly adapted, is wholly appropriate. It speaks of evangelizing, perhaps even of a missionary evangelizing ("feet" implying travel?). The "good things" include, not least, "salvation" (Isa 52:7, 10). More important, the good news is for Zion—"Your God reigns"; the message is one of assurance to Jerusalem of the Lord's mercy, of God's deliverance of his people for all the world to see. And probably already at this time the passage was understood eschatologically, as a reference to the age to come, when God would reverse Israel's present inferior and oppressed state. This eschatological note may also be present in the word "timely," with its overtones of the harvest season. Clearly then the good news to be announced to Israel in the last days is for Paul the good news of God's eschatological act in Christ. And clearly, too, the quotation well sustains and carries forward a train of thought dealing with Israel's response to that good news.

16–17 Paul's immediate reaction to the Isaiah quotation is to recall that not all have obeyed the good news—the first time in this section that he has brought himself to express Israel's failure so bluntly. Only some Jews have given the response of faith to the gospel, which Isaiah predicted. As indeed Isaiah also predicted—"Who has believed our report?" (Isa 53:1) This sudden interjection reveals that the thought of the remnant, and the anguished puzzle of why all of Israel have not believed the good news of Christ, is still uppermost in Paul's mind. Also breaking the surface of Paul's thought once again is the equation between faith and obedience, Paul's conviction that faith in Christ is the obedience the law now calls for. But probably the main reason for the abrupt comment is that Paul saw a corollary to the Isaiah quotation which came from the same context and which strongly buttressed his conclusion that only a small proportion of Israel would accept his gospel. Isaiah here too predicted a response of disbelief on the part of Israel.

However, this is not the line of thought Paul had intended to develop. The rhetorical chain of vv 14–15 most naturally invited a possible explanation of Israel's unbelief in terms of their not having heard, or of their not having had preachers sent to them. And that indeed is the way Paul develops the point in v 18. So v 16 is something of an interruption. The link between Isa 52:7 and 53:1 causes him to short-circuit the more sequential response to vv 14–15 and to formulate the first open statement of Israel's disobedience in failing to believe the evangelists' message. He could have reverted to the chain of questions by asking, "Why have they not believed? Have they not heard?" But instead he uses the link word ("report") given him by Isa 53:1 to summarize the progression leading to faith in a way which also draws in the earlier exposition of Deut 30:11–14: "So then faith comes from (hearing) the report, and hearing (the report) through the (preached) word of Christ." "The word of Christ" is "the report" of the preachers, "the gospel," "the word of faith" which directs faith to Christ.

18   If the chain connecting the law of righteousness understood in terms of faith with faith in Christ is thus reduced to one link (hearing the report), then one possible explanation of most of Israel's unbelief is that they have not recognized that link; they have not heard or understood the word of faith. Paul no doubt recalled the effect of "the revelation of Christ" in his own understanding, not only as opening his eyes to who Christ is, but also as transforming his understanding of the law, the realization that the law was the word of faith which called for faith in Christ. It is that link which most of his fellow Jews have missed. Why so? Could it be simply that they have never had the kind of experience which had proved so effective for Jewish Christians, that experience of hearing with understanding which brought a whole new insight into and perspective on the so familiar law? Have they not heard?

But Paul will not accept that as an adequate reason. They *have* heard. He can put the point in the well-known language of Ps 19:4: "their sound has gone out to all the earth, and their words to the ends of the inhabited world." The psalmist refers, of course, to the testimony of the heavens to the glory of their creator. But the fact that the passage speaks of a revelatory testimony at all is sufficient to explain Paul's use of it. For he is not quoting it as a proof text or citing it as a prophecy fulfilled, and the absence of an introductory formula ("as it is written," or some such) may be significant here. It could be simply that Paul's answer slips easily into the language and rhythm of scripture, his thought and very consciousness on such matters shaped by a lifelong familiarity with the sacred text. Clearly, however, he uses the words to refer to the Christian mission to the diaspora. This outreach had been going on for about 20 years, and since the Jerusalem agreement in a more systematic way (Gal 2:9—probably about 7 years earlier). And if his own tactics as apostle to the Gentiles were typical of the gentile mission as a whole (Jew first and also Gentile), the outreach to the diaspora must have been considerable (the implication of Rom 15:20–24 is that in Paul's view only the western regions of the Roman Empire remained so far untouched). Consequently there must have been few diaspora synagogues within the Roman Empire or Parthia which had not heard something of the claims made about Messiah Jesus. Allowing for an element of hyperbole in the psalmist's language, Paul's answer is clear and justified: it cannot be said that Israel has not heard the gospel; the bulk of Israel's unbelief cannot be explained or excused on the grounds that they have never had the opportunity to believe.

19   Paul will not leave it at that. For it is not simply that Israel has heard the word of faith, but failed to grasp the connection between the law and Christ which it provided; not simply that Israel's misunderstanding of the law has caused most of Paul's fellow Jews to mis-hear the gospel. It is also a fact that Israel has ignored so many of its own scriptures which are now being fulfilled in Israel's rejection and the nations' acceptance of the word of faith. He has already used such scriptures to demonstrate that the acceptance of the gospel by the Gentiles and by only a remnant of Israel had long been part of God's overall purpose (9:25–29). Now he reverts to the same theme to underline the point that Israel ought to have recognized that this was what was to happen. So he asks again, "Have they not known?" Their unbelief cannot be excused on the grounds that they have not heard the gospel. They have. And their knowledge of their own scriptures ought to have informed their hearing. They should have known what to expect. So they are doubly without excuse: they have heard the gospel, and they should have grasped the significance of such scriptures as the following.

Deut 32:21—Moses' song had spoken of God's response to Israel's unfaith (Deut 32:20) in particularly striking terms: God would provoke his wayward sons to jealousy over a "no nation"; he would make them angry over a foolish nation. The future tenses encouraged the readers of Paul's day to treat the passage as a prophecy, and to see in the phrase "no nation" a reference to other nations of later days—Philistines, Samaritans, Babylonians, and so on. Paul refers it to the current situation, either because he thinks the first claim to fulfillment of such a prophecy has to be eschatological—that is, it refers to the end period or the new age; or because he sees in Deut 32:21 prophecy of a recurring pattern in God's dealings with his people. Either way, Israel ought to have seen in the positive response of the Gentiles to the gospel of Messiah Jesus a fulfillment of Deut 32:21 (not to mention Hos 1:10 [LXX 2:1]; 2:23 [LXX 25]—Rom 9:25–26).

What is still more significant about Deut 32:21 for Paul is that it also provides him with a clear indication of how God intends to resolve the so distressing riddle of Israel's failure to believe: he will provoke them to jealousy. This is a first hint of the full resolution Paul will shortly unveil (11:11–16). As with the exposition in 9:14–23, so here he touches briefly on themes which together will provide as complete as possible an answer to the puzzle of Israel's unfaith and demonstrate even more clearly God's faithfulness and his righteousness from faith to faith.

20 Paul's favorite prophet, Isaiah, also gives him another text whose significance Israel ought to have recognized—Isa 65:1–2. For it speaks with surprising boldness of the Gentiles' discovery of God (by implication, once again, in the end time), despite their previous history of ignorance of God and of failure to seek him out. It speaks also of the Gentiles enjoying one of the primary privileges of the covenant people (experience of the self-revelation of God), despite their not even asking for God as Moses had (Exod 33:18). The passage probably had Israel itself in view originally, but as its wording went, it could be understood as a reference to the Gentiles, especially when read in conjunction with Hos 1:10; 2:23; and Deut 32:21. Within the wider context of the scriptures and "intertestamental" literature as a whole, the expectation was fairly well established that in the end time the Gentiles would recognize Yahweh to be the only God, despite their previously having thought of him no doubt as merely the God of Israel. So Paul's interpretation is hardly forced and would not be dismissed as an unjustified interpretation of Isaiah even by his more critical readers.

21 Moreover, when so understood, Isa 65:1–2 can be seen to express clearly just the contrast between Gentile belief and Jewish unbelief which is the cause of all Paul's joy and anguish. For Isa 65:2 speaks without question of Israel's disobedience and obstinate refusal (in contrast to Gentile obedience and willing confession, vv 16, 9–10)—again as something not short-lived or unusual, but as a persistent response to God. Isaiah speaks also of God's continued persistence in appealing to unfaithful Israel—a reminder, like 3:3, that God remains pledged to his people and will not give up on them, despite Israel's persistence in disbelief. Here again Israel ought to have recognized the perfect match between such a scripture and the situation now resulting from the Gentile mission of the believers in Jesus Messiah. Those who rejoice in the scriptures cannot put forward the excuse that they never knew what is so plainly prophesied therein.

In short, having expounded the way in which God's call and purpose comes into effect (9:6–29), Paul has now exposed the fact and character of Israel's unbelief in increasingly explicit terms (9:30–10:21). He has explained it as a failure to understand the law as the word of faith pointing to the eschatological significance of Christ (9:30–10:13) and has refused to excuse Israel on grounds that they had never heard the word of faith or had insufficiently clear indication of how God would achieve his purpose in the final days (10:14–21). Presumably it was the interlocking of these two elements in his thought, the way his understanding of the law in terms of faith meshed into these prophecies of Jewish unbelief and Gentile belief, which provided Paul the Jew with one of the central supports for his faith in the Christ.

D. The Mystery of God's Faithfulness   (11:1–32)

1. The Remnant according to Grace—and the Others   (11:1–10)

Bibliography

See also 9:1–11:36 *Bibliography*.

Clements, R. E. "'A Remnant Chosen by Grace' (Romans 11:5)." In *Pauline Studies,* FS F. F. Bruce, ed. D. A. Hagner and M. J. Harris. Exeter: Paternoster, 1980. 106–21. **Cranfield, C. E. B.** "The Significance of διὰ παντός in Romans 11:10." *SE* 2 (1964) 546–50. **Dreyfus, F.** "Le passé et le présent d'Israel (Rom 9:1–5; 11:1–24)." In *Israelfrage,* ed. Lorenzi. 140–47. **Hanson, A. T.** "The Oracle in Romans 11:4." *NTS* 19 (1972–73) 300–302. **Hasel, G. F.** *The Remnant: The History and Theology of the Remnant Idea from Genesis to Isaiah.* 2d ed. Berrien Springs: Andrews University, 1974. **Luz, U.** *Geschichtsverständnis.* 80–83. **Müller, C.** *Gottes Gerechtigkeit.* 44–47. **Müller, K.** *Anstoss.* 13–31. **Zeller, D.** *Juden.* 126–29.

Translation

¹ *I ask, therefore, has God repudiated his people?* ᵃᵇ *Not at all! For I too am an Israelite, of the seed of Abraham, of the tribe of Benjamin.* ² *God has not repudiated his people whom he foreknew. Or do you not know what the scripture says in the section about Elijah, how he appeals to God against Israel?* ³ *"Lord, they have killed your prophets, they have torn down your altars, and I alone have been left and they seek my life."* ⁴ *But what says the divine answer to him? "I have kept for myself seven thousand men, who have not bowed the knee to Baal."* ⁵ *Thus therefore also in the present time, there is a remnant in accordance with the election of grace.* ⁶ *But if by grace, no longer* ᶜ *from works, since otherwise grace would no longer be grace.* ᵈ

⁷ *What then? What Israel sought for, that it did not obtain; but the elect obtained it. And the rest were hardened—* ⁸ *as* ᵉ *it is written,*

> *God gave to them a spirit of torpor,*
> *eyes that they should not see*
> *and ears that they should not hear,*
> *until this very day.*

⁹ *And David says,*

> *Let their table become a snare and a net,*
> *a trap and a retribution for them;*
> ¹⁰ *Let their eyes be darkened so that they cannot see,*
> *and bend their backs continually.*

Notes

ᵃ Some witnesses, including P⁴⁶, read τὴν κληρονομίαν instead of τὸν λαόν—probably an assimilation to Ps 94 [LXX 93] :14 (Metzger).

ᵇ A tendency to assimilate v 1 to v 2 is also indicated in the addition of ὃν προέγνω (again including P⁴⁶).

ᶜ Some witnesses, once again including P⁴⁶, read οὐκ instead of οὐκέτι, presumably to prevent the latter being read with temporal force and so allowing the implication that the election had previously been "from works."

ᵈ After the final χάρις someone felt it appropriate to add a balancing saying: εἰ δὲ ἐξ ἔργων οὐκέτι ἐστὶ χάρις ἐπεὶ τὸ ἔργον οὐκέτι ἐστὶν ἔργον—an expansion which became established in B and א², hence TR and AV/KJV.

ᵉ Here again the regular confusion between καθώς and καθάπερ (see on 3:4 *Notes*).

Form and Structure

The section functions both as a summing up of the argument to date of chaps. 9–11, and as an important transition to the final phase of the argument (11:11–32). Thus the underlying issue of God's faithfulness already posed in 9:6 is reexpressed (vv 1–2a) in still more uncomfortable terms (uncomfortable not least for Paul the Jew): "Has God rejected his people?" And the key arguments of 9:6–13, 27–29, and of 9:31–33, 10:18–21 are recalled in vv 2b–6 (a remnant, by grace, not works) and vv 7–10 (the rest rejected by

God) respectively, with vv 1–6 more apologetic and vv 7–10 more polemical in character. Vv 7–10 are not simply a conclusion, but, as so often with Paul's conclusions, introduce and point forward to the next stage of the argument (see on 5:20–21 *Form and Structure*).

Worthy of note is the use of passages from all three sections of the OT in vv 8–10—Torah (Deut 29:4 [LXX 3]), Prophets (Isa 29:10), and the Writings (Ps 69:22–23)—in line with Jewish hermeneutics (see Müller, *Anstoss*, 13–21). That Paul here makes use of an already traditional testimonium or florilegium is possible (Käsemann, Wilckens). The form maintains the argumentative style of this whole section (10:18–11:12) in which semi-rhetorical questions predominate, each answered by an appropriate scripture.

Question	Scripture
10:18a	10:18b
10:19a	10:19b–21
11:1a	11:2a
11:2b	11:3
11:4a	11:4b
11:7a	11:8–10
11:11	

The opening question (11:1) is a natural conclusion (οὖν) to the preceding answers (10:18b, 19b–21).

Comment

1 λέγω οὖν, μὴ ἀπώσατο ὁ θεὸς τὸν λαὸν αὐτοῦ; "I ask, therefore, has God repudiated his people?" The force of λέγω depends on the context—so, here, "ask"—with the μή pointing to a negative answer. Although Paul uses ἀπωθέομαι only here, the usage "push away, repel, spurn, reject," is well enough known (LSJ); in the NT elsewhere only Acts 7:27, 39; 13:46; and 1 Tim 1:19. But Paul clearly has in mind the regular OT usage, where the thought of God rejecting his people was entertained as a prospect, or question or conclusion (Judg 6:13; 2 Kgs 23:27; Pss 44:9, 23 [LXX 43:10, 24]; 60:1, 10 [59:3, 12]; 74 [73]:1; 78 [77]:60, 67; 108:11 [107:12]; Jer 7:29; 31:37 [not in LXX]; Lam 2:7; 5:22; Ezek 5:11; 11:16; Hos 9:17); in view of the use about to be made of the idea of the remnant, 2 Kgs 21:14 is particularly notable. Beside or within this possibility and prospect so frequently and so uncomfortably posed, the assurance that God has *not* rejected or will not reject his people was voiced much less frequently, at least in the same terms (1 Sam 12:22; Ps 94 [LXX 93]:14; 95 [94]:3(?); Lam 3:31). In picking up and using the OT theme in this way Paul indicates that this is no new issue for Israel. Previous crises had posed the same question before, and Israel's previous failures had not prevented positive answers being given in the past (cf. particularly 2 Macc 6:12–16).

Paul's use of the concept "God's people" strongly reflects Jewish usage, with its distinctive features: λαός as denoting an ethnic or national entity, and in particular Israel as God's people (λαός) as thus marked out from other nations (ἔθνη); so 1 Chron 17:21—οὐκ ἔστιν ὡς ὁ λαός σου Ἰσραὴλ ἔθνος ἔτι ἐπὶ τῆς γῆς (*TDNT* 4:32–35). Paul's own usage is striking: (1) he uses λαός only in OT quotations (9:25–26; 10:21; 11:1–2; 15:10–11; 1 Cor 10:7; 14:21; 2 Cor 6:16); (2) on each occasion, in Romans at least, the passage quoted is one which provides a sharp challenge to any comfortable assumption that Israel can rest on the fact of being "God's people." Paul's avoidance of the term on his own account and quotation of just these passages adds strongly to the impression that Paul was both reacting against the more typically Jewish idea of God's people as an ethnic or national entity and attempting by these passages to redefine the people of God and to redraw its boundaries (cf. the comparatively isolated precedent of Amos 9:7–10). All this is lost sight of by the classic view which takes "God's people" as a "spiritual" entity.

μὴ γένοιτο, "not at all!"; see on 3:4. Paul's confidence is thoroughly Jewish (e.g., Jer 31:36–37; 2 Macc 6:16), but on different terms.

καὶ γὰρ ἐγὼ Ἰσραηλίτης εἰμί, ἐκ σπέρματος Ἀβραάμ, φολῆς Βενιαμείν "for I also am an Israelite of the seed of Abraham, of the tribe of Benjamin." Paul's claim to the covenant name of his people (see on 9:4) is, of course, deliberate (he does not say ἐγὼ Ἰουδαῖος εἰμί). His concern is to maintain continuity even while redefining "the people of God" (see above), and to avoid any suggestion that in opening up his promises to the Gentiles God has abandoned "his people" or changed his original purpose for Israel. The point is further underscored by the ἐκ σπέρματος Ἀβραάμ, which naturally echoes the argument of 4:13–18 and 9:7–8. Paul speaks from within "Israel," but as one who sees that the promise was to *all* the seed. The contrasting points Paul draws from the same relationship to Abraham (9:7; 11:1) illustrate the tension within Paul's own thought as both Jew and Christian. The usual suggestion (e.g., F. W. Maier, 105; Vischer, 112–14; Gaugler; Barrett; Leenhardt; Black; Mayer, 246–47; Schlier; Villiers, 209; Harrisville) that Paul puts himself forward in a representative capacity (God has not rejected his people because he has not rejected me!) both misses and cheapens the point (cf. SH, Denney, Knox, Zeller). As in 2 Cor 11:22 and Phil 3:5–6 what is at stake is Paul's claim to express an authentically Jewish viewpoint and understanding of God's workings, to be speaking *as* a Jew. Understood this way the sentence becomes less of an argument for the Gentile character of the Roman Christian community (against Althaus, Schmidt, Kuss with bibliography).

Why he adds φυλῆς Βενιαμίν (as in Phil 3:5) is less clear. More elaborate suggestions based on the later traditions that Benjamin was the first of the tribes to enter the Red Sea (Str-B, 3:286–88; Käsemann), or that Benjamin as one of the two continuing (southern) tribes (Ezra 4:1; 10:9) could represent the hope of the restoration of the lost tribes (Michel), seem unnecessarily contrived from such a brief allusion. More likely Paul simply echoes a more extended self-identification or self-introductory formula, in which tribe as well as father was given; there is sufficient indication that tribal identity, particularly of Judah and Benjamin, was regarded as worth maintaining by some at least (see Jeremias, *Jerusalem*, particularly 275–83). Paul shows that he is as firmly located within Judaism as anyone can be; he is no first- or even tenth-generation proselyte. Maccoby's counter suggestion (*Mythmaker,*

95–96), that Paul was a Gentile whose claim here is totally invented and fictitious, is wildly fanciful and shows no sensitivity to Paul's whole argument in Romans (see also *Introduction* §1).

2 οὐκ ἀπώσατο ὁ θεὸς τὸν λαὸν αὐτοῦ, "God has not repudiated his people." The quotation, whose wording has already determined the question of v 1, is from both 1 Sam 12:22 and Ps 94 [LXX 93]:14:

1 Samuel/Psalms:	ὅτι οὐκ ἀπώσεται κύριος τὸν λαὸν αὐτοῦ
Romans:	οὐκ ἀπώσατο ὁ θεὸς τὸν λαὸν αὐτοῦ.

The change of tense ("has not rejected" from "will not reject") simply indicates Paul's confidence that the scriptural assurance has not been falsified by the present disobedience (10:21) of God's people. The replacement of ὁ θεός for κύριος may be occasioned by the fact that Paul liked to keep κύριος for Christ, and so chose to use ὁ θεός in v 1, following suit in the actual quotation itself in v 2. See further on 11:1. This firm assertion will be elaborated in two parts: (1) the remnant (vv 3–6) and (2) the final conversion of "all Israel" (vv 7–32).

ὃν προέγνω, "whom he foreknew"—that is, the whole people, not just part (SH; Lagrange; Murray; Dreyfus, 142; Kuss). The language is firmly rooted in the Jewish concept of Israel's election (see on 8:29). Paul shares the confidence of other Jews that nothing could alter the basic fact of God's choosing Israel to be his own (cf. Mayer, 247–48). This was to reach classic expression in *m. Sanh.* 10.1: "All Israelites have a share in the world to come." Paul differs from this not in the matter of the assurance which derives from the belief in election, but in the self-definition of the elect; see further below 11:5.

ἢ οὐκ οἴδατε, "or do you not know?"—a variant on ἢ ἀγνοεῖτε (6:3; 7:1).

ἐν Ἠλίᾳ, "in Elijah"—a familiar way of referring to a passage = in the section about Elijah (cf. Mark 12:26; Rom 9:25; see further SH, Str-B 3:288). The connection of thought would be strengthened if Paul shared the view attested in some later rabbinic traditions that Elijah was of the tribe of Benjamin (Str-B 4:782).

τί λέγει ἡ γραφή, "what the scripture says"—"the scripture" probably referring here to the individual passage about to be cited (BGD, γραφή 2a); but a collective designation, scripture as a whole, is also quite possible (see on 4:3).

ὡς ἐντυγχάνει τῷ θεῷ κατὰ τοῦ Ἰσραήλ, "how he appeals to God against Israel." For ἐντυγχάνω in this sense cf. 1 Macc 8:32; 10:61, 63; 11:25; and *3 Macc* 6.37; "pleads with God against Israel" (RSV, NEB) is less satisfactory (Black). The specification of Israel as the object of Elijah's complaint is not given by the Elijah story itself (in the Elijah sequence "Israel" occurs only in 1 Kgs 17:1, 14, and 18:36, in positive formulations); Paul's use of it here is thus determined more by his own line of thought. In which case it functions as an expression of his dialectic of continuity/discontinuity: Paul as an Israelite (11:1) echoes Elijah's complaint against Israel. To that extent Paul sees himself, with a mixture of self-assertion and self-mockery, as a latter-day Elijah (cf. Munck, *Christ,* 109; Käsemann), appealing to God to vindicate his understanding of Israel's role within God's saving purpose over against the bulk of his fellow countrymen, and expecting a similar rebuke and reassurance that God's purpose for Israel is still "on course." But Wilckens rightly notes that the whole reference to the Elijah story serves to undergird the thesis of v 2a, not to explicate v 1b (cf. Luz, *Geschichtsverständnis,* 81; Zeller, *Juden,* 126–27). For Ἰσραήλ see on 9:4.

3 κύριε, τοὺς προφήτας σου ἀπέκτειναν, τὰ θυσιαστήριά σου κατέσκαψαν, κἀγὼ ὑπελείφθην μόνος, καὶ ζητοῦσιν τὴν ψυχήν μου, "Lord, they have killed your prophets, they have torn down your altars, and I alone have been left, and they seek my life." The quotation is of Elijah's repeated complaint in 1 Kgs 19:10, 14, with the κύριε perhaps drawn unconsciously from Elijah's first self-pitying lament in 19:4. The first two clauses are inverted (perhaps since threat to life is the more pressing for Paul [Käsemann]), the third expressed differently but with the same effect, and the fourth abbreviated. That Paul here quotes from memory (Cranfield) is quite likely.

4 ἀλλὰ τί λέγει αὐτῷ ὁ χρηματισμός; "but what says the divine answer to him?" The use of the unusual χρηματισμός at this point (only here in the NT) is striking. Used of a decree or ordinance made by a sovereign or public authority, or of a public document, it is also attested in the sense of an oracular or divine utterance (see LSJ; *NDIEC* 4:176), often in a dream (cf. Matt 2:12, 22; Acts 10:22). In this sense it occurs in 2 Macc 2:4 of a divine injunction given to Jeremiah that he should go to Mount Sinai. It probably is not accidental that these two usages (2 Macc 2:4 and here) are both linked with visits to Mount Sinai (Jeremiah and Elijah): there may have been some tendency in Jewish circles to use this word in connection with the divine injunction which recalled Judaism to the revelation given at Sinai (cf. *1 Clem.* 17.5; see further Hanson, "Oracle"); moreover, it was at Sinai that Moses received the fundamental salvation-history revelation of God as "merciful" (Harrisville; see on 9:15). In form and effect the phrase is parallel to τί λέγει ἡ γραφή (v 2).

κατέλιπον ἐμαυτῷ ἑπτακισχιλίους ἄνδρας, οἵτινες οὐκ ἔκαμψαν γόνυ τῇ Βάαλ, "I have kept for myself seven thousand men, who have not bowed the knee to Baal." The sense is clearly that of 1 Kgs 19:18, but the Greek shows no dependence on the LXX, and is only slightly closer to the MT. If Paul is quoting from memory (see on 11:3) it shows both that the memory could produce a version quite divergent in detail and that such divergence would presumably cause Paul no qualms. For κατέλιπον in the sense "left over, seen to it that something was left (for the future)" cf. Sir 24:33; the first person follows the Hebrew rather than the LXX (BGD, καταλείπω). The addition of the reflexive (ἐμαυτῷ) strengthens the sense both of divine act and of covenant faithfulness (cf. Lietzmann)—a good example of elaborative or paraphrastic translation.

Since the number seven probably bore the connotation of completion (the seven days of creation) it may be that the number used in 1 Kgs 19:18 had this overtone—the 7,000 as representing the completeness of Israel (*TDNT* 2:628–29; Cranfield; otherwise Hübner, *Israel,* 101)—though it poses the key issue of remnant theology with some sharpness (whether the faithful few *are* the complete number or constitute a *promise* of some *larger* whole [Israel] being preserved or restored in the future; see further on 11:5). Cranfield draws attention to Matt 18:22—the seventy times seven indicating a forgiveness which knows no limit. If such overtones were present to Paul it would serve his own apologetic well—7,000 as an open, not closed, number indicating the open-endedness of God's covenant promise ("apocalyptic wholeness" [Michel]). But since Paul merely quotes and makes nothing of the number here, we cannot be sure that such overtones were present to him or intended by him. Only men are named, as in Mark 6:44 (Michel); contrast Matt 14:21.

The use of the feminine (τῇ Βάαλ), unlike LXX (τῷ) probably reflects the Hebrew custom of reading בֹּשֶׁת (= αἰσχύνη, "shame") instead of בַּעַל (Dillmann in Munck, *Christ*, 109). Paul may indeed have had in mind the two examples of this in the Elijah stories (1 Kgs 18:19, 25). For examples of the feminine form with Βάαλ see in the LXX 2 Kgs 21:3, Jer 2:8, and 12:16 (BGD); see further SH and Str-B 3:288). Paul uses the scriptural text as one accustomed to reading aloud and making such alterations in the process.

5   οὕτως οὖν καὶ ἐν τῷ νῦν καιρῷ, "thus therefore also in the present time." The initial tripling of connectives is found only here in Paul. The force of the οὕτως is to indicate that the preceding verses do not merely provide a compelling argument (οὖν), but also a typical example of God's dealings. When ἐν τῷ νῦν καιρῷ, "in the present time," is added, a specifically eschatological note is sounded (see on 3:26), giving the typical case of Elijah typological significance. That is to say, the present phase of God's purpose (involving a reaffirmation of election but in "remnant" terms) is understood not simply as one further example of God's way of working, far less as an afterthought, or adjustment of God's plans to take account of an unexpected turn of events. Rather it is the eschatological point of all his dealings up till "the now time": election and remnant as "now" being experienced in and through Paul's ministry are part of the climax of salvation-history thus foreshadowed in the Elijah episode. It is in terms of the eschatological outcome that such a puzzling episode can be at last fully understood ("puzzling" since "election" of Israel and "remnant" do not cohere in an obvious way). See further Goppelt, *Typos*.

λεῖμμα κατ᾽ ἐκλογὴν χάριτος γέγονεν, "there is a remnant in accordance with the election of grace." The fact that λεῖμμα is cognate with κατέλιπον (v 4) cannot be reproduced in English; Barrett helpfully translates, "there has come into being such a remnant." λεῖμμα as such occurs only here in the NT, and in the LXX only in 2 Kgs 19:4. But underlying it is the much more common "remnant" idea (שְׁאֵרִית, variously translated into Greek). See on 9:27b–28, Hasel, *IDBS* 735–36, and Wilckens. It came particularly into prominence at the great Assyrian and Babylonian crisis points of Israel's (Judah's) history (2 Kgs 19:4, 31 = Isa 37:4, 32; frequently in Jer [6:9; 15:9; 23:3; 24:8; etc.]; Ezek 9:8; 11:13; Ezra 9:8; Neh 13:15; see further particularly Clements). Since the "crisis of faith" now confronting Israel was of a similar order, and more critical in eschatological terms, Paul would recognize the typological parallels. The aggressively positive character of such promises as Mic 5:7–8 and Zech 8:12 would cause Paul less problem, since the concept here is governed by that of election (κατ᾽ ἐκλογήν) which he was in process of redefining (v 7). For ἐκλογή see on 9:11; cf. 1QS 8.6—"those chosen by divine benevolence"

(Fitzmyer). After a long absence χάρις reappears (last used in this sense in 6:15), reminding Paul's listeners that Israel only understands its election when it understands it as an act of God's free and unconditional choice (9:11); see on 1:5 and 3:24. The concept of "remnant" is in accordance with *that* understanding of election; the emphasis on God's grace reinforcing the κατέλιπον ἐμαυτῷ of the Elijah quotation (v 4). The perfect tense (γέγονεν), as usual, indicates an original action (God's choice of Israel) establishing a situation which still pertains. God's original choice of Israel still holds true into the "now time," precisely because it was an election of grace; that is, it did not depend on Israel's performance of covenant obligations, and so it was not restricted by them either. Michel's observation that "the understanding of the doctrine of justification in terms of grace interprets also that of election" puts Paul's point somewhat in reverse. Paul's argument is rather that the understanding of righteousness is determined by the fact that Israel's election was in terms of grace (rightly Dahl, "Future," 156). On the issue of who is to be counted as Israel, the elect, see on 9:6, 27b–28, and Dreyfus.

6 εἰ δὲ χάριτι, οὐκέτι ἐξ ἔργων, ἐπεὶ ἡ χάρις οὐκέτι γίνεται χάρις, "but if by grace, no longer from works, since otherwise grace would no longer be grace." For χάρις see on 1:5 and 3:24. οὐκέτι provides a logical rather than temporal connection, as in 7:20, 14:15, and Gal 3:18 (BGD). ἐξ ἔργων is, of course, short for ἐξ ἔργων νόμου (see on 4:2). The point is polemical, as are the earlier uses (3:20, 27–28; 4:2, 6; 9:12, 32), which Paul clearly recalls in summary fashion; NEB's very varied rendering of the phrase considerably obscures its leitmotif function in the letter. The context here confirms the earlier observation that the "works" referred to are a way of understanding election which Paul firmly rejects (election of grace, not from works)—"works" understood as the hallmark of election, as that which marks out the elect as such. The point being that the remnant is not constituted as a group within Israel by their faithfulness to the law ("the righteous" of the Psalms of Solomon, or the covenanters at Qumran; see on 1:17 and 9:6), but as a group sustained by God's grace; *that* is how election is to be understood and how it is sustained. NJB's rendering of ἔργα as "good actions" perpetuates the classic misunderstanding that Paul is objecting to a belief that justification can be earned by good works (which also wholly determines Gaugler's discussion, responding to Lagrange). See further on 3:20 and 9:32. ἐπεί here has the sense "since otherwise"—as in 3:6 and 11:22 (see BDF, §456.3). The fourfold repetition of χάρις in vv 5–6 puts it beyond doubt where the key to Paul's understanding of Israel and of the gospel is to be found; χάρις by definition precludes the kind of limitation which ἐξ ἔργων involves.

7 τί οὖν; "what then?"; see on 6:15.

ὃ ἐπιζητεῖ Ἰσραήλ, τοῦτο οὐκ ἐπέτυχεν, "what Israel sought for, that it did not obtain." The thought is in effect a rephrasing of 9:31, with διώκω replaced by ἐπιζητέω and φθάνω by ἐπιτυγχάνω. The ἐπι- prefix in ἐπιζητέω intensifies the idea of seeking, but does not import the idea of "striving" (against BGD, Schlier); cf. particularly Paul's other use of it in Phil 4:17. ἐπιτυγχάνω means properly "hit the mark," hence "attain, obtain"—usually with the genitive (as in its other NT occurrences: Heb 6:5; 11:33; James 4:2), but occasionally with the accusative (LSJ, BGD), which makes possible the neat ὃ . . . τοῦτο construction. Ignatius was to make much use of it in reference to martyrdom as an attaining to God (θεοῦ ἐπιτυχεῖν); see references in BGD.

ἡ δὲ ἐκλογὴ ἐπέτυχεν, "but the elect attained it." As the former clause echoes 9:31, so this clause echoes 9:30. Because of the parallel, ἐκλογή is usually taken as a reference to the Gentile Christians (cf. also 10:20), but since v 5 is also being taken up, and ἐκλογή is balanced by οἱ λοιποί (cf. v 20), there is an equally strong argument for ἐκλογή to be referred to the *Jewish* Christians (F. W. Maier, 112; Nygren—ἡ ἐκλογή = τὸ λεῖμμα; Wilckens; Heil). Certainly it cannot but be significant that the word occurs in Romans only within chaps. 9–11 (9:11; 11:5, 7, 28) and so is closely related to the particular issue of these chapters (What then of Israel?). So the primary reference is most likely the Jews who have believed in Jesus Messiah. But since Paul undoubtedly regarded the opening of the gospel to the Gentiles as part of God's purpose of election, and had already transferred the closely related category ἐκλεκτοὶ θεοῦ to the new reality of believing Jews *and* Gentiles (see on 8:33), it would be unjustified to argue that *only* Jewish Christians are in view here.

What was sought and (not) obtained is not expressed here. Obviously it is not "election" itself (= initial acceptance by God), but must be something like the benefits of a sustained covenant relationship, including final vindication (= righteousness in that sense, or νόμος δικαιοσύνης [9:31]).

οἱ δὲ λοιποὶ ἐπωρώθησαν, "but the rest were hardened." The substantive οἱ λοιποί of course means simply "the others," without indication of whether "the others" are a small or large proportion of the whole (cf. Matt 22:6; 27:49; Luke 18:9; Eph 2:3). So it is not entirely fair to accuse Paul of concealing the fact that the reference is to the overwhelming majority of the people (Käsemann; though note the use of τινες in 3:3 and 11:17). On the other hand, Paul might well be aware that the LXX occasionally used οἱ λοιποί for the remnant (particularly Jer 43:5 [LXX 50:5 A]; 52:16 S); so there may be a deliberate play on words here, perhaps with the further implication that in the final count οἱ λοιποί will be also counted among the λεῖμμα κατ' ἐκλογὴν χάριτος (so 11:26–32).

πωρόω, from πῶρος (a kind of marble), means basically "petrify," or in medical terms "cause a stone to form (as in the bladder) or a callus" which unites a fractured bone (LSJ; J. A. Robinson, *Ephesians,* 2d ed. [London: Macmillan, 1907] 264; TDNT 5:1025–26). The metaphorical application of the passive ("become insensible or deadened") is particularly biblical, as in all its NT usage, usually of the heart (Mark 6:52; 8:17; John 12:40; 2 Cor 3:14). John 12:40 uses it when citing Isa 6:10, where the LXX (as also Matt 13:15 and Acts 28:27) uses the near synonym παχύνομαι ("become impervious, insensitive, dull"). As these last three NT references indicate, the Isa 6:10 passage was much used by the first Christians as they sought illumination from the scriptures to explain the puzzling obtuseness of most Jews' response to the gospel (see also Mark 4:12 // Luke 8:10). Here a "divine passive" is certainly intended (Barrett; Mayer, 255–56; Cranfield; Barth, *People,* 41; Wilckens; see particularly Hofius, "Evangelium," 303–4; though see also Michel). The thought is obviously similar to that of σκληρύνω in 9:18, reinforcing the character of v 7 as a summary of the earlier argument but also providing a thematic link between God's treatment of Pharaoh (Exodus) and God's dealings with "the rest (of Israel)," as foreshadowed in Israel's own scripture, including Isa 6:10. By translating, "The rest were made blind to the truth," NEB reinforces the link with v 8 at the expense of the link back to 9:18. See further on 9:18, 11:8, and 11:25.

8 καθὼς γέγραπται, "as it is written"; see on 1:17. The texts as usual round off the argument.

The text cited is basically a reworked citation of Deut 29:4 [LXX 3], quoted quite properly once again from memory.

Deuteronomy: καὶ οὐκ ἔδωκεν κύριος ὁ θεὸς ὑμῖν καρδίαν εἰδέναι καὶ ὀφθαλμοὺς
Romans: ἔδωκεν αὐτοῖς ὁ θεὸς πνεῦμα κατανύξεως ὀφθαλμοὺς
(Deut): βλέπειν καὶ ὦτα ἀκούειν ἕως τῆς ἡμέρας ταύτης
(Rom): τοῦ μὴ βλέπειν καὶ ὦτα τοῦ μὴ ἀκούειν ἕως τῆς σήμερον ἡμέρας

The change from negative to positive, as well as the genitive and infinitive construction, certainly strengthens the sense of deliberate intent. The modification of the final words hardly alters the sense, but by citing the verse as from his own perspective the obtuseness of Israel in the wilderness is presented as continuing to characterize the bulk of the people till his own day; the element of eschatological correspondence is still in play (see on 11:5). For the phrase ἕως τῆς σήμερον ἡμέρας cf. particularly Matt 28:15 and 2 Cor 3:14 (see further BGD, σήμερον). Cranfield suggests that the phrase may also imply a time limit set to this divine hardening (up to, but not beyond); cf. 11:11–32.

The major departure from the Deuteronomy text is the insertion of πνεῦμα κατανύξεως from Isa 29:10, the only place where the phrase occurs in the LXX. κατάνυξις itself is very rare (in the LXX only otherwise in Isa 60:3 [LXX 59:5]), and probably means something like "stupefaction" or "torpor" (see SH, Cranfield). Müller, *Anstoss,* 19–20 argues that v 8 is not a mixed citation, but is drawn exclusively from Isa 29:10a in a form not preserved for us in the LXX. But the closeness of v 8 to Deut 29:4 [LXX 3], and the likelihood that v 9a also contains an insertion from another passage (see on 11:9–10) suggest otherwise (so also Hübner, *Israel,* 104, who dismisses Müller's arguments as "highly artificial"). The note of divine judgment is more strongly marked in Isa 29:10 than in Deut 29:3, so that the insertion of the phrase underscores the claim that the rest of Israel's present failure is the result of divine action and part of God's purpose. We should also note that Isa 29:10 comes from the middle of a section of the prophet much used in early Christian reflection regarding Jewish blindness: 28:16 (Rom 9:33; 1 Pet 2:6), 29:13 (Mark 7:6–7 par.), 29:14 (1 Cor 1:19); also 28:11 (1 Cor 14:21) (Lindars, *Apologetic,* 164). There is no specific allusion to Isa 6:9–10 as such here, but the theme is so close, the ἐπωρώθησαν of v 7 probably contains an allusion to it, and with the importance of the apologetic theme in earliest Christianity's self-understanding (see on 11:7) it would be surprising if Isa 6:9–10 was not in Paul's mind at this point (see Dodd, *Scriptures,* 38; Maillot).

9–10 καὶ Δαυὶδ λέγει, "and David says"; see on 4:6 and 10:5.

γενηθήτω ἡ τράπεζα αὐτῶν εἰς παγίδα καὶ εἰς θήραν
καὶ εἰς σκάνδαλον καὶ εἰς ἀνταπόδομα αὐτοῖς,
σκοτισθήτωσαν οἱ ὀφθαλμοὶ αὐτῶν τοῦ μὴ βλέπειν,
καὶ τὸν νῶτον αὐτῶν διὰ παντὸς σύγκαμψον,

"let their table become a snare and a net,
a trap and a retribution for them;
let their eyes be darkened so that they cannot see,
and bend their back continually."

The quotation is more or less from Ps 69:22–23 [LXX 68:23–24], with *καὶ εἰς θήραν*, "and for a trap," replacing *ἐνώπιον αὐτῶν*, "before them," in the first line, and the prepositional phrases in line 2 inverted. The *καὶ εἰς θήραν* may have been drawn in deliberately or subconsciously from the very similar maledictory passage in Ps 35 [LXX 34]:8—

ἐλθέτω αὐτοῖς παγίς . . .
καὶ ἡ θήρα . . . συλλαβέτω αὐτούς,
καὶ ἐν τῇ παγίδι πεσοῦνται ἐν αὐτῇ.

That Paul is following the Greek here rather than translating directly from the Hebrew is probably indicated by the fact that the fourth line of the Greek differs from the Hebrew:

Hebrew: "and make their loins tremble continually";
Greek/Paul: "and bend their back continually."

Ps 69 seems to have been greatly used in early Christian apologetic: specific quotations—

Ps 69:9	John 2:17; Rom 15:3;
Ps 69:22–23	Rom 11:9–10;
Ps 69:25	Acts 1:20;

with a number of allusions also probable—

Ps 69:4	John 15:25	Ps 69:24	Rev 16:1
Ps 69:8	Mark 3:21	Ps 69:25	Luke 13:35
Ps 69:9	Heb 11:26	Ps 69:28	Phil 4:3; Rev 3:5
Ps 69:21	Mark 15:23 pars.		

(see also on 15:3).

There is disagreement on how much weight should be given to the specific details of the text. Is it cited for its overall polemical thrust, or did Paul intend his readers to see significance in the terms used? The most likely example of heavy overtone would be the word *τράπεζα*. Is Paul alluding to the cultic table, the altar (Müller, *Anstoss,* 23–27; Käsemann; Wilckens)? On the one hand, such an allusion would depend more on pagan parallels, which we see also reflected in 1 Cor 10:21 (*TDNT* 8:211, 213–14; BGD, *τράπεζα*

2); prior to the destruction of the temple τράπεζα seems to have been used only for the table of showbread (so particularly Exod 39:36 [LXX 18]; 1 Chron 28:16; 2 Chron 29:18; 1 Macc 1:22); the transfer of the function of atonement from altar to table (see particularly *b. Ber.* 55a; Str-B, 3:289) is a solution to the problem of the temple's destruction. At the same time, the association of ideas was natural since sacrificial meat was so regularly consumed in all sacrificial systems, and we can already see the association elsewhere (particularly 1QM 2.4–6 and 1 Cor 10:18). So such an allusion certainly cannot be excluded. In which case Paul would be alluding to the central importance of the cult in the Judaism of his time. His fellow Jews' dependence on atonement through the sacrificial system, and assumption that atonement was assured for those living within the covenant, had become a snare and delusion to them. (Käsemann's further onslaught on "pious works" and "religiosity," however, moves well beyond the point.) On the other hand, a more general allusion to the meal table (Barrett, Michel, Schlier) would gain its force from the importance of table fellowship for Paul's fellow Pharisees in particular (see on 14:2 and further Dunn, "Pharisees"). It was just that attempt to maintain purity and standing within the covenant by emphasis on such "works" and the halakoth which undergirded them, which was proving a stumbling block for the typical Jewish piety that Paul remembered so well. The issues of 14:1–15:6 may already be in view (Minear, *Obedience,* 78–79).

Only in Ps 35 [LXX 34] :8 does the LXX use θήρα to translate רֶשֶׁת ("net"), which is used elsewhere as a figure of divine judgment (Ezek 12:13; 17:20; 32:3; Hos 7:12). παγίς ("trap, snare"), elsewhere used to translate רֶשֶׁת, quite often refers to a trap made for oneself, as in the two psalms cited here (see also Pss 9:15 [LXX 16]; 57:6 [LXX 56:7]; Prov 6:2; 12:13; 18:7; 29:6; Tob 14:10; Sir 27:26, 29; 1QH 2.29); but it is also used in reference to divine judgment (Jer 48 [31]:43–44; Ezek 29:4), on Israel as well (Isa 8:14). For σκάνδαλον see on 9:33; as a translation of וּלְמוֹקֵשׁ, εἰς σκάνδαλον may be translated "as a lure or trap" and appears quite often in the LXX (Josh 23:13; Judg 2:3; 8:27 A; 1 Sam 18:21; Ps 106 [105]:36; Wisd Sol 14:11; 1 Macc 5:4). The thought of "recompense, repayment," is more clearly in ἀνταπόδομα, in the LXX usually referring to punishment (e.g., Gen 50:15; Ps 28 [LXX 27]:4; Lam 3:64; Joel 3 [LXX 4] :7; Jud 7:15; Sir 14:6). See further Müller, *Anstoss,* 27–31. The piling up of the four εἰς phrases (including the inserted εἰς θήραν) is particularly effective, and heightens the note of intended judgment. Paul in effect is attacking the confidence of the "righteous" among the Jews that they would be saved from such snares (*Pss. Sol.* 4.23) or that they would be a snare or recompense to hostile sinners (1QH 2.8; 1QM 4.12).

For the different ways of taking the last line (backs bent under slavery, a heavy burden, cowering with fear, bowed with grief, too weak to stand, groping through blindness) see Cranfield. Whether Paul would have wanted an allegorical meaning to be read out from the line, or at least a specific allegorical meaning, is far from clear. But presumably it would be the other side of his "liberty" theme: it is such a bowed-down-ness from which the believer has been liberated (e.g., 8:2; Gal 5:1; see also on 6:18). διὰ παντός is better translated "continually" than "for ever" (Cranfield; against RSV, NIV, NJB), though either

way the phrase provides the best case for the view that Paul was not particularly
interested in the details of the text (since he is about to stress his confidence
that Israel's blindness will be short-lived) (Gaugler).

Explanation

1 Paul, caught up as ever in the flow of his argument, and sensitive to
how his readers would respond, asks the obvious question. If Israel has shown
itself so ignorant of the righteousness of God according to its own scriptures,
and so oblivious to the word of Christ as preached to it, does that mean
that God has in fact repudiated Israel? The implication being either that
God's patience will last only so long with such a recalcitrant people, or that
God has now pushed Israel aside irrevocably in favor of the Gentiles. Not
for the first time an Israelite posed this fearful possibility which cut so deeply
at his self-understanding. God's choice of Israel to be his people was so fundamental to everything which the typical Jew stood for that he could contemplate
nothing more terrible. As most of his readers would have no difficulty in
recognizing, Paul here deliberately picks up the language so often used at
times of Israel's deepest shame, particularly prior to and during the exile
(e.g., 2 Kgs 21:14; Jer 7:29). Has what the prophets spoke of generations
ago happened again, or rather happened now at last with eschatological finality? Has God rejected his covenant people once and for all?

Paul poses the possibility only to reject it—"Not at all! For I too am an
Israelite, of the seed of Abraham, of the tribe of Benjamin." The answer at
first seems rather ludicrous, as though Paul was saying, "The fact that *I*
have understood and believed the word of faith is sufficient proof that God
has not rejected Israel," as though Paul was setting himself up as a representative of his whole people, or even as progenitor of a reconstructed people!
But that is almost certainly not what Paul meant. The effect of such posturing,
in studied disregard for all the other Jewish Christians, not an insignificant
number, would be to trivialize the assertion. Certainly what comes to expression
is Paul's consciousness of being one of the covenant people ("Israelite"—
9:4), of being one of the seed of Abraham in whom God's promise and
purpose is fulfilled (4:13–18; 9:7–8), of his tribal identity (cf. Phil 3:5). But
this is not an expression of egotistical aggrandizement, rather of indignation
that a Jew could conceive of such a horrifying outcome. This is the utterance
not of one self-confident in his own status over against his people, but of
one confident in God on behalf of his people. Not as one outside the covenant,
one for whom the covenant is no longer of significance, does Paul here speak,
but precisely as a member of the covenant people. It is not because he is a
Christian that Paul can dismiss the suggestion that God has repudiated his
people (by implication, in favor of the Gentiles), but because he is an Israelite,
because he is so conscious that he belongs to God's people. It is precisely as
a Jew that Paul reaffirms God's faithfulness to the Jews.

2 The real answer to the question of v 1 is given in the direct rebuttal
which uses precisely the same words as the question: "God has *not* repudiated
his people." Paul does not introduce the words as a quotation of scripture,
but those of his first readers familiar with Israel's oft-repeated fear of divine

repudiation would probably recognize here that Paul was using the language of other scriptures which rendered the fear groundless: "the Lord will not repudiate his people" (1 Sam 12:22; Ps 94:14). The promise would be particularly appropriate since it came as a reassurance to Israel despite its sin (1 Sam 12:20) and despite the Lord's chastening (Ps 94:12).

Paul adds "whom he foreknew." God knew the character of his people before he chose them as his people, and that means also foreknew their frequent unfaithfulness to God, including now their large-scale rejection of the gospel. That is why their rejection of the gospel makes no difference to God's commitment to them. Had it been the case that their unfaithfulness was going to make any difference to God's faithfulness, he would never have chosen them in the first place. Paul's confidence is twofold: that Israel is not acting in any way unforeseen by God; and that consequently God remains faithful to Israel notwithstanding Israel's failure. Just as the choice of Jacob and rejection of Esau was without regard to their future conduct (9:10–13), so Israel's status as God's people remains unaffected by Israel's latest and most serious failure.

2b–4 To substantiate his point Paul once again focuses on the theme of the remnant, not because that is the whole answer (as he will soon reveal), but because it is the first part of the whole. The prophecies of Isaiah had already shown that as at the destruction of the Northern Kingdom, so now, God could maintain and fulfill his purpose for his people as a whole through a remnant (9:27–29). Another example is the famous episode in the Elijah cycle, where Elijah at Mount Horeb, full of self-pity, laments the fact that only he remains faithful to God, while Israel under Ahab and Jezebel has turned against both prophets and sanctuaries of the Lord, and where God reassures Elijah that he is not alone, there are still 7,000 faithful men, a substantial minority. Significant here is the modification Paul makes at the beginning of the second part of the abbreviated quotation, "I have kept for myself. . . ." The emphasis once again, as consistently in 9:6–29, is on the divine initiative. The assurance to Elijah is not simply that 7,000 men have retained their faith in the Lord, but that the Lord has sustained their faith; their continuing faithfulness is a demonstration of God's continuing faithfulness to his covenant promise and people. As God sustained and carried out his covenant purpose through such a minority then, so now.

Paul introduces the quotation with quasi-legal language, as an appeal or petition to the sovereign authority *against* Israel. He clearly sees himself in a position very similar to that of Elijah at Horeb—not for the first time had an Israelite taken a stand which seemed to isolate him from and put him on the defensive over against the rest of Israel. Again the implication is probably not that Paul felt himself to be the only Jew faithful to the covenant God. To divert the firm assurance that God had not repudiated his people (v 2) into a rebuke of his own presumption would weaken the force of his argument. The protestation of his own membership of the covenant people (v 1) is not an expression of vainglorious pride (God has not repudiated his people because his purpose still continues in me), far less an echo of Elijah's self-pitying lament. It is rather an expression of firm assurance that as an Israelite he could rest confidently on Israel's scriptures and draw deductions about

God's faithfulness to Israel from the precedents clearly attested in the scriptures.

5 Paul proceeds to draw out the parallel. The situation confronting Elijah was typical of God's dealings with his people. Paul sums it up with the word "remnant," no doubt intending to remind his readers also of the Isaiah passage already quoted (9:27 = Isa 10:22). In the face of these two witnesses no Jew or Gentile sympathizer could deny that in the past God had preserved his covenant faithfulness to his people through a remnant, or deny the possibility of his doing so again in the present. Moreover, as one conscious of living in the new epoch introduced by Christ ("in the present time"; cf. 3:26), Paul no doubt saw such patterns in God's previous dealings with Israel as having not merely typical, but typological significance—prefiguring the way in which he would deal with his people at the end time, at the climax of the ages (cf. 1 Cor 10:1–11). It may even be that he specifically mentioned "Elijah" in v 2 precisely because the name would evoke thought of the eschatological events (Mal 4:4–5; Sir 48:9–10). For Paul then the parallel is soundly based: as then, so now. That only a minority of Jews have believed the word of faith about Messiah Jesus is only to be expected by those who can read the ways of God in the history of his people.

But the parallel is even closer, the type more complete. As the 7,000 at the time of Elijah were preserved by God himself ("I have kept for myself"), so the covenant principle is reaffirmed (again typically and typologically). God's covenant always has depended on God's electing power. By reintroducing this strong word ("election") Paul no doubt intends to recall his readers to its use earlier in the argument (9:11), where he had pointed out that the line of covenant promise through Jacob rather than Esau was a matter of divine selection. Here too then the reference to Elijah has the effect of recalling and confirming a key point made earlier: that God's covenant is a matter of election from start to finish.

So too the reintroduction of the word "grace" recalls its important role at a still earlier stage of the argument (3:24–6:15; 12 times), particularly its prominence in the climax to the first main theme (5:15–6:1). For the first time Paul introduces the word "grace" in his treatment of God's faithfulness to Israel; for the first time he links the two concepts, "election" and "grace." Clearly there is here on Paul's part a deliberate attempt to bring together these two key concepts which between them could be said to sum up the two main thrusts of his overall argument: "election" which quintessentially expresses Israel's self-understanding as the chosen people of God; "grace" which so richly expresses Paul's understanding of his experience of the gracious power of God through faith in Christ. The fact that Paul did not describe divine election in terms of "grace" earlier in chaps. 9–11 should not be misunderstood, as though he somehow wanted to deny that grace had effected God's electing purpose prior to Christ (however well such an interpretation might seem to fit 6:14–15, it would run counter to 4:16). On the contrary, there is no real distinction in Paul's mind between the merciful God (9:15–18) and the gracious God (cf. 11:30–32; 15:9). Nevertheless, it is probably true that for Paul and for many other Jewish Christians, belief in Jesus Christ had been a rediscovery of the experience of the grace of God which had been obscured for them while they remained within the limits of more traditional Judaism. But for Paul conversion was precisely a rediscovery of what he now realized more clearly had always been at the heart of Judaism rightly understood—a rediscovery of God's choice not on the basis of good or evil deeds (9:11) but as an act of sheer generosity. Conversion to Jesus Messiah was not a moving away from the faith of patriarchs and prophets, but a rediscovery of its pristine power.

6 If v 5 reaffirms the continuity between God's election of Israel and the Jewish Christians' experience of grace now through Christ, v 6 highlights once again the element of *dis*continuity—discontinuity, that is to say, not between God's original choice of Israel and his present call of the Gentiles (that is an element of continuity, provided by the remnant), but discontinuity between Israel's present understanding of that original choice and Paul's awakened understanding of it through his new faith in Christ. The discontinuity lies in Israel's *mis*understanding of its election, Israel's failure to recognize that it was always a matter of sheer grace on God's part. The bulk of Paul's Jewish contemporaries had (in Paul's view) made the mistake of understanding their status as God's chosen people in terms of works, in terms of the national customs and ritual acts which defined their identity as God's holy people, both ethnically and religiously (circumcision, sabbath, food laws, etc.). For Paul the mistake is self-evidently a mistake, for if God's choice of Israel was a matter of election, of sheer grace (as he had already demonstrated from scripture—9:6–18), then it cannot in any sense depend on such works, it cannot depend in particular on a Gentile having to assume the ethnic and religious identity of a Jew by committing himself to observe the customs and ritual obligations peculiar to the Jews—"otherwise grace would not be grace."

The reintroduction of the phrase "of works," as with the reintroduction of the word "grace" in v 5, recalls important statements of Paul's argument earlier in the letter (3:20, 27–28; 9:32). Clearly in vv 5–6 Paul is trying to achieve a summary statement which draws together the most important elements of his whole thesis so far. In so doing, for the first time, somewhat surprisingly, he brings "works" and "grace" into direct antithesis. Thereby we are given confirmation that Paul's understanding of divine grace is not antithetical to *law* as such (despite the possible implication of 6:14–15), but to law understood in terms of "works." "Law" after all can be linked in Paul's mind with grace's correlates, "faith" and "righteousness" ("law of faith"— 3:27; "law of righteousness"—9:31), in a way inconceivable for "works" (contrast 3:27–28 and 9:30–32). Likewise, precisely because "of works" summarizes Israel's misunderstanding of the law *within* the election of grace, we are also given confirmation that "works" for Paul do *not* denote "works of merit" which "earn" God's favor (despite the possible implications of 4:4). Rather what Paul objects to is "works" understood as a qualification for God's favor simply because it is they which qualify for membership of the covenant people and which sustain that identity as God's elect. It is this *reduction* of God's election to matters of ethnic and ritual identity which Paul sees as the fatal misunderstanding and abandonment of God's grace and of the election of grace.

7–10 This neat synthesis and summary of his argument so far (vv 5–6) now provides Paul with a platform on which to build his definitive answer to the problem posed to his own faith by Israel's disobedience and even antagonism to the gospel. Here at last he evidently feels able to develop the various hints already dropped and to build up to the final denouement, the climactic unveiling of the divine mystery. First of all (vv 7–10), the hint dropped in 9:22–23 and 9:33 that Israel's failure was not only foreseen by God, but rather intended by God, and in fact actually brought about by God.

7 Verse 7 looks at first simply like a (further) summing up of the argument. But, as so often earlier, Paul makes his conclusion the first step into the next stage of his exposition, and here he begins to draw together the threads into his final pattern. "What Israel sought for, it did not attain" picks up and repeats what Paul had already said in 9:31 and 10:3. "But the elect attained it" draws together 9:30 and 11:5—"the elect" being first and foremost the remnant within the chosen people (11:5—the Jewish Christians), but also by implication the Gentiles who without pursuing righteousness came upon it and grasped it (9:30)—Jew first and also Gentile. However, these earlier assertions are recalled only in order to take the exposition that further final step—the sting coming in the tail. "But the others were hardened, became insensible." What had been hinted in 9:22–23, 33 is now spelled out. The readers would now realize why it was that Paul had persisted in developing both sides of the doctrine of election in 9:13 and 9:18, even when it seemed unnecessary to the point then being made, and even despite the awkward questions it raised for his understanding of judgment. The reason is now clear. Paul insisted that the corollary of election of one was hardening of another because it helped explain Israel's present obtuseness in the face of the gospel. Now that election is to be seen as election of the remnant, the corollary this time applies to the rest of Israel apart from the remnant. The misunderstanding and unbelief of most of Paul's fellow Jews is no accident; it is *God's* doing; it is the obverse of his extending his electing grace to Gentile as well as Jew, just as rejection of Esau and hardening of Pharaoh was the obverse of his election of Israel.

8 Paul does not draw back from this awkward corollary, any more than he drew back in chap. 9. But he has reached his conclusion simply as a logical deduction both from the way God's election has worked in history and from the identification of Jewish Christians with the remnant spoken of by the prophets. Now he seeks to confirm and establish it not simply as a corollary, but as something directly spoken of as such in scripture.

The first scriptural proof is basically a quotation of Deut 29:4, elaborated consciously or unconsciously with a phrase from Isa 29:10 ("spirit of torpor") and perhaps a sideways glance to Isa 6:9–10. Rather more striking is the way Paul has turned what was presented as an excuse for Israel's obtuseness ("the Lord God has not given you . . . eyes to see . . .") into an act of deliberate intent ("God gave them eyes that they should not see"). However, Paul's audiences would hardly think of this as an unjustified modification, particularly in the light of the supplementation from Isaiah. "Spirit of torpor" is a phrase unique to and within the LXX, so that at least those well versed in the LXX would not fail to pick up the cross-reference. Moses *does* ascribe

Israel's obtuseness to God, even if as an act of omission rather than of commission. And Isaiah speaks of God's part in his own generation's dullness in terms every bit as forceful as Paul's: "the Lord has poured out on you a spirit of sleep and will close their eyes . . ." (LXX).

The effect of the conflated text is to reinforce the point that what is happening to the rest of Israel now is no different from what happened more than once in the past. Israel now is showing no greater obtuseness than it did in the past. And each time it was God's doing. Israel cannot deny the testimony of its own scriptures that within God's election purpose for Israel there have been times when God himself prevented Israel from recognizing the course and character of God's purpose. Moreover, the implication which Paul no doubt intended by continuing the quotation to the last line is that it is the *same* obtuseness ("until the present day"). Israel's misunderstanding of and disobedience to the word of faith is but the continuation and eschatological climax of a sustained lack of perception on Israel's part. At the same time the Jews (Jewish Christians) among Paul's first readership might also justifiably infer that if God so dealt with his people while they were indeed the exclusive focus of his covenant concern, then there can be good hope that his present punitive action toward Israel does not signify a complete change in God's purpose for Israel or abandonment of Israel. Here too the last line could be fairly taken to imply that the obtuseness laid upon Israel was only "until the present day" and would as part of the end events soon be lifted. Whether Paul himself intended all this wealth of meaning is less clear, but it certainly accords with the view he develops throughout this chapter.

9–10 The second scriptural proof is a straight quotation from the LXX of Ps 69:22–23 with (possibly subconscious) conflation from Ps 35:8. Some of Paul's earliest readers might well be puzzled by the use of this text, for the original psalm was directed against David's enemies, a curse invoked on Israel's opponents (the same applies to Ps 35:8). As in 3:10–18, Paul turns David's imprecations against his own people! However, those familiar with the more atomistic exegesis of the rabbis would probably consider the interpretative use of the psalm acceptable. Just as the link provided by the appearance of "snare" in both psalms made possible their conflation, so the link provided by talk of "unseeing eyes" would constitute a validation for drawing in Ps 69:22–23 as a way of elaborating and clarifying Deut 29:4. More important, those more fully instructed in the new faith in Jesus Messiah would be aware that Ps 69 was widely regarded in Christian circles as a prophetic text which spoke beforehand of the sufferings of their Messiah, David himself presaging in experience and word what his greater son would undergo (Paul himself was certainly aware of this Christian understanding of the psalm, as Rom 15:3 demonstrates). As Israel by its liturgical use of the psalms over the centuries had taken David's words as an expression of their own distress and of their own hostility to Israel's enemies, so now in the eschatological transposition effected by Christ, Christians felt justified in taking David's words as an expression of the sufferings endured by Messiah Jesus, albeit ironically at the hands of his own people.

Yet even for those who were more familiar with the traditional Jewish reference of the psalm and less familiar with its Christian interpretation,

Paul's use of it would by no means lack sense or justification. For in the argument of chaps. 9–11 Paul has now clearly established the point, that what Israel earlier thought was true of the Gentiles (as a corollary to Israel's election) is now proving true of Israel itself (as a corollary to that same election focusing upon the remnant within Israel, as well as broadening out to include the Gentiles). And this includes the curse Israel invoked upon its enemies: by their resistance to "the election of grace" (v 5) the rest of Israel had put themselves in the position of those on whom David originally invoked his curse; they turned their own imprecation back upon themselves.

As to the details of the text, Paul may well be content to understand them in general terms, without specific reference. But it is possible that he would take "their table" as a reference to the cult (cf. 1 Cor 10:21), and so would think of Jewish devotion to their distinctive cultic rituals, or of the importance Pharisees placed on the ritual purity of table fellowship, as the stumbling block. And the last line would quite likely evoke in him the sense of oppression and even slavery with which he now looked back on his own Pharisaic zeal for works and scrupulosity in things of the law (cf. Gal 4:21–5:1; Phil 3:6–9). Christ became a stumbling block to most of the Jews (9:33) only because they had already tripped and ensnared themselves in a ritual practice which handicapped rather than helped them in the pursuit of righteousness (9:31–32) and which so reinforced their religious self-identity in nationalistic terms that they were unable to recognize the eschatological and universal significance of the word of Christ.

2. The Hope of Israel's Restoration   (11:11–24)

Bibliography

See also 9:1–11:36 *Bibliography*.

Baxter, A. G., and **Ziesler, J. A.** "Paul and Arboriculture: Romans 11:17–24." *JSNT* 24 (1985) 25–32. **Berger, K.** "Abraham in den paulinischen Hauptbriefen." *MTZ* 17 (1966) 47–89 (here 83–86). **Bourke, M. M.** *A Study of the Metaphor of the Olive Tree in Romans 11*. Washington, D.C.: Catholic University of America, 1947. **Dahl, N. A.** *Das Volk Gottes*. 2d ed. Darmstadt: Wissenschaftliches, 1963. **Davies, W. D.** "Paul and the Gentiles: A Suggestion concerning Romans 11:13–24." In *Studies*. 153–63, 356–60. **Dreyfus, F.** "Le passé et le présent d'Israel (Rom 9:1–5; 11:1–24)." In *Israelfrage*, ed. Lorenzi. 148–51. **Fridrichsen, A.** *The Apostle and His Message*. Uppsala, 1947. **Gale, H. M.** *Analogy*. 205–15. **Johnson, D. G.** "The Structure and Meaning of Romans 11." *CBQ* 46 (1984) 91–103. **Luz, U.** *Geschichtsverständnis*. 274–79, 392–94. **Rengstorf, K. H.** "Das Ölbaum-Gleichnis in Röm 11:16 ff." In *Donum Gentilicium*, FS D. Daube, ed. C. K. Barrett et al. Oxford: Clarendon, 1978. 127–64. **Zeller, D.** *Juden*. 215–18, 238–45.

Translation

[11] *I ask, therefore, have they stumbled so as to fall? Not at all! But by their trespass salvation is coming to the Gentiles in order to provoke them to jealousy.*

[12] *And if their trespass means riches for the world, and their failure riches for the Gentiles, how much more will their fullness mean.*

[13a] *I am speaking to you Gentiles. So then,*[a] *inasmuch as I am apostle to the Gentiles, I magnify*[b] *my ministry,* [14] *in the hope that I might provoke my kindred to jealousy and might save some of them.* [15] *For if their rejection means reconciliation for the world, what shall their acceptance mean other than life from the dead?* [16] *If the initial offering is holy, so is the mixture as a whole; and if*[c] *the root is holy, so also are the branches.*

[17] *But if some of the branches have been broken off, and you, a wild olive, have been grafted among them and have become sharer in the richness of the olive tree's root,*[d] [18] *do not boast over the branches. If you do boast, it is not the case that you sustain the root, but the root sustains you.* [19] *You will say, then,*[e] *"Branches were broken off in order that I might be grafted in."* [20] *Quite so: they were broken off on the ground of unbelief, but you stand through faith. Do not cherish proud thoughts,*[f] *but fear.* [21] *For if God did not spare the natural branches,*[g] *neither will he spare you.* [22] *Consider then the goodness and severity of God: to those who fell, severity; but to you the goodness of God,*[h] *provided that you continue in that goodness—otherwise you too will be cut off.* [23] *Whereas, they too, if they do not continue in unbelief, shall be grafted in; for God is able to graft them in again.* [24] *For if you were cut off from the natural wild olive tree and grafted unnaturally into the cultivated olive tree, how much more shall those who belong to it naturally be grafted into their own olive tree.*

Notes

[a] Variation of conjunction in some MSS indicates scribal uncertainty as to how vv 13–14 were to be related to the preceding context. Similarly with the slightly awkward μὲν οὖν.

[b] P[46] and others read the future, strengthening the note of Paul's determination.

[c] The omission of εἰ in P[46] and some MSS must be accidental (Metzger).

[d] Omission of τῆς ῥίζης and introduction of a καί following ῥίζης attest attempts to improve Paul's awkward Greek.

[e] The insertion of οἱ by D and others makes the reference to all the branches cut out.

[f] Some MSS amend ὑψηλὰ φρόνει to the more explicitly negative ὑψηλοφρόνει.

[g] It is difficult to decide whether μή πως belongs to the original text or not. BGD, μήπως 1b, suggest it gives a less certain note ("perhaps he will not spare you either"). That hardly sounds right in the context: Paul's warning is much more threatening (cf. Cranfield). However, we could take the double negative as strengthening Paul's assertion: "neither will he somehow spare you" (cf. Black). See discussion in Metzger.

[h] The omission of θεοῦ at a secondary stage is understandable, since it disrupts the balance of the chiasmus; see also Lietzmann.

Form and Structure

The awkwardness in the structure of this section (e.g., Schmidt divides it between vv 15 and 16, Kuss between vv 12 and 13, while Johnson argues that the paragraphing should be 11:1–6 and 11:7–16) probably stems from the fact that with each sentence Paul is ready to go at once into the final mystery (11:25–32), so that he seems to repeat himself unnecessarily. In fact Paul uses the restatements to gather together the threads of the previous argument, ready to unveil the completed pattern: in particular, vv 11–12 pick up the talk of Israel's stumbling (9:32–33) and of divine provocation

(10:19). In the apparent digression of vv 13–14, elaborating the key word παραζηλῶσαι (v 11), Paul makes a point of reminding the Roman congregations of his own very personal involvement and critical role in this final drama of salvation history, underlining once again the degree to which the personal letter is integrated with the theological treatise, and reinforcing the impression that the body of the letter serves in large degree as Paul's personal apologia (see *Introduction*). V 15 not merely reformulates the thought of v 12 but heightens the exhilarating sense of imminent end which spurred Paul's mission on.

Vv 17–24 constitute a pause for exhortation (cf. Luz, *Geschichtsverständnis*, 34) prior to the climactic denouement (vv 25–32), with v 16 serving as a bridge into it. The resumption of the diatribe style with repeated second person singular address (vv 17, 18, 20, 21, 22, 24) is directed to the presumptuous boasting of gentile believers (vv 17–18a). The echo of the earlier rebukes of Jewish presumption is deliberate, since the danger is the same—of assuming that a portion within the people of God (the same tree!) is a matter for which the "haves" can boast over the "have-nots." The warning is reinforced by a threefold argument: you (Gentiles) are still dependent on your Jewish roots (v 18b); if you fall into the same error as the unbelieving Jews you will share the same fate (vv 19–22); and they can be more easily reinstated into God's saving purpose than you (vv 23–24). The exhortation thus comes back to the same point as vv 12 and 15 and so leads naturally into vv 25–32.

Other stylistic features include: the frequency of the εἰ δέ (vv 12, 16, 17, 18) and εἰ γάρ (vv 15, 21, 24) formula; *qal waḥomer* (πόσῳ μᾶλλον) in vv 12 and 24; the frequent use of -μα forms in v 12 (these three features all make v 12 strongly reminiscent of 5:16–17); the balance of v 12

τὸ παράπτωμα αὐτῶν	πλοῦτος κόσμου
τὸ ἥττημα αὐτῶν	πλοῦτος ἐθνῶν
τὸ πλήρωμα αὐτῶν;	

and the neat chiastic structure of v 24.

Comment

11 λέγω οὖν, μὴ ἔπταισαν ἵνα πέσωσιν; "I ask therefore, have they stumbled so as to fall?" Paul's confidence in his understanding of God and of God's purpose makes the answer certain (Michel). πταίω in the sense of "stumble, trip, fall" is well known (LSJ). The sense "suffer defeat" is the majority usage in the LXX (1 Sam 4:2, 10; 7:10; etc.), so that a heavy note of blameworthiness should not be assumed. But the imagery of 9:33 is obviously still in mind, and the closer parallels in Jewish thought would be Sir 37:12, *T. Gad* 4.3, Philo, *Leg. All.* 3.66, and James 2:10, 3:2—πταίειν in the sense "fail, slip into sin" (see also *TDNT* 6:883–84). Note also Deut 7:25, where πταίειν translates the niphal of שׁקץ ("be ensnared") from which שׁקוּץ ("snare" = σκάνδαλον, Ps 69:22 = Rom 11:9) comes. Since σκάνδαλον also occurs in 9:33 it is evident that Paul is drawing out a connected train of thought from a familiar sequence of interrelated imagery. The implication of divinely intended outcome is hard to escape (cf. 9:33 and 11:7–10; see, e.g., Mayer, 263; Kuss; and Schlier), but ἵνα in a consecutive sense, to represent the result of the preceding clause, is well attested (BGD, ἵνα II.2) and makes excellent sense of the imagery here employed—a stumble resulting in a fall—so that the translation should be left more open (SH, Lagrange, Cranfield). πίπτω can be used as more or less synonymous with πταίω ("fall"; in *T. Gad* 4.3 they are variant readings); but the clear implication here is of πίπτειν as something consequent upon and more serious than πταίειν. Hence "fall" in some complete or final sense, "fall to rise no more" (so usually in Homer [LSJ]; Isa 24:20; *Pss. Sol.* 3.10; Heb 4:11; *1 Enoch* 48.10), or the sprawling on one's face which puts a runner out of the race (so, e.g., *TDNT* 6:164, Cranfield, Schlier, Zeller). See also 11:22 and 14:4.

μὴ γένοιτο, "not at all!"; see on 3:4.

ἀλλὰ τῷ αὐτῶν παραπτώματι ἡ σωτηρία τοῖς ἔθνεσιν, "but by their trespass salvation is coming to the Gentiles." παράπτωμα can mean "false step, or slip," so Paul may consciously or unconsciously be continuing within the same circle of imagery (Munck, *Christ*, 118; Barrett). But if πταίειν allows a slackening of the note of blameworthiness (see above), with παράπτωμα the balance is very much the other way (cf. particularly 5:15–18); so here "trespass, transgression, sin" is best (see on 5:15; Cranfield; though NJB's "failure" is a good compromise). It is not necessary to specify more closely what "trespass" Paul had in mind. Israel's rejection of the gospel is the usual answer (10:16–21), on grounds that it was Jewish hostility to the Christian message, at least according to Acts, which resulted in the opening to the Gentiles (Acts 11:19–21; 13:45–48; 18:6; 28:24–28); so, e.g., Michel, Wilckens. But a reference also to the cross is possible, since in Paul's thought that is the basis of salvation (5:9–10; 1 Cor 1:18); see particularly Cranfield. Most likely, however, Paul has in mind the more general point that Israel's endeavor has been misdirected (9:31–32; 10:3; 11:7): this maintains the coherence of the imagery Paul has been using—in "pursuing" ἐξ ἔργων they have erred and in thus "slipping up" have failed to obtain their goal—see on 9:31 (as with the indictment of 2:1–3:20 Israel's failure to understand its role in God's purpose of salvation is a matter for condemnation); and from this more basic failure Israel's particular mistake of rejecting Christ has followed (9:31–33).

It should not be assumed that σωτηρία, "salvation," lacks its usual future orientation here (see on 1:16). On the contrary, Paul can use it here precisely because he has the process of the final climax so clearly in view (see particularly on 11:15). It is a more accurate reflection of Paul's thought therefore to provide a future-oriented present tense for the unexpressed verb than a past tense ("has come"—RSV, NEB, NIV; "has brought"—NJB); so "is coming," that is, with the same force as the present tense of the verb in 1 Cor 1:18 and 2 Cor 2:15. For ἔθνεσιν see on 1:5.

εἰς τὸ παραζηλῶσαι αὐτούς, "in order to provoke them to jealousy." The εἰς τὸ + infinitive clearly denotes divine intention (10:19). The sense "provoke to jealousy" for the little-used παραζηλόω is biblical (1 Kgs 14:22; Ps 78 [LXX 77]:58; Sir 30:3). Since the idea of God provoking rather than being provoked is so unique, Paul must intend to recall 10:19 with its quotation of the unique Deut 32:21b (Hübner, *Israel*, 107; see on 10:19). The thought constitutes a neat reversal of *T. Zeb.* 9.8, ἐπιστρέψει πάντα τὰ ἔθνη εἰς παραζήλωσιν αὐτοῦ. It might be said that this is the Christian variation on the more typically Jewish reflection that God chastises (not rejects) Israel for Israel's benefit (as in Prov 3:11–12; Wisd Sol 11:1–14; 2 Macc 6:16; *Pss. Sol.* 10, 13; Philo, *Det.* 144–46). Althaus appropriately compares Matt 21:31–32. NEB's "stir to emulation" unnecessarily introduces the thought of human effort.

12 εἰ δὲ τὸ παράπτωμα αὐτῶν πλοῦτος κόσμου,
καὶ τὸ ἥττημα αὐτῶν πλοῦτος ἐθνῶν,
πόσῳ μᾶλλον τὸ πλήρωμα αὐτῶν,
"But if their trespass means riches for the world,
and their failure riches for the Gentiles,
how much more will their fullness mean."

The rhetorical structuring of the verse is clearly marked (see *Form and Structure*) and must be borne in mind in exegeting the individual elements, particularly the three -μα words.

For παράπτωμα αὐτῶν, "their trespass," see on 11:11. πλοῦτος used metaphorically for wealth or abundance of something is quite frequent in Paul, usually contrasting by implication the relative poverty of a current condition with a transcendent or eschatological abundance (2:4; 9:23; 11:33; Phil 4:19; Col 1:27; also Eph 1:7, 18; 2:7; 3:8, 16; the nearest to a literal usage is 2 Cor 8:2). Once again in this rhetorically shaped phrasing Paul is not attempting a specific meaning, but simply seeking a way to contrast the deprived condition of Israel in the final buildup to the climax of God's purpose for the world, with the blessings of salvation newly opened up to the Gentiles. It is a measure of the richness of Paul's experience and hope that he should use this word as a way of imaging the benefit brought by the gospel (cf. 1 Cor 1:5; 2 Cor 6:10; Col 2:2). For κόσμος, see on 3:6 (here in parallel to "Gentiles"). Note again the lack of precision—"world" in contrast to the rest of Israel who trespassed—though this reflects more characteristic Jewish usage, Israel as distinguished from "all the nations of the world" (Luke 12:30; Str-B, 2:191).

The word ἥττημα, "loss, failure," is attested (LSJ) only in biblical Greek (Isa 31:8; 1 Cor 6:7; and here). On that basis the sense "defeat" would be possible (see SH, Gaugler, Knox, Murray, MM, and ἡττάομαι [e.g., Epictetus 2.18.6]), but see also Lietzmann and Barrett. How much can be drawn from the parallel with παράπτωμα (so a culpable failure; e.g., Käsemann, Schlier) or the contrast with πλήρωμα (so diminution of fullness; see discussion in Wilckens) must remain unclear. As with δικαίωμα in 5:18 the words are chosen more for rhetorical reasons than for precision of meaning. ἥττημα was chosen because Paul wanted a -μα word which would serve as another expression of Israel's plight by virtue of its wrong-headed pursuit (9:31–32; 11:7) and consequent refusal of the gospel (9:32–33; 10:21). For ἔθνη see on 1:5.

πόσῳ μᾶλλον, "how much more," is a variation of πολλῷ μᾶλλον (see on 5:9); so also 11:24 (BGD, μᾶλλον 2b). With τὸ πλήρωμα αὐτῶν, "their fullness," the broad idea is again clear, and whether a more detailed meaning is intended is again more open to question. Certainly it would be unwise for exegesis to strain for a narrowly focused meaning, since rhetorical considerations have played at least some part in determining the words used. πλήρωμα in itself can be used to denote a range of meaning from "that which fills or makes full," "that which is full," "that which is brought to fullness, completion, sum total," "fulfilling, fulfillment," to "the state of being full" (BGD). No doubt an element of contrast with παράπτωμα and ἥττημα is intended, but pressing it to give the sense "their fulfilling of the divine command" (BGD, πλήρωμα 4) probably pushes too far (despite 13:10; see Zeller, *Juden*, 239 n.2); so too NJB's paraphrase, "when all is restored to them." More likely it is the broader contrast between remnant and Israel as a whole, so between the rest's failure and the prospect of all Israel being saved (v 26); so most (see, e.g., *TDNT* 6:305, Black, Wilckens with bibliog.). This certainly fits with the immediate context: the rest who stumbled (v 11) and their final acceptance (v 15); and the hope of a "fullness" of Gentiles being matched by a fullness of Israel to which the whole argument is building up (vv 25–27). However, since Paul strives more for effect than for precision, a more open translation like "fullness" is desirable (so NIV); see also on 11:25. At all events it is clear that Paul cannot rest content in the thought of only a remnant saved (cf. Hofius, "Evangelium," 305–6).

Here too we can speak of a Christian variation of the more familiar Jewish hope that gentile blessing depended on gentile conversion, on the eschatological pilgrimage to Zion of gentile proselytes (for references see on 9:26); here note particularly Isa 60:5 ("the wealth [πλοῦτος] of the nations shall come to you"; Paul would be especially conscious of this if his forthcoming journey to Jerusalem with the collection was also in his mind (Munck, *Christ*, 120–22; see also on 11:25). The new order of precedence (Gentiles, then Jews) maintains a similar balance, but the terms have changed (no longer on Judaism's terms but as equal partners and heirs of the promise to Abraham [4:13–18]).

13 ὑμῖν δὲ λέγω τοῖς ἔθνεσιν, "I am speaking to you Gentiles." The specific address (ὑμῖν is emphatic) does not necessarily mean that the Roman congregations were exclusively Gentile, since Paul could intend by this phrase to catch the attention specifically of the Gentile members of the Christian groups to whom his letter would be read (Cranfield). But a gentile majority is probably envisaged (so most), otherwise Jewish rejection would not be such a contrast to Gentile conversion and there would be less occasion for Gentile boasting over Jewish failure (vv 17–24); Hort, cited by SH, also draws attention to the fact that Jews are spoken of in third person terms in chaps. 9–11, whereas from here on Gentiles are directly addressed in second person terms. See also on 1:6 and *Introduction* §2.

ἐφ᾽ ὅσον μὲν οὖν εἰμι ἐγὼ ἐθνῶν ἀπόστολος, "so then, inasmuch as I am apostle to the Gentiles." As is generally agreed, ἐφ᾽ ὅσον carries no sense of temporal restriction ("for as long as"), but means rather "to the degree that = insofar as" (cf. Matt 25:40, 45; BGD, ἐπί III.3); so here, "in my capacity as" (Cranfield). μὲν οὖν probably has the force of summarizing what has been said in moving to a new subject (BDF §451.1): the following clauses (vv 13–15) gathering up (and repeating) the point of vv 11–12, with the point now directed firmly at Paul's Gentile audience. Cranfield's suggestion that the sense is "contrary to what you may be inclined to think," would have greater force if Paul had written μενοῦνγε (see on 9:20). The ἐγώ is partly rhetorically determined (to balance the ὑμῖν), but partly also expresses strong self-consciousness that he in particular had been chosen as apostle to the Gentiles. He did not, of course, regard himself as the only apostle to the Gentiles (the absence of the definite article should be observed). At the same time we should not underestimate the crucial role and task he saw himself as having been given: his sphere of ministry to the Gentiles had been clearly marked out and accepted (Gal 2:9); in the event no one else seems to have engaged in or contemplated such a geographically wide-ranging ministry as Paul's (15:19, 23–24); and his task of provoking his own people to jealousy (v 14) was an absolutely crucial factor in the final act of the world drama (1 Cor 4:9) in bringing about the fullness of the Gentiles (v 25) and so also the fullness of Israel (vv 12–14). See further on 1:1 and 11:15; cf. Fridrichsen and Käsemann. On the word order, ἐθνῶν ἀπόστολος, see BDF §474.4.

τὴν διακονίαν μου δοξάζω, "I magnify my ministry." διακονία has a quite general sense here; it should not be rendered "office" (Käsemann; against AV/KJV). If, however, a more technical overtone is preferred ("diaconal ministry"), the corollary for Paul would be that all service is "diaconal." See further on 12:7; and cf. Schlier. δοξάζω should not be understood simply in the sense "speak highly of," "take pride in" (NJB); as 1:21 in particular implies, what is in view is a harmony of word and act, so a praise which is expressive of commitment of life (praise expressed in a quite concrete way [Michel]); Paul "glorified" his ministry by giving himself to it wholly and unreservedly (cf. 1:5). At the same time he was by no means unwilling to speak out and make much of his ministry (as here and Gal 2:1–10), though not for any vainglorious end: the ἐφ' ὅσον and εἴ πως (v 14) show clearly a restricted or specific purpose in view. Cf. his prayers of thanksgiving in 1 Cor 1:4; Phil 1:3; Col 1:3; 1 Thess 1:2; 2:13; and 2 Thess 2:13; also Eph 1:16 (Schlier).

14 εἴ πως παραζηλώσω μου τὴν σάρκα, "in the hope that I might provoke my kindred to jealousy." For εἴ πως as an expression of expectation see BDF, §375. The phrase hardly indicates that this is "the true aim of his Gentile mission," so that talk of a "subsequent rationalization" is uncalled for (against Räisänen, "Römer 9–11," 2913). παραζηλώσω clearly picks up the thought of v 11 with its recall of 10:19 (see on 11:11)—an interpretive "master-stroke" (Lindars, "Universalism"). But now Paul makes bold to describe his own ministry as the means by which this reaction might be engendered in his fellow Jews. In his use of σάρξ here Paul shows his instinctive familiarity with the Hebrew use of בָּשָׂר in the sense "kindred, blood relations" (e.g., Gen 29:14; Judg 9:2; 2 Sam 5:1; Neh 5:5). As usual with Paul there is no strictly "neutral" use of σάρξ, since even here it denotes particularly the "rest" of Israel who have been "hardened," whose "trespass" and "failure" had opened the door to the Gentiles (see on 1:3, 2:28, 4:1, and 9:3); but here it seems impossible to retain the breadth of meaning of σάρξ in translation, since to translate "my flesh" would be misleading. There is, of course, nothing that can be called anti-Semitic at this point: Paul speaks as one who gladly acknowledges and highly values his ethnic identity as a Jew.

καὶ σώσω τινὰς ἐξ αὐτῶν, "and I might save some of them." That this is a transferred sense of σώζω used as a missionary term is implied by 1 Cor

9:22 (see, e.g., Wilckens with other references). But the sense of salvation as an eschatological blessing should not be wholly lost (as Barrett and Cranfield when they give it the meaning "convert"); Paul "saves" as himself an agent of God's eschatological salvation whose ministry is actually part of the final act leading into the climax of salvation (see on 11:15). Why Paul says only τινὰς ἐξ αὐτῶν is unclear—a realistic assessment of the results of his ministry (Cranfield; not such "a great optimist" as Dodd thinks), "diplomatic caution" (Käsemann, referring to εἰ πως), the recognition that others were involved in the mission to the Gentiles (see on 1:1); see also Munck, *Christ*, 123–24. Whatever the reason, the more modest hope expressed here should not be seen as a diminishing of Paul's eschatological vision, as an actor on the world stage in the final scene of the drama of human history (1 Cor 4:9; see further on 11:15 and 11:26). See also Lübking, 120–22.

15 εἰ γὰρ ἡ ἀποβολὴ αὐτῶν καταλλαγὴ κόσμου, "for if their rejection means reconciliation for the world." The structure is precisely the same as v 12a. But Paul does not simply repeat v 12: he expresses the same contrast in more positive terms of divine action (rejection and acceptance [Kuss]); and he explains (γάρ) why he is so keen to provoke Israel to salvation (the ultimate success of the Gentile mission depends on Israel's acceptance [see further below]). ἀποβολή probably has the active sense of "throwing away, jettison, rejection" (LSJ, BGD), rather than the passive "loss" (as in its only other occurrence in biblical Greek [Acts 27:22]), since it stands here in opposition to πρόσλημψις (cf. Wilckens); the same contrast (ἐκβολή/πρόσλημψις) is found in the addition to Sir 10:20 (= 10:21). Paul probably has in mind the same complex of divine intention and human culpability as in 9:31–33 (see also on 11:11 and 11:12). For καταλλαγή see on 5:10. The thought is closely parallel to 5:10 in form and sequence of thought.

5:10	*11:15*
εἰ γὰρ ἐχθροί	εἰ γὰρ ἡ ἀποβολὴ αὐτῶν
yet καταλλαγή	yet καταλλαγή
πολλῷ μᾶλλον	τίς . . . εἰ μή
→ ζωή	→ ζωή
Note also σωθήσεσθαι (vv 9, 10)	σωτηρία, σώζω (vv 11, 14)

So Paul no doubt has in mind the death of Christ (5:10), though here once again we should avoid either-or exegesis (as in Cranfield), since it is unlikely that if the point was put to him, Paul would want to exclude the idea of reconciliation accepted (2 Cor 5:18–20 [SH]) or of a world reconciled as including the reconciliation of Jew and Gentile (Eph 2:16 [Barrett]); in Paul's gospel and theology these strands are too closely interwoven to be easily separated (here not least). For κόσμος see on 3:6 and 11:12.

τίς ἡ πρόσλημψις εἰ μὴ ζωὴ ἐκ νεκρῶν; "what shall their acceptance mean other than life from the dead?" For πρόσλημψις, only here in biblical Greek, "acceptance" may be too passive a translation, since it can have the more active sense of "taking in addition, taking to oneself, acquisition" (LSJ, *TDNT* 4:15), and that matches the divine initiative implied in the ἀποβολή more closely. Either way, it is clearly a *final* acceptance which is in view. As Wilckens rightly notes, not only the extension of the gospel to the Gentiles was mediated through Israel, but the final act of salvation is also mediated through Israel; the fullness of eschatological life for which Paul looked (see below) will only come through God's once again taking Israel to himself (F. W. Maier, 124); "the final act of all history rests upon the Jews" (Davies, "Gentiles," 154). As throughout this section, so here Paul retains his emphasis on divine initiative without diminishing the culpability of human trespass; within the overall sweep of the divine purpose there is still plenty of room for individual human responsibility (cf. Schmidt, 189). For εἰ μή cf. Rom 7:7 and Gal 1:19.

ζωή as divine gift usually has an eschatological character (even when αἰώνιος is not added)—the life of the new age already experienced in this age and continuing into the new age (as in 5:17, 8:2, 6, 10; for ζωὴ αἰώνιος see on 2:7; see further BGD, ζωή 2bβ). The eschatological force here is put beyond dispute by the ἐκ νεκρῶν (cf. Schlier), which elsewhere always denotes resurrection (in 6:13 note the ὡσεί; see on 6:13). Moreover, as in the πολλῷ μᾶλλον contrasts of 5:9–10, the rhetorical structure demands that the final phrase should describe something which outstrips the earlier: in 5:9–10, eschatological salvation (in the final judgment) presented as the climax of reconciliation/justification; here "life from the dead" presented as something more wonderful still than "reconciliation of the world." Paul therefore must mean by ζωὴ ἐκ νεκρῶν the final resurrection at the end of the age/history (so most); a symbolical sense (spiritual blessings already enjoyed [Gaugler, Murray, Hendriksen]; the conversion of Israel [Leenhardt; Stanley, *Resurrection*, 197; Fitzmyer]) would be an anticlimax after καταλλαγὴ κόσμου. That Paul could thus think of the end of history as so close is very striking, and he could evidently assume that the language and conviction would be familiar to his Roman audiences. Even more striking that he could see his own work as triggering off that final sequence: fullness of Gentiles (v 25), fullness of Jews (v 12) = reconciliation of the world → the final resurrection. Zeller notes that in Jewish thought resurrection of the dead was usually a presupposition for the restoration of Israel (*Juden*, 242–43); once again Paul reiterates a Jewish hope but in reworked Christian terms where Israel's priority in salvation-history is fully recognized but not in any exclusive terms.

16 εἰ δὲ ἡ ἀπαρχὴ ἁγία, καὶ τὸ φύραμα, "but if the initial offering is holy, so is the mixture as a whole." For ἀπαρχή see on 8:23. An allusion to the law requiring an offering of a portion of dough (made into cakes) is probably intended (Num 15:17–21—ἀπαρχὴν φυράματος, vv 20, 21; referred to by Philo, *Sac.* 107; *Spec. Leg.* 1.132; Josephus, *Ant.* 4.71). ἁγία denotes the holiness of the sacrifice, "holy" because dedicated to God, reserved for him in his cult—a usage familiar to both Jew and Gentile (LSJ; see particularly the frequent usage in Exod-Num). The idea of this cultic holiness extending to the rest of the dough/harvest etc. is not present in the OT, and can hardly be read from Philo, *Spec. Leg.* 1.131–44 (Lietzmann, Lagrange, and particularly Bourke, 68–72; despite Berger, "Abraham," 84, and Käsemann). But the holiness of the temple was frequently thought of as extending to Jerusalem and its hills (e.g., Neh 11:1, 18; Isa 11:9; 48:2; 66:20; Jer 31:23, 40; Ezek 20:40; BDB, קֹדֶשׁ 2e). The Qumran community regarded themselves as a "community of holiness" (עצת (ה)קדש—1QS 2.25; 8.21; 1QSa 2.9; 1QH 7.10;

CD 20.25). And the Pharisees, or at least a significant portion of them, evidently saw it as their objective to extend the holiness of the temple throughout the land, at least in that they observed in daily life the level of purity/holiness required in the law only in relation to the temple (see Neusner, e.g., *Politics*; also *Judaism*, 70; Dunn, "Pharisees"). Likewise the whole people could be regarded as "saints" (ἅγιοι; see on 1:7) and "consecrated" (ἡγιασμένοι; see on 15:16). So the logic of Paul's assertion here would be widely recognized and accepted even though formal justification for it was lacking (cf. also 1 Cor 7:14, and Schmidt).

The reference of ἀπαρχή/φύραμα is disputed. Most assume that the patriarchs are meant by the former and so, naturally, Israel as a whole by the latter (which would certainly fit with vv 12b and 18); less relevant is the later rabbinic reference to Adam as the firstling of the world (Str-B, 4:667–68; Rengstorf, 130–35), since in Paul Adam is hardly a type or source of holiness (5:12–19). But Paul's more regular reference in identifying ἀπαρχή with people is to the first Christian converts (16:5; 1 Cor 16:15; 2 Thess 2:13) and it fits his argument better here to see ἀπαρχή as those who have first responded to the gospel in this final stage of salvation-history, both Jews (the remnant, vv 2–6) and Gentiles (vv 7, 11–15); so that φύραμα consists of *all* the seed of Abraham (see further Cranfield, with bibliog.); cf. Philo, *Spec. Leg.* 4.180 (Israel as the firstfruits of the whole human race). There is no reason why the two halves of v 16 should be synonymous rather than complementary (cf. particularly Leenhardt). On the contrary, Paul probably intended to bring both ideas together in this verse (early converts, including Gentiles, as promise of the complete harvest, including Jews [v 12a]; promise to patriarchs as assurance that God is still faithful to Israel as a whole [v 12b]). In this way v 12 provides a transition from the argument of vv 11–15 (v 16a) to the warning against Gentile boasting over Jew in vv 17–24 (v 16b). Despite 1 Cor 15:20, 23, a reference to Christ as ἀπαρχή is unlikely; that is a different application of the same metaphor.

καὶ εἰ ἡ ῥίζα ἁγία, καὶ οἱ κλάδοι, "and if the root is holy, so also are the branches." Paul here evokes a similar relationship (quantitative—part to whole; organic—root to plant), and thus, slightly awkwardly (because the relationship is similar but not identical; e.g., the trunk is not mentioned in the second), leads into the extended metaphor of vv 17–24. For the dependence of branches on root cf. Job 18:16; Jer 17:8; Ezek 31:7; Hos 9:16; Sir 1:20 and 40:15. Paul is certainly drawing here on a long-established imagery of Israel as God's planting (Ps 92:13; Jer 11:17; *Pss. Sol.* 14.3–4; *1 Enoch* 84.6) or specifically as a "righteous plant" (*Jub.* 1.16; 7.34; 16.26; 21.24; 36.6; *1 Enoch* 10.16; 93.2–10), and often in eschatological terms (Isa 60:21; 61:3; Jer 32:41; Amos 9:15; *Jub.* 1.16; *1 Enoch* 93.10); in the DSS referred to the Qumran community (1QS 8.4–5; 11.8; CD 1.7). Closely related is the imagery of Israel as a spreading vine (Ps 80:8–18; Jer 2:21; Ezek 17; *4 Ezra* 5.23, 28), and the eschatological overtones of the messianic hope of a branch from the root of Jesse (Isa 11:1, 10; Jer 23:5; 33:15; Zech 3:8; 6:12; *T. Jud.* 24.5; 4QPat 3–4; 4QFlor 1:11; cf. 1QH 6.14–17; 8.4–11). See also *TDNT* 6:986–88. The root of this planting, where identified, is thought of as Abraham (*1 Enoch* 93.5, 8; Philo, *Heres.* 279) or Isaac (*Jub.* 21.24); see also on 4:1 and 4:2 and Rengstorf,

140–43. Paul probably has this sense also in mind (root = patriarchs, branches = their descendants), since that leads naturally into the next paragraph—some of (these) branches have been broken off (so most; see above). Even so we should note that ῥίζα can be used in parallel to λεῖμμα (as Sir 47:22 shows; so also 2 Kgs 19:30; Isa 37:31; 1 Esd 8:75, 84–86), so that the sense of "(remaining) shoot" = the (Jewish Christian) remnant need not be wholly excluded (cf. Gaugler; Barth, *Shorter*; Barrett). But probably decisive here is the realization that Paul has shifted his thought from the idea of election which breaks earthly continuity (9:7–13; 11:5–6) to that of God's faithfulness expressed in the continuity of his promise to Israel (Käsemann). Gentile Christians cannot be in view since they are the newly grafted-in branches in the following allegory (Lietzmann); here the parallel between ἀπαρχή and ῥίζα certainly breaks down. And a reference to Christ as the root (Wright, *Messiah*, 186) is hardly obvious. The problematic conception of "corporate personality" should not be drawn in here (against, e.g., Schmitt, 105); see on 5:12.

How much of a "theology of sanctification" can be drawn from this verse is unclear. It is hardly likely that the metaphors should be pressed to give an allegorical meaning—holiness transmitted from first offering/patriarchs to eschatological believers in the same way as it is transmitted from offering to whole lump or from root to branches. Paul certainly would not want to frame a doctrine of transmission of holiness in strict genetic terms (9:6–8); this must be borne in mind in the interpretation of 1 Cor 7:14. At the same time some connection is implied, presumably at least in some measure, in analogy to 5:19. That is to say, Paul was thinking in terms of a salvation-history certainty that what God had begun he would complete, which must include Israel in some substantial sense. In other words, any doctrine of sanctification drawing on this verse must observe the tension in Paul's thought regarding the promise which is to Israel (9:4; 11:28–29) but which also comes to expression through grace (11:5–6). An interesting comparison is Philo, *Praem.* 152—root need *not* determine fruitfulness—but only in relation to the proselyte!

17 εἰ δέ τινες τῶν κλάδων ἐξεκλάσθησαν, "but if some of the branches have been broken off." The εἰ δέ maintains the structural unity of the passage (see *Form and Structure*). For the surprising τινές see on 3:3; but cf. also the τινάς of v 14. In Paul's estimates in these verses vision and hope jostle with a sobering realism which provides the necessary basis for the warning against presumption. The passive of ἐκκλάω is part of the horticultural image but maintains the emphasis of the act as God's (cf. vv 7, 8, 10, 15). Paul, of course, does not pursue the usual corollary—discarded branches are burnt (e.g., Matt 3:10; John 15:6); see 11:23.

σὺ δὲ ἀγριέλαιος ὢν ἐνεκεντρίσθης ἐν αὐτοῖς, "and you being a wild olive have been grafted among them." ἀγριέλαιος is really an adjective, but it can be taken as a substantive (BGD). Paul's use of the olive tree in his extended metaphor will have been due only partly to the fact that Israel had occasionally been likened to one (Jer 11:16; Hos 14:6), since other "plant" images for Israel are more frequent in Jewish literature (see on 11:16) (despite Walter, 180–81, it can hardly be doubted that Paul has Israel as a people in view). Equally important would have been the fact that the olive tree was the most widely cultivated fruit tree in the Mediterranean area. Paul's choice was determined by the appropriateness of well-known procedures in olive culture, including that of grafting wild shoots on to cultivated trees (see *OCD* 749–50; Str-B 3:291; Cranfield; though see Munck, *Christ,* 128–30); ἐγκεντρίζω is in fact a t.t. for tree grafting (BGD). Baxter and Ziesler note that the purpose of such grafting in olive culture would be to rejuvenate the tree (against Munck, 130). Davies develops the suggestion that the imagery of the olive may have been derived from the name of one of the synagogues in Rome (συναγωγὴ Ἐλαίας; so, e.g., W. L. Knox, *Jerusalem,* 254, 258 n.17, and Kirk; details in Leon, 145–47) to note that the olive in the cultured pagan world would naturally evoke Athens and Greek culture (see also Siegert, 168). Paul abruptly turns the tables on such Gentile pride by representing the Gentile believers as a *wild* olive, since the wild olive was notoriously *un*productive. To represent *Israel* as the cultured olive would clearly imply the superiority of the Jewish spiritual heritage as over against the non-Jewish (Davies, "Rom 11:13–24," 158–63). Paul turns the tables on Gentile pride as effectively as he had on Jewish pride in chap. 2. ἐν αὐτοῖς must obviously mean "among (the remaining) branches" (Cranfield; otherwise Davies, "Rom 11:13–24," 356 n.6). Paul's ambiguity on the point arises out of the fact that he still regards even the broken-off branches as still properly part of, or at least belonging to, the tree. That Paul is drawing on traditional material is certainly possible, but can hardly be demonstrated from *b. Yebam.* 63a (Ruth and Naomi grafted into Abraham; see Ruth 1:4, 16), despite Rengstorf, 143–46. Bourke properly raises the issue of the correlation between the metaphors of the body of Christ and the olive tree (79 ff.), but resolves the tension in Paul's understanding of salvation-history continuity (e.g., 9:6; 11:28) too easily by simply taking up the traditional identification of the olive tree with "the mystical body of Christ" (103; "the olive tree is . . . the Church" [111]).

καὶ συγκοινωνὸς τῆς ῥίζης τῆς πιότητος τῆς ἐλαίας ἐγένου, "and have become sharer in the riches of the olive tree's root." συγκοινωνός is very characteristically Pauline: nearly 70 percent of the κοινων- words in the NT come in the Pauline corpus; and for συν- see on 6:4. For συγκοινωνός/έω see 1 Cor 9:23, Eph 5:11; Phil 1:7; and 4:14. Fundamental to Paul's soteriology is this emphasis on "sharing with"—sharing with Christ (6:4; 1 Cor 1:9; 10:16; Phil 3:10), sharing in the Holy Spirit (2 Cor 13:13; Phil 2:1), sharing with fellow Christians (e.g., 12:13; 15:26; 2 Cor 1:7; Phil 1:7), and here not least Gentile sharing with Jew (see also 15:27). Paul would have no time for an individualism which ignored the horizontal solidarity of either ecclesiology or salvation-history. πιότητος can be either adjectival ("the rich root"—e.g., BGD, Lietzmann, Barrett), or appositional ("in the root, its fatness, of the olive tree"—Michel, Cranfield). Current English translations do not cope with the phrase very well: RSV and NJB concentrate on the thought of richness and ignore the "root"; NEB paraphrases "same root and sap," diminishing the note of "richness"; best is NIV, "the nourishing sap from the olive root." The fatness or richness of the olive was almost proverbial (cf. Judg 9:9; *Jos. As.* 5.7; and *T. Lev.* 8.8).

18 μὴ κατακαυχῶ τῶν κλάδων, "do not boast over the branches." In this little used compound the κατά brings out the element of competitive superiority expressed in the boasting; cf. the only other NT occurrences, James 2:13 and 3:14 (*TDNT* 3:653–54). καυχάομαι, of course, was a crucial word in Paul's indictment of his fellow Jews for their presumption (see on 2:17). It is highly significant that it is precisely this danger which Paul is anxious to warn gentile Christians against—of making the same mistake as had most Jews—that is, of forgetting that their place within the saving purpose of God depended solely on his grace. It is just this sin (ceasing to live out of a creaturely dependence on God alone) which is the fundamental sin of Jew as well as Greek (1:18–3:20); see also on 12:16 and 14:16. The ambiguity already in 11:17 is preserved here in τῶν κλάδων: it can include both unbelieving Jews (broken-off branches) and Jewish Christians (natural branches still remaining in the tree); so SH, Kühl, Lagrange, Schlatter, Michel. Whether there is also a reflection here of gentile anti-Semitism, such as we find among Roman intellectuals (see *Introduction* §2.3.1) is less clear: Christianity was not yet sufficiently distinct from Judaism, so that few were likely to be attracted to Christianity who cherished anti-Jewish feelings; the Gentile Christians in Rome were most likely drawn in large part, initially at least, from the ranks of those Gentiles attracted to Judaism (see *Introduction* §2.2.2); so the thesis that Romans was written to combat anti-Semitism (Lütgert, *Römerbrief*, 79–90; Bartsch, "Gegner"; Minear, *Obedience*, 79; Maillot, 287) cannot build too much on this verse (see also *Introduction* §3). The danger Paul is addressing may have been chiefly local (Schlier), arising in large part out of the ejection of Jews from Rome several years earlier: that could have encouraged feelings that God's purpose had now moved on from the Jews, bringing a status-reversal which some welcomed (Jews were now the adherents and fringe members); and such feelings could have been strengthened by problems arising over the return of some Jewish Christians after a few years' absence (see *Introduction* §2.4.4). This would give sufficient ground for Paul's exhortation, without the further hypothesis that Paul was contesting *enthusiastic* tendencies in Rome (against Michel). One way or other, however, the verse does strengthen the likelihood that Paul was quite well aware of the circumstances of the Christian congregations in Rome.

εἰ δὲ κατακαυχᾶσαι, οὐ σὺ τὴν ῥίζαν βαστάζεις ἀλλὰ ἡ ῥίζα σέ, "if you do boast, you do not support the root, but the root supports you." The οὐ is emphatic. βαστάζω here probably denotes not simply a physical holding up or carrying but also the idea of fruit bearing (cf. LSJ II.5; Luke 11:27). The language possibly strengthens the speculation outlined above: gentile Christians who had been exempt from the political pressures brought against the Jews in Rome would naturally tend to feel that the vulnerable Jewish Christians had become more dependent on them. Paul's answer is unequivocal: gentile Christians are beneficiaries of the rich spiritual heritage which stems from Abraham through the Jews (cf. 15:27) and that relationship continues unbroken (whatever the particular circumstances at Rome); "the church rests on God's covenant and history with Israel, not on what the gentile Christians bring with them" (Althaus; see also F. W. Maier, 132). A church which is not drawing upon the sustenance of its Jewish inheritance (including the OT, but not only the OT) would be a contradiction in terms for Paul. A Christianity composed only of Gentiles would be a grief to Paul and an end to his most cherished hopes (cf. Eph 2:11–22). See also particularly Käsemann.

19 ἐρεῖς οὖν, "you will say, then"; see on 9:19. Paul shows his even-handedness between Jew and Gentile by addressing Gentile objections in the same style as he used to meet Jewish objections (2:1–5, 17–27); the danger confronting them being the same (see on 11:18).

ἐξεκλάσθησαν κλάδοι ἵνα ἐγὼ ἐγκεντρισθῶ, "branches were broken off in order that I might be grafted in." For the terms used see on 11:17. Paul allows the interlocutor to follow out the logic of the metaphor. Here again the danger is of making the same mistake as had so many Jews before them—of assuming that what happened to others was primarily for their sake as such. The ἐγὼ contrasted with the plural κλάδοι heightens the note of presumption: "several branches removed to make room for me." Despite what was said on 11:18, it is regrettably true that the sentiments here were used to express the logic of Christian anti-Semitism in later centuries.

20 καλῶς, "quite so." The diatribe style is maintained. Cf. Mark 12:32, and see BGD, 4c. Paul is not being ironic (against Michel, Manson, Schmidt, Black); the agreement is real, but qualified. The tension of continuity and discontinuity between the phases of salvation-history is maintained.

τῇ ἀπιστίᾳ ἐξεκλάσθησαν, σὺ δὲ τῇ πίστει ἕστηκας, "they were broken off on the ground of unbelief, but you stand through faith." The first dative is causal (BDF, §196), but the second is more instrumental; the neatness of the contrast in Greek therefore cannot be easily reproduced in translation. For ἀπιστία see on 3:3; since the sense can again include "unfaithfulness" Paul can maintain his even-handed rebuke of both Jewish and Gentile presumption (see on 3:3 and 11:17). For ἐκκλάω see on 11:17. The perfect ἕστηκας has the force of past action resulting in a continuing state maintained by the faith through which the past action was brought about. The sense is given by translating "stand firm" (cf. RSV); see 1 Cor 7:37; 10:12; and particularly 1 Cor 15:1–2 and 2 Cor 1:24; cf. Rom 5:2 (see also *TDNT* 7:651). By πίστις Paul of course means "faith" as he has defined it on chap. 4 = dependent trust in God.

μὴ ὑψηλὰ φρόνει, ἀλλὰ φοβοῦ, "do not cherish proud thoughts, but fear." ὑψηλὰ φρονεῖν can have a positive meaning, "to think lofty thoughts," as in Philo, *Ebr.* 128 (BGD, ὑψηλός 2; cf. Schmidt). But the image of height (high mountains, etc.) can naturally be given the connotation "too high = (unjustifiably) proud," as in 1 Sam 2:3 and Eccl 7:8; so here and 12:16; also 1 Tim 6:17. The pride here is that voiced in 11:19; but the warning example continues to be Israel whose presumption transformed πίστις into ἀπιστία. In advocating "fear" Paul draws on a strong strand of Jewish piety prominent in the wisdom tradition, the fear of the Lord as the beginning of wisdom (e.g., Pss 2:11; 34:9, 11; 111:10; 112:1; Prov 1:7; 3:7; Sir 1:11–14, 16, 18, 20, 26–27, 30; 2:7–10, 15–17); so in Paul himself particularly 2 Cor 5:11; 7:1; Phil 2:12; and Col 3:22. Cf. also 3:18 and 13:7. Only fear of God can keep faith from deteriorating into presumption, since only in trembling creatureliness does faith retain its character as dependent trust (see also Althaus on 11:22). The words are frequently quoted in the patristic period.

21 εἰ γὰρ ὁ θεὸς τῶν κατὰ φύσιν κλάδων οὐκ ἐφείσατο, "for if God did not spare the natural branches." Still using the εἰ formulation (see *Form and Structure*) Paul gives a second reason why his Gentile reader should not boast (the first in v 18). For κατὰ φύσιν (also in v 24) see BGD, φύσις 1, and on

2:14; and cf. Gal 2:15. φείδομαι (here the opposite of ἐκκλάω [vv 17, 19, 20])
usually appears in negative formulations; cf. Acts 20:29; Rom 8:32; 2 Cor
13:2; 2 Pet 2:4–5; and Ign. *Rom.* 1.2 (BGD, Michel).

μή πως οὐδὲ σοῦ φείσεται, "neither will he spare you." The warning is based
partly on the logic of the metaphor (natural branches have a better prospect
of survival than grafted branches) but partly also on the logic of salvation-
history. Paul's insistence throughout is that whatever the present state of
affairs (Israel's rejection of the gospel and "hardness"), Israel still retains
the advantage of being the people first called by God—a priority of grace,
not a right. The seriousness of the warning should not be underestimated.
If Jewish branches could be cut off, then gentile branches could certainly
suffer the same fate (note the future tense rather than subjunctive—"will"
rather than "might" [NJB]). If even the promises to Israel could not prevent
such an outcome, then gentile Christians should not assume that they were
exempt from a similar outcome. The possibility of believers "falling away"
(= failing to stand firm; v 20), apostatizing, is one which Paul certainly did
not exclude. On the contrary, he reckoned with it in all seriousness. Cf. the
"eschatological reservation" typical in the structure of chaps. 6–8 with the
more clear-cut "already" statements of the first part of each chapter balanced
by the "not yet" emphasis of the second half (always with the implication
that an exhortation ignored could constitute a critical denial of the "already"
indicative); see chaps. 6–8 *Introduction*. See particularly 8:13; 8:17 ("provided
that"); 9:3; 11:22; 14:15, 20. Elsewhere note particularly 1 Cor 3:17; 8:11;
9:27; 10:1–12; 15:1–2; 2 Cor 13:5; Gal 5:4; Col 1:22–23; Heb 3:14; 6:4–8;
10:29. A doctrine of "perseverance of the saints" which does not include
the lessons of salvation-history has lost its biblical perspective. Even more
than in 8:13 the personal singular address (σοῦ) gives the warning more pressing point.

22   ἴδε οὖν χρηστότητα καὶ ἀποτομίαν θεοῦ, "consider then the goodness and
severity of God." For χρηστότης, "goodness, kindness, generosity," see BGD,
and on 2:4. Schlier maps out its semantic range by listing the words elsewhere
associated with it. ἀποτομία (*hapax legomenon* in NT) continues the imagery
(literally, "cutting off"), but otherwise is a surprising word for Paul to use
since hellenistic usage referred it to the law with the sense "judicial strictness"
or even "pitiless severity" (MM, *TDNT* 8:107; see e.g., Philo, *Flacc.* 95). But
Paul is probably more influenced by wisdom usage, as also in 11:20 (see on
11:20); Rengstorf's suggestion (158–63) that behind it lies the Hebrew judicial
term for family division has less to commend it. Only in Wisd Sol 5:20, 22;
6:5; 11:10; 12:9; and 18:15 do the correlatives ἀπότομος and ἀποτόμως occur
in the LXX; there they refer to the judicial strictness of God (especially 6:5
and 11:10); see *TDNT* 8:108. Is Paul aware of Wisd Sol 12:8–10 which talks
of God sparing (ἐφείσω) pagans and withholding the destruction of his stern
word (λόγῳ ἀποτόμῳ; cf. Wisd Sol 18:15 and Heb 4:12) to give them opportunity for repentance despite their evil nature (ἔμφυτος κακία)? If so, Paul once
again turns the tables on Jewish presumption: God's judicial severity is directed
toward Jews, not Gentiles. Perhaps also he reminds those who build their
hopes too much on the law (ἐξ ἔργων νόμου) that the corollary is judgment
on the basis of the law (cf. particularly 2:12 and the following argument

2:12–27). The possibility of an *ad hominem* dimension to the argument should tell against any suggestion that Paul intended God's "judicial severity" and "goodness" to be reckoned of equal weight in his thought at this point, since the stronger emphasis is on grace and mercy (11:5–6, 22, 29, 30–32); cf. on 9:22. Cf. also the rabbinic texts in Str-B, 3:292.

ἐπὶ μὲν τοὺς πεσόντας ἀποτομία, "to those who fell, severity." The πεσόντας reverts to v 11, the mixture of metaphors underlining the looseness with which Paul handles the tree metaphor. The allusion back to the earlier language also includes a note of blameworthiness which the "breaking off" imagery as such had not allowed for (though cf. of course v 20); cf. Paul's use of the "fall" metaphor in 14:4 and 1 Cor 10:12; also Heb 4:11. Paul thus continues to maintain a balance between human responsibility and divine act (cf. again 9:22). On ἀποτομία see above.

ἐπὶ δὲ σὲ χρηστότης θεοῦ, ἐὰν ἐπιμένῃς τῇ χρηστότητι, "but to you the goodness of God, if you continue in that goodness." The triple χρηστότης strengthens the implication that this is the dominant divine characteristic for Paul; see above. The ἐάν clause should not be underplayed; Paul's whole point is that presumption is fatal, whether of Jew or of Gentile. ἐπιμένω has the force of "persist in, persevere" (BGD, 2); cf. 6:1 and 11:23. Once again Paul underlines the point that perseverance is a Christian responsibility rather than an unconditional promise; "throughout the New Testament continuance is the test of reality" (Bruce); see also on 11:21, and note the comparable εἰ clauses in 8:13, 17 and particularly Col 1:23 (εἴ γε ἐπιμένετε τῇ πίστει). In the balance of the μέν and δέ clauses we might note that the severity is consequent on the unfaith, whereas the divine goodness precedes the human response.

ἐπεὶ καὶ σὺ ἐκκοπήσῃ, "otherwise you too will be cut off." As in v 6 ἐπεί has the sense of "since otherwise" (BDF, §456.3). ἐκκόπτω, usually used when describing cutting down the whole tree (as in Matt 3:10; 7:19; Luke 13:7, 9), also v 24, is simply a variation on ἐκκλάω (vv 17, 19, 20).

23 κἀκεῖνοι δέ, ἐὰν μὴ ἐπιμένωσιν τῇ ἀπιστίᾳ, ἐγκεντρισθήσονται, "but they too, if they do not continue in unbelief, shall be grafted in." The third person indicates that Paul does not envisage the presence of unbelieving Jews among his listeners; thus confirming that the second person style of chap. 2 was a matter of rhetoric. The ἐπιμένω is deliberately chosen to balance v 22: it is not a once-for-all refusal of belief (or act of faith) which is decisive for condemnation (or salvation) but the persistence in that attitude (cf. 8:6). For ἐγκεντρίζω see on 11:17. This is a third reason why Gentiles should not boast.

δυνατὸς γάρ ἐστιν ὁ θεὸς πάλιν ἐγκεντρίσαι αὐτούς, "for God is able to graft them in again." The logic of salvation-history has here left the logic of olive culture behind (cf. Dodd's typically pungent comment; "Paul is a city boy" [Lietzmann]). If the point were to be pressed the implication would be that the cut-off branches were somehow preserved and prevented from withering so that a regraft would be possible to conceive. Alternatively Paul could mean that the power of God can rejuvenate withered branches (cf. 4:19–21). In using δυνατός of God here Paul may have been mindful that גִּבּוֹר, regularly translated by δυνατός, was used of God, not least in his covenant faithfulness to his people (Neh 9:32; Ps 24 [LXX 23]:8, δυνατός twice; Isa 10:21—the remnant of Jacob returning to the mighty God; Jer 32:18; cf. Luke 1:49).

For Gentile Christians to assume otherwise would be as false as Israel's older assumption that Gentiles were excluded from the covenant as Gentiles. The power of God evoked here is the same power as in 4:21: it was the character of that power as calling nonentity into life (4:17), not as an automatic prejudice in favor of the Jew, which the Jew of chap. 2 had misunderstood. Gentile believers must not make the same mistake. See further on 4:21. We might contrast 2 *Apoc. Bar.* 84.2, where the hope of being planted is dependent on keeping the law.

24 εἰ γὰρ σὺ ἐκ τῆς κατὰ φύσιν ἐξεκόπης ἀγριελαίου καὶ παρὰ φύσιν ἐνεκεντρίσθης εἰς καλλιέλαιον, "for if you were cut out from the natural wild olive and grafted unnaturally into the cultivated olive." The κατὰ φύσιν / παρὰ φύσιν contrast does not imply that the process of grafting was unnatural; the point focuses rather awkwardly on the surprising fact that a branch from one subspecies can be successfully grafted into another (see Michel, Schmidt, and Cranfield). The metaphor continues to be strained since the unnaturalness Paul has in mind is that of Gentiles being counted as full members of the covenant people while still Gentiles (that is, not becoming Jews). The language reflects a Jewish view of Gentiles even while seeking to undermine that view. The point is that, notwithstanding God's long cultivation of Israel, "nature," or as we might say here, ethnic identity has no bearing on membership of the people of God. On ἀγριέλαιος / καλλιέλαιος see on 11:17; Israel is as a cultured olive because it has been tended over centuries by the master gardener.

πόσῳ μᾶλλον οὗτοι οἱ κατὰ φύσιν ἐγκεντρισθήσονται τῇ ἰδίᾳ ἐλαίᾳ, "how much more shall those who belong to it naturally be grafted into their own olive tree." For πόσῳ μᾶλλον see on 11:12; here it corresponds to the πρῶτον of 1:16 and 2:10 (Schlatter). ἴδιος gains its force from the metaphor (cf. Luke 6:44), as the complement of κατὰ φύσιν; not here with the negative sense of 10:3, but still with the note "distinctively theirs."

The parenetic point is that gentile Christians' own experience of grace should be enough to show them that if they can be accepted by Israel's God, how much more ethnic Israel. The theological point is that God's election includes both Jews and Gentiles, not as Jews and Gentiles, but as a people constituted as such by God's call (9:11, 24). See also Wilckens, 2:248–50.

Explanation

The next stage of the argument is to develop the hints dropped in 10:19–21. Having shown that Israel's hardening at this stage in the history of salvation was purposed by God just as much as Pharaoh's at an earlier stage, Paul now hastens to add that this is not the whole story. God's punitive action against the majority of Israel is not his last act in the history of salvation; these menacing scriptures are not his last word concerning Israel.

11 So Paul returns to the question of 11:1 and replaces it: "They have not tripped so as to fall into ruin, have they?" They surely have not gone completely to pieces? Is their mistake any more than a momentary stumble? They have not gone sprawling on their face so as to be unable to complete the course, have they? And his immediate reply, "No indeed!" "Far from it!" The forcefulness of both question and answer recalls the similar indignant rebuttals earlier in the letter—Paul's frequent denial that his gospel devalues the place of either Israel or the law within the purpose of God (3:3–4; 3:31; 7:7, 13; 11:1). It is almost as though Paul had been restraining himself on this point with mounting impatience until the appropriate place in his argument, and now he can hold back no longer. His first hearers may well have experienced a tingle of anticipation as they realized that they were approaching the climax to the whole argument, Paul's exposition of how he saw the continuity between Israel and the Christ-believers working out. The very wording of the question itself, with its distinction between a (mere) trip and a (complete) fall, suggests not only that there is an answer to the problem of Israel's unbelief, but what that answer will be. The effect of even asking the question is to relativize and soften the harsher sentences from Moses and David (vv 8–10). However obtuse Israel has been up till now, it will not be permanent; however mistaken they have been, it is not fatal.

How can this be so? Verse 11b sums up Paul's answer with the same brevity of expression as in v 7. "By their transgression salvation has come to the Gentiles. . . ." What Paul intended his readers to understand by "their transgression" is not clear. The context strongly implies that it was the bulk of Israel's characteristic and sustained misunderstanding of the law (in terms of works) and so also their failure to respond to the word of faith (he has already demonstrated their inexcusableness on this latter point in 10:16–21). But Paul may also be casting a glance further back to 9:33 as well. Their sin was particularly to stumble at Christ, so to misunderstand him as to hand him over for crucifixion and to reject the word in its witness to him. In what way did this transgression mean salvation for the Gentiles? If Paul is referring to the crucifixion of Jesus, then presumably he would be thinking in terms of 5:6–11, 15–19: it was the Jewish authorities' rejection of Christ which brought about the death and resurrection of Jesus, that death and resurrection which introduced the new stage in God's dealings with humankind (3:21–26) and which made possible the wider offer of God's righteousness to all who believe. But if the reference is simply to Israel's abuse of its covenant privileges (by treating them at too superficial a level), Paul may simply be thinking of the actual historical sequence of events: it was the Hellenists' reaction to a faith too narrowly circumscribed by continuing loyalty to temple and circumcision which resulted directly in the Gentile mission (cf. Acts 6:8–8:4; 11:19–21; Gal 2:1–10). Probably Paul also intends to continue the thought that Israel's failure was divinely intended—an implication hard to exclude in the light of vv 7–10. The clause would then be a further expression of the logic of election: Israel's rejection of Christ and of the gospel was as essential in God's scheme of things as his rejection of Esau and hardening of Pharaoh; Israel's fall is the obverse of the coming of salvation to the Gentiles. In this case what would be significant is the use of the strong word "transgression." Paul is able to attribute the same failure both to the punitive act of God and to the reprehensible error of Israel; that God intended a particular outcome does not remove human responsibility for it. In other words, this passage expresses the same tension between election and judgment already hinted at less clearly in 9:22–23.

". . . salvation to the Gentiles so as to provoke them to jealousy." The purpose of God now extended to the Gentiles does not end with the salvation of the Gentiles. Indeed the salvation of the Gentiles is not an end in itself; it also has in view the salvation, the restoration, of Israel. God has not abandoned his people even in the act of hardening them. He has not torn up his covenant with Israel and started again. Even his punitive action against the bulk of Israel has Israel's salvation in view as well. Herein Paul's earlier conviction, that Israel's unfaithfulness has not nullified God's faithfulness (3:3–4), begins to achieve coherent expression. Paul the Jew at last begins to show how even his own people's unbelief and disobedience provides a double source of comfort for his anguish expressed earlier (9:1–3; 10:1); it is precisely that unbelief and disobedience which led to the gospel being offered to the Gentiles, which in turn will spur his fellow Jews to faith. So too what was implicit in 9:14–24 becomes at last clear: that God's outreach in wrath is bound up *within* his purpose of mercy. In the mysterious workings of divine providence God uses human reactions one to another, even when motivated by protective self-interest, to further his own larger outreach of grace.

12   Lest his predominantly gentile readers draw the conclusion that their salvation is only a means to the end of Israel's reinstatement, Paul goes on to reexpress the point in terms which show that his vision is larger than either and richer than both. Since Israel's transgression has brought riches to humankind as a whole, their defeat or failure riches to the Gentiles, how much more their fullness. The force of the contrast is clear enough in broad terms, but greater precision is difficult to achieve. Judging by the deliberate use of unusual words to form similar-sounding phrases (their transgression, their defeat, their fullness) Paul is striving more for a resonant statement than for precise definitions. Thus he may intend to evoke the contrast between Israel's sins of commission and of omission, on the one hand, and Israel's fulfillment of its election destiny as a whole, on the other; or the intention may be rather vague—a contrast in broad terms between Israel's present lapsed state and its future restoration. Either way the meaning is plain: Israel's rejection brought benefit to the rest of humankind; Israel's acceptance will bring still more benefit to humankind. And the point is clear too: Israel's future conversion does not mean that the benefits which have accrued to the Gentiles will be withdrawn; on the contrary, Gentiles will enjoy still greater benefits along with Israel. Israel's spiritual prosperity and the rest of world's are not antithetical; "the wealth of nations" means wealth for all.

Paul can make the point so firmly presumably because for him it was always part of Israel's vocation from God, to bring blessing to the world, to mediate the promise of Abraham to "many nations" (4:13–18), to share the riches of its covenant heritage (9:4–5) with all who believe. Israel's mistake is precisely that it failed to realize both the character and the purpose of its election. When that realization finally dawns, then of course not just Israel but the whole world will benefit and together they will rejoice in the fullness of eschatological blessing. For then the wealth of the covenant heritage will cease to be a bone of contention between Jew and gentile believer, the covenant promise will no longer be regarded as the exclusive right or possession of any, and so only then will it be *fully* experienced and *fully* enjoyed by all.

13–14 Lest the twin thrust of the last two sentences had been misheard or not fully appreciated Paul repeats them. The solemnity of the first person formulation recalls that of 9:1–3 and 10:1–2, and underlines the depth of concern and conviction behind these words; Paul evidently feels that his insight at this point is crucial. He has spent so much time explaining that the gospel is continuous with and the fulfillment of Israel's covenant promise, so much time justifying his own awkward and seemingly anomalous position, so much time trying to mollify his fellow countrymen, as it must have seemed. But he is equally conscious that the gentile believers need to understand *their* place within the divine purpose, how their blessing not only contributes to but also depends upon the blessing of Israel now in the eschatological present. Both partners in this eschatological minuet must learn to acknowledge the role of the other.

So he addresses the gentile members of the Roman congregations specifically, who probably outnumbered the Jewish believers (but not the Jews) in Rome. And he addresses them precisely as one who is apostle to the Gentiles. He cannot claim to be *their* apostle as such (contrast 1 Cor 9:1–2), but he can appeal on the broader basis of being apostle to the Gentiles as a whole or in general. Even those in Rome who have never met him will know how much they owe to him: he is the one who most unreservedly identified himself with the gentile believers, took their part, fought for their cause (cf. Gal 2:3–9); for their sake he had been regarded as a renegade and a heretic by many of his fellow Jews. So the gentile believers in Rome could be in no doubt that he had their spiritual good firmly at heart.

Thus they would probably realize that when he goes on to say "I magnify my ministry in the hope that I will provoke my flesh to jealousy . . .," he wants to place some weight on the verb ("magnify"). He does not say that the sole or main purpose of his ministry to the Gentiles is the provocation of his fellow countrymen. Rather he hopes to achieve that provocation by *magnifying* his ministry. In other words, Paul is explaining why he has not been content to work away on behalf of the Gentiles quietly and without fuss. They will no doubt be aware how much trouble his advocacy of Gentile freedom from the law has caused, both among Jews as a whole and Jewish Christians too. He had made a public issue of it, spoken out loud and clear over against those who regarded the gentile mission as an aberration or an anomaly or who would rather it was given no prominence. And he continues so to champion the cause of the gentile Christians as a matter of deliberate policy, so that the Jews (not least the Jews back home in Palestine) could not ignore it.

His aim is to provoke that people who are his people, to make them so uncomfortable over the success of the gentile mission that they will be forced to recognize how God is working and how God's purpose of mercy is being effected among the "no people" of the Gentiles. Paul feels the tension in himself, the tension between his complete identity as a Jew and his conviction regarding the gospel. His hope is to provoke a similar tension in his fellow countrymen, a tension between covenant nationalism and report of Gentile blessing, which will be resolved by their acceptance of Jesus as Messiah and all that follows from that. Presumably what gave him that hope was the scripture he had quoted earlier (10:19 = Deut 32:21) and which he here echoes. It is a measure of the boldness of Paul's vision that he could conceive of his mission as that which in God's good purpose might suffice to provide that final spur which would at last goad his fellow Jews into seeing what they had so far missed—though his confidence perhaps falters a little as he recalls how firmly set and how deeply rooted was the conviction of most of his fellow Jews as to the privileged status of their nation before God. His success would surely stir some from their stupor (v 8), but would it take others to complete the "fullness" (v 12)? or would "some" be enough, perhaps with an ironic backward glance to the way he had initially played down Jewish opposition to the gospel (3:3—"some did not believe")?

15 If vv 13–14 reemphasized the point of v 11, v 15 reemphasizes the point of v 12. However much or little depends on Paul's own ministry, Paul's confidence is firm that the rest of Israel will come to accept the gospel and that their acceptance will be for the good of all who believe. Now, however, he puts the point once again in terms of *God's* doing—"their rejection (by God) . . . their acceptance (by God)." What could be described from one angle as Israel's transgression (v 12) can from another angle be described as God's rejection. Paul maintains the tension implicit in 9:19–23 between a mercy-motivated purpose of election and a transgression deserving judgment of wrath. Moreover, where in v 12 he spoke of "riches for the world," here he speaks of "reconciliation of the world"; and where in v 12 he was content with a "how much more" formula, here he expresses the "how much more" as "nothing other than life from the dead." The balance between "reconciliation" and "life from the dead" recalls the somewhat similar balance of 5:10 and suggests that Paul is again thinking of the death of Christ as the means of reconciliation (as in 5:10). And "life from the dead" could hardly be understood by Paul's readers as anything other than a reference to the final resurrection. Here more clearly than anywhere else so far in the letter Paul expresses a sense of the nearness of the final consummation of God's purpose for the world. The "more than" the riches of reconciliation is the resurrection of the body, the complete redemption of the world (8:21–23). Nothing less than this is Paul's goal, the goal of his mission to the Gentiles: to (help) trigger off that final crescendo, when Gentile "riches" will result in Jewish "fullness," will result in "life from the dead." However the tension between election and judgment is resolved, Paul is sufficiently confident that life will be the winner, life which triumphs over death, the fullest possible sharing in the life of him who has already broken through (5:10, 17, 21; 6:5, 8, 23).

How Paul understood the divine rationale in all this is not clear. Was the casting off of Israel really necessary at this stage in salvation-history? Why could not the Gentiles have come in without the bulk of the Jews being thrown out, albeit temporarily? Paul's answer presumably might once again be in terms of the cross—that it was precisely Israel's rejection of its Messiah which was God's means of reconciliation—reprehensible, but divinely willed for the world's good. But the dominant thrust of his overall argument suggests that he might also have maintained that it had become necessary to break the identification between covenant promise and Jewish nation, so long and so firmly established in Jewish self-understanding, if the promise was indeed to be to *all* the seed (4:16). Without such a break in the continuity of Israel's covenant status any broadening out to embrace the Gentiles would inevitably have been misunderstood in terms of Jewish self-aggrandizement or religious imperialism. Consequently there had to be this initial stage in the outreach to the Gentiles which distanced itself from Israel as such in order that its character of grace might become clear both to the Gentiles (their being freely offered the riches of the Jewish heritage without having to become Jews) and to the Jews (provoked by the influx of Gentiles to recognize once again the wholly gracious nature of their own election). It is the magnificence of Paul's vision that he could see himself as called to such a crucial role in thus uniting Jew and Gentile under grace as the climax of God's purpose for creation.

16 To express the strength of his hope Paul once again rings the changes on his metaphors: "If the first offering is holy, so also is the mixture; if the root is holy, so also are the branches." The metaphor of the firstling or firstfruits dedicated to God would certainly be familiar to Paul's readers, since it was common enough parlance in the sacrificial practice of Gentiles as well as Jews. And an allusion to Num 15:20–21 in particular was probably in Paul's mind, where the phrase "first offering of the mixture" is twice used.

The deduction drawn by Paul ("so also is the mixture") would be less obvious however, since the point of dedicating part of something to *God* was to make the rest available for *ordinary* use. But perhaps we see something of Paul's Pharisaic background emerging here; for one of the Pharisees' chief aims was precisely to break down the distinction between sacred and secular which the practice of the firstfruits and tithing could easily encourage, and to extend the sphere of cultic purity as expressed in the temple ritual to the whole of life. Where "holiness" tends to be equated with ritual purity, then not only the tithe is "holy" but the tithed foodstuff also, precisely because it does not render the user unclean (precisely because it has been tithed). Paul of course no longer thinks in such terms of ritual purity, but the idea of a "holiness" which pervades all of life by virtue of an act and attitude of dedication is certainly fundamental to his thought (1:7; 6:19, 22; 12:1; cf. 1 Cor 6:11; 1 Thess 4:3–4, 7). In this sense we can speak quite properly of Paul's "deritualized Pharisaism."

More likely, however, the sacrificial connotation of the metaphor has fallen into the background of Paul's thought, dominated as it is at this point by his eschatological perspective ("life from the dead," v 15). As in 8:23 the implication is that the "firstfruits" are the first sample of the whole, whose presence already on the stage of salvation-history gives foretaste and guarantee of the eschatological harvest soon to be completed (cf. 1 Cor 15:20, 23), the first sheaf or portion demonstrating the character and quality of the future whole. Either way the implication is that those who have already believed in Christ, both Jew and Gentile, are the first of a much larger whole, whose sanctification as "saints" gives clear promise that the complete "fullness" will share the same sanctification (cf. particularly 2 Thess 2:13). But the logic of v 16a is not so much the logic of offering and tithe, but of Paul's firm assurance that God has already revealed the character of his eschatological people, that when the fullness of Israel is accepted once more it will manifest the holiness of those already "called to be saints" through the gospel (rather than, he might also imply, the cultic holiness of nationalistic Judaism).

The second metaphor evokes a rather different image ("if the root is holy so also the branches"). But its logic would be more apparent to Paul and his readers: the root obviously determines the vitality and quality of the branches. Moreover the image of Israel, not least eschatological Israel, as a planting of the Lord cannot have been far from Paul's mind. As the next few verses confirm, this in fact is where Paul's thought is focused—the branches are eschatological Israel. The logic is the logic of salvation-history as well as of nature. In which case, in line with the imagery of Israel as God's planting, the root must be Abraham or the patriarchs in general. It is the setting apart of Israel's forefathers, Abraham in particular, which ensures that eschatological Israel will also be holy to the Lord, for they will be heirs of and participants in the same promise (vv 28–29).

The recipients of the letter would probably feel no compulsion to interpret both metaphors of v 16 in precisely the same way; as metaphors all they have in common is the chronological sequence of the two halves in each case. On the contrary, indeed, it is important to recognize the *different* reference of the two metaphors, for they are complementary rather than synonymous. "The mixture" and "the branches" certainly have the same reference—the people of God in its final composition. But "the first offering" and "the root" refer precisely to the two different elements which will constitute God's elect in the end: on the one hand, the Jews and Gentiles who have already believed, and, on the other, historical Israel. The holiness of the end-time saints is dependent both on their continuity with the original Israel and on the word of faith which constitutes the remnant and the gentile mission. In this way Paul maintains his double loyalty, flesh of Abraham's flesh, faith of Abraham's faith, a Jew who is also apostle to the Gentiles, called to proclaim the gospel of God's Son to Jew first but to Gentile as well.

17–24 The last image of root and branches also provides Paul with the transition to the next paragraph, a more extended reflection on the relation of the different branches to each other and to the tree itself. Lest the gentile believers think that the image of Israel as God's planting refers only to the Jews he shows how the metaphor can be elaborated to include them. But lest the Gentile believers think God has now jettisoned the Jews, Paul leaves them in no doubt that the tree in question is Israel itself.

17 The tree is identified as an olive, but in a casual, by-going way. Paul presumably had at the back of his mind the passages which likened Israel to an olive (Jer 11:16; Hos 14:6), but he makes nothing of them. The olive is presumably chosen because it facilitates the metaphor of grafting, not because it is a particularly appropriate image of Israel.

"Some of the branches were broken off"; again the euphemistic use of "some," perhaps to cover any embarrassment at Israel's large-scale rejection of the gospel (cf. 3:3), but perhaps also because in the perspective of salvation-history as a whole it is indeed only "some" (albeit the majority of the present generation) who have been unfaithful and whose salvation he hopes to secure (v 14). Once again the implication is present that prior to this time (the Christ event) the understanding of God's purpose as focused upon and coterminous with Israel was justified. But God has now brought that stage of salvation-history to an end (3:21–22; 10:4). The metaphor necessitates the picture of the branches being broken off by a force external to the tree, and Paul would not flinch from the implication that he is speaking of God's punitive act against Israel, any more than he did in vv 8 and 15, otherwise he could easily have used less punitive imagery such as withering or blight.

"You, a wild olive, were grafted in among them. . . ." Paul uses the singular, turning as it were to address each gentile believer individually, or the typical representative gentile Christian (like the typical spokesman of Jewish presumption in 2:1). Whether or not Paul was aware of the possibility of grafting a wild shoot into a cultivated tree is no more relevant than the identity of the tree as an olive in the first place. What matters is the point being clearly made. Gentile Christians have been given to participate in an established growth, one long cultivated by God while they grew wild. It is only branches which have been cut off, not the whole tree which has been cut down; God has not started afresh from the beginning. The blessings they share with Jewish Christians must be seen therefore as stemming from the source of Israel, from those to whom the covenant promises were first given; it is the same election, the same promises, the very blessings in fact itemized at the beginning of this whole section (9:4–5).

18 The fact that more Gentiles than Jews seem to be accepting the gospel should not be misinterpreted, as though God's choice of Israel was no longer relevant, part of a bygone age. Whatever may be true of some of the branches, God has not abandoned the tree as a whole. He has not reversed the roles, lavishing his horticultural care on the Gentiles while leaving Israel to run wild. He has not turned the tree upside down, as though the Gentiles were now the main support and starting point for his purposes of salvation. Everything all still goes back to his promise to Abraham, his choice of Israel; that still determined the course of his purpose and the character of his call.

19 The gentile interlocutor replies by taking up Paul's own line of thought developed in vv 11–15. The fact that the removal of Jewish branches and ingrafting of Gentile branches are contemporaneous processes is not accidental; rather the one leads to the other, the one was necessary for the sake of the other. Once again Paul does not shirk the hard questions posed by his own convictions. If it is indeed the case that the extension of the call of God and word of faith to the Gentiles was made possible only by Israel's transgression and rejection, does that not imply that God has given the Gentiles higher priority than the Jews? And is that not a ground for at least some gentile boasting over the rejected Jews? Whether Paul was aware of such claims to gentile superiority on the part of the gentile Christians in Rome is not clear; the question can be explained wholly as arising from Paul's own line of thought.

20 Paul does not refute the premise: Jewish rejection was indeed the presupposition of gentile acceptance. But the conclusion is false. An analysis of what is happening solely in terms of God's purpose as perceived from the limited perspective of one's own involvement within that purpose is bound to be inadequate. Man's response to that purpose is also part of the picture, and it is here that attention should be focused. The reason why so many Jewish branches were lopped off is not to be grasped solely in terms of divine fiat, but is rather to be explained from Israel's unfaith. And gentile believers must never forget that their own insertion into the covenant/tree came about through their own faith, and that their continuance within the covenant/ tree is dependent on their continuing faith; Paul here echoes an exhortation with which his readers may well have been already familiar (cf. 1 Cor 15:1; 16:13; 2 Cor 1:24). To rest solely on a partial grasp of God's overall purpose is to make the same mistake as Israel—to presume God's favoritism. Such presumption is not only short-sighted and ill-informed—the one forgets that the election of Israel always had the nations in view from the first, the other is unaware that the call of the Gentiles now has the recall of Israel equally in view for the imminent future; but it is also itself a lapse into unfaith, a failure to maintain that responsive obedience from the heart to divine grace through which God sustains the believer within the covenant. Paul is quite clear that the tension between God's sovereign purpose and human responsibility must never be slackened into presumption, whether the presumption that the law is a platform which lifts Israel above the nations (chap. 2), or the presumption that the dethroning of the law makes obedience irrelevant (chap. 6). For such presumption is the very opposite of the humble trust which relies only on God's power for the fulfillment of his promise (chap. 4).

20c–21 Consequently the appropriate response for the gentile believer to the present stage of salvation-history is not pride in status, but fear—fear not of the Potter (the inscrutable ways of divine providence, or whatever), but fear of the Creator who is also Judge, and whose response to the pride and presumption of the creature will always be one of wrath and condemnation (chaps. 1–2). This is what so many Jewish branches have found to their cost. And if God's electing purpose for Israel can comprehend within it the rejection of so many Jews, if this is the way election and judgment can be seen actually to work out in practice, how much more easily could a few Gentile branches be lopped off without modifying God's overall purpose one whit, and how much more should the individual Gentile be on his guard against the fatal pride.

22 Paul presses home his point in a way which recalls the double aspect of God's electing purpose (9:13–23) and shows still more clearly how fundamental that earlier exposition was for his resolution of the dilemma of Israel's failure to respond to the gospel: "Note then the goodness and severity of God. . . ." Here too we can also see more clearly the extent to which the presuppositions of Jewish presumption have been reversed. The comfortable assumption which Paul exposed in 1:18–3:20, that God's righteousness is to Israel and his wrath to the nations, is now turned completely on its head. God's strict enforcement of his covenant righteousness is now directed against those members of the covenant people who have failed to respond in faith and fallen in the blindness of their false covenant assurance. Whereas his kindness is directed toward the gentile believer—though only so long as he avoids the mistake of the Jewish majority. Paul does not attempt a deeper analysis of the twin aspects of God's outreach to his human creation at this point. It is enough for him to recognize that the two aspects cannot be isolated from each other, that both are in play in the current situation, that Israel's failure is thus still within the scope of God's dealings with humankind, and that therefore faith can indeed trust in God by this double operation to achieve his own purpose in his own time.

The key for Paul is the interlock of grace and faith: to "continue in God's kindness" (v 22) is obviously synonymous with "standing in faith" (v 20) and the opposite of "continuing in unbelief" (v 23). It is when faith responds to God's gracious outreach and remains within that alone (5:2), under that alone (6:14), that it can do its work within the believer. But when grace is met by a faith which (contradiction in terms) no longer depends solely on God's kindness, which ceases to be open to God's reaching out to the other (Gentile or Jew), which assumes grace as a right, hereditary or national, institutional or ritual, then faith has become unfaith, a claim upon God rather than a trust in God, a boasting of presumption rather than a boasting of the creature in humble thanksgiving to its Creator. In this way Paul underlines the precariousness of the gentile believers' situation—precarious because the history of Israel shows how quickly faith can be corrupted into unfaith, how easily grace can be perverted into human presumption. Individual gentile Christians should not assume that what has happened to them is something final and irreversible; the only security derives from a sustained and unreserved reliance on God's grace alone.

23–24 Not surprisingly, given Paul's train of thought, the conclusion to his extended metaphor of the olive tree of Israel is a reversion to the hope of his kinsfolk's restoration to their former place within God's covenant purpose. Not only can the gentile branches be lopped off (if they turn from faith to unfaith), but the old branches can be grafted in again (if they turn from unfaith to faith). For God is able to do it. Paul recognizes how far his exposition is straying from the metaphor, but the horticultural impossibility becomes a way of emphasizing the power of God. Here again grace needs only faith as the opening through which it can pour its life-giving energy to revitalize even branches withered by Israel's false assurance. For if God can perform the physiological impossibility of making Gentiles full members of the covenant people, seed of Abraham and heirs of the promise, how much more easily can the natural seed and heirs be reincorporated into what is actually their own people and their own inheritance. Once again, Paul implies clearly, what he has in mind is by no means a wholly new beginning, but rather a concept of the people of God whose basis and character has been obscured by Israel's misunderstanding, is being discovered afresh through the gospel not least by the Gentiles, and will shortly be reestablished among the rest of Israel as well.

3. The Final Mystery Revealed   (11:25–32)

Bibliography

See also 9:1–11:36 *Bibliography.*

Aus, R. D. "Travel Plans." **Brown, R. E.** *The Semitic Background of the Term "Mystery" in the New Testament.* FBBS 21. Philadelphia: Fortress, 1968. **Davies, W. D.** "People of Israel." 138–43. **Dibelius, M.** "Vier Worte." 14–17. **Feuillet, A.** "L'espérance de la 'conversion' d'Israel en Rom 11:25–32: L'interpretation des versets 26 et 31." In *De la Tôrah au Messie, FS* H. Cazelles, ed. J. Dové et al. Paris: Desclée, 1981. 483–94. **Glombitza, O.** "Apostolische Sorge. Welche Sorge treibt den Apostel Paulus zu den Sätzen Röm 11:25ff." *NovT* 7 (1965) 312–18. **Grässer, E.** *Der Alte Bund im Neuen.* Tübingen: Mohr, 1985. 20–25. **Hahn, F.** "Zum Verständnis von Römer 11:26a: '. . . und so wird ganz Israel gerettet werden.'" In *Paul and Paulinism, FS* C. K. Barrett, ed. M. D. Hooker and S. G. Wilson. London: SPCK, 1982. 221–36. **Hofius, O.** "Die Unabänderlichkeit des göttlichen Heilsratschlusses." *ZNW* 64 (1973) 135–45. **Hübner, H.** *Law.* 81–82. **Jeremias, J.** "Einige vorwiegend sprachliche Beobachtungen zu Römer 11:25–36." In *Israelfrage,* ed. Lorenzi. 193–203. **Luz, U.** *Geschichtsverständnis.* 286–300. **Müller, U. B.** *Prophetie.* 225–32. **Mussner, F.** "'Ganz Israel wird gerettet werden' (Röm 11:26): Versuch einer Auslegung." *Kairos* 18 (1976) 241–55. **Plag, C.** *Israels Wege.* 36–47, 55–61. **Ponsot, H.** "Et ainsi tout Israël sera sauvé: Rom 11:26a: Salut et conversion." *RB* 89 (1982) 406–17. **Refoulé, F.** ". . . *Et ainsi tout Israel sera sauvés": Romains 11:25–32.* Paris: Cerf, 1984. **Reicke, B.** "Um der Väter willen (Röm 11:28)." *Judaica* 14 (1958) 106–14. **Sänger, D.** "Rettung der Heiden und Erwählung Israels: Einige vorläufige Erwägungen zu Römer 11:25–27." *KD* 32 (1986) 99–119. **Schaller, B.** "ΗΞΕΙ ΕΚ ΣΙΩΝ Ο ΡΥΟΜΕΝΟΣ: Zur Textgestalt von Jes 59:20f." In *De Septuaginta, FS* J. W. Weavers (1984). 201–6. **Spicq, C.** "ΑΜΕΤΑΜΕΛΗΤΟΣ dans Rom 11:29." *RB* 67 (1960) 210–19. **Stuhlmacher, P.** "Zur Interpretation von Röm 11:25–32." In *Probleme biblischer Theologie, FS* G. von Rad, ed. H. W. Wolff. Munich: Kaiser, 1971. 555–70. **Stuhlmann, R.** *Das eschatologische Mass im Neuen Testament.* FRLANT 132. Göttingen: Vandenhoeck & Ruprecht, 1983. Esp. 164–88. **Wright, N. T.** *Messiah.* 197–210. **Zeller, D.** *Juden.* 130–37, 245–67.

Translation

²⁵ *For I do not want you to be unaware, brothers, of this mystery, lest you be wise in* [a] *your own estimation, that a hardening in part has come over Israel, until the full number of the Gentiles has come in;* ²⁶ *and so all Israel shall be saved, as it is written:*

> *Out of Zion will come the deliverer;*
> *he will turn away ungodliness from Jacob.*

²⁷ *And this will be my covenant with them,*
> *when I take away their sins.*

²⁸ *With regard to the gospel they are enemies because of you,*
> *whereas with regard to the election they are beloved for the sake*
> *of the fathers;*

²⁹ *For the gifts and the call of God are irrevocable.*

³⁰ *For just as you were once disobedient to God,*
> *but now have received mercy by their disobedience,*

³¹ *So also they have now been disobedient for your mercy,*
> *in order that* [b] *they also might receive mercy.*

³² *For God has confined all* [c] *in disobedience*
> *in order that he might have mercy on all.*

Notes

[a] παρ' was probably introduced in the light of 12:16 and the underlying Prov 3:7; otherwise the replacement of παρά by ἐν (A B) would be the result of a scribe reckoning ἐν the more suitable preposition, and the omission (P⁴⁶ etc.) would have been accidental.

ᵇℵ B D etc. read a third νῦν, "in order that they also might now receive mercy." Others, including P⁴⁶, omit it. Some minuscules read ὕστερον, "later," or better, as superlative, "finally"; but that is an obvious attempt to maintain the sequence: "once," gentile disobedience; "now," Gentiles receiving mercy and Israel disobedient; "finally," Israel receiving mercy. The νῦν would not greatly affect the sense (the "now" time includes two phases; see on 11:31) and is not inappropriate structurally, but is still slightly awkward. A clear-cut decision either way is not possible (Lietzmann, Metzger).

ᶜThe substitution of τὰ πάντα for τοὺς πάντας by some witnesses may have been occasioned by a glance forward to 11:36 or by a recollection of Gal 3:22 (Metzger).

Form and Structure

Paul maintains the style of personal address, but with the second person singular of vv 17–24 reverting to second person plural, retained throughout (vv 25–31). Vv 25–27 have the character of denouement, with the introduction of the revealed mystery as resolution to the problem of divine hardening (πώρωσις), which Paul deliberately introduced and emphasized at an early stage in the discussion (9:18) and reasserted at 11:7, and the reuse of πλήρωμα (11:12). The hope of Israel's salvation (11:26) answers to the thematic statement of 1:16. Plag's counterarguments that vv 25–27 are a secondary insertion misperceive this climactic character of the passage and carry little weight (*Wege*, particularly 41–47); see also Wilckens.

Vv 28–32 are formulated with particular care, both as to rhetorical structure (9 lines laid out, apart from line 3, in a sequence of epigrammatic contrasts; see *Translation* and on 11:28 and 11:30–31) and to provide a fitting summing up and climax to the whole of the preceding argument. The use of ἐκλογή, κλῆσις, and ἐλεέω/ἔλεος gather together the key elements and main thrust of chaps. 9–11 (ἐκλογή—9:11; 11:5, 7; καλέω/κλῆσις—9:7, 12, 24–26; ἐλεέω/ ἔλεος—9:15–16, 18, 23). The repeated contrast between ἀπειθέω/ἀπείθεια and ἐλεέω/ἔλεος (4 times in vv 30–32) rehearses in summary form the indictment of 1:18–3:20 ("shut up in disobedience") and the resolution of 3:21–5:11 ("have mercy"). And v 32 repeats with breathtaking brevity the conclusion of 5:12–21, with the status and role of Israel within the world-wide and history-long purpose of God finally clarified, by an ironic eschatological reversal of the salvation-history pattern of "Jew first and also Greek." Thus the individual and cosmic tension between the epochs of Adam and Christ (chaps. 6–8) is seen to be reflected also in Israel, the people of God divided between disobedience and mercy (chaps. 9–11); and as the resolution of the one is the resurrection (8:19–23), so the resolution of the other is the salvation of Israel, completing the at-last-truly-ecumenical wholeness of God's people likewise in resurrection (11:15).

Comment

11:25 οὐ γὰρ θέλω ὑμᾶς ἀγνοεῖν, ἀδελφοί, "for I do not want you to be unaware, brothers"; see on 1:13. Since vv 23–24 bring the movement of the argument back to the point reached in vv 12 and 15 (see 11:11–24 *Form and Structure*) the γάρ quite naturally picks up not only v 24 as such, but also vv 11–24 as a whole (Cranfield).

τὸ μυστήριον τοῦτο, "this mystery." The most common meaning for μυστήριον in the Greco-Roman world would be in reference to the mystery cults ("the mysteries"—usually in the plural), their secret teachings and rituals, known only to initiates, and kept secret so effectively that we today know little about them; see LSJ, MM, BGD, *TDNT* 4:803–8. Wisd Sol 14:15, 23 and *3 Macc* 2.30 show how widespread would be knowledge of such mysteries; and Philo does not hesitate to use the language of the cults when he speaks of the mind being initiated in the mysteries of the Lord (*Leg. All.* 3.71, 100; *Cher.* 42, 48, 49; *Sac.* 60, 62; *Gig.* 54, 61; *Praem.* 121); cf. Wisd Sol 8:4 and 12:6. Writing from Corinth, Paul would be well aware of the most famous of the Mysteries—that celebrated at Eleusis in Attica. The cult of Attis had been given official status at Rome under Claudius, and we know that the mysteries of Isis were carried out both at Rome and near Corinth (*OCD*; see also on 6:3). But, unlike Alexandrian Judaism, Paul's usage shows no knowledge whatsoever of or interest in the vocabulary of the mysteries. The background which informs his language is exclusively Jewish, and specifically Jewish apocalyptic. For in Jewish apocalyptic language, "mystery" has the sense not of undisclosed secrets, but rather of divine secrets now revealed by divine agency. The sense first occurs in Dan 2:18–19, 27–30 ("God is . . . a revealer of mysteries") and 4:9 Theod. (revealed by the holy spirit of God); so typically also in the classic apocalyptic writings (*1 Enoch* 41.1; 46.2; 103.2; 104.10, 12; 106.19; *2 Enoch* 24.3; *4 Ezra* 10.38; 12.36–38; 14.5; *Gk Ap. Ezra* 1.5; *2 Apoc. Bar.* 48.3; 81.4; *3 Bar.* [*Greek*] 1.8; *3 Bar.* [*Slav.*] 17.1; Rev 1:20; 10:7; 17:5); also *T. Levi* 2.10; *T. Jud.* 16.4; *Par. Jer.* 9.22. In the DSS note particularly 1QS 3.23; 4.18; 9.18; 11.3, 5, 19; 1QH 1.21; 2.13; 4.27–28; 7.27; 11.10; 12.13; 1QpHab 7.5, 8, 14; 1Q27 1.3–4. The divine secrets thus revealed were by no means only about the end of the world (see Brown, 1–30; Rowland, *Open Heaven*) but predominantly so. The means by which the mysteries were unveiled (ἀποκάλυψις) were various: typically by vision or heavenly journey; at Qumran characteristically by interpretation of scripture (F. F. Bruce, *Biblical Exegesis in the Qumran Texts* [London: Tyndale, 1960]); cf. *1 Enoch* 104.12.

In Paul the mystery is the mystery of God's purpose, his intention from the first to include at the last Gentiles with Jews as his people (so recognized by the redactor in 16:25–26); or as he elaborated it subsequently, the mystery is Christ, in whom Gentile as well as Jew is united (Col 1:26–27; 2:2; 4:3; and more explicitly still in Eph 1:9–10; 3:3–6). Paul does not indicate when or how this mystery was revealed to him. But since it is so explicitly related to the problem which Paul himself posed so sharply and gives an answer so distinctive of Paul (vv 25c–26a), it makes best sense to conclude that Paul understood it as a revelation given particularly to himself to make known (cf. 1 Cor 4:1; Eph 3:1–6, 7–9; also 1 Cor 15:51–52 and 1 Thess 4:15); quite possibly through the scriptures, as at Qumran (cf. vv 26–27 and 16:26), but even so with the charismatic givenness which ἀποκάλυψις implies (cf. Michel; Schmidt; Müller, *Prophetie*, 225–32; Dunn, *Jesus*, 212–22; *pace* Cranfield); see also below. Certainly the parallel of Jewish apocalyptic literature is of a revelation given to an Enoch or Ezra or Baruch in order that he might make it known (*1 Enoch* 37.4–5; 91.18; *4 Ezra* 12.36–38; *2 Apoc. Bar.* 81.4–82:1; *3 Bar.* [*Slav.*] 17.1; *Par. Jer.* 9.22–23). The parallel is even stronger since the revelation given in apocalyptic writing was so often in response to the same kind of mystery, the puzzle of Israel's defeat or failure or chastisement (cf.

particularly 1QM 14.9; 16.11; 17.9; 1QH 5.36; 9.23). As the apocalyptist's revelation was a response to the anguished cry "How long?" (Dan 8:13; 9:20–27; 12:6–8; *4 Ezra* 6.59; *2 Apoc. Bar.* 26; and cf. particularly the sequence in *4 Ezra* 10.38–39 and *2 Apoc. Bar.* 81.3–4), so the mystery revealed by Paul provides an answer to the anguish he expressed in 9:1–3 and 10:1. That Paul was moving in the same circle of thought is sufficiently indicated by such parallels as Isa 6:10–13 (see on 11:8); Zech 1:12–17; Rev 6:10–11; *4 Ezra* 4.33–37 and *Apoc. Abr.* 28.3–29.2 (see also Zeller, *Juden,* 249–50; Müller, *Prophetie,* 229–32; Wilckens). The fact that Paul has prepared for this conclusion throughout chaps. 9–11 in no way weakens these parallels (*pace* Sänger, 110–16), since the revelation of the mystery was no doubt given to Paul some time before he wrote this letter and was in part at least the reason for the fervency of his work as "apostle to the Gentiles." NEB's "deep truth" does not catch the full sense of what should therefore be regarded as a technical term.

ἵνα μὴ ἦτε παρ' ἑαυτοῖς φρόνιμοι, "lest you be wise in your own estimation." The text is in doubt (see *Notes*), but the echo of Prov 3:7 may well be deliberate (see on 12:16). For παρά meaning "in the sight or judgment of someone" see BGD, II.2b. As might be expected in a Hellenistic culture which prized rationality, φρόνιμος is a very positive attribute (LSJ). A similar attitude is characteristic in biblical Greek, particularly in the wisdom literature with its commendation of prudence and good sense (e.g., Prov 17:27–28; 18:14–15; Wisd Sol 6:24; Sir 21:24–26; *T. Naph.* 8.10; Matt 25:1–12). But Paul in particular picks up the more jaundiced note of 1 Sam 2:10 (LXX) and Prov 3:7 in his warning against reliance on human wisdom here and elsewhere (12:16; 1 Cor 4:10; 2 Cor 11:19). Here he clearly echoes the warning of v 20 (see on 11:20, and also Barrett), though a reference to Jewish confidence attacked in 2:17–24 is likely too (Wilckens, n.1125), and underscores the implication that the "mystery" about to be unveiled was neither humanly contrived nor perceived by rational power but rather given by divine revelation (cf. 1 Cor 1:18–2:16). Paul may have been aware that what he was about to say would strain credibility.

ὅτι πώρωσις ἀπὸ μέρους τῷ Ἰσραὴλ γέγονεν, "that hardening in part has come over Israel." As with πωρόω (see on 11:7), the metaphorical application of the process by which the extremities of fractured bones are reunited by a callus is biblical, denoting dullness, insensibility, obstinacy (the only three biblical references are Mark 3:5, Eph 4:18 and here). As in its other occurrences in Paul ἀπὸ μέρους should be taken adverbially, that is, with πώρωσις rather than Ἰσραήλ—so "partial hardening or blindness" (BGD, NEB; cf. NIV) rather than "part of Israel" (RSV, NJB); cf. 15:15; 2 Cor 1:14; 2:5. It is not unimportant that Paul still retains a concept of Israel as a unified whole: the people suffering partial blindness, rather than only part of the people suffering blindness; even in his criticism of his people Paul still feels himself to be part of a single people. Likewise, even as "apostle to the Gentiles" he does not hesitate still to use "Israel" in contrast to "the Gentiles," even the believing (fullness of the) Gentiles. See further on 11:7, and for Ἰσραήλ see on 9:4. The perfect tense denotes the continuing state which has afflicted Israel since the new age was brought in by Christ.

ἄχρι οὗ τὸ πλήρωμα τῶν ἐθνῶν εἰσέλθῃ, "until the full number of the Gentiles has come in." ἄχρι οὖ certainly suggests a temporal sequence ("until the time when"), implying that once the full number of the Gentiles has come in Israel's blindness will cease. It does not follow, however, that Paul had a clear perception of the final events as happening in strict sequence or of how the Parousia of Christ was related to Israel's final conversion (vv 26–27). His conviction is simply of a mounting climax with the incoming of the Gentiles as the trigger for the final end in which Israel's conversion, Christ's Parousia, and the final resurrection (v 15) would all be involved. The thought once again is characteristically apocalyptic, expressive of the certainty that events on earth are following a schedule predetermined by God (e.g., Dan 11:36; *Jub.* 1.29; *2 Apoc. Bar.* 48.2–3, 6; see further Russell, *Apocalyptic*, 230–34). In particular, the idea of the number of the elect as planned by God and awaiting completion was one which came strongly to the surface in the second half of the first century A.D. (see particularly *2 Apoc. Bar.* 23.4; 30.2; 75.6; *4 Ezra* 4.36–37; *Apoc. Abr.* 29.17; Rev 6:11; 7:4; 14:1; *1 Clem.* 2.4; 59.2; *5 Ezra* 2.40–41; Stuhlmann, chap. 3). That such an emphasis need not and should not serve as any excuse for human indolence and passivity is sufficiently indicated by the example of Paul himself (11:13–14; 15:14–15; 16:25–26).

For πλήρωμα see further on 11:12. By using the same word Paul presumably intended to indicate that the incoming of the Gentiles would be equivalent to that of Israel (cf. particularly Murray). This is not necessarily an exact numerical equivalence—no attempt is made to specify what "the full number" might amount to (cf. Munck, *Christ*, 133–35; though, as Barrett notes, " 'the number intended by God' might be identical with the 'total number' "; in Revelation the figure 144,000 is, of course, symbolical)—but sufficiently equivalent (as many, or as few) for ethnic origins (Jew or Gentile) to be unimportant (see also Stuhlmann, 173–78). For Jewish expectation of an eschatological conversion and pilgrimage of the nations to Zion, see on 9:26; it is certainly possible that Paul had in mind as part of the Christian variation of this Jewish hope his forthcoming journey to Jerusalem with the collection (so particularly Aus, 242; Hübner, *Israel*, 112–13; see also on 11:12).

The frequency of the verb εἰσέρχομαι in the Jesus tradition in talk of entering into the "kingdom" or into "life" (Mark 9:43, 45, 47 par.; 10:15, 23–25 pars.; Matt 5:20; 7:21; 19:17; John 3:5), its distinctiveness as one of Jesus' characteristic idioms (Jeremias, *Theology*, 32–33), and its infrequency in Paul (only three times elsewhere) make it likely that Paul is drawing here on pre-Pauline tradition which stems from Jesus (Michel, Käsemann, Schlier, Wilckens; but see also Munck, *Christ*, 132; Aus, 251–52; Schmitt, 110, Räisänen, "Römer 9–11," 2922—εἰσέρχομαι from the motif of the incoming of Gentiles to Zion [though none of the passages cited under 9:26 use εἰσέρχομαι]; a continuation of the metaphor of grafting, as Fitzmyer, is less natural). If that is the case, however, it is a tradition charismatically reshaped (see further on 12:14) as part of the revelatory answer given to Paul (see above on μυστήριον); cf. Käsemann (with bibliography). Moreover, Paul has used the spatial imagery of Jesus' formulation to transform the traditional Jewish expectation that the final acceptance of the Gentiles would be a physical pilgrimage to Jerusalem. What marks out Paul's view from that of his fellow Jews (and Jewish Christians?)

is that for him the gentile "incoming" would not establish Jewish superiority (on Israel's terms in effect), but rather the character of God's election, so that in an important sense Israel's restoration is on Gentiles' terms (that is, in terms of grace alone). It is in this way that Paul resolves what Davies rightly calls "Paul's quandary . . . : how to do justice to the historical role of his own people without thereby, *ipso facto*, elevating their ethnic character to a position of special privilege" ("Israel," 147).

26 καὶ οὕτως πᾶς Ἰσραὴλ σωθήσεται, "and so all Israel shall be saved." Following the ἄχρι οὗ, some temporal weight cannot be excluded from καὶ οὕτως (Stuhlmann, 165); but the basic sense of οὕτως is "thus, in this manner," referring to Paul's conviction that conversion of the Gentiles will be the means of provoking Israel to jealousy and converting them; cf. particularly 1 Thess 4:17 (so Zeller, *Juden,* 251; Schlier; Sänger, 107–8; NJB, but obscured in NEB; see brief review of the discussion in Hübner, *Israel,* 110–11; see also on 11:25 ἄχρι οὗ); Feuillet, "L'espérance," 486–87, argues for both modal and temporal significance, citing also 1 Cor 11:28 and 14:25. A reference forward to καθὼς γέγραπται ("and so . . . as it is written") is much less likely (e.g., Müller, *Prophetie,* 226–27; Jeremias, "Beobachtungen," 198–99; Mussner, *Tractate,* 32; against BGD; Plag, 37; C. Müller, *Gerechtigkeit,* 43 n.88; and Stuhlmacher, "Interpretation," 560).

There is now a strong consensus that πᾶς Ἰσραὴλ must mean Israel as a whole, as a people whose corporate identity and wholeness would not be lost even if in the event there were some (or indeed many) individual exceptions (see, e.g., Luz, *Geschichtsverständnis,* 292 and n.114; Mayer, 287–89; Kümmel, *Theology,* 244; Hofius, "Evangelium," 316–18; against the older view that Paul means "all spiritual Israel," still maintained by Ponsot, and Refoulé's consistent attempt to argue that "all" here can only mean "all the remnant"). The idiom is well enough known and should not cause confusion (cf. 1 Sam 25:1; 1 Kgs 12:1; 2 Chron 12:1; Dan 9:11; *Jub.* 50.9; *T. Levi* 17.5; *T. Jos.* 20.5; *T. Ben.* 10.11; Ps. Philo 22.1; 23.1; etc.; and the much-quoted *m. Sanh.* 10.1; see also Plag, 46–47, 58; Hübner, *Israel,* notes particularly Isa 45:25, not to mention the typical hyperbolic description of other Christian writers— e.g., Mark 1:5; Luke 3:21; and Acts 13:24). Here it clearly functions in contrast to λεῖμμα (11:5), and τινές (11:17; Schlier), and indeed ἀπὸ μέρους (11:25), and as parallel to πλήρωμα (11:12) as a broad characterization rather than a specific enumeration (Stuhlmann, 178–81; cf. also the parallel in 5:18–19 between "all" and "the many"). For Paul, who has stressed the power of his gospel to *all* who believe (1:16), that his apostleship was for the obedience of faith among *all* the Gentiles (1:5), and that the promise to Abraham was to *all* the seed (4:16), it was clearly important to be able to say *all* Israel. For other (unlikely) ways of understanding πᾶς Ἰσραὴλ, see Michel, Schmidt, and Cranfield.

The salvation of Israel in the sense of the restoration of those scattered throughout the Diaspora was a common enough theme of Jewish expectation (Deut 30:1–5; Neh 1:9; Jer 23:3; 29:14; Ezek 11:17; 36:24; Mic 2:12; 4:6–7; Zeph 3:19–20; Zech 10:8–10; Sir 36:11; Bar 4:37; 2 Macc 2:18; *Jub.* 1.15; *Pss. Sol.* 17.26–28; 1QSa 1.1–6); the closest parallels in language link the hope of Israel's salvation with the expectation of a royal messiah (Jer 23:5–

6 and 4QFlor 1.11–13). Note again, however, that Paul has inverted the more typically Jewish expectation that the eschatological pilgrimage of the Gentiles would be the final climax and would underscore the triumph of Israel's faith (see references on 9:26); here the restoration of Israel is to be a consequence of the incoming of the Gentiles (see further on 11:25); see also Stuhlmann, 166–73. For σωθήσεσθαι, see on 5:9; here it is climactic of the confidence and prayers which have characterized this section—9:27; 10:1, 9–10, 13; 11:13–14, 26 (Heil). It is, of course, final salvation which is in view, including the redemption of the body and of creation itself (8:19–23; 11:12; Cranfield, against SH).

καθὼς γέγραπται, "as it is written"; see on 1:17, and above on οὕτως. The first three lines of the quotation are more or less verbatim from Isa 59:20–21 LXX.

ἥξει ἐκ Σιὼν ὁ ῥυόμενος, "out of Zion will come the deliverer." The most significant difference from the LXX is that Paul writes ἐκ Σιών instead of ἕνεκεν Σιών, "from Zion" instead of "for the sake of Zion" (MT reads לְצִיּוֹן, "to Zion"; Schaller suggests that a translation of εἰς Σιών was corrupted in transmission to ἐκ, ΕΙΣ being easily misread as ΕΚ). But a deliberate alteration by Paul is quite conceivable: even though he quotes the passage as a foundation or confirmation of his hope of Israel's salvation, he does not wish to rekindle the idea of Israel's national primacy in the last days (Zion either as the physical focus of or sole reason for the redeemer's coming); and, as just noted above, he is in process of transforming—not merely taking up—the expectation of an eschatological pilgrimage of Gentiles to Zion. The point remains valid even if Paul has drawn the phrase ἐκ Σιών from Pss 14 [LXX 13]:7 and 53:6 [LXX 52:7] or from Isa 2:3 (Hübner, Israel, 115–16); these passages simply provide some justification for a modification of Isa 59:20, which had importance for Paul.

A second difference did not involve any textual modification: for Paul ὁ ῥυόμενος is to be understood as a reference to Christ in his Parousia (cf. 7:24, and particularly 1 Thess 1:10), whereas the original reference was probably to Yahweh himself (cf. particularly Jub. 22.14–15); the rabbinic reference of the passage to the Messiah attested in b. Sanh. 98a (Str-B, 4:981; Michel; Cranfield) cannot be traced back to our period with any confidence (see also Zeller). It was specifically Christian faith in Jesus as God's eschatological agent which would give Paul his particular messianic interpretation of the passage. In using ἐκ Σιών, therefore, Paul will have been thinking not of Jesus' origin as a Jew, and so of his incarnation (so rightly Wilckens; against Luz, Geschichtsverständnis, 294–95; Schmidt, Zeller, Räisänen, "Römer 9–11," 2920), but of his eschatological appearance in (and so "from") Jerusalem (cf. 2 Thess 2:4, 8) or of his coming from heavenly Jerusalem (cf. Gal 4:26; Heb 12:22; Rev 3:12; 21:2; Käsemann; Jeremias, "Beobachtungen," 200; Davies, "Israel," 141–42), that is, of Jesus' Parousia (see Hübner, Israel, 114, with bibliography). Since the thought in this section is focused so clearly on the final climax, this is almost certainly the way Paul will have understood the future, ἥξει, as referring to an event (the Parousia) which he expected to play a decisive role in the final turning again of Israel.

ἀποστρέψει ἀσεβείας ἀπὸ Ἰακώβ, "he will turn away ungodliness from Jacob."

ἀποστρέφω, only here in the undisputed Paulines, can have the stronger sense of "remove" (BGD). Paul presumably had in mind the revelatory impact of Christ's second coming which would open Israel's eyes to recognize the nature and climax of God's saving plan. This would also fit well with the typical apocalyptic idea of a secret concealed in the interim to be revealed at the end (see on 11:25). It is partly accidental that ἀσέβεια occurs only here and in 1:18 in the undisputed Paulines, but the result is effective since 1:18 was the heading for the indictment in 1:18–3:20: it is just the ungodliness which characterizes Jew as well as Gentile which will be removed; the impiety which first caused the breach between God and man will be removed, the end achieving the purpose of the beginning. Ἰακώβ is an un-Grecized form of the OT, used quite often in the OT as variant for the more frequent Ἰσραήλ, but used by Paul only in the two OT quotations, here and 9:13; however, Barth, *People*, 43, takes Jacob "of the alienated (northern) part of Israel, viz., of the Jews who stumbled over their Messiah Jesus."

In all this, the suggestion particularly of Plag (49–61) and Mussner ("Ganz Israel," 245–53; also *Tractate*, 34 [qualified in "Heil," 210–13]; cf. Rese, "Römer 11," 430; Gager, *Origins*, 252, 261; Gaston, *Paul*, 148) that the passage envisages a special way of salvation for Israel (the way of the redeemer as distinct from the way of conversion) poses a false and quite unnecessary antithesis (rightly rejected by Mayer, 293–300; Hahn, "Röm 11:26a," 228–29, who notes that banishment of ἀσέβεια = banishment of ἀπιστία = πίστις; Luedemann, *Judentum*, 33–34, who refers to vv 14 and 23; Sanders, *Law*, 196; Schmitt, 221–22 n.765; Hübner, *Israel*, 120; Grässer, *Bund*, 227–29; Hofius, "Evangelium," 319–20—"Israel will come to faith in the same way as Paul himself!" i.e., through a personal encounter with the exalted Christ; Lübking, 125–28—Paul is emphasizing the divine initiative in this saving process, as consistently throughout chaps. 9–11; Sänger, 116–19). At the same time it is nevertheless significant that Paul expresses his confident hope in characteristically Jewish terms, not in terms which were to become distinctive of Christianity. He avoids emphases which might be unnecessarily offensive and offputting to his fellow Jews, and throughout this closing section he expresses his hope in more all-embracing *theo*logical (rather than specifically *Christo*logical) language (see also on 11:36), just as he took care in chap. 4 to express faith in Christ in terms of faith in the creator God (4:17, 24–25; the tension at this point is not so sharp as Räisänen, "Römer 9–11," 2934–35, maintains). "Paul was not thinking in terms of what we normally call conversion from one religion to another but of the recognition by Jews of the final or true form of their own religion" (Davies, "Israel," 142; cf. Feuillet, "L'espérance," 491–92). See also on 9:6.

27 καὶ αὕτη αὐτοῖς ἡ παρ' ἐμοῦ διαθήκη, "and this will be my covenant with them." In Isa 59:21 the talk of teaching given to children and children's children would naturally recall the exhortation attaching to the covenant given at Sinai (Deut 4:9–10; 6:6–7). In this context, the hope of new covenant is probably more accurately described as of renewed covenant, or of old covenant at a more effective level of operation (Jer 31:33; Ezek 36:27). But the language and hope was sufficiently open for Paul and the first Christians to give the concept "new" a more transforming character. At the same time he would want to insist on the *continuity* that the theology of covenant embodied. Not least in importance is the fact that he uses the concept of covenant in Romans only when talking of his own people (cf. particularly Grässer, 23–25; see also *Introduction* §§5.1 and 5.3, and on 9:4; and cf. the uncertainty as to whether or in what sense the sect who wrote the Damascus Document regarded themselves as the community of "the new covenant in the land of Damascus"). Against the view of Zeller and others that διαθήκη should retain the sense of "decree," see Schmidt and Wilckens. The omission of the subsequent lines of Isa 59:21 was not because of any difficulty they caused: Paul would certainly have found talk of God's Spirit and of God's word in their mouth (cf. 10:8–10) amenable to his more explicitly eschatological interpretation.

ὅταν ἀφέλωμαι τὰς ἁμαρτίας αὐτῶν, "when I take away their sins." This last line of the quotation is almost certainly derived from Isa 27:9 with the plural ("their sins") replacing the singular ("his sin"). This interpretative merging of two texts would be quite acceptable in view of the close similarity of theme between the two passages, the previous line of 27:9 also talking about the taking away (ἀφαιρέω) of Jacob's guilt or breach of the law. The association of forgiveness of sins with Israel's final vindication or specifically with renewal of the covenant was sufficiently well established in Jewish expectation (e.g., Isa 4:4; *Jub.* 22.14–15; *Pss. Sol.* 18.5) (see further Str-B, 1:162–65; *TDNT* 4:991–92, 998–99) for Paul's adaptation of it here to be reckoned a justifiable variation (cf. Plag, 50–52). The distance between Paul and more characteristic views of Judaism should not be exaggerated: the cult underlined both the seriousness of sin and the divine provision of forgiveness; warning against presumption on these points was a feature not simply of Jewish prophecy (cf., e.g., Sir 5:4–7; 7:8–10). So once again it is unlikely that Paul was inveighing against a Jewish view of merit earning (as Cranfield); though we may assume that his transposition of the hope of forgiveness from its characteristically cultic and ritual context to the eschatological was a way of reinforcing the crucial interlock of grace and faith in nonnational, nonethnic terms.

28   κατὰ μὲν τὸ εὐαγγέλιον ἐχθροὶ δι' ὑμᾶς,
     κατὰ δὲ τὴν ἐκλογὴν ἀγαπητοὶ διὰ τοὺς πατέρας,
     "with respect to the gospel they are enemies because of you,
     whereas with respect to the election they are beloved for the sake of
       the fathers."

The formulation obviously has a deliberate and strong rhetorical structure. One consequence is the lack of a linking phrase or particle, which would have disrupted the symmetry; but the summary and summing up effect of vv 28–32 is clear enough without it. A more important consequence for exegesis, however, is that precision of form takes precedence over precision of meaning: the prepositions are chosen not because they necessarily mean the same thing each time, but, on the contrary, because their range or diversity or indeed ambiguity of meaning can be expressed in the same preposition + accusative form. Hence the κατά specifies the fact of a relation (to gospel and election) but not the precise nature, and the two διά phrases can be translated differently (as above).

By εὐαγγέλιον Paul most likely has in mind the gospel of which Christ is the content and himself the apostle, as elsewhere in Romans (1:1, 9, 16; 2:16; 10:16; 15:16, 19, 29; 16:25; see further on 1:1). Since the contrast (κατὰ τὴν ἐκλογήν) looks to the original choice of Israel in the age before Christ, the opening phrase κατὰ τὸ εὐαγγέλιον is hardly more specific than as a way of referring to this final phase of God's dealings introduced by Christ in which the proclamation of the gospel has the top priority for Paul. It is less likely that Paul intended his readers to think that Israel's hostility was part of the gospel ("in accordance with the gospel"): the "mystery" which had been revealed to him Paul did not regard as part of the gospel but as a solution to the puzzle regarding the gospel's reception. Most consider ἐχθροί as passive in view of the parallel with ἀγαπητοί (bibliography in Kuss), though an active sense is not excluded (Käsemann; Mayer, 301–2; Wilckens); in which case it is the strong language already used (9:13) which Paul has in mind (cf. 9:18; 11:7–10, 25; and for the idea of God as Israel's enemy see particularly Isa 63:10 and Jer 30:14). But Paul could have intended the active sense to predominate (Zahn, Lagrange, Barrett, Schmidt, Black, Schlier; others in Zeller, *Juden,* 131 n.200), as in his usage elsewhere (5:10; 8:7; 12:20; 1 Cor 15:25–26; Gal 4:16; 5:20; Phil 3:18; Col 1:21; 2 Thess 3:15), since, as already noted, the parallelism is more of form than of meaning (note also Beck's protest, 68–69). δι' ὑμᾶς, of course, sums up the chief thrust of the preceding verses (11–25): in the mystery of the divine purpose it was necessary for Israel to stand outside the gospel for some time, and to experience that hostility to God which is characteristic of humankind in this age (5:10; 8:7), in order that the gospel might be offered to Gentiles as God's free grace to man, not as the gospel of the Jews defined in ethnic terms. Only so could it be open to man as the free gift of forgiveness to an enemy rather than a right of nationality or race; and only so, of course, could Israel rediscover it in its character of free grace to all.

κατὰ τὴν ἐκλογήν, "as regards election," refers not simply to the fact of Israel's election, but to the character of God's choice of Israel as a free and gracious choice (9:11; 11:5; so rightly SH; see further on 9:11 and 11:7). The Israel of Paul's day, in his view, was not beloved of God simply because it was Israel, the physical descendants of the fathers (see again 9:6–7 and 11), but precisely because God's promise to the fathers had this gracious character which regarded even "enemies" as "beloved" (Dodd's criticism of Paul for "trying to have it both ways" misses the point; contrast Barrett; not brought out clearly enough in Zeller, *Juden,* 133–37). To the extent that ethnicity is a factor it is a factor on both sides of the contrast: being seed of Abraham sets them within the sphere of God's love; the false evaluation of that inheritance sets them in opposition to God. For ἀγαπητός see further on 1:7; it is God's faithfulness to his chosen, despite their hostility to his fuller purpose of grace, which is being stressed here (the bald assertion of 3:3–4 has now been explained); Israel's election is a fundamental axiom for Paul which the gospel has not revoked (cf. Haacker, "Evangelium," 71). As most recognize, the διά in the final phrase should not be translated "on account of the fathers," since the parallelism is rhetorical (see above). Hence there are no grounds for seeing any reference to or expression of a doctrine of merits (as implied already in *2 Apoc. Bar.* 78.7 and 84.10) since that would be completely at odds with Paul's conception of election (see also on 2:5 and 4:4–5). For οἱ πατέρες see on 9:5.

29 ἀμεταμέλητα γὰρ τὰ χαρίσματα καὶ ἡ κλῆσις τοῦ θεοῦ, "for the gifts and the call of God are irrevocable." ἀμεταμέλητος, in biblical Greek occurring only here and in 2 Cor 7:10, means initially "not to be regretted" (as 2 Cor 7:10; LSJ), and so "irrevocable," as of something one does not take back (BGD; Spicq 72–74—"force of a legal axiom"). It is given the place of emphasis: once again the stress is on God's faithfulness (Cranfield). The assertion does not run counter to the OT talk of God's "repenting," which is an anthropomorphic way of expressing God's dissatisfaction with human conduct (Gen 6:6–7; 1 Sam 15:11, 35), or most frequently God's withdrawal of a threatened punishment (Exod 32:14; Deut 32:36; 2 Sam 24:16; 1 Chron 21:15; Pss 90:13; 106:45; 135:14; Jer 15:6; 18:8; 26:3, 13, 19; 42:10; Joel 2:13; Amos 7:3, 6; Jonah 3:9–10; 4:2). In contrast, when the biblical writer wants to stress the constancy of God's purpose, he emphasizes the contrast between God and man: God is not like man that he should repent = change his mind (Num 23:19; 1 Sam 15:29; Ps 110:4; cf. Jer 4:28; Ezek 24:14; Zech 8:14); so here (cf. Heb 6:17–18). See further *TDNT* 4:627. Still less can the language be related easily to the Greek ideal of the immutability of God (cf. Philo, *Immut.* 21–22); the Judeo-Christian understanding of God is too essentially personal for that. Here in particular we should note that it is specifically "the gifts and call of God" which are so described, not some property of the divine nature: as always in the OT, the language is used of God in his relation to his creation and in his purpose with regard to his creatures. The link with 9:6 is closer than Zeller, *Juden,* 133, allows, since Paul's whole endeavor is to clarify the character and objective of God's "call" of Israel. Not least, we should recognize an important variation on the central theme of God's faithfulness (πίστις and ἀλήθεια).

For χαρίσματα see on 1:11. Here the concrete enactments of divine grace no doubt refer to or at least include those listed in 9:4–5. κλῆσις (only here in Romans) is correlated with καλέω and κλητός. Paul refers back to his argument in 9:6–29 where the idea of God's call was of thematic importance (9:7, 12, 24–26), including the thought that God's call of Isaac and Jacob (9:7, 11) was characteristic of his summons as Creator (4:17) and of all whom he accepts (8:30), and so of Gentiles as well (9:24–26); see further on 1:1; 4:17; and 8:30. The phrase χαρίσματα καὶ κλῆσις can be taken variously: as two distinct categories (Cranfield); with κλῆσις as the particular and most important of these χαρίσματα (Michel); or as a hendiadys in the manner of Käsemann ("It is the power of God's address and claim which takes place with every charisma. . . . God does not give gifts without calling and vice-versa"). There is no reason to choose between these: Paul would no doubt have been happy to own all three. Since the statement is made as a general principle, the gentile (and subsequent) readers would be justified in applying it more broadly to their own call (1:6, 7) and foundational gifts of grace (5:15-16; 6:23); the continuity of election always includes but is not limited to Israel, since it is a continuity of grace.

30	ὥσπερ γὰρ ὑμεῖς	ποτε	ἠπειθήσατε	τῷ θεῷ
		νῦν δὲ	ἠλεήθητε	τῇ τούτων ἀπειθείᾳ,
31	οὕτως καὶ	οὗτοι νῦν	ἠπείθησαν	τῷ ὑμετέρῳ ἐλέει,
	ἵνα καὶ	αὐτοὶ (νῦν)	ἐλεηθῶσιν.	
	"for just as	you were once	disobedient	to God
		but now have	received mercy	by their disobedience,
	so also	they have now	been disobedient	for your mercy
	in order that	they also might	(now) receive mercy"	

(following Wilckens' layout).

This is the most contrived or carefully constructed formulation which Paul ever produced in such a tight epigrammatic form, with so many balancing elements (ὥσπερ/οὕτως, ὑμεῖς/οὗτοι, ποτέ/νῦν, ἀπειθέω/ἐλεέω [twice] and τῇ τούτων ἀπειθείᾳ/τῷ ὑμετέρῳ ἐλέει) set within a basic chiastic structure. In such a tightly drawn and inevitably somewhat artificial formulation rhythm of clause and balance of phrase is as important as meaning and a degree of ambiguity can be tolerated. Cranfield in particular is unwise to strain for sharply defined alternative renderings, since the construction is precisely one which does *not* press reader or listener to such either-or decisions. Had precision of meaning been important for Paul he would no doubt have readily sacrificed structure for the sake of meaning. But at the climax of a carefully outlined argument there is little fear of a reader being much misled, so that priority can be placed on rhetorical effect.

It is no surprise that the other passage where the ὥσπερ/οὕτως formula is prominent is 5:12, 19 21, since it is such an appropriate means of stating a final balanced conclusion. The point here is that now the place and role of Israel within the larger two ages view of history (Adam/Christ) has been clarified and can be summed up in similar terms: the period of disobedience (Adam's, the world's) includes that of Israel; the period of divine mercy (through Christ, to all/the many) will likewise include Israel.

The ποτέ/νῦν antithesis highlights the salvation-history division of epochs, but with the complicating factor that the eschatological "now" (see on 3:21 and 5:9) includes the period of Israel's disobedience, so that "the now time" (3:21) is subdivided into the two phases: mercy to Gentiles and Jewish disobedience; followed by mercy to Jew as well (hence the problem of the second νῦν in v 31; see *Notes*). If part of the original text, the second νῦν was probably a way of highlighting the eschatological imminence of this second and final phase of "the now time" (Lietzmann; Michel; Stuhlmacher, 567 n.49; Käsemann; otherwise, Cranfield; Zeller, *Juden*, 263; and Schlier).

The emphasis on disobedience (ἀπειθέω [twice], ἀπείθεια) in this final summary formulation is certainly intended to recall not simply 10:21, but also once again the Adamic disobedience expressed in the earlier climax of 5:12–21 by means of the synonym παρακοή (5:19; cf. 2:8) and the preferred antonym ὑπακοή (so also 10:16). Note also that Paul sums up his own mission in terms of bringing Gentiles to "the obedience of faith" (1:5; 15:18; also 16:26). The choice of ἀπείθεια to sum up the epoch of Adam in its continuing effect on Israel even in the epoch of Christ is therefore deliberate: it reinforces the thematic unity of the letter and underlines the fact that the eschatological tension of this overlap of the epochs period is not simply an individual experience (chaps. 6–8) but afflicts whole nations as such.

For ἐλεέω/ἔλεος see on 9:15; as a fundamental category of Jewish covenant confidence its summary use for both Paul's gentile readers and "all Israel" is a further indication that Paul retains his whole comprehension of God's saving purpose for Gentile and Jew within the covenant categories God first laid down in Exod 34:6, properly understood, as Paul would insist, as grace and not as right. In asserting God's "lack of repentance" over his calling of Israel (v 29) was Paul mindful that the much-used formula of Exod 34:6 (see on 9:15) had been expanded in Joel 2:13 and Jonah 4:2 to further describe the mercy of God as a "repenting of evil"?—God's "repenting" of the hardening he inflicted on Israel (v 7) was an expression of the "unrepentance" of his initial choice of Israel.

The τῷ ὑμετέρῳ ἐλέει should certainly be taken with the preceding verb rather than the following ἵνα clause (Dibelius, 15–16; Lagrange). Cranfield's careful argument to the contrary (with SH; Munck, *Christ*, 140; Murray; RSV; NIV; NJB) fails to reckon with two decisive factors: (1) the clear inner chiasmus within the overall chiastic structure of vv 30–31, which is most naturally understood as making synonymous assertions:

$$\text{ἠλεήθητε τῇ τούτων ἀπειθείᾳ}$$
$$\text{ἠπείθησαν τῷ ὑμετέρῳ ἐλέει.}$$

(2) In striving for a more precise parallelism of meaning between the dative phrases, he does not give enough weight to the recognition that the parallel is precisely in the fact of the dative form rather than its meaning, and has the elegantly contrived formulation (vv 30–31) ending with a very awkward ἵνα clause. The two datives can be given different force without disturbing the elegance of the formulation (the difference comes only in translation): the former as instrumental ("by means of their disobedience")—the logic has been clearly explained in the preceding verses (particularly vv 11–12, 15); the latter as dative of advantage ("for your mercy"), completing the synonymous chiastic parallel (so Käsemann; Schlier; Wilckens; Siegert, 174; against BGD, ἔλεος 2b; BDF §196; Lietzmann; Kuss).

The ἵνα of course indicates divine purpose. The most explicit formulation of purpose (ἵνα rather than datives) indicates that it is just this climax to which the divine purpose has been driving throughout.

32 συνέκλεισεν γὰρ ὁ θεὸς τοὺς πάντας εἰς ἀπείθειαν, ἵνα τοὺς πάντας ἐλεήσῃ, "for God confined all in disobedience in order that he might have mercy on all." συγκλείω, "confine or imprison" someone in (εἰς) something (BGD; see also Michel n.18); NIV's "bound over to" is not forceful enough. The closest parallel is Gal 3:22–23; in both cases Paul may have had in mind the language of Pss 31:8 [LXX 30:9] and 78 [LXX 77]:50, 62. To the end, Paul does not relax the strong note of divine initiative in Israel's failure to respond to the gospel, a note which has not slackened throughout chaps. 9–11 (9:13–23, 33; 11:7–25). At the same time he retains the emphasis on human disobedience and so of human responsibility (ἀπείθεια; see on 11:30–31). The echo of the indictment of 1:18–32 with its triple παρέδωκεν is deliberate. For ἐλεέω see on 11:31; as with v 31 the ἵνα indicates that the final and ultimately controlling purpose of God is one of mercy; the puzzle of unbelief and disobedience cannot be resolved except from an eschatological perspective (see also on 9:13). As the ἀπείθεια sums up the first part of Paul's exposition (1:18–3:20), so the ἐλεέω sums up the second (3:21–5:11) (Wilckens); 11:32 thus restates the conclusion of 5:12–21 while reworking its terms to include and resolve the problem of Israel.

The force of the definite article is to contrast the whole or totality with the preceding parts (BDF, §275.7). The πᾶς, so insistent a feature of Paul's expression of the gospel (see particularly 1:5, 16, 18; 2:9–10; 3:9, 19–20, 22–23; 4:11, 16; 5:12, 18; 10:4, 11–13) now provides a fitting element in the final concluding statement: the "all" includes both parties in the preceding verses (you Gentiles, and Israel); Israel has been included in the blanket condemnation of humankind in order that humankind as a whole, including Israel, might be recipients of his mercy in its character as unconditional grace. "The total sweep of the argument of Romans is held together by the theme of the peculiar interaction between Israel's particularity and the universality of the gospel for the Gentiles" (Beker, "Faithfulness," 14). This continuing orientation to the issue of Israel's national distinctives and ethnic differentiation should not be lost sight of: Käsemann continues to operate with a primarily individualistic conception of justification, with the fundamentally corporate dimension of Paul's argument drawn in only in a secondary and awkward way. To Paul here cf. the openness of Wisd Sol 11:23, and contrast the more restricted and less attractive vision of *4 Ezra* 7.20, 59–61 and 8.38, 55 (Zeller). A Christianity which takes the "all" seriously cannot operate with any kind of ethnic, national, cultural, or racial particularism or exclusiveness. In particular the inclusiveness includes Israel (not just the remnant of Israel, as again Refoulé, 229–35): the eschatological people of God does not exclude Israel; a universal (catholic) church without Israel would be inconceivable for Paul (cf. particularly Wilckens); or, more accurately in terms of Paul's whole apologia, "the church has no existence apart from Israel and has no separate identity" (Richardson, *Israel*, 130). While "the all" does not necessarily include every single individual (cf. "all Israel," 11:26), it certainly does not exclude universalism (see particularly Dodd's moving exposition and diagram; also Kuss's brief review of the classic alternatives). It is the openness and inclusiveness of "the all" (not just "both"—Denney; Zeller, *Juden,* 264; against Jeremias, "Beobachtungen," 203), which is more important than a numerical specification (see also on 5:19). With the double emphasis (Cranfield) on the final two words—mercy to all—a highly fitting conclusion is achieved.

Explanation

So far there has been a degree of hesitancy about the arguments pursued by Paul, as though he had been only exploring answers to the pressing problem of Israel's failure. But now as he moves into the last section the tentativeness disappears, and the argument takes on a note of full-blooded conviction. What he had posed simply as a hypothesis on 9:22–23 and more definitely as a possibility of divine power in the sequence of "if" clauses in 11:12–24, he now states as an assured fact. Having so carefully encouraged his readers to recognize the possibility of God's mercy and wrath working together to effect his larger purpose, he now claims boldly that this possibility is what God is actually doing.

11:25 Paul turns as it were from addressing his single gentile interlocutor to address once again the whole community. That it is primarily the gentile majority of the Roman congregations which he has in view, is probably implied by the repetition of his stated concern that they should avoid thinking too much of themselves (cf. Prov 3:7), which echoes the dominant warning of the preceding metaphor (vv 17–24)—though it is by no means impossible that he had the Jewish Christians in view as well, since they would readily assume what is not actually stated in the metaphor, that they were original branches of the olive tree which had *not* been broken off. Either way Paul's concern is to remind them once again of the danger of lapsing into the sort of pride and presumption which (in Paul's view) had cost the majority of their Jewish contemporaries so dearly.

With a fine sense of dramatic climax Paul at last unveils his answer to the problem which has lain unresolved since it first became obvious in 1:18–3:20. Paul calls it "this mystery," a description which would almost certainly give many of those who first listened to his letter a sense of privileged belonging and thrill of anticipation. For the word would inevitably conjure up the idea of a secret known only to those who had been initiated—an overtone not confined to the mystery cults (cf. 1QS 4.6; 1 Cor 2:6–7). By letting them share in this mystery Paul was opening to them one of the deeper secrets of Christianity which was still hidden to those outside the circle of Christ-believers. However, those familiar with Jewish apocalyptic, or indeed with Paul's own usage (as in 1 Cor 15:51), would recognize that Paul intended the word "mystery" in a more specialized sense—not just a religious secret (far less a secret rite), but mystery as *eschatological* mystery, mystery as insight into the events of the end time, into how salvation-history is going to reach its destined climax, into how God is soon to fulfill his final purpose for his people. In Jewish thought such a mystery was unveiled through direct revelation from God (e.g., Dan 2:28–29; *1 Enoch* 103.2; 1QS 11.3–4), perhaps as a revelation of the correct interpretation of scripture (as in 1QpHab 7.4–5). Paul clearly stands wholly within this apocalyptic tradition. He had not solved the puzzle of Israel's lapse by his own intellectual ability or by his skill as an exegete. God had revealed the solution to him, perhaps through the scripture he is about to cite, though it is equally possible that the verses were seen to have such a full eschatological significance only in the light of this revelation received independently of them. Either way, Paul's claim is that God had resolved the puzzle of Israel's failure by revealing to him that Israel's fall always had been part of God's purpose for the climax of history.

The mystery he now invites them to share is precisely the confirmation of the possibility already envisaged. "A hardening has come in part on Israel . . . ." Paul does not attribute the hardening here to God, but in the light of what he has already said (9:18; 11:7) he does not need to. In this summary fashion the mystery of the dark side of election is again affirmed, and again with firm reference to Israel itself. The blindness is partial as both temporary and as afflicting what Paul hopes will in the end be a relatively small proportion of his people.

". . . until the fullness of the Gentiles has come in. . . ." The harshness of God's punitive action against Israel is ameliorated by the setting of a time limit. What had been only implicit prior to this is now spelled out: God's severity against those who fell is limited to a specific purpose and period. As elsewhere in apocalyptic, the specification of a definite time limit (though not in terms of days or weeks or years) heightens the emphasis on divine control: everything is working out in accord with the original plan of God. Within this penultimate phase the object is the incoming of the Gentiles. What was previously expressed in terms of "salvation," "riches," and "reconciliation" (vv 11, 12, 15) is now expressed in terms which echo the typical Jewish hope that in the last days there will be a mass conversion and pilgrimage of the Gentiles to Zion (e.g., Isa 2:2–3; Tob 13:11). The time limit is specified more precisely as the incoming of the *"fullness"* of the Gentiles. In repeating the word used of Israel in v 12 Paul almost certainly implies a degree of complementarity between Jew and Gentile within the eschatological assembly of God's people. But the word also has the advantage of implying an apocalyptic precision which is not yet visible to the recipient of the mystery, and so a (somewhat convenient) degree of vagueness in the details of the future foreseen (cf. *4 Ezra* 4.35–36). Certainly there will be a full measure of the Gentiles, the full number intended by God, but how many that would be Paul does not say—all, many, or only some; he is content simply to specify all that God will call.

26–27 ". . . and so all Israel shall be saved." The climax will be the fulfillment of his heart's prayer (10:1)—Israel's salvation, Israel's restoration to full communion with its God. Whatever is happening to Israel now, Paul has been given the divinely revealed assurance that all will come out right for Israel in the end, that God's faithfulness to his first love will be demonstrated for all to see. Again in this summary statement Paul does not say how it will all come about, but again he does not need to. The way in which the pendulum had swung from Israel to the Gentiles and would swing back again to Israel had already been clearly enough articulated (10:19; 11:11–14): Israel would be saved by being made jealous at the sight of Gentiles enjoying what had been their privileges (9:4–5), and so provoked into abandoning their unbelief in Jesus their Messiah and into acceptance of the gospel (1:16). Paul specifies *"all* Israel," by which he presumably means "Israel as a whole," since it is unlikely that he is now offering a greater definition or more comprehensive hope than that already expressed by the word "fullness" (vv 12, 25). His assured hope and prayer is that those who have tripped over the stone of stumbling have not fallen into irretrievable ruin (9:33; 11:11), but his vision of God's future is not so clear that he can exclude the possibility that some will remain firm in their unbelief (9:23; 11:23).

The scripture he quotes as proof is Isa 59:20–21 fused with a line from Isa 27:9. Whether or not the former was already given a specifically messianic interpretation at the time of Paul, it would certainly be understood to refer to the new age introduced by Israel's rescue and restoration to divine favor. And Paul would obviously link the talk of God making or reestablishing his covenant with the Jeremiah prophecy of a new covenant (Jer 31:31–34; cf. 2 Cor 3:3). Paul would also certainly identify the redeemer as Christ (cf. 1 Thess 1:10), and since he refers the scripture to the eschatological climax he would not be thinking of Jesus' previous historical association with Jerusalem, rather of his Parousia from heaven to Jerusalem or from heavenly Jerusalem (cf. again 1 Thess 1:10; also Gal 4:26). This is the first and only time Paul speaks of Christ's second coming in this letter. He could no doubt assume that it was a well known element in the new movement's teaching (cf. 13:11–14) which needed no fuller exposition in this final summary dealing with a different issue. What role Christ's return would actually play in the end events is by no means clear, not least how it would "turn away ungodliness from Jacob" and how this fitted in with Israel's being provoked to jealousy by the gentile influx. But a lack of clarity and precision on the interrelation of the end events is a feature of the early Christian eschatology and Paul presumably was no wiser on these matters. His contribution to the early Christian eschatological thought at this point is simply in the revelation given to him that Israel's salvation is to be the climax of salvation-history, not a precise schedule or agenda of coming events.

As throughout this brief section, Paul picks up Jewish hopes and language in a marked degree. We have already noted the characteristically apocalyptic expression of Jewish hope in v 25 (the set time for the fulfilling of God's purpose, the incoming of the intended number of Gentiles). In quoting Isa 59:20–21, especially as supplemented by Isa 27:9, he catches hold of two other still more strikingly characteristic features of the faith and hope cherished by many Jews. The one is the confident hope that in the last days the dispersed of Israel would return to the promised land and those who had fallen into error would be restored to righteousness. The other is the emphasis, unusual in Paul but deliberately heightened by the fusion of the two Isaiah passages, on God's forgiveness of sins. This is all the more noticeable because it is not Paul's own preferred way of expressing the gospel (he never speaks of forgiveness as such on his own account, and in this letter at least, "sin" is usually a personified power); Paul here shows himself to be well aware of the strong Jewish assurance that the covenant God of Israel is one "who takes away sins" (Exod 34:7; Num 14:18; Sir 2:11), just as he forgave the sins of David (Ps 32:1–2, already cited at 4:7–8; Sir 47:11). There is no suggestion here, or anywhere else in Romans, that Paul accused his ancestral faith of teaching the need to earn salvation, to merit forgiveness. On the contrary, Paul himself affirms on his own behalf the basic Jewish conviction that in giving the covenant to Israel God had made provision for the covering of sins, and that God would manifest his covenant faithfulness in the last days by rescuing Israel from its impiety and by taking away its sins once and for all.

This complete reversion to characteristic Jewish language and hope might have surprised some of Paul's first readers, but only if they had failed to perceive the degree to which Paul has already transformed both language and hope. For the hope of Israel's restoration as it finally emerges at this conclusion to his theological exposition is now significantly different from anything his non-Christian Jewish contemporaries cherished. For one thing, the covenant is no longer to be defined in nationalistic terms or in terms of observing the works of the law (the Torah rituals and customs distinctive of Israel), as is strikingly expressed in the book of Jubilees (e.g., 15.26–28), or by the Qumran community (particularly 1QSa and 1QM), or later among the rabbis (for whom an intention to obey all the Torah was to be the one real condition for entering the covenant). The other main difference is that for Paul the Gentiles are no longer a lesser breed without the law, either to be exterminated or to come in at the last to learn from Israel and in effect to acknowledge Zion's primacy (as in Isa 2:2–3; *Pss. Sol.* 17.33–35; *Sib. Or.* 3.710–20). The incoming of the Gentiles is now envisaged as *preceding* the restoration of Israel and in such a way that the Gentiles' incoming is educative of Israel, establishing not Israel's superiority but the character of God's election. It is precisely this transposition in order of precedence which, Paul hopes confidently, will make Israel see that the covenant is a matter of grace and faith throughout, not of nationality or cultic ritual, and not something designed to bring renown to any particular nation or city as such. Perhaps this is the point of Paul's alteration of the phrase about Zion: Israel has a precedence in salvation-history which no one can gainsay, but Israel has no claim on an eternal primacy—the deliverer comes "from (heavenly?) Zion," but not "for the sake of (earthly) Zion." It is thus precisely because Israel's hope has been so transformed by the gospel that Paul can take up this characteristic Jewish language at the last: his hope for Israel even when expressed in traditional terms is a hope transformed by the coming of Christ, by the reassertion of grace and by the incoming of the Gentiles already under way.

28 Having thus revealed the mystery of God's eschatological dealings with Israel in clear-cut terms Paul now draws the discussion to an end with a sequence of summary statements in which he seems to be striving for a tightness of epigrammatic expression which both restates the puzzle of Israel's present status and resolves it in a comprehensive overview of God's saving purpose. In a finely balanced antithesis he first poses the paradox of Israel's double status as viewed from different perspectives within salvation history. "As regards the gospel . . . , as regards the election . . . ," denote the two main phases of the divine purpose, or more precisely a defining characteristic of each phase. "The gospel" is Paul's watchword for the phase introduced by Christ, the phase of gentile outreach and Jewish disobedience (1:1–5, 9, 16; 10:16). "The election" characterizes the phase of God's commitment to Israel, only apparently suspended during this time of gospel outreach and gentile incoming, but in fact still sustained in the remnant (11:5, 7), and soon to be fulfilled in its character as an election of grace (9:11; 11:5).

The sharpness of the paradox is expressed in the second element of the antithesis—"enemies/beloved." Paul does not hesitate to express himself in polemical terms. At this time God counts (the bulk of) Israel as his enemies. In part at least, Paul will refer here to the hostility of most of traditional Judaism to the movement which sprang from Messiah Jesus; Paul of all people could hardly avoid thinking of that (cf. Phil 3:6; 1 Thess 2:14–16). But probably his main thought is again of the divine initiative (as regularly in this chapter—

vv 7–8, 15, 17, 19–22). Israel's present languishing under divine disfavor is "for your sake"; for a reason not part of the revealed mystery the extension of the gospel to the Gentiles has depended on Israel's rejection of it and on God's cutting off the Jewish branches. But at the same time, seen from the perspective of election the same Israel is "beloved." Even though the election has been narrowed to the remnant (and believing Gentiles) for the present (11:5, 7), it still has "all Israel" in view. The reason given is "for the sake of the fathers": God has not abandoned the promises given to the fathers; they have not been nullified by Israel's unbelief; God is still faithful.

29 It is this latter half of the paradox which Paul reemphasizes: "for irrevocable are the gifts and the call of God." Paul had expressed his conviction as to God's faithfulness to Israel as long ago as 3:3, but there as a question. The same conviction has clearly been at the base of the whole discussion of this last main section (chaps. 9–11), Paul's unwillingness to concede that God could have abandoned Israel first raising the question regarding Israel's rejection of the gospel and finally overwhelming it. But now at last he states in clear and unambiguous terms what is obviously one of the basic postulates of his faith as both Jew and Christian, reaffirmed no doubt by the mystery revealed to him—that God is faithful to the covenant relationship he first established with Abraham and his seed. God has not withdrawn from the commitment to Israel into which he entered at his own initiative. The word "irrevocable" is given particular emphasis, not as a description of God's character or dealings in general, but with specific reference to his purpose of salvation. He who foresees the end from the beginning does not need to tailor his election to the changing circumstances of Israel's belief and unbelief; rather the course pursued by Israel has to be seen as falling within that original election, part of the original purpose.

By "gifts" Paul presumably refers again to the covenant privileges listed in 9:4–5, but as a general word for all the enactments and manifestations of divine grace his readers might justifiably give it a wider reference (cf. 1:11; 5:15–16; 6:23; 12:6). The word "call" is no doubt deliberately intended to recall the main thrust of the argument in 9:6–29: a call defined in terms of promise and election, not of works; directed to a "no-people," Gentiles as well as Jews; not determined by the ethnic and cultic boundaries of the people Israel. This is the call which Israel first received and which has never been withdrawn. It is this character of God's original call which the incoming of the Gentiles will force Israel to recognize, and in recognizing it they will respond once again unto salvation. Paul no doubt deliberately chooses words ("gifts," "call") which his gentile readers both claimed and rejoiced in and emphasizes that God's original decision to bestow them first on Israel is still in force; for he wants the gentile Christians never to forget that they have entered into Israel's privileges, just as he wants the Gentiles' entering into them to correct the Jewish misunderstanding and misappropriation of them.

30–31 The chiasmus of these verses is even more carefully constructed than the antithesis of v 28, and despite a degree of ambiguity, the meaning is clear. The summing up is posed deliberately in terms of (human) disobedience and (divine) mercy, two concepts at the heart of Jewish self-understanding, and expressed in such a way as to bring out how these concepts have been transformed by the final eschatological sequence of events inaugurated by Christ. The situation of the gentile believers had previously been characterized by disobedience to God—this is the characteristic Jewish view of the Gentiles which Paul shares in common with his fellow Jews at this point. He does not thereby rule out the possibility envisaged in chap. 2 of Gentiles keeping the requirements of the law (2:26), since he refers here to his gentile readership as such. Whether some of them would think of disobedience in general terms (cf. 2:8) or specifically of their time as God-worshipers, when they knew the law but did not submit wholly to it, is not clear. Whatever the precise reference, no one (Paul, his readers, or the Jews at large) would now dispute that his gentile readership's starting point had been a state properly characterized as disobedience.

But that previous situation has now been totally transformed. The gentile members of the Roman congregations have now received mercy, and have done so as a result of *Jewish* disobedience. Paul is here not merely repeating in summary fashion the argument of vv 11–15, but doing so in what some of his fellow Jews would regard as deliberately provocative terms. For the tables have now been completely turned; Jewish assumption of monopoly on divine mercy and of gentile exclusion through disobedience has been turned on its head. Gentile disobedience did *not* disqualify from mercy, and, irony of ironies, what did "qualify" the Gentiles was *Jewish* disobedience.

However, at this point the other half of the chiasmus comes into play. Jewish disobedience leading to the receiving of mercy by Gentiles becomes the pivot on which the course of salvation-history swings back to take in Israel once again. Here too the summary statement of the main thrust of vv 11–27 in the characteristic Jewish language of "disobedience" and "mercy" heightens the paradox and irony. For what Paul calls Jewish disobedience would be regarded by most of his Jewish contemporaries as Jewish obedience. So the turning of the tables is by no means simply a case of Jew and Gentile exchanging roles, but also of Jewish misunderstanding being set right thereby. Paul's confident hope is that the fact of "disobedient" Gentiles receiving mercy will shock his fellow Jews into a recognition that their "obedience" is in fact disobedience to the word of faith (10:16, 21). By coming to see that their exclusive claim to God's covenanted mercy was what was actually *dis*qualifying them from that mercy, they would become open once again to receiving that mercy as sheer mercy, mercy to the *dis*obedient. This interaction of Jewish disobedience, resulting in Gentiles receiving mercy, resulting in Jews at large receiving the same mercy, is already in play, part of the eschatological "now" already in train, and shortly to reach its consummation just as soon as the sound of the gospel already winging its way to the limits of the inhabited world (10:18) has resulted in the incoming of the full number of Gentiles.

32   V 32 appears at first to be simply an even tighter and more comprehensive epigrammatic climax to the final statement (vv 25–32), what might be called, since it uses the terms of vv 30–31, the summary of the summary. "God has made all prisoners in disobedience. . . ." Here again the gentile readers would presumably think of their preconversion state outside the range of God's covenant promise, either through ignorance or choice (God-worshipers not willing to take on the complete works of the law), and of how hearing the gospel had made them aware that they were being disobedient to the truth of God in ways they had not appreciated. This period of being shut up in disobedience like a prison they can now recognize to have been God's means of preparing them for mercy. So too the clause speaks of Jewish disobedience in language which summarizes the preceding statement of Jewish rejection of the gospel, both as an act of transgression and yet as also an act intended by God to open up God's covenant mercy to the Gentiles and so in turn to open up Israel to that same mercy (vv 11–24).

In fact, however, in a quite extraordinary way (extraordinary since only twelve words are involved) the verse actually sums up the principal themes of the whole letter. (1) God's wrath as a handing over of man to his own desires and passions = God's shutting all up to disobedience. Without detracting from man's responsibility for his own acts, without preventing man from pursuing his own ends, God has nevertheless so ordered things (the way things work out at individual and social, human and natural levels) that persons who decide to go their own way regardless of God find themselves more and more confined and hemmed in by the consequences of their decision. A path of disobedience freely chosen becomes more and more shut in and enclosed by that very disobedience. (2) God's justification of the ungodly = God's mercy to the disobedient. In a way never quite so clearly articulated before (most clearly in the earlier summing up in 5:20–21) Paul now indicates how the first two major stages of his argument relate to each other theologically (1:18–3:20 and 3:21–5:21). God has confined human beings to disobedience precisely because it is only to the disobedient that he can show mercy. Men and women cannot receive God's mercy so long as they rely on anything else, their own wisdom or status (by virtue of ethnic identity or cultic practice), so long as they think they are being obedient. To shut them up in disobedience is to bring home to them their own creatureliness, is to open them to mercy. (3) The sustained use of the characteristic Jewish terminology of mercy and obedience into this last verse underscores the claim implicit throughout the first half of the letter and developed most fully in chaps. 9–11, that Israel's peculiar covenant privileges, summed up as God's mercy to Israel, have been extended to all. Now at last we can see the argument of the whole letter set within the full sweep of salvation-history. This is the eschatological "now," the final "in order that," which God always had in view when he first gave his promise to Abraham all these centuries ago—the broadening out of his covenant blessing to all the nations of the world. (4) The twin aspects of God's purpose of election are reaffirmed in one final breathtaking summary— wrath as well as grace, severity as well as kindness, hostility as well as love, confined to disobedience as well as subject to mercy. The history of Israel, as much as that of the Gentiles, reveals the pattern of God's dealings with humankind, shows that it is necessary to recognize both faces of God if any sense and continuity of purpose is to be found in history, confirms that it is possible to contain the most negative of situations within a faith in the one God. The double emphasis of 9:18–23 is thus shown to be not an embarrassing diversionary corollary but actually the key to the whole. And the mystery which resolves the paradox is the revelation that the ultimate purpose is one of mercy: God hardens some in order to save all; he confines all to disobedience in order to show mercy to all. (5) No less striking is the absence from this final summary of any mention of human faith. Of the two notes struck so firmly in the first thematic statement, "from faith to faith" (1:17), it is the note of God's faithfulness which sounds out most loudly and clearly in this final majestic chord—God's faithfulness to Israel sustained through the transposition from the minor key of disobedience to the major key of divine mercy, and in the process revealed and reaffirmed in its original character of grace as faithfulness of the Creator to all his creation, as the final triumph of mercy to all, to Gentile as well as Jew. It is the magnificence of this vision of the final reconciliation of the whole world to God which makes it possible to see here the expression of a hope for universal salvation ("universalism"). But precisely because it is so summary in its expression and so grandiose in its sweep it would probably be wiser to assume that Paul is speaking simply in general terms.

E. A Concluding Hymn of Adoration   (11:33–36)

Bibliography

See also 9:1–11:36 *Bibliography*.

Barth, M. "Theologie—ein Gebet (Röm 11:33–36)." *TZ* 41 (1985) 330–48. **Bornkamm, G.** "The Praise of God: Romans 11:33–36." *Experience*. 105–11. **Deichgräber, R.** *Gotteshymnus und Christushymnus in der frühen Christenheit.* SUNT 5. Göttingen: Vandenhoeck & Ruprecht, 1967. 61–64. **Dupont, J.** *Gnosis*. 91–93, 329–47. **Jeremias, J.** "Einige vorwiegend sprachliche Beobachtungen zu Röm 11:25–36." In *Israelfrage*, ed. Lorenzi. 203–5. **Norden, E.** *Agnostos Theos*. 240–50. **Zeller, D.** *Juden*. 267–69.

Translation

^{33}O the depth of the riches
  and^a the wisdom and the knowledge of God.
  How unfathomable are his judgments
  and incomprehensible his ways.
^{34}For who has known the mind of the Lord?
  or who has been his counselor?
^{35}Or who has given in advance to him
  and it shall be repaid?
^{36}Because from him and through him and to him are all things.
  To him be glory for ever. Amen.

Notes

^{a}The omission of καί in 321 and lat was probably the result of a scribe assuming that Paul intended the phrase to read ". . . the riches of the wisdom and knowledge of God" (so NIV); see also Murray.

Form and Structure

Appropriately, the hope of a truly universal salvation leads into a hymn in praise of the Creator, the unknowability of his ways, and the certainty that he cannot be deterred from the accomplishment of his purpose. Character-istic of the carefully composed nine-line hymn are the exclamatory expressions at the beginning of lines 1 and 3, the rhetorical questions in lines 5–7 and the doxology (Deichgräber, 61). Since there is no Christological reference in the hymn (somewhat surprisingly), it should be classed as a hymn to God, whose closest parallels would be in Rev 4:11; 7:12; 15:3–4; and 16:7. Cf. also the Hellenistic synagogal prayers preserved in the *Apostolic Constitutions* (e.g., 8.5.1–2). The use of triads—the threefold structure (vv 33, 34–35, 36), three words dependent on βάθος, three rhetorical questions in parallel possibly answering chiastically (Jeremias, "Chiasmus," 284) to the three words (γνώσεως —ἔγνω, σοφίας—σύμβουλος, πλούτου —προέδωκεν), and the three prepositional formulae of v 36 (Michel; Deichgräber, 62)—confirm the careful composition of the passage, but afford no foothold whatsoever for a trinitarian interpreta-tion of any part of the hymn such as we find in many of the Fathers (so rightly SH; Lagrange; Bornkamm, "Praise," 109; Murray; Cranfield). The *theo*logical breadth of the assurance expressed at the end of chaps. 9–11 appropriately matches the *Christo*logical focus of the assurance expressed at the end of chaps. 6–8 (cf. Luz, *Geschichtsverständnis*, 300; Morris, "Theme"; Davies, "Israel," 148; Lübking, 153—"the dominating theocentric aspect in Rom 9–11"; note also Beker, *Paul*, 363—"the climax of the history of salvation is not the resurrection of Christ . . . but the impending glory of God"; Hüb-ner, *Israel*, 123–24; M. Barth, "Theologie," 345–46).

The style is Jewish through and through (even v 36a) with v 33 entirely modeled on scriptural language and assertions. Particularly prominent are the links with Job: note especially σοφία—Job 28; κρίμα—Job 40:8; (ἀν)εξιχνίαστος —Job 5:9; 9:10; 13:9; 28:27; God's ὁδός—Job 21:14; 26:14; 28:13, 23; v 34— Job 15:8; v 35 = Job 41:3. The combination of motifs in the OT, in apocalyptic literature, in wisdom traditions, and in Hellenistic Judaism is very striking (cf. Leenhardt). Paul may be making a deliberate attempt to hold together as many different strands of Judaism as possible, and thus to demonstrate both the Jewishness of his message and the breadth of its appeal within Judaism.

There is nothing to show whether the passage was taken over by Paul from a pre-formed Jewish or Jewish-Christian hymn. But there is no reason why he should not have composed it himself, using familiar phrases, texts, and formulae. This latter is made more probable by the number of echoes of language which was evidently much in Paul's mind in dealing with the church at Corinth (βάθος—1 Cor 2:10; σοφία, only here in Romans, and γνῶσις —regularly in the Corinthian correspondence; v 34 = 1 Cor 2:16; v 36 = 1 Cor 8:6). Since Romans was probably written from Corinth such parallels strongly suggest some influence from Paul's involvement at Corinth in his framing this hymn of adoration.

Comment

11:33 ὦ βάθος πλούτου καὶ σοφίας καὶ γνώσεως θεοῦ, "O the depth of the riches and the wisdom and the knowledge of God." For ὦ as an exclamation expressing strong emotion see BDF, §146.2, and BGD, ὦ 3; it should not be regarded as a personifying address to βάθος (against Deichgräber, 62). βάθος here clearly denotes the inexhaustible depths of what follows; cf. particularly 1 Cor 2:10; Rev 2:24; and *1 Clem.* 40.1 (see further BGD); contrast the technical usage in 8:39. For πλοῦτος see on 11:12 and 9:23. The combination of the two metaphors (depth and riches) jars at first, but increases the force of the imagery (a treasury which has no bottom); cf. particularly Eph 2:7 and 3:8. "The thought expressed is of profundity and immensity" (Cranfield). As in Col 1:27 and Eph 3:8 the thought is primarily of the "mystery" unveiled in vv 25–27; cf. particularly 1QS 11:19.

σοφία (only here in Romans; contrast 1 Corinthians, 17x; Colossians, 6x) clearly denotes the wisdom of God in the way he operates in reference to the world, or specifically in the way he brings about man's salvation (1 Cor 1:21; Eph 3:10; *Herm. Vis.* 1.3.4). The thought is still of the mystery of God's saving purpose for all. Paul links here into a deeply rooted Jewish tradition. The wisdom of God in creation, revelation, and redemption is a focal topic particularly in the Jewish wisdom literature (e.g., Job 12:13; 38:36–37; Ps 104:24; Prov 2:6; 3:19; Wisd Sol 7:15, 25–26; 9:2, 4, 6, 9, 17–18; 10:1; etc.; Sir 1:1–10; 15:18; 42:21; also Jer 10:12; 51:15; Dan 2:20–23; *2 Enoch* 30.8; 33.3 [11.21–22]). It is noticeable here that Paul takes up the thought of the hiddenness of divine wisdom (see below) but not that of the personification of divine wisdom (as in Prov 8 and Sir 24; see further Dunn, *Christology*, 168–73), which elsewhere he identifies with Christ (1 Cor 1:24; see further on 11:36). This is presumably because he has in mind the very specific expression of divine wisdom in the "mystery" of vv 25–27.

γνῶσις occurs more frequently in Romans (2:20; 15:14), but again the Corinthians usage dominates (1 and 2 Corinthians, 16x). As an attribute of God it is a natural associate of divine wisdom (Prov 2:6; 30:3; Eccl 2:26; Col 1:9; 2:3; *4 Ezra* 14.40; see further Dupont, *Gnosis*, 92 n.2). Here again the focus will be specific, referring particularly to God's (fore)knowledge of his own, as in 8:29 and 11:2 (see also *TDNT* 1:706, Cranfield, Schlier, Wilckens; and further on 8:29).

ὡς ἀνεξεραύνητα τὰ κρίματα αὐτοῦ καὶ ἀνεξιχνίαστοι αἱ ὁδοὶ αὐτοῦ, "how unfathomable are his judgments, and incomprehensible his ways." For ὡς used in exclamation (as in 10:15), as a feature of hymnic style, see already Pss 8:1, 9; 66:3; 84:1; 104:24; Sir 17:29 (Deichgräber, 61 n.3). ἀνεξεραύνητος occurs only here in biblical Greek (though also in Prov 25:3 and Jer 17:9 Symm.); see also BDF, §30(4). ἀνεξιχνίαστος is almost as rare—only in Job 5:9; 9:10; 34:24; Pr Man 6; also Eph 3:8 and *1 Clem.* 20.5. Both words are taken up in the patristic period (see LPGL). Characteristically Jewish is the talk of God's "judgment" (מִשְׁפָּט)—the axiomatic assumption that God acts justly, as Creator and covenant God, that what he does is right, even when hard to understand (e.g., Gen 18:25; Deut 32:4; Job 40:8; Pss 10:5; 36:6; 111:7; 119:75; Isa 30:18; 40:14; Wisd Sol 17:1; see also *TDNT* 3:924–33; also on 2:2 and 3:8). Käsemann notes that "the righteousness of God and not, as commonly assumed, his love, is the central concept in Paul's theology." ὁδός as a way of acting, conduct, and specifically as "the way [דֶּרֶךְ] of the Lord" is also characteristically Jewish (e.g., Gen 18:19; Exod 33:13 MT; Deut 26:17–18; Pss 81:13; 103:7; Prov 8:22; Jer 32:39; Ezek 18:25–29; Rev 15:3).

The overarching thought of a divine purpose whose wisdom and justice is beyond human comprehension is also characteristic of Jewish thought. So of the hiddenness of divine wisdom (Job 28; Prov 30:1–4; Sir 24:28–29; Bar 3:29–31; Wisd Sol 9:13–16); the link to the next verse is natural, as Sir 42:21 shows. So too the inscrutable character of God's way (Isa 45:15; 55:9; 1QH 7.31–32; *4 Ezra* 3.30–31; 4.2, 10–11; *2 Apoc. Bar.* 14.8; 20.4; 44.6). The thought was particularly common in apocalyptic (*pace* Leenhardt), understandably when so much of it was a response to crisis in Israel's history, when the ruling purpose of God must have appeared especially obscure; in addition to the above, see also *1 Enoch* 63.3; 93.11–14; *4 Ezra* 4.21; 5.36–40; 8.21; *2 Apoc. Bar.* 14.8–11; 75.1–5 (Wilckens rightly criticizes Käsemann and Schlier for describing *2 Apoc. Bar.* 14.8–11 as an expression of resignation [but vv 12–15] and thus contrasting it with Paul). Of course the Jewish wisdom writer believed he had the key to divine wisdom, since wisdom had been given to Israel in the law (Sir 24:23; Bar 4:1) (*TDNT* 7:518). And the apocalyptist had been given his revelation (cf. particularly Dan 2:20–23; and see on 11:25). But all would accept an unknowability about God and his purposes: to accept his judgment and follow his way was not always to understand them. Philo likewise can rejoice in knowing God (through the Logos) while recognizing how little can be known of God (Dunn, *Christology*, 226–27). So here with Paul: even though the mystery has been revealed (v 25), it is the recognition that there is far, far more to God's purposes and actions than human mind can ever take in which is the fitting final thought. "This description of the divine wisdom represents not so much the conclusion of the argument as the assumption that underlies it" (Schlier).

34 The quotation is directly from Isa 40:13 with only minor alteration, though it may show knowledge of a targumic version (Wilckens):

Romans: τίς γὰρ ἔγνω νοῦν κυρίου   ἢ τίς σύμβουλος αὐτοῦ ἐγένετο;
Isaiah: τίς   ἔγνω νοῦν κυρίου, καὶ τίς αὐτοῦ σύμβουλος ἐγένετο;

Similar thoughts are expressed in Job 15:8; Isa 55:8–9; and Jer 23:18. Paul might well have had in mind the whole of the magnificent Isa 40:12–26, with its similar assertion of God's faithfulness and righteousness in the face of bewildering historical circumstances. The γάρ both strengthens what was a natural and appropriate transition of thought and indicates Paul's awareness that he is now citing scripture to give added weight to the thoroughly biblical thought of the preceding four lines. The rhetorical question in this form is characteristic, particularly in post-exilic Judaism (Ps 106:2; Jer 10:7; Sir 16:20; Wisd Sol 9:16–17; 11:21; *Pss. Sol.* 5.3, 12; 15.2; *1 Enoch* 93.11–14; *2 Apoc. Bar.* 14.8–9; see further Deichgräber, 61 n.4). The sentiment is characteristically Jewish and provides no ground for seeing here an implied criticism of claims made by pneumatics (against Michel). Paul may indeed be influenced by the situation in Corinth (see *Form and Structure*), but his use of Isa 40:13 in 1 Cor 2:16 is differently directed, and here once again the lack of Christological focus marks a significant difference (contrast 1 Cor 1:23–24, 30; 2:8). Of course, "wisdom" is God's counselor (as in Wisd Sol 9:4, 9, 17–18); but see on 11:33 (last para.).

35 ἢ τίς προέδωκεν αὐτῷ, καὶ ἀνταποδοθήσεται αὐτῷ: "or who has given in advance to him, and it should be repaid?" "who has given anything to him, so that his presents come only as a debt returned?" (njb)—"a clear climax (vv 34–35) of absurd assumptions" (Bornkamm, "Praise," 107). The quotation from Job 41:3 LXX [EV 41:11a] is markedly different from the LXX, but clearly enough a rendering of the not-altogether-clear Hebrew. Paul's quotation of Job 5:13 in 1 Cor 3:19 also diverges markedly from the LXX, which suggests that Paul either made his own translation of the Hebrew or knew a different Greek translation from the LXX (Lietzmann, Michel). Cranfield, however, notes that his reminiscences of Job 1:1, 8 in 1 Thess 5:22 agree with the LXX. The v.l. of Isa 40:13 is taken from here. προδίδωμι means properly "give beforehand, pay in advance." Paul may intend this meaning since it underscores the impossibility of the thought: even if there was a strongly legalistic strand in the Judaism Paul was opposing (which we have questioned), it would never have gone so far as asserting that good works *preceded* God's covenant grace (cf. Str-B, 3:295). So a polemic against a rabbinic view along these lines (so Michel, Schmidt) is unlikely (rightly Zeller, *Juden,* 268 n.113). At the same time it is possible that he was using this agreed theologoumenon of Jewish theology as a way of underlining his own insistence on grace as a matter of divine initiative from start to finish. ἀνταποδίδωμι, "give back, repay, return," can be used in both a good sense (so here, as also Luke 14:14; 1 Thess 3:9; cf. Luke 14:2 and Col 3:24), or with reference to punishment or revenge (as in the rest of the NT usage—12:19; 2 Thess 1:6; Heb 10:30; cf. Rom 11:9).

36 ὅτι ἐξ αὐτοῦ καὶ δι' αὐτοῦ καὶ εἰς αὐτὸν τὰ πάντα, "for from him and through him and to him are all things." For ὅτι see BDF, §456.1. The use of prepositions like "from," "through," and "to" when speaking of God and the cosmos ("all things") was widespread in the ancient world and typically Stoic. Cf. particularly (1) Pseudo-Aristotle, *De Mundo* 6 (see Nilsson, *Religion,* 297 n.1); (2) Philo, *Spec. Leg.* 1.208; (3) Philo, *Cher.* 125–26; (4) Seneca, *Ep.* 65.8; (5) Marcus Aurelius, *Medit.* 4.23; (6) and the Hermetic *Asclepius* 34; with (7) Rom 11:36, (8) 1 Cor 8:6 and (9) Col 1:16–17.

(1) ὅτι ἐκ θεοῦ πάντα καὶ διὰ θεοῦ συνέστηκε
(2) ἐν τᾷ πάντα ἢ ... ἐξ ἑνός τε καὶ εἰς ἕν
(3) πρὸς τήν τινος γένεσιν πολλὰ δεῖ συνελθεῖν,
   τὸ ὑφ' οὗ, τὸ ἐξ οὗ, τὸ δι' οὗ, τὸ δι' ὅ
(4) Quinque ergo causae sunt, ut Plato dicit:
   id ex quo, id a quo, id in quo, id ad quod, id propter quod
(5) ἐκ σοῦ πάντα, ἐν σοὶ πάντα, εἰς σὲ πάντα
(6) omnia enim ab eo et in ipso et per ipsum
(7) ἐξ αὐτοῦ καὶ δι' αὐτοῦ καὶ εἰς αὐτὸν τὰ πάντα
(8) εἷς θεὸς ὁ πατὴρ ἐξ οὗ τὰ πάντα καὶ ἡμεῖς εἰς αὐτόν
   καὶ εἷς κύριος ... δι' οὗ τὰ πάντα καὶ ἡμεῖς δι' αὐτοῦ
(9) ἐν αὐτῷ ἐκτίσθη τὰ πάντα ... τὰ πάντα δι' αὐτοῦ
   καὶ εἰς αὐτὸν ἔκτισται ... καὶ τὰ πάντα ἐν αὐτῷ συνέστηκεν

See further Norden, 240–50; Dupont, 335–45; Lietzmann; Michel; Wilckens. The use of such typically Stoic language does not, of course, indicate that Paul here becomes a spokesman for Stoic pantheism (rightly Althaus). The language is appropriate to a variety of theistic beliefs, and had already been domesticated within Jewish monotheism, as the use of it by Philo demonstrates. Similarly the referring of τὰ πάντα to God in such passages as Sir 43:27; 1QS 3.15; Philo, *Heres* 36, *Som.* 1.241; 1 Cor 15:28; Eph 3:9; and Rev 4:11; and the use of instrumental language (διά, ἐν or dative) to express God's creative act through, in, or by wisdom (as in Ps 104:24; Prov 3:19; Philo, *Det.* 54; *Fuga* 109; see further Dunn, *Christology*, 165, 189–90, 225, 227). Note also the Christian usage in (7)–(9) and cf. John 1:3; Acts 17:28; Eph 4:6; Heb 1:2; and 2:10. It is unlikely that there is any significance in Paul's use of διά here rather than ἐν, in view of the variations in the above formulations; "in"—(4), (5), (6), (9); "through"—(1), (3), (6), (7), (8), (9) (so also Wilckens; against Käsemann and Schlier).

More striking, once again, is the way Paul confines all the prepositions to God, despite the Christological reference of διά in (8) and (9). This must indicate that Paul saw no conflict whatsoever between ascribing agency in creation to God and ascribing it also to Christ. Presumably therefore they were simply variations of the same formula so far as Paul was concerned. Rom 11:36 thus confirms the implication of 1 Cor 8:6 that ascribing agency in creation to Christ did not conflict at all with his belief in God as one and alone creator, and that the Christology thus expressed was contained within his (Jewish) monotheism. This further implies that the wisdom Christology thus emphasized was basically an assertion of the one Creator God's saving action in, through, and (in a fundamental sense) as Christ; see further Dunn, *Christology*, chap. 6. The absence of a Christological focus in this closing hymn of praise strengthens the view that the preceding doxology (9:5) was likewise retained within uncontroversial Jewish categories.

αὐτῷ ἡ δόξα εἰς τοὺς αἰῶνας, ἀμήν, "to him be glory for ever, Amen." The doxology is a variation on the benedictions used earlier (see on 1:25 and 9:5), and reappears at the end (see on 16:27); elsewhere in the Pauline corpus at Gal 1:15; Phil 4:20; Eph 3:21; 1 Tim 1:17; 2 Tim 4:18; and regularly in Revelation in several variations (see particularly 1:6; 4:9; 5:13; 7:12; 15:3, 7; 19:1). For δόξα see on 1:21 and 9:4. Praise to God in response to insight given into the ways of God is also typically Jewish (e.g., Sir 39:14–16; *1 Enoch* 22.14; 25.7; 27.5; 36.4; 1QS 11.15 ff.; 1QH 7.26–27; *4 Macc* 18.24; Matt 11:25–26 // Luke 10:21).

Explanation

The majestic vision of the full sweep of God's sovereign purpose of mercy in the final summary of the argument (vv 25–32) draws most fittingly from the apostle a paean of praise to this God. The nine-line hymn, which may well reflect its Corinthian origin, does not seek to penetrate more deeply into the mystery of God's purpose. Paul, having caught a glimpse of the measureless majesty of God's mercy, falls back in an awe and wonder which struggles to find expression.

11:33 The first two lines exalt the inexhaustibility of God's riches both of his wisdom and of his knowledge. Paul is very conscious that the divine wealth of goodness and glory previously referred to (2:4; 9:23) is a far from complete picture of God's treasury. The resources which God can draw on for human benefit are limitless and neither Jew nor Gentile Christian has begun to experience their full potential. The hymn speaks particularly of God's "wisdom and knowledge," words hardly used in this letter (contrast 1 Cor). Presumably the problems which focused in this language at Corinth were not evident at Rome, and Paul can use the words simply of God's insight and instruction without fear of stirring up similar misunderstandings. Whatever wisdom and knowledge the believer might claim (cf. 1 Cor 3:18; 8:1; 12:8) he has not even begun to know what God knows or to see what God sees.

Even without reference to v 35, the third and fourth lines seem to echo themes characteristic of Job, and the whole central section of the hymn may well have been originally inspired by meditation on that profound work. The celebration of God's judgments is particularly appropriate at the conclusion of an argument which has strongly affirmed the certainty and justice of God's final judgment (2:2–3, 16; 3:4–6) and the double aspect (wrath and mercy) of his saving purpose. Again the feeling is of one who has been permitted to perceive something of God's ways with humankind, but whose overwhelming impression is that the something is only a passing glance into mysteries too deep to begin to penetrate, too vast even to begin to comprehend. Paul also was quite probably aware of the echoes from Job and may have felt himself, like the ancient poet, as one who had caught a glimpse only of parts of God's ways (the mere edge of his doings), who had heard but a faint whisper of him (Job 26:14).

34 If Job is without peer in his expression of the mystery of divine sovereignty, the majesty of God in his saving purpose is nowhere more magnificently expounded than in the second half of Isaiah. This profound and astonishing proclamation of faith in the God of Judah as the one God (astonishing in face of the disasters to Judah which it presupposes) not surprisingly provides the hymn writer with a further powerful statement of the mystery and self-sufficiency of God's purpose. Where in 1 Cor Paul uses the text to celebrate the privilege of having been given insight into the depths of God and into the mind of the Lord (1 Cor 2:10, 16), here it celebrates the mysteries of God's purpose which mere man can never hope to understand. The very idea of man being able to offer advice to God, let alone to understand enough of God's judgments and ways to be able to evaluate them as more appropriate or less appropriate, is not even worth considering.

35 The dominant influence of Job is reasserted in the quotation from Job 41:11, a saying which would be given particular meaning by the custom of returning favors previously given (cf. Luke 6:32–35; 14:12). The point then is that God owes no one anything, for any favor previously done to him (since everything under heaven is God's in the first place, Job 41:11b). The thought is particularly appropriate in the epilogue to an argument intended to confront and refute the assumption of most of Paul's Jewish contemporaries that God's mercy was their national prerogative, for such an assumption too easily becomes the presumption that God's mercy is Israel's right, something God owes to them, as some later rabbinic statements show.

The most fundamental aspect of Paul's exposition of God's righteousness from faith to faith is well summed up in the slogan, "God is no man's debtor."

36 Where the focus is so exclusively on the supreme majesty and self-sufficiency of God, the Stoic type formula provides a fitting climax: he is the source, medium, and goal of *everything*, the beginning, middle, and end of all that is. In using the same prepositional formulation in 1 Cor 8:6, Paul had divided the functions thus expressed between the "one God the Father, from whom all things and we to him," and the "one Lord Jesus Christ, through whom all things and we through him" (in Col 1:16 he was to use them all of Christ). But here Paul thinks only of God without further definition in terms of Christ—not unnaturally since here it is the impenetrable and incomprehensible nature of God's dealings with man that he celebrates, whereas there his thought was on the revelation of the wisdom of God precisely in, through, and as Christ. Consequently v 36 is probably better seen as an echo more of 1 Cor 15:27–28 despite the closer verbal links with 1 Cor 8:6. Like ben Sira two centuries earlier, Paul wants to bring his attempts to expound the mystery of God's purpose to a conclusion.

> Though we speak much we cannot reach the end,
> and the sum of our words is, "He is the all" (Sir 43:27).

In an argument which began with man's rebellion against God as creator (1:18–25), what could be more appropriate than a final acclamation of God the creator? In the final analysis the election of Israel, the gospel outreach to the Gentiles, the whole course of salvation-history itself, are simply aspects of the most fundamental relation of all, that of the Creator with his creation. To him alone be the glory forever. Amen.

VI. The Outworking of the Gospel for the Redefined People of God in Everyday Terms (12:1–15:13)

Introduction

Paul has now effectively redrawn the boundaries of the people of God—the one God of Jew and Gentile, no longer the boast of Jew as Jew (2:17; 3:29); the covenant promise to all Abraham's seed, not determined by physical descent (4:16; 9:8); "works of the law" in flesh and outward form marking an ethnic identity set aside in favor of "the work of the law written in the heart" by gracious call which knows no social boundaries (2:15, 28–29; 3:20; 9:12; 11:6); a gospel open to all who believe, Jew first but also Gentile (1:16–17), a mercy which embraces all, Jew as well as Gentile (11:30–32). Intrinsic to the older definition of the people of God was the imperative "This do and live" (Lev 18:5), the practical outworking of life lived within the covenant people. With the people of God thus redefined, an equivalent rule of life needs to be formulated, the "walk in newness of life" as over against the walk in the ordinances of Israel's law (6:4), the service in newness of Spirit as over against oldness of letter (7:6), the obedience of faith in accord with the Spirit fulfilling the requirement of the law unconfused with Jewish "works" (8:4). To sketch out such a way of living with particular reference to characteristic and critical issues likely to confront the Roman congregations is the task of this section. In other words, chaps. 12–15 follow naturally from and constitute a necessary corollary to the overall argument of chaps. 1–11; they should not be regarded as a piece of standard parenesis which has no direct material or thematic connection with what has gone before and could have been discarded or wholly reordered without loss (cf. Furnish, *Theology,* 98–106, and Ortkemper, 1–4; against Dibelius, *Tradition,* 238–39; Fitzmyer; Schmithals, *Römerbrief*—originally separate letters; non-Pauline—O'Neill; Minear, *Obedience,* 83–85, thinks chaps. 12–13 continue the address of 11:30–31 particularly to "the strong" in preparation for the appeal to the same group in 14:1 f.).

Seen as corollary to the preceding chapters, the subjects and sequence of chaps. 12–15 become more coherent and meaningful. The obedience called for is taken out of cultic context and cannot be reduced to written formulae (12:1–2). The corporate identity of the eschatological people of God is transposed from the category of ethnic Israel to that of the body of Christ, Paul naturally taking it for granted that inheritance of the promises will have communal and not merely individual expression (12:3–8). The ethic of 12:9–21 reflects the wisdom of Israel set within the context of Jesus' call for a love which knows no barriers. A redefined people of God, no less than ethnic Israel, must address the question of how it should relate to the power structures within which it must live in the age of Adam (13:1–7). The sober advice there offered is undergirded by a reaffirmation of love of neighbor as the sum and substance of the law (13:8–10) and reinforced by the reminder of the imminence of final salvation (13:11–14), where the teaching and character of Jesus is clearly the key to eschatological life yet lived within the realities of the old age. Nor is it any surprise that the most sustained piece of parenesis focuses on the issues of food laws and sabbath, since together with circumcision these two practices most clearly marked out Jews as different from others, a people apart. The confusion of social identity caused by the redrawing of the boundaries of the people of God is well mirrored in 14:1–15:6. There is a rough and unbalanced *abcdcba* structure in the section:

12:1-2	the basis for responsible living, by implication, other than the law;
12:3-8	(the body of) Christ as the social expression of God's people;
12:9-21	love as the fundamental moral imperative in human relationships;
13:1-7	Christians and the powers that be;
13:8-10	love of neighbor as the fulfilling of the law in human relationships;
13:11-14	Christ as the pattern of Christian living;
14:1-15:6	the basis for social intercourse, by implication, other than the law.

Note also the bracketing references to God's mercies/mercy (12:1; 15:9) that link the whole back into the central and concluding emphasis of chaps. 9–11 (particularly 11:30–32), the echoes of 5:3–5 in 12:12 and of 11:20, 25 in 12:3, 16, and the use of link words in the transition between paragraphs: διώκω (12:13, 14), κακός/ἀγαθός (12:21; 13:3–4), ὀφειλή/ὀφείλω (13:7, 8). In view of 13:1–7, the contrast between the more general parenesis of chaps. 12–13 and the more specific issues of chaps. 14–15 should not be exaggerated (Donfried, "False Presuppositions," 127). The echoes of Jesus' teaching (particularly at 12:14, 18; 13:7, 8–10; and 14:10, 13, 14, 17, 18; 15:1, 2) indicate not only a greater dependence of Christian parenesis on the Jesus tradition than is usually recognized (cf. Allison, "Pattern"; *pace* Furnish, *Theology*, 53–58), but also the greater coherence of the section (12:1–15:13) as a whole.

The final paragraph (15:7–13) confirms that the underlying theme of the preceding parenesis has still focused on Jew-Gentile relationships; it also provides an effective conclusion to the body of the letter as a whole, with Christ as the crucial junction between God's continuing faithfulness to his people Israel and the extension of his covenant mercy to the Gentiles. At the same time, the paragraph serves as a transition back to the more personal letter format.

A. The Basis for Responsible Living—the Christian's Worship (12:1–2)

Bibliography

Betz, H. D. "Das Problem der Grundlagen der paulinischen Ethik (Röm 12:1–2)." *ZTK* 85 (1988) 199–218. **Bindemann, W.** *Hoffnung.* 99–105. **Blank, J.** "Zum Begriff des Opfers nach Röm 12:1–2." *Paulus.* 169–91. **Casel, O.** "Die Λογικὴ θυσία der antiken Mystik in christlich-liturgischer Umdeutung." *JLW* 4 (1924) 37–47. **Daly, R. J.** *Christian Sacrifice.* Washington: Catholic University of America, 1978. 243–46. **Deidun, T. J.**

Morality. 97–99. **Dunn, J. D. G.** *Jesus.* 223–25. **Evans, C. F.** "Rom 12:1–2: The True Worship." In Lorenzi, *Dimensions.* 7–33. **Furnish, V. P.** *Theology.* 101–6, 188–89. **Grabner-Haider, A.** *Paraklese und Eschatologie bei Paulus: Mensch und Welt im Anspruch der Zukunft Gottes.* Münster: Aschendorff, 1968. 116–28. **Hooker, M. D.** "Interchange in Christ and Ethics." *JSNT* 25 (1985) 3–17. **Käsemann, E.** "Worship in Everyday life: A Note on Romans 12." In *New Testament Questions of Today.* London: SCM, 1969. 188–95. **Merk, O.** *Handeln.* 157–58. **Mullins, T. Y.** "Petition as a Literary Form." *NovT* 5 (1962) 46–54. **Ortkemper, F. J.** *Leben.* 19–41. **Radl, W.** "Kult und Evangelium bei Paulus." *BZ* 31 (1987) 58–75. **Schlier, H.** "Vom Wesen der apostolischen Ermahnung nach Römerbrief 12:1–2." *Zeit* 74–89. **Schrage, W.** *Einzelgebote.* 49–53, 163–74. **Schweizer, E.** "Gottesdienst im Neuen Testament und Kirchenbau heute." *Beiträge zur Theologie des Neuen Testaments.* Zürich: Zwingli, 1970. 249–61. **Seidensticker, P.** *Lebendiges Opfer (Röm 12:1).* Münster: Aschendorff, 1954. See Esp. 2560–63. **Stoessel, H. E.** "Notes on Romans 12:1–2." *Int* 17 (1963) 161–75. **Walter, N.** "Christusglaube und heidnische Religiosität in paulinischen Gemeinden." *NTS* 25 (1978–79) 422–42; here 437–38. **Weiss, K.** "Paulus—Priester der christlichen Kultgemeinde." *TLZ* 79 (1954) 355–64. **Wenschkewitz, H.** "Die Spiritualisierung der Kultusbegriffe Tempel, Priester und Opfer im Neuen Testament." *Angelos* 4 (1932) 71–230. Esp. 189–91.

Translation

¹*I appeal to you, therefore, brothers, through the mercies of God, to present your bodies a sacrifice, living, holy,* ᵃ*acceptable to God,*ᵃ *which is your spiritual worship.* ²*Do not be conformed*ᵇ *to this age, but be transformed*ᵇ *by the renewal of your*ᶜ *mind, so that you may ascertain what is the will of God, what is good, acceptable, and perfect.*

Notes

ᵃSome manuscripts, including ℵ* read τῷ θεῷ εὐάρεστον, but the sense is very little altered if at all.

ᵇThe imperative rather than the infinitive (συσχηματίζεσθαι, μεταμορφοῦσθαι) has the stronger attestation (including 𝔭⁴⁶ and B*).

ᶜὑμῶν seems to have been added to earlier versions lacking it in order to fill out the sense (see also Metzger).

Form and Structure

Paul begins with an exhortation which summarizes the claim of his gospel (Grabner-Haider, 116–17), which sets out the basis for all Christian lifestyle and relationships, and which deliberately indicates the balance necessary between personal commitment and divine enabling. The opening παρακαλῶ is typical of Paul's style, but also of private and official letters of antiquity, and prepares for his personal requests in 15:14 ff. At the same time the verses pick up previous threads of the discussion in a parenesis which reflects the course of the complete discussion to this point (Furnish, *Theology,* 103–5).

1:24	ἀτιμάζεσθαι σώματα	12:1	παραστῆσαι σώματα
1:25	ἐλάτρευσαν τῇ κτίσει	12:1	τὴν λογικὴν λατρείαν
1:28	ἀδόκιμον νοῦν	12:2	ἀνακαινώσει νοός
2:18	γινώσκεις τὸ θέλημα καὶ	12:2	εἰς τὸ δοκιμάζειν τί
	δοκιμάζεις		τὸ θέλημα

(cf. Evans, "Romans 12:1–2," 31).

The echo of language and categories prominent in chaps. 6–8 is also strong—παραστῆσαι recalling 6:13, 16, 19, σώματα recalling 6:6, 12; 7:4, 24; and 8:10, 11, 13, 23, and the renewed νοῦς recalling 7:23, 25; this is how Christians must live as those being transformed, yet within this age, and within the consequent eschatological tension (cf. Leenhardt). More striking is the sudden use of cultic language (sacrifice, worship), but transformed, and the contrast with 2:18: the service God looks for transcends the bounds of cult—it is the commitment of every day (Käsemann; Ortkemper, 40); and the mode of life illustrated in what follows is determined not by reference to the law, but with an immediacy of perception of God's will.

Comment

12:1 παρακαλῶ οὖν ὑμᾶς, ἀδελφοί, "I appeal to you, therefore, brothers." The weight of the οὖν should not be discounted (as Lietzmann). By using it Paul indicates that the exhortation follows from what has gone before—from chaps. 9–11 as much as from chaps. 5–8 (against Schlier). For a Jew it would be self-evident that faith and theology must come to expression in daily living. What follows is instruction on how the newly redefined people of God should live as such (see further 12:1–15:13 *Introduction*). For ἀδελφοί, see on 1:13. παρακαλῶ has a wide range of usage (BGD, "summon, invite, exhort, encourage, request, entreat, comfort"), as is evident in Paul's own usage (e.g., Schlier). In the sense clearly intended here, it features regularly in the correspondence of the age, being a natural formulation in the direct personal address of a letter ("ask, beseech, urge"—see MM; Mullins compares *P. Oxy.* 292). Since it is such a natural formula, too much should not be made here of its use also in diplomatic correspondence (cf. Ortkemper, 21; see further on 15:30). It may be Paul's polite way of hinting at his apostolic authority "to the Gentiles" to a church which he had not founded, but the disclaimer of 15:20 undercuts that possibility (contrast 1 Cor 9:2). Probably more relevant here is the use of such language in Hellenistic Judaism as evidenced by Sir prologue and particularly 2 Macc (e.g., 2 Macc 2:3; 6:12—παρακαλῶ οὖν; 9:26—παρακαλῶ οὖν ὑμᾶς = diplomatic usage; 12:42). The fact that Paul regards "exhortation" as a ministry which was more widespread within the Christian congregations (12:8; 1 Thess 5:11—παρακαλεῖτε ἀλλήλους; it is not only "apostolic exhortation") should warn us against seeing the language here as a subtle means of exercising extra leverage; the imperative follows from the logic of the gospel (οὖν) rather than from Paul's apostolic commission as such (see further Dunn, *Jesus,* 271–99, particularly 275–80, 291–93, 298–99).

διὰ τῶν οἰκτιρμῶν τοῦ θεοῦ, "through the mercies of God." The plural may partly indicate the different concrete expressions of God's mercy (cf. BDF, §142), but more likely reflects the Hebrew plural רַחֲמִים (as in 2 Sam 24:14; 1 Chron 21:13; Pss 25:6; 40:11; 51:1; etc.; Isa 63:15; Dan 2:18; 9:9, 18; Hos 2:19; so in Paul's other usage—2 Cor 1:3 and Phil 2:1; singular, Col 3:12; see also Lietzmann). The emphasis on divine mercy confirms the connection of thought with the preceding section (11:30–32; e.g., Gaugler, Leenhardt), despite the different Greek words used (in the prophets the root רחם is rendered by both words), and reinforces the οὖν (otherwise, Evans, 10–12). The διά could therefore have the force of "with appeal to" or "in the name of" (cf. 15:30) (Käsemann), but as with the similar διά appeals elsewhere in Paul (12:3; 15:30; 1 Cor 1:10; 2 Cor 10:1), διά here probably has more of an instrumental force (Furnish, *Theology*, 102; see also Schmidt): Paul's authority in making the appeal is grounded in and expressive of his own experience and role as agent of God's mercy (11:13–14, 22, 30–31) (but against Furnish, this strengthens the link with the preceding context); cf. 12:3—διὰ τῆς χάριτος τῆς δοθείσης μοι; and see also Schlier, "Wesen," 78–80.

παραστῆσαι τὰ σώματα ὑμῶν θυσίαν, "to present your bodies a sacrifice." παρίστημι here is certainly drawn from the technical language of sacrifice = "offer or present a sacrifice" (παριστάναι θυσίαν), a usage already well established in Greek literature and inscriptions (see MM, BGD, παρίστημι 1d, Lietzmann, Lagrange, Michel, Cranfield). The sacrificial allusion helps explain the use of σώματα rather than μέλη ("limbs, parts"), as in 6:13, 19: the sacrifice is the body in its wholeness and not just its individual elements. But, of course, the exhortation amounts to the same thing: the σῶμα is the collectivity of the μέλη (v 4; 1 Cor 12:12, 14). This parallelism with 6:13 also underlines the regularly made observation that σῶμα clearly stands here for the person: παριστάνειν ἑαυτούς (6:13, 16) = παραστῆσαι τὰ μέλη ὑμῶν (6:13, 19) = παραστῆσαι τὰ σώματα ὑμῶν (12:1). σῶμα in this sense (almost = reflexive pronoun, "your very selves" [NEB]) does occur in Greek literature (BGD, 1b; *TDNT* 7:1026, 1030, 1039–40), despite the more dualistic character of Greek anthropology, though for that reason it is usually regarded as more typical of the wholistic character of Hebrew anthropology, despite the fact that σῶμα has no consistent Hebrew equivalent (*TDNT* 7:1045); but in the LXX cf. Prov 11:17, Job 6:4; 19:26 (A); 33:17; Sir 51:2; Dan 3:95 (*TDNT* 7:1048); and in the Pauline corpus cf. particularly Phil 1:20 and Eph 5:28; also untypically Greek is the thought of σῶμα as an acceptable sacrifice to God (Wenschkewitz, 191). The point to be emphasized, however, is that σῶμα denotes not just the person, but the person in his corporeality, in his concrete relationships within this world; it is because he is body that man can experience the world and relate to others (Käsemann; Grabner-Haider, 122–27; Schlier; Wilckens; Ortkemper, 23–24). It is not to be thought of in contrast to an "inner consecration" (cf. Gundry, *Soma*, 35; Deidun, 98–99), but as the physical embodiment of the individual's consecration in the concrete realities of daily life (Seidensticker, 258; Schrage, 49), a "somatizing" rather than a spiritualizing (Radl, 62; see also on 6:6). It is as part of the world and within the world that Christian worship is to be offered by the Christian (cf. Bindemann, 102–3).

θυσίαν ζῶσαν ἁγίαν εὐάρεστον τῷ θεῷ, "a sacrifice, living, holy, acceptable to God." The figurative use of sacrificial language is widely attested, both in Jewish and wider hellenistic literature, often in criticism, implicit or explicit, of reliance on a superficial ritual performance (e.g., Pss 50:14, 23; 51:16–17; 141:2; Prov 16:6; Isa 1:11–17; Mic 6:6–8; Sir 35:1; Tob 4:10–11; 1QS 9.3–5; 2 Enoch 45.3; see further TDNT 3:186–89). There is an important difference, however. In Jewish critique of a false reliance on sacrifice it was assumed that ritual sacrifice was still necessary: the importance of the cult is clearly indicated in such passages as 2 Macc 1:19–22; 3:32–39; Jub. 50.11; Ep. Arist. 88; Sib. Or. 3.573–79; and by the flow of temple tax from the diaspora to maintain the daily sacrifice in Jerusalem; the Qumran sect had by no means rejected the cult itself (see the Temple Scroll!), and even after the destruction of the temple the rabbis show by their continuing concern to regulate for qodašin ("hallowed things") that they regarded the current state of affairs as essentially temporary. Likewise, hellenistic critique of bloody sacrifice was basically a sophisticated attitude among the intelligentsia and continued alongside the regular sacrificial practice of state, city, and cult (TDNT 3:188), or expressed an anthropological dualism foreign to Christian and to Jewish thought as well (see below on λογικήν). The earliest Christian groups in the cities of the diaspora, however, must have stood out as strangely distinctive by the fact that they practiced no sacrificial ritual, named no one as priest, and looked to no temple like that at Jerusalem (cf. Walter, "Christusglaube," 437; contrast inter alia the five examples of ἱερεύς, "priest," in the Jewish inscriptions from Rome—Leon, 192–93). In other words, unusually their use of sacrificial imagery implies a replacement of ritual sacrifice and indicates an assumption that the death of Jesus had been a final sacrifice to end all sacrifices (but see also on 3:25), though a reference to Christ's sacrifice as such does not seem to be present here (pace Seidensticker, 262). The subsequent dominance of θυσία in reference to the Eucharist in the Fathers (see LPGL, θυσία 6) represents something of a regression from Paul's eschatological perspective. See also on 15:16.

The ζῶσαν is probably chosen to contrast the thought of a sacrifice which consists in the quality of daily living, "a constant dedication" (Murray), with a sacrifice which consists in killing an animal (Denney, Kirk, Gaugler, Ortkemper, 24; cf. Sib. Or. 8.408). Here we should recall that σῶμα is not used with reference to sacrifice in the LXX, nor does it occur in Paul in the quite proper Greek sense "corpse" (TDNT 7:1048, 1060). Both points underline the implied contrast being made by Paul: the thought of sacrifice has been transposed across a double line—from cultic ritual to everyday life, from a previous epoch characterized by daily offering of animals to one characterized by a whole-person commitment lived out in daily existence. So a cross-reference to 6:4 is quite in order—ἐν καινότητι ζωῆς—in contrast, we might add, to 10:5.

ἁγίαν maintains the cultic imagery, the sacrifice as essentially set apart to God (see on 1:7). For the thought of the sacrifice as God's property see particularly Philo, Spec. Leg. 1.221 (cited by Cranfield, 599 n.3). ἁγίαν as such does not have ethical content (Käsemann); that comes rather from the context and as a consequence of "belonging-to-God-ness."

εὐάρεστος, "acceptable, pleasing," almost always with reference to God;

this is the case in its only two LXX references (Wisd Sol 4:10; 9:10; also *T. Dan.* 1.3; classically of Enoch—cf. Gen 5:22, 24; Sir 44:16; Wisd Sol 4:10) and in its other Pauline references (12:2; 14:18; 2 Cor 5:9; Phil 4:18; Col 3:20; also Heb 11:5–6; 12:28; 13:16, 21; only Titus 2:9 otherwise). Cf. particularly Phil 4:18 and 1 Pet 2:5, not obviously baptismal in character (despite Käsemann). Paul perhaps would have in mind those prophetic passages which speak of the unacceptability of sacrifice to God (Hos 8:13; Amos 5:22; Mic 6:7; Mal 1:8, 10, 13).

τὴν λογικὴν λατρείαν ὑμῶν, "your spiritual worship," "your reasonable religion." The phrase stands in apposition to the whole preceding phrase (as almost all agree). The continued use of cultic language is clearly deliberate: of the nine occurrences of λατρεία in the LXX, eight refer to Jewish cultic worship (*TDNT* 4:61; Schlier; see on 9:4). λογικός does not occur in the LXX, but is a favorite expression of Greek philosophical, particularly Stoic, thought, in the sense of "belonging to reason, rational." As such it marks out what is appropriate to man, in distinction from beasts, and what relates him to God; cf. particularly Epictetus 1.16.20–21: "If I were a nightingale, I should be singing as a nightingale; if a swan, as a swan. But as it is, I am a rational being (λογικός εἰμί), therefore I must be singing hymns of praise to God." This sense naturally lends itself to a spiritualizing antithesis between rational and physical; Philo's blend of Stoic and mystical emphases provides a number of examples (e.g., *Opif.* 119; *Leg. All.* 1.41, 70–72; 2.22–23; *Det.* 82–83), not least in his treatment of the laws of sacrifice in *Spec. Leg.* 1.201, 277 (see further in Cranfield, and Evans, "Romans 12:1–2," 18–19); note also *T. Levi* 3.6 (the worship in heaven is a rational and bloodless offering), and *Ap. Const.* 7.34.6, 7.35.10, 7.38.5, 8.9.8, 8.12.17, 8.15.7, 8.41.4. All these probably indicate Jewish usage prior to Christian appropriation (note particularly that 8.9.8 thinks of man as a rational being by virtue of the law given him, implanted and written). Elsewhere the language is more explicitly Christian, often framed in the light of Rom 12:1 (see *Ap. Const.* 2.25.7 and 6.23.5; and further *LPGL*, λατρεία 8; also the intense spirituality of *Odes Sol.* 20.1–3). The Hermetic writings also take up the same language, including not least the talk of "spiritual sacrifice" (λογικὴ θυσία: 1.31; 13.18, 21—texts in Lietzmann, 133–34, and Cranfield; ET in R. M. Grant, *Gnosticism: An Anthology* [London: Collins, 1961]), but it is doubtful whether Lietzmann and Reitzenstein (*Mystery Religions*, 415–16) are justified in the conclusion that Paul is using specifically Hermetic technical terms here. A broader usage in Hellenistic Judaism has already been indicated ("Stoic language mediated through the Hellenistic synagogue"—Barrett; also Gaugler). More to the point, Paul has in view *not* simply a worship offered by the mind, but, in *contrast* to the Hermetic devotion, a worship expressed in the bodily reality of everyday living (Schlier; cf. Leenhardt); similarly *mutatis mutandis* in contrast to Philo (Ortkemper, 33). The implied contrast with ritual worship (Murray) should again not be overplayed (Cranfield, Wilckens), but again not be disregarded (cf. particularly Käsemann, and see above on θυσίαν ζῶσαν . . .); if Paul is indeed trying to set out alternative identity markers for the new community of Christians (see 12:1–15:13 *Introduction*), the worship here will be *distinct* from the cultic hallmarks of traditional Judaism (against Casel, 45). The distinctively comparable language of 1 Pet 2:2, 5 (τὸ λογικὸν ἄδολον γάλα . . . πνευματικὰς θυσίας εὐπροσδέκτους τῷ θεῷ) may well have been influenced by Paul (Käsemann). The thought of "spiritual worship" as that which is consistent with the truth revealed in Christ (Cranfield) reads too much into the wording here, though of course it follows from the overall context and from διὰ τῶν οἰκτιρμῶν τοῦ θεοῦ (TDNT 4:143) in particular. At this point, however, it would be closer to Paul's thought to say that the worship he calls for is λογική as being proper for man the creature—the logical expression of his creatureliness properly understood, and lived out (in contrast to 1:21, 25). Evans, "Romans 12:1–2," 20–22, and Betz, "Problem," 212, understandably resist the rendering "spiritual" and prefer "rational"; but NEB ("by mind and heart") and NJB ("as sensible people") lose more than they gain.

2   καὶ μὴ συσχηματίζεσθε τῷ αἰῶνι τούτῳ, "and do not be conformed to this age." There has been considerable discussion (see, e.g., Lagrange) as to whether the verb formed round the root σχῆμα carries the implication of a superficial, external transformation, with a large consensus strongly of the opinion that the two verbs συσχηματίζεσθαι and μεταμορφοῦσθαι are more or less synonymous in Koine Greek (cf. particularly 2 Cor 3:18, μεταμορφούμεθα . . . εἰς δόξαν, with Phil 3:21, μετασχηματίσει τὸ σῶμα . . . σύμμορφον τῷ σώματι τῆς δόξης αὐτοῦ; and see further especially Cranfield). More note, however, should have been taken of the typically Pauline compounding of σχηματίζεσθαι with συν-, which has the force of "form oneself after another, be formed like" (LSJ, BGD); cf. 1 Pet 1:14. What is warned against therefore is not so much the superficiality of such a transformation as the fact that it is a transformation which takes something else (other than Christ?) as its pattern, in this case this present age. Even less is there the thought of the superficiality of this age (which we find in 1 Cor 7:31). The passive form (though NEB, NIV, and NJB, and also Evans, "Romans 12:1–2," 27, take it as middle) indicates recognition of a power or force which molds character and conduct and which "this age" exercises; Paul in effect recognizes the power of social groups, cultural norms, institutions, and traditions to mold patterns of individual behavior. The present imperative, however, indicates that human responsibility is also involved—that the individual can accept or resist such power structures, can acquiesce in or resist such behavior patterning: "stop allowing yourself to be conformed . . ." (Cranfield). Harrisville's formulation is helpful: "'conform' refers to a posture or attitude that may be changed at will, whereas 'form' at the heart of 'transformed' refers to what grows out of necessity from an inward condition."

ὁ αἰὼν οὗτος, "this age," is used a number of times by Paul (1 Cor 1:20; 2:6, 8; 3:18; 2 Cor 4:4; also Eph 1:21; with other variations, cf. especially Gal 1:4; 1 Cor 3:19; 5:10; and 7:31). Clearly implied is the contrast of Jewish eschatology between the present age and the age to come. But that inference must at once be qualified by several facts: Paul does not himself use the antithetical term "the age to come" (only in Eph 2:7); there is some question as to whether Jesus used the contrast (Matt 12:32; Mark 10:30 // Luke 18:30; Luke 20:34–35; but lacking in the parallels); the contrast only seems to become explicit in Jewish apocalyptic writing in the classic post-A.D. texts (עלמא—4 Ezra 6.9; 7.12–13, 50, 113; 8.1; 2 Apoc. Bar. 14.13; 15.8; 44.11–15; cf. Sim.

Enoch = *1 Enoch* 48.7; 71.15); and the earliest rabbinic attestation is in *m.* *'Abot* 2.7 (but attributed to Hillel) and *Gen. Rab.* 44 (attributed to Johanan ben Zakkai) (see fuller data in Dalman, *Words,* 147–56; *TDNT* 1:204–7). All this suggests a formulation which came to prominence in the second half of the first century A.D., of which Paul is one of our earliest witnesses. At all events, the language is clearly Jewish in origin (cf. LSJ, αἰών II.2).

It should be noted that what Paul calls for here is *not* some sort of escape from or abandoning of "this age/world"; such an interpretation would fly in the face of v 1 ("when God claims our bodies in and with them he reaches after his creation"—Käsemann; see on 12:1, and see also Schlier). But it could invite a nonconformity to ecclesiastical structures if and when it became clear that they themselves had come to conform too much to the structures and character of this age.

ἀλλὰ μεταμορφοῦσθε τῇ ἀνακαινώσει τοῦ νοός, "be transformed by the renewal of the mind." The idea of metamorphosis is common to many religious strands of the ancient world, including the classic myths about the gods changing into earthly form, and accounts of individuals being transformed through mystery ritual or gnostic release (as in Apuleius, *Met.* 11.23–24; *Corp. Herm.* 13.3; fuller details *TDNT* 4:756–57). But that should not be taken to imply that Paul here is using "mystery-conceptions" (as again Reitzenstein, 390). For the language could be used in the sense of a moral transformation (as in Seneca, *Ep.* 6.1), a stronger form of μετανοεῖτε (Lietzmann). Moreover, the idea is equally found in Jewish apocalyptic, initially with regard to the resurrection (Dan 12:3; *1 Enoch* 104.6; 1 Cor 15:51–53; Phil 3:21; Mark 12:25; *4 Ezra* 7.97; *2 Apoc. Bar.* 51.5), but also as something consequential upon one being taken up to heaven while still alive, particularly Enoch (*1 Enoch* 71.11; *2 Enoch* 22.8; *Asc. Isa.* 9.9). The eschatological context of Paul's thought already indicated by his talk of "this age" (see above) indicates that the Jewish apocalyptic usage is the more likely source of his language.

All this simply highlights the transformation in the ideas themselves which early Christian and Pauline thought effected. (1) It is a transformation already in train, as also in 2 Cor 3:18; 4:16–5:5; and Phil 3:10–11; this is a fundamental aspect of the Christian reshaping of Jewish eschatology to take account of the eschatological significance (the Already) of Christ's own death and resurrection, resulting in the overlap of the ages in which Christians found themselves (see further chaps. 6–8 *Introduction*). (2) Consequently it happens, in accordance with Jewish eschatological hope, as part of the future age, but at the same time, in accordance with the Christian reshaping of that hope, *within* this age as well—not by seeking to escape from it (in some mystical ascent; hence 2 Cor 12:1–10). To reexpress the thought here in the slogan "Become what you are" (as *TDNT* 4:759; Schlier) forgets the character of tension and not-yetness which is the consequence of this overlapping of the ages and which is expressed here in the present tense. The passive is the usual voice in the whole range of usage, but here, of course, it indicates that the source and power of such a transformation is wholly and solely God's.

ἀνακαίνωσις, "renewal," occurs only in Christian literature (that is, first in Paul; see *TDNT* 3:452–53). The combination of the ideas of "transformation" and "renewal" may indicate some sort of balance of continuity and discontinuity with what was before. There is a continuity of the subject; but fundamental attitudes must be changed and new perspectives taken up. In view of the εἰς τό . . . clause, the renewal is necessary for Jew as well as Gentile (see below). The fact that the parallel uses of the verb in Paul (2 Cor 4:16 and Col 3:10) are in the present tense reinforces the observations of the preceding paragraph. The immediate source of the renewal is not specified, but if asked Paul would almost certainly have referred to the Spirit (2 Cor 3:18; 4:16 bracketed by 4:13 and 5:5; Titus 3:5, the only other NT usage; cf. *Herm. Vis.* 3.8.9). It is not very helpful to ascribe the language to "cultic-sacramental thought" (Michel; so Schlier, Ortkemper 37), since Paul's thought is of a continual activity of the Spirit on the mind.

With νοῦς, Paul (21 of the 24 NT occurrences come in the Pauline corpus) once again uses terminology which had specific value in Stoicism, Philo, and the Hermetica (*TDNT* 4:954–58). Paul, however, uses it in the still more widespread sense to denote man's rationality (understanding, mind, attitude, way of thinking, . . . —BGD; see also Schlier), as that which distinguishes human beings from the rest of creation. Unlike these other systems, the higher or divine order is not to be summed up merely in terms of reason. There is no mind/body dualism in Paul; "renewal of mind" is bound up with "presenting of bodies" (v 1). Although a higher part of humanity's created-ness, νοῦς, like ψυχή ("soul"), is a more neutral term which can express man's fallenness (1:28; Col 2:18; Eph 4:17; also all three references in the Pastorals— 1 Tim 6:5; 2 Tim 3:8; and Titus 1:15) as much as his renewal (cf. 7:23, 25; 14:5; 1 Cor 1:10; 2:16). It is the πνεῦμα ("spirit") which is the Godward side of man, more than νοῦς (cf. 1 Cor 14:15 and Eph 4:23 [also Phil 4:7], though elsewhere they do overlap—cf. Rom 1:9; 7:6 and 25; in Paul the πνεῦμα/ νοῦς distinction is equivalent to Philo's understanding of a higher and lower mind in man; see also on 7:23). This emphasis on inner transformation, or better, on a transformation which works from inside outwards (to that extent there may be some thought of contrast between μορφή and σχῆμα; see on συσχηματίζεσθε above), is characteristic of prophetic parenesis; but in Paul it becomes a way of distinguishing the Christian emphasis from the too ethnic, law-centered spirituality of contemporary Judaism (see on 2:28–29, and fur-ther below—δοκιμάζειν). The contrast with and reversal of the more sweeping indictment of 1:28 (see *Form and Structure*) is also notable (Furnish, *Theology*, 103–4). Here again the too quick referral of the thought to baptism can obscure the point.

εἰς τὸ δοκιμάζειν ὑμᾶς τί τὸ θέλημα τοῦ θεοῦ, "so that you may ascertain what is the will of God." The outworking and test of inward renewal is ethically responsible conduct (εἰς τό . . .). δοκιμάζειν usually has the sense of "test, examine, approve" (see on 1:28; "test and approve"—NIV; "discern"—NEB, NJB). Here what is in view is something more charismatically immediate than formal—"the capacity of forming the correct Christian ethical judgment at each given moment" (Cullmann, *Christ and Time*, 228; cf. Dodd, 189); cf. particularly Phil 1:9–10 and 1 Thess 5:21; so also Eph 5:10, 17. At this point it overlaps with διακρίνειν as used in 1 Cor 14:29 (cf. 1 Cor 2:13–15; 12:10; *Did.* 11.7), as the equivalent use of δοκιμάζειν in 1 John 4:1; *Did.* 12.1; and

Herm. Man. 11.7, 16 confirm. This probably also indicates that Paul has in mind a corporate and not merely individualistic process (cf. Ortkemper, 38); hence the continuity to the next section. It must be judged highly probable that in this opening basic statement of the foundation for Christian ethics Paul intends to pose a contrast with the equivalent claim of his fellow Jewish religionists as characterized in 2:18—γινώσκεις τὸ θέλημα καὶ δοκιμάζεις . . . — the point being that the more characteristically Jewish claim rests on the law— . . . κατηχούμενος ἐκ τοῦ ἱέῦ νόμου. The central thrust of v 2 therefore coheres with that of v 1: Paul holds forth a different (eschatological) spirituality (not cult-focused) and ethic (not law-determined) for the Roman congregations. That is not to say that he encourages an antinomian ethic: the objective is still "the will of God"; and the emphasis is parallel to that of Jer 31:31–34; Ezek 36:26–27; and Wisd Sol 9:9–10, 17–18. Rather, like these writers, Paul recognizes that a personally prescriptive motivation has to come from constant inward renewal, without, however, denying the law its role as moral yardstick and norm (see further Dunn, *Jesus*, 222–25). See also 14:22. For θέλημα see on 2:18.

τὸ ἀγαθὸν καὶ εὐάρεστον καὶ τέλειον, "the good and acceptable and complete." As in 2:10 and 7:12–13, 18–19, Paul uses ἀγαθός as signifying what all people of spiritual and moral sensibility would approve; in view of the other wisdom parallels in this verse (see above and below) Paul may have in mind particularly its frequent use in wisdom literature (cf. Michel; see HR). ἀγαθός becomes something of a link word in what follows (vv 2, 9, 21; 13:3–4). τὸ εὐάρεστον is probably substantive here (so most; against Dodd)—that is, not an adjective describing God's will, since εὐάρεστος elsewhere almost always means "acceptable to God" (see on 12:1), but another way of describing what God wants. τέλειος (only here in Romans; elsewhere in Paul of persons, except 1 Cor 13:10) has the force of "having attained the end or purpose, complete, perfect" (BGD). Here too Paul will have been conscious of the widespread use of this category in Greek thought, and of the equivalent concept in the OT ("unblemished, undivided, complete, whole") (see *TDNT* 8:67–72). Given the charismatic thrust of Paul's thinking here he may be distancing himself somewhat from both the Greek attitude (as does Wisd Sol 9:6) and the idea of a blamelessness which is either cultically characterized (the unblemished sacrifice) or which consists in walking according to the statutes of the law (contrast the DSS references in *TDNT* 8:73 with 2:28–29 and 7:6). Since what is in view here is also described as "God's will," we should cf. particularly Matt 5:48, and note the sense of τέλειος in reference to the gods as "having power to fulfill, efficacious" (LSJ II; *TDNT* 8:68).

Explanation

With chaps. 9–11 Paul has completed his main theological exposition. What should follow? Those in the Roman congregations who already knew his style would expect him to turn to some practical counsel. For obvious reasons. All the major religious and philosophical systems recognized the need to provide practical guidance for daily living: the need to cope with the mysterious

and frightening and unexpected, and with the realities of power and powerlessness in the first-century Mediterranean and Middle Eastern world was a principal driving force in these systems. And Judaism in particular was as much
or more a way of life than a system of belief ("faith" = faithfulness). For
Paul, however, it was not simply a matter of stringing together a set of moral
imperatives, as so often in the Jewish wisdom tradition (though there will
be an element of that—12:9–21). Nor could a simply personal or individual
ethic serve. In the letter so far Paul's chief concern has been to redefine the
relation between Jew and Gentile within the saving purpose of the one creator
God. And that has involved a redrawing of the boundaries and redefining
of the characteristics which mark out the people of God. Since ethics and
communal relationships were part of these boundaries and distinctive characteristics, his task cannot be completed unless he carries on the process of
redefinition into the sphere of ethics.

For the great mass of the Jewish people it was the law which served both
as the *ethnic* boundary and as the *ethical* framework: the people of God were
those who lived "within the law," "under the law," performing the works of
the law as maintaining their membership of the covenant ("covenantal
nomism"). Paul had called this understanding of the law in question: the
boundary marked by the law and by the physical rite of circumcision no
longer existed for him (2:28–29); works of the law which demonstrated Jewishness no longer counted (2:23; 3:20, 27–30). Faith in Christ is the new boundary,
circumcision of the heart by the Spirit is the real mark of the true Jew, of
eschatological membership of God's people (2:28–29; 3:21–26; chap. 4). The
line of the covenant is by election, not by flesh, through God's call, not through
works of the law (9:6–13). Righteousness is not exclusive to Israel over against
the Gentiles, but is *God's,* to all who believe (10:3–13), to Jew first but also
Gentile, to Jew as well as Gentile (11:17–32).

But the law served also as an *ethical* framework: "the man who does these
things shall live his life by them" (10:5). To live within the boundary of the
law meant also following the rules laid down by the law, the rules for life,
for social relationships within the boundary and also for relationships with
those outside the boundary. In calling into question the role of the law in
defining Israel's *ethnic* boundary had Paul not also destroyed it in its role as
providing an *ethical* framework? Having redrawn the boundaries of the people
of God, what redefinition of the ethical characteristics of the people of God
is also required?

It is this sort of logic which evidently governs the movement of Paul's
thought as he turns from theological exposition to parenesis. His task now:
in the light of that exposition, to redraw some of the principal ethical guidelines,
to provide a sufficient indication of the ethical and social expression of the
corporate identity of the eschatological people of God.

12:1 Paul signals his concern and objective by immediately resorting to
cultic and sacrificial terminology: "hand over yourselves as sacrifices . . . your
spiritual worship." For ritual is an important part of group identity: in the
ancient world too, cultic and sacrificial ritual regularly served to express national identity and loyalty, and participation in a group's distinctive cultic
rituals marked the participant as belonging to the group. So Israel's sacrificial
system was one of the main ritual expressions which marked out and main-

tained Israel's covenant distinctiveness as the people of God. But Paul's redefinition of the people of God had in effect removed that boundary marker. In reworking the role of the law in reference to the eschatological people of God what was to be done with the extensive sections of the law which deal with sacrifice and the centrality of the Jerusalem cult? Paul immediately provides the answer: he takes up cultic terms in order to redefine them too. The sacrifice God looks for is no longer that of beast or bird in temple, but the daily commitment of life lived within the constraints and relationships of this bodily world. The boundary of cultic ritual is transposed from actual cultic practices to the life of every day and transformed into nonritual expression, into the much more demanding work of human relationships in an everyday world.

Roman congregations would see Paul's point without much difficulty. They could hardly help but be aware of their own distinctiveness over against the typical *collegia* and synagogues of Rome precisely on this very issue. In their case it was the *lack* of a sacrificial ritual (not even a libation), or of obligation to a national temple in Jerusalem, which marked them out. Paul's use of cultic language was nicely calculated to reassure his readers that despite what other groups had in the way of cult and sacrifice they themselves were not disadvantaged: they could render the sacrifice which God wanted and the appropriate worship. The emphasis on a spiritual sacrifice was of course not new, but in Paul's case and that of the early Christian congregations, it was not a matter of "both . . . and" (observe the sacrificial system, but recognize that God wants something more), but rather of encouraging the idea of a different kind of community, marked by self-giving *without* an accompanying sacrificial cult. At the same time Paul's insistence that such sacrifice must take concrete bodily expression prevents his thought degenerating into a mere unworldly pietism or enthusiastic dualism.

2 Nor is it surprising that the main concern of the second exhortation is knowledge of the will of God. For to live in tune with the divine, however conceptualized, was a fundamental objective for all religious and quasi-religious systems of the age. And again, particularly in Judaism, life in accordance with the will of God was as good a summary of the overall obligation of the people of God as any other. For Judaism, however, that meant simply walking in the ways of God, that is, according to the commandments and statutes of God, or, in a word, in accordance with the law.

Here too, then, Paul spells out the equivalent obligation of the redefined people of God. In particular the echo of 2:18 is hard to ignore. Paul had characterized "the Jew" as confident that he knew God's will and could discern the right order of priorities by virtue of his being instructed in the law. Here, no doubt deliberately, he uses the same language: the objective is still discerning the will of God. But no longer is that a matter of observing all the statutes of the law. For the eschatological people of God it is rather a matter of recognizing the eschatological tension of living between the two ages: on the one hand, resisting the danger of adapting too much to the norms and values of this age, and on the other, of submitting to the power of the risen one to renew from within. As earlier (particularly 6:4; 7:6; and 8:4) the alternative to dependence on written formulations is a charismatic immediacy of dependence on God.

To Paul's readership, living in Rome itself, the pattern of "this age," both the quality of personal ethics and the working of social and political and religious power would be obvious, at least in broad outline. The alternative model for transformed living is not specified here, but that Christ was both the pattern and source of this renewal and transformation is clear enough and had been indicated with sufficient clarity in chaps. 6–8. The renewal which gives insight into God's will is described as "renewal of the mind"— once again, not in antithesis to practical everyday living ("present your bodies . . . be transformed by renewal of your mind . . ."), but as a reminder that for Paul spiritual renewal of the people must begin in the inwardness of a person (cf. 2:29) and must include not least the person's power of thought and reason. Neither Paul nor his readers would see this as a soft option or open door to irresponsibility: to ascertain the will of God is never easy, and far less so when it is recognized that God's will cannot be reduced to a set of rules and regulations; the key, however, is the willing and eager submission of the creature to live out of his dependence on God—to seek to *know* God's will as the first objective, and his enabling for the still harder task of *doing* it.

With this combined emphasis on commitment to and dependence on God, marked out in distinction from the more typical Jewish reliance on cult and law, Paul has set out the basis for responsible living and for the more specific parenesis which follows.

B. The Body of Christ as the Social Context of Faith   (12:3–8)

Bibliography

Aune, D. *Prophecy in Early Christianity and the Ancient Mediterranean World.* Grand Rapids: Eerdmans, 1983. **Baumert, N.** "Charisma und Amt bei Paulus." In *L'apôtre Paul,* ed. A. Vanhoye. Leuven University, 1986. 203–28. **Best, E.** *One Body in Christ.* London: SPCK, 1955. **Bosch, J. S.** "Le Corps du Christ et les charismes dans l'épître aux Romains." In Lorenzi, *Dimensions.* 51–72. **Brockhaus, U.** *Charisma und Amt: Die paulinische Charismenlehre auf dem Hintergrund der frühchristlichen Gemeindefunktionen.* Wuppertal: Brockhaus, 1972. **Cranfield, C. E. B.** "μέτρον πίστεως in Romans 12:3." *NTS* 8 (1961–62) 345–51. Repr. in *Bible.* 203–14. **Dubarle, A. M.** "L'origine dans l'Ancient Testament de la notion paulinienne de l'église corps du Christ." *SPCIC* 1:231–40. **Dunn, J. D. G.** *Jesus.* 211–12, 227–33, 236–38, 249–52, 262–65, 285–86. **Forbes, C.** *Prophecy and Inspired Speech in Early Christianity and Its Hellenistic Environment.* Macquarie University Ph.D., 1987. **Grau, F.** *Der neutestamentliche Begriff χάρισμα, seine Geschichte und seine Theologie.* Tübingen Ph.D., 1946. **Greeven, H.** "Propheten, Lehrer, Vorsteher bei Paulus: Zur Frage der 'Ämter' im Urchristentum." *ZNW* 44 (1952) 1–43. **Hainz, J.** *Ekklesia.* 181–93, 259–65. **Hanson, P. D.** *The People Called: The Growth of Community in the Bible.* San Francisco: Harper & Row, 1986. 438–51. **Hemphill, K. S.** *The Pauline Concept of Charisma.* Cambridge University Ph.D., 1976. 164–96. **Herten, J.** "Charisma— Signal einer Gemeindetheologie des Paulus." In *Kirche im Werden,* ed. J. Hainz. Munnich: Schöningh, 1976. 57–89. **Jewett, R.** *Anthropological Terms.* 201–50, 302–4. **Judge, E. A.** "Demythologizing the Church: What Is the Meaning of 'The Body of Christ'?" *Interchange* 11 (1972) 155–67. **Käsemann, E.** "Ministry and Community in the New Testament." *Essays on New Testament Themes.* London: SCM, 1964. 63–94. ———. "The Theological Problem Presented by the Motif of the Body of Christ." *Perspectives.* 102–21. **Klaiber, W.** *Rechtfertigung.* **Menoud, P. H.** "Church and Ministry According to the New Testament." *Jesus Christ and the Faith.* Pittsburgh: Pickwick, 1978. 363–435. **Meuzelaar, J. J.** *Der Leib des Messias.* Assen, 1961. **Oepke, A.** *Das Neue Gottesvolk.* Gütersloh: Gütersloher, 1950. **Ortkemper, F. J.** *Leben.* 41–85. **Percy, E.** *Der Leib Christi (Σῶμα Χριστοῦ) in den paulinischen Homologoumena und Antilegomena.* Lund: Gleerup, 1942. **Ridderbos, H.** *Paul.* 369–76, 393–95, 438–67. **Robinson, J. A. T.** *Body.* 55–58. **Schrage, W.** *Einzelgebote.* 136–40, 141–44, 179–86. **Schulz, S.** "Die Charismenlehre des Paulus." In *Rechtfertigung,* FS E. Käsemann, ed. J. Friedrich et al. Tübingen: Mohr, 1976. 443–60. **Schürmann, H.** "Die geistlichen Gnadengaben in den paulinischen Gemeinden." *Ursprung und Gestalt.* Düsseldorf: Patmos, 1970. 236–67. ———. ". . . und Lehrer: Die geistliche Eigenart des Lehrdienstes und sein Verhältnis zu anderen geistlichen Diensten im neutestamentlichen Zeitalter." In *Dienst der Vermittlung.* Erfurter Theologische Studien 37. Leipzig: St. Benno, 1977. 107–47; and published separately. **Schweizer, E.** *Church Order in the New Testament.* London: SCM, 1961. Esp. 99–104, 181–89. ———. "Die Kirche als Leib Christi in den paulinischen Homologumena." *Neotestamentica.* Zürich: Zwingli, 1963. 272–92. **Unnik, W. C. van.** "The Interpretation of Romans 12:8: ὁ μεταδιδοὺς ἐν ἁπλότητι." In *On Language, Culture and Religion,* FS E. A. Nida, ed. M. Black and W. A. Smalley. The Hague: Mouton, 1974. 169–83. **Wedderburn, A. J. M.** "The Body of Christ and Related Concepts in 1 Corinthians." *SJT* 24 (1971) 74–96.

Translation

3 *For I say, through the grace given to me, to all who are among you, that you should not think too highly of yourselves beyond what you ought to think, but observe proper moderation, as God has measured to each a measure of faith.* 4 *For just as in one body we have many members, and all the members do not have the same function,* 5 *so we all are one body in Christ, and individually members of one another—* 6 *having charisms which differ in accordance with the grace given to us, whether prophecy in proportion to faith,* 7 *or service*[a] *in service, or he who teaches*[a] *in teaching,* 8 *or*[b] *he who encourages in encouraging, he who shares with sincere concern, he who cares with zest, he who does acts of mercy with cheerfulness.*

Notes

[a] Some later scribes substituted ὁ διακονῶν for διακονίαν for obvious reasons, whereas A goes the opposite way by reading διδασκαλίαν in place of ὁ διδάσκων.

[b] p[46] apparently and others certainly follow the same natural trend of attempting to achieve greater consistency, by dropping the last εἴτε.

Form and Structure

Significantly, the first example Paul gives of living by immediacy of divinely given discernment is the mutuality of charismatic ministry within the body of Christ, the eschatological equivalent to the cultic assembly of Israel. The opening recalls 1:5 and the grounds on which Paul makes the appeal (as apostle to the Gentiles). The emphatic warning against inflated thinking (v 3) recalls the similar warning against Gentile presumption in 11:7–24 (particularly 11:20), but also the similar theme of the earlier diatribes against Jewish presumption (chaps. 2–4): the "us" over "them" attitude which Paul saw as the heart of Jewish failure and as a potential danger for Gentile Christians must not be allowed to characterize the eschatological people of God. The "measure" is always the faith which all can exercise. The body imagery of vv 4–5 summarizes the lengthier treatment of 1 Cor 12, with the charismatic functions of the body put in more general terms of acts of ministry regularly offered than the more targeted lists of 1 Cor 12.

There is a rhythmic structure in vv 3–5 (two sets of four lines) which probably indicates a pattern of parenesis worn smooth by regular use. In vv 6–8 the exhortation regarding the seven kinds of charisms listed becomes increasingly telegraphic in style. Again it will not be accidental that the first of the seven replaces the old tension between prophecy and law with a prophecy expressive of faith, while the list climaxes in the gift of showing mercy (reflecting in the everyday life of human relationships the salvation-history climax of 11:30–32).

Comment

12:3 λέγω γάρ, "for I say." As is generally recognized, the formula has an imperative ring (BGD, λέγω II.c, Lietzmann, Michel, Schmidt, Käsemann); cf. particularly 2:22 and 12:1 with 12:3, and 1 Cor 7:8 with 7:10. But perhaps it would be more accurate to speak of a warning note spoken with prophetic authority or authority of divine revelation, as in Gal 1:9 and 5:2; also Matt 3:9 // Luke 3:8 and Luke 13:3, 5; cf. *Jub.* 36.11, *1 Enoch* 91.18; 94.3, 10; 102.9 (see further Müller, *Prophetie*, 132–36).

διὰ τῆς χάριτος τῆς δοθείσης μοι παντὶ τῷ ὄντι ἐν ὑμῖν, "through the grace which has been given to me, to all who are among you." "Grace given to me" is a regular Pauline usage (15:15; 1 Cor 3:10; Gal 2:9; also Eph 3:2, 7; cf. also Rom 12:6—"grace given to us"). It expresses the dynamic quality of χάρις—a sense of commission and enabling. Paul uses it appropriately here, since in this sense it begins to overlap with χάρισμα—χάρις as the divine commission and enabling which comes to concrete expression in χάρισμα (see on 12:6). Here too he clearly has in mind the χάρις already spoken of in 1:5— the grace which came to expression in his apostleship—hence again the note of authority (see on λέγω above). But hence also is the courteous indication that his "grace" is no different in kind from the "grace given" to them too (12:6; cf. 1:11–12). Paul speaks as a charismatic to charismatics. See further on 1:5; also Schlier. The παντί is emphatic, and the emphasis heightened by the slight awkwardness of the phrase. It suggests that Paul at least sees the possibility of factional tension (compounding the Jew-Gentile tensions), such as he knew too well in the Corinthian church on the subject of charisms; cf. particularly 1:7, and the slight polemical or apologetic edge in 1:16; 2:1; 3:9, 22–23, etc.

μὴ ὑπερφρονεῖν παρ᾽ ὃ δεῖ φρονεῖν ἀλλὰ φρονεῖν εἰς τὸ σωφρονεῖν, "not to think too highly of yourselves beyond what you ought to think, but to think sensibly."

In a classic formulation which would find a ready echo with the more literate members of the Roman churches Paul plays on the φρονεῖν root, and nicely distinguishes a self-understanding which goes beyond what is fitting from one which displays good judgment. The basic meaning of φρονεῖν is "to think, form or hold an opinion, have an understanding," but the term can be given a more particular and often negative force by its context (LSJ, BGD). In the NT this is almost wholly Pauline; see on 8:5; elsewhere in Romans—11:20; 12:16; 14:6; 15:5 (for some unexplained reason Heil translates it by "strive"). It is especially frequent in the phrase μέγα φρονεῖν, "to be high-minded" (LSJ, φρονέω II.2b) as in 11:20 and 12:16. Here it can have a properly neutral sense since the negative force is given by ὑπερφρονεῖν (only here in the NT), denoting an understanding which goes beyond proper bounds, so "(too) proud, haughty." The παρά has a comparative sense, so "beyond" what is necessary, and reinforces the ὑπέρ (cf. Plutarch, *Mor.* 83F; BGD, παρά III.3); cf. 8:26 καθὸ δεῖ (BGD, δεῖ 6). σωφρονεῖν is the contrast the readership would expect since σωφροσύνη features regularly in popular hellenistic philosophy denoting modesty and restraint, in classical terms the golden mean between license and stupidity, and one of the four cardinal virtues (Spicq, 868 n.1). This usage has already influenced hellenistic Judaism, including Wisd Sol 8:7, *4 Macc* (e.g., 5.23), *T. 12 Patr.*, Philo (e.g., *Immut.* 164) and Josephus (see further in *TDNT* 7:1098–1102). Here the wordplay shows that Paul too is conscious of this wider usage. So here the verb (σωφρονεῖν) can be translated "observe proper moderation or discretion, exercise self-control," "with sober judgment" (RSV, NIV), with ὑπερφρονεῖν as the antonym, just as classically σωφροσύνη is the antonym of ὕβρις (*TDNT* 7:1098). For Paul, of course, it is moderation as expressed by the renewed mind (v 2) and as measured in terms of faith (see below) which is in view. So while it is true that he warns here against the sort of extreme which an unbalanced spirituality can produce (cf. particularly the other Pauline use in 2 Cor 5:13), he does so not simply by appealing to philosophical categories (as Michel, Käsemann) but to a common consensus regarding the desirability of moderation as drawn into a Christian evaluation (v 2). There is nothing to show here whether Paul has a specific group in mind or is simply warning against what he knows to be a common danger in any charismatic circle (cf. Ortkemper, 43–44).

ἑκάστῳ ὡς ὁ θεὸς ἐμέρισεν μέτρον πίστεως, "as God has measured to each a measure of faith." The thought is rather compressed (Cranfield), but the meaning is clear enough so far as syntax is concerned. Despite Cranfield's strong and repeated advocacy (followed by Fitzmyer, Wilckens; cf. also Jewett, *Tolerance*, 61–62, and Harrisville; against most—e.g., *TDNT* 4:634; Lietzmann; Barrett; Murray; Schmidt; Schlier; Ortkemper, 45–46; Zeller), it is very unlikely that μέτρον here has the sense of "standard by which to measure, means of measurement." (1) Following μερίζω the phrase is more naturally taken as an apportioning of *different* measures—as is the case in 1 Cor 7:17 and 2 Cor 10:13 (the nearest parallel—apostles have been apportioned different spheres of service [NEB]). (2) The fact that the μέτρον is given to *each* does not imply that all have the same μέτρον. The thought is parallel to that in 1 Cor 12:7 (each has been given some measure of faith), as is clear from v 6a and indeed v 3a itself (cf. also the very Pauline 1 Pet 4:10); see also on

12:4–5. (3) Cranfield's concern lest Paul be understood to commend a reliance on "fluctuating subjective feelings" is understandable, but it rather misses the point. The sober self-assessment just called for has in view the rich diversity of the expressions of faith (and grace): by recognizing that each is graced in some measure and each expression is indispensable to the community of faith a false sense of superiority will be effectively avoided (as Paul argued at length in the parallel passage, 1 Cor 12:14–26). Cf. particularly Schlatter.

(4) All this confirms what we would have had to deduce anyway from the use of πίστις, since throughout the letter Paul uses this key word of the human act and attitude of believing, as the means through which God effects his saving work (δικαιοσύνη), in contrast to a more objectively or externally ascertained pattern of conduct (ἔργα νόμου). This trust, which is the common denominator of all Christians (= believers), Paul clearly sees as variable in different believers (4:19–20; 14:1; Leenhardt compares the concept of maturity, as in 1 Cor 2:6; 3:1; and Phil 3:15). Here there is no sharp distinction in fact between "saving faith" and "miracle-working faith" (as in 1 Cor 12:9). Both indicate that measure of reliance on God which enables χάρις to come to expression in χάρισμα. It is the confident trust in God which recognizes that all faith and grace is from God which prevents the misjudgment of ὑπερφρονεῖν. Paul's vision is that such reliance needs to be strengthened since it is the basis of Christian conduct and relationship (see further on 14:23). Black's suggestion that πίστις here should have the sense "responsibility" is really a variation on πίστις = "faithfulness" and does not fit with Paul's whole train of thought in the letter.

4–5 καθάπερ γὰρ ἐν ἑνὶ σώματι πολλὰ μέλη ἔχομεν, τὰ δὲ μέλη πάντα οὐ τὴν αὐτὴν ἔχει πρᾶξιν, οὕτως οἱ πολλοὶ ἓν σῶμά ἐσμεν ἐν Χριστῷ, τὸ δὲ καθ᾽ εἷς ἀλλήλων μέλη, "for as in one body we have many parts, and all the parts do not have the same function, so we all are one body in Christ, and individually parts of one another." The two verses consist of a parallel (καθάπερ . . . οὕτως) between the self-evident fact that a single body (ἓν σῶμα) has many constituent parts (μέλη; see on 6:13) which do not have the same function (πρᾶξις), and the diverse membership of the Christian community which all together forms one body in Christ. The range of alternative origins for this conceptuality has been thoroughly reviewed by Jewett, *Anthropological Terms*, 210–50, and briefly in Käsemann and Ortkemper, 50–58; see also Wedderburn, "Body."

(1) Underlying the usage is Paul's recognition that acceptance of the gospel is bound to have a corporate expression. Though much of what Paul has so far argued could be reduced to an individualistic concept of salvation, it now becomes clear that Paul was simply assuming the inevitability of its communal character. The basic point was evidently noncontroversial: there was no need to develop a theological argument for it in the main body of the exposition (chaps. 1–11); it could be simply assumed in the parenesis, as the unavoidable outworking of justification by faith and of the being ἐν Χριστῷ (Klaiber, 58, 74, 95, 103, 192–93). But why the imagery of the body in particular?

(2) An influence from the common comparison of the polis with the human body (the body politic), of which the fable of Menenius Agrippa is the best known example (Livy, *Hist.* 2.32; Epictetus 2.10.4–5, cited by Dodd; see further Lietzmann on 1 Cor 12:12 and *TDNT* 7:1038–39, 1041), is hard to dispute

(e.g., *TDNT* 7:1069, Cranfield, Wilckens, Zeller). But while that explains the parallel, community = body, it leaves unexplained why Paul speaks in 1 Cor 12 of "the body *of Christ*," or more precisely here, as "one body *in* Christ" (though the distinction should not be overemphasized at this point, as by Jewett, 303–4).

(3) The previously much-promoted view that the origin lies in a (gnostic) primal man myth (individuals as pieces of an original heavenly man) has now fallen almost wholly by the wayside (but still in Kümmel, *Theology*, 210); see, e.g., Ortkemper, 52–53, 54–55, 57–58. The earlier ideas of, e.g., a Philo are not gnostic and to describe them as "pre-gnostic" is as helpful and as unhelpful as describing the medieval church as pre-Reformation (see further Dunn, *Christology*, particularly 98–100, 123–26, 229–30, 248, 252–53).

(4) The thought of Christ as eschatological Adam is not immediately evident, but must lie in the background, since it is of a piece with the εἰς Χριστόν and σὺν Χριστῷ language which elaborates the Adam Christology of chap. 5 in 6:3–8, climaxing in the ἐν Χριστῷ formula in 6:11. "The motif of the church as the body of Christ cannot be isolated from the characteristic Pauline Christology of the second Adam" (Käsemann, "Motif," 112). See further Barrett and on 6:11 and 9:1; cf. also Jewett, 237–45; but a solution in terms of Christ as "corporate personality" (particularly Best) is as problematic as the term itself (see again Rogerson at 5:12).

(5) Likewise following on from chaps. 4 and 9–11 is the implication (though no more than that) that a body (politic) in Christ is the equivalent corporate expression of the seed of Abraham/Israel/people of God in the new era introduced by Christ, as Israel κατὰ σάρκα was the corporate expression of the previous era (cf. the more elaborate theories of Oepke and Meuzelaar).

(6) In view of 1 Cor 10:16–17, an allusion to the community as expressing the corporate unity in the Lord's Supper can hardly be excluded. But it is less likely that that is the sole or chief origin (against, most recently, Goppelt, *Theology* 2:146; Ortkemper, 49–50, 56), since the exposition of the body imagery in 1 Cor 12 and Rom 12 (as also Eph 4) seems to have worship as a whole in view, and not just sacramental worship (see also Dunn, *Unity*, 129–30).

(7) Much less convincing is the further deduction of Percy, *Leib*, 44 and Robinson, *Body*, 55–58, that for Paul the community is identical with the (crucified and) resurrected body of Christ, which creates more confusion than clarity, and which certainly seems to make nonsense of Phil 3:21.

(8) A probably stronger influence is the actual *experience* of community, of common participation (κοινωνία). This again is used of the Eucharist in 1 Cor 10:16, but the more typically Pauline thought is of the shared experience of the Spirit (2 Cor 13:13/14; Phil 2:1) as effecting the unity of the church, the oneness of the body (1 Cor 12:12–13; Eph 4:3, 7–13). Such an emphasis ties in with (4) above: 1 Cor 15:45—sharing in (the image of) the last Adam is the work of the life-giving Spirit. More important, it fits fully into the strongly charismatic emphasis of the immediate context: the simple fact is that Paul uses the body of Christ as an ecclesiological concept only in connection with charisms (Rom 12; 1 Cor 12; also Eph 4); the Christian community as the body of Christ exists for him only as the charismatic community (Born-

kamm, *Paul*, 195: "Only in this context of the effects and gifts of grace does the apostle utilize the ancient world's figure of the one body and the variety of its members"; contrast Ridderbos, *Paul*, 372–73, who again makes too much of an either-or: "the one body is not conceived in the first instance as a pneumatic but . . . as a redemptive-historical 'objective' unity"). To this extent the often-made point that "the picture of the body is more than a mere metaphor" (e.g., Käsemann, "Motif," 102–3; Nygren; Ortkemper, 48) is sound: the body imagery is actually an expression of the consciousness of community and oneness experienced by the first Christians as they met "in Christ."

To search for a single origin for the body of Christ imagery is therefore probably too much of an oversimplification; several influences can be traced in it. Consequently also the significance of the imagery should not be reduced to a single point or too quickly dogmatized. For example, Käsemann is right to stress that the members do not constitute the body, but Christ constitutes them as such; though to describe the church as the earthly sphere of his power is in danger of forgetting that the Spirit, though given to the church, is not confined within it. Similarly with Klaiber's insistence that the body of Christ is the earthly body of the exalted Christ (41–48, 53–59): a comparison of 12:5 ("one body *in* Christ") with 1 Cor 12:12 (Christ is like a body) with Eph 4:15 (Christ the head of the body) shows just how flexible the imagery was (note the important caveats of Judge, "Demythologizing"); the worshiping community can certainly claim to be a focal point of Christ's earthly presence, but as soon as a church thinks it has an exclusive claim to represent Christ, as soon as "in Christ" is identified with "in the church" (Maillot), that church is making the same mistake as Israel κατὰ σάρκα—the very mistake against which Paul pits himself in this very letter.

Too little noted is the use of πρᾶξις, "acting, activity, function" (as in Matt 16:27; BGD), which in the parallel expanded into v 6 is χάρισμα—ἔχει πρᾶξιν = ἔχοντες χαρίσματα (see further on 12:6). οἱ πολλοί is the same Semitism as in 5:19, meaning "all." Here it refers to all the recipients, "all you" (v 3), with whom Paul identifies—the all of any worshiping community. That is to say, as explicitly in 1 Cor 12 (Rom 12:5 is closely parallel to 1 Cor 12:27), so here, "the body" has in view the local Christian congregation(s) (despite Bosch, 56–57). For τὸ δὲ καθ' εἷς = "individually, with relation to each individual," see BDF, §305, and BGD, εἷς 5e. ἀλλήλων μέλη, "members of one another" is a slightly odd variation of the body metaphor, but serves very effectively to bring out the degree of interdependence which Paul regards as the most important point to draw from the body imagery (here as in 1 Cor 12; also Eph 4—note v 25; "each member belongs to all the others"—NIV), thus underlining the fact that the body language is primarily for Paul an ecclesiological rather than Christological concept (hence again the variation in terminology as between 1 Cor 12:12–13 and Rom 12:4–5). The consequence for ecclesiology also needs to be borne in mind: as Käsemann notes, "No ecclesiastical hierarchy can be deduced as constitutive from the motif of Christ's body."

Particularly notable is the repeated correlation (not contrast) between the oneness of the body and the diversity of its members: "one body . . . many parts . . . all the parts do not have the same function . . . we the many are one body . . . individually parts of one another." The point is that the body is *one* not despite its diversity, but is *one body* only by virtue of its diversity; without that diversity the body would be a monstrosity (1 Cor 12:17–20); "the unity of the body consists in the diversity of the members" (Hainz, 183).

6 ἔχοντες δὲ χαρίσματα κατὰ τὴν χάριν τὴν δοθεῖσαν ἡμῖν διάφορα, "having gifts different in accordance with the grace given to us." It is almost universally assumed that v 6 begins a new sentence (e.g., NEB, Barrett, Michel, Käsemann), with the second halves of the subsequent phrases filled out with imperatival force—so particularly RSV: "Having gifts that differ according to the grace given to us, let us use them" (the last four words having been added to the text). This forces the sense too much in one direction (a "somewhat harsh ellipse," as SH recognize). The sentence reads more naturally as a continuation of the body imagery of vv 4–5 with the meaning of ἀλλήλων μέλη spelled out in terms of different charisms. The point then of the following phrases is that they are a description of the Christian congregation functioning as "one body in Christ": the one who teaches, exhorts, etc., is the member (μέλος) of the body; the act of teaching, exhorting, etc., is the function (πρᾶξις) of the limb/organ, the member of the body functioning as such. Vv 6–8 are a description of how the body of Christ functions. That Paul's description of his vision or "in principle" ideal of the body of Christ as charismatic community has prescriptive force is no doubt the case. But as Paul actually sets it out it is simply a description of what being one body in Christ involves so far as Paul is concerned. Cf. particularly Denney and Schlatter.

The ἔχοντες is determined by the imagery of the body, since it refers to organs and limbs with fixed functions. And Paul follows through the logic of the imagery by characterizing the subsequent charisms in terms of regular ministries ("he who teaches . . ."). But the point should not be pressed to exclude charism in the sense of spontaneous act of ministry: in 1 Cor 14:26 he uses the same verb (ἔχει) to describe those who come together for worship ("each has a psalm, a teaching, a revelation, a tongue, an interpretation") where it is clear from the context that that can include a Spirit-prompted impulse to speak out experienced during the period of worship itself (14:13, 30); and in what follows here Paul thinks of charism as the function of the member, as the act of ministry rather than as a latent gift which the gifted individual can call on at will (see further below).

For χάρισμα see on 1:11. Particularly evident here is the character of χάρισμα as the embodiment, concrete manifestation in word or action, of χάρις (Grau, 12; Käsemann, "Ministry," 65; Baumert's counterargument is a non sequitur). The essential balance between the two words is maintained if we see χάρις as the resource which comes to particular expression in χάρισμα, the fountainhead from which the particular draft or more regular stream is drawn (cf. Herten, 84). Brockhaus's assertion that χάρισμα is not a central concept in Pauline theology and is best translated simply as "gift" (*Gabe* or *Geschenk*—141, 238) does not give enough weight to this link with χάρις (which certainly is a central concept for Paul) or to its dynamic character (1:5). He is on sounder ground when he notes (238–39) that the essential role Paul gives to charisms in 12:3–8 does not extend to a general concept of Christian ethics: as becomes evident in 12:9–21, Paul appeals to other factors in his parenesis (Jewish wisdom and Jesus tradition); and the charisms have their validity and role within the Christian community, while the concept of charism is not used in discussing the believer's relation to the state or to the non-Christian neighbor. The fact remains, however, as Brockhaus also recognizes, that the Spirit as power and norm provides the unifying factor behind both ethical parenesis and Christian community: χάρισμα = manifestation of the Spirit (1 Cor 12:7); ethics as a walking κατὰ πνεῦμα (cf. also Schulz, 456–57). Moreover, once again, the fact that vv 3–8 follow vv 1–2 should not be forgotten: there is obviously a conceptual but also a theological link between the σῶμα of v 1 and the σῶμα of v 5; membership of the body of Christ is not to be separated from the daily service involved in human relationships (cf. Schweizer, "Leib," 292).

Here again ἔχοντες should not be pressed to give the sense of possession: grace is experienced only as *given* (see further on 12:3); the resource is "available" only as the reality of the living relationship between God and man, Creator and creature, Lord and servant (Schrage, 142–43, notes that charisms cannot be commanded, unlike even love). So too the concreteness of χάρισμα (in relation to χάρις) is lost when χάρισμα is defined as "the potential or ability to serve" (Hemphill, 181–82). χάρισμα is the reality of χάρις coming to visible expression in the actual being and doing of members of the body one for another in their mutual interdependence; "not possessions, which the individual can have for himself, but the activities which take place within the community and are indispensable if it is to thrive, . . . through which a living body emerges out of the community" (Schlatter); "the Church becomes a Church not by tradition in itself, but by the repeated action of the Spirit . . ." (Schweizer, *Church Order,* 99). Paul does not elaborate this point here, but it is implicit in the imagery itself, and here particularly with the use of διάφορα ("different"), since that together with ἀλλήλων μέλη (v 5) shows that Paul has in mind the more elaborate exposition of 1 Cor 12: (1) *all* are members of the body, and *as such* all are therefore charismatics (organs having functions; see also on 5:15); (2) all are different as members, that is, as having different charisms; (3) on these differences functioning as such and their mutually beneficial interaction the oneness and well-being of the body depends—one (body in Christ) by virtue of (this) diversity. The main difference with 1 Cor 12 is that the relative importance of the various charisms is not pursued here (see also Herten, 82–83). From this it becomes clear that Paul is not simply echoing 1 Cor 12–14, which is much more sharply focused on particular problems at Corinth, but is in fact providing a more generalized picture of the earliest Christian congregations (Brockhaus, 198–202; against Lietzmann and Michel). It is a striking fact, worth noting once again, that Paul can so confidently take it for granted that congregations he had neither founded nor visited would be charismatic ("Paul knows only the charismatic community"—Schulz, 447). This must imply that the pattern was widespread at least in the diaspora churches. (Brockhaus, 89–90, also notes that quite a strong consensus in modern scholarship is prepared to speak, with various qualifications, of a charismatic beginning of the church.) See further Dunn, *Jesus,* particularly 253–57, 262–65.

εἴτε προφητείαν, "whether prophecy." The old dispute as to whether prophecy is best described as "forth-telling" (almost = preaching, "the announcing of the word"—Maillot) or as foretelling (predictive) has obscured the more basic character of prophecy as inspired speech, words given as from "without" (by the Spirit) and not consciously formulated by the mind. This is also a distinctive feature of Judeo-Christian prophecy as over against wider Greek use, where προφητεία does not yet appear in non-Jewish literature (*TDNT* 6:784; though it is used in first-century inscriptions for the office of prophet at Didyma and other shrines—LSJ, Forbes, 230), and where προφήτης and μάντις are distinct, with the latter denoting immediate inspiration and the former the spokesman who declares the message thus received or who acts as official spokesman for the shrine (LSJ, *TDNT* 6:790; Forbes, 237–38); though προφητεύειν can be used to include the idea of inspiration (the much cited Plato, *Phaedrus* 244; Philo, *Heres* 259–61; Plutarch, *De defectu oraculorum* 438a). The regularly repeated claim that Christian prophecy was distinct from the more ecstatic forms of *prophecy* prized in the wider hellenistic world has therefore to be severely qualified (Forbes, particularly chap. 8 and 11; cf. Aune, 230). The distinctiveness of Christian prophecy has to be more carefully defined: distinct in its spontaneous and unstructured immediacy of inspiration (cf. 1 Cor 14:30), as over against the more formalized prophetic ritual and procedures of the recognized shrines; and distinct in the Pauline emphasis on rationality (1 Cor 14:12–19), as over against the ecstatic experiences prized in manticism, in the frenzy of the Dionysiac festivals and also evidently within the church at Corinth (1 Cor 12:2; 14:12).

Prophecy is mentioned only here in Romans. But Paul's placing of it at the head of the list of charisms is consistent with the prominence he gives to it elsewhere (especially 1 Cor 14:1, 39; 1 Thess 5:19–20); in two lists which speak of person rather than of gift itself, "prophets" come second only to "apostles" (1 Cor 12:28; Eph 4:11; cf. Eph. 2:20). The reasons are spelled out in 1 Cor 14: prophecy "builds up" or benefits the congregation more than other charisms (14:3–5) by virtue of bringing encouragement and consolation (14:3, 31; see also on 12:8), fresh revelation (1 Cor 14:6, 26, 30) and humbling self-knowledge (14:24–25). It should not be forgotten that women were also expected to exercise this gift (1 Cor 11:5; cf. Acts 2:17; 21:9). The use of the noun "prophecy" rather than "prophet" in v 6 underlines the point already made that Paul has in mind here the function of prophesying, χάρισμα as the actual speaking of words given by inspiration. See further Dunn, *Jesus*, 227–33; cf. Ortkemper, 67–72; both with further literature.

κατὰ τὴν ἀναλογίαν τῆς πίστεως, "in proportion to faith." ἀναλογία has the force of "right relationship or proportion," and κατ᾽ ἀναλογίαν is familiar, typically in mathematical formulations, in the sense "proportionately, in proportion to" (LSJ, MM, *TDNT* 1:347, Michel). A strong body of opinion maintains that the phrase here must have an objective reference to the content (or rule) of faith, since only an objective standard of faith could serve as a criterion by which to judge prophecy—*fides quae creditur* (so recently Käsemann; Schlier; Ortkemper, 72–74; Wilckens; Aune, 204–5, 235; Zeller; Maillot; earlier discussion reviewed in Lagrange). But this is unlikely (SH; Denney; Schlatter; Althaus; Gaugler; Leenhardt; Schmidt; Bosch, 63; cf. Murray): (1) κατὰ τὴν ἀναλογίαν τῆς πίστεως stands in parallel to and as an elaboration of κατὰ τὴν χάριν τὴν δοθεῖσαν ἡμῖν—clearly implying that the faith is the faith exercised by the one who prophesies (cf. *TDNT* 1:347–48). (2) The mistake of reading the sequence of phrases as virtual imperatives (see on 12:6, first paragraph) is compounded here by understanding πίστις as a norm by which the community could test the prophetic utterance. But when the phrases are recognized to be elaborations of the imagery of the body and therefore as descriptive rather than prescriptive (see again above), it becomes clear that the κατὰ τὴν ἀναλογίαν τῆς πίστεως describes how the prophet functions, or, more precisely, how the act of prophecy comes about—that is, by the prophet speaking forth in proportion to his faith = his dependence on God (the usual sense of πίστις throughout Romans; see on 12:3). NJB's "as much as our faith tells us" is equally unsatisfactory. (3) Hence Zahn and Michel are correct to understand ἀναλογία πίστεως as a variant or near synonym of μέτρον πίστεως (v 3); Lagrange, Michel, and Cranfield note that μέτρον and ἀναλογία are translated by the same word in the Peshitta Syriac.

On this understanding Paul does leave his teaching open to the abuse of false prophecy—a danger of which he is acutely aware whenever he speaks on the subject of prophecy elsewhere (1 Cor 12:10; 14:29; 1 Thess 5:19–20; see Dunn, *Jesus*, 233–36; also "Prophetic 'I'-Sayings and the Jesus Tradition: The Importance of Testing Prophetic Utterances within Early Christianity," *NTS* 24 [1977–78] 175–98). But the danger he sees confronting the Roman congregations is not so much of charismatic abuse and overenthusiasm, but of not giving enough weight to the immediate dependency of faith, and of superseding it or devaluing it by placing higher value on Jewish (or non-Jewish) identity (cf. again 12:3 with 3:27–30 and 11:18–20). Hence the appropriate check here is that of a proper (that is, creaturely) sense of dependence and reliance on God to give the words without which prophecy cannot happen (cf. Leenhardt—"The expression should neither fall short of nor exceed the controlling inspiration"; and see further Dunn, *Jesus*, 211–12).

7 εἴτε διακονίαν ἐν τῇ διακονίᾳ, "whether service in serving." Paul can use διακονία in a wide range of meaning: to embrace and characterize all charisms as acts of service (χαρίσματα = διακονίαι—1 Cor 12:4–5; also Eph 4:12); for his own ministry as a whole (Rom 11:13; 2 Cor 3:8–9; 4:1; 5:18; 6:3; cf. 1 Tim 1:12; 2 Tim 4:5); for specific acts or periods of ministry (1 Cor 16:15; 2 Cor 11:8; Col 4:17), including participation in the collection for the church in Jerusalem in particular (Rom 15:31; 2 Cor 8:4; 9:1, 12–13; see also on 15:25). Here it probably falls somewhere in the middle of the spectrum, denoting neither an isolated and individual act of service, nor a lifelong ministry, but various kinds of "*ad hoc* service" (Bornkamm, *Paul*, 183) or regular acts of ministry undertaken by the same persons (see further Dunn, *Jesus*, 249–50; cf. particularly Schlier); but not necessarily "administration" (NEB) and not yet in the technical sense of "diaconal office" (so rightly Ortkemper, 74–75; against Lietzmann, Murray), or denoting a concrete office (so rightly Hainz, 187–88); cf. on παρακαλῶν (12:8). Its placement after προφητεία need not indicate a narrow sense = service to the poor and needy (Cranfield): that would overlap too much with the last three items on the list (v 8); prophecy is placed first not to indicate that the list is a sequence of closely defined charisms but because it is the most important and that which most typifies a manifestation of the Spirit (an inspired utterance which involves the whole person and benefits others). Wilckens suggests that "prophecy" covers the third and fourth items on the list (teaching, exhorting), and "service" the last three. But while that does recognize the main areas of overlap in the list, it does not really fit with the εἴτε . . . εἴτε . . . structure.

The ἐν τῇ διακονίᾳ is not simply tautologous, but underlines the basic character of a charism for Paul as grace (χάρις) coming to visible expression (χάρισμα); SH's "let him minister and prophesy or exhort" reads too much into the text. The different διακονίαι in view are not particular abilities, far less the responsibility of an office (cf. Käsemann), but the actual acts of ministry, the bodily organ functioning as such. This observation is strengthened by the fact that Paul speaks here of διακονία rather than of ὁ διακονῶν: the focus is wholly on the act and not on the actor. See also on 12:6.

εἴτε ὁ διδάσκων ἐν τῇ διδασκαλίᾳ, "whether he who teaches in teaching." The fact that Paul thinks of teaching also as a charism should indicate sufficiently that Paul did not think of teaching merely as a conveying and passing on established tradition (cf. 6:17 and 16:17). The implication is that he recognized an interpretative role for the teacher, in which the teacher must depend (equally as the prophet) on the Spirit for insight into the traditional formulae and for the significance he draws from them for his own context and congregation. Consequently the line between teaching and prophecy becomes very thin—the latter characterized more as new insight into God's will (see on 12:6), the former more as new insight into old revelation (cf. Gaugler); Paul's own reworking of older Jewish wisdom and of the Jesus tradition in the parenesis of 12:9 ff. well exemplifies the balance Paul himself maintained. See further Dunn, *Jesus*, 236–38; Schürmann, "Lehrer." That Paul recognizes the importance of *both*, but prizes prophecy the more highly, needs to be remembered: "teaching preserves continuity, but prophecy gives life; with teaching a community will not die, but without prophecy it will not live" (Dunn, *Jesus*, 284).

The switch from the gift to the one who exercises the gift (ὁ διδάσκων) could be stylistic in motivation in order to avoid too much repetition (hence v 8b–d). But it may well also indicate that Paul saw teaching here as a more regular ministry—though he also thought of it in terms of particular teachings given by those not necessarily regarded as teachers (1 Cor 14:6, 26; Col 3:16; see also Dunn, *Jesus*, 284). Certainly the need to instruct in the traditions regarding Jesus and his teaching and to do so in an orderly way would be present in all the earliest Christian congregations from the beginning (cf. Acts 2:42; 1 Cor 11:2, 23; 15:3; 1 Thess 4:1; 2 Thess 2:15; 3:6) so that one of the earliest regular ministries (proto-offices) to emerge would inevitably be that of teacher (Gal 6:6; cf. Acts 13:1; 1 Cor 12:28; Heb 5:12; James 3:1)—the teacher fulfilling a vital social function in preserving and passing on the traditions which gave the first Christian communities their distinctive identity. Even so, as in the other phrases, the addition of ἐν τῇ διδασκαλίᾳ continues to place primary emphasis on the act of teaching as the Spirit-inspired (charismatic) functioning of the bodily organ. Throughout, the focus is on the functions themselves rather than on the status of those who exercise them (Meeks, *Urban Christians*, 134–35).

8 εἴτε ὁ παρακαλῶν ἐν τῇ παρακλήσει, "whether he who encourages in encouraging"; cf. the sequence in 1 Tim 4:13. Both the main words here have a range of meaning: "urge, exhort" (e.g., 1 Cor 4:16; 2 Cor 10:1; 1 Thess 5:11); "request, entreat" (e.g., 1 Cor 16:12; 2 Cor 12:18; Philem 10); "comfort, cheer up" (e.g., 2 Cor 1:4; 7:6–7; 1 Thess 3:7), or possibly also "console, conciliate" (1 Cor 4:13) (BGD). Of these the first and third would appear to be most appropriate here; but Paul no doubt chose the words precisely because of their breadth of meaning (as with διακονία). Hence the overlap with prophecy (1 Cor 14:3, 31) is unimportant: Paul does not have in mind a set of clearly differentiated charisms (as would be necessary if they denoted offices with demarcated "job descriptions"); individuals would speak out under inspiration and it would neither be clear, nor would it matter, whether the utterance was described as a "prophecy" or an "exhortation." In view of the significance now seen in the use of παρακαλέω as a polite way of exercising authority in 12:1 and particularly 15:30 (also 16:17) (see on 12:1 and 15:30), the fact that Paul numbers this among one of the charisms ministered regularly by (other) members within the congregation should not be ignored (cf. 1 Thess 4:18; 5:11, 14).

ὁ μεταδιδοὺς ἐν ἁπλότητι, "he who shares in sincere concern" (cf. BGD, ἁπλότης 2). μεταδιδούς means not just "giving," but "giving a share of, sharing." As indicated by the context (and confirmed by the ἁπλότητι), it is what the individual has to share functioning as a member of the body which is in view. Since the sharing here *is* the charism, the thought is different from 1:11, where the charism is *what* is shared (see on 1:11). Here, then, it is probably sharing of food or wealth or possessions which is in view (as in Job 31:17 LXX; Ep Jer 27 [EV 28]; Philo, *Jos.* 144; *Spec. Leg.* 2.71, 107; 4.74; Luke 3:11; Eph 4:28; cf. Acts 2:45; 4:34–37; see also Ortkemper, 79–81); but a sharing of one's own goods, as the ἐν ἁπλότητι more likely implies, not a distributing the community's alms (SH, Lagrange, Murray; against Käsemann, Schlier; despite 15:27 and van Unnik, the thought of sharing in the riches of the gospel hardly fits so well with the ἐν ἁπλότητι or with the immediate context). The basic meaning of ἁπλότης is "simplicity" (as in 2 Sam 15:11 and Josephus, *War* 2.151; in *T. 12 Patr.* ἁπλότης is the main theme of *T. Iss.*, reflecting the Stoic and Cynic idealization of the simple life and character of the former—*T. Iss.* tit.; 3.2, 4, 6, 7, 8; 4.1, 6; 5.1, 8; 6.1; 7.7; see Hollender and de Jonge, 233–34). The sense here may be extended to embrace the thought of "generosity, liberality" (so rsv, niv; Spicq, 127; as also in 2 Cor 8:2 and 9:11, 13; cf. particularly *T. Iss.* 3.8; also James 1:5); though if so it should be remembered that it is a liberality which arises out of and expresses the simplicity and single-mindedness of the person of faith (cf. the regular phrase ἁπλότης καρδίας: 1 Chron 29:17; Wisd Sol 1:1; *T. Reub.* 4.1; *T. Sim.* 4.5; *T. Levi* 13.1; *T. Iss.* 7.7; Eph 6:5; Col 3:22; so here neb, "with all your heart"; njb , "generously, from the heart"), who is generous simply because he relies so completely on God and therefore can sit wholly loose to personal possessions, "a self-forgetful attitude, entirely innocent of any ulterior motive" (Black). Although the sequence of thought has begun to move beyond the more straightforward description of organs of the body and their functions (12:6), that imagery is still a controlling force: the ἁπλότης is the mode of the charism's function, the character of the sharer as expressed in his sharing; to insert an imperative (μεταδιδότω—as Michel, Cranfield) obscures this point.

ὁ προϊστάμενος ἐν σπουδῇ, "he who cares with zest" (similarly RSV). προΐστημι means literally "set before," and one of the most obvious and frequent uses for the passive is to denote the act of being "set over or at the head of" (LSJ). Hence the possible sense for ὁ προϊστάμενος of "he who rules," "leader" (NEB), favored by most (e.g., SH; Lietzmann; Barrett; Schmidt; Borsch, 69–70; NIV, NJB); so also 1 Tim 3:4–5, 12; 5:17; and *Herm. Vis.* 2.4.3. But it is also found quite frequently in the sense "be concerned about, care for, give aid" (as in Epictetus 3.24.3; Josephus, *Ant.* 14.196—"protect"; cf. Titus 3:8, 14; 1 Thess 5:12 could be taken either way). Here the latter is the more probable: (1) "leader" is more likely to be expressed with the perfect tense (ὁ προεστώς), as consistently in the LXX (2 Sam 13:17; Prov 23:5; 26:17; Amos 6:10; Dan LXX Bel 7; *4 Macc* 11.27; cf. LSJ, προΐστημι B.II.1; MM); (2) it would be surprising if a regular leadership function were placed so far down the list (cf. Ortkemper, 82–83), given that a degree of ranking seems to be involved in this list (prophecy first because it is most important—see on 12:6), whereas in 1 Cor 12:28 κυβερνήσεις ("giving guidance") probably refers to a series of individual acts of ministry rather than to the regular ministry of particular individuals (Dunn, *Jesus,* 252–53; for identification of προϊστάμενος with κυβέρνησις see, e.g., Bosch 69–70); (3) almost certainly decisive is the fact that προϊστάμενος here is set between two forms of aid giving (μεταδιδούς and ἐλεῶν), and so would most naturally be read as denoting one of a sequence of three kinds of "welfare service" (see further Kühl; Dunn, *Jesus,* 251–52, with bibliography). If the sense is "protector" then the thought is of some member in the congregation who by virtue of his or her wealth or social status within the local community (city) was able to act as a champion of the rights of the little congregation or its socially vulnerable members (cf. Michel, Cranfield, Wilckens), as probably Phoebe (see on 16:2).

σπουδή means "eagerness, earnestness, diligence," and in religious matters "zeal" (BGD); the word is found elsewhere in Paul in Rom 12:11; 2 Cor 7:11–12; and 8:7–8, 16 (in a similar context). To avoid confusion with ζῆλος ("zeal") an alternative translation is desirable. "Zest" is useful in that capacity since it conveys the sense of vitality Paul envisages as the expression of such concern and avoids the element of ruthlessness in religious commitment which ζῆλος even then could imply (see on 10:2). Once again we should note that, following on from ἔχοντες, Paul's language is intended to be as much descriptive of how the body works (when working properly) as prescriptive.

ὁ ἐλεῶν ἐν ἱλαρότητι, "he who does acts of mercy with cheerfulness." This is the only occasion in the Pauline literature in which ἐλεέω is used of human rather than divine mercy (9:15–16, 18; 11:30–32; 1 Cor 7:25; 2 Cor 4:1; Phil 2:27; 1 Tim 1:13, 16). It can mean acts of mercy in general (cf. particularly Prov 14:21, 31; *T. Iss.* 5.2; *T. Zeb.* 7.2; 8.1; *T. Ben.* 4.4; Philo, *Mut.* 40; so RSV, NEB, *TDNT* 2:483, Käsemann, Cranfield—"tend the sick, relieve the poor, or care for the aged and disabled"; Schlier and Wilckens compare Luke 10:37); but if Paul intended to distinguish this third "welfare ministry" from the preceding two, which may not be the case, we could narrow its meaning to

almsgiving in particular (Michel; cf. ἐλεημοποιός—Tob 9:6 S; ἐλεημοσύνη—
e.g., Sir 7:10; 35:2; Tob 1:3, 16; 4:7–8 BA; Matt 6:2–4; Acts 9:36). This is
made more likely by the fact that giving "cheerfully" is a fairly common
theme in Jewish piety (Prov 22:8a LXX, cited in 2 Cor 9:7; Sir 35:9; Philo,
Spec. Leg. 4.74; *T. Job* 12.1; *Lev. Rab.* 34.9—in Str-B, 3:296). This in turn
strengthens the impression that Paul still has in mind a picture of the Christian
congregation functioning as a body: the ministry of "poor relief" functions
as an organ of the body when it is done with gladness. All three qualifying
clauses (ἐν ἁπλότητι, ἐν σπουδῇ, ἐν ἱλαρότητι) are simply aspects of the χάρις
which comes to expression in these χαρίσματα.

Explanation

12:3   Having stated the basis for the social identity and lifestyle of the
Christian congregation—a cultic dedication in daily life apart from any particular cultic focus, and a discernment of God's will springing from the immediacy
of relationship with God not dependent on the written law—Paul turns at
once to the social reality of the Christian congregation in its interrelationships.
Whereas the moral exhortations of chaps. 6–8 were directed to the individual,
the concern here immediately focuses on mutual relationships. This is further
confirmation, if such were needed, that the intervening chapters (chaps.
9–11) were no parenthesis or later insertion: since the corporate identity of
the elect was no longer to be defined in terms of physical descent and works
of law, it was essential that the new corporate identity be clearly defined.
Similarly, it would occasion no surprise that Paul should make his first piece
of specific counsel a call for each to avoid any thoughts of superiority in
these mutual relationships and to maintain a proper sense of one's place
within God's scheme of things. For it was precisely such presumption on
the part of "the Jew" which Paul had attempted to undermine and indict in
chaps. 2–4, and equally such a dangerous tendency on the part of the Gentile
"branches" against which he had warned in chap. 11. That which had divided
Jew and Gentile and hindered the promises of God reaching their climactic
fulfillment was the first and most serious danger to be avoided. Whether it
was pride in race or in loyalty to tradition or in seeming favor by God or in
charismatic prowess, such pride should be resisted and brought low, for it
was the greatest danger to the unity and oneness of corporate identity as
God's people—hence the carefully formulated call to "all who are among
you." All are in danger of harboring such false and divisive notions of self-
esteem—none more so than the one who thinks the exhortation is addressed
to others.

Significantly, Paul begins and ends this initial appeal by using once again
the language of "grace" and "faith." The former ("through the grace given
to me") has exhortative force but is not intended as an attempt to "pull
rank." Like the appeal in v 1 ("through the mercies of God"), it refers rather
to the outworking of God's merciful will and gracious power as the *only* criterion
for any claims or appeals within the people of God—thus preparing for the
description of the Christian community's functioning charismatically as a corporate unity (vv 4–8). Paul's claim on the Roman congregations is not of a

piece with the presumptive assessments he had previously attacked and now warns against; it belongs with the claim of grace (*charis*) coming to expression in gift (*charisma*) by means of which the new corporate identity is constituted and functions as Christ's body.

So too with the reminder that a proper self-esteem is only possible in terms of the faith which makes no claims but simply opens itself to God's grace. Such receptivity is the other side of the coin from grace. Only so can God's grace come to expression as grace and without being corrupted into presumption. This is the message Paul has been emphasizing throughout the letter—that God works through faith, and faith alone; unconditional creaturely trust alone as the basis of relationship not only of man to God but of God's people to one another. The unusual thought of such faith as itself also something for which man depends on God simply underscores the point: not only in doxology (11:33–36) but in daily life, the Creator alone makes possible and sustains all things.

4–5 Having alerted his listeners once again to the faults which were so destructive of the older corporate outworking of God's grace, Paul immediately turns to a description of the new corporate identity appropriate for the eschatological people of God. In place of nationality and ethnic unity as the form of God's people, Paul puts forward the image of a body. The image would have been familiar to his Roman audiences: the body of a single entity made up of diverse members mutually interdependent was obvious and common enough in popular philosophy. Paul's choice was no doubt deliberate: it would give his readers a sense of coherence and identity which could sustain them over against the larger body politic in which they lived and worked, without that depending on a sense of national or racial solidarity. At the same time he prevents its being assimilated to a too vague idea of world citizenship or a too narrow concept of civic politics: they are one body *in Christ*; only "in Christ" do they function as a body; the "in Christ" provides a countermodel of social identity no longer reducible to merely ethnic or cultural categories.

From the fact that Paul made so much of the image of the church in Corinth as the body of Christ (in Corinth) in his first letter to Corinth (1 Cor 12; also Eph 4), we can deduce that Paul saw it as one of the best means of encouraging the right sort of community spirit in the diaspora congregations. Although the metaphor is not developed here, the emphases it brings to the fore are clear enough: a Christian believing, which could be no private matter or solitary piety, but which involved as of its essence a belonging to a larger body, an indispensable corporeality; an active membership—each having its different function as part of the body; a practice of mutual support in both giving and receiving without overdependence on any one member or function ("members one of another"). The fact that the imagery was well known to describe the body politic probably implied also that for Paul the Christian congregation's functioning as a body could itself serve as a model for the functioning of the wider (secular) society. And as the body of Christ the members could think of themselves so functioning as the principal medium of Christ's continued presence in human society. That this was to be no mere "spiritual" presence within, far less a withdrawal from that wider society in a completely separate identity, was already implicit in the exhortation of v 1: their functioning as one body in Christ included the daily embodiment of the life of the Spirit in the all-too-physical realities of human existence.

6–8 For Paul the reality of being Christ's body (or one body in Christ) was "fleshed out" by reference to charisms. As in 1:11, the recipients of the letter would understand from the formation of the word and by the description which follows that "charism" denotes any word or action which brings to concrete expression God's gracious outreach to humankind, which serves as "a means of grace." This emphasis on grace (*charis*) as the source and measure of these gifts (*charisms*) ("having charisms in accordance with the *charis* given to us") highlights once again a crucial point always in the background in this letter: the mode of life acceptable to God is never one lived out of one's own resources but always lived in dependence on God. This point needs ever to be borne in mind in discussing whether charisms are wholly "supernatural" or utilize "natural" abilities. Whatever the answer, the point for Paul is that words and actions are only charisms insofar as they express and convey grace.

Paul clearly envisages the body of believers functioning charismatically: "members having charisms. . . ." Indeed "charism" and "body of Christ" are inextricably intertwined in Paul's thought: in only three passages within the Pauline corpus is the concept of the body of Christ developed, and always in terms of charisms or gifts of ministry (Rom 12:4–8; 1 Cor 12; Eph 4:7–16). For Paul the body of Christ is by definition a charismatic community. In this case he identifies the functions of the body as the charisms themselves; the congregation functions as Christ's body when its members let the grace of God come to diverse expression through them. As the first items of the list of charisms show, what is in view is not a matter of office or status, but the act itself of prophesying and serving. And even when the list goes on to mention persons ("he who teaches," "he who encourages," . . .) the emphasis is still on the action (in this case, regular ministry—present participle) of teaching and exhorting ("in teaching," "in encouraging"). And in the final grouping likewise it is the character of the regular ministry of sharing, caring, and showing mercy on which the thought focuses ("with sincere concern," "with zest," "with cheerfulness").

It is clear too that Paul thinks of every member of the Roman churches as, properly speaking, charismatic. "The many" of v 5 does not leave out any member of the Roman house groups, however more extensive the phrase may be. Paul evidently did not conceive of a congregation made up of charismatics and noncharismatics: all are charismatics, for that is what being a member of one body in Christ means. Since such an assertion was hardly based on firsthand knowledge of the different Roman congregations, it must mean that this is simply a description of how Paul understands and defines any congregation as Christ's body, or as one body in Christ. Implicit here is an ecclesiology of the church as charismatic community, not overly dependent on any one or two particularly gifted individuals, but mutually interdependent each on everyone else, on the living interplay of charisms and regular ministries, without the necessity of a particular structure (as of its essence) beyond that of the body of Christ itself.

The range of charisms illustrated probably has some significance. Paul says nothing of the gifts which seem to have caused most controversy at his place of writing (Corinth), viz., speaking in tongues (1 Cor 14) and "miracles" (2 Cor 11:21–12:13). And clearly his list in 1 Cor 12:8–10 was drawn up with a view to the particular situation in Corinth, not as some kind of universally applicable, far less exhaustive, list of charisms. That could hardly be the case anyway, since, as we have seen, "charism" denotes any word or action which brings grace to expression. The absence of these more controversial gifts presumably means that Paul did not know of similar problems at Rome. That is to say, his treatment here can hardly be directed against "charismatics" or enthusiasts: the warning of v 3 can certainly point up that danger but was hardly directed against enthusiasts alone (cf. 4:2 and 11:18); and a description of the body as functioning charismatically can hardly be seen as directed against charismatics.

The significance of mentioning the gifts which he does is that they all fall into the categories of speaking and serving (as in 1 Pet 4:11). This presumably means that for Paul at any rate the most characteristic expression of the grace/*charis* of God was in these two areas—words which speak to will and mind and heart, acts which serve the needs of the more disadvantaged members of any congregation. Paul did not regard communication at rational and intellectual level as something dispensable; he sought to maintain a balance between words which encourage and words which instruct; it was evidently important to him to pass on and hold firm to the founding traditions of the faith, though he always gave higher priority to the immediacy of dependence on the Spirit expressed in prophecy. He did not think of spiritual gifts as synonymous with the eye-catching and very physical; the charismatic Spirit came to expression characteristically for him in service, no doubt often hidden from the public eye, in the humdrum maintenance of others in the basics of everyday living, as the Spirit of the crucified.

The degree of overlap between the different charisms (prophecy can include exhortation; the last three fall within the broader category of service) confirms that Paul did not have in view a set of clearly defined ministries but a regular response to the promptings of grace which allowed a less restricted expression, as, no doubt, occasion demanded. So too with the first member of the list (prophecy) Paul emphasizes once again that it is a gift expressed in proportion to faith, to the individual's receptivity and readiness to be used by God's grace for the benefit of others. And with the final trio the emphasis likewise is on the simple, open-hearted character without which the charism cannot come to full expression as the enactment of grace. With such emphases Paul seeks to bring his major theological insights of the earlier part of the letter into practical everyday expression.

C. Love as the Norm for Social Relationships (12:9–21)

Bibliography

Allison, D. C. "Pattern." **Bindemann, W.** *Hoffnung.* 107–12. **Daube, D.** "Participle and Imperative in 1 Pet." In Selwyn, *1 Peter.* 467–88. ———. "Jewish Missionary Maxims in Paul." *ST* 1 (1948) 158–69. Repr. in *Rabbinic Judaism.* 336–51. **Dunn, J. D. G.** "Paul's Knowledge of the Jesus Tradition: The Evidence of Romans." Forthcoming in FS W. Trilling, ed. T. Holtz et al. **Furnish, V. P.** *Love Command.* Particularly 102–8. **Jewett, R.** *Tolerance.* 92–114. **Kanjuparambil, P.** "Imperatival Participles in Rom 12:9–21." *JBL* 102 (1983) 285–88. **Klassen, W.** "Coals of Fire: Sign of Repentance or Revenge?" *NTS* 9 (1962–63) 337–50. **Leivestad, R.** "ΤΑΠΕΙΝΟΣ—ΤΑΠΕΙΝΟΦΡΩΝ." *NovT* 8 (1966) 36–47. **Merk, O.** *Handeln.* 159–61. **Morenz, S.** "Feurige Kohlen auf dem Haupt." *TLZ* 78 (1953) 187–92. **Munro, W.** *Authority in Paul and Peter: The Identification of a Pastoral Stratum in the Pauline Corpus and 1 Peter.* SNTSMS 45. Cambridge University Press, 1983. 56–67. **Neirynck, F.** "Sayings of Jesus." 295–303. **Ortkemper, F. J.** *Leben.* 85–125. **Perkins, P.** *Love.* 89–95. **Piper, J.** *"Love Your Enemies": Jesus' Love Command in the Synoptic Gospels and the Early Christian Paraenesis.* SNTSMS 38. Cambridge University Press, 1979. **Ramaroson, L.** " 'Charbons ardents': 'sur la tête' ou 'pour le feu' (Prov 25:22a—Rom 12:20b)." *Bib* 51 (1970) 230–34. **Sauer, J.** "Traditionsgeschichtliche Erwägungen zu den synoptischen und paulinischen Aussagen über Feindesliebe und Wiedervergeltungsverzicht." *ZNW* 76 (1985) 1–28. **Schnabel, E. J.** *Law.* 299–342. **Schottroff, L.** "Non-violence and the Love of Enemies." *Essays on the Love Commandment.* Philadelphia: Fortress, 1978. 9–39. **Stendahl, K.** "Hate, Non-Retaliation, and Love." *HTR* 55 (1962) 343–55. **Synofzik, E.** *Vergeltungsaussagen.* 48–49. **Talbert, C. H.** "Tradition and Redaction in Romans 12:9–21." *NTS* 16 (1969–70) 83–94. **Unnik, W. C. van.** "Die Rücksicht auf die Reaktion der Nicht-Christen als Motiv in der altchristlichen Paränese." In *Judentum, Urchristentum, Kirche,* FS J. Jeremias, ed. W. Eltester. Berlin: Töpelmann, 1960. 221–34. **Walter, N.** "Paulus und die urchristlichen Tradition." *NTS* 31 (1985) 498–522. **Wenham, D.** "Paul's Use of the Jesus Tradition: Three Samples." In *The Jesus Tradition Outside the Gospels.* Gospel Perspectives 5. Sheffield: JSOT, 1985. 7–37.

Translation

[9] *Let love be without pretense. Hate* [a]*what is evil, be devoted to what is good.* [10]*Show family affection to one another in brotherly love; show the way to one another in respect.* [11]*Be not negligent in eagerness; be aglow with the Spirit; serve the Lord.* [b] [12]*Rejoice in hope; be steadfast in affliction; be persistent in prayer.* [13]*Share in the needs* [c] *of the saints; aspire to hospitality.*

[14]*Bless those who persecute you,* [d] *bless* [e] *and do not curse.* [15]*Rejoice with those who rejoice;* [f]*weep with those who weep.* [16]*Live in harmony among yourselves; do not cherish proud thoughts but associate with the lowly. Be not wise in your own estimation.* [17]*Repay no one evil for evil; take into consideration what is noble* [g] *in the sight of all.* [18]*If possible, so far as it depends on you, live at peace with everyone.* [19]*Do not take your own revenge, beloved, but give opportunity for God's wrath; for it is written,*

"Vengeance is mine, I will repay," says the Lord.

[20]*But* [h] *if your enemy is hungry, feed him; if he is thirsty, give him to drink;*

for in so doing you will heap coals of fire on his head.
²¹ *Do not be overcome by what is bad, but overcome the bad with the good.*

Notes

ᵃ Some witnesses read the slightly softer μισοῦντες (see Lietzmann).

ᵇ There is strong support for the reading κυρίῳ (p⁴⁶ ℵ A B etc.), but the regular Western combination (D* F G etc.) reading καιρῷ has some support (Lagrange, Leenhardt, Schmidt, Käsemann; others in Ortkemper, 93 n.91). κυρίῳ certainly accords with Paul's normal use of δουλεύω with a personal object (cf. particularly 14:18; 16:18; Col 3:24; 1 Thess 1:9; Eph 6:7; even in Rom 6:6 and 7:25 ἁμαρτία and νόμος are personified). But for that very reason καιρῷ could be regarded as the *lectio difficilior*. On the other hand, it appears too difficult: even given the significance Paul puts upon καιρός (see on 3:26), the thought of "serving the time" cannot be Pauline (contrast Col 4:5; Eph 5:16); on the contrary, it had something of the same pejorative ring (opportunist) which the English "time-server" still has (see Lagrange, Michel). Metzger notes how easy it would have been for an abbreviation for κυρίῳ to be misread at transcription level. See also Lietzmann and the full discussion by Cranfield.

ᶜ A similar Western combination supports the reading μνείαις (D* F G etc.)—"sharing in the remembrance/commemoration of the saints." But the Pauline corpus normally uses ἔχειν or ποιεῖσθαι with μνεία (1:9; Eph 1:16; 1 Thess 1:2; 3:6; 2 Tim 1:3; Philem 4; cf. Phil 1:3; nowhere else in the NT); and χρεία is the more natural companion for κοινωνέω. μνείαις probably entered the MS tradition as a scribal error (confusing a poorly written ΧΡ with ΜΝ—WH, Lietzmann), and perhaps reflecting the beginning of a practice of intercession for the dead (Käsemann; see further Lagrange).

ᵈ p⁴⁶ and B omit the ὑμᾶς. It may have been added to make explicit what is clearly implicit.

ᵉ p⁴⁶ also omits the second εὐλογεῖτε—an understandable attempt to polish.

ᶠ Some add καί—more polishing.

ᵍ The expansion by F G etc. to read οὐ μόνον ἐνώπιον τοῦ θεοῦ ἀλλὰ καί is a typical attempt to harmonize this verse to Prov 3:4 and 2 Cor 8:21 (see further Metzger).

ʰ The adversative force of ἀλλά caused puzzlement among those who understood the Proverbs quotation as also speaking of divine judgment; hence various emendations—ἐὰν οὖν, ἐάν, καὶ ἐάν, ἐὰν δέ—but none so strongly supported as the text.

Form and Structure

As in 1 Cor 12–13, Paul's thought moves from talk of the body of Christ to the theme of love (e.g., SH; Knox; Furnish, *Theology*, 100), subsumed under the appeal of vv 1–2 (Piper, 103–6). This is the most loosely constructed of all the paragraphs, consisting mainly of individual exhortations (stringing pearls) held together in part by particular words and thematic links (especially love: ἀγάπη, φιλαδελφία, φιλόστοργος, φιλοξενία—vv 9, 10, 13; bad: πονηρός, κακός—vv 9, 17, 21; good: ἀγαθός, καλός—vv 9, 17, 21). Paul will not have been unmindful that the indictment of 2:1–11 worked with similar broad categories of good and bad: the implication is that only love which flows from the commitment and enabling of vv 1–2 can perform the good which accords with God's good will. Vv 9–13 run together structurally, the implied imperative of the initial call for love expanded in a series of participial clauses. The parallels with other first-century Christian parenesis, particularly 1 Thess 5:12–22 and 1 Pet 3:8–12 (Selwyn, 408–410), indicate both that Paul was drawing on a common style of parenetical material, but also that the individual elements could be formulated in different permutations and combinations (see further Piper, 4–18, 119–22; against the redactional theories of Talbert, and of Munro who is overconfident in reconstructing an earlier stratum consisting of 12:4–8, 11b–12 and 13:11–14; but analysis of this kind requires tighter methodological control than is provided by criteria such as "credible sequence" and "feasible point of attachment").

Michel (also Talbert, 84–85, and Black) see in vv 10–13 a sequence of five pairs, but this depends somewhat on reading καιρῷ instead of κυρίῳ. When κυρίῳ is read (see *Notes*) the sequence is better taken in a 2, 3, 3, 2 grouping, as the verse division recognizes (so Käsemann). Either way, the rhetorical parallelism of the sequence of nine clauses beginning with the dative is striking. The whole paragraph (vv 9–13) could be set out in note form:

> [9]Genuine love: hating what is evil, devoted to what is good;
>> [10]family affection in brotherly love for one another,
>> showing the way to one another in respect;
>> [11]not negligent in eagerness, aglow with the Spirit,
>> serving the Lord;
>> [12]rejoicing in hope, steadfast in affliction,
>> persistent in prayer;
>> [13]sharing in the needs of the saints, aspiring to
>> hospitality.

See also Bultmann, *Stil*, 75–76.

Whereas vv 9–13, following on from vv 3–8, are directed more to the internal relationships within the body of Christ, vv 14–21 seem to focus more on relationships with the wider world, leading into 13:1–7. Paul evidently was particularly mindful of the fact that the little congregations in Rome were an endangered species, vulnerable to further imperial rulings against Jews and societies. He therefore urges a policy of living quietly, and of nonresponse to provocation. The counsel is chiefly rooted in Jewish traditional wisdom regarding human relationships (v 15—Sir 7:34; v 16—Prov 3:7 and Isa 5:21; v 17—Prov 3:4; v 18—Ps 34:14 [LXX 33:15]; v 19—Lev 19:18 and Deut 32:35; v 20—Prov 25:21–22; v 21—*T. Ben.* 4.3). The "imperatival participles" which are a feature of the whole section also indicate use of Jewish material (Daube, "Participle"; Kanjuparambil; though see also Talbert). The unusually heavy concentration of OT allusions indicates a strong concern on the part of Paul to root this most demanding of ethical obligations in the tried and tested wisdom of Jewish scripture and experience (cf. Piper, 113–14). But the echo of Jesus' teaching on the theme of love of neighbor is also strong in v 14 (cf. Matt 5:44 // Luke 6:27–28) and is probably intended to set the keynote for the verses which follow (12:14–13:7) before being picked up again more explicitly in 13:8–10. Allison in particular has noted how many of the echoes of the Jesus tradition come from the central section of the "Sermon on the Plain" (12:14—Luke 6:28; 12:17—Luke 6:27–36; 12:21—Luke 6:27–36; 14:10—Luke 6:37) and deduces that Paul must have been familiar with this collection of Jesus' sayings on the theme of love of neighbor and of enemy ("Pattern," 11–12). See also the broader analysis of Schnabel, 299–342.

Vv 15–16 seem to break the pattern of an exhortation directed to Christian relationships with the wider society. But they partially reflect the use of a traditional Jewish parenesis which could embrace a whole social ethic within the mutual relations of the covenant people, whereas in a Christian and diaspora context the boundary lines fell differently. Perhaps more to the point, these verses were probably addressed to some of the tensions within the Roman congregations, particularly between Jewish and Gentile Christians, which were a result of the persecution already suffered by the Roman Jews (see Introduction §§2.3 and 2.4).

Comment

12:9 ἡ ἀγάπη ἀνυπόκριτος, "let love be sincere." The absence of a joining particle and the change of style probably indicate that the reader should take a pause and so make a new beginning (cf. 9:1). The phrase then would function almost as a heading (cf. Schlier, 373; against Käsemann)—"love sincere"; and with the sequence of participial clauses following (vv 9b–13), it would be clear that they should be understood as an elaboration of these opening words—"this is what love is like" (Nygren). The translation by means of an imperative (implied) slightly obscures this "thesis character" of v 9a, but is a legitimate way of bringing out the imperatival force of the participles.

ἀγάπη has been used so far only of divine love—of God (5:5, 8; 8:39) or of Christ (8:35); later of the Spirit (15:30; cf. 5:5). Here it is of human love (as in 13:10 and 14:15). It is a long-familiar fact that the word appears only exceptionally in nonbiblical Greek before the second or third century A.D. (but see BGD, ἀγάπη; Spicq, 22–27, with bibliography, 27–30), and that the occurrence in the LXX (20x) usually refers to conjugal love between man and woman (11x in Canticles). The frequent use of the word in the NT (116x; 75x in the Pauline corpus) therefore gives weight to the often-made claim that this is a word seized and taken over by the first Christians as they sought to find language to express their new experience of grace, a word filled with new content and significance by earliest Christian experience of God's love (see further on 5:5; see also SH, 374–76). The claim should not be overstated: ἀγάπη had already been used for divine love (cf. Wisd Sol 3:9; *Ep. Arist.* 229) and of human love for God (Jer 2:2; Wisd Sol 6:18— Wisdom); and the verb, ἀγαπᾶν, was already much more widely used (Furnish, *Love Command*, 220–22). Nevertheless, the sudden explosion of usage in the earliest Christian author (Paul) is sufficient indication that the Christians found it necessary to make a fresh minting of a previously little-used word; the subsequent use of ἀγάπη by Christians for their common meal ("love feast"; see BGD, II; *LPGL* E.4) underscores the Christians' own consciousness of its distinctiveness (see also on 12:10). Moreover, the fact that talk of human ἀγάπη appears only now after the earlier strong talk of God's love and Christ's love is probably sufficient indication that Paul took it for granted that human ἀγάπη was possible only as an expression of divine ἀγάπη (cf. 5:5; and again Wisd Sol 3:9 and *Ep. Arist.* 229; also *T. Gad* 5.2 and *T. Ben.* 3.5, where the usage probably betrays Christian influence; so too *T. Reub.* 6.9; *T. Gad* 4.2, 6, 7; *T. Ash.* 2.4; *T. Jos.* 17.3; and *T. Ben.* 8.1–2). See also Dodd.

ἀνυπόκριτος means literally "without hypocrisy," so "genuine, sincere." The word is found also with reference to love in 2 Cor 6:6 and 1 Pet 1:22; with regard to "faith" in 1 Tim 1:5 and 2 Tim 1:5; elsewhere in biblical Greek only Wisd Sol 5:18; 18:16; and James 3:17. The ὑποκριτής was the "play-actor" who projects an image and hides his true identity behind a mask. Paul would be conscious no doubt of the danger of deceit, including self-deceit, not least in the matter of spiritual gifts and enablings (cf. Cranfield; and see below).

ἀποστυγοῦντες τὸ πονηρόν, κολλώμενοι τῷ ἀγαθῷ, "hating the evil, devoted to the good." ἀποστυγέω is a strong word, "hate violently, abhor" (LSJ, SH). Hence it is no accident that Paul chooses πονηρός (the only time in Romans) as the antithesis to ἀγαθός, instead of the usual κακός, since πονηρός is the stronger word ("wicked, evil") as against the less forceful κακός ("bad"). κολλάω is equivalently strong on the other side—"join closely together, unite." In the passive, with the dative, as here, it has the force of "cling to, enter into a close relation with" (Ps 119 [LXX 118]:31; T. Iss. 6.1; T. Dan. 6.10; T. Gad 5.2; T. Ash. 3.1; T. Ben. 8.1; Did. 5.2; and Barn. 20.2 echo this passage; BGD; Schlier refers also to 1QS 1.4–5). ἀγαθός is the more regular member of the antithesis (2:7, 10; 3:8; etc.). Although the form of the contrast is distinctive (particularly the ἀποστυγέω), the contrast itself is not untypical (e.g., Pss 34:14; 37:27; Amos 5:15; 1QS 1.4–5); see further on 2:10.

The parallel with 1 Thess 5:21–22 is particularly worth noting:

Romans: ἀποστυγοῦντες τὸ πονηρόν, κολλώμενοι τῷ ἀγαθῷ·
Thessalonians: τὸ καλὸν κατέχετε, ἀπὸ παντὸς εἴδους πονηροῦ ἀπέχεσθε·

Moreover, both exhortations follow immediately upon teaching related to charisms (Rom 12:6–8; 1 Thess 5:19–20—Spirit, prophecy), with the former introduced by a warning against deceit (12:9) and the latter introduced by a call for discernment (5:21—πάντα δοκιμάζετε). Add to this the fact that the sequence of vv 6–9a follows that of 1 Cor 12–13 (charisms, love). Taken together it suggests that Paul's thought was following a familiar track: charisms as vital to the reality of the Christian church, but as always needing to be checked and monitored in relation to love (cf. Michel, Wilckens, and see particularly Käsemann), with discrimination always necessary to discern what was good and worthwhile in any claim to charismatic authority and what may need to be rejected as evil. The latter sequence (charisms–discrimination) is regular in Paul (1 Cor 2:12–15; 12:10; 14:29; 1 Thess 5:19–22; see also 12:11c below) and becomes an established feature in earliest Christianity (1 John 4:1; Did. 11.11; Herm. Man. 11.7.16; cf. Matt 7:22–23). And love as the chief mark of Christian discipleship is strongly attested in the Synoptics and John as well as in Paul (see further on 13:8–10).

10 τῇ φιλαδελφίᾳ εἰς ἀλλήλους φιλόστοργοι, "in brotherly love showing family affection to one another." Both φιλ- words denote the love which is characteristically expected in a family: φιλαδελφία, love for brother or sister; φιλοστοργία, typically, love of parent for child (as almost always in Philo, Abr. 168, 198; Mos. 1.150; Spec. Leg. 2.240; Virt. 91, 128, 192; Praem. 158; cf. Legat. 36), but also of other family ties. In some contrast the Christian usage extends well beyond the immediate bonds of family (φιλαδελφία—1 Thess 4:9; Heb 13:1; 1 Pet 1:22 [cf. 3:8]; 2 Pet 1:7; 1 Clem. 47.5; 48.1; φιλόστοργος—only here in the NT). But here too (as with ἀγάπη in 12:9) the transition should

not be exaggerated. ἀδελφός was more broadly used for members of a religious association (see on 1:13; and further Lagrange); and φιλάδελφος could also denote a wider fraternal concern, for which love for brother was the pattern (as in 2 Macc 15:14; and note its frequent use as a title for kings, particularly the Ptolemies—see LSJ). Likewise more generalized uses of φιλόστοργος are well enough attested, where the type of family affection can be understood as capable of being extended fittingly to such as country or king or a pet animal (e.g., Polybius 16.17.8; Josephus, *Ant.* 4.135; LSJ; Spicq, 500–505; *NDIEC* 2:100–103; 3:41–42). Michel notes the reputation the Essenes had for loving one another (Josephus, *War* 2.119; borne out, e.g., by 1QS 1.9–10; 5.25; 10.26; CD 6.20–21). Nevertheless, the Christian use of these typically family words does rather stand out in its consistency, and the combination of both words underscores the point. This too is part of the redefinition of boundaries in which Paul engages—a sense of family belongingness which transcended immediate family ties and did not depend on natural or ethnic bonds. The organic imagery of the interrelatedness of the body requires to be supplemented by the emotional bond of family affection ("your feelings of deep affection for one another"—NJB).

τῇ τιμῇ ἀλλήλους προηγούμενοι, "showing the way to one another in respect." τιμή clearly has its normal sense of "honor, respect" (LSJ, BGD; cf. particularly 13:7 and 1 Pet 1:17), here presumably the honor due not in terms of any status or intrinsic quality (cf. Ortkemper, 90–91, though he probably pushes too hard for clear distinctions between Jewish and Christian concepts here), but in terms of membership of the same body (vv 3–8) and of the eschatological family of God (v 10)—that is, as accepted by God (cf. 14:3–4, 6–8). The description of synagogue archons as πάσης τιμῆς, of which four examples occur in *CIJ* (Leon 176–8), probably does not shed extra light for us. προηγέομαι is almost always taken in the sense "esteem more highly": "give pride of place to one another in esteem" (NEB; see SH, Cranfield); and the sense certainly gains much support from Phil 2:3. The versions took it in the sense "outdo" (BGD): "outdo one another in showing honor" (RSV). But sense and context would be served equally by the more characteristic sense of "go before, lead the way": "show the way to one another in respect" (so particularly Kirk; Jewett, *Tolerance,* 107–8; cf. *m. ʾAbot* 4.15—"be first in greeting every man"). The use of τιμή in 1 Cor 12:23–24 and the echo of the chief theme of 1 Cor 12:14–26 suggests that Paul is still thinking of the typical Roman congregation in terms of charismatic relationships, which need always to be sustained within love, and by constant recall of the nature of charism as something given and therefore as conferring no honor on the charismatic as such other than his or her being used to minister grace to others. What is required is a genuine recognition and acceptance each of the other and of the part of each in the life and worship of the congregation (cf. 1 Thess 5:13).

11 τῇ σπουδῇ μὴ ὀκνηροί, "not negligent in eagerness," "with unflagging energy" (NEB). ὀκνηρός describes a person showing hesitation (ὄκνος) through weariness, sloth, fear, bashfulness, or reserve (*TDNT* 5:166; Spicq, 615—"culpable nonchalance"). The fault is often warned against in wisdom literature (Prov 6:6, 9; 20:4; 21:25; 22:13; 26:13–16; 31:27; Sir 22:1–2; 37:11; Philo,

Heres 254; Matt 25:26; elsewhere in biblical literature only Phil 3:1). Cf. *m.* *'Abot* 2.15. For σπουδή see on 12:8. The striking combination of language ("not indolent in eagerness') is clearly deliberate and reinforces the point (cf. 12:10—φιλαδελφίᾳ . . . φιλόστοργοι).

τῷ πνεύματι ζέοντες, "aglow with the Spirit." The precise force of ζέω is uncertain, but the imagery is clear enough. The basic sense is "bubble, boil" (as of water, as in Ezek 24:5), with the thought of heat a natural correlation (so of the process of fermentation, as in Job 32:19, and of glowing iron, as in Josephus, *War* 5.479). The metaphorical application to burning passion (Plato, *Republic* 4.440C; Philo, *Sac.* 15; *Heres* 64) or rage (*4 Macc.* 18.20; Philo, *Migr.* 210; *Mos.* 2.280) is natural; see further LSJ and *TDNT* 2:875–76. The association with πνεῦμα is a feature of the only two NT occurrences of ζέω (Acts 18:25 and here) and is distinctive to the NT. By πνεῦμα Paul most probably means the (Holy) Spirit (RSV; otherwise NEB, NIV, NJB): such emotive imagery he regularly uses of the Spirit (e.g., 5:5; 1 Cor 12:13c; 1 Thess 1:6)—he seems indeed concerned to keep the human emotional/ spiritual dimension correlated to the Spirit (8:15–16, 26; 1 Cor 14:14–16; Gal 5:22–23); and the association of fire with the divine רוח/πνεῦμα is well rooted in Jewish and Christian thought (Isa 4:4; 30:27–28; Matt 3:11 // Luke 3:16; Acts 2:3; 1 Thess 5:19; Rev 3:15; *4 Ezra* 13.10–11; cf. Michel and Black). It may be of some significance that the close parallel in Acts 18:25 (the only other NT reference) proffers a bridge between the influence of the Baptist (baptism of John, baptism in Spirit and fire) and Paul (Acts 18:24–19:7); cf. Dunn, "Birth of a Metaphor."

τῷ κυρίῳ δουλεύοντες, "serving the Lord." For a possible variant reading see *Notes.* For κύριος see particularly on 10:9. The combination is natural (master, slave), but to describe it as "unusually flat" (Käsemann) ignores the vivid sense of committedness both terms evidently expressed for Paul (e.g., 6:17; 7:6, 25; 10:9; 14:18; also Acts 20:19; and see further on 1:1 and 6:16). Here we should note particularly the element of control the phrase exercises on the one preceding: "bubbling with the Spirit" needs always to be checked by and channeled into service of the Lord Christ (cf. on 12:9).

12 τῇ ἐλπίδι χαίροντες, "rejoicing in hope"; "let hope keep you joyful" (NEB). As earlier, ἐλπίς has its usual Hebraic sense of confident trust (sure hope) rather than the more Greek sense of tentative expectation (hoping for better things); see on 4:18. Since the dative can contain both senses, we should not push for a choice between a local dative ("rejoice in"—*TDNT* 9:369 n.91; Schlier) and an instrumental dative ("rejoice by virtue of"—BDF, §196; Michel). Paul here may be deliberately recalling earlier and more developed words of encouragement, or was following familiar parenetical sequences: in vv 12a and 12b the thought is obviously very close to that of 5:2–5 (χαίρω/καυχάομαι, θλῖψις, ὑπομονή/ὑπομένω); and a similar progression of thought to that in 8:24–27 is evident in vv 12a, 12c (hope, prayer). Clearly implicit also is both the sense of eschatological excitement ("rejoicing") and the note of eschatological reserve ("in hope"); cf. 15:13 and 1 Thess 2:19. For joy as a characteristic of earliest Christianity, cf. also, e.g., 14:17; 15:15; 2 Cor 6:10; Gal 5:22; Phil 1:4, 25; 2:17–18; 3:1; 4:1, 4; 1 Thess 3:9; 5:16; Acts 2:46; 13:52; 1 Pet 1:8; 1 John 1:4.

τῇ θλίψει ὑπομένοντες, "steadfast in affliction." The sequence again echoes

1 Cor 12–13 (here 13:7); see *Form and Structure*. For θλῖψις see on 5:3. ὑπομένω occurs regularly in earliest Christian literature in the sense "endure, hold out, stand one's ground" in trouble, affliction, persecution—e.g., Mark 13:13; 1 Cor 13:7; 2 Tim 2:10; Heb 10:32; 12:2; James 1:12; 1 Pet 2:20; *1 Clem.* 45.8; *Did.* 16.5; *Mart. Pol.* 2.2 (see further BGD). The translation "endure" should not be given a too passive connotation: as with its correlate ὑπομονή, ὑπομένω implies a positive attitude to suffering (*TDNT* 4:586–87); as also does the connection with the preceding phrase (cf. 2 Cor 7:4; 8:2; 13:9; Col 1:24; 1 Thess 1:6). The degree to which Paul successfully integrates suffering into his understanding of the process of salvation is one of the strongest features of his soteriology (see further on 5:3 and 8:17; Dunn, *Jesus*, 326–88).

τῇ προσευχῇ προσκαρτεροῦντες, "persisting in prayer." προσκαρτερέω is an even stronger, or more positive, word—"to busy oneself with, be devoted to, hold fast to or persevere in something" (BGD). It is particularly so with reference to prayer (Acts 1:14; 2:42; 6:4; Col 4:2); cf. the equivalent thought of unceasing prayer (Luke 18:1; Eph 6:18; 1 Thess 5:17); and contrast the more sober rabbinic advice in Str-B, 2:237–38. As in 8:26–27, prayer is the natural expression of the eschatological tension: only by maintaining a constant "open line" to God in the Spirit can the tension be experienced as a positive sign and recreative force.

13 ταῖς χρείαις τῶν ἁγίων κοινωνοῦντες, "sharing in the needs of the saints." χρεία can mean "need" in general (e.g., Matt 3:14; Mark 11:3; Luke 15:7; John 2:25; 1 Cor 12:21; 1 Thess 1:8; 5:1; Heb 5:12), but here personal difficulties, particularly financial and daily necessities are probably in view (cf. Acts 2:45; 4:35; 6:3; 20:34; 28:10; Eph 4:28; Phil 2:25; 4:16; Titus 3:14; 1 John 3:17; see further BGD). The more general sense of "share" for κοινωνέω can likewise have more specifically the sense "give or contribute a share in" with reference to financial or material contributions (as in the other Pauline uses—Gal 6:6 and Phil 4:14–15; and note Rom 15:27). Paul's talk later and elsewhere of a "sharing" (κοινωνία) in the sense of "gift or contribution" "for the saints" (15:26; 2 Cor 8:4) suggests strongly that Paul has the collection particularly in mind (e.g., Furnish, *Love Command*, 105; see further on 15:26), but that would only be a particular example of a more general involvement in common concern for the bodily needs of one another (Jewett, *Tolerance*, 110, suggests the reference is to taking up the burdens of those deported under Claudius and even then returning to Rome; this is much more plausible than Minear's [87] characteristically tendentious suggestion that Paul is requesting the Gentile house churches to give aid to the Jewish house churches). The first Christians carried on the strong social concern of Jewish provision for widows, orphans, strangers, and the community's poor in general. For ἅγιοι see further on 1:7.

τὴν φιλοξενίαν διώκοντες, "aspire to hospitality." The obligation to provide hospitality to the stranger was deeply rooted and highly regarded in ancient society: e.g., the tradition is very old of temples and altars being places of asylum; Zeus was frequently called Ζεὺς Ξένιος, protector of the rights of hospitality (as in 2 Macc 6:2); the legend of Philemon and Baucis (Ovid, *Met.* 8.613–70) characterizes the ideal. Within Judaism the memory of Israel's experience as "strangers in Egypt" was a powerful reinforcement of the impulse to hospitality (especially Lev 19:34 and Deut 10:19). Abraham was extolled as the model of hospitality because of his entertaining the three heavenly visitors in Gen 18 (Philo, *Abr.* 107–114; Josephus, *Ant.* 1.196; *1 Clem.* 10.7; probably Heb 13:2, the only other NT occurrence of φιλοξενία), and Job also (Job 31:32; *T. Job* 10.1–3; 25.5; 53.3). See further Spicq, 932–35; *TDNT* 5:17–20; Str-B, 1:588–89; 4:565–71. Hospitality was a key feature of Jesus' ministry, both in his dependence on it (Mark 1:29–31; 14:3; Luke 10:38–42) and in his practice and commendation of it as a model of divine generosity (Mark 2:15–17; Matt 11:19 // Luke 7:34; Luke 14:1–24). The early mission would likewise depend on such hospitality (e.g., Mark 6:8–11 pars.; Acts 16:15; 18:3; see also 16:1–2, 13, 23). Since inns were often held in bad repute (cf. Plato, *Laws* 918D) travelers and merchants would obviously hope for hospitality from fellow countrymen. The demand on the ethnic subgroups in Rome in this connection would probably be considerable, hence perhaps the need to press the obligation on his readers (διώκω—"pursue, strive for, seek after, aspire to"); cf. 1 Pet 4:9. Subsequently hospitableness is regarded as a desirable characteristic in a bishop (1 Tim 3:2; Titus 1:8; *Herm. Sim.* 9.27.2).

14 εὐλογεῖτε τοὺς διώκοντας (ὑμᾶς), εὐλογεῖτε καὶ μὴ καταρᾶσθε, "bless those who persecute (you), bless and do not curse." εὐλογέω is another word whose force in earliest Christian thought derives much more from Christianity's Jewish heritage than from its Greek context. In Greek usage the sense is the obvious one, "speak well of" (someone), and so "praise" or "eulogize." The idea "bless" comes wholly from the Hebrew בָּרַךְ and gains its distinctive character from the distinctively Jewish idea of God blessing his human creatures, where "bless" has a much stronger force than the Greek εὐλογεῖν—"bless" in the sense of bestow grace and peace, sustain and prosper (as in the classic formulation of the Aaronic benediction—Num 6:24–26). When one person blesses another, the clear implication is that he calls on Yahweh to bestow his favor on the other, although a particular blessing (expression of that favor) could of course be requested (as in Gen 27:27–29; 49:28; Deut 33; 1 Sam 2:20). By way of antithesis καταρᾶσθαι obviously means to call on God to withhold his favor (both specific and providential), and, possibly, also to act as a power for ill in the life and circumstances of the one cursed (e.g., 2 Sam 16:5–13; 2 Kgs 2:24). See also *TDOT* 2:284–95; *TDNT* 2:754–63; and on 1:25.

The thought of returning blessing for cursing is a feature of Christian teaching and consolidates something of an advance on the more characteristic *lex talionis* attitude of the covenant as previously understood (Gen 12:3; 27:29; Num 24:9—though in fact Balaam is in some sense an antitype of one who is called on to curse and who finds he can only bless, Num 22–24; 1QS 2.1–10; cf. Matt 5:43), although the "advance" is prefigured in Exod 23:4–5, *T. Jos.* 18.2 and *T. Ben.* 4.3 (Christian influence?), and 1QS 10.17–18 (but note 10.19–21) (see further on 12:17, 19, and 20); Zeller notes also Papyrus Insinger 19. That Christians could already expect persecution is implied in a wide range of NT texts (Matt 5:10–12, 44; 10:23; 23:34; Luke 11:49; 21:12; 1 Cor 4:9; 2 Cor 6:4–5; 11:24–25; Gal 4:29; 5:11; 6:12; 1 Thess 2:14; Heb 10:32–33; 1 Pet 3:13–17; 4:12–19) as Paul himself only too well recalled (Acts 22:4; 9:4–5 // 22:7–8 // 26:14–15; 1 Cor 15:9; Gal 1:13, 23; Phil 3:6).

The issue of whether Paul's language here was influenced by the tradition of Jesus' saying something similar is frequently left merely as an uncertain possibility (even in Cranfield). However, the probability that the Pauline parenesis does reflect the exhortation of Jesus must be judged to be very strong: (1) The parallel with Luke 6:27–28 is close, with Matt 5:44 as a variant version:

Romans:	εὐλογεῖτε τοὺς διώκοντας (ὑμᾶς),	εὐλογεῖτε καὶ μὴ καταρᾶσθε·
Luke:	ἀγαπᾶτε τοὺς ἐχθροὺς ὑμῶν . . .	εὐλογεῖτε τοὺς καταρωμένους ὑμᾶς·
Matthew:	ἀγαπᾶτε τοὺς ἐχθροὺς ὑμῶν καὶ	προσεύχεσθε ὑπὲρ τῶν διωκόντων ὑμᾶς.

That Jesus was remembered as having said something along these lines seems clear (note also *Did.* 1.3). The fact that his exhortation was remembered in different versions simply underlines the extent to which Jesus' sayings formed a living tradition where the expression of the sense was more important than a particular form of words ("a targumic paraphrase"—Michel, Schlier). Paul's failure to cite them as words of Jesus should occasion no surprise: Paul's letters are not the medium for passing on the Jesus tradition, but can evidently assume knowledge of tradition already passed on and adaptable to different situations (cf. Goppelt, *Theology* 2:45–46; Allison, 21–22); the Jesus tradition had evidently entered into the living stream of Christian parenesis and was shaping the thought and aspiration as many a cherished scriptural formulation did also (see e.g., 12:15). The same influence is evident in 1 Cor 4:12, influence at the level of shaping thought rather than as formally recalled; note also 1 Pet 3:9. See further J. D. G. Dunn, *The Living Word* (London: SCM, 1987). (2) Add to this the points made in the previous paragraphs: the fact that the language and sentiment are hardly drawn from Greek thought; and that the counsel constitutes something of a step beyond the more typically Jewish assumption that God would curse those who cursed his people. The inescapable conclusion is that the attitude inculcated here is distinctively Christian. And since the contrast between blessing and cursing appears in this form only in Luke 6:28 and Rom 12:14 (Paul nowhere else uses καταράομαι), the obvious corollary is that the one who provided this decisive moral impetus was Jesus himself, as the Synoptic tradition attests. "Paul's teaching is the same as Jesus' " (Stuhlmacher, "Law," 100); Walter, 501–2, questions whether the teaching was remember as *Jesus* traditon. For other examples of probable influence on early Christian parenesis from the remembered tradition of Jesus' teaching see 1:16; 2:1; 11:25; 12:18; 13:7, 9; 14:13, 14, 17, 18; 15:1, 2; 16:19; see also on 2:27; 6:16, 17; and 15:3. See further Dunn, "Paul's Knowledge."

15 χαίρειν μετὰ χαιρόντων, κλαίειν μετὰ κλαιόντων, "rejoice with those who rejoice, weep with those who weep"—an example of the imperatival infinitive, much used by Homer; also Phil 3:16 (BDF, §389). This is first of a sequence of exhortations where Paul draws on the maxims of traditional Jewish wisdom (see *Form and Structure*). Here the closest parallel is Sir 7:34: μὴ ὑστέρει ἀπὸ κλαιόντων, καὶ μετὰ πενθούντων πένθησον, "Do not fail those who weep, but mourn with those who mourn." See also Job 30:25 LXX; Philo, *Jos.* 94; *T. Iss.* 7.5; *T. Zeb.* 6.5; 7.3–4; *T. Jos.* 17.7. For later rabbinic parallels see Str-B,

3:298. As with the echo of Jesus' teaching in v 14, it is the sentiment which is traditional rather than a particular form of words. And as so often with wisdom material, it is not particularly distinctive of Jewish and Christian thought. Here cf. particularly Epictetus 2.5.23: "Where a man may rejoice with good reason, there others may rejoice with him" (see also Michel, n.27). The parallel with 1 Cor 12:26 and Phil 2:17–18 suggests that Paul had the internal relationships of the Christian congregations particularly in view, but there is no reason he should not have had wider associations in view as well (*TDNT* 9:369 n.93; Furnish, *Love Command*, 106; Cranfield; Wilckens). There was certainly some ambivalence within earliest Christianity on the degree to which Jesus encouraged his disciples to feel a sense of solidarity with the poor and oppressed; cf. particularly Matthew's handling of the first beatitude (Matt 5:3 // Luke 6:20) and of the parable of the sheep and the goats (Matt 25:31–46). But Paul's other counsel on social relationships suggests an openness to the nonbeliever which would encourage a broader application of his words here (cf. 1 Cor 10:27; 14:23–25). Such genuine empathy (feeling with; cf. particularly Gaugler) with those benefiting or suffering from the ups and downs of daily existence would be seen as distinct from the Stoic ideal of ἀταραξία, "impassiveness" (Käsemann). For χαίρειν, see also on 12:12. Paul uses κλαίω elsewhere only in 1 Cor 7:30 and Phil 3:18. For the contrast with eschatological overtones, cf. John 16:20 and *Herm. Vis.* 3.3.2; also Luke 6:21, 25.

16 τὸ αὐτὸ εἰς ἀλλήλους φρονοῦντες, "live in harmony among yourselves." τὸ αὐτὸ φρονεῖν means literally "to think the same thing." Paul is certainly not calling for a rote uniformity of thought, but for a common attitude and purpose (Käsemann, Schlier); "be in agreement, live in harmony" (BGD); so also 15:5; 2 Cor 13:11; Phil 2:2 (which includes an alternative formula— τὸ ἓν φρονεῖν); 4:2; 2 Clem. 17.3; cf. the alternatives used by Josephus—τὸ αὐτὸ φρονεῖν (*War* 2.160) and ὅμοια φρονεῖν (*Ant.* 19.58). Similarly, τά τινος φρονεῖν can denote agreement in opinion, or more broadly, "be on someone's side or party" (LSJ, φρονέω II.2c). At the same time we should not weaken its force too much: Paul would want Christian congregations to decide as far as possible by consensus, by seeking the mind of the Spirit on matters affecting their life and worship together (cf. 1 Cor 2:16; 6:5; 7:40; 14:37–38), even if in matters of personal lifestyle different views and practices were quite acceptable (see chap. 14). At any rate the εἰς ἀλλήλους certainly seems to imply a perspective limited to the inner relations of and between congregations (Wilckens; Ortkemper, 104), though the thought of the effect of such harmony on outsiders would be a natural corollary (Cranfield).

μὴ τὰ ὑψηλὰ φρονοῦντες, "do not cherish proud thoughts"; see on 11:20. The thought is probably the same as 11:20, rather than a warning against ambition (Cranfield; against BGD, ὑψηλός 2). It is still the tensions within the congregations that Paul has in view—probably still the temptation on the part of Jewish and Gentile Christians to claim a more favored status before God (2:17–20; 11:18–20), rather than an assumed overenthusiasm for more striking charisms (against Michel, Schmidt). "Rom 12:16 offers an exposition of σωφρονεῖν" (Luck, *TDNT* 7:1102, referring to 12:3).

ἀλλὰ τοῖς ταπεινοῖς συναπαγόμενοι, "associate with the lowly." With ταπεινός we meet once again a Jewish rather than a Greek attitude. For the typical Greek mind with its idealization of the free man, ταπεινός denotes someone or something servile, menial, petty, and base—even in Epictetus, who elsewhere comes close to Christian sentiment (*TDNT* 8:2–3). But in Jewish thought God is characterized precisely as the one who chooses and favors the ταπεινός (Judg 6:15; Job 5:11; Pss 10:18; 18:27; 34:18; 82:3; 102:17; 113:7; 138:6; Prov 3:34; Isa 14:32; 25:4; 49:13; 54:11; 61:1; 66:2; Zeph 2:3; 3:12; Jud 9:11; Sir 3:20; 10:15; 35:17; *Ep. Arist.* 263; Luke 1:52; James 4:6; 1 Pet 5:5; the Qumran covenanters regarded themselves as "the lowly"—see further *TDNT* 8:12–14; and for Hellenistic Judaism 8:14–15; Leivestad's qualifications do not affect the basic point). Here again Paul takes it for granted that Christians should live in accordance with this insight, as also commended and exemplified by Jesus (in particular Matt 5:3–5; 11:29; 18:4; 23:12; cf. Mark 10:42–45). The ambiguity of ταπεινοῖς (neuter or masculine) cannot be resolved, and may have been deliberate (Barrett), and is usually left open— menial or lowly tasks, or people held in low esteem by the influential and powerful (see, e.g., BGD, συναπάγω; Schlatter; Lagrange; Wilckens). The verb is somewhat surprising and could quite properly be translated "be led or carried away" (cf. its only two other NT uses—Gal 2:13 and 2 Pet 3:17; also the ecstatic overtones of 1 Cor 12:2). Paul presumably intended to encourage an uninhibited wholeheartedness in lifestyle, not a grudging or calculating act. That he was conscious of the missionary potential in such a policy (Daube, "Missionary Maxims," 346–37) is certainly possible, as also in the main thrust of the paragraph (Schottroff, 23–24).

μὴ γίνεσθε φρόνιμοι παρ' ἑαυτοῖς, "do not be wise in your own estimation"; "do not keep thinking how wise you are" (NEB). Note the ringing of changes in the φρον- word group (3 times in v 16). Since so much of this section is clearly a pulling together of related motifs in Jewish wisdom (see *Form and Structure*), we may assume that the emphasis here was drawn from Prov 3:7, and that Paul would have been aware of it and have expected his listeners who were well versed in the LXX likewise to recognize the scriptural force of the injunction: Prov 3:7—μὴ ἴσθι φρόνιμος παρὰ σεαυτῷ (cf. Isa 5:21; cf. also Prov 26:5, 12; 28:26). The plural formulation suggests that Paul had a corporate self-esteem in mind—once again, that of Jew over against Gentile or Gentile over against Jew. See further on 11:25, where he gives the same warning in more or less the same terms.

17 μηδενὶ κακὸν ἀντὶ κακοῦ ἀποδιδόντες, "repay no one evil for evil." This qualification (or clarification) of the *lex talionis* is closer to Jewish thought (Prov 20:22; 24:29; *Jos. As.* 23.9; 28:5, 10, 14; 29:3; *Apoc. Sed.* 7.9; cf. Exod 23:4–5; 2 Chron 28:8–15; Str-B, 1:368–70; cf. also the warning against returning good with evil—Prov 17:13 and Jer 18:20), than the exhortation to return evil with good which is presented as more distinctively Christian (Matt 5:38– 48 // Luke 6:27–36; see further on 12:14, but also on 13:10). It quickly became a firm part of Christian parenesis (1 Thess 5:15; 1 Pet 3:9; Pol. *Phil.* 2.2). See further Piper, chap. 2, Wenham, 17–23, and Sauer, 17–28).

προνοούμενοι καλὰ ἐνώπιον πάντων ἀνθρώπων, "take into consideration what is noble in the sight of everyone." The basic meaning of προνοέω is "think beforehand," so "take into consideration" or "take thought for," blending into the proactive sense "provide for" (LSJ). Both here and in 2 Cor 8:21 the thought seems to be more of the need for sensitivity to the views of others than of active material provision, as in 1 Tim 5:8; though in Pol. *Phil.* 6.1 the context suggests that the same sentiment should be taken of action rather than of thought. Like ἀγαθός (vv 9, 21), for which it serves here as a variant (as in 7:12–21), καλός is chosen because it denotes a quality of beauty (physical or moral) which would receive general approbation in people of sensibility (so "honorable," NEB; see also on 7:16). As earlier, by choosing such general words as "good" and "bad," Paul shows himself ready to appeal to a widespread sense of what is morally right and fitting (see also on 1:26 and 28; 2:7 and 10; cf. particularly Phil 4:8 and 1 Thess 4:12).

These considerations are probably sufficient to settle the meaning of ἐνώπιον πάντων ἀνθρώπων—not as equivalent to the dative (Michel, Schmidt, Wilckens), but in the most natural sense: "(noble) in the sight or opinion of all." Confirmation comes from the clear echo of Prov 3:4, here and in 2 Cor 8:21 (Prov 3:4 was also taken up by Philo, *Ebr.* 84 and by the rabbis, Str-B, 3:299):

Proverbs: προνοοῦ καλὰ   ἐνώπιον κυρίου   καὶ   ἀνθρώπων·
2 Corinthians: προνοοῦμεν καλὰ οὐ μόνον ἐνώπιον κυρίου ἀλλὰ καὶ ἐνώπιον ἀνθρώπων.

Since ἐνώπιον κυρίου clearly means "what God regards as noble," ἐνώπιον ἀνθρώπων can hardly be taken in a different sense. Despite the absence of ἐνώπιον κυρίου in v 17 Paul is hardly likely to have intended the exhortation here to be read differently from the claim made in 2 Cor 8:21 (cf. 4:2); against Cranfield, who takes the prepositional phrase with the verb and gives the clause the forced sense, "aim at in the sight of all men those things which (actually) are good (as determined by the gospel)."

18   εἰ δυνατὸν τὸ ἐξ ὑμῶν, μετὰ πάντων ἀνθρώπων εἰρηνεύοντες, "if possible, so far as it depends on you, live at peace with everyone." For εἰ δυνατόν, cf. *Ep. Arist.* 9; Josephus, *Ant.* 4.310; 13.31; Mark 13:22 par.; Gal 4:15; in full form εἰ δυνατόν ἐστιν—Mark 14:35 par. (BGD, δυνατός 2a). BGD cite no parallels to τὸ ἐξ ὑμῶν, but ἐκ as indicating a reason which is a presupposition is well within the range of its usage (BGD, ἐκ 3f). εἰρηνεύω is used rather than εἰρηνοποιέω, "make peace" (as in Col 1:20). Even so there may be influence from Matt 5:9 (μακάριοι οἱ εἰρηνοποιοί), or, more likely, Mark 9:50 (εἰρηνεύετε ἐν ἀλλήλοις; see also on 14:13), with clearer echoes in 2 Cor 13:11 and 1 Thess 5:13 (see on 12:14); cf. also Heb 12:14. The ideal is more widely cherished: Sir 6:6; Epictetus 4.5.24—εἰρήνην ἄγεις πρὸς πάντας ἀνθρώπους. Piper, 112, draws attention particularly to Ps 34:14 [LXX 33:15]. For the richness of the concept of peace against a Jewish background, however, see on 1:7 and 5:1.

The double qualification (if possible, so far as depends on you) is striking. Paul clearly recognizes that such harmonious living with neighbors might not be possible nor lie within their own power: hostility and persecution was too familiar a rule for any such assumption to be made (see references on 12:14; and *Introduction* §2.3). Paul neither presses an unrealistic ideal upon them nor expects them to compromise their faith for the sake of a quiet life (cf. Murray; Schlier; Ortkemper, 108).

19 μὴ ἑαυτοὺς ἐκδικοῦντες, ἀγαπητοί, ἀλλὰ δότε τόπον τῇ ὀργῇ, "do not take your own revenge, beloved, but give opportunity for (God's) wrath." ἐκδικεῖν occurs regularly in the OT: outside the prophets it is used as much of human vengeance as of divine—referring to times when Israel had a leadership where striking back was a real option (Moses, Joshua, Samuel, Saul, the Maccabees—e.g., Num 31:2; Judg 15:7; 1 Sam 14:24; Sir 46:1; 1 Macc 13:6). In the prophets however, the thought is almost always of divine punishment—on Israel's enemies, or on Israel itself (e.g., Jer 5:9; 23:2; Hos 4:9; Joel 3 [LXX 4]:21; Amos 3:2, 14; Nah 1:2). It is this prophetic language which Paul has in mind, as the λέγει κύριος following the scriptural quotation shows (Deut 32:35), since many of these threats of punishment are expressed in first-person prophetic speech with a λέγει κύριος added, whereas it does not occur in the Deuteronomy passage itself. In the context of Rome, the advice may not seem to have been very necessary for politically powerless Christian churches, but the growing and increasingly desperate activity of the Zealots in Palestine was warning enough of how an oppressed people or persecuted minority might turn to acts of revenge, and the Christian congregations would not need reminding of how vulnerable they were to hostile pressures (see *Introduction* §2.3). And there was always the alternative danger of a small group, particularly if apocalyptic in orientation, retreating into ghettolike sectarianism protected by a pessimistic dualism (cf. Bindemann, 109–110). The ἀγαπητοί functions both as an encouragement to those who might easily find themselves under extreme provocation (the fire of Rome and Nero's persecution of the Christians was to follow in less than ten years) and as a reminder that it is none other than God who is their champion (see on 1:7).

Although the actual phrase διδόναι τόπον ὀργῇ is most closely paralleled in Plutarch, *De cohibenda ira* 14, and although τόπος in the sense of "room for something, occasion" is well enough known in Greek usage (BGD, τόπος 2c; *TDNT* 8:190), Paul more probably derived the idiom from Jewish wisdom (Wisd Sol 12:10, 20; Sir 4:5; 13:22; 16:14; 19:17; 38:12; so also Eph 4:27 and Heb 12:17; cf. Rom 15:23). ὀργή of course denotes divine wrath (as most recognize, e.g., *TDNT* 8:206 n.144; Althaus; Hanson, *Wrath*, 92–93; Murray; Leenhardt; *pace* Dodd), but we should not assume that Paul has in mind only future judgment here (as does Schlier), in view of 1:18 ff. (see on 1:18).

γέγραπται γάρ, "for it is written"; see on 1:17. The following quotation is from Deut 32:35:

Paul = Heb 10:30	ἐμοὶ ἐκδίκησις ἐγὼ ἀνταποδώσω
MT	לִי נָקָם וְשִׁלֵּם ("vengeance is mine and recompense")
LXX	ἐν ἡμέρᾳ ἐκδικήσεως ἀνταποδώσω
Tg. Neof. = *Frg. Tg.*	Vengeance is mine, and I am he who will repay
Tg. Onq. = *Tg. Ps.-J.*	Punishment is before me, and I even I will repay (Str-B, 3:300).

Since the text of Paul and Heb agrees in part with the MT and in part with the LXX and is closest to the Targums, we should assume that a different text from the LXX was current among the diaspora churches. By speaking of "the day of judgment" the LXX seems to refer to the last judgment (cf. Jer 46 [LXX 26]:10; Philo, *Leg. All.* 3.106; Luke 21:22); but the Hebrew is not so specific in content or context, and elsewhere in the OT the thought of divine retribution is not regularly eschatological. Paul's departure from the LXX at this point leaves open the issue of whether he referred the text to the last judgment (see on ὀργή above). For ἐκδίκησις cf. particularly Isa 59:17–18; for ἀνταποδίδωμι cf. Rom 11:9 and 2 Thess 1:6. Since he is echoing prophetic language (see first paragraph above) Paul in effect treats λέγει κύριος as part of the quotation and therefore κύριος as referring to Yahweh (Ortkemper, 111–12; cf. 14:11; 1 Cor 14:21; 2 Cor 6:17–18); see further Ellis, *Paul's Use,* 107–112.

The taking of vengeance, that is, acting independently of or beyond the law, is denounced in the OT (Lev 19:18; Prov 20:22; 24:29; Sir 28:1–7), with the specific thought sometimes added in postbiblical Judaism that vengeance can be left to the Lord (*T. Gad* 6.7; 1QS 10.17–18; CD 9.2–5; Ps. Phoc. 77; *2 Enoch* 50:4), but already implicit in the prophets' frequent talk of divine punishment (as the use of Nah 1:2 in CD 9.5 shows; see references in first paragraph above). The closest parallels, however, seem to have in view an intracommunity ethic (*T. Gad* 6.7; CD 9.2–5; 1QS 10.17–18, but see 2.5–10 and 10.19–21), so that here again we see the effect of Christianity's redefining the boundaries of the people of God as resulting in a greater openness and wider application of this principle (contrast e.g., Ps 149:7; Mic 5:15; Sir 35:18); cf. Michel, Käsemann, Schlier, Wilckens; and see also on 12:14.

20 ἀλλὰ ἐὰν πεινᾷ ὁ ἐχθρός σου, ψώμιζε αὐτόν· ἐὰν διψᾷ, πότιζε αὐτόν· τοῦτο γὰρ ποιῶν ἄνθρακας πυρὸς σωρεύσεις ἐπὶ τὴν κεφαλὴν αὐτοῦ, "but 'If your enemy is hungry, feed him; if he is thirsty, give him to drink; for in so doing you will heap coals of fire on his head.'" The quotation follows the LXX of Prov 25:21–22 almost exactly (Ramaroson's suggested emendation of the Hebrew leaves the Greek unaltered—and unexplained), with ἀλλά as introduction and the more or less synonymous translation ψώμιζε in place of the LXX's τρέφε (both = "feed"); the B reading of ψώμιζε at Prov 25:21 is almost certainly derived from Romans. The force of the ἀλλά is disputed. The most obvious way to take it is as adversative to v 19b–c rather than to v 19a (Zeller; against Wilckens). But that still leaves it unclear as to exactly how Paul intended the quotation from Prov 25:21–22 to qualify v 19b–c: either as envisaging some act of vengeance which Prov 25 allows; or, more likely, as inculcating a positive response to hostility (as against an attitude of resignation which "leaves it all to God"). The question is bound up with the tricky issue of how the last part of the Prov 25 quotation should be understood: what did Paul understand by "heaping coals of fire on his head"? The dispute is ancient: eschatological judgment (Chrysostom; and in this century Spicq, *Agape* 2:155–56; Stendahl, "Hate," 348; and particularly Piper, 115–19); a burning shame leading to repentance (Augustine, Jerome; the majority view today, e.g., Cranfield, Wilckens). The former is certainly supported by the obvious imagery portrayed (Pss 18:8, 12; 140:10 [LXX 11]; Amos 3:4, 7; Obad 15; 2 Esdr = 6 Ezra 16.53; cf. Prov 6:27–29 and Sir 8:10; 11:32). But a more positive sense is probable. (1) Such a negative tone (do good to your enemy so that his punishment will be all the more severe) fits ill with the context: the spirit of the Sermon on the Mount breathes through these verses (cf. Dodd, Schmidt) with a consistent call to open-handed goodness and generous response unmotivated by malice—vv 14, 17, 19, 21. In particular the ἀλλά sets v 20 in some contrast to the idea of leaving the enemy to God's judgment; to read the contrast as "Leave your enemy to God, but try to increase his guilt by your acts of kindness" strikes a jarring note. And it hardly fits comfortably either with the positive thrust of v 20a–b (cf. 2 Kgs 6:22) or with the final call to "overcome evil by good" (Furnish, *Love Command,* 108). As already noted, therefore, the ἀλλά is best taken as calling for a positive response to hostility (by meeting it with acts of kindness) and not simply as a passive response (leave it to God). (2) The suggestion of Morenz that the original imagery of Prov 25:22 can gain illumination from an Egyptian repentance ritual, in which carrying coals of fire (in a dish) on the head was evidence of the genuineness of repentance, has gained a good deal of support in recent years (see particularly Käsemann, Michel, Cranfield). It is of course not necessary to suppose that Paul knew of such a ceremony. Since so much of Proverbs is derived from or shared with Egyptian wisdom (see, e.g., W. McKane, *Proverbs* [London: SCM, 1970] 51–150) it may be sufficient that the original awareness that something positive was meant by the metaphor was transmitted with the metaphor itself (otherwise, Stendahl, "Hate," 352). (3) Here too the Targum of Prov 25:21–22 is probably important since it adds: ". . . on his head and God will hand him over to you" or "will make him your friend" (Str-B, 3:302), that is, "you will win him" in a missionary sense (*TDNT* 7:1095 n.5). This seems to confirm that this particular metaphor ("put coals of fire on someone's head") was recognized as a positive and beneficial act. It also calls in question whether the metaphor should be allegorized (burning shame, remorse), since that is simply a more refined form of revenge (Ortkemper, 122, citing A. Juncker), and we may be dealing simply with a very vivid metaphor for a sharp change of mind brought about by an act of love (Klassen, 349). (4) Finally, we may note that Paul's omission of the final line of the proverb (Prov 25:22b—"and the Lord will reward you") suggests that Paul is seeking to avoid any sense of self-seeking in the action advocated. If so, this would confirm that Paul understood it as an expression of outgoing love seeking only good for the enemy in line with v 14 (Matt 5:44 // Luke 6:27).

Without being able to specify the meaning precisely therefore we probably have sufficient reason to conclude that Paul would have intended the Proverbs citation to bear a positive meaning: that is, as explicating and underlining the importance of meeting an enemy with hospitality and kindness. Such prudent counsel was not untypical of ancient wisdom (see above on 12:17; Zeller), but the impulse from the memory of Jesus' teaching and example gives it a more powerful thrust and motivation.

21 μὴ νικῶ ὑπὸ τοῦ κακοῦ ἀλλὰ νίκα ἐν τῷ ἀγαθῷ τὸ κακόν, "do not be overcome by what is bad, but overcome the bad with the good." The epigrammatic character of the exhortation reinforces its clear function as rounding off and summarizing the principal thrust of vv 14–21. The present tense indicates a call for dedicated persistence. The use once again of the most general and widely recognized contrast between "good" and "bad" (see on 2:10) would increase its appeal and commend those who truly tried to live in accordance with it to all people of good will. As such it is not exclusively Christian (cf. again *T. Ben.* 4.3; 1QS 10.17–18; in Greek literature, particularly Polyaenus, *Strategemata* 5.12, in Michel and Schlier; but see also on 2:14 and 17; Knox sets 1 Macc 2:67–68 in contrast) and shares with 13:1–7 an element of pragmatic prudence for the vulnerable minority (see also 12:18). And Zeller is justified in drawing attention to the traditional character of the exhortation against those who insist too quickly on "the christological basis of the parenesis" (against Cranfield and Wilckens). Nevertheless, while the material is largely traditional, the consistent emphasis on love in the preceding paragraph (vv 9–13) and the influence of the Jesus tradition in the heading to this paragraph (vv 14–21) strongly suggest that Paul would be the first to say that the motivation for such a lifestyle comes from the example of Christ and its enabling from the Spirit of Christ (cf. particularly 5:5, 10).

Explanation

12:9 In describing the Christian congregation as a charismatic body in Christ, Paul would hardly be unmindful of the charismatic realities of the congregation to which he at that time belonged (Corinth). In addressing it some years earlier he had made a point of stressing that love was the indispensable medium through which the charisms must be exercised, for otherwise they are useless (1 Cor 13). So here Paul's teaching moves in an accustomed sequence of thought from charism to love. Not that they are opposites or alternatives (love without charisms): as was clear in vv 5–8, charisms are simply the functions of the body (without charisms the body is paralyzed); but love determines the character of the body's functioning (charisms without love are counterproductive to their purpose, and so are rendered grace-less). The sequence of thought implies that Paul saw a danger that charisms become merely mechanistic, reflex actions patterned on remembered spontaneities, routinized by regularity—a danger threatening all regular ministries, of service as well as of speech (vv 6–8). To be effective they need to be exercised in love. The problem, as Paul no doubt also saw all too well, is that love itself can become formalized in expression, a cloak of pretense hiding an insensitive lack of genuine concern, a pretentious claim as manipulative as any coercive (pseudo-)charism, an outward form for a judgmental and condemnatory spirit. Hence the call for a love which is genuine, in deed as well as word, in mutual relationships as well as creed, as fully accepting of the brother (and the enemy) as God in Christ has accepted them (5:6–10). That this opening exhortation stands as a heading for all that follows and has in mind both Christ as model and the quality of love expressed in 1 Cor 13:4–7 is indicated by the word itself, so distinctive in its Christian usage, by the echoes of Christ's own teaching, particularly in vv 14, 17, and 18, and by the echoes of 1 Cor 13:4–7 in vv 12, 16, and 17.

The immediate corollary is somewhat surprising—"hating the evil, united with the good." There is a vehemence in the first phrase which suggests Paul was no stranger to the dangers of both charism and love being corrupted. The more "spiritual" the claim, the more dangerous and demonic the corruption. The fact that Paul uses the most general categories (evil, good) indicates an awareness that unbalanced emphasis on spiritual factors can result in attitudes and conduct which others can see to be evil (by generally accepted standards) but which the devout claim to be able to justify; although the Christian is not to be conformed to this world (v 2), there is a level of moral sensibility in the wider community which the Christian congregation ignores at its peril. As elsewhere Paul evidently sees a need to correlate talk of charisms with an open-eyed and level-headed love which recognizes evil for what it is. But to be an effective check there must be a passion both in the revulsion against evil and in the commitment to what is good.

10 With v 10 the body imagery gives way to that of the family. The love Paul calls for and sees to be essential if the Christian congregation is to function as one body in Christ has the quality of family love. By that Paul will mean the kind of love which recognizes and can speak about (in the intimacy of the family) weaknesses and failings, but which has a quality of loyalty that outlasts repeated disappointments. If the new communities which have cut across the usual divisions of nation and class can experience the reality of such love, they have a bond which will hold them together through thick and thin.

Another side of such love is the readiness to recognize strengths and to praise attainments of family members. Paul will no doubt already have had sufficient experience of congregations where some members were unwilling to extend a genuine respect across the full range of membership, but cherished doubts and questions about the reality of others' commitment or charism. Where "brotherly love" and "family affection" are in effective interaction, each will be ready to take the lead in showing respect for others, including those whose understanding of commitment and practice of charism is different from one's own. Love without respect for the other is hollow and self-defeating.

11 The next three exhortations become less specific, focusing on matters of basic attitude and motivation. A quality of zestful eagerness and vibrant spirituality is desirable as an expression of the love which binds together the family of Jesus and motivates the functions of the body of Christ. Paul may be thinking of a weariness of spirit and stultifying sameness which can soon characterize even the most charismatic of congregations. There is something slightly artificial in the idea of "working at being eager"; but it is accompanied by the thought of a heat or glow generated by the Spirit. The two evidently hung together, the one emphasizing the elements of human discipline necessary if the inner fire of the Spirit is to maintain the temperature of the body at normal vitality. The double emphasis ("not indolent . . . fired by the Spirit") suggests that the life of the Spirit in the Christian community has an uncomfortable character—an inner drive matched by a personal discipline.

The third phrase in what seems to be a triplet ("serving the Lord") probably functions once again as something of a control or check on what might otherwise be interpreted as an invitation to unbridled enthusiasm. The love which binds a congregation together needs that inner spontaneity bubbling up within if it is to remain fresh and personally real, but it can easily become too experiential and "frothy" unless it expresses also the fundamental commitment to Christ as Lord and is motivated by the desire to serve him. The imagery of the slave is a reminder that what is in view is not personal satisfaction or flights of spirituality, but the will and command of the master.

12 The next three phrases seem to hang together also as a triplet: the association of hope, rejoicing, affliction, and patient endurance is one which came naturally to Paul (cf. 5:2–5), and "persistence in prayer" as an expression of "endurance in affliction" was equally natural (cf. 8:18–27). The sequence from v 10 could have been run in different ways (v 12 could have come before v 11 without greatly diminishing the effect), but the link of Spirit and hope was also part of 5:2–5 and the progression of Spirit to the themes of suffering, hope, and prayer was a major element in the structure of chap. 8. Indeed it is characteristic of Paul's spirituality of eschatological tension to qualify the talk of life in the Spirit now with the awareness of the not yet of hope and the reality of suffering. Christians can be called on to rejoice, not so much in what has already been accomplished in them, but in their firm confidence in God. Such hope sustains the patient endurance in suffering and the persistence in prayer. Likewise it is itself sustained by prayer; for in the midst of suffering only an uninhibited crying out to God can provide sufficient safety valve for the pressures of potential despair.

13 The more individual exhortations of vv 11–12 are framed by the emphasis on mutual interdependence and communal support (vv 10, 13). Zestful spirituality and patient hope cannot be sustained by the individual on his or her own, but only with the support of the congregation functioning as body and family. And such spirituality cannot be maintained apart from practical concern for the physical well-being of all members of the congregation. By describing the members of the churches as "saints" Paul reminds his listeners once again that they are the eschatological equivalent to the Israel of old. And though the boundaries of the people of God have been redrawn in terms of grace and faith rather than of physical descent and law, the ancient obligations of Israel to care for the disadvantaged within the wider community have not been withdrawn or redefined, but still remain part of the scriptural definition of the will of God. Within Rome in particular the importance of offering hospitality to traders and travelers would be considerable. Paul does not commend it for its evangelistic opportunities, but simply as an obligation of good-neighborliness—the sort of "good" which would be universally recognized. At the same time, since the demand for hospitality at Rome would be so great, Paul was probably conscious that the practice of unstinting hospitality would be likely to put a considerable strain on the Roman congregations' resources, and was therefore a highly appropriate item with which to round off this sequence of exhortations to love without pretense. Apart from anything else, Paul was hoping to enjoy that hospitality on his own account in the not too distant future (15:28).

In this paragraph (vv 10–13) the strong emotive element should not be ignored—"love . . . hating . . . clinging to . . . brotherly love . . . family affection . . . eagerness . . . aglow . . . rejoicing . . . aspire   to . . . ." Paul was not afraid to make an appeal in such emotional terms. He is careful to build in an element of check and control, as we have seen. But at the same time he seems to recognize that without a deeply rooted motivation and passion the kind of commitment he calls for here cannot be sustained, particularly in the face of suffering and human need.

14–21 In vv 14–21 Paul broadens his perspective from the internal relationships within and among the Christian congregations to take in their relationships with the wider community within which they had to live and make their living. Paul evidently was mindful of the political realities which confronted these new small groups within the cities of the Roman Empire in the eastern Mediterranean. In particular he would be aware of the fact that the little churches in Rome were an endangered species, vulnerable to further imperial ruling against Jews and societies. His first concern therefore is to urge a policy of avoiding trouble by refusing retaliation to provocations and by responding with positive good to all hostile acts directed against them. This latter concern is the linking theme, being repeated with variations no less than four times (vv 14, 17, 19, 21), buttressed by scripture (v 20) and given the place of emphasis at both beginning and end (vv 14, 21). The fact that he takes for granted that persecution and acts of malice would be directed against the small house gatherings is significant enough. It speaks eloquently of the atmosphere of threat and intimidation within which these Christians had to live out their discipleship. All the more striking it is therefore that he advocates such a positive outgoing goodness in response (not merely passive resistance). It was no doubt a policy of prudence: a reputation for kindliness might well help ensure the support of the citizenry at large in any confrontation with the authorities. But even more important, it was a policy which Jesus had advocated by word and deed and was a characteristic expression of that same love which should characterize relationships within the congregation of faith (vv 9–10, 13).

This is a second striking feature of this paragraph—the degree to which it builds on characteristic themes of Jewish wisdom, but with emphases drawn from the teaching of Jesus integrated and giving the whole a more distinctively Christian positive outward-lookingness. The whole effect would be to remind his readers of the extent to which this new faith in Jesus Christ was firmly rooted in its Jewish heritage, in its praxis as well as its beliefs; also of the extent to which Jesus' own teaching on matters of social ethics was an elaboration of centuries-old Jewish wisdom. The echo of the Jesus tradition is strong particularly in v 14, but since that verse sets the theme for what follows, that echo pervades the whole—by implication in vv 17 and 21, and more explicitly in v 18. The fact that Paul does not quote any exhortation as a word of Jesus as such does not diminish the echo of Jesus' words one whit—any more than his failure to cite Proverbs and Leviticus in vv 16, 17, and 19 diminishes the clear echo of that earlier instruction. In both cases we are evidently dealing with a parenesis whose authority and relevance gave it an immediacy and force which did not depend on chapter and verse. This sense of a living tradition of direct authority, which included both OT and Jesus tradition, effectively prevented the emergence of a new "written code" (7:6) so long as it lasted.

The fact that vv 15–16 seem to focus attention back once again more on the internal relationships of the Christian congregations should not be seen merely as a disruption of the wider concern. On the contrary, these verses should be taken as some indication of the degree to which Paul saw the life of the Christian churches as integrated into the wider life in the city. The call for sensitive sympathy with those caught in the ups and downs of daily life (v 15), for a proper modesty of self-esteem and for a genuine solidarity with the most lowly ranked or disadvantaged within the congregation (v 16) is of a piece with the positive will to bless the persecutor (v 14) and to do good to the malicious and spiteful (v 17). Paul did not see a Christian's life as divided neatly into two sets of attitudes and obligations—one to fellow believers, the other to nonbelievers. The same sympathetic concern and positive outgoing love should be the rule in all cases—a love which does not reckon or depend on receiving a positive response in turn. For this not only Jesus' words but Jesus' example provided the model which would be not far from the surface of Paul's mind (here too the same sequence of thought as in 5:1–11 and 8:18–39 probably reflects a regular pattern in Paul's theology).

Also significant is the extent to which Paul takes for granted actual contact of his listeners with the wider city community, and awareness of the moral standards prized by others: they must live at peace (v 18) and seek to have as positive relations with their unbelieving neighbors and associates as possible; they must be mindful of what others value and hold in high regard and be sure not to let their ethical and aesthetic standards leave them open to the criticisms of Stoic or Cynic (v 17); they should be known for their whole-hearted committal to oneness with the deprived (v 16), they should show hospitality to enemy as well as fellow believer (v 20), and their relationships within the wider community could result in persecution (vv 14, 17, 19–21). All in all Paul has no thought of the Roman Christians as compartmentalizing their lives (into spiritual and ordinary affairs) or of living their lives cut off from contact with the wider community. He takes it for granted that Christians will live out their daily lives and wider relationships motivated by the same love as in their relationships with fellow believers.

At the same time Paul shows himself to be under no illusions: the prospect of persecution is the recurring motif in these verses; and in v 18 Paul shows that he has no intention of commending an overenthusiastic or too impractica-ble ideal in these wider relationships ("if possible, insofar as it depends on you"). The eschatological tension is not only a matter of living the life of the Spirit through a mortal body on the way to death, but also a matter of living as the body of Christ within the body politic where the same forces of death are dominant. This essentially is the speech of the oppressed, who need to be warned against responding to malevolence in kind lest evil simply feed on itself and spawn greater evil, who need to be reminded that vengeance in human hands is a treacherous commodity which destroys the good it is meant to defend and must perforce be left to God alone, and who need to be encouraged repeatedly that Christ's answer to evil is always and never other than a positive act of good. Only so will good outlast and gain the victory over evil (v 21). And if such warning needs to be given to communities under threat or reality of oppression, how much more need it be given to the triumphalist church.

D. Live as Good Citizens (13:1-7)

Bibliography

Aland, K. "Das Verhältnis von Kirche und Staat in der Frühzeit." *ANRW* II.23.1 (1979) 60–246. Bammel, E. "Romans 13." In *Jesus and the Politics of His Day*, ed. E. Bammel and C. F. D. Moule. Cambridge University Press, 1984. 365–83. Barrett, C. K. "The New Testament Doctrine of Church and State." *New Testament Essays*. London: SPCK, 1972. 1–19. Blank, J. "Kirche und Staat im Urchristentum." In *Kirche und Staat auf Distanz*, ed. G. Denzler. Munich, 1977. 9–28. Borg, M. "A New Context for Romans 13." *NTS* 19 (1972–73) 205–18. Bornkamm, G. *Paul*. 210–15. Bruce, F. F. "Paul and 'the Powers that be.'" *BJRL* 66 (1983–84) 78–96. Campenhausen, H. von. "Zur Auslegung von Römer 13." *Aus der Frühzeit des Christentums*. Tübingen: Mohr, 1963. 81–101. Carr, W. *Angels and Principalities*. SNTSMS 42. Cambridge University Press, 1981. Esp. 115–18. Cranfield, C. E. B. "Some Observations on Romans 13:1–7." *NTS* 6 (1959–60) 241–49. Cullmann, O. *The State in the New Testament*. London: SCM, 1957. Delling, G. *Röm 13:1–7 innerhalb der Briefe des Paulus*. Berlin: Evangelische, 1962. Dibelius, M. "Rom und die Christen im ersten Jahrhundert." *Botschaft und Geschichte II*. Tübingen: Mohr, 1956. 177–228. Dunn, J. D. G. "Romans 13:1–7—A Charter for Political Quietism?" *Ex Auditu* 2 (1986) 55–68. Eckstein, H.-J. *Syneidesis*. 276–300. Friedrich, J., W. Pöhlmann, and P. Stuhlmacher. "Zur historischen Situation und Intention von Röm 13:1–7." *ZTK* 73 (1976) 131–66. Furnish, V. P. *Moral Teaching*. 115–41. Goppelt, L. "Die Freiheit zur Kaisersteuer: Zu Mark 12:17 und Röm 13:1–7." *Christologie und Ethik*. Göttingen: Vandenhoeck & Ruprecht, 1968. 208–19. Hanson, A. T. *Wrath*. 93–96. Heiligentahl, R. *Werke*. 93–114. ———. "Strategien konformer Ethik im Neuen Testament am Beispiel von Röm 13:1–7." *NTS* 29 (1983) 55–61. Jewett, R. *Anthropological Terms*. 439–41. ———. *Tolerance*. 114–20. Käsemann, E. "Principles of the Interpretation of Romans 13." *New Testament Questions of Today*. London: SCM, 1969. 196–216. Kallas, J. "Romans 13:1–7: An Interpolation." *NTS* 11 (1964–65) 365–74. Kosnetter, J. "Röm 13:1–7: Zeitbedingte Vorschichtsmassregel oder grundsätzliche Einstellung?" *SPCIC I*. 347–55. Kruijf, T. C. de. "The Literary Unity of Rom 12:16–13:8a: A Network of Inclusions." *Bijdragen* 48 (1987) 319–26. Kuss, O. "Paulus über die staatliche Gewalt." *Auslegung I*. 246–59. Laub, F. "Der Christ und die staatliche Gewalt: Zum Verständnis der 'Politischen' Paränese Röm 13:1–7 in der gegenwärtigen Diskussion." *MTZ* 30 (1979) 257–65. Merk, O. *Handeln*. 161–64. Morrison, C. D. *The Powers That Be*. London: SCM, 1960. Neirynck, F. "Sayings of Jesus." 286-91. Neugebauer, F. "Zur Auslegung von Röm 13:1–7." *KD* 8 (1962) 151–72. Perkins, P. *Love*. 97–103. Pierce, C. A. *Conscience in the New Testament*. London: SCM, 1955. 66–74. Ridderbos, H. *Paul*. 320–26. Riekkinen, V. *Römer 13: Aufzeichnung und Weiterführung der exegetischen Diskussion*. Helsinki: Suomalainen Tiedeakatemia, 1980. Schelkle, K. H. "Staat und Kirche in der patristischen Auslegung von Röm 13:1–7." *ZNW* 44 (1952–53) 223–36. Schlier, H. "Die Beurteilung des Staates im Neuen Testament." *Zeit*. 1–16. Schmithals, W. *Römerbrief*. 191–97. Schrage, W. *Einzelgebote*. 222–28. ———. *Die Christen und der Staat nach dem NT*. Gütersloh: Gütersloher, 1971. Strobel, A. "Zum Verständnis von Röm 13." *ZNW* 47 (1956) 67–93. ———. "Furcht, wem Furcht gebührt: Zum profangriechischen Hintergrund von Röm 13:7." *ZNW* 55 (1964) 58–62. Thrall, M. E. "The Pauline Use of συνείδησις." *NTS* 14 (1967–68) 118–25. Unnik, W. C. van. "Lob und Strafe durch die Obrigkeit hellenistisches zu Röm 13:3–4." In *Jesus und Paulus*, FS W. G. Kümmel, ed. E. E. Ellis and E. Grässer. Göttingen: Vandenhoeck & Ruprecht, 1975. 334–43. Walker, R. *Studie zu Römer 13:1–7*. Munich: Kaiser, 1966. Wengst, K. *Pax Romana and the Peace of Jesus Christ*. London: SCM, 1987. 80–84. Wilckens, U. "Röm

13:1–7." *Rechtfertigung als Freiheit*. Neukirchen: Neukirchener, 1974. 203–45. = "Der Gehorsam gegen die Behörden des Staates im Tun des Guten: Zu Römer 13:1–7." In Lorenzi, *Dimensions*. 85–130. **Wink, W.** *Naming the Powers I*. Philadelphia: Fortress, 1984. Esp. 45–47.

Translation

¹ *Let every person* ª *be subject to the governing authorities. For there is no authority except given by* ᵇ *God, and the powers* ᵇ *that be have been established by* ᵇ *God.* ² *So then, he who opposes the authority has resisted the ordinance of God; and those who resist shall receive judgment on themselves.* ³ *For rulers are not a cause of fear to good* ᵇ *but to bad.* ᵇ *Do you want to be without fear of the authority? Do good, and you will have his commendation.* ⁴ *For he is God's servant to you* ᵇ *for good. But if you do wrong, be afraid. For he does not bear the sword to no purpose. For he is God's servant, an avenger for wrath* ᶜ *against the evildoer.* ⁵ *Wherefore it is necessary* ᵈ *to be subject, not only on account of wrath, but also on account of conscience.* ⁶ *For that is why you also pay tribute. For they are ministers of God engaged in this very task.* ⁷ *Render to everyone their dues: tribute to whom tribute is due, tax to whom tax; fear to whom fear is due, respect to whom respect.*

Notes

ª Instead of πᾶσα ψυχή ᴾ⁴⁶ and several Western authorities read πάσαις ("Be subject to all governing authorities"), perhaps to avoid the semitic idiom involved in the former (Metzger).

ᵇ Various tidying-up emendations have been made at later stages in the manuscript tradition which do not affect the sense of the text.

ᶜ εἰς ὀργήν is omitted by D F G, probably because of some hesitation at some stage on the part of some scribes to attribute agency of divine wrath to a human ruler.

ᵈ ᴾ⁴⁶ D F G and others omit ἀνάγκη and read ὑποτάσσεσθε, perhaps to avoid the implication of an impersonal cosmic necessity which διὸ ἀνάγκη may have suggested (see on 13:5).

Form and Structure

Despite the change to third-person format, these verses are really a continuation of the preceding exhortation and should not be regarded as "an independent insertion" (so correctly Friedrich et al., 150–53; Cranfield; Wilckens; Riekkinen, esp. chaps. 1 and 2; against Michel, Käsemann—"an alien body in Paul's exhortation"), or as a non-Pauline insertion (against most recently O'Neill and Schmithals, *Römerbrief*, 191–97)—as is clearly indicated by the continuation of influence from Jewish wisdom and the carryover of basic categories at beginning (ἀγαθός/κακός—12:21; 13:3–4; ὀργή—12:19; 13:4–5; ἐκδικέω/ἔκδικος—12:19; 13:4; πάντων ἀνθρώπων/πᾶσιν—12:17–18; 13:7) and end (ὀφειλή/ὀφείλω—13:7, 8; Friedrich et al., 148–49; Wilckens; Bruce, 80–83; Kruijf). Note also the common themes shared by 2:7–11 and 13:3–4:

	good work/the good	2:7, 10; 13:3-4
	honor/praise	2:7, 10; 13:3
	the evil	2:9; 13:3-4
	wrath	2:5, 8; 13:4
also	condemnation	2:3; 13:2
	conscience	2:15; 13:5

(Heiligenthal, *Werke*, 108).

The theme of quietist response and legitimate authority links 12:14–21 and 13:1–7 firmly together, and guidance on how to cope with opposition and hostility naturally leads into consideration of the political realities within which the Roman Christians had to live (see further 12:1–15:13 *Introduction*). Although the changing identity of the people of God (no longer simply Jews identified in ethnic categories) was part of the problem (Wright, *Messiah*, 225), Paul again draws here on the sound political wisdom of an Israel tested by oppression and dispersion (e.g., vv 1, 4—Wisd Sol 6:3–4) to counsel a policy of political quietism. Paul's recognition of the need to function within the realities of this age is underlined by his heavy use of the language and categories of Hellenistic administration (see particularly Strobel). Parallels with other first-century Christian writings (particularly 1 Pet 2:13–17) indicate that this policy of political prudence was widespread among the earliest Christian congregations (Selwyn, *1 Peter*, 427; Wilckens, "Römer 13:1–7," 212–13). The point is driven home here by repetition of key concepts—ἐξουσία (vv 1–3), τάσσεσθαι and compounds (vv 1, 2, 5), ἀγαθός/κακός (vv 3–4), φόβος/φοβεῖσθαι (vv 3, 4, 7) and ὀργή (vv 4, 5). The use of such language "tells the reader that the Christian is willing to belong to the larger society, and that he/she is not out to subvert the social order" (Perkins, 98; see also Moxnes, "Honour," 65–68). The pragmatic quality of Paul's counsel is also indicated by the fact that Paul speaks not of the state as such but of political and civic authority as it would actually bear upon his readers. His rounding off the exhortation with specific advice about the paying of taxes almost certainly reflects a knowledge of current affairs in Rome (vv 6–7; Dunn, "Romans 13:1–7," 66). The merging of the categories of civil servant and cultic office-holder (v 6—"ministers of God") again reflects the blurring of older boundaries caused by the redefinition of the people of God by transformation of cultic (cf. 12:1) and ethnic categories.

Comment

1 πᾶσα ψυχὴ ἐξουσίαις ὑπερεχούσαις ὑποτασσέσθω, "let every person be subject to the governing authorities." The abruptness of the transition is marked by the lack of a conjunction or joining particle (cf. particularly 9:1) and by the switch to third person. But neither this nor the subject of this paragraph is sufficient reason to regard it as an independent insertion, unrelated to the context: on the contrary, the structure of chaps. 12–15 suggests that the counsel given here stands very much at the center of Paul's concerns; the theological redrawing of the boundaries of the people of God, which has been the effect of the argument in 1:18–11:36, made some consideration of this subject inescapable (see further 12:1–15:13 *Introduction*); and the political context of the Christian house churches in Rome would have made some guidance on the theme imperative (see further *Introduction* §§2.3–4). The lack of connection therefore simply signifies that Paul has been unable to achieve a smoother connection (though note the connecting links outlined in *Form and Structure*); his concern to take up this subject causes him to do so in a sudden and somewhat brusque way. In the urgency of his concern he simply states his advice in blunt fashion, to serve as the thesis which he elaborates and repeats for emphasis in v 5.

πᾶσα ψυχή is semitic (כָּל־נֶפֶשׁ), with the soul as the center of the earthly life, the lower half as it were of the πνεῦμα (cf. Philo's conception of a higher and lower mind in man), standing for the whole person by metonymy; see further on 2:9. The counsel is all-embracive, though here naturally the Christian audience is primarily in view: in the old age of Adam, states and kingdoms are part of the social corporeality of humankind, and given the character of the old age, that includes ruler and ruled (contrast the different model of Mark 10:42–44). So long as believers yet belong to that age (as chaps. 6–8 made clear) they must live in terms of its political composition (cf. Dibelius, "Rom," 184; Nygren), just as the individual must live the life of the Spirit while yet in the body of death (7:24–8:10).

ἐξουσία is used here in the restricted sense of "official power or authority" (cf. Luke 7:8; 19:17; 20:20; see further Leenhardt), which by natural usage comes to mean also the bearers of such authority, thus "authorities, government officials" (so also Luke 12:11; Plutarch, *Philopoemen* 17; Josephus, *War* 2.350; see also BGD, *TDNT* 8:29–30 and *NDIEC* 2:83–84). This is confirmed by the accompanying participle: οἱ ὑπερέχοντες = "those in authority, superiors" is well enough attested in such writers as Polybius and Artemidorus (BGD; see also LSJ, ὑπερέχω II.4c). In the LXX see Wisd Sol 6:5, and cf. 2 Macc 3:11; also Philo, *Agr.* 121. The language seems to have become established in Christian parenesis on attitudes to the power of kings and rulers: 1 Pet 2:13—ὑποτάγητε . . . βασιλεῖ ὡς ὑπερέχοντι; 1 Tim 2:2—prayer to be made ὑπὲρ βασιλέων καὶ πάντων τῶν ἐν ὑπεροχῇ ὄντων (the latter phrase = τῶν ὑπερεχόντων).

There is nothing therefore in the usage to support the suggestion that ἐξουσίαι here mean also angelic powers behind and acting through the political authorities. This once quite popular view (see especially Cullmann, 95–114; Morrison; and most recently, Wink; for patristic interpretation, see Schelkle) has now become something of a historical curiosity (see particularly the careful discussions of Cranfield, who has become much less enamored of the view since his earlier study, and of Riekkinen, 133–70; also, e.g., Gaugler; Delling, 20–34; Carr; and Bruce, 88–90). Not surprisingly, the consideration now generally regarded as decisive (but not considered by Wink) is the extreme unlikelihood of Paul's calling for submission to heavenly powers (contrast 8:37–39; 1 Cor 15:24–27; Gal 4:8–11; Col 2:15); "a heavenly rule with the help of angelic powers is unthinkable in Paul" (Käsemann); the use of ἄρχοντες and ἐξουσία in v 3 also tells against it (see on 13:3). In fact such a suggestion probably runs counter to one of the main thrusts of Paul's theology. For rule by angels was part and parcel of the nationalism to which Paul's apostleship to the Gentiles ran counter (cf. Deut 32:8–9 LXX; Dan 10:13, 20–21; 12:1; Sir 17:17; *Jub.* 15.31); whereas the mission to the Gentiles aimed to break down such barriers (3:29–30 leading up to 4:13–17 and 5:12–21) and to bring to wider realization the eschatological rule of the one God through Christ over all creation (8:31–39; 11:33–36). Certainly no apotheosis of the state is even hinted at: "not divine [*göttlich*], but God-intended [*gottgewollt*]" (Schrage, *Christen,* 56).

ὑποτάσσω (ὑπό—"under"; τάσσω—"place, order") has the clear sense "subject, subordinate," and in the middle or passive, "subject oneself, be subjected,

subordinate" (stronger than ὑπακούω, which has more the sense of "respond").
It is thus the natural correlative of ἐξουσία and ὑπερέχω, whatever the authority
in question—whether of husband (Eph 5:22 *v.l.;* Col 3:18; Titus 2:5; 1 Pet
3:1, 5—a patriarchal society being of course assumed), of parents (Luke 2:51),
of masters (Titus 2:9; 1 Pet 2:18; *Did.* 4.11; *Barn.* 19.7), or of secular authorities
(1 Chron 29:24; Titus 3:1; 1 Pet 2:13; *1 Clem.* 61.1; and here); the thought
of ecclesiastical submission appears only in the apostolic fathers (BGD)—1
Cor 16:16 has in view charismatic authority (the household of Stephanas
"appointed themselves to ministry"!), and in 1 Pet 5:5 it is more a call for
respect for age (against Schlier; cf. Eph 5:21). Given its prominence in these
Christian texts, we may deduce that such counsel to disciplined acceptance
of the realities of social status and of what that entailed for the social inferior
was a regular part of early Christian parenesis (cf. particularly Selwyn,
1 Peter, 419–37); and though social relationships are different today, it may
well be the case that such submission is an inevitable or inescapable outworking of the Christian grace of humility (*TDNT* 8:45; cf. particularly Phil
2:3—τῇ ταπεινοφροσύνῃ . . . ὑπερέχοντας ἑαυτῶν). Cranfield's argument that
ὑποτασσέσθω has the sense of "recognizing that one is placed below the authority
by God . . ." tries to import too much theological freight into the word.
The thought that the subjection is limited by the terms of the ruler's God-
given authority is correct, but is the point of the clauses which follow. "Be
subject" is the principle (vv 1, 5) to which the qualifications are added. For
ὑποτάσσειν as due to God see on 8:7.

  οὐ γὰρ ἔστιν ἐξουσία εἰ μὴ ὑπὸ θεοῦ, αἱ δὲ οὖσαι ὑπὸ θεοῦ τεταγμέναι εἰσίν, "for
there is no authority except given by God, and the powers that be have
been established by God." Here again Paul draws on the resources of Jewish
wisdom (see particularly Schrage, *Christen*, 14–28; Friedrich et al., 145–46).
Prov. 8:15–16—"By me kings reign, and rulers decree what is just; by me
princes rule, and nobles govern the earth"; Wisd Sol 6:3 reminds boastful
rulers, "Your dominion was given you from the Lord, and your sovereignty
from the Most High"; similarly Sir 10:4; 17:17; *Ep. Arist.* 224; Josephus,
War 2.140. It was a theologoumenon which had carried weight in the days
of Israel's own sovereignty (2 Sam 12:8) and one to which Jews clung in the
darker days of threat and oppression by the superpowers (Isa 41:2–4; 45:1–
7; Jer 21:7, 10; 27:5–6), not least in apocalyptic (Dan 2:21, 37–38; 4:17, 25, 32;
5:21; *1 Enoch* 46.5; *2 Apoc. Bar.* 82.9); for rabbinic references see Str-B,
3:303–4. It would no doubt have been particularly important in diaspora
synagogues (cf. Laub, 264: "The Paul who speaks in Rom 13:1–7 is not the
'apostle of Jesus Christ' but the diaspora Jew"). Lietzmann also notes the
passages which indicate a longstanding Jewish acceptance of the obligation
to express loyalty to the foreign ruling power by offering sacrifice and prayer
on behalf of the ruler. It is unlikely, however, that the Caesar cult was as
yet provoking any clash of loyalties. There is some parallel here with 12:6–
8 (Schlatter): authority properly so described (of charism or political power)
derives from God. "Paul refuses all Manicheism or the slightest dualism"
(Maillot).

  The implication of ὑπὸ θεοῦ τεταγμέναι, of course, is of an authority ordered
by God, (1) subject to the limits of that ordering (cf. Matt 8:9 // Luke 7:8;

Acts 15:2; 22:10; *1 Clem.* 20.2; 61.1–2), and (2) commensurate to the submission called for (v 1a; cf. Schlier, "Beurteilung," 10). The corollary, that those who abuse their God-given authority or call for greater submission than God has ordered will come under the judgment of God, is spelled out explicitly in the same passages (especially Wisd Sol 6:4–5; *2 Apoc. Bar.* 82.4–9), with Nebuchadnezzar a fearful warning (Dan 4:13–17, 23–25; 5:20–21); see also *4 Macc.* 12.11. The further corollary that a subject's submission is determined by the same God-ordained limits naturally follows (though of course Paul is hardly concerned to draw it out here) and allows a fair amount of reworking of this counsel in the light of changed political systems and conditions. It is noticeable that Paul makes no effort to add a specifically eschatological qualification to his assertion (the authority of earthly rulers will soon be at an end) (cf. particularly Kuss, "Gewalt," 257–58). But if there is some dependence on Jesus tradition here (see on 13:7), a Christian audience would probably recognize that any restatement of the first half of the principle of Mark 12:17 carries with it also the second (cf. Goppelt, "Freiheit," 216–18; in the same way in vv 8–10 Paul does not need to remind his readers that the call for love of neighbor presupposes the prior obligation of love of God).

2 ὥστε ὁ ἀντιτασσόμενος τῇ ἐξουσίᾳ τῇ τοῦ θεοῦ διαταγῇ ἀνθέστηκεν, "so then, he who opposes the authority has resisted the ordinance of God." For ὥστε in this usage see on 7:4. For ἀντιτάσσομαι, "oppose, resist" a person, cf. 1 Kgs 11:34, Hos 1:6 and James 5:6. ἀνθίστημι is nearly synonymous ("set oneself against, oppose, resist, withstand") and may be introduced for reasons of stylistic variation. But it is probably significant that its typical usage in the LXX is for a resistance which was unavailing before superior strength (Lev 26:37; Deut 7:24; 9:2; 11:25; Josh 1:5; 7:13; 23:9; Judg 2:14; 2 Chron 13:7; Jud 6:4; 11:18) or for a resistance to God which was inconceivable (Job 9:19; Ps 76:7; Jer 49:19 = 50:44; Jud 16:14; Wisd Sol 11:21; 12:12) (see on 9:19). The clear implication is of a state of affairs, a structure of society, that cannot be changed, so that resistance is not only against God's ordering of society, but wasteful of time and energy. διαταγή occurs in only two other passages in biblical Greek—Ezra 4:11 and Acts 7:53 (also *1 Clem.* 20.3), but it is well attested in papyri and inscriptions (MM, *TDNT* 8:36), though the customary word for an official decree is διάταγμα (in the NT only in Heb 11:23); see further Strobel, "Röm 13," 86, and Friedrich et al., 136–40.

οἱ δὲ ἀνθεστηκότες ἑαυτοῖς κρίμα λήμψονται, "and those who resist shall receive judgment on themselves"; "those who so resist have themselves to thank for the punishment they will receive" (NEB). The perfect participle indicates a determined and established policy: "those who have set themselves to resist." The words are directed more against anarchy than single-issue protest. For κρίμα see on 2:2; 3:8; and 11:33. The idiom, λαμβάνεσθαι κρίμα, "to receive judgment" is semitic (Mark 12:40 pars.; James 3:1) and simply means "be condemned" (BGD, κρίμα). As in 9:19, Paul may, consciously or unconsciously, have been influenced by the language of Job 9:19 LXX and Wisd Sol 12:12: τίς ἀντιστήσεται τῷ κρίματι (θεοῦ). Divine judgment is clearly in view, and presumably eschatological, as the end result of such a deliberate policy (ἀνθεστηκότες), as in 2:2–3. But just as divine wrath works through the make-up of the human species (1:18–32), so Paul could readily conceive of divine judgment working through the structures of (divinely ordained) human society (cf. Murray, Cranfield, Käsemann); cf. 13:4.

3 οἱ γὰρ ἄρχοντες οὐκ εἰσὶν φόβος τῷ ἀγαθῷ ἔργῳ ἀλλὰ τῷ κακῷ, "for rulers are not a cause for fear to good work but to bad." The γάρ indicates that Paul intends this as a further elaboration of what he means by a divinely ordered society. Here there can be no dispute that ἄρχοντες means human rulers (rather than angelic powers; NJB translates "magistrates"), even though the only other Pauline uses are open to other interpretation (1 Cor 2:6, 8; otherwise in the Pauline corpus only Eph 2:2; Titus 1:9 is attested only by 460); outside Paul cf. particularly Matt 20:25; John 7:26; 12:42; Acts 3:17; 4:5, 8, 26; 13:27; 14:5; 16:19; see further MM and Strobel, "Röm 13," 79–80. φόβος here clearly means "that which arouses fear" (BGD, 1)—here understood as something desirable for the good ordering of society; the different situation and counsel of Isa 8:12–13 and 1 Pet 3:13–15 is not in view. Once again the ἀγαθός/κακός antithesis signals that Paul is expressing himself in terms which would gain the widest approbation from men and women of good will (see on 2:10); for "good work," as something desirable in Paul's eyes, see on 2:7 (the parallel between 2:1–16 and 13:1–7 [see *Form and Structure*] is no accident). Whatever the abuses perpetrated on the system by corrupt rulers, this statement of principle would be widely accepted (see material collected by Strobel, "Furcht," 59–60, and van Unnik). That good citizenship may be particularly in view is suggested by the following clauses (Käsemann, Schlier), but in societies where religious performance and piety were part of good citizenship that indicates an already broad reference.

θέλεις δὲ μὴ φοβεῖσθαι τὴν ἐξουσίαν; "do you want to be without fear of the authority?" For a few lines Paul reverts to diatribe style (as in 1 Cor 7:21, 27–28), a simple way of varying the rhythm and of keeping attention; the line could be read as a conditional clause ("if you wish . . ."—e.g., Barrett), but assuming punctuation for a question would read better. The use of ἐξουσία here, where civic authority or officialdom is clearly in view, confirms the limited reference of ἐξουσίαι in v 1 (see on 13:1), though here the sense may be more of the authority vested in ruler or official.

τὸ ἀγαθὸν ποίει, καὶ ἕξεις ἔπαινον ἐξ αὐτῆς, "do good and you will have its commendation." More clearly than in anything so far said, Paul appeals to the general sense that good citizenship and moral caliber are to be commended: "do right" (NEB, NIV), "live honestly" (NJB). For ἔπαινος, "praise, approval, applause," is a characteristic goal of Greek wisdom and philosophy and includes particularly the idea of public commendation (*TDNT* 2:586; Strobel, "Röm 13," 81–84), not least for "good works" (Heiligenthal, *Werke*, 104–7). Hence it is found also in the sense "complementary address, panegyric" (LSJ 2), synonymous with ἐγκώμιον ("encomium, eulogy") in at least one aretalogy of Isis (*NDIEC* 1:15). Characteristic of Jewish values is the conviction that the only desirable praise is from God (Ps 22:25 [LXX 21:26]; Wisd Sol 15:19; Philo, *Leg. All.* 3.77; *Heres* 90; *Abr.* 190), but the more typical Greek idea is evident in the famous Sir 44:8, 15, and in Philo, *Post.* 141. In 2:29 Paul displayed the same typically Jewish distrust of human praise (cf. 1 Cor 4:5), a clear reminder that the scope of his remarks here is limited and directed to a particular context (Phil 4:8 makes a similar appeal to a consensus instinct for what is true, honorable, just, pure, lovely, gracious, excellent, and praise-worthy). Here again 1 Pet 2:14 walks in close company with our passage.

4 θεοῦ γὰρ διάκονός ἐστιν σοὶ εἰς τὸ ἀγαθόν, "for he is God's servant to you for good." διάκονος is well enough attested in inscriptional evidence in the sense "(civic) official or functionary" (MM); so in Esth 1:10; 2:2; and 6:3 for royal attendants, with no indication of a sacral or cultic reference (*TDNT* 4:231). In any case, such usage would chime in with Paul's concern to desacralize the idea of divine service (1:9; 12:1; 15:16), and for a broader understanding of what counts as service acceptable to God (12:7). Breaking down the barrier between cult and everyday, between "chosen" and Gentile, remains a preoccupation in the back of his mind. The overtone is strengthened by the explicit assertion that such officials are "servants of God," although anticipated in Isa 45:1; Jer 25:9; and particularly Wisd Sol 6:4. The σοί of course refers to the Christian readership, but in their status as residents of Rome rather than as believers, with τὸ ἀγαθόν once again more general (see on 2:10), more civic well-being (Michel; Leenhardt; Käsemann; Wilckens; Riekkinen, 208) than spiritual well-being, as in 8:28 (against Walker, 37–39; Cranfield), though Paul would not hold the two in sharp distinction.

ἐὰν δὲ τὸ κακὸν ποιῇς, φοβοῦ, "but if you do wrong, be afraid"—applying the rationale of v 3a. Again the language is unspecific—τὸ κακόν referring to what everyone with a sense of responsibility and obligation would recognize as against the common interest.

οὐ γὰρ εἰκῇ τὴν μάχαιραν φορεῖ, "for he does not bear the sword to no purpose." φορέω is the frequentative of φέρω, implying repeated or habitual action (LSJ), hence "wear" (BGD); the thought is of an established order (thus serving as the antinomy to the perfect οἱ ἀνθεστηκότες—v 2). εἰκῇ can have the sense "without cause, in vain, to no avail, to no purpose" (BGD, *NDIEC* 2:81); cf. its other Pauline/NT use—1 Cor 15:2; Gal 3:4; 4:11; and Col 2:18 (otherwise only Matt 5:22 *v.l.*). The full phrase most obviously has in view the power of life and death which was then, as for most of human civilization, the ultimate sanction for government. Cranfield (cf. Friedrich, 142–44) seems justified in calling in question the older assumption (Lagrange, Michel, Barrett, Leenhardt) of an allusion to the *ius gladii* (the right of the sword) as such, since during the first two centuries it referred only to the power of provincial governors in connection with Roman citizens under their command (A. N. Sherwin-White, *Roman Society and Roman Law in the New Testament* [Oxford: Clarendon, 1963] 8–11); but he is probably less so in doubting a reference to capital punishment (the sword represents capital not corporal punishment) (cf. Murray). The reminder would be all the more potent in Rome, since there too even Roman citizens, who elsewhere had the right of appeal to a higher court and as far as the emperor (cf. Acts 25:11), were confronted by the Empire's ultimate authority (see *OCD*, "Appelatio," 86–87).

θεοῦ γὰρ διάκονός ἐστιν, ἔκδικος εἰς ὀργὴν τῷ τὸ κακὸν πράσσοντι, "for he is God's servant, an avenger for wrath against the evildoer." The opening words of v 4 are repeated, with the emphasis once again on the genitive: "*God's* servant he is" (Black). ἔκδικος has been assimilated to ἐκδικάζω ("decide a legal process, avenge") and so gains the sense of "avenger" (*TDNT* 2:444; NJB). It is used in a less forceful sense, "legal officer, advocate" (frequently in the papyri—MM, *TDNT* 2:444–45). But Jewish usage elsewhere supports the stronger sense (Wisd Sol 12:12; Sir 30:6; Josephus, *War* 5.377), as also the only other NT/Pauline use (1 Thess 4:6); and the εἰς ὀργήν here puts the question beyond dispute. "The state thus is charged with a function which has been explicitly forbidden to the Christian (12:17a, 19)" (Bruce). As in 12:19, ὀργή denotes divine wrath (as "avenger" he is "God's servant"), but not the final eschatological wrath of 2:5 (more clearly in view in v 2). As in 1:18 ff., Paul's point is that the structures of the world are God-given—there the moral structures, here the social structures (cf. 13:2); see further on 1:18. The thought of nations being used by God as agents of his wrath is, of course, firmly rooted in Jewish history (particularly Isa 5:26–29; 7:18–20; 8:7–8; 10:5–6, 25–26; 13:4–5; though Paul would not be unmindful of the warnings which accompanied such references—10:7–19; 14:4–6; 16:6–7).

5 διὸ ἀνάγκη ὑποτάσσεσθαι, "wherefore it is necessary to be subject." The phrase is formed with ἀνάγκη + infinitive, as in Matt 18:7 and Heb 9:16, 23. The reason for the "necessity" is given in the following clause. The use of ἀνάγκη here is striking, since its philosophical use in reference to divine or immanent necessity—the way things are (laws of nature) and have to be (fate, destiny)—would be well known (LSJ, *TDNT* 1:345). Paul appeals to this sense of the (divine) givenness of things. For ὑποτάσσεσθαι see on 13:1. The opening assertion is repeated with the added force of the intervening argument (διό).

οὐ μόνον διὰ τὴν ὀργήν, ἀλλὰ καὶ διὰ τὴν συνείδησιν, "not only on account of wrath but also on account of conscience." For ὀργή see on 1:18 and 13:4. For συνείδησις see on 2:15. Here the thought is that the morally responsible person and good citizen will recognize the need for government in society as a divine ordinance (so most): resistance to this divinely ordered authority will provoke in such a person a pang of conscience (διά); and prospect of such moral discomfort should dissuade from civil disobedience. In this role conscience can serve as a positive guide of moral conduct, hence "sense of responsibility, consciousness of obligation" (see Eckstein, 287–300; the disagreement between Pierce and Thrall is somewhat pedantic). Indeed "conscience" serves at this point as a more positive monitor to balance the more serious and severe threat of "wrath"; "a Christian's political conduct should not be motivated by fear alone" (Käsemann); "if obedience is a matter of conscience, then it is no longer servile; when conscience is introduced as the motive of obedience, the latter can no longer be counted on!" (Leenhardt). It is to be noted that here as in 2:15 Paul does not conceive the operation of conscience as something distinctively Christian (Wilckens, though rightly noting the continuity of thought into 13:8–10; against, e.g., SH; Lagrange; Walker, 47–48; Cranfield); see particularly the closely parallel tombstone inscription cited by Pierce, 72 (*CIG* 2:3518); and note the use of ἀνάγκη in v 5a. Once again, then, as often in 1:18–2:16, Paul appeals to the moral sensibility of the ancient world (see on 1:28); the specifically Christian guide to social conduct is provided by love (13:8–10) and faith (see on 14:22 and 23). The counsel would be seen both as socially responsible and as sound common sense (pragmatic). And once again Paul does not separate moral or spiritual obligation from civic responsibility and political reality: civic duty (here subjection to the governing authorities) has the force of moral obligation (similarly 1 Pet 2:13, 19). "We cannot escape daily life. We meet the will of God there" (Käsemann).

6 διὰ τοῦτο γὰρ καὶ φόρους τελεῖτε, "for that is why you also pay tribute." This is evidently the climax of the discussion (see particularly Furnish, *Moral Teaching*, 126, 131–35) and not just an illustration (as Gaugler, Barrett, Käsemann) or third argument (as Wilckens). It was not simply that taxation is the point at which the power of the state most rudely impinges on daily life (as then, so now). Nor was it simply that taxes and tax collectors were a constant source of injustice and embitterment (Philo, *Spec. Leg.* 2.92–95; 3.159–63; Josephus, *Ant.* 16.45, 160–61; Mark 2:15–16 pars.; Matt 11:19 // Luke 7:34; Matt 18:17; 21:31–32; Luke 18:11; 19:7), and raised theological questions for many Jews in occupied Palestine (Mark 12:13–17 pars.; Josephus, *Ant.* 18.4, 23; cf. Acts 17:7). Paul must have been aware that the subject was a particularly sensitive matter in Rome itself. We know from Tacitus (*Ann.* 13) that the year A.D. 58 saw persistent complaints against the companies farming indirect taxes and the acquisitiveness of tax collectors (see *OCD*, "Publicani"), so that some reform became essential. Presumably these complaints had been building up, or at least the occasion for them, in the years preceding 58, during the period when Romans was written. Moreover, it was precisely in the matter of taxation that individuals who might otherwise have hoped to avoid contact with political authorities would have had to deal with government officials. Jews by reason of their special privileges, above all in the matter of taxation (the unique provisions regarding the temple tax), would have been in an especially sensitive position (as is illustrated by the antagonism of Cicero, *Flacc.* 28.67; Tacitus, *Hist.* 5.5.1, and the Josephus references above). And Christians, still largely identified with Jews, would share that vulnerability. Hence in this matter above all the counsel of prudent citizenship would come to sharp focus. See also Friedrich et al., 156–59; Furnish, *Moral Teaching*, 133–35; Bammel, 369–75; and *Introduction* §2.4.5; Wengst's criticisms of Friedrich (*Pax*, 82) do not weaken the case.

The γάρ shows that τελεῖτε must be taken as indicative, rather than imperative. The distinction between φόρος and τέλος (v 7) corresponds to the difference between *tributum* (direct taxes from which Roman citizens would have been exempt in Rome) and *vectigalia* (direct taxes comprised initially of revenue from rents on state property but in Paul's time also including customs duty, tax on slave sales and manumissions, death duties) (see *OCD*, "Vectigal"); see *TDNT* 9:80–81 and Schlier, who notes other passages where φόρος and τέλος come together. Josephus uses both the phrases employed by Paul— φόρους τελεῖν, "pay tribute" (*Ant.* 5.181; 12.182; see also BGD, τελέω 3), and φόρον/φόρους ἀποδοῦναι (v 7), also "pay tribute" (*Ant.* 14.203; *Ap.* 1.119). The implication of φόρος ("tribute") and ἀποδιδόναι (properly "give back") is that in a context of government, whether by right of conquest or not, taxation is an inescapable obligation on the members of the community so governed. φόρον/φόρους δοῦναι, "to pay tribute," also appears in 1 Macc 8:4, 7; Luke 20:22; 23:2; and Josephus, *War* 2.403.

λειτουργοὶ γὰρ θεοῦ εἰσιν εἰς αὐτὸ τοῦτο προσκαρτεροῦντες, "for they are ministers of God engaged in this very task." Despite the strong cultic background of the verb λειτουργέω and of the noun λειτουργία in the LXX (both technical terms for the priestly cult), it is generally agreed that the context here is that of the secular technical usage in Hellenistic society, where λειτουργεῖν and λειτουργία refer to the rendering of public services to the body politic, traditionally the obligation which well-to-do citizens undertook for the benefit of the community (see LSJ; *TDNT* 4:216–22). With λειτουργός itself the case is even stronger (MM; *TDNT* 4:229–30; Strobel, "Röm 13," 86–87; Spicq, 479)—more or less equivalent to "public servant." In the present context, where the obligations of good citizenship are at the heart of Paul's parenesis, this is most naturally the sense which stands at the forefront of Paul's mind. At the same time he does call them "ministers of *God*" (cf. SH; Barrett; *TDNT* 4:231; Schrage, *Christen,* 57; Wilckens, "Römer 13:1–7," 221; Maillot; see further on 15:16). This is not simply an extension or application of the argument made in vv 1–5 (even tax collectors serve the divinely ordered structure of human society—Riekkinen, 214), but it contains a further reminder that the division between sacred and secular for Paul has been broken down: where in 12:1 the language of the cult is extended to everyday life, here he does not hesitate to describe the obligations and functions of the state as ministry commissioned by and on behalf of God (note also the still stronger overtone in Paul's two other uses of λειτουργός—15:16 and Phil 2:25); cf. Lagrange, Schmidt, Black. εἰς αὐτὸ τοῦτο is most naturally referred to collection of taxes (Cranfield, Wilckens). προσκαρτερέω, "occupy oneself diligently with, pay persistent attention to" (*TDNT* 3:618; see further Spicq, 758–60; cf. on 12:12). Strictly speaking, εἰς αὐτὸ τοῦτο should not serve as object (προσκαρτερέω takes the dative), but it is difficult to translate more precisely without being pedantic—"thoroughly engaged in their task for this very purpose"; "to these duties they devote their energies" (NEB). The use of this word reinforces the impression that Paul has in view the ideal of civil service as dedicated public service (a high view of public service, even collection of taxes, as a vocation can clearly be developed on the basis of this text). But by that very token he implies also a recognition that tax collectors in particular may not in practice be so dedicated to the public good. Riekkinen (215) suggests that εἰς αὐτὸ τοῦτο προσκαρτεροῦντες should be taken with v 7—"remembering all this, give everybody what is due them"; but with such a linking clause the absence of a joining particle would be surprising.

7 ἀπόδοτε πᾶσιν τὰς ὀφειλάς, "render to everyone their dues." ὀφειλή occurs elsewhere in the NT only in Matt 18:32 and 1 Cor 7:3. Such a sweeping injunction indicates not only the moral recognition that obligations should be paid (or repaid), but also the attitude of the social inferior or powerless minority who are only too aware that an obligation not honored can quickly become an occasion for scrutiny or retribution on the part of a suspicious or watchful officialdom.

τῷ τὸν φόρον τὸν φόρον, τῷ τὸ τέλος τὸ τέλος, "tribute to whom tribute is due, tax to whom tax is due." See on 13:6.

τῷ τὸν φόβον τὸν φόβον, τῷ τὴν τιμὴν τὴν τιμήν, "fear to whom fear is due, respect to whom respect is due." A distinction between "fear" and (the weaker) "respect, honor" may be intended, as 1 Pet 2:17 ("fear God; honor the emperor") probably implies (so most); see also *TDNT* 9:193 and Str-B, 3:305. But the suggestion that Paul would use "fear" only in reference to God (as in 1 Pet 2:17; see particularly Cranfield's misgivings) probably takes too little account of the stark political realities in Rome (cf. *m. ʾAbot* 3.2); cf. Wilckens, "Römer 13:1–7," 222–23. Given the theology of good government, "fear" is a proper response to *God*-appointed authority (cf. Prov 24:21; *Ep. Arist.* 194); cf. Murray. There is no conflict with v 3: the "fear" owed to those who bear the sword is what ensures prompt fulfillment of obligation as well as avoidance of wrongdoing. Like "conscience" (v 5), such "fear" can have a positive effect. "Respect" is too weak a translation, in 1 Pet 2:18 and Eph 6:5 (with τρόμος) as well (against BGD, rsv, niv, njb). For τιμή, "(public) honor," see LSJ; BGD, 2; and on 2:7.

An allusion to the saying of Jesus preserved in the Synoptics (Mark 12:17 pars.) cannot be ruled out (e.g., SH; Dodd; Goppelt; Delling, 16–19, and *TDNT* 8:44; Schmidt; Cranfield; Riekkinen, 86–94—"yes" and "no"). The theme is the same—the necessity of paying tribute; the sequence of 13:7, 8–10 is paralleled by the sequence Mark 12:13–17, 28–34 (Allison, "Pattern," 16–17); and Luke renders the tradition in terms of φόρον (ἀπο)δοῦναι (Luke 20:22, 25). This could well be the form, then, in which this important counsel of Jesus was remembered, particularly in the Diaspora. And it would be in just such a manner (that is, as loosely and with broad application) that the saying would have entered and continued to influence the stream of Christian parenesis (see further on 12:14).

13:1–7 has naturally served as an important basis for a general theology of the state. For centuries it validated the state as the secular arm of the one divinely ordered commonwealth (*Corpus Christianum*) or as an essential expression of the order of creation, being taken both to justify use of state power in suppression of Baptist and other radical groups at the time of the Reformation, and by German Christians as the ground for their support of the Third Reich (see further Wilckens 3:43–66). But it should be clear from the above that the discussion in these verses is context-specific. Paul may not have been aware of the situation in Rome in detail, but he would have been aware that the Jewish community with whom the Christian groups were still largely identified had not long before been expelled (see *Introduction* §§2.3–4). And he was probably aware of the mounting unrest regarding the taxation system (see on 13:6), at least in general terms. He writes here with the reality of his readers' political context very much in view. "What we have here is not a dogmatic treatise on the government and the State, but a demand for loyal conduct in order to avoid a fresh edict" (Marxsen, *Introduction,* 100). That this was also good missionary strategy (cf. 12:21) should not be forgotten (Heiligenthal, "Strategien"). Moreover, his exhortation is more closely related to the larger argument of Romans itself than has usually been appreciated. It is the relationships of the newly redefined people of God which he works out in these chapters (see further 12:1–15:13 *Introduction*). And it is the tensions this redefinition set up between Jew and Gentile and in the political self-identity of the Christian groups which evidently motivated the treatment here rather than a fear of charismatic enthusiasm (against Althaus, Michel, Käsemann), or of chiliastic hostility to the world (against Lietzmann) or of zealotic tendencies (against Schmidt, Borg); for none of which is there any evidence in the letter itself. Any attempt to integrate 13:1–7 into a more systematic Christian doctrine of the state must needs recall this context specificity (to Rome and within Romans) of the passage. Moreover, it should not leave out of account the hidden or implied qualifications, which would be present to anyone who knew the Jewish tradition (in wisdom, prophecy, and apocalyptic) on which Paul was drawing (see above on the implications of ὑπὸ θεοῦ τεταγμέναι [v 1] and προσκαρτερέω [v 6]), as well as those involved in any echo of the logion preserved in Mark 12:17 pars.

Explanation

13:1 "Let every person be subject to the governing authorities." The abruptness of the transition and the starkness of the command can be properly appreciated only if we recognize the force of two factors. One is what we have described as Paul's attempt to redraw the boundaries of the redefined people of God. The other is the political realities confronting the Christian groups in Rome.

Under the previous definition, the heirs of Abraham, Isaac, and Jacob had been able to mark out and defend clear guidelines for relations with the state. Ideally Judaism was a state and national religion, with the law allowed to govern the whole range of relationships, political as well as social and religious. And even when that ideal was impossible to realize, it was still possible for the Jewish people to live within the covenant by maintaining their distinctive ethnic identity. They had special privileges allowing the continuation of ancestral customs, including the right to send the temple tax each year to Jerusalem; and in cases of large Jewish population, as particularly in Alexandria, they were able to function for most purposes almost as a state within the state, with their own administrative and judicial powers. One of the principal concerns of diaspora Judaism was to maintain the freedom to live their lives as wholly in terms of the Torah distinctives as possible—to live within their own boundaries as Jews, even in an often hostile environment. And much of the political maneuvering of Jewish communities in the diaspora, as attested by Philo and Josephus, was directed precisely to that end.

But Paul's redefinition of the people of God no longer made that possible. A community which no longer identified itself in ethnic terms could therefore no longer claim the political privileges accorded to ethnic minorities. Paul must have been very conscious that by redrawing the boundaries of the people of God in nonethnic terms he was putting the *political* status of the new congregations at risk. Whatever he might claim about Gentiles being grafted into the olive tree of Israel, the political reality was that the new congregations were in process of shedding the identity of ethnic Israel, and the sociological reality was that the believers in Jesus as the Christ were breaking down or ignoring the very boundaries which had given the Jews their distinctiveness and thus their protection. Consequently, any attempted overview of the group identity and of the social relationships of Christian congregations in the diaspora would have to address the issue of their political status and what that meant in the reality of daily existence—and particularly in Rome, the very seat of imperial government.

Within the political structures of the Roman state the responsibilities and powers of government were clear. These responsibilities and powers were exercised by a few by right of birth, or connection, or wealth, or ruthless self-advancement. For the rest, the great majority, there was no political power and no realistic hope of wielding it. For modern commentators accustomed to a centuries-old tradition of developing democracy, the political realities of ancient society, including not least the Roman Empire, are hard to grasp. It would not even have occurred to Paul and his readers that they could exercise political power in a Roman city, far less that they by their efforts might change its structures. All they could do was to live within the structures which existed, accommodate to them—as everyone had to—and seek to benefit from whatever rules or rights the governing authorities granted, such as Julius Caesar had granted the Jewish synagogues.

So Paul's opening exhortation was simply the common-sense wisdom of the great mass of the powerless living within the power structures of the corporate state. Since politics was the business of so few, the rest who wanted to be about their own business naturally took it for granted that they must operate within the constraints laid down by the ruling authorities. For any exposition of how the eschatological people of God should live within the political realities of the Roman state, this was the obvious first thing to be said. Little gatherings of Christians, living in the capital city, without political power, dependent on the good will of the authorities, who could be very arbitrary and unpredictable in their rulings regarding minority ethnic or religious groups, were only acting prudently if they sought to avoid giving any cause for offense. Paul states it as an exhortation not so much because his readers might think otherwise, but rather because the recent history of Jews in Rome made them that much more vulnerable. Paul's reminder is, in effect, to say: since you cannot change the terms under which you live, and since your position is already hazardous, remember the political realities of the politically powerless and live accordingly.

1b   The rationale for this basic exhortation is also clear: political authority is from God. Here again Paul enunciates no new principle. On the contrary, it was one which was familiar in Jewish wisdom. More to the point, it was a principle to which prophet and apocalyptist clung when confronted by the overwhelming might of a Nebuchadnezzar or faced by Syrian oppression: in Daniel's repeated declaration, "The Most High rules the kingdom of men and gives it to whom he will" (Dan 4:17, 25, 32). Such assertions must have been particularly meaningful for Jews living in the diaspora, as aliens living under a foreign power, and often as slaves and dispossessed. To be able to affirm that God is one, *their* God is one, and so also God of the Gentiles, meant in the logic of the times that *all* rule and authority must have come from that one God, *their* God.

The comfort of such a belief was not that it made them any less vulnerable to the whims of such rulers—the Maccabean crisis had been proof enough of that. The comfort was rather that such rulers were by definition responsible before God, and so were under the constraint of God's final judgment. That particularly Jewish belief would, of course, have little impact on the rulers themselves, but at least it gave their oppressed Jewish subjects the assurance that rulers who flouted their responsibility before God would come under his judgment sooner or later—as Nebuchadnezzar had found to his cost in the Daniel story (4:13–25; 5:20–21). So, too, the whole point of the assertion of the Wisdom of Solomon that kings receive their dominion from the Lord was to warn them that the Most High would inflict severe judgment on those who "did not rule rightly, nor keep the law, nor walk according to the purpose of God" (6:4).

This line Paul takes up in the second half of v 1. The point had double importance. For one thing, it gave a solid theological undergirding to the practical wisdom restated in the first half of the verse. But just as important in this instance, it constituted a reaffirmation of Jewish wisdom, a taking over of the practical faith by which ethnic Israel had lived under the rule of regional superpowers of the time. That is to say, in redrawing the boundaries of the people of God, Paul nevertheless retains the older boundaries between the people of God and the secular authorities. The perspective from which the people of God were to view the political powers-that-be remained the same even when the definition of the people of God itself was being altered. The continuity of the chosen of God under an authority which determined the structures of political existence, and might do so in an oppressive way, remained through the discontinuity between ethnic Israel and eschatological Israel.

2–5 In the following four verses the logic of this basic restatement of Jewish wisdom is pressed home in what might be termed a theology of the orderly state, of good government. The principle is simple and would have commanded wide assent: regularity in nature and orderliness in society is something provided for by nature and commended by divine reason; a society needs constraints in order to ensure "the good"; and it is one of the chief roles of a ruler that he is responsible for administering such constraints, for commending the "good" and punishing the "bad" (vv 3–4). In theological terms, the corollary of asserting that God gives dominion to kings and rulers is that he does so for the good of his creatures. In the matter of exercising political authority, rulers are "servants of God" (another echo of Wisd Sol 6:4). Their power is not their own; it comes from God. To resist them, therefore, in the exercise of their God-given responsibility is to resist God and so to incur his judgment and wrath (vv 4–5). Hence Paul can even say that submission to political authority should be motivated not simply by fear of retribution but by concern for a good conscience—not simply a matter of accepting the harsh realities which cannot be changed, but a matter of theological principle. Such orderliness is part of the creative purpose of God. To cooperate in and submit to its working is all of a piece with the creature's acknowledgment of the Creator.

It should be noted here too that this is not a specifically Christian line of reasoning. There is no implication here that Christ has overcome the "authorities" or anything like that. The argument does not depend on the assumption that a new state of affairs exists by virtue of Christ's ministry. These are rather the conditions under which the people of God has operated for centuries. Indeed, since the theology of good government applied also to the Jewish state during its years of independence (as in 2 Sam 12:8), it can be said that this is the condition under which the people of God always exists. In other words, the argument is theological, not Christological; it is expressed in terms of the normal circumstances of social order, not in terms of salvation-history. Nor is it particularly eschatological, as indicating a state of affairs which is temporary and from which the people of God will soon be delivered. It is simply a recognition that this is the way society operates, always has and always will, but given a crucially theological and moral dimension by repeating the Jewish affirmation that God has so ordered it for the good of humankind in society and with the corollary that both ruler and ruled are responsible to God in consequence.

6–7 It is a striking fact that the discussion builds up to its climax on the subject of paying taxes. This is unlikely to be accidental, and these verses should not be regarded as an anticlimax or simply another argument. Nowhere else does Paul include such instruction in any of his letters, and there must have been some reason for his doing so here. Those listening to his letter read out in Rome itself would know well enough what that reason was—the abuses, particularly of indirect taxation, which were causing increasing unrest in the capital at that very time. Paul must have been reasonably well informed of current affairs in Rome and would be well aware that Christian merchants and traders associated with the Jewish "superstition" were in a particularly vulnerable situation. Failure of a number of Christians to pay even an inflated tax might draw the authorities' attention to the little congregations and put them at risk. Paul's advice is not entirely clear as to whether he would have his readers pay excessive taxes without protest; but certainly his intention is clear that what the state could levy as a tax, indirect or direct, ought to be paid faithfully.

But Paul does not hesitate to undergird this policy of political prudence with firm theological assertion. The authorities in their function of levying taxes are "ministers *of God*" (v 6); taxes could be regarded as the secular equivalent of the offerings and sacrifices brought to the altar; within the state as ordered by God, tax officials are the equivalent of priests within the cult! As in 12:1–2, the boundary that separated the cult (of Israel) from the daily business of living in a busy city has been broken down. Whether it is a case of sacralizing the state or rather of desacralizing the cult is left open. And here again in his final exhortation Paul echoes the traditional Jewish commendation of reverence for the king (Prov 24:21), drawing on the inherited wisdom of his native faith to give guidance to the newly redefined people of God, still living under alien and potentially repressive rulers.

The strangeness of all these assertions to modern ears should only make us more conscious of the need to imagine ourselves sympathetically into the situation of these first Christians in Rome. Apart from anything else, the divine legitimacy of royal or imperial rule was still an unquestioned axiom (even if it did not always prevent assassinations and rebellions); indeed "the divine right of kings" was an axiom of government which survived into the modern period. Moreover, we should not forget that the Roman authorities had a well-developed system of spies and informers (the notorious episode of Sejanus was well within living memory—A.D. 27–31). In repeating the platitudes of good citizenship in the familiar Hellenistic public terminology of the time, Paul may well have been mindful of the need to avoid arousing suspicions in any of the more than casual visitors to one of the little Christian house meetings. Simply to ask how Paul could counsel such submission to a tyrannous and unpredictable power, as though such unqualified support for the powers-that-be was naively optimistic, is wholly to ignore the mind-set of the age, the harsh political realities of the particular situation in Rome, and the important qualification that threat of judgment was a constraint on ruler as well as ruled.

Paul does not idealize the situation he is addressing. He does not pretend the authorities of whom he speaks are models of the good ruler. His advice does not particularly arise out of his own experience of Roman protection and the *pax Romana*. He and his Jewish readers in Rome knew well enough the arbitrary power of Rome. The tradition of Jewish wisdom on which he draws had already been well tested by the fires of persecution. Paul would have no illusions that a quiet subservience would be sufficient to guarantee peace. But his advice is not conditional on Roman benevolence. It is simply a restatement of the long-established Jewish recognition of the reality and character of political power.

Paul's political realism also meant that he gave no thought to the Zealot option which was currently gaining strength within Palestine itself. Nor is there any indication that his readers were in any danger of being seduced by that option: however realistic it might appear to be in Palestine, it could hardly be entertained, even on theological grounds, within Rome itself. But neither did he advocate a policy of withdrawal from the corruption of the metropolis, as though the desert or the Qumran alternative could provide a model for Christians in general or for Roman Christians in particular. That too was a nonstarter. Political realism for Paul meant living *within* the political system even if that meant living to a large extent in the terms laid down by that system.

In short, this passage does provide a basis for a theology of political power. The fact and inevitability of political power is affirmed and validated—for *every* person. The state on the corporate scale is the equivalent of the body on the individual scale; it is the means of corporate existence in this world. As there is no basis for a spirit/body dualism in Paul, so there is no basis for a social dualism, whereby political power and political activity is regarded as evil or antithetic to religion. On the contrary, Paul seems to go out of his way to eliminate any such division. State officials not simply *can* be, but properly speaking *are,* "servants of God." For Paul who lived his whole life as one of priestly ministry (15:16), there was no clear division between sacred and secular. Christians could be involved in the political structures of the time and wield political power without ceasing to be Christians, and indeed as part of their Christian service.

Beyond that we cannot go with confidence. Paul does not envisage the possibility of a Christian political party or a Christian state. At that point a different set of theological principles would probably come into play. For Paul would certainly be fearful lest any other political or national entity made the same mistake as his fellow countrymen had—that of identifying God's purpose of salvation with one particular nation's well-being and political dominance. Nor does he speak to the issue of whether civil disobedience or nonviolent resistance can be Christian. Here we must recall that his advocacy of political quietism is in the context of the political powerlessness of most members of the ancient state. In contrast, our modern democratic traditions make it possible for individuals to exercise some political power and to pass judgment on whether rulers are operating for the good of their citizens. At the same time there has been a decrease in the typical ruler's sense of responsibility toward God, or the gods, and so a drastic reduction of the constraint on a ruler's freedom to abuse the ruled, which belief in (a final) judgment provided. Where there is no longer any effective self-constraint on the oppressor provided by a theology of political power, it is wholly legitimate that such a theology should come to expression in the defense of civil rights and democratic principles on behalf of the oppressed. At the same time it would have to be said that where a government was *not* serving God for the good of its citizens, any appeal to this passage as a way of maintaining their subservience would be a complete distortion and an abuse both of Paul's purpose and of its continuing scriptural significance.

E. Love of Neighbor as the Fulfillment of the Law   (13:8–10)

Bibliography

Abrahams, I. "The Greatest Commandment." *Studies in Pharisaism and the Gospels.* 1st series. Cambridge: Cambridge UP, 1917. 18–29. **Berger, K.** *Die Gesetzesauslegung Jesu I.* WMANT 40. Neukirchen: Neukirchener, 1972. 50–55, 80–136. **Borgen, P.** "The Golden Rule: With Emphasis on Its Use in the Gospels." *Paul Preaches Circumcision and Pleases Men.* Trondheim: Tapir, 1983. 99–114. **Dülmen, A. van.** *Theologie.* 225–30. **Furnish, V. P.** *Love Command.* 108–111. **Hübner, H.** *Law.* 66–67, 83–85. **Lyonnet, S.** "La charité plénitude de la loi (Rom 13:8–10)." In Lorenzi, *Dimensions.* 151–63. **Marxsen, W.** "Der ἕτερος νόμος Röm 13:8." *TZ* 11 (1955) 230–37. **Merk, O.** *Handeln.* 164–65. **Mohrlang, R.** *Matthew.* 94–110. **Moule, C. F. D.** "Obligation in the Ethic of Paul." In *Christian History and Interpretation,* FS J. Knox, ed. W. R. Farmer et al. Cambridge: Cambridge UP, 1967. 389–406. **Neirynck, F.** "Sayings of Jesus." 291–94. **Nissen, A.** *Gott und der Nächste im antiken Judentum: Untersuchungen zum Doppelgebot der Liebe.* WUNT 15. Tübingen: Mohr, 1974. **Ortkemper, F.-J.** *Leben.* 125–32. **Perkins, P.** *Love.* 12–25, 78–88. **Räisänen, H.** *Law.* 26–27, 64–66. **Sanders, E. P.** *Law.* 93–112. **Schrage, W.** *Einzelgebote.* 97–100, 249–71. **Wischmeyer, O.** "Das Gebet der Nächstenliebe bei Paulus." *BZ* 30 (1986) 161–87.

Translation

⁸*Owe* ᵃ *nothing to anyone except to love one another; for he who loves the other has fulfilled the law.* ⁹*For the commandment, "You shall not commit adultery," "You shall not kill," "You shall not steal,"* ᵇ *"You shall not covet," and any other*

commandment, is summed up in this word, in the command,[c] *"You shall love your neighbor as yourself."* [10] *Love does no wrong to the neighbor; therefore the fulfillment of the law is love.*

Notes

[a]The continuity with v 7 is strengthened in ℵ Ψ and some other witnesses by reading the participle ὀφείλοντες.

[b]ℵ and other witnesses demonstrate the natural impulse to insert the missing ninth commandment, "You shall not bear false witness."

[c]B F G omit the awkward ἐν τῷ, without appreciating the force of the τό in both v 8 and v 9.

Form and Structure

Paul brings the whole discussion of social relationships back under the rule of love (12:9) with the implicit acknowledgment that such a demanding lifestyle could hardly be sustained without such a model and resource. The initial emphasis on love as a debt provides an effective link with the preceding verse (ἀπόδοτε πᾶσιν τὰς ὀφειλάς . . . μηδενὶ μηδὲν ὀφείλετε), as also the further play on the theme of doing evil in v 10 (v 4—κακὸν ποιεῖν, κακὸν πράσσειν; v 10—κακὸν ἐργάζεσθαι). It is hardly accidental that explicit reference to the letter's subtheme (the law) reemerges at this point, since the theological treatment of the law in 1:18–11:36 was bound to raise the question of its continuing role as norm for personal and social ethics in the redefined people of God, and since the parenesis so far had both used and transformed Torah themes. With the people of God redefined in nonethnic categories it was obviously important that the law, so much identified with ethnic Israel as such, be similarly redefined—not abandoned or attacked (against Käsemann); otherwise continuity between the two epochal phases of the people (and purpose) of God would be lost. This he was able to do because the Christian tradition of Jesus' teaching had already shifted the focus of the law regarding human relationships to Lev 19:18 (Mark 12:31, etc.), and so provided a new center around which the rest of the law could cohere and by means of which the reference of competing principles and relevance of ethnically restrictive rules could be determined (differently Hübner, *Law,* 85). The triple emphasis on love of neighbor (vv 8, 9, 10) and bracketing emphasis on fulfilling the law (vv 8, 10) effectively gathers together and sums up the earlier scattered references on these themes (love—5:5; 8:28; 12:9; fulfillment—8:4; cf. 1:5; 3:31; 9:31–32; 10:6–8). Räisänen, *Law,* 65, misses the continuity of Paul's thought here, as elsewhere, and leaves it in confusion. Note also the chiastic structure of v 10—ἡ ἀγάπη . . . ἡ ἀγάπη.

Comment

13:8 μηδενὶ μηδὲν ὀφείλετε εἰ μὴ τὸ ἀλλήλους ἀγαπᾶν, "owe nothing to anyone except to love one another." The precise force of ὀφείλετε εἰ μή is difficult to pin down: particularly whether ὀφείλετε should be taken in the double sense of indebtedness ("Be in debt to no one") and obligation ("except that you

ought to love . . .") (see BGD, ὀφείλω 2); also whether εἰ μή should be taken
as "but" rather than "except" (cf. BDF §448.8; BGD, εἰ VI.8); see e.g., the
discussion in Michel, Black, Cranfield, Schlier, and Ortkemper, 126–27. In
fact, it is questionable whether Paul formulated the phrase with such precision
in mind; the exhortation has the force of an epigram (with an epigram's
formal ambiguity); and the form is determined by the conjunction of two
familiar ideals—the conventional desire to avoid debt (see examples cited by
Strobel, "Röm 13," 88, and Wilckens n.372), which also picks up from v 7
(repeating v 7a in negative form), and "the (well-known command to) love
one another" (BDF §399.1). The effect of the conjunction of the two clauses
thus linked by εἰ μή, where "except" is the most natural meaning (BDF
§§376, 428.3), is to bring out the idea that love of the other is not merely
an obligation but a responsive obligation, an obligation which arises from
what those addressed have received. Paul, of course, would have in mind
the fact of having been loved and accepted by God in Christ (5:8) through
the gift of the Spirit (5:5). The likelihood is that he has thus reverted immediately to the teaching and example provided by Jesus: it was Jesus who spoke
of love as gratitude for forgiveness received (Luke 7:41–43, 47); and it was
he who gave the determinative force to "love your neighbor" so far as Christians
were concerned—"the well-known command to love one another" (see on
13:9).

The double negative (μηδενὶ μηδέν) as usual reinforces the command. It is
generally agreed that ἀλλήλους means not just "fellow believers" (though see
Lietzmann) but embraces all with whom the Roman Christians would come
in contact. This certainly follows from the whole of the preceding section,
at least from 12:17–13:7, where relationships with the wider community are
wholly in view. It is consistent too with the emphasis on love of neighbor
which follows (vv 9–10). And although the exhortation elsewhere would normally refer to fellow Christians, the wider obligation would hardly be strange
to Paul (see particularly 1 Thess 3:12; cf. Gal 6:10 and 1 Thess 5:15). Perhaps
it would be best to say that Paul has fellow believers particularly in view but
not in any exclusive way. At all events, the emphasis is typically Christian,
as the close parallel of 1 John 4:11 confirms.

ὁ γὰρ ἀγαπῶν τὸν ἕτερον νόμον πεπλήρωκεν, "for he who loves the other
has fulfilled the law." ἕτερον could be taken with νόμον ("the other law"; so,
e.g., Zahn, Marxsen, Leenhardt, Maillot). But the great majority rightly assume
that Paul intended it as the object of ἀγαπᾶν: νόμος (even without the definite
article [Lyonnet, 154]) consistently means the Torah in this letter (even 7:23
and 8:2), so the thought of different laws here is unlikely; an allusion to the
state law (as the first law) is unlikely, since Paul has nowhere mentioned it
in vv 1–7 (against Marxsen, 234–36; approved by Merk, 165); and νόμος
here must have the Torah in mind (as v 9 shows) rather than "the law of
Christ" (cf. Gal 6:2) or the twofold command to love (against Gutbrod, TDNT
4:1071); to take "the other law" as a reference to the second table of the
law might be justified by v 9, but it is a convoluted rendering of the phrase;
and nowhere else does Paul use ἀγαπᾶν absolutely (see particularly Michel
n.5; Cranfield; Wilckens; Ortkemper, 128 n.17). The article before ἕτερον is
important as particularizing the obligation: "Fulfillment of the law involves

not just loving someone other than oneself, but loving *each* man whom God presents to one as one's neighbor by the circumstances of his being someone whom one *is in a position to* affect for good or ill. The 'neighbor' in the NT sense is not someone arbitrarily chosen by us; he is given to us by God" (Cranfield); see also 2:1; 1 Cor 6:1; 10:24, 29; 14:17; and Gal 6:4 (BGD, ἕτερος 1be).

πληρόω here probably has the sense of "properly perform," do what the law really asks for. "Fulfill" in the sense of "exhaustively complete" is a possible meaning of πληρόω (cf. NEB, "has satisfied every claim of the law"), but by no means necessary. It has gained credence more from the traditional view of rabbinic Judaism as insisting on a legalistically aggregated obedience and from a misunderstanding of Gal 5:3 (where "do the whole law" means in effect "take on a completely and exclusively Jewish identity"). But what the Judaism of Paul's time sought was the keeping or performing of the law (including the provision of atonement), not some ideal of sinless perfection (Sanders, *Paul;* and *Introduction* §5.1). The dispute between Paul and his fellow Pharisees therefore was about what fulfillment = performance of the law really involves; see also on 8:4. In fact, it was open to *both* to see the law thus "fulfilled" in love of neighbor (see on 13:9). Paul is almost certainly following, consciously or unconsciously, language already established in the Jewish-Christian debate with the Pharisees (cf. Matt 5:17–20), and the use of the perfect (πεπλήρωκεν) probably reflects the same debate (cf. James 2:10–11; 1 John 2:5). Here again (as particularly in 3:31 and 8:4) Paul shows a very positive attitude to the law—the law as something he expects Christians to "fulfill"; there are no seeds of antinomianism here (so rightly Moule, "Obligation"; against Knox, *Life,* 153–54). To accuse Paul of having an "unschematic" (Lietzmann) or inconsistent (Räisänen, *Law,* 65) view of the law by contrasting 3:20 is to miss and misunderstand all this.

9 τὸ γὰρ οὐ μοιχεύσεις, οὐ φονεύσεις, οὐ κλέψεις, οὐκ ἐπιθυμήσεις, "for the 'You shall not commit adultery,' 'You shall not kill,' 'You shall not steal,' 'You shall not covet.' " τό again signifies "the well-known (commandments)," as in v 8. Paul cites the ten commandments, numbers 7, 6, 8, 10. The order (of the first two) is different from the Hebrew of Exod 20:13–17 and Deut 5:17–21, but accords with the order found in the LXX B of Deut 5, the Nash papyrus (pre-Christian, from Egypt—see *IDB* 3:510), Philo, *Decal.* 36, 51, 121–37, 168–71; *Spec. Leg.* 3.8; Luke 18:20; James 2:11; and Clement, *Strom.* 6.16 (also omitting number 9), which strongly suggests that this was the order in which the commandments were widely known in the diaspora (see also Berger, 272–73). Of the first three commandments mentioned here, Paul cites numbers 7 and 8 (in reverse order) in 2:21–22; number 8 is also echoed in Eph 4:28; otherwise he never mentions them again. James 2:11 refers to numbers 6 and 7 in a similar context, with Lev 19:18 also cited in James 2:8. In the episode of the rich young man (Mark 10:17–22 pars.) all five commandments from number 5 to number 9 are listed, but only Matt 19:19 includes a reference to Lev 19:18. The implication is fairly strong that this was a regular topic of discussion within earliest Christian circles. In Paul's case the use of just these commandments here and in 2:21–22 (and nowhere else) strongly suggests that they had some importance in the dialogue between

Jew and Gentile regarding the appeal of Judaism and Christianity. It was just these commandments which were most likely to commend the code containing them to those of moral sensibility (see further on 2:21–23). They were of broader appeal and less distinctively Jewish than the earlier commandments, including particularly the sabbath law, which Paul never commends (see further on 14:5). Consequently any failure in these areas by Jews would be regarded as more blameworthy by morally responsible Gentiles (hence 2:21–22). And here it is just these commands which he cites as summed up in the love command. For οὐκ ἐπιθυμήσεις see on 7:7. That a distinction between the first five commandments (dealing with the "divine") and the second five (dealing with human relations) was already present in Jewish though is confirmed by Philo, *Decal.* 121; but that is not the same as a distinction between ritual and moral commands; see on the next phrase and 13:10.

καὶ εἴ τις ἑτέρα ἐντολή, "and if there is any other commandment." Paul makes an all-embracing reference to indicate that the commandments just cited are not the only ones he could refer to, though, as we have just noted, the actual choice made was hardly arbitrary. But by adding this generalized reference he can retain the widest possible sympathy for his point: the devout Jew, who would think of the rest of the ten commandments and others fundamental to covenant Judaism, needs to be reminded of the centrality of the love command (see also on the next phrase); and the Gentile attracted by the broader moral appeal of such commands as those just cited needs to be reassured that so far as the gospel is concerned any other commandments involved in Christianity come to focus in the love command just as do the four cited. That is to say, Paul can make his point with reference to the commandments usually understood as distinctive of Israel, without limiting his point to these commandments.

ἐν τῷ λόγῳ τούτῳ ἀνακεφαλαιοῦται ἐν τῷ, "it is summed up in this word, in the (command)." λόγος here is the word of divine revelation, as in 9:6, 9, 28 (from Isa 10:23). Paul may be mindful of the fact that the ten commandments were referred to in Greek-speaking Judaism as οἱ δέκα λόγοι (Exod 34:28; Deut 10:4; Philo, *Heres* 168; *Decal.* 32; Josephus, *Ant.* 3.138). The ἐν τῷ continues the pattern of the τό in vv 8 and 9—"the (well-known command)." ἀνακεφαλαιόομαι is a rare word, but the sense is clear: "bring everything to a head" (an intensive form of κεφαλαιόω), hence "sum up" the argument of an orator (so Dionysius of Halicarnassus, *De Lysia* 9; LSJ; see further BGD and *TDNT* 3:681–82); elsewhere in the NT it occurs only in Eph 1:10 (in taking Eph 1:10 as his starting point Irenaeus strengthens the sense of repetition in his famous theory of "recapitulation"—*TDNT* 3:682).

It is important to appreciate the fact that the idea of the law being summed up in a single formulation is not new or distinctively Christian. According to *b. Šabb.* 31a, Hillel summed up the law in the negative form of the golden rule: "That which you hate do not do to your fellows; this is the whole law; the rest is commentary; go and learn it"; note also Luke 10:26–28 and Mark 12:32–33. More striking still, Rabbi Akiba spoke of the same passage (Lev 19:18) as "the greatest general principle in the Torah" (*Sipra* on Lev 19:18) (Abrahams, 20; Str-B, 3:306). And later still Rabbi Simlai (third century) maintained that Amos and Habakkuk had each reduced the law to one principle: "Seek me and live" (Amos 5:4); "The righteous man lives by his faith" (Hab 2:4) (*b. Mak.* 23b–24a; Abrahams, 23; Str-B, 1:907). In so arguing, therefore, Paul is not making an anti-Jewish point; on the contrary, it is one that many Jews would readily accept (see also on the previous phrase). The difference would be that Hillel and the others would see the fundamental principle as one from which all the other commands could be deduced. Hillel certainly did not mean to discourage the would-be proselyte from observing the law: "Go and learn it!" ("the accent lies on the 'Go, learn' "—Wischmeyer, 166; see also Nissen, 396–99, 400–401). Paul, on the other hand, evidently saw the love command as so much the substance of the law that such love could stand in place of much of that law. If the law is performed in loving the other (v 8), then it does not require further supplementation (the point is overstated and pressed to an antithesis by Wischmeyer, 183–87). Of course, the love command would come to expression in not committing adultery, not murdering, etc.; but not necessarily in rules regarding the sabbath and diet. On the contrary, Paul would no doubt say, insistence on such rules had offended against the law of love or prevented its coming to expression. Presumably on this point the influence of the Jesus tradition was considerable (see next paragraph).

ἀγαπήσεις τὸν πλησίον σου ὡς σεαυτόν, "you shall love your neighbor as yourself." The passage cited is itself from "the law"; despite its very positive expression, here picked up by Paul, Nygren can still speak of "the negative quality which always characterizes the law"! It is true, however, that explicit references to Lev 19:18 are lacking in Jewish literature prior to Paul, and the allusions to it show that it was given no particular prominence (Sir 13:15; *Jub.* 7:20; 20:2; 36:4, 8; *T. Reub.* 6.9; *T. Iss.* 5.2; *T. Gad* 4.2; *T. Ben.* 3.3–4; 1QS 5.25; 8.2; see Wischmeyer, 162–68, summarizing Nissen and Berger). In contrast, Lev 19:18 is the passage in all the Pentateuch most frequently cited by NT writers—Mark 12:31 pars.; 12:33; Matt 5:43; 19:19; Gal 5:14; James 2:8 ("the royal law"). Consequently it must be judged almost certain that Paul is drawing here on the tradition that Jesus himself summed up the law by reference to Lev 19:18. The fact that he does not cite Jesus as the authority for the assertion is explained partly by the character of earliest Christian remembering of the Jesus tradition (living tradition; see on 12:14), and partly by the fact that the assertion was by no means controversial for many Jews (see preceding paragraph).

Nor should it be assumed that all Jews inevitably took ὁ πλησίον as the fellow Israelite. Certainly the original context of Lev 19:18 is thus circumscribed; the Qumran usage presupposes a closed fellowship (Berger, 117–20); Matt 5:43 presupposes that some Jews (of Matthew's time?—post-A.D. 70) drew the conclusion that it did *not* include the enemy; and the parable of the good Samaritan implies a similar rebuke (Luke 10:25–37) (see also Nissen, 304–29). But ὁ πλησίον can be used equally of "the fellow man" (BGD; cf. *TDNT* 6:312–15), and there are some indications of a greater openness on this point elsewhere in Jewish writings: Lev 19:34 itself; Prov 6:1; the translation of רע by ὁ πλησίον in the LXX (Berger 100–105); Sir 13:15 (Berger, 112–14); *1 Enoch* 99.15; Philo, *Spec. Leg.* 2.63; *Virt.* 116; Josephus, *War* 7.260; *T. Iss.* 7.6. Moreover, the negative form of the "golden rule," which is the other side of this command, is also attested in Jewish literature as of universal scope (see on 13:10). Paul would no doubt be opposed to any restriction of the love command to fellow Israelite; and this is certainly implicit in all his argument thus far. But the point here may rather be that love of neighbor will be its own fulfillment of the law (v 10), not as determined (and restricted) by the full range of the Torah, nor as a means to drawing them into observance of the law (contrast Hillel in *m. ʾAbot* 1:12—". . . loving mankind and bringing them nigh to the Law"; cf. Wisd Sol 6:18—"love of her (Wisdom) is the keeping of her laws"). ὡς σεαυτόν of course does not make love of self the basis of love of neighbor (Wilckens) and should probably not be seen as a concession to human fallenness (against Cranfield), since self-love is a narrowing, excluding, self-engrossed kind of love. Rather, it implies a recognition of the importance of self-respect, so can be coordinated with the call for sober self-esteem (12:3) and ensure that the reckoning of others better than self (Phil 2:3) has nothing cheap in it (cf. particularly Murray).

10 ἡ ἀγάπη τῷ πλησίον κακὸν οὐκ ἐργάζεται, "love does no wrong to the neighbor." This is in fact the negative form of the "golden rule." Its roots may be very early (cf. Ps 15:3) and the sentiment was widely current in proverbial wisdom (cf. Zech 8:17; Sir 10:6; *Ep. Arist.* 168, 207; *Jos. As.* 23.12). The actual "rule" itself is already in Tob 4:15 (καὶ ὃ μισεῖς, μηδενὶ ποιήσῃς) and attested of Hillel (*b. Šabb.* 31a; see on 13:9), as indeed quite outside Judeo-Christian thought (see Abrahams, 21; Borgen, 100–101, 103–4). A sharp contrast between the positive form of the rule (Matt 7:12) and the negative should *not* be pressed, as though the former was distinctively Christian and the latter characteristically Jewish. The positive demand for a pro-active concern for the well-being of others (particularly the poor, the widow, the orphan and the stranger) is too characteristic of prophetic and Jewish piety generally. The negative form is simply the converse of the positive, as indeed here (13:9–10). This two-sided exposition of the love command arises immediately from Lev 19:18 anyway and is reflected elsewhere in Jewish thought (e.g., *Jub.* 36.7–8; *Tg. Yer.* on Lev 19:18 [Abrahams, 21]; cf. Philo, *Spec. Leg.* 4.186). In commending love of neighbor in this way, therefore, Paul's exhortation both in v 9 and here is thoroughly Jewish. However, see also on 12:14 and 12:17. Schmidt's reference to "the absoluteness, totality and perfectibility of love" is not untypical of an "over the top" idealism the passage seems to inspire in commentators.

For ἀγάπη see on 12:9. As typically in this section (12:17, 21; 13:3–4) κακός is used in broad reference to what would generally be regarded as "bad, evil, wrong." As in 2:10 ἐργάζεσθαι κακόν/ἀγαθόν means simply "doing evil/good." It is frequently pointed out that 1 Cor 13:4–7 provides a clear indication of what Paul has in mind here.

πλήρωμα οὖν νόμου ἡ ἀγάπη, "therefore love is the fulfillment of the law" (NIV; so NJB). πλήρωμα is usually taken in an active sense—"fulfilling" (RSV); thus love in action is what fulfills the law (so, e.g., SH, Lietzmann, *TDNT* 6:305, Michel, Cranfield). The sense is unusual (πλήρωσις would have been the more natural choice), but it may simply reflect Paul's liking for -μα words (see 5:15–16 and 11:12); and the context certainly makes some degree of active force inescapable (πλήρωμα = ἐργάζεσθαι ἀγαθόν τῷ πλησίον; cf. 2:13).

The -μα formulation probably matches the equally surprising use of the perfect (πεπλήρωκεν) in v 8. For the sense of "fulfill" see further on 13:8; "love is not the *completion* but the *performance* of the law" (Barrett).

The thought here and in v 8 is obviously very close to that of Gal 5:14:

Galatians: ὁ πᾶς νόμος ἐν ἑνὶ λόγῳ πεπλήρωται, ἐν τῷ (Lev 19:18);
Romans: . . . νόμον πεπλήρωκεν . . . ἐν τῷ λόγῳ τούτῳ ἀνακεφαλαιοῦται ἐν τῷ (Lev 19:18).

Hübner's attempt to argue for a "significant divergence" between the two letters at this point (*Law*, 83–85) is forced (Wilckens): Paul envisages a fulfilling = a meeting of the law's demands in both letters, since in both letters his endeavor is to separate the law from its too restrictive function of setting Jew apart from Gentile. Hence also the normal recourse to the assumption that Paul can only have the moral law in view here is also slightly off target: it is the *whole* law, in its function of promoting love of neighbor, which is in view. In Jewish thought that meant bringing mankind "nigh to the law" (Hillel—*m. ᾽Abot* 1.12), that is, bringing them within the bounds of Judaism. But for Paul the love command meant an opening out of Judaism itself, to lose its ethnic distinctiveness; and that meant that the rituals which set Jew apart from Gentile become an unjustified restriction of the love command (this was the point of 2:25–29) (cf. Sanders, *Law*, 100–103, 114). The love command is not opposed to ritual per se; in Paul's hands it simply questions the assumption that love of neighbor must (or will inevitably) be expressed in certain rituals, and it warns that some cherished rituals may come to prevent love of neighbor (see also Dunn, "New Perspective," 115–16).

Explanation

13:8–10 Paul sums up his exhortation regarding Christians' relationships with the wider community by focusing the whole on a repeated call to love— "love one another," "love the other," "love your neighbor"—where the context makes clear that for Paul the embrace of Christian love must not be limited to the community of faith, but must include also the neighbor who is the enemy (12:14, 17, 21) or the state official (13:1–7)—an interesting variation, in effect, of the parable of the good Samaritan, where it was the (religious) state officials (priest and Levite) who failed to offer neighborly love (Luke 10:30–35).

The exhortation consists of taking up the everyday pragmatism of popular morality of both Greek and Jew, no doubt familiar to his readers as such, and bringing it all to the touchstone and summation of love. First the negative guideline of petit bourgeoisie economics ("Never get into debt") is transposed into the much more positive obligation to active concern for one another (v 8). Then the basic rules that make possible relationships of trust ("Don't take unfair advantage—no adultery, no killing, no stealing, no envious coveting") are gathered up into the ancient Mosaic command to "love your neighbor as yourself" (v 9). And the whole is summed up in a chiastic definition of love in negative terms as avoiding doing wrong to the neighbor and in positive terms as fulfilling the law (v 10).

The triple emphasis on love is matched by a triple emphasis on love of neighbor as the fulfillment and summation of the law: "he who loves the other has fulfilled the law"; no commandment is not covered by the summary, "Love your neighbor as yourself"; "love is the fulfillment of the law." These are the first references to the law since the somewhat dismissive statements of 10:4–5; and indeed, as his readers would soon realize, these are the last references to the law in the letter as a whole. They therefore fulfill a crucial role: they would reassure that Paul's gospel was not antinomian—on the contrary, he counts fulfillment of the law as something important. Equally important, he reasserts the continuity with the revelation previously given to Israel, not least in the law—the fulfillment is a fulfillment of God's purpose in giving the law to Israel in the first place. For those who had been attracted to Judaism by its strong moral structure, this would be of crucial importance. It would provide vital confirmation that Paul was not so much in the business of abandoning the firm guidelines of the Torah, as of transforming and transposing them by freeing them from their specifically ethnic context.

It is not simply coincidental that he focuses on the command to love the neighbor. This in itself would be enough to set him within a liberal Judaism which was willing to differentiate between primary and secondary, between fundamental and consequential in matters of the law. The talk of love as an obligation (v 8) and the uncontrived rendering of the love command in negative as well as positive form (vv 9–10) would strike many of his audience as characteristically Jewish. But Paul nevertheless is evidently moving beyond this characteristic emphasis drawn from the law, and he would probably expect his readers to recognize a more specific allusion to the teaching of Jesus as such. Certainly the tradition was no doubt well enough known in Christian congregations that Jesus too had summed up the law, or the second table of the law, in terms of Lev 19:18. It is this allusion to the Jesus tradition, set within the context of his discussion to this point, which would help his readers to recognize the distinctiveness of this otherwise impeccably Jewish sentiment. For on Jesus' lips Lev 19:18 became a word which validated his concern for sinner and esteem for Samaritan (Luke 10:33–37). It was a word which broke through the boundaries which had become a feature of so much contemporary Judaism—boundaries within Israel, between "righteous" and "sinner," boundaries surrounding Israel, between Jew and Gentile. And that would seem to be its force also in the context of Paul's understanding of a love of neighbor which expands God's covenant love outward rather than draws the non-Jew into a covenant love more narrowly focused on Israel. Moreover, it would probably be recalled in the Jesus tradition treasured among the different churches that Jesus himself had shown by his own example how love of neighbor operated as a fulfillment of the law—as a principle to be applied in the light of the circumstances rather than a rule to be imposed whatever the circumstances (e.g., Mark 2:23–3:5). Paul certainly was shortly to call his readers to "put on Christ" (13:14) and subsequently to evoke Jesus as a pattern for his readers in 15:2–3 and 5; and the discussion in chap. 14 echoes another of Jesus' major controversies with the guardians of the law, in which other teaching of Jesus is recalled; so the thought lies near to hand. And no doubt he intended the implication to be taken here also that the love he spoke of was dependent on the gift of the Spirit (cf. 5:5) and could be sustained only as fruit of the Spirit (Gal 5:22).

With such repeated emphasis on the central importance of love it would be easy to lapse into a sentimental but unrealistic idealism which would be productive more of guilt than of grace. The point has frequently been drawn from v 8 that Paul presents the obligation to love as the one debt which the believer can never repay; "The debt of charity is permanent, and we are never quit of it; for we must pay it daily and yet always owe it" (Origen). That is true, though it may make too much of the imagery Paul uses to provide the transition from the preceding paragraph. But when it is added to the thought that the neighbor for Paul is *not* to be limited to the fellow Jew (far less to the person in physical proximity) but includes anyone, that can easily become an impossible and (for that reason) oppressive burden for believers who find themselves obligated to love everyone. Either that, or the love called for becomes so superficial and dissipated that it becomes a mere word which may provide cheap comfort for a conscience but hardly carries the weight of either Jewish or Jesus' or Pauline concern.

It is important to note therefore that there are in effect two limiting features in the exhortation. The call to love the other is in fact *limited* to the neighbor. This still does not involve a restriction by physical proximity or ethnic acceptability, but it does not broaden the outreach of love to everyone. The neighbor is the person encountered in the course of daily life who has a need which lays claim to the believer's resources—a claim, it should also be said, which can never be regulated or limited by rules or code of practice and that often has an unexpected quality for which no forward planning is possible. And it calls for an actual output of love in action. But it is also in effect limited by the qualification "as yourself." The call is not to a love which would, if words mean anything, go far beyond the resources of any individual. A realistic self-esteem recognizes limits to what may be said or done on one's behalf, does not dissipate vital energies in a wide range of involvement which stretches personal resources too far and too thinly. The call is for a love which is equally responsible and which recognizes that in most cases a more intensely focused active concern, limited in scope, is likely to be more beneficial than a general assertion of love for all which ends by actually loving nobody and only diminishes oneself.

The point is, then, that a realistic and active love which seeks the good of the other without necessarily being bound by convention meets the requirements of God's law more than a love constrained by legal precedent and conditional on acceptance of ethnically limiting customs and rituals.

F. The Imminence of the End as Spur (13:11–14)

Bibliography

Barr, J. *Biblical Words for Time*. London: SCM, 1962. **Baumgarten J.** *Paulus*. 209–13. **Dautzenberg, G.** "Was bleibt von der Naherwartung? Zu Röm 13:11–14." In *Biblische*

Randbemerkungen, FS R. Schnackenburg, ed. H. Merklein and J. Lange. Würzburg: Echter, 1974. 361–74. **Grabner-Haider, A.** *Paraklese und Eschatologie bei Paulus.* Münster: Aschendorff, 1968. 84–85. **Lövestam, E.** *Spiritual Wakefulness in the New Testament.* Lund: Gleerup, 1963. 25–45. **Merk, O.** *Handeln.* 166–67. **Müller, U. B.** *Prophetie.* 142–48. **Ortkemper, F.-J.** *Leben.* 132–48. **Ridderbos, H.** *Paul.* 487–97. **Vögtle, A.** "Röm 13:11–14 und die 'Nah'-Erwartung." In *Rechtfertigung,* FS E. Käsemann, ed. J. Friedrich et al. Tübingen: Mohr, 1976. 557–73. ———. "Paraklese und Eschatologie nach Röm 13:11–14." In Lorenzi, *Dimensions.* 179–94.

Translation

[11] *And this, knowing the time, that it is already the hour for you*[a] *to wake up from sleep, for now is our salvation nearer than when we believed.* [12] *The night is far advanced, and the day is at hand. Let us therefore put off*[b] *the works of darkness, and*[c] *let us put on the weapons*[d] *of light.* [13] *Let us conduct ourselves decently as in the day, not in revelry and drunkenness, not in debauchery and sexual excess, not in quarreling and selfish envy.*[d] [14] *But put on the Lord*[e] *Jesus Christ and make no provision for the flesh to satisfy its desires.*

Notes

[a] ἡμᾶς has strong support (including P[46] vid), but in view of the ἡμῶν in the following line ὑμᾶς must be regarded as the more difficult reading, and is supported by ℵ B et al. (see Metzger; otherwise, Gaugler).

[b] P[46] and various Western authorities read ἀποβαλώμεθα instead of ἀποθώμεθα. Since the former is unique in Paul and the latter conforms to the more typical usage elsewhere, the usual canons of text criticism tend to favor ἀποβαλώμεθα as the original (so Cranfield; against Metzger); but the sense is hardly affected.

[c] On the inconsequential variant καί instead of δέ, see Metzger.

[d] Typical scribal polishing variants are the replacement of ὅπλα by ἔργα in A and D (v 12) and the replacement of the singular ἔριδι and ζήλῳ by plurals (v 13).

[e] P[46] has modified the less usual "Lord Jesus Christ" to the more usual "Jesus Christ our Lord."

Form and Structure

The opening phrase recalls the recipients to the eschatological perspective so basic to Christian self-understanding—not only a new but the final age of God's purpose (3:26; 8:18; 11:5). The theme is no doubt prompted, like the preceding emphasis on love, by the harshness and hazards of the situation which called forth the advice of 12:14–13:7. The emphasis on salvation to faith (v 11) recalls the opening thematic statement (1:16), and the exhortation recalls the earlier counsel in 6:12–13 (vv 12, 14) and 8:13 (v 14) in particular. The imagery of putting off/putting on was common in earliest Christian parenesis (Selwyn, *1 Peter,* 394–95), perhaps reflecting a widespread pattern of exhorting new converts and baptisands; vv 11b–12 in fact fall without strain into a four-lined hymn form (Schlier) which Paul may well be quoting with elaboration; and parallels with other first-century Christian writings again suggest a common parenetical sequence (cf. particularly 1 Thess 5:4–9 and Eph 5:8–14). The imagery of night and day, darkness and light, echoes the sharper dualism of the first verses in each of chaps. 6, 7, and 8; but the recognition that the night is not yet over and that continually renewed commitment is necessary equally echoes the eschatological tension of the second half of these chapters. The characterization of nighttime revelry (v 13) probably reflects not so much a fear on Paul's part that this was true of the Roman congregations as it does a knowledge of Roman society. Striking is the mixture of first and second person exhortation, the triple mixed metaphor of v 12b, and the contrast of three double negatives (v 13) with the single call to "put on Christ" (v 14). The summary climax of the exhortation in terms of the character of Christ (v 14) is obviously as deliberate as the summary of the law in the love of neighbor command (vv 8–10). In the sweep of its embrace vv 11–14 make as effective a summing up of this phase of parenesis as the opening summary of 12:1–2 (cf. Merk, 166).

Comment

13:11 καὶ τοῦτο εἰδότες τὸν καιρόν, "and this, knowing the time." The καὶ τοῦτο is awkward to translate. The nearest parallels suggest that the phrase is resumptive or recapitulative, gathering up what has already been said; cf. particularly 1 Cor 6:6, 8 and Eph 2:8 (BDF, §442.9). To regard it as an ellipse with verb omitted (BDF, §480.5) is less satisfactory, since choice of a particular verb ("do this" [Leenhardt, Schlier, NIV]) rather weakens the breadth of the reference back. NEB's "in all this" is probably best. But καὶ τοῦτο could also be understood as adding a further thought—"besides this" (RSV, NJB), "in addition"—providing a transition to a regular section of parenesis (cf. Ign. *Eph.* 11.1). Either way, Paul is keen not to move on from his more general parenesis without specifically underscoring the eschatological context of all Christian ethics.

The εἰδότες indicates an allusion to something well known and accepted by Paul's audience (cf. particularly 5:3; 6:9; 1 Cor 15:58; 2 Cor 5:6; Gal 2:16; etc.). It need not indicate an appeal to a well-established tradition as such; it would satisfy the force of εἰδότες that Paul is referring to a generally accepted emphasis (as present, e.g., in Jewish-Christian apocalyptic or early Christian prophecy [Ortkemper, 133 n.56]), from which he draws equally acceptable conclusions. But it is true that many of the following elements are well spread across the NT, indicating if not a fixed tradition as such, at least a common emphasis and illustrative or supportive metaphors (see below). For καιρός see on 3:26 and 5:6; here cf. particularly 1 Cor 7:29. In Jewish apocalyptic cf. particularly 2 *Apoc. Bar.* 85.10. Still important are Barr's warnings against the danger of constructing and imposing a theological "kairos concept" on the text.

ὅτι ὥρα ἤδη ὑμᾶς ἐξ ὕπνου ἐγερθῆναι, "that it is already the hour for you to wake up from sleep." ὥρα + infinitive is a familiar construction in Greek to indicate the right time to do something (LSJ, ὥρα B.3; see further BGD, ὥρα 3). The ἤδη naturally increases the sense of urgency: the hour has already struck. In questioning the eschatological overtone of the phrase itself, Cranfield does not give enough weight to this note of urgency. And as linked with the metaphor of transition from sleep to waking, and so conjoint with the transition from night to day (v 12), it is hard to avoid the sense of "God's appointed eschatological hour," as in Dan 8:17 (εἰς ὥραν καιροῦ); 8:19 (εἰς ὥρας καιροῦ συντελείας); 11:35 (καιρὸς εἰς ὥρας); 11:40 (ὥρα συντελείας); John 4:23; 5:25; 1 John 2:18 (ἐσχάτη ὥρα); Rev 3:3, 10. "The waking up is the renewal described in 12:2" (Althaus).

Sleep as a negative image is familiar in Greek philosophical tradition, since it symbolizes abnegation of the νοῦς, or inactivity and weakness (e.g., Epictetus 2.20.15; see further *TDNT* 8:547–48; Schlier). So, naturally, in Jewish thought also—e.g., Prov 6:4, 9; Sir 22:8; *4 Macc* 5.11; *T. Reub.* 3.1, 7; Philo, *Som.* 1.121; 2.162 (see further Lövestam, 35–37, 40–41; *TDNT* 8:551–52). Christian usage follows suit (Eph 5:14; 1 Thess 5:6–10; Mark 13:35–6; Matt 24:43 // Luke 12:39; cf. Matt 25:5; Luke 12:37; 1 Cor 15:34; Eph 6:18; Rev 3:2–3; 16:15). Although the imagery lends itself to a more characteristically Hellenistic or dualistic scheme (see particularly H. Schlier, *Der Brief an die Epheser* [Düsseldorf: Patmos, [5]1965] 241), it clearly belongs to a much more universal currency (against Gaugler). Here obviously, as characteristically in the other NT references, the connotation is eschatological and moral.

νῦν γὰρ ἐγγύτερον ἡμῶν ἡ σωτηρία ἢ ὅτε ἐπιστεύσαμεν, "for now is our salvation nearer than when we (first) believed." σωτηρία is, as usual, future—the completed wholeness to be achieved by God's grace (see on 1:16); cf. here particularly 1 Thess 5:8–9. As in 10:9, 14, 16, Paul uses πιστεύειν in the aorist, to indicate the act of commitment which began their Christian experience. It should not be ignored that Paul's most common definition of what we now call "Christians" is in terms of believing. It was the act of belief (with the concomitant gift of the Spirit) which best characterizes that beginning (10:9; see also 1 Cor 3:5; 15:2; Gal 2:16; 2 Thess 1:10; 2:12; also Eph 1:13), as also the same attitude of believing which best characterizes (from the human side) the continuing divine human relationship (see on 1:16). The emphasis is, of course, determined in large part by his polemic against the position of most of his fellow Jews, who saw membership of the covenant people in terms of circumcision and other such works of the law as being equally important (see on 3:20). But Paul's emphasis on "believing" as the common and distinctive denominator of the new movement needs to be given more weight. Cf. on 6:3–4.

The νῦν is again eschatological (see on 3:21 and 5:9): the whole between-time, between the "already" of commitment in conversion-initiation and the "not yet" of salvation, is pregnant with the about-to-be of God's purpose coming to full term (NJB's "by now" weakens this sense). Despite Dodd, Black, and Cranfield, it is difficult to avoid the overtone of heightened imminence in the use of ἐγγύτερον, though it is true that Paul does not specify any terminus (see Vögtle, "'Nah'-Erwartung," and Ortkemper, 136, 138–39; cf. Murray; Kümmel, *Theology*, 186; Baumgarten, 210; Grabner-Haider, 85; Gaugler ["had the apostle reckoned in terms of two thousand years, he could hardly have so spoken"]; Beker, *Paul*, 145 ["apocalyptic undergoes a profound modification in Paul, but this does not affect the intensity of its expectation"]). His words share the same character as the sayings of Mark 1:15 par. and 13:28–29 pars.—as indeed of v 12: ἡ δὲ ἡμέρα ἤγγικεν (also James 5:8; 1 Pet 4:7). An echo of what was remembered as a characteristic emphasis of Jesus' proclamation can hardly be dismissed; but it cannot be proved, since it was also characteristic of Jewish Christian apocalyptic generally (cf. particularly *4 Ezra* 4.33–50; 8.61; 11.44; *2 Apoc. Bar.* 23.7; 82.2; Mark 13:29–30 pars.; Rev 1:1, 3; 3:11; 22:10, 20). The ἡμῶν goes more naturally with σωτηρία, left to the end of the phrase for emphasis ("our salvation" [NIV, NJB, Michel]), than with ἐγγύτερον ("nearer to us" [RSV, NEB, Lagrange, Lietzmann, Barrett, Cranfield]); elsewhere Paul does not hesitate to personalize the hope of salvation (2 Cor 1:6; Phil 1:28; 2:12).

12 ἡ νὺξ προέκοψεν, ἡ δὲ ἡμέρα ἤγγικεν, "the night is far gone, and the day is near." Somewhat surprisingly, the metaphorical or spiritual contrast between night and day is not strongly attested, occurring only infrequently in the biblical tradition (Ps 139:12; Isa 21:11–12; John 9:4; 11:10), though the negative overtone of "night" in such a contrast is self-evident (as also in a phrase like "thief of/in the night" [Jer 49:9; Obad 5; 1 Thess 5:2]). It naturally lent itself to apocalyptic, but even there only occasionally functions to characterize the supersession of the old age by the new (Zech 14:7; Rev 21:25; 22:5; *2 Enoch* 65.9). Paul's usage therefore may be distinctively his own (the closest parallel is again 1 Thess 5:5–8) or at least a feature of very early Christian parenesis expressive of its eschatological perspective. Müller sees it as a typically prophetic admonition and compares Isa 43:19; 55:6; and Matt 3:10 (*Prophetie*, 142). For the more typical emphasis on the day as the day of judgment see on 2:5 and *TDNT* 2:951–53; cf. particularly Heb 10:25. But here "day" has a very positive overtone in contrast to "night" (as in v 13; cf. 2 Pet 1:19). See further below on the parallel contrast between darkness and light.

προκόπτω in this connection can mean simply "advance," but the aorist when paralleled with the second half of the saying must mean "well advanced" (cf. *TDNT* 6:716 n.85); "the night is nearly over" (NJB). For ἤγγικεν see on 13:11 and cf. Phil 4:5 (ὁ κύριος ἐγγύς). The imagery clearly indicates that the night is not yet over and the day has not yet come (Lövestam, 30)—a clear Not-yet emphasis to put alongside the Already emphasis in v 13—a reversal of Paul's normal way of posing the Already/Not-yet tension of Christian experience (see chaps. 6–8 *Introduction*); see also on 13:13. Early morning, before the heat of day, was and is a period of great activity in the east (see Black).

ἀποθώμεθα οὖν τὰ ἔργα τοῦ σκότους, ἐνδυσώμεθα (δὲ) τὰ ὅπλα τοῦ φωτός, "let us therefore put off the works of darkness, and let us put on the weapons of light." The contrasting imagery of taking off and putting on clothes is again obvious and would be familiar to Paul's readers in metaphorical usage: putting off vices (a more Greek than Hebrew metaphor—e.g., Demosthenes 8.46; Plutarch, *Coriolanus* 19.4; *Ep. Arist.* 122; in the NT—Eph 4:22, 25; Col 3:8; James 1:21; 1 Pet 2:1); and putting on virtues (more characteristically Hebraic—e.g., Job 29:14; Pss 93:1; 132:9, 16; Prov 31:25; Isa 51:9; 61:10; Wisd Sol 5:18; Bar 5:1; Philo, *Conf.* 31; and cf. particularly Isa 59:17; in the NT—Eph 6:14; Col 3:12; 1 Thess 5:8; and here particularly Eph 6:11; see further on 13:14); see BGD for both terms. Although we should not assume a practice of changing clothes for night wear and day wear (Michel, Cranfield), the context in this case does suggest a change of clothes related to the transition from night to day; and the fuller phrases here suggest some divesting of ordinary (night?) wear in order to clothe oneself with the accoutrements of war. The stronger the eschatological note, the more the imagery of preparation for the (decisive) final battle (between the forces of darkness and those of light) comes to the fore; see further on 13:13.

ἔργον /ἔργα is essentially a neutral word, but it is not surprising that Paul chooses to use it (in contrast to ὅπλα) on the negative side of the equation. For though it can be used with a qualifying word in a positive sense (as in 2:7, 15 and 13:3), when it stands alone it is more likely than not to have a negative connotation (cf. Luke 11:48; 1 Cor 5:2; 2 Cor 11:15; 2 Tim 4:14; 3 John 10; but the point does not emerge from any Pauline antipathy to "works" as a concept, let alone to "good works," since the negative force of the word standing alone is more widely attested; see further BGD). Here, of course, there is a qualifying word which makes the negative tone explicit; cf. particularly Isa 29:15 and Eph 5:11. The imagery is probably elaborated in v 13, since v 13b also functions as an antithesis to what is appropriate for the day (ἡμέρα). For ὅπλα see on 6:13. The idea of "putting on weapons" sounds somewhat stilted to us, but like the similar phrase "to be in arms," it is a natural idiom (Herodotus 1.13; 7.218; LSJ, ὅπλον III.6); what is clearly in view is dressing for battle, being kitted out with the full panoply of war (weapons and armor; cf. Eph 6:11).

The third contrast meshes in more immediately to the preceding contrast of night and day. It was a popular antithesis in Job (12:22, 25; 17:12; 18:6, 18; 22:11; 24:16; etc.) and Isaiah (5:20; 9:2; 42:6–7, 16; 59:9; 60:1–3), and naturally lends itself to a contrast between inability to see and enlightenment in a spiritual or moral sense (e.g., σκότος—Deut 28:29; Ps 82:5; Isa 42:7; φῶς —Pss 36:9; 97:11; Mic 7:8–9). For the contrast in Jewish wisdom see further Eccl 2:13, Wisd Sol 17:20–18:4, Philo, *Som.* 2.39, *Spec. Leg.* 1.288, 3.6, and particularly the quite closely parallel sequence in Prov 4:14–19 (walk, sleep, drink, light of dawn leading to full day, darkness). In *T. 12 Patr.* note the interesting parallel with *T. Levi* 19.1: "choose for yourselves either darkness or light, either the law of the Lord or the works of Belial" (cf. also *T. Naph* 2:10; *T. Gad* 5:7; *T. Jos.* 20:2; *T. Ben.* 5:3). The contrast lends itself particularly to the eschatological dualism of apocalyptic (cf. already Amos 5:18, 20; also Isa 60:19–20): *1 Enoch* 10.5; 92.4–5; 108.11–15; *2 Enoch* 65.9–10; *2 Apoc. Bar.* 18.2; 48.50; and particularly the sharp antithesis in the DSS between "the sons of light" and "the sons of darkness" (1QS 1.9–10; 3.24–5; 4.7–13; with the same talk of girding for war, for final battle, found in 1QM, especially 1.1, 8–14 and 13.5–16; bibliography in Wilckens, n.411). See also on 2:19. The NT makes good use of the antithesis also, not least for the event of conversion (Matt 4:16; Acts 26:18; 2 Cor 4:6; Eph 5:8; Col 1:12–13; 1 Pet 2:9; also *1 Clem.* 59.2), but also in more typically wisdom categories (Matt 6:22–23 // Luke 11:34–36; 1 John 1:6; cf. *Barn.* 18.1—"the two ways"). Jewish consciousness of the privilege of election is evident in Rom 2:19. The use of light and darkness as eschatological categories is reflected in John 3:19 and 2 Cor 6:14 as well as in 1 Thess 5:4–5 and here. For both terms, see further BGD and the full treatment in *TDNT* 9:310–58.

13 ὡς ἐν ἡμέρᾳ εὐσχημόνως περιπατήσωμεν, "let us behave decently as in the day." For περιπατέω, "conduct oneself," see on 6:4. εὐσχήμων signifies what would generally be regarded as decent, proper, presentable in responsible society. The element of (mere) appearance (literally, "of good [εὖ] external appearance" [σχῆμα]) has disappeared from the word by this time. It is not a Jewish concept (cf. only Prov 11:25; *4 Macc* 6.2) but quite familiar in a Greek scale of values. In the NT εὐσχήμων (Mark 15:43; Acts 13:50; 17:12; 1 Cor 7:35; 12:23–24); εὐσχημόνως (1 Cor 14:40; 1 Thess 4:12). See further BGD; *TDNT* 2:770–71; LSJ, εὐσχημόνως, "with grace and dignity, like a gentleman"; Barrett, "with nothing to be ashamed of"; Spicq, 333–35. To be noted, once again, is the fact that Paul has no hesitation in calling on his readers to observe the conventional respectability of his day; he does not press for a Christian ethic distinctive in every element; see also on 1:28; 2:7, 10; 12:17; 13:3, 5, 10.

Recent commentators have emphasized that the ὡς does not reinforce any sense of mere appearance—ὡς in the sense of "as is actually the case," rather than "as though" (Käsemann, Cranfield, Schlier, Wilckens; against, e.g., Lietzmann and Barrett). But the Already/Not-yet tension needs to be expressed more carefully. In fact the double use of ἡμέρα in v 12 and v 13 reflects very much the same Already/Not-yet tension which is evident in the Jesus tradition regarding Jesus' proclamation of the kingdom of God. Indeed, we could almost replace ἡμέρα by the word βασιλεία: for the Not-yet, cf., e.g., Mark 1:15 (ἤγγικεν ἡ βασιλεία) and 1 Cor 6:9–10; Gal 5:21; for the Already, cf., e.g., Matt 12:28; Luke 17:21; Rom 14:17; and Col 4:11. The point in all cases is that those who look for the coming of the kingdom/day must live as citizens of that kingdom, in the light of that (coming) day (see also on 13:11 and 13:12).

μὴ κώμοις καὶ μέθαις, "not in revelry and drunkenness"—the plurals probably indicating frequency. κῶμος, originally a festal procession in honor of Dionysus, carries the overtone of uninhibited revelry to excess; so in the only two LXX passages (Wisd Sol 14:23 and 2 Macc 6:4), as in the only other two NT references (Gal 5:21 and 1 Pet 4:3). μέθη, "drunkenness" (as in Luke 21:34; see also Eph 5:18 and 1 Thess 5:7); but in association with κῶμος (as also in Gal 5:21) it may have more the sense of "drinking bout," or suggest that the two words be translated as a hendiadys—"drunken revelry." See BGD, on both words. Petronius' vivid account of Trimalchio's banquet in *Satyricon,* written quite probably within about ten years of Paul's letter to Rome, gives a fair idea of what Paul must have had in mind. This and the following phrases hang, of course, on the main clause (v 13a): "more than in our own times it was believed among the Romans that during the night everything was permitted" (Lagrange).

μὴ κοίταις καὶ ἀσελγείαις, "not in debauchery and sexual excess." By natural association and progression the meaning of κοίτη moves from "bed," through "marriage bed," to "sexual intercourse" (see on 9:10), and in association with ἀσέλγεια to "sexual excess" (BGD). ἀσέλγεια denotes "debauchery, licentiousness, sensuality"—an obvious member of any list of vices (Mark 7:22; 2 Cor 12:21; Gal 5:19; 1 Pet 4:3; cf. also Eph 4:19; 2 Pet 2:2, 7, 18; Jude 4); as in Wisd Sol 14:26 and Philo, *Mos.* 1:305 especially of sexual excess (BGD). Perhaps again translation as a hendiadys is appropriate; "debauched sexual excess."

μὴ ἔριδι καὶ ζήλῳ, "not in quarreling and envy." For ἔρις see on 1:29. While ζῆλος is itself a neutral term (see on 10:2), in close association with ἔρις (as in 1 Cor 3:3; 2 Cor 12:20; Gal 5:20; *1 Clem.* 5.5; 6.4; 9.1; cf. James 3:14, 16) it obviously has a strongly negative sense. Perhaps here too a hendiadys, "rivalry, party attachment" (see further BGD, ζῆλος 2), with a stronger allusion to the political and social factions and infighting characteristic of Rome, at this period no less than others. As Stumpff notes, in such vice lists "it is doubtful whether . . . we can or should try to fix with precision the meaning of each individual word. ζῆλος here denotes the kind of zeal which does not try to help others but rather to harm them, the predominant concern being for personal advancement" (*TDNT* 2:881–82). For such vice lists see on 1:29–31.

14 ἀλλὰ ἐνδύσασθε τὸν κύριον Ἰησοῦν Χριστόν, "put on the Lord Jesus Christ." To "put on" someone is not necessarily "grotesque" (Gaugler). It is a not unnatural extension of the metaphorical usage already noted under 13:12 (Cranfield, Harrisville): "let Christ Jesus himself be the armor that you wear" (NEB; so NJB). Change of clothes may have been part of initiation ceremonies elsewhere, though it is only clearly attested for the mysteries by Apuleius, *Met.* 11.14 ff. (*TDNT* 7:687–88), and there is no indication that a change of robes was already part of Christian initiation. But a similar phrase is already attested in the first century B.C. by Dionysius of Halicarnassus 11.5, used of acting: τὸν Ταρκύνιον ἐνδύεσθαι, "to play the role of Tarquin" (LSJ, ἐνδύω; *TDNT* 2:319). In context-of-meaning terms, the parallel should not be dismissed as irrelevant to what Paul could expect his hearers to understand by the phrase: the intensity of concentration needed by an actor to "live a part" is the sort of intensity of dedication required by the believer to live "as in the day" (v 13).

However, Paul no doubt had in mind a richer, more mystical (or better) spiritual meaning in a double sense. (1) The call is of a piece with his Adam christology/soteriology (cf. *TDNT* 2:320). Hence the closest parallels come in talk of the final "putting on" of the incorruptibility and immortality (1 Cor 15:53–54) which is "the image of the heavenly," "the last Adam" (15:45–49), and of "putting on the new man" (Col 3:9–10; Eph 4:24). So it is part of the important Pauline understanding of the process of salvation as a becoming conformed to the image of Christ (see further on 8:29) and it speaks of the believers' responsibility within that process, the determined cooperation with the outworking of grace in this time of eschatological tension (see also Schlatter). (2) Talk of human responsibility, however, should not be sharply distinguished from the divine enabling and power by which the "putting on" is accomplished. It is no accident that the LXX uses "putting on" language for the endowment and empowering of the Spirit: "the Spirit put on Gideon/Amasai/Azariah" (Judg 6:34; 1 Chron 12:18/19; 2 Chron 24:20); so also Luke 24:49. And it ties into the Adam soteriology referred to above (cf. particularly 8:29; 2 Cor 3:18; and the indicative/imperative balance noted below). Outside the NT, cf. Job 29:14 (Heb.); *Herm. Sim.* 9.24.2; and the more intense spirituality of *Odes Sol.* 33.12.

Most see baptismal terminology here (e.g., Michel; Schmidt; Käsemann; Müller, *Prophetie,* 147; Schlier; Ortkemper, 146; Maillot; but see Barrett on

13:12; Leenhardt's attempt to link the εὐσχημόνως of v 13 into the same thought is very strained). Of course, it is not a description of baptism or of what baptism as such does; Paul is hardly calling for a further baptism (this needs to be borne in mind in cross-referencing to Gal 3:27). It is, rather, a way of describing the spiritual transformation which has a decisive beginning in conversion-initiation, but which is hardly completed or final. The indicative needs to be held in tension with the imperative (hence Col 3:3/5; 3:10/12 and Eph 4:24). It is because the primary reference of the metaphor is to a spiritual transformation effected by the Spirit rather than to a once-for-all act (see further Dunn, *Baptism,* particularly 109–111) that Paul must balance indicative (Gal 3:27) with imperative (here). Here is a further reminder that the aorists of 6:2–4 should not be taken in isolation. We should not assume that Paul has enthusiasts or pneumatics in view at this point (as once again Michel and Käsemann); the danger of a slackening of moral resolve would be much more widespread. Vögtle, "Paraklese," 194, rightly notes that the qnormative content of this exhortation is neither grounded in nor dependent on the imminent expectation of v 11.

The κύριος Ἰησοῦς Χριστός is formulaic (1:7), but the setting of κύριος first may reflect Paul's characteristic exhortation to act ἐν κυρίῳ (see further on 16:2).

καὶ τῆς σαρκὸς πρόνοιαν μὴ ποιεῖσθε εἰς ἐπιθυμίας, "and make no provision for the flesh to satisfy its desires." πρόνοιαν (only here in Paul) ποιεῖσθαί τινος is an established phrase in Greek, "to make provision for something, be concerned about something," not least in the popular Greek of the papyri (MM; BGD, πρόνοια); cf. Dan 6:19; *Ep. Arist.* 80; Josephus, *Life,* 62; *Ap.* 1.9; and for the phrase here Philo, *Ebr.* 87. The present tense could have the force of "stop doing" something (so NJB and NEB). For σάρξ see particularly on 1:3 and 7:5; for ἐπιθυμία see on 1:24; and for the phrase (ἐπιθυμία σαρκός) see Gal 5:16, 24; Eph 2:3; 2 Pet 2:10, 18; and 1 John 2:16. What Paul is calling for is not precisely clear and depends on how the εἰς ἐπιθυμίας is related to the rest of the clause. He could be understood to mean "do not care for the flesh in such a way that desires arise" (*TDNT* 4:1012), or as a much sharper polemic against the flesh as such: "no rights must be accorded at all to the flesh and its tendencies" (Käsemann). The issue hangs on the degree to which Paul sees "flesh" and Christ/Spirit as mutually exclusive categories (see again on 7:5). However negative the weight of σάρξ, here it is clear that a life lived habitually in terms of satisfying the natural/animal appetites is to be resisted; that would be life κατὰ σάρκα (8:4 ff). At the same time, it is equally clear that the "flesh" is not something which Paul regards as having been left behind by the believer; the believer is still ἐν σαρκί (7:5) and must continually refuse to walk κατὰ σάρκα, an all-too-realistic possibility (8:12–13).

Explanation

13:11–14 Paul could have gone straight to his next major concern (the problem of deep differences among the Roman congregations on the lifestyle appropriate to the gospel), since "love of neighbor" (13:8–10) is also the main thrust of his counsel to "the strong" in the following chapter (14:15).

But evidently he felt the need to add some further exhortation to remind his readers of the eschatological constraints upon their daily conduct. Despite the longer-term perspective implicit in vv 1–7, and the clear enunciation of the basic principle of all Christian conduct and relationships which remains in force whatever the time span of its operation (vv 8–10), Paul evidently thought it necessary or desirable to underscore the fact that with the step of faith/commitment his readers had entered upon a completely new phase of historical existence. It was not that the new had completely left the old behind; on the contrary, the conditions of the old still held sway. The point was rather that even though they lived still within the old they had resources from the new which enabled them to live by its power.

The imagery used has two features. (1) It is strongly temporal—"time," "hour," "near," "far advanced," "at hand" (vv 11–12). (2) It is strongly contrasting—"wake up from sleep," "night"/"day," "put off"/"put on," "darkness"/"light," "decently"/"revelry, drunkenness," etc., "put on Christ"/"make no provision for flesh." The combined effect is powerful. The readers are left in no doubt that there is a sharp "either-or" confronting them, not only in their original decision to accept the gospel, but precisely as a result of their decision to accept the gospel. A choice once made has to be confirmed and lived out in a whole sequence of repeated decisions.

The eschatological tension is strongly marked. His readers, even those who have taken the decisive step of faith, can be described as asleep (v 11); the circumstances in which they live as night still prevailing (v 12); there are "works of darkness" which they must yet "put off" (v 12); the desires of the flesh are still strong and to be contested (v 14). The sequence of unsavory couplets, "drunken revelry, debauched sex, envious rivalry" (v 13) may simply be a way of characterizing the conduct of the night in the extreme terms which most inhabitants of Rome would know about, at least from the gossip and rumor of the marketplace. But since some members of the church in Corinth had to be rebuked for similar licentiousness (1 Cor 5–6) and not dissimilar disorder (1 Cor 12:2; 14:12, 23, 33, 39), the possibility cannot be excluded that Paul saw these as real temptations and threats to his Roman readers. Either way, the sequence of Paul's imagery and the intensity of his concern underline the extent to which Paul saw the circumstances and character of the old age of Adam (5:12–21) as still a powerful factor influencing the conduct of these first generation Christians. In their still belonging to the old unredeemed epoch, both in their own natural appetites and in their social context, there are forces to be reckoned with and guarded against lest the darkness close in again and once more shut out the light.

The note of imminent expectation is equally strong. The final salvation is much nearer (v 11)—that is, the completed transformation of the whole person into the image of Christ, in body as well (8:11, 23). The daylight which wholly dispels the darkness of night is close at hand (v 12). The urgency and compulsion of the exhortation arises immediately from this sense of imminence: "it is already the hour for you to wake up . . . Let us therefore put off. . . ." The twentieth-century scholar, nineteen and a half centuries later, and still the darkness of the old age lingers on, cannot help wondering whether the force of the moral imperative is critically weakened by this delay. But it need not be so. The sensitivity to the problem caused by the delay for moral earnestness has only emerged in relatively recent times. Even in the nineteenth century, before infant mortality was so dramatically reduced and life expectancy so dramatically increased, a passage like this could be readily interpreted in the light of the ever-present threat of a life cut short in its prime. A society for whom the finality of death has been pushed back to the margins of concern and largely ignored as a factor influencing lifestyle and conduct can easily sneer at the improving pieties of Victorian sentimentality about death. Such an attitude invites a fearful rejoinder in terms of new and unlooked-for viruses or nuclear catastrophe. Ironically, in a modern nuclear age, it becomes possible to believe more realistically in the imminence of the end, without the passing of the decades reducing the foreboding or expectation, but rather intensifying it for each new generation. The words which resulted in Augustine's conversion (13:13–14) may not yet have lost their power to correct the still too casual and selfish readers of a much later age.

More to the point here is the positive side of the antitheses, the power of the Already: the decisive act of commitment has been made (v 11); there are "weapons of the light" which can be donned (v 12); Paul and his readers belong to the day and can live in its light, even though the hours of darkness still linger (v 13); the Lord Jesus Christ is himself a factor and power who can fully overcome the desires of the flesh and prevent the natural appetites from becoming too dominant a factor in the period before the body is finally and fully redeemed (v 14). For the Christian even in "the darkest hour before dawn" the decisive fact is what has already happened—not just the Christian's own conversion, but much more important, the Lordship of Jesus Christ. It is the critical turn of the ages, which happened in Christ's resurrection, the new humanity and the resources it brings for those still caught up in the old, which make all the difference. Believers can be exhorted to wake up, put off, put on, etc., not because their future depends solely on such strength of purpose, but as the way to open themselves to the eschatological rule of God in Christ.

The imagery is frequently understood as derived from baptismal parenesis. This may be so, and many clearly find helpful the thought of "renewal of baptism" or "living the baptismal life." But the reference back to baptism is less justified exegetically and less helpful than it might be. Paul's pointing backwards here is to the step of faith (which would normally be expressed in baptism), and that act of commitment is clearly an important presupposition of the moral exhortation at this point. Elsewhere he defines the Christian in terms of the Spirit received (as in 5:5 and 8:9), and that recall to the actuality of the original spiritual renewal and source of continuing moral enabling is equally important in such exhortation. The baptismal ritual was part of that whole, but to refer the whole to the ritual moment would run the danger of losing sight of these other more typically Pauline emphases. Moreover, baptism as a once-for-all act speaks well of the decisive initial stage of the life of faith, but it has neither the flexibility of the concept "faith" itself (Paul can use it in the present as well as in the aorist tense: those who continue to believe, as well as once made the act of commitment), nor the potential to encourage repeated acts of commitment of the same kind (as Paul achieves in his talk of putting off and putting on). Here too Paul finds it necessary to express the ongoing reality of sharing in Christ's death and risen life with a richer and more diverse range of images than many of those who succeeded him in the life of discipleship.

G. The Particular Problem of Food Laws and Holy Days (14:1–15:6)

Bibliography

Allison, D. C. "Pattern." Black, M. "The Christological Use of the Old Testament in the New Testament." *NTS* 18 (1971–72) 8. Cambier, J.-M. "La liberté chrétienne est et personnelle et communautaire (Rom 14:1–15:13)." In *Freedom and Love: The Guide for Christian Life (1 Cor 8–10; Rom 14–15)*, ed. L. de Lorenzi. Rome: St. Paul's Abbey, 1981. 57–84. Carson, D. A., ed. *From Sabbath to Lord's Day*. Grand Rapids: Zondervan, 1982. Donfried, K. P. "The Kingdom of God in Paul." In *The Kingdom of God in Twentieth-Century Interpretation*, ed. W. Willis. Peabody, Mass.: Hendrickson, 1987. 175–90. Dunn, J. D. G. "Jesus and Ritual Purity: A Study of the Tradition History of Mark 7:15." In *A Cause de L'Évangile*, FS J. Dupont. Lectio Divina 123. Paris: Éditions du Cerf, 1985. 251–76. Dupont, J. "Appel aux Faibles et aux Forts dans la communauté romaine (Rom 14:1–15:13)." *SPCIC I* 357–66. Evans, O. E. "What God Requires of Man—Rom 14:14." *ExpT* 69 (1957–58) 199–202. Furnish, V. P. *Love Command.* 115–18. Haufe, G. "Reich Gottes bei Paulus und in der Jesus tradition." *NTS* 31 (1985) 467–72. Jewett, R. *Tolerance.* Johnston, G. "'Kingdom of God' Sayings in Paul's Letters." In *From Jesus to Paul*, FS F. W. Beare, ed. P. Richardson and J. C. Hurd. Waterloo, Ontario: Wilfrid Laurier University, 1984. 143–56. Karris, R. J. "Romans 14:1–15:13." Kleinknecht, K. T. *Gerechtfertigte.* 356–64. Kreitzer, L. J. *Jesus and God in Paul's Eschatology.* JSNTSup. 19. Sheffield: Academic, 1987. Esp. 107–12. Lacey, D. R. de. "The Sabbath/Sunday Question and the Law in the Pauline Corpus." In *Sunday,* ed. Carson. 159–95. Lincoln, A. T. "From Sabbath to Lord's Day: A Biblical and Theological Perspective." In *Sunday,* ed. Carson. 343–412. Mattern, L. *Verständnis.* 115–18, 158–62. Meeks, W. A. "Judgment and the Brother: Romans 14:1–15:13." In *Tradition and Intepretation in the New Testament,* FS E. E. Ellis, ed. G. F. Hawthorne and O. Betz. Grand Rapids: Eerdmans; Tübingen: Mohr, 1987. 290–300. Merk, O. *Handeln.* 167–73. Minear, P. S. *Obedience.* 6–35. Müller, K. *Anstoss.* 32–45. Nababan, A. E. S. *Bekenntnis und Mission in Römer 14 und 15.* PhD, Heidelberg, 1963. Newton, M. *Purity.* 98–102. Neirynck, F. "Sayings of Jesus." 306–8. Nieder, L. *Die Motive der religiös-sittlichen Paränese in den paulinischen Gemeindebriefen. Ein Beitrag zur paulinischen Ethik.* MThSt 12. Munich: Karl Zink, 1956. 71–77. Rauer, M. *Die "Schwachen" in Korinth und Rom nach den Paulusbriefen.* Freiburg: Herder, 1923. Rordorf, W. *Sunday.* London: SCM, 1968. Schmithals, W. *Römerbrief.* 95–107. Schrage, W. *Einzelgebote.* 150–61. Schulz, A. *Nachfolgen und Nachahmen.* SANT 6. Munich: Kösel, 1962. Segal, A. F. "Romans 7 and Jewish Dietary Law." *SR* 15 (1986) 361–74. Stanley, D. M. *Resurrection.* 198–99. Synofzik, E. *Vergeltungsaussagen.* 45–48. Theissen, G. "The Strong and the Weak in Corinth: A Sociological Analysis of a Theological Quarrel." *Social Setting.* chap. 3. Thüsing, W. *Per Christum.* 30–41. Watson, F. *Paul.* 94–98. Willis, W. L. *Idol Meat in Corinth: The Pauline Argument in 1 Corinthians 8 and 10.* SBLDS 68. Chico: Scholars Press, 1985.

Introduction

The lengthy treatment of one specific issue is insufficiently explained by the thesis that Paul sought to draw some general lessons from the experience of congregations elsewhere, particularly Corinth (cf. 1 Cor 8–10) (against SH 399–403; Knox; Leenhardt; Furnish, *Love Command,* 155; Karris, 83; Aune, *Literary Environment,* 220; see also on 14:2); apart from anything else, key motifs in each exposition are lacking in the other (Rom—unclean/clean; 1 Cor—idol meat, conscience, knowledge). Equally inappropriate is Knox's claim that 14:1–15:13 is something of an appendix to the ethical section. More likely the section evidences Paul's knowledge of circumstances in Rome itself, at least in broad terms, with tensions between those who saw themselves as part of an essentially Jewish movement and therefore obligated to observe the characteristic and distinctive Jewish customs, and those who shared Paul's understanding of a gospel which transcended Jewish particularity. The issue also follows from Paul's earlier treatment of the law, almost as inevitably as his treatment of circumcision in 2:25–29 and 4:9–12, as also his preceding treatment of social ethics, since the Jewish law was nowhere else more distinctive and determinative of social relationships than in the food laws and laws regarding sabbaths and festivals (e.g., *Ep. Arist.* 139, 142; Philo, *Mos.* 1.278). The nature of the theological transformation Paul has effected with regard to the law's relationship to the people of God is clearly indicated in what Paul says here; for on issues where the law had specific rulings Paul nowhere refers to the law; that boundary-defining role of the law is at an end; a much greater diversity of opinion and practice can now be envisaged within the people of God (vv 2, 5–8). As in chap. 2, the day of judgment is still the final test to which all will be subjected, but the criterion of judgment on these matters is the individual's charismatic apprehension of the will of God (as in 12:2), or, in a word, faith (14:5, 22–23). And in direct continuity with 13:8–14 the arbiter is love (14:15) and the norm is Christ (14:4, 6–8, 14, 15, 18; 15:3, 5).

A stylistic feature of the section is the switch back and forth from plural (14:1, 7–8, 13, 16, 19; 15:1–2, 4–6) to singular (14:4, 10, 15, 20–22; 15:2); cf. Wilckens. As so often in this letter, both sections of the argument/exhortation are clinched with scriptural quotations (14:11; 15:3).

1. The Problem Posed: The Challenge to "the Weak" (14:1–12)

Bibliography

See 14:1–15:6 *Bibliography.*

Translation

[1]*But welcome the one who is weak in faith, though not with a view to settling disputes.* [2]*Someone has faith to eat everything; but the weak person eats*[a] *(only)*

vegetables. ³*Let the one who eats not despise the one who does not eat, and let not the one who does not eat pass judgment on the one who eats, for God has welcomed him.* ⁴*Who are you who condemns the slave of someone else? In relation to his own master he stands or falls. And he shall stand, for the master*ᶜ *is able*ᵇ *to make him stand.* ⁵ᵈ*Someone judges one day to be more important than another; another judges every day to be alike. Let each be fully convinced in his own mind.* ⁶*The one who holds an opinion on the day does so to the Lord.*ᵉ *And the one who eats does so to the Lord, for he gives thanks to God; and the one who does not eat does so to the Lord and gives thanks to God.* ⁷*For no one of us lives for himself and no one dies for himself.* ⁸*For if we live, we live for the Lord; and if we die, we die*ᶠ *for the Lord. So whether we live or whether we die, we are the Lord's.* ⁹*For it was for this purpose that Christ died and lived again,*ᵍ *in order that he might be lord over both dead and living.* ¹⁰*So you, why do you judge your brother? Or you, why do you despise your brother? For we shall all stand before the judgment seat of God,*ʰ ¹¹*for it is written:*

As I live, says the Lord, to me shall bend every knee
and every tongue shall give praise to God.

¹²*So then*ⁱ *each of us will give account of himself to God.*ʲ

Notes

ᵃThe imperative ἐσθιέτω in P⁴⁶ and Western texts may simply reflect a too casual assimilation to the imperatives in v 3 or some antipathy on the part of Gentile Christian congregations to the weaker Jewish Christian congregations diminishing in number (cf. Cranfield).

ᵇP⁴⁶ and others read δυνατὸς γάρ ἐστιν—probably an attempt to amend the text to the more regular usage (Metzger; and cf. on 14:4).

ᶜThe θεός of D F G etc. was probably accidental, an understandable slip in view of the interplay between κύριος and θεός in these verses; but see *Note* h below.

ᵈγάρ is read by א* et al., but omitted by P⁴⁶ אᶜ B etc. Since other arguments are equally divided (Paul could have linked this example by γάρ to the preceding case as a continuation of the same problem or further example of the same dispute, or it could have been added by scribes who recognized the continuity), it is probably better to follow the somewhat stronger MS evidence in favor of its absence (Metzger, Cranfield).

ᵉFailure to recognize that v 6a could include both groups resulted in the addition of καὶ ὁ μὴ φρονῶν τὴν ἡμέραν κυρίῳ οὐ φρονεῖ in an attempt to achieve a similar balance to that in the second half of the verse.

ᶠSome MSS, taking the second ζῶμεν as a subjunctive, read the subjunctive ἀποθνῄσκωμεν, turning Paul's indicative into an edifying exhortation (Käsemann).

ᵍThe less usual ἔζησεν was replaced or supplemented in some MSS by ἀνέστη (cf. 1 Thess 4:14); see further Lietzmann, Cranfield, 708 n.1.

ʰAt an early date θεοῦ was replaced by Χριστοῦ, probably under the influence of 2 Cor 5:10 (Lietzmann, Metzger).

ⁱWhether οὖν should be read or not is difficult to judge (see Cranfield, 711 n.1), but it makes very little difference.

ʲτῷ θεῷ could have been added in the light of v 11, but it is supported by a strong combination of MSS (א A C D etc.) and versions (lat sy co) (Metzger).

Form and Structure

Following the initial statement of the problem (vv 1–2), the main thrust of the first paragraph (vv 3–12) is directed chiefly to "the weak in faith" and against the tendency to judge the less scrupulous brother (κρίνω [vv 3–

5, 10]). The parallel with the sequence of thought in chap. 2 is striking and probably deliberate (cf. Meeks, "Judgment," 296)—rebuke against judging (κρίνειν) others (2:1–3; 14:3–4, 10), followed by a reminder that all must face the judgment of God (2:16; 14:10–12); see also on 14:4. The implication is thus strengthened that what is in view is a typically Jewish perspective of the believer who wants to stay firmly within the law as traditionally understood.

Notable features of this paragraph are the emotional impact achieved by the affective use of diatribe style in vv 4 and 10 and the theme of living and dying drawn out with some style in vv 7–9, perhaps reflecting some confessional (cf. 2 Cor 5:14–15 and Gal 2:20—Nababan, 54–62), liturgical or hymnic underlay; cf. 2 Tim 2:11–13 (Schmidt, Black, Schlier).

Comment

1 τὸν δὲ ἀσθενοῦντα τῇ πίστει προσλαμβάνεσθε, "but welcome the one who is weak in faith." The force of the δέ should not be lost. Paul was able to use such a lightly adversative conjunction because he intended a continuity of thought from the preceding exhortation (cf. Schlatter, 362–63). The connection is threefold. (1) The particular problems outlined in what follows are the climax of his attempt to redefine the people of God and its corollaries (see 12:1–15:13 *Introduction*). For Jews, not least in the diaspora, the boundaries which marked them off in their distinctiveness as the elect people of the one God were most emphatically and visibly drawn in the daily lifestyle expressed in diet and festivals (see further on 14:2 and 14:5). Consequently the parenesis builds up to these issues, and the discussion of them is given what would otherwise be a disproportionate amount of space. (2) The golden rule of love of neighbor which has knit together the earlier exhortation (12:3, 9–10, 13, 14–17, 21; 13:8–10) continues to be the leading principle governing relationships strained by differences on important matters affecting faith and communal lifestyle (particularly 14:15). (3) The immediate carryover from chap. 13 is given by the connection between "flesh" (13:14) and being "weak in faith" (14:1; both with particular reference to social eating habits [13:13; 14:2ff.]). As has been clear from several of the previous references, σάρξ combines the thought of human weakness (the subjection of the physical to decay and corruption, the power of the human appetites to exercise a crippling and destructive fascination for the individual; see on 7:5), and Paul's critique of his fellow Jews for their false trust in their ethnic identity expressed not least in the outward ritual of circumcision (see on 2:28–29; also 4:1 and 9:3; and again on 7:5). The implication of the δέ is that "weakness in flesh" is an example of such σάρξ-ness: "do not make provision for the flesh . . . , but welcome the weak in faith." That is to say, "weakness in faith" is an expression of a "fleshly" attitude, but of a less serious nature that it can be accepted within the spectrum of Christian liberty (see further on 14:2).

ὁ ἀσθενῶν τῇ πίστει, "the one who is weak in faith," is of course a somewhat pejorative description—a nickname given by others, rather than by the individuals in view (Michel, Cranfield, Wilckens; "specifically Paulins"—Nababan, 30–34). The contrasting phrase, ἡμεῖς οἱ δυνατοί, "we, the strong," does not appear till 15:1, but it is already evident in the very use of the phrase that Paul numbers himself with "the strong" (14:14, 20). It is not that Paul regards "weakness" per se as something defective (though cf. 5:6). On the contrary, he elsewhere regards human or physical weakness as the very locus of divine power in this present epoch (particularly 2 Cor 4:7–11; 11:30; 12:5, 9–10; 13:4, 9). What is defective here is the faith—"weak *in faith.*" What he means by that is already clear from 4:19: to be "weak in faith" is to fail to trust God completely and without qualification (cf. Barrett; the two passages are not so far apart as Cranfield thinks). In this case the weakness is trust in God *plus* dietary and festival laws, trust in God *dependent* on observance of such practices, a trust in God which leans on the crutches of particular customs and not on God alone, as though they were an integral part of that trust. So also 1 Cor 8:7, 9–10 and 9:22. Kirk suggests the best rendering of the contrast is "adaptable" and "rigid" (on 15:1).

The use of the singular may be significant. It is partly stylistic (see 14:1–15:6 *Introduction*), and does not contradict the clear implication that a group is involved (see particularly Wilckens, 3:110). But it may also reflect the situation of the Roman congregations when Jewish Christians who had been expelled in 49 were returning in ones and twos to pick up the threads of their old life, and where the temptation was for the majority Gentile Christians to act in condescending fashion to them (see further *Introduction* §2.4.4, and on 14:2).

προσλαμβάνομαι has the force of "receive or accept into one's society, home, circle of acquaintances" (BGD: 2 Macc 10:15; Acts 28:2; Philem 17; so also 15:7). What is in view is the everyday recognition and practice of brotherhood, not an official act of reception (rightly Rauer, 81–82; Nababan, 35; Käsemann; against Schlatter, Lagrange, Kirk [referring to baptism]). See also on 14:3.

μὴ εἰς διακρίσεις διαλογισμῶν, "though not with a view to settling disputes," "without attempting to settle doubtful points" (NEB). For the μή cf. Matt 26:5. διάκρισις in its only other Pauline usage denotes the process of deliberation (or insight) whereby a decision is reached about the validity of inspired utterances (1 Cor 12:10; cf. 1 Cor 2:13, 15; 14:29; = δοκιμάζειν, 1 Thess 5:19–21, so that Rom 12:2 and 14:22 come into play here as parallels; cf. the only other NT use [Heb 5:14]). It can have the sense, "quarrel, dispute" (BGD, LSJ III; so Nababan, 36, and NJB here); but that is not attested elsewhere in the NT except Acts 4:32 D. διαλογισμός derives from the imagery of balancing accounts, and so gains the sense of "consideration, discussion, debate, argument" (LSJ); in the Pauline literature cf. particularly Phil 2:14 and 1 Tim 2:8 ("scruples," as Moffatt, Barrett, Murray, Cranfield, is already imposing a negative interpretation on the word). The precise meaning of the two words thus conjoined is difficult to express in a simple translation. But what is in view seems to be the possibility that the majority group in a congregation would see the reception of "the weak in faith" as an opportunity to engage in an argument which, as the majority (and "the strong"), they would be able to arbitrate in favor of the majority opinion (cf. SH, NIV); that the advice is directed to the welcoming majority rather than to all is clear enough (rightly Cranfield and Wilckens; against Käsemann). What comes to expression, then, is a keen pastoral concern: that newcomers should not be subjected to demanding discussion about their common faith and its outworking (certainly not while they were settling down and certainly not as a first priority of community concern, though Michel is right in noting that a healthy congregation must engage in some such διάκρισις); and that the majority should not seek to impose their views and practice as being the majority and the more established. The liberty of the Christian assembly should be able to embrace divergent views and practices without a feeling that they must be resolved or that a common mind must be achieved on every point of disagreement. All this stands, even though Paul does regard some opinions held by fellow Christians as immature, and in the course of this very chapter seeks to engage in some further education toward greater maturity (vv 14, 20). Nevertheless, the overarching concern and priority in what follows is that a church should be able to sustain a diversity of opinion and lifestyle as an integral aspect of its common life.

2 ὃς μὲν πιστεύει φαγεῖν πάντα, "someone has faith to eat everything." πιστεύειν + infinitive occurs in Greek in the sense "believe that, feel confident that" something is, will be, or has been (LSJ, πιστεύω I.3; Lagrange = θαρρῶ); elsewhere in the NT it occurs only in Acts 15:11 (Michel). The usage here is unusual, but the sense is clear enough: the one so described has sufficient faith ("strong in faith") to eat everything. This "believing" should not be taken in a different sense from the regular use of πιστεύειν already established in the letter: it is the same trust in God so powerfully expounded in 4:17–22. (Cranfield's paraphrase, "has the assurance that his faith permits him to eat" [697–98; cf. NIV], is too stilted and loses the dynamic sense of a trusting relationship; see further on 14:22 and 23). And by implication and context the contrast is the same: a trust in God which is measured by and therefore too much limited to faithful practice of works of the law (in chap. 4, circumcision; here, food laws and festivals; see below and on 14:5). Such trust in God is not, of course, a carte blanche for an unlimited range of social behavior (cf. chaps. 6 and 12–13), but the limitations will not be determined by race or national tradition ("everything" meaning "every potential food," in contrast to a restricted diet). On the use of φαγεῖν see also 14:21.

ὁ δὲ ἀσθενῶν λάχανα ἐσθίει, "but the weak eats (only) vegetables." It is significant that Paul does not repeat the πιστεύειν in this clause: whereas "eating everything" *is* an expression of faith (unconditional trust in God), to eat only vegetables Paul does not regard as an expression of faith as such. λάχανον, mostly in the plural, refers to "garden herbs," in distinction from wild plants, and so "vegetables" (LSJ, MM). In the OT—Gen 9:3; 1 Kgs 21 [LXX 20]:2; Ps 37 [LXX 36]:2; and Prov 15:17; in the NT—Mark 4:32 par. and Luke 11:42. The practice of vegetarianism for religious or philosophic reasons was quite well known in the ancient world; e.g., the (neo-)Pythagoreans as attested by Diogenes Laertius 8.38 and Philostratus, *Vita Apol.* 1.8 (see material collected in *TDNT* 2:690; Lietzmann; Rauer, 138–64; Michel, 419–20; Cranfield, 693 n.5; Wilckens, 3:112). On the basis of these data a specifically Jew-Gentile controversy is disputed (e.g., by Gaugler; Kümmel, *Introduction*, 310–11; and Vielhauer, *Geschichte*, 180–81), and Rauer, 164–69, argues that "the weak" are gentile Christians still influenced by their previous background in Gnostic, Hellenistic mystery religions. But here Paul must have at least the dietary rules of Jews and Jewish Christians in view, whatever other practices can be included within its sweep.

(1) The whole letter is oriented to the issue of Jew and Gentile, and how they stand in relation to the gospel and to each other (see *Introduction* §4.2). We have seen that this is true not only of chaps. 1–11 but also of chaps. 12–15 (see chaps. 12–15 *Introduction*); it would be odd indeed were Paul to give so much attention to the particular issue of diet were it not related to this central and sustained concern. This is confirmed in the way Paul leads into the discussion, by using key words of the earlier discussion, "flesh" and "believe" (see on 14:1), and in the way he rounds it off, by repeating his call for mutual acceptance (cf. 14:1) with explicit reference to the larger thematic Jew/Gentile issue (15:7–13). Note also the parallel between 2:1–16 and 14:1–12 (see *Form and Structure*).

(2) The terms of the discussion itself (14:1–15:6) are most clearly applicable to particularly Jewish concerns. The talk of "clean" (καθαρός—v 20) and especially "unclean" (κοινός—v 14) is characteristically and in the latter case distinctively Jewish (see on 14:14 and 14:20; with regard to abstinence from wine see on 14:21). And the concern about festivals is equally characteristic of Judaism (see on 14:5). Set alongside these characteristic emphases of "covenantal nomism," Paul's counteremphasis on faith (14:1, 2, 22–23) is not at all surprising and fits into the overall argument of the letter far more closely than has usually been perceived.

(3) Too little appreciated in discussions of the passage is the considerable importance of dietary laws for Jews of this period. It was not simply that the laws of clean and unclean food were so clearly stated in the Torah (Lev 11:1–23; Deut 14:3–21). Also and even more important was the fact that the Maccabean crisis had made observance of these laws a test of Jewishness, a badge of loyalty to covenant and nation (1 Macc 1:62–63; cf. 2 Macc 5:27; and with reference to an earlier period Josephus, *Ant.* 11.346). This was reinforced by the accounts of heroes of the faith popular in the diaspora. Their success was in large measure dependent on their faithfulness in the matter of the food laws, their loyalty to God as expressed in their refusal to eat the food of Gentiles (Dan 1:3–16; 10:3; Tob 1:10–12; Jud 12:2, 19; Add Esth 14:17; *Jos. As.* 7.1; 8.5); for other references see, e.g., Schlier and Wilckens. Jewish scruples on these matters were well known in the ancient world, with Jewish refusal to eat pork quite frequently commented on (e.g., Diodorus 34–35.1.4; Philo, *Legat.* 361; Erotianus, frag.; Plutarch, *Quaest. Conviv.* 4.5; Tacitus, *Hist.* 4.2; Juvenal, *Sat.* 14.98; texts apart from Philo in *GLAJJ* §§63, 196, 258, 281, 301). That is to say, dietary rules constituted one of the clearest boundary markers which distinguished Jews from Gentiles and which were recognized as such; so also observance of the sabbath (see on 14:5); see further *Introduction* §5.3.1. It was precisely this departure from such widely recognized social norms and identity markers which must have caused considerable heart searching and dispute (διαλογισμός—v 1) among Jewish Christians and those previously most influenced by Jewish traditions. That such heart searching and dispute were important in earliest Christianity's bursting the wineskins of Jewish ancestral traditions is indicated with sufficient clarity in Acts 10:13–16; 11:3; and Gal 2:11–14 (see further Dunn, "Incident"). What is

in view here is much more than irrational food taboos (against Dodd, 219–20), or "unimportant" and "minor questions" (Fitzmyer). The issue is more sharply focused than Jewett allows (*Tolerance*, 31–32), and to characterize it as a discussion of "unessentials" (R. Dederen in Jewett, 32) misses the centrality and crucial nature of the issue for earliest Christianity's self-understanding.

Which food laws were in mind is not made clear. The Jewish law of clean and unclean foods did not, of course, require vegetarianism. There were also the kosher laws to be considered, requiring that the blood be properly drained from the animal (Lev 3:17; 7:26–27; 17:10–14; Deut 12:16, 23–24; 15:23; and see Acts 15:20, 29). And probably more important in a diaspora environment was the fear of eating food tainted by idolatry, which seems to have been a motive in the case of some Jewish priests imprisoned in Rome, of whom Josephus speaks, who "had not forgotten the pious practices of religion and supported themselves on figs and nuts" (Josephus, *Life* 14); see further SVM 2:81–83, Str-B 3:54–55 and 4:366–72. The problem of idol meat (τὸ εἰδωλόθυτον) was certainly pressing for the church in Corinth (1 Cor 8–10; see Willis), and later in Asia Minor (Rev 2:14, 20); and see again Acts 15:20, 29; also *Did.* 6.3 and Justin, *Dial.* 34.8–35.1.

Paul, however, is probably thinking of the whole complex of food laws together, and so expresses the issue in terms which would cover them all (see also 14:21). (1) A similar tie-up is indicated, e.g., in Dan 1:16; 2 Macc 5:27; *Jos. As.* 8.5; Josephus, *Life* 14; and *4 Macc.* 5.2; and cf. *T. Reub.* 1.10; *T. Jud.* 15.4, and traditions of vegetarian practice attributed to the Therapeutae (Philo, *Vit. Cont.* 37), to James the brother of Jesus (Eusebius, *HE* 2.23.5) and to the Ebionites (Origen, *In Matth.* 11.12; Epiphanius, *Haer.* 30.15.3; see further Schmithals, 98 nn.16, 17). Certainly wherever there was a fear of breaching the important sequence of food laws, the simplest and safest course would be to avoid meat altogether (as Segal, 367, notes, the same logic is still followed by some pious Jews today). (2) There are many points of overlap and echo between this section and 1 Cor 8–10 (listed by Karris, 86–87; Cranfield, 691–92; and Wilckens, 3:115) but no mention of the particular issue addressed in 1 Cor—viz., idol meat (see also on 14:14 and 14:1–15:6 *Introduction*). The best explanation of both features is that Paul was generalizing from the more specific issue of Corinth to address a broader issue which, however, could well have included the specific issue of idol food (see also on 14:21; for how much Paul knew of the situation in Rome see *Introduction* §2). (3) We should not forget the importance of social factors. In particular Barrett's assumption that kosher meat would be readily available in Rome because the Jewish community was so large neglects the fact that (most of?) the Jewish community had been expelled less than ten years previously (see *Introduction* §2.2.3; cf. Watson, *Paul*, 95–96). In the interval, provision for proper slaughter of clean animals would probably have become much more limited, and may even have been closed down as part of the means of achieving the expulsion. Jewish Christians returning to Rome in small numbers may well have hesitated to draw attention to their being Jews by insisting on proper techniques of slaughter and have preferred to avoid meat altogether (cf. Wilckens, n.547; Josephus, *Ant.* 14.261, indicates that provision for dietary observances would require official permission). Meeks recognizes the importance of the issue of diet here in boundary-defining terms (*Urban Christians*, 97–98; see further *Introduction* §5.3). For other social factors (including occasions when ordinary individuals might expect to eat meat) which may have contributed to the situation envisaged by Paul, see Theissen, *Social Setting*, chap. 3.

Finally we should note that a straightforward identification of "the weak" as Jewish Christians, and "the strong" as Gentile Christians may not be assumed. No doubt "the weak" included Gentiles who had previously been attracted to Judaism (proselytes and God-worshipers; see *Introduction* §2.2.2), and "the strong" included Jews like Paul himself, or Prisca and Aquila (so rightly Wilckens, 3:107, 114). But in view of the above, it is much more likely that the issue relates to the continuing significance of the law in regulating the practice of Jewish Christians, proselytes, and God-worshipers, than to the influence of pagan syncretism on Jewish Christians brought in through God-worshipers (against Käsemann, and those cited by him): the primary attraction for the God-worshiper and proselyte was the distinctive character of the Jewish traditions (the situation addressed in Col 2:16 and 1 Tim 4:3 is different; there is no indication that syncretism was an issue among the Christian congregations in Rome, so far as Paul was aware; against Rauer and Barrett). It should also be remembered that there would (no doubt) be others in the Roman congregations who did not fall readily into either category ("weak" or "strong") (cf. Minear).

3 ὁ ἐσθίων τὸν μὴ ἐσθίοντα μὴ ἐξουθενείτω, "let the one who eats not despise the one who does not eat." It is evident from such references as 2 Kgs 19:21; 2 Chron 36:16; Ezek 22:8; Wisd Sol 4:18; and Luke 23:11 that ἐξουθενεῖν can convey a strong note of contempt (cf. BGD); "hold in contempt" (NEB). It is the characteristic temptation of those who see themselves as "strong" to *despise* those whom they regard as "weak." In view of the likely influence of the whole Maccabean period on questions of Jewish self-identity and Jewish/Gentile relations (see on 14:2), the description of 2 Macc 1:27 may be relevant: the faithful rigorists of the Maccabean heritage felt despised by Gentiles.

ὁ δὲ μὴ ἐσθίων τὸν ἐσθίοντα μὴ κρινέτω, "and let the one who does not eat not pass judgment on the one who eats." The weight of the verb used in the second clause (κρίνω) and its difference from ἐξουθενέω in the first clause has been often missed (but cf. Schlatter, Lagrange, Althaus, Leenhardt, Murray, Harrisville). Consistently in Paul κρίνω has the sense of "make a judgment regarding" (see also on 14:5), with the stronger note frequently of "condemn" (2:1, 3, 12, 27; 3:7; 14:4, 10, 22; 1 Cor 5:3, 12–13; 11:31; 2 Thess 2:12; here cf. particularly Col 2:16); so here NIV. What seems to be in view is the condemnation by "the weak" of the conduct of "the strong"; that is, the firmly held judgment that the conduct is unacceptable, which in this context means "unacceptable to God" (v 4). The one who does not eat evidently regards *not* eating as of crucial importance in maintaining the relationship with God, so that *eating* becomes an act unacceptable to God, an act, that is to say, which merits divine condemnation. This is fully equivalent to the attitude of "the righteous" within the various sects of Judaism at the time, who regarded the nonobservers of such customs as "sinners" (see Dunn, "Sinners"; and on 1:17 and 9:6) and confirms the probability that what was in view here was an understanding of covenant loyalty among the Jewish Christians in Rome which still counted observance of dietary traditions as of fundamental importance in maintaining the distinctiveness of the people of God's favor. Their list of essential marks of the people of God included items which others regarded as matters of indifference (cf. v 5). The temptation facing them was that they would actually regard the nonobservers as non-Christians (cf. particularly Nababan, 39–40).

The verbs in the two clauses should not therefore be regarded as synonymous (NJB surprisingly translates ἐξουθενέω as "condemn"). Paul catches well the different vices to which more scrupulous and more liberal temperaments are liable in their attitudes to each other: the liberal who regards the scruples of the traditionalist as tolerable but worthy only of contempt; the conservative who regards the free-er practice of the liberal as intolerable and as putting him beyond the bounds of acceptable conduct (cf. Barrett, Schmidt).

ὁ θεὸς γὰρ αὐτὸν προσελάβετο, "for God has welcomed him." The use of the verb may echo deliberately its use in Pss 26:10; 64:4; and 72:24 (MT 27:10; 65:4; 73:24). But more important here is the fact that it is the same verb which Paul used in v 1: the attitudes of the different groups toward each other should reflect the much more important attitude of God himself. This reflection leads Käsemann to the assumption that the exhortation here is addressed to both groups (followed by Jewett, *Tolerance,* 129). But both Käsemann and Jewett have missed the importance of the distinction between the two preceding verbs and clauses in v 3, and so fail to appreciate that Paul's exhortation here (v 3c) is a rebuke particularly to the condemnatory attitude of the weak (vv 3b, 4): the one with the much tighter understanding of what is acceptable conduct for God's people would think that God has *not* accepted the other (Jewett reads 14:1–15:6 too much in the light of the more even-handed exhortation of 15:7; but see on 15:7).

Potentially significant is that Paul speaks of *God* accepting, rather than Christ. Throughout this chapter God is consistently presented as the one with whom ultimate authority and judgment lie, and Christ is a more subordinate figure (14:3, 6, 10–12, 17–18, 20, 22; 15:5–6)—κύριος indeed (14:4, 6, 8, 11[?]; 15:6), but with God as the final validator (hence the formulation of 14:6, 10, 18 and 15:6); see also on 14:10; 11; 15:6; and 15:7, where *Christ* accepts to the glory of *God.* Thüsing recognizes the importance of this interplay but does not pick up all the nuances.

4 σὺ τίς εἶ ὁ κρίνων ἀλλότριον οἰκέτην; "who are you who condemns the slave of someone else?" The echo of 2:1, 3 is probably deliberate (κρίνω is used twice as often in chaps. 2 and 14 as in any other chapter of the NT; see also *Form and Structure*). Paul has in view the attitude of the Jew(ish Christian) who is confident that conduct falling outside the rules and boundaries laid down by the law *ipso facto* puts the individual concerned outside the covenant, "without God in the world" (Eph 2:15). The οἰκέτης is the house or domestic slave, with the implication of a more immediate relationship between slave and particular master, the slave answerable only to his own master (δεσπότης—Prov 22:7; Philo, *Immut.* 64; 1 Pet 2:18; κύριος—Philo, *Post.* 138; Luke 16:13; *2 Clem.* 6.1; cf. also the only other NT use [Acts 10:7]; BGD; Spicq, 215–16). The idea of claiming rights with regard to "another person's slave" as an example of something inadmissable and ridiculous would be widely recognized (cf. especially Dio Chrys. 31.34); cf. particularly 2 Cor 10:15 and 1 Pet 4:15 where p72 reads ἀλλοτρίοις ἐπίσκοπος, "meddling in other people's affairs" (BGD).

τῷ ἰδίῳ κυρίῳ στήκει ἢ πίπτει, "in relation to his own master he stands or falls." The dative is usually taken as a "dative of advantage" (BDF, §188(2); e.g., Lagrange, Schlier). But the master's benefit does not seem to be in view. The issue is rather whether the master regards the slave's conduct as acceptable or unacceptable. In the case of a personal house slave the master's approval or disapproval counts for everything, and the judgment of others on the slave's behavior is irrelevant. Moral failure is not in view (Nababan, 43; against SH). The imagery of standing or falling clearly expresses the alternatives of a harmonious relationship (between master and slave) maintained or breached, or, in larger terms, preservation and/or persistence in some responsibility over against some failure in discharging that responsibility (for the contrast cf. particularly Prov 24:16; Rom 11:22/24; 1 Cor 10:12; for ἵστημι/στήκω in this sense cf. 1 Cor 15:1; 16:13; 2 Cor 1:24; Gal 5:1; Phil 1:27; 4:1; 1 Thess 3:8; 2 Thess 2:15; Eph 6:14; for πίπτω in a less serious sense than 11:11 see 11:22 and *1 Clem.* 59.4). A reference to final judgment as such is not in view (Murray).

σταθήσεται δέ, δυνατεῖ γὰρ ὁ κύριος στῆσαι αὐτόν, "and he shall stand, for the master is able to make him stand." It is probably better to translate σταθήσεται so, rather than as a passive (cf. Matt 12:25), since the following clause would then become repetitive. Even so the "standing" is not absolute, but a standing τῷ κυρίῳ = still approved by his master. In the imagery used, δυνατεῖ denotes the legal power of the master over his slave; so equivalent to δυνατὸς εἶναι + infinitive, "to be in a position to" (cf. 2 Cor 9:8 and 13:3; see *Notes*). The issue is solely about what behavior is acceptable to the master. There is no implication that a fall has preceded the στῆσαι (Kühl, Käsemann). On the contrary, the point is that whereas "the other" thinks some particular conduct constitutes a "fall," the master regards it as acceptable and *not* as a fall. στῆσαι, then, in the sense of "sustain in his position" rather than "restore him to his previous position." Is there an echo here of 10:3?

5 ὃς μὲν κρίνει ἡμέραν παρ᾽ ἡμέραν, ὃς δὲ κρίνει πᾶσαν ἡμέραν, "someone judges one day to be more important than another, someone else judges every day to be alike." This is a rather compressed sentence and difficult to translate. The key is not so much to distinguish different meanings of κρίνειν ("prefer"/ "approve" [BGD]) as to recognize the force of the παρά as indicating preference (BDF §236.3 and especially *TDNT* 5:734–35), though in translation the result is the same. κρίνειν still has the basic sense of "make a judgment regarding" (14:3), with the indication of preference given by παρά, and the force of the πᾶσαν given by its contrast to the παρά.

What the disagreement amounts to is hardly clear from the formulation. But no doubt Paul can express it so concisely and imprecisely because his readers would know well what he was referring to. This clearly implies that the issue is related to the overall situation among the Christian congregations in Rome and no doubt also to the main theme of the letter. That is to say, it is a disagreement which sprang in large part at least from or was expressive of the tensions in Rome between the Gentile- and Jewish-Christian members (so most now). This deduction is obviously strengthened by the way in which Paul sets out the disagreement in precise parallel to the issue of diet (v 2). Almost certainly the same two groups are involved (see further on 14:2). If confirmation were needed it comes from v 6, where opinions about particular days are set alongside the different eating practices as all of a piece (cf., e.g., the association of the two issues in CD 6.17–18, Josephus, *Ant.* 11.346, and Juvenal, *Sat.* 14.96–100, not to mention Col 2:16). Had different factions been involved it is unlikely that Paul would have focused so exclusively on the foods issue; in that case he must have said more about the days issue as addressing the problem of a different group. The fact that he says so little about (special) days indicates both that it was the lesser problem (in Rome) and that the advice he gives on foods was advice to the two groups sufficient to cover both issues; that the days issue had arisen previously and been already resolved (de Lacey, 181–82) is less likely since Paul clearly regards the resolution of both to be the same (vv 5–6).

From this we may deduce that the problem arose because many Jewish Christians (and Gentile Christians influenced by Jewish tradition) regarded the continued observance of the special feast days of Judaism (particularly the sabbath) as of continuing importance (since the new movement of which they were a part was, of course, simply a fulfilled or eschatological form of Judaism). This is just as we might expect, since observance of the feast days, particularly of the sabbath, was a sensitive issue within Judaism at this time, and since the sabbath in particular was widely recognized as one of the distinctive features or boundary markers of diaspora Judaism. The sabbath, after all, was part of the decalogue and rooted in creation itself (Gen 2:2–3; Exod 20:8–11); so the issue of v 5 was no issue for devout Jews (Sir 33:7–9). More important, it was bound up with Israel's self-understanding as the elect people of God (Exod 31:16–17; Deut 5:15; Neh 9:13–14; Ezek 20:16; 1 Macc 1:43; in Josephus, *Ant.* 11.346, note how already before the Maccabees "eating unclean food and violating the sabbath" ranked together as the two chief hallmarks of covenant disloyalty). Acceptance of the sabbath was to be a mark of proselytes and of their participation in the covenant (Isa 56:6). Within Palestine the increasing importance of the sabbath is clearly indicated in *Jub.* 2.17–33; 50.6–13; CD 10.14–11:18; and Mark 2:23–3:5 pars.; and the sensitivities over the proper observance of the feast days are indicated by the bitter calendrical disputes of the post-Maccabean period reflected particularly in *Jub.* 6.32–35; *1 Enoch* 74.10–12; 75.2; 82.4–7; 1QS 1.14–15; 1QH 12.8–9; and CD 3.14–15. Within the diaspora the importance of the sabbath, as a badge of ethnic identity and devotion to ancestral custom, is underlined both by the concern of Josephus and Philo to document the right of sabbath observance granted to Jewish communities in Asia (Josephus, *Ant.* 14.241–46, 258, 263–64) and Rome (Philo, *Legat.* 155–58), and by the glorification of the sabbath which was quite a feature of diaspora Jewish apologetic (*Aristob.* frag 5, in Eusebius, *Praep. Evang.* 13.12.9–16; Philo, *Abr.* 28–30; *Decal.* 102; *Spec. Leg.* 2.59, 70). The attractiveness to Gentiles of the sabbath (unusual as such a regular day of rest) claimed by Philo (*Mos.* 2.21) and Josephus (*Ap.* 2.282), even if exaggerated, is confirmed by Col 2:16, Juvenal, *Sat.* 14.96, 105–6, and subsequently by Tertullian, *Ad Nationes* 1.13; see also Leon,

12–14, and *TDNT* 7:32–34. The importance of the feasts for Roman Jews is also indicated by the frequency of the *lulab* and *etrog* (palm branch and citron used in the Feast of Tabernacles) in the inscriptions of the Jewish catacombs in Rome (Leon, 196, cites 34 and 27 examples respectively).

Against this background, in the context of what we know about Jewish and Christian presence in Rome at this time (see *Introduction* §2), and within the argument of the letter itself (see *Introduction* §4.2 and chaps. 12–15 *Introduction*), the most obvious reference for v 5 is to a concern on the part of some Jewish Christians and others who had been proselytes or God-worshipers lest they abandon a practice of feast days and sabbath commanded by scripture and sanctified by tradition, a central concern lest they lose something of fundamental importance within their Jewish heritage, something close to the heart of the distinctiveness of the whole Jewish (and now Jewish-Christian) tradition and identity (cf. particularly Gal 4:10; and for the continuing importance of the Jewish festivals at this period of Christian development, cf. 1 Cor 16:8; Acts 20:6, 16 and 27:9; see also on 15:16 ἡγιασμένη). This makes better sense than assuming a reference to fast days as such (e.g., Kühl; Rauer, 180–84; Gaugler; Leenhardt; Nababan, 50–53; cf. *Did.* 8.1), which seem to have been neither so central in Jewish self-understanding nor so sensitive an issue within earliest Christianity (Matt 6:16–18; Mark 2:20 pars.; 9:29 par.; Acts 13:2–3; 14:23; cf. 2 Cor 6:5; 11:27); or to days regarded as propitious or unpropitious (Lagrange, Käsemann; cf. Str-B 3:308), which is too far from the central concerns of this letter; or to any question regarding Sunday (Schlatter), which does not yet seem to have become an issue and was not yet (for a long time) thought of as taking over or continuing the traditions of the sabbath (Rordorf) (but Murray's attempt to exempt Sunday observance from what Paul says here [257–59] smacks too much of special pleading).

ἕκαστος ἐν τῷ ἰδίῳ νοὶ πληροφορείσθω, "let each be fully convinced in his own mind." For πληροφορέω see on 4:21. Notice that it is a way of speaking of πίστις (4:21), so that what Paul calls for here is further described in 14:22–23—viz., a settled conviction (opposite διακρίνομαι, Schlier) that the pattern of conduct followed is in accord with the will of God. The implication is that such πληροφορία is the end result of the δοκιμάζειν of 12:2. It is to be noted that Paul does not expect differences of opinion within the Christian congregations to result in these differences being held less firmly or with less assurance; in this Paul may consciously be echoing a wisdom motif (Sir 5:9–10 [Michel]; cf. James 1:6–8); liberty of opinion does not mean endless vacillation or the death (of a clear judgment) by a thousand qualifications.

6 ὁ φρονῶν τὴν ἡμέραν κυρίῳ φρονεῖ, "the one who holds an opinion on the day does so to the Lord." Translated thus the clause could refer to both opinions outlined in v 5 (see on 8:5). Alternatively, φρονεῖν could be taken in a stronger way, "set one's mind on, be intent on," and thus be restricted to the view of "the weak": "the one who is intent on the day (that is, a particular day rather than others)" (BGD). The dative is like that of 14:4 and strengthens the clear implication that Paul is thinking in terms of 12:2. The liberty of opinion which he has clearly in view is a liberty within and under the lordship of Christ (Paul takes it for granted that that is the same as "in accordance with the will of God"). See particularly Käsemann.

καὶ ὁ ἐσθίων κυρίῳ ἐσθίει, εὐχαριστεῖ γὰρ τῷ θεῷ, "and the one who eats does so to the Lord, for he gives thanks to God." The freedom which Paul commends here is not anything like a complete license of opinion (a point well expressed by Schlier on v 5). Paul has in view only a responsibly reached and responsibly held opinion and practice—"to the Lord"—and one which is consciously maintained in thankful dependence on God (NEB's "has the Lord in mind" is not strong enough). The thanksgiving in view, of course, is particularly the blessing spoken at meals (*TDNT* 2:760–61; 9:410; in the NT cf. Mark 8:6 par.; 14:23 pars.; John 6:11, 23; Acts 27:35; 1 Cor 11:24); it is important that the Jewish Christian who believes his practice is more in accord with sacred tradition should recognize that the one who sits loose to that tradition in respect of diet gives just the same thanksgiving. But beyond the context of the meal itself Paul may be mindful of 1:21: it is the attitude of thankful dependence on God which marks out the one who belongs to the age of Christ (in contrast to Adamic man [1:21]; see also on 14:11), not particular rules and practices seen as the essential expression of that thanksgiving. Note again the connection between κύριος and θεός; to do something κυρίῳ, enables and is enabled by thanksgiving τῷ θεῷ (see on 14:3, last paragraph).

καὶ ὁ μὴ ἐσθίων κυρίῳ οὐκ ἐσθίει καὶ εὐχαριστεῖ τῷ θεῷ, "and the one who does not eat does so to the Lord and gives thanks to God." Paul accepts that a negative action or refusal can also be "to the Lord." The καί is presumably used instead of γάρ since he gives thanks not for his abstaining, but for what he does eat (vegetables); see also Murray. Paul probably has in view the fact that gatherings for the common meal (cf. 1 Cor 11) would include both groups (Schlatter, Gaugler, Michel), where a mutual acceptance (not merely tolerance) of diverse views and practices would be essential.

7 οὐδεὶς γὰρ ἡμῶν ἑαυτῷ ζῇ καὶ οὐδεὶς ἑαυτῷ ἀποθνῄσκει, "for no one of us lives for himself and no one dies for himself." The idea of living for someone's (or something's) benefit is quite familiar in Greek (see references in BGD, ζάω 3b), with the clear implication that to live "for oneself" is to live selfishly; the closest verbal parallels (live for/die for) are in Plutarch, *Cleomenes*, 31 (cited by Cranfield) and Alciphron 4.10.5 (cited in BGD, ἀποθνῄσκω 1aα). But for Christians (vv 8–10 show that Paul only has Christians in view) Christ is the model to be followed (2 Cor 5:14–15; Phil 2:5–11); the "we" is "the we of the community" (Nababan, 64). The saying underlines the impossibility of a genuine or complete autonomy. In practice even the most "free" are caught in and dependent on a network of relationships, not to mention things. Christian liberty should certainly never be classified as a kind of autonomy.

8 ἐάν τε γὰρ ζῶμεν, τῷ κυρίῳ ζῶμεν, ἐάν τε ἀποθνῄσκωμεν, τῷ κυρίῳ ἀποθνῄσκομεν, "for if we live, we live for the Lord, and if we die, we die for the Lord." For the idea of living and dying for someone/something see on 14:7. But the idea of living (or dying) for *God* is much more typical of Jewish and Christian thought: with reference to the dead, compare particularly *4 Macc.* 7.19 and 16.25 with Luke 20:38 and Rom 6:10 (cf. 1 Thess 4:14); but also to the living, Philo, *Mut.* 213, *Heres* 111, and the particularly Christian application of Rom 6:11; 2 Cor 5:15; and Gal 2:19 (cf. 1 Thess 5:10).

ἐάν τε οὖν ζῶμεν, ἐάν τε ἀποθνῄσκωμεν, τοῦ κυρίου ἐσμέν, "so whether we live or whether we die, we are the Lord's." κύριος has here a stronger than usual sense of "master" (in relation to slave), as in v 4; so here, "we belong to the

Lord" (cf. 1 Cor 3:23). The relation of believers to their Lord takes precedence over any difference of opinion between believers; how he disposes of his own is his affair. Life and death are much more important differences than disagreement over diet and days; and not even they disturb the relation between believers and their Lord.

9 εἰς τοῦτο γὰρ Χριστὸς ἀπέθανεν καὶ ἔζησεν, "for it was for this purpose that Christ died and lived again." This seems to be a variation on a more typical formula, "Christ died and rose/was raised again" (see on 8:34), with ζάω preferred to ἐγείρω because of the preceding thrice-repeated ζάω of v 8 (Kramer, *Christ*, 29–30; see also *Form and Structure*). When used thus with ἀποθνῄσκω, ζάω of course has the force "become alive again" (BGD, ζάω 1ab; BDF, §331); cf. particularly 2 Cor 13:4; (a reference to Jesus' life on earth is hardly likely [rightly SH]). This dialectic between a living beyond death and a living now which can nevertheless partake of the character of that life beyond death (see on 14:7) is a characteristic expression of the eschatological tension for Paul (cf. 6:4 and 8:10).

ἵνα καὶ νεκρῶν καὶ ζώντων κυριεύσῃ, "in order that he might be lord over both dead and living." The word order ("dead and living") is presumably determined by the preceding phrase ("died" and "lived"), though its unusualness (instead of the otherwise more natural "living and dead") helps bring out Christ's power even over the world of death (Stanley, *Resurrection*, 199). The doubly emphasized purpose (εἰς τοῦτο, ἵνα) ought not to be ignored. It is characteristic of Paul's Christology and soteriology that he sees the primary thrust of Christ's death and resurrection as directed toward his becoming lord of all things, including dead as well as living (part of his Adam Christology; e.g., 5:21; 1 Cor 15:20–25; Phil 2:9–11; and see further on 10:9). No view is expressed about where the dead are or what form of existence they might have (cf. 1 Cor 15:18; 2 Cor 5:3; 1 Thess 4:14; 1 Pet 3:19–20; 4:6; see also on 10:7). It is the completeness of the lordship which is in view here: no condition known or imaginable to humankind escapes his rule (cf. 8:38–39); see also Nababan, 27–28, 79. The object is clearly to relativize the disputes on food and days within the perspective of God's overarching purpose in Christ.

10 σὺ δὲ τί κρίνεις τὸν ἀδελφόν σου; ἢ καὶ σὺ τί ἐξουθενεῖς τὸν ἀδελφόν σου; "so you, why do you judge your brother? or you too, why do you despise your brother?" In the diatribe format, using the same verbs as in v 3, the fact that Paul is addressing different groups and their identity is clear. For ἢ καί see Lietzmann. For κρίνω and ἐξουθενέω see on 14:3. The repeated use of κρίνειν (8 times in chap. 14) helps set the (condemnatory) judgment of "the weak" in perspective. Christian judgment of *things* is valid and indeed essential (v 5), but judgment of *people* must give place to the judgment of God (vv 10–12); see particularly v 11 and cf. 1 Cor 2:15 and James 4:12. The *repeated* use of ἀδελφός (for the first time since the beginning of the parenesis, 12:1, and then again in vv 13, 15, and 21) presses home the point: *each* is treating shamefully a fellow believer, a member of the new family of Christ (cf. 8:14–17, 29; for ἀδελφός see on 1:13). Synofzik, 45–46, draws attention particularly to the close parallel of 1 Cor 4:1–5.

πάντες γὰρ παραστησόμεθα τῷ βήματι τοῦ θεοῦ, "for we shall all stand before the judgment seat of God." παρίστημι is well known in the papyri in the judicial technical sense of appearing in court before a judge (MM, BGD, 1e, 2aα); so in the NT, Acts 27:24 as well as here (cf. 1 Cor 8:8; 2 Cor 4:14; also 2 Tim 4:17). The βῆμα is a raised place or tribune for delivery of speeches in public assembly (LSJ II.2; as in Neh 8:4; 2 Macc 13:26; and Acts 12:21), and hence the tribunal of a magistrate or judge (again very common in the papyri [MM, BGD]); in the NT—Matt 27:19; John 19:13; Acts 18:12, 16–17 and 25:6, 10, 17. The extension of the language to the final judgment (here and 2 Cor 5:10) is natural. That the βῆμα is in a public place underlines the openness of this judgment (Michel) in implied contrast to the more insidious carping and snide comments made in the "in-group" language of one group about the other. For Paul, evidently, there is no essential difference between the judgment seat of *Christ* (2 Cor 5:10) and that of *God* (here). Christ acts as God's representative (Käsemann, Schlier; "the salvation act of Christ and the future judgment . . . two sides of the same motif" [Merk, 169]), but see further on 14:3 and 14:11. As so often in Paul, the πάντες has weight (given the place of emphasis): *no* one can or should assume that he or she is exempt from final judgment (see also on 14:12). "The Christian will not only be asked whether he was a Christian, but he must also answer *how* he was a Christian" (Mattern, 162). The standing before one's Lord to give account of one's stewardship both now (vv 4–6) and at the end (vv 10–11) (cf. 1 Cor 4:1–5) matches the present and future tenses of δικαιοῦσθαι (see on 2:13).

11 γέγραπται γάρ, "for it is written"; see on 1:17. The following quotation is a mixed form. Paul either quotes from memory and runs two passages together without realizing it, or he does so deliberately. Either way it underlines the point that use of (OT) scripture for its authoritative teaching was not simply mechanical: the substance of divine(ly inspired) utterance was more important than a pedantic exactness of form (cf. Justin, *Apol.* 1.52.6).

ζῶ ἐγώ, λέγει κύριος, "as I live, says the Lord"—a formula which occurs quite frequently in the prophets (Num 14:28; Isa 49:18; Jer 22:24; 46 [LXX 26]:18; Ezek 5:11; 14:16; 16:48; 17:16; 18:3; 20:31, 33; Zeph 2:9), though not in Isa 45:23. However, since it is such a regular introductory formula, no violence is done to either text when Paul thus uses it in its regular function.

ὅτι ἐμοὶ κάμψει πᾶν γόνυ, καὶ πᾶσα γλῶσσα ἐξομολογήσεται τῷ θεῷ, "that to me shall bend every knee, and every tongue shall give praise to God." This is verbatim from the LXX of Isa 45:23 with only ἐξομολογήσεται and πᾶσα γλῶσσα in reverse order. The oracle is used in its original sense: all who would contest the supreme and final authority of the one God will in the end-time judgment bow and acknowledge that there is no other God than Yahweh, "a righteous God and a Savior" (Isa 45:21). The implication is there to be drawn that those who take upon themselves to pass judgment on others are usurping the authority of God alone, falling into the same old trap of idolatry and putting themselves in the place of God (1:21–25; see also on 14:6).

ἐξομολογέω almost certainly is intended in its usual LXX sense, "acknowledge, confess, praise" (as in its only other uses in Paul [15:9 and Phil 2:11]; also Matt 11:25 // Luke 10:21); so BGD; against the suggestion of *TDNT* 5:215 that confession of sins is (also) in view. That the text envisages the conversion of the Gentiles would increase its significance: a further reminder to Jewish Christians that God's final purpose had always embraced the Gentiles; and to Gentile Christians that their conversion was one of submission to the one God proclaimed by Israel and its scriptures.

The fact that Paul retains the τῷ θεῷ here, whereas in Phil 2:10–11 the same passage (Isa 45:23) is used to speak of confession of *Christ's* lordship, is in keeping with the general balance Paul seems to wish to maintain in this chapter between the lordship of Christ and the ultimate authority of God. For this reason it is also more likely that in this instance Paul follows his usual practice (cf., e.g., 12:19; 1 Cor 14:21; 2 Cor 6:17, 18; see further *TDNT* 3:1086–87) in referring the κύριος of the first part of the citation to God and not to Christ (Cranfield; against Nababan, 85–88, Black and Wilckens). In passages where the κύριος of the OT is referred to Christ (see on 10:9 and 10:12) it is the status and role of the risen and exalted Christ which is in view; to refer such a regular revelation formula ("as I live, says the Lord") to Christ has no precedent or parallel at this time. Hence the talk of the "Ineinander" of Christocentricity and theocentricity (Wilckens; also Zeller and Kreitzer; Thüsing, 30–38, is more circumspect), although justified by a more systematized presentation of Paul (v 10 and 2 Cor 5:10; v 11 and Phil 2:10–11), is less justified as an exegesis of Rom 14 itself (see also on 14:3).

12   ἄρα (οὖν) ἕκαστος ἡμῶν περὶ ἑαυτοῦ λόγον δώσει τῷ θεῷ, "so then each of us will give account of himself to God." λόγον (ἀπο)δοῦναι is an established phrase, "to give an account or make an accounting" (see BGD, λόγος 2a); in the NT—Matt 12:36; Luke 16:2; Acts 19:40; Heb 13:17; 1 Pet 4:5; cf. 1 Pet 3:15. Each word is emphatic (Denney, Cranfield): "each"—neither side will be exempt; "for himself"—not for his brother; "give account"—openly; "to God"—not to the fellow members of his faction. It is clearly important for Paul that faith did not exempt any, far less every, believer from the final reckoning of God's judgment (see especially 2:6–16; 1 Cor 3:12–15; 2 Cor 5:10).

Explanation

It would not surprise Paul's audiences in Rome that his sequence of mainly more general exhortation reaches its climax and most detailed treatment on the issues of dietary traditions and special (feast) days. For these were two of the most sensitive issues which could confront this still essentially Jewish movement as it began to develop its own distinctive character and identity. Next to the practice of circumcision, nothing marked out the Jewish diaspora communities so clearly as their observance of the dietary rules and special days laid down in the Torah. It was not that such laws were intrinsically more important than other parts of the Torah. But the events of the Maccabean crisis and the subsequent factional disputes within Judaism had given these laws in particular special prominence. Devotion in the matter of food laws had been a test of loyalty to the covenant at that time, and the devotion of such heroes as Daniel, Tobit, and Judith had no doubt impressed the issue deeply on the self-understanding of the typically devout Jew; the calendrical disputes which were still a feature of Palestinian Judaism underscored the importance of the feast days; and the growing concern to observe the sabbath as a mark of devotion was evident not only among Pharisees. And in the Diaspora it was the peculiar Jewish habits regarding food and the regular one day of rest in seven which particularly marked them out as different from other sects and societies, since these customs affected their social and business relationships and would catch the eye of the Gentile most frequently. In other words, food laws and sabbath were among the clearest boundary markers which set Jews apart from Gentiles as a people.

The issue then which confronts Paul here is no slight or casual one. Those today who think he was making too much fuss over some peculiarities of diet (simply a matter of a few vegetarians), or particular feast days (one or two more holy days), have completely missed the point. The issue was far more serious than that. Nor was it simply a matter of the convenience or inconvenience for social life of a few food fads or a too-ardent piety, though the restriction caused by such beliefs on wider social relationships did cause Paul concern elsewhere (1 Cor 10:23–30). The issue here, however, was much more fundamental. What was at stake was nothing less than the whole self-understanding of the new movement of which Paul was a chief apostle, in other words, the definition of Christianity itself. Were those who had acclaimed Jesus as Lord still simply part of Judaism, who had therefore to locate themselves within Judaism? For the typical Gentile as well as the typical Jew a yes answer could have only one consequence: the observance of the traditional food laws and sabbaths. Most of the gentile Christians within the diaspora congregations, particularly those founded by Paul, seem to have already moved beyond that position. The breaking down of the barrier between Jew and Gentile, which was so much a part of Paul's mission, had resulted in an abandoning of the hitherto characteristic hallmarks of the diaspora Jew (how slowly or quickly we cannot tell, but Gal 2:11–19 and 4:8–11 were obviously important stages along the way for the Pauline congregations at least).

The abandonment of or refusal to adopt such important identity markers probably caused few problems for gentile Christians; the response to the gospel and commitment in baptism was the more fundamental change of life. But for Jewish Christians, or Gentiles who had long been associated with Judaism before they heard the gospel ("judaizing" God-worshipers or proselytes), much more was at stake. Nothing less than a crisis of identity. Had they not been the people of God as Jews, as those who lived within the limits clearly marked out by the law? How then could they become or remain part of the eschatological assembly of God if they abandoned these very hallmarks and removed these very boundary markers? Hitherto the realm of holiness within which salvation functioned had been demarcated by such purity rituals; the area beyond, outside, had been clearly identified as "unclean." But now these rituals were being challenged (vv 14, 20) and the realm within which they could be confident of salvation was losing its previous clarity of definition. The depth of the sociopsychological problem which the practice of the gentile and freer thinking Jewish Christians caused the more traditional Jewish and judaizing Christians should not be underestimated or played down. And when this was compounded by the political pressures under which Jews (and Jewish Christians) in Rome had recently found themselves, the crisis must have been severe. In these circumstances to abandon food laws and sabbaths was to betray everything which had been most compelling and moving in the Jewish history of the past two centuries. And to use the excuse of threatened persecution from the state would simply make the act of treachery all the more shameful.

This seems to be the situation to which Paul turns at this point. In other words, he is not simply drawing together a few apposite lessons of general reference from his experience elsewhere; in which case he would hardly have given the issue the climactic and inordinately lengthy treatment which he devotes to it (four times as long as any other single subject in these chapters). On the contrary, he recognizes a crisis confronting the congregations in Rome of some magnitude: the danger of a split which could have Jewish believers so alarmed by the abandonment of the old yardsticks of covenant loyalty that they lost their faith in Christ; the danger that a law-free Christianity might cut itself off from its Jewish roots and influence by crass insensitivity. The advice Paul gives is marked by great pastoral sensitivity and is of much wider relevance than to this issue alone—of relevance wherever concerns to maintain old traditions come into conflict with concerns for a less traditional expression of the gospel.

1–2 Paul's initial advice sets the tone. The more dominant group, who already sit light to food laws and sabbaths, should not attempt to impose their views on "the weak in faith." To be noted at once is the characterization of those who feel the traditional Jewish customs to be too important to give up, as "weak." They might well feel somewhat insulted by the label. Were they not rather demonstrating the *strength* of their principles?—the same strength of devotion as had been shown by Daniel and the Maccabees. But Paul is quite clear that the position they hold to is one characterized by a deficiency in faith. By implication they are putting too much weight on the outward form of the covenant people (2:17–29); too much weight on their physical (fleshly) membership of Israel (13:14); they are not living out of complete dependence on God like father Abraham (4:19–21). Paul is in no doubt: the attitude thus expressed is deficient, "weak."

We would expect no less forthright an opinion on the matter from Paul. Some of his readers indeed might well have been surprised that he was not more forthright. Any who knew the fierceness of his polemic in Galatians against very similar attitudes might well wonder at the difference in tone. The reason for that difference is not clear. But a large part of it at least probably lies in the difference between the situations addressed. In Galatians Paul was fighting furiously to maintain the viability of his law-free mission and the very existence of some of his earliest churches, or at least the very existence of his "gospel for the Gentiles" within some of his earliest churches. Had the missionary zealous traditionalists won there, the whole expression of the gospel for which he stood might have been eclipsed, or (in many respects worse) set completely adrift from its Jewish foundation. But in Rome it was the more liberal understanding of the gospel which was dominant, and the Jewish Christians trickling back to Rome following the expulsion of Jews some years earlier were in a much more vulnerable position both in numbers and in their sociopolitical circumstances. The danger, however, was the same—of a rift between the two main groupings, with the consequent danger of Paul's gentile movement losing its Jewish roots.

Paul's counsel was clear. The more liberally minded should not take advantage of their position (both their majority numbers and their so far less exposed position as non-Jews). They should not exploit their own readiness to discuss their differences as a way of making the more inhibited newer members feel inferior. They should not pressure them to accept the will of the majority and conform to the dominant ethos. The liberty claimed by the more liberal should be accorded to the traditionalists—liberty to be less liberal. Thus is the tone set for the major thrust of Paul's guidance to those who regarded themselves as "strong in faith."

But Paul builds up to this more sustained plea by stages.

3 He starts by warning both sides of the danger each stands in with respect to the other. The more liberal practitioner is in danger of *despising* the traditionalist. The traditionalist is in danger of *condemning* the liberal. Paul here displays a keen psychological insight into the character of almost any social grouping, where there will always be some who are more conservative than the rest, or, alternatively, others who will be more liberal than the rest in the policies and practices they pursue. And where the natural tendency will be for those who think of themselves as more liberated and mature to despise the narrow-minded, pedantic traditionalists; while the traditionalists will regard the more liberated as having abandoned too many important parts of the tradition, and indeed as having put themselves outside what the tradition represented and safeguarded.

3c–4 It is this latter danger on which Paul focuses and to which he devotes most of the first half of the chapter (vv 3c–12). He calls first of all (vv 3c–4) for a genuine recognition and acceptance of the other's status as a Christian. This is addressed particularly to the traditionalist. For "the weak" are traditionalists precisely because they regard these traditions as fundamental to their faith. They cannot conceive of that faith without or apart from these traditions. That is why their natural inclination is to "condemn" the liberal (v 3)—because their understanding of Christianity is more tightly defined and because the liberal falls outside Christianity as they understand it. For the more traditional Christian, the more liberal Christian is not actually to be reckoned as a Christian.

Paul's response is to challenge just that presupposition, to challenge the traditionalists to recognize that Christianity is larger than their definition of it, to recognize that *God* accepts people whose views and practices *they* think are unacceptable. With repeated emphasis Paul presses home the point: "God has welcomed him . . . he is God's servant . . . he will stand because it is precisely and solely God's prerogative and power to make him stand" (vv 3–4). This is a crucial step in Paul's pastoral tactic: to get the traditionalists actually to accept that someone who differs from them, and differs from them in something they regard as fundamental, is nevertheless acceptable to God and accepted by God. With genuine recognition that the spectrum of Christian opinion on such crucial matters is broader than any particular expression of Christian opinion, there can be a real respect among fellow believers across the spectrum of Christian liberty. Without such recognition and respect the gospel itself has been abandoned and the traditionalists fall back into the ancient trap of dictating to God and setting up their own judgment in place of God's.

5 Paul's second piece of counsel is that each should be fully convinced in his or her own mind on such contentious subjects. Not that such definite opinions need to be reached on the whole range of issues affecting Christian belief and conduct. But these particular issues did make all the difference to social lifestyle and to the harmony of the Christian congregation. The point is that the strength of conviction with which one held his or her view should not intimidate the other. Each should weigh such issues before God and reach her or his own judgment, even if it meant differing, and differing quite fundamentally, with the other. Here clearly implied is Paul's firm recognition that Christians will disagree with one another on important issues, and yet each can be convinced of the rightness of his or her position. They can disagree, and *both* be *right* (that is, accepted by God). It was not necessary for one to be wrong for the other to be right. The richness of Christian truth and its expression could allow a range of views and lifestyles and all be legitimate, strongly held in good faith.

6 But lest his readers think he is advocating complete liberality and cannot distinguish liberty from license, Paul is careful to add a crucial qualification. He is taking it for granted that both of the parties in the dispute have indeed reached their conclusions before the Lord, and live out their different patterns of conduct in honor of that Lord and in thankfulness to God. That is to say, the range of acceptable liberty is restricted to what is appropriate as Christian obedience and as the expression of the creature's dependence on the creator (1:21). Only what can be received from and offered to God in humble thankfulness is Christian conduct. This is the *real* foundation for Christian faith and lifestyle, not particular expressions in traditional or ritual form. Whoever can lay claim to such obedience and hold her or his conduct before God in thanksgiving to God should be accepted as a Christian, even if that conduct is controversial or what others might count as inappropriate for their discipleship. Christian faith will have clear enough lines of expression (all that has been said in chaps. 12–13), but not as determined by limitations of race, culture, or national tradition.

7–9 The point is that the Christian is not a law unto himself or herself. But neither is any Christian a law unto someone else. One cannot claim freedom for oneself without allowing freedom to the other. What is right for one cannot be a sure guide to what is right for another. If the strong should not try to force the weak into a frightening liberty where guidelines are far less clearly drawn, neither should the weak seek to restrict the strong within the limits of their own more tightly defined liberty. The convictions of one should not be used as a stick to beat the other or as a yardstick by which to judge the other. Such issues lie wholly with the Lord. It was in order that he might have such rights and claims over individuals that he died and lived again. For anyone else to lay claim to the authority to determine conviction and conduct of another would be to usurp the exclusive rights of Christ and to fall again into the primeval sin of trying to do God's work for him.

10–12 The conclusion is clear. Neither of the different groups in Rome have any right to pass judgment on the other, any right to make slighting or condemnatory remarks about those who disagree with them within the circle of believers. Each must answer for himself or herself and not for any other. And each *will* answer for herself or himself in the final judgment; the citation of one of the most powerful monotheistic passages in the scriptures (Isa 45:23) would have a powerful effect particularly on those seeking to be loyal to Jewish traditional beliefs. And one of the things each will have to give account of is precisely such condemnatory or slighting attitudes to those whom God had already accepted. Thus ends the first part of Paul's charter of Christian liberty and mutual tolerance.

2. The Responsibility of "the Strong" (14:13–23)

Bibliography

See 14:1–15:6 *Bibliography*.

Translation

^{13} *Let us therefore no longer pass judgment on one another, but decide this rather: not to put an occasion for offense or downfall in the brother's way.* ^{14} *I know and am convinced in the Lord Jesus that nothing is profane in itself,*[a] *except that to the one who reckons something profane, to that person it is profane.* ^{15} *For if your brother is deeply upset on account of food, you are no longer conducting yourself in terms of love. Do not by your food destroy that one for whom Christ died.* ^{16} *Therefore*[b] *do not let your*[c] *good be brought into contempt.* ^{17} *For the kingdom of God is not a matter of eating and drinking, but of righteousness, peace, and joy in the Holy Spirit.* ^{18} *For he who serves the Christ in this*[d] *is pleasing to God and approved*[e] *by people in general.* ^{19} *So then we pursue*[f] *what makes for peace and*[g] *for the building up of one another.* ^{20} *Do not for the sake of food destroy*[h] *the work of God. Everything is clean,*[i] *but it is quite wrong for the person who eats with offense.* ^{21} *It is a fine thing not to eat meat nor drink wine nor anything by which your brother stumbles.*[j] ^{22} *The faith which*[k] *you have keep to yourself before God.*[l] *Happy is the man who does not condemn himself by what he approves.* ^{23} *But the man who doubts is condemned if he eats, because it is not of faith. Everything which is not of faith is sin.*[m]

Notes

[a] The δι' αὐτοῦ, "through him" (that is, Christ), of later MSS, is clearly an attempted correction or improvement.

[b] The omission of οὖν by a few witnesses is occasioned by the fact that the other μή injunctions (vv 15b, 20) are introduced without a conjunction. But the correction misses the structural character of the οὖν here (see *Form and Structure*).

[c] The weight of MS evidence clearly supports ὑμῶν, with ἡμῶν as a very understandable variant.

[d] Another improving correction changes the singular to the plural (to embrace more clearly all 3/4 items in v 17b).

^e B G* and a few others give evidence of some unhappiness at the thought that the approval of the general public should be a factor in weighing Christian conduct; hence the alteration to δοκίμοις, "and to approved men."

^f The indicative διώκομεν is probably original; it has the weightier textual support (including א and B), and alteration to the subjunctive to give an exhortation is more likely than the alternative change from the clear exhortation to the more surprising indicative (so SH, Käsemann, with others listed; against Cranfield, Schlier, Wilckens, Metzger).

^g In a further improving amendment Western witnesses add φυλάξωμεν ("let us safeguard") to give two balanced clauses.

^h In conscious or unconscious assimilation to v 15, א* reads ἀπόλλυε for κατάλυε (see also Note j).

ⁱ Likewise א² assimilates the text to Titus 1:15 by adding τοῖς καθαροῖς.

^j At quite an early stage the text was expanded by the addition of ἢ σκανδαλίζεται ἢ ἀσθενεῖ, probably under the influence of 1 Cor 8:11–13 (see, e.g., Metzger, Wilckens n.475). א* again assimilates to v 15 by reading λυπεῖται (see also Note h).

^k ἦν has the strong support of א B and others, but its omission is assumed in almost all the versions (Lietzmann, Metzger). If lacking, the text would be best construed as a question, "Do you have faith? Keep it to yourself." It is difficult to decide between the alternatives (hence Aland²⁶ sets ἦν in brackets).

^l א* omits "before God."

^m The doxology (16:25–27) appears at this point alone in L Ψ the Byzantine text and elsewhere, and both here and after 16:23 in A P the Armenian version and in some minuscules (the evidence is laid out fully and clearly in Metzger). Almost certainly the appearance of the benediction here is the result of the text of Romans having been abbreviated in some subsequent recensions. See further on 16:25–27 Notes.

Form and Structure

The main thrust of the second paragraph (vv 13–23) is directed chiefly to the other attitude (the "strong" [15:1]), with continued use of κρίνω in v 13 making an effective transition. The exhortation falls neatly into three sections:

vv 13–15	consider the weaker brother;
vv 16–18:	take account of the effect on outsiders;
vv 19–21:	build up the church.

Each section opens with an οὖν and features bluntly expressed negative warnings ("Do not . . ."). The degree to which Paul repeats himself is indicative of his desire to press upon the strong their responsibility. Vv 13–23 in fact revolve around vv 14 and 20b (the law of unclean foods is no longer operative for believers), but with each qualified (vv 14b, 20c) to show that the principal weight is on love (Michel; even if love is mentioned specifically only at v 15, it is clearly also the governing motivation in the negative terms of vv 13a, 13b, 15b, 16, and 20). The roughly chiastic structure of the paragraph also helps reinforce this theological concern, and by giving double emphasis to the counsel, puts the greater weight of responsibility on "the strong":

13a	22–23
13b	21
14	20b
15	20a
16–18	19

Other features include the wordplay on κρίνω in vv 22–23 (as well as in v 13) and the consistent echoes of Jesus' teaching in vv 13, 14, 15, and 17. The closing verses of chap. 14 pick up the themes of the opening:

v 1 — v 23
v 2a — v 22a
v 3 — v 22b

Comment

13 μηκέτι οὖν ἀλλήλους κρίνωμεν, "let us therefore no longer pass judgment on one another." The exhortation is probably to both groups (Althaus, Gaugler, Cranfield), drawing the necessary conclusion (οὖν) from vv 10–12, and with κρίνειν used to characterize both attitudes previously distinguished; see also on 14:3 and 14:10. Some dependence on the attitude commended in the Jesus tradition retained in Matt 7:1 par. is certainly possible.

ἀλλὰ τοῦτο κρίνατε μᾶλλον, "but decide this rather." The wordplay on κρίνειν is obvious (see particularly Barrett), and we should have no qualms in translating the verb differently here. κρίνειν clearly has a range of meaning which no single English equivalent matches (but see NEB). For the meaning here see BGD, κρίνω 3, and for the construction compare particularly 1 Cor 7:37 and 2 Cor 2:1. It quickly becomes apparent that the change from first person to second person, and shift in meaning of κρίνειν signals a narrowing of the focus of address to "the strong." For μᾶλλον = "rather" in the sense "instead (of something)," see BGD, μᾶλλον 3a.

τὸ μὴ τιθέναι πρόσκομμα τῷ ἀδελφῷ ἢ σκάνδαλον, "not to put an occasion for offense or downfall in the brother's way." For πρόσκομμα see on 9:32, and for σκάνδαλον see on 9:33. The connection of both words with idolatry in Jewish thought (πρόσκομμα—Exod 23:33; 34:12; Jer 3:3; 1QS 2.11–12, 17; *TDNT* 6:749; σκάνδαλον—Judg 2:3; 8:27; Ps 106 [LXX 105] :36; Hos 4:17 LXX; Zeph 1:3 Symm.; Wisd Sol 14:11) explains the use of πρόσκομμα in 1 Cor 8:9 and probably of σκανδαλίζειν in 1 Cor 8:13. But here Paul does not seem to have the problem of idolatry as such in mind, but partly reuses the line of argument formulated in 1 Cor 8 (but no doubt used in varied forms elsewhere) and partly echoes the πρόσκομμα/σκάνδαλον link which had already become established in Christian thought through the use made of Isa 8:14 (Rom 9:33; 1 Pet 2:8). The words are near synonyms anyway (Müller, *Anstoss*, 32–35). The use of σκάνδαλον here is closer to that in Jud 12:2—offense caused by eating gentile food (cf. *Pss. Sol.* 4.23; 1QH 16.15). σκάνδαλον seems to be the more emotive word (see BGD). The echo of 9:33 ties the offense into the Jewish failure to acknowledge Christ and anticipates the Christological plea of v 15: Jewish-Christian offense over the foods issue is of a piece with Jewish failure to recognize the eschatological significance of Christ for Gentile as well as Jew. A reference to the conservative (weak) enticing the liberal (strong) to give up their principles (Murray; Jewett, *Tolerance*, 135) is much less likely. As Gaugler notes, more than mere "tolerance" of alternative viewpoints and practices is clearly in view.

In view of the other echoes of Jesus' teaching in these chapters (see on 12:14) it is by no means unlikely that here too we have an echo of teaching preserved in Mark 9:42 pars. (Dodd, Cranfield; though see also Müller, *Anstoss*, 42–45). The echo becomes stronger when it is recalled that in the Matthean parallel to Mark 9:42 the "little one" is clearly understood as a "brother" (Matt 18:6; cf. vv 15, 21) and that in the 1 Cor parallel to Rom 14:13 the verbal form is used ("lest I put an occasion for offense [σκανδαλίσω] before my brother" [1 Cor 8:13]). Since the transitive form of the verb is very rare (Allison, 15), the probability must be judged substantial that the Pauline exhortation and the Jesus tradition are directly related, and indeed that the Pauline parenesis has been influenced by the Jesus tradition shared by both Gentile (Mark) and Jewish (Matthew) churches. Allison is able to make a strong case for recognizing that Paul probably knew the collection of Jesus traditions that Mark has incorporated in Mark 9:33–50 (Allison, 13–15), though surprisingly he ignores the echo of Mark 9:50 in Rom 12:18.

14 οἶδα καὶ πέπεισμαι ἐν κυρίῳ Ἰησοῦ, "I know and am convinced in the Lord Jesus." The triple emphasis (I know, am convinced, in the Lord) is very forceful and makes it clear that the following ὅτι statement is one on which Paul puts great stress; the nearest parallels have only two out of the three elements used here—Gal 5:10; Phil 1:25; 2:24; and 2 Thess 3:4 (Cranfield). It is a particularly strong expression of the faith/conviction he wants his readers to enjoy (vv 5c, 22–23). The emphasis would have the double effect of demonstrating his complete conviction about the cleanness of all foods to "the weak" and of making "the strong" more amenable to the teaching which follows. For πέπεισμαι see on 8:38. For the ἐν formula see on 6:11, and for ἐν κυρίῳ see on 16:2; here cf. particularly Gal 5:10; Phil 1:14; and 2:24. The addition of Ἰησοῦ (in distinction from the more regular ἐν κυρίῳ) may reflect Paul's awareness that the following dictum stemmed originally from Jesus during his earthly ministry (Lagrange, Leenhardt, Cranfield, Harrisville), but was understood pneumatically (ἐν κυρίῳ; cf. Schmidt, and see below); however, 1 Thess 4:1 shows that this need not be the case (cf. Käsemann—"in virtue of the authority of the Lord Jesus").

ὅτι οὐδὲν κοινὸν δι' ἑαυτοῦ, "that nothing is profane in itself." The reference of οὐδέν is, of course, limited by the context—no kind of food (cf. Cranfield). For δι' ἑαυτοῦ see BGD, ἑαυτοῦ 1b. κοινός is almost indisputable proof that the discussion moves within the context of distinctively Jewish concerns and sensitivities (the weight of the case is hardly recognized by Rauer [105, 129], who builds too much on the δι' ἑαυτοῦ as indicating a dualistic content and gnostic origin for the phrase [165–66]). (1) κοινός in ordinary Greek means simply "common, ordinary." The sense "profane, unclean" derives from the use of κοινός as equivalent to the biblical אְמֵט (e.g., Lev 11:4–8; Deut 14:7–10; Judg 13:4; Hos 9:3) or לֹח (Lev 10:10; Ezek 22:26; 44:23), a step taken subsequent to the LXX rendering of the OT, but reflecting the increasing purity concerns of the Maccabean and post-Maccabean period (see further below). There are no real parallels in non-Jewish Greek: the parallel in Plutarch, *Eroticus*, cited by Lietzmann is simply an extended use of the normal meaning—"common," in contrast to more refined (cf. BGD, κοινός 2). (2) The importance of ritual purity, not least in matters of food in the Judaism of this period, is well illustrated by the use of the word: 1 Macc 1:47, 62 (the faithful of Israel refused to eat "unclean food"); Mark 7:2, 5 (Mark has to explain the unusual use of κοινός = defiled, to his Greek readers): Acts 10:14 and 11:8 (Peter reacts as a devout Jew, registering horror at the thought of eating anything profane or unclean). (3) This evidence coheres closely with the wider evidence of a deep concern to maintain purity laws in the Judaism of the time: e.g., Jud 12:7; *Jub.* 3.8–14; *Pss. Sol.* 8.12, 22; 1QS 3.5; CD 12.19–20; for the Pharisees see particularly Neusner, *Judaism,* 70 (cf. *TDNT* 3:418–23); and for the Essenes see, e.g., Newton, *Purity,* chap. 2; see also on 14:20. That such concerns were also prevalent in the Diaspora is indicated by *Sib. Or.* 3.591–92, the evidence cited under 14:2, and some archaeological indications that water facilities were available at diaspora synagogues (Trebilco, chap. 8).

The picture already sketched in 14:2 and 14:5 therefore gains a further dimension. For purity rituals are one of the clearest means by which a community can define itself and mark itself off from others (M. Douglas, *Purity and Danger* [London: Routledge, 1966]; in reference to Judaism of the time cf., e.g., Ezek 42:20; *Ep. Arist.* 139, 142, 315; 1QS 5.20; and Josephus, *Ant.* 13.4). So what was at issue here is not simply observance of the Torah and the unity of the community (Käsemann). At stake was the whole Jewish conception of holiness and whether a clear line of demarcation must not be drawn between the holy community and those outside. By removing such an important boundary marker Paul would seem to many Jewish Christians to be threatening their sacred space and leaving the community with its defenses down and exposed to all sorts of corrupting influences (cf. Wilckens). Nor is there any thought of the ceremonial law pointing to Christ and having been fulfilled by him and so rendered nonobligatory in its literal expression (Cranfield). Such a line of thought is completely imported into the text and misses entirely the socioreligious dimension of the discussion.

The issue of whether v 14 reflects the saying of Jesus in Mark 7:15 ("there is nothing from outside a person . . . which is able to defile him"—οὐδέν ἐστιν . . . ὃ δύναται κοινῶσαι αὐτόν) is usually answered in the affirmative, at least to the extent that Paul reflects a Christian tradition referred elsewhere back to Jesus (otherwise Lietzmann). The issue is more complex, however, in view of the "weaker" version of the saying in Matt 15:11 and *Gos. Thom.* 14, and in view of the surprising unwillingness of the earliest community of Jesus' disciples in Jerusalem to follow what, according to Mark 7:15, was unequivocal teaching (cf. Acts 10:14; 11:2–3; Gal 2:12). It is best resolved by assuming that Jesus' original words had been more ambiguous than Mark represents (closer to Matthew's version) and that Mark 7:15 *and* Rom 14:14 express the use made of it and interpretation given to that saying when the question of clean and unclean foods emerged as an issue in the gentile mission (see further Dunn, "Mark 7:15"). This would also help explain why Paul does not cite Jesus as his authority on such an important issue; "the phrase ἐν κυρίῳ Ἰησοῦ in Rom 14:14 is not a quotation formula" (Neirynck, 308; see also below). In other words, v 14 is a good example both of the pneumatic character of Paul's use of the Jesus and kerygmatic traditions (see also Dunn, *Unity,* 77–79), and of the character of the passing on, or better living in and through, what was not merely a remembered but also a reexperienced tradition of Jesus still heard as the word of the Lord (ἐν κυρίῳ Ἰησοῦ) to his disciples (see on 12:14).

εἰ μὴ τῷ λογιζομένῳ τι κοινὸν εἶναι, ἐκείνῳ κοινόν, "except that to the one who reckons something profane, to that person it is profane." Here εἰ μή has the force of ἀλλά ; cf. 1 Cor 7:17 and Gal 1:7 (BDF, §448.8). λογίζεσθαι is used here at the weightiest end of its range of meaning (cf. 3:28; 8:18; Phil 3:13 [BGD, 3])—hence not a passing fancy or lightly held opinion, but a conviction bound to the truth of God (Michel). The emphatic use of ἐκεῖνος here and in v 15 (unusual in Paul) may just possibly be some reflection of its analogous use in Mark 7:20 (see further above). To be noted is that Paul does not so much call for the abolition of the law of clean and unclean as for shifting the basis on which such a distinction may be regarded as relevant in the Christian community; that is, not as a boundary dividing one group from another and preventing communion, but as an issue affecting the expression of liberty *within* a community which embraces diverse viewpoints. As Käsemann rightly points out, Paul is not formulating a doctrine of *adiaphora* here (as, e.g., SH): actual conduct in such a sensitive area is *not* a matter of indifference; the fact that a brother is sensitive on this issue (though not the belief in clean and unclean) is a factor which determines conduct.

15 εἰ γὰρ διὰ βρῶμα ὁ ἀδελφός σου λυπεῖται, οὐκέτι κατὰ ἀγάπην περιπατεῖς, "for if your brother is deeply upset on account of food you are no longer conducting yourself in terms of love." The γάρ is usually referred back to v 13b, probably rightly, with v 14 as a parenthesis (see, e.g., Cranfield). βρῶμα is the suitably general word used twice in v 15 and again in v 20, and also 1 Cor 8:8, 13; cf. βρῶσις (v 17). For ἀδελφός see on 14:10. The reappearance of the second person singular (see 14:1–15:6 *Introduction*) indicates the intensity of Paul's personal appeal to each of "the strong" (cf. v 20). λυπεῖσθαι can have a stronger meaning than merely "be grieved" (cf. the discussion in Müller, *Anstoss*, 39–41). In nonbiblical Greek λυπέω can be used of cavalry or light troops harassing or annoying an army (LSJ, λυπέω I.3), and in the LXX it occurs quite often in the sense "angered" (1 Sam 29:4; 2 Sam 13:21; 2 Kgs 13:19; Neh 5:6; Esth 1:12; 2:21; Jonah 4:1, 4, 9). So a stronger translation is needed to bring out the degree of hurt implied ("distressed" [NIV], "outraged" [NEB]); "a euphemism" (Spicq, 518). What Paul has in view is not merely a passing sense of irritation or momentary pang of grief, but an actual wounding of conscience (Käsemann) which destroys the whole balance of the brother's faith (cf. vv 13, 15b, 21).

For ἀγάπη see on 12:9. This is the only place in 14:1–15:6 at which Paul uses the key motive which links together all his parenesis in these chapters; however, the concern which Paul wants his readers to feel and live out for their fellow believers is clear throughout even when expressed in different terms. For περιπατέω referring to daily conduct see on 6:4. κατὰ ἀγάπην obviously belongs with κατὰ πνεῦμα over against κατὰ σάρκα and κατὰ ἄνθρωπον (cf. 8:4; 1 Cor 3:3; 2 Cor 10:2–3; Gal 5:16); cf. also 1 John 2:10. The tension Paul maintains between the liberty of personal conviction (vv 5, 14a, 22–23) and the exercise of liberty through love is noteworthy. As explicitly in Eph 5:2, so here it is implied that the pattern for this love is Christ who gave himself to death for us when we were "weak" (5:8) (Wilckens). "Correct faith immediately becomes wrong when it violates love" (Gaugler).

μὴ τῷ βρώματί σου ἐκεῖνον ἀπόλλυε ὑπὲρ οὗ Χριστὸς ἀπέθανεν, "do not by your food destroy that one for whom Christ died." As all recent commentators agree, what is in view in ἀπόλλυμι is final eschatological ruin, the opposite of the final judgment of acquittal. To appreciate the full force of the reference here, however, its use to describe the fate of the unfaithful Israelite (repeatedly in Deuteronomy) has to be borne in mind (see on 2:12). Paul is referring precisely to that obligation to covenant loyalty which determined the life pattern of the devout Jew, and to the conviction that failure so to live would result in being put out of the covenant, with loss of share in Israel's final destiny (hence also the force of the much cited parallel in *m. Sanh.* 4.5—"if any man has caused a single soul to perish from Israel ["from Israel" lacking in some texts] scripture imputes it to him as though he had caused a whole world to perish" [Danby]). As in 2:12, therefore, Paul is expressing himself in the terms that "the weak," the devout Jew(ish Christian), would regard as appropriate—viz., the fear that by abandoning the touchstones of covenant loyalty they would put themselves outside the realm of saving grace. Consequently it is less clear than at first appears that Paul himself accepts the logic of that understanding of covenant obligation. The real, or at least more immediate, danger which Paul has in mind is that "the weak," presumably by being persuaded (cf v 1) against his better judgment to abandon food law and sabbath (cf. 1 Cor 8:10), will in the event believe that he has broken the covenant with God and that he has thus condemned himself to eternal loss (hence the near synonyms: ἀπόλλυμι/καταλύω—v 20, λυπεῖν—v 15a, τιθέναι πρόσκομμα/σκάνδαλον—vv 13, 20, προσκόπτω—v 21) (cf. particularly Murray, and Ladd, *Theology*, 523). It may also be implicit, of course, that such a belief could become self-fulfilling by driving "the weak," who has thus abandoned his convictions, to abandon entirely his faith in Christ and membership of the "one body in Christ." See further 14:23; cf. the argument very close in spirit in 1 Cor 8:10–12.

For the echo of the well-established creedal and evangelistic formula "Christ died for the sake of," see on 5:6. The comment on Bengel is apposite: "Do not value your food more than Christ valued his life."

16 μὴ βλασφημείσθω οὖν ὑμῶν τὸ ἀγαθόν, "therefore do not let your good be brought into contempt." Here too the use of characteristic in-house covenant language must be noted: "blasphemy" as that which Gentiles do by failing to recognize Israel's specially favored position before God (see on 3:8; this is a case where the thematic language of 1 Cor 8 and 10, here 10:30, is reworked and given a slightly different thrust). Accordingly ἀγαθόν is probably best understood in a broad sense, "the good" which sums up all God's covenanted blessings (righteousness, salvation—cf. 8:28, 10:15) and not merely the freedom of "the strong" (so Michel, Nababan, 94, Cranfield, Schlier; against SH, Lagrange, Barrett, and others cited by Käsemann, comparing 1 Cor 8:9); principal alternatives listed by Hendriksen n.387; Kirk sees it as a t.t of Greek ethics ("the ends that you may legitimately pursue"). And ὑμῶν will refer to *all* the recipients of the letter, including "weak" as well as "strong" (marked by the return of the second person plural from the singular of v 15), and not just "the strong" alone (against the great majority). What is in view is the likelihood that such insensitive conduct will cause such hurt to "the weak" and disharmony among the Roman congregation(s) that the gentile onlookers and casual acquaintances will gain a low opinion both of the community who claim to be recipients of this covenanted good and of the God they claim to serve. Since the fault, as envisaged here, would be primarily that of "the strong," Paul is once again warning the majority (Gentiles) within the Roman congregations not to let their sense of "strength" lead them into the same mistake as the devout Jew had fallen into in his boasting in the law (2:23–24); see also on 11:18 and 12:16.

17 οὐ γάρ ἐστιν ἡ βασιλεία τοῦ θεοῦ βρῶσις καὶ πόσις, "for the kingdom of God does not consist of eating and drinking." βασιλεία is unusual in Paul; where it does occur it is usually in the formulaic talk of "inheriting the kingdom" (1 Cor 6:9–10; 15:50; Gal 5:21; cf. Eph 5:5; James 2:5; in the Jesus tradition cf. particularly Matt 5:5 and 19:29, and further Haufe, 470–71; see on 8:17), or with similar future eschatological reference (1 Thess 2:12; 2 Thess 1:5; cf. Col 4:11; 2 Tim 4:1, 18; of Jesus' eschatological but present reign—1 Cor 15:24; cf. Col 1:13). The only close parallel is 1 Cor 4:20:

Romans:	οὐ γάρ ἐστιν β· κ· π· ἡ βασ· τ· θεοῦ ἀλλὰ	. . .	ἐν πνεύματι ἁγίῳ·
1 Corinthians:	οὐ γάρ ἐν λόγῳ ἡ βασ· τ· θεοῦ ἀλλ'		ἐν δυνάμει.

This suggests that the category of "the kingdom of God" lay to hand in the common Christian tradition (Paul can take it up as an obviously familiar concept), but that Paul chose to make little use of it (perhaps for the simple reason that a preacher traveling through the Roman Empire speaking of another kingdom could leave himself open to charges of sedition; cf. Acts 17:6–7, Mark 15:26 pars., John 18:33–37). The inverse ratio of βασιλεία references to πνεῦμα (ἅγιον) and δικαιοσύνη references in the Synoptic tradition as compared with the Pauline letters is striking:

	Jesus-Synoptics	Pauline corpus
βασιλεία	c. 105	14
δικαιοσύνη	7	57
πνεῦμα (ἅγιον)	13	>110

An obvious inference is that Jesus' emphasis on the kingdom has been effectively replaced by Paul's emphasis on righteousness (Jüngel, *Paulus,* 267) and on the Spirit (Dunn, *Jesus,* 310–11). Used thus "the kingdom of God" becomes a way of describing "what Christianity is all about" (cf. Black)—"the essence of Christianity" (Schmidt). Cf. *2 Clem.* 12.1.

In fact Paul's usage here reflects an equivalent emphasis in the Jesus tradition—that God's eschatological rule was already being manifested in the present, particularly in Jesus' exorcisms (Matt 12:28 // Luke 11:20) and table fellowship (Luke 14:12–24 // Matt 22:1–10). Two points of contact are noteworthy (insufficiently recognized by Haufe). (1) In both cases it is the powerful activity of the Spirit which is regarded as the manifestation of God's final rule. Hence the thought here is very much of a piece with the eschatological tension so characteristic of Paul's thought—the Spirit, indeed, as the first installment of the inheritance which is the kingdom (1 Cor 6:9–11; Gal 4:6–7; also Eph 1:13–14; see further on 8:17; cf. also 8:23). For both Jesus and

Paul the Spirit *is* the presence of the kingdom, still future in its complete fulfillment (see further J. D. G. Dunn, "Spirit and Kingdom," *ExpT* 82 [1970–71] 36–40). For both Jesus and Paul the character and power of the still future rule of God can provide inspiration and enabling for the present.

(2) At first sight Jesus' likening the kingdom to a banquet seems to be at odds with Paul's denial that the kingdom should be understood in terms of eating and drinking. Not so! Jesus' parable of the banquet was a protest against the sort of restrictions on table fellowship which Pharisees, and in that case particularly Essenes, practiced (cf. Luke 14:13, 21 with 1QSa 2.3–9). Paul is making precisely the same sort of protest against a measuring of what is acceptable in God's presence in terms of rules governing eating and drinking. It is very likely therefore that Paul's language here is a further example of the influence of the Jesus tradition on Paul's teaching, but at the level of shaping his thought rather than as a formal yardstick (see on 12:14; cf. Johnston, "Kingdom," 152–55). In fact Paul uses this inextricable link between kingdom and Spirit (probably derived originally from Jesus) as a principle of discrimination on both fronts on which he was engaged: against those too much influenced by Hellenistic ideas of wisdom (1 Cor 14:20; cf. 1 Cor 2:4); and against those too much dependent on the traditional customs of Judaism (here). The parallel should not be taken to support the conclusion that Paul is combating enthusiasm here (cf. 1 Cor 4:8!), since the consistency of Paul's focus on the Jew/Gentile tensions in the letter is clear beyond reasonable dispute (against Käsemann).

The ἐστίν can be variously paraphrased: "does not consist in," "is not a matter of," "does not depend on." βρῶσις and πόσις should both be taken of the act of "eating" and "drinking" (BGD), not as "food" and "drink" (rsv). It is the harm done by the too insensitive eating habits of "the strong" which Paul has in mind, more than the inhibitions of the weak about certain foods (though cf. 1 Cor 8:8; whether "the weak" had scruples regarding drink is not clear; see on 14:21). The implications of Paul's teaching here for the theology and the administration of the Eucharist are rarely noted, but should not be ignored.

ἀλλὰ δικαιοσύνη καὶ εἰρήνη καὶ χαρὰ ἐν πνεύματι ἁγίῳ, "but righteousness, peace, and joy in the Holy Spirit." The key word of the whole letter, δικαιοσύνη, used here for the last time, is unlikely to have a different sense from what has been a consistent but broad usage—God's gracious power reaching out to renew and sustain the believer (see on 1:17, and the closest parallel, 8:10). Indeed it could be argued that because of its use of this key thematic term, v 17 is the "theological center" of chaps. 12–15 (Jüngel, *Paulus*, 26 n.1; cited also by Kertelge, *Rechtfertigung*, 298, and Reumann, 91). The focus is on the divine enabling which comes to expression in conduct (in relation to others) κατὰ πνεῦμα/ἀγάπην (v 15), not on the conduct itself (so rightly Käsemann, Michel, and Schlier; against SH and Barrett). εἰρήνη too is first and foremost God-given (and corporate) and embodies the same eschatological tension as is present in δικαιοσύνη and πνεῦμα ἅγιον (see further on 1:7 and 5:1). χαρά also is not to be conceived of merely as frothy feeling of delight, but as the confidence of God which can be sustained even in persecution (cf., e.g., Matt 5:12; Rom 5:3–5; 2 Cor 7:4; 1 Thess 1:6; 1 Pet 1:6). The subjective element in the thought can certainly be maintained (Barrett), so long as the corporate dimension is also kept in view. Elsewhere in Paul see 15:13 (joy and peace); 15:32; 2 Cor 1:15, 24; 2:3; 7:13; 8:2; Gal 5:22 (fruit of the Spirit); Phil 1:4, 25; 2:2, 29; 4:1, etc.; see also on 12:12. The final phrase, ἐν πνεύματι ἁγίῳ, can be taken either with all three preceding terms (cf. 8:10 and Gal 5:22; so, e.g., Zahn, Schlatter, Lagrange, Schmidt, Wilckens), or solely with χαρά (cf. 1 Thess 1:6; e.g., Michel, Black, Cranfield). The ἐν will have its usual sense of "in the power of" (embracing both a locative and instrumental sense), as in 2:29; 7:6; 8:9; 9:1; and 15:16 (so explicitly, 15:13, 19)—"Christianity as a supernatural life lived in the holy Spirit" (Dodd).

18 ὁ γὰρ ἐν τούτῳ δουλεύων τῷ Χριστῷ, "for he who serves the Christ in this." ἐν τούτῳ is best taken in a recapitulative sense but without a more specific reference = "in this matter" (cf. particularly 1 Cor 11:22; 2 Cor 8:10; Michel; Cranfield reviews the range of options; Wilckens's n.463 pressing for a reference to ἐν πνεύματι ἁγίῳ [cf. Black] is unnecessarily pedantic). For δουλεύειν see on 1:1, 6:16, 7:6, and 12:11. Talk of the "moral autonomy" of the individual is wholly inappropriate in exposition of Paul's thought in this section (cf. Schmidt), since, as always for Paul, the individual is always a dependent being (cf. 1:23, 25; 6:16). The use of the definite article with Χριστός is unusual in Paul but is consistently maintained to the end of this section (15:3, 7); so we should probably see here a deliberate attempt to express himself in terms closest to those of the Jewish Christian minority = "the Messiah" (as in 9:3, 5). It is not impossible that here too Paul's language has been uncontrivedly shaped by the Jesus tradition, since the redefinition of participation in the kingdom in terms of slavery is reminiscent of the saying of Jesus about true greatness as servanthood, much reflected on in the earliest Christian communities (Mark 9:35 par., and particularly 10:42–44 pars.; see J. McDermond, *"The Slave of All": A Tradition-Historical Study of a Synoptic Saying*, Diss., Durham, 1987).

εὐάρεστος τῷ θεῷ καὶ δόκιμος τοῖς ἀνθρώποις, "pleasing to God and approved among men." For εὐάρεστος see on 12:1. ἄνθρωποι is generic—men and women, people generally. Unusually δόκιμος refers to approval in relation to other people (contrast the only other NT usages [16:10; 1 Cor 11:19; 2 Cor 10:18; 13:7; 2 Tim 2:15; James 1:12]; *TDNT* 2:260; see also on 1:28, ἀδόκιμος). But here, once again, Paul does not hesitate to set as one of his norms for conduct what the generality of people of good will would recognize to be acceptable and praiseworthy behavior (as in 1:28; 2:7, 10; 12:17; and 13:3, 5, 10, 13). The contrast with v 16 is evident (Cranfield): conduct which limited personal freedom in consideration for others is the opposite of the selfish insensitivity which was careless of the hurt caused; and both would be observed and remarked upon by neighbors, visitors, and associates.

19 ἄρα οὖν τὰ τῆς εἰρήνης διώκομεν, "so then we pursue what makes for peace." For ἄρα οὖν see on 5:18. εἰρήνην διώκειν seems to be an idiom well established in earliest Christian speech (2 Tim 2:22; Heb 12:14; 1 Pet 3:11), probably in dependence on Ps 34:14 [LXX 33:15] (so explicitly 1 Pet 3:11). For the imagery of "pursuit" see further on 9:30. Since εἰρήνη has a corporate and not merely individual dimension in Jewish thought (on which Paul is here drawing; see on 1:7), it is not necessary to argue that the sense here is different from that in v 17; there can be no "peace with God" when a Christian congregation is divided (see also BGD, εἰρήνην 1b).

καὶ τὰ τῆς οἰκοδομῆς τῆς εἰς ἀλλήλους, "and what makes for the edification of one another." The metaphor of building (up) has an obviously positive meaning and reference (cf. Epictetus 2.15.8), which would be familiar not least from the OT where Jeremiah in particular makes repeated use of it (Jer 12:16; 31 [LXX 38]:4, 28; 33 [LXX 40]:7; 42 [LXX 49]:10; 45:4 [LXX 51:34]); see also on 14:20. The imagery was especially important for Paul: he used it for his own ministry (15:20; 1 Cor 3:9–10; 2 Cor 10:8 and 13:10 [deliberate echo of Jeremiah]; 12:19), and the imagery lent itself to the conviction of a building together of Jew and Gentile (Eph 2:19–21; 1 Pet 2:5). Its most frequent usage, however, was in his counsel to the churches to which he wrote: that "upbuilding" should be a crucial criterion in determining relationships and mutual interdependence (15:2; 1 Cor 8:1; 10:23; 1 Thess 5:11; so too Eph 2:22; 4:12, 16, 29; see also *TDNT* 5:140–42); and particularly in a congregation's discerning the relative value of different charisms (1 Cor 14:3–5, 12, 17, 26; see Dunn, *Jesus,* 295–96). What is in view is once again not some sense or feeling of "edification" (in pietistic terms), as a too casual reading of passages like 15:2 and Eph 4:29 might suggest, but whether the congregation is actually benefiting and being built up—that is, developing in harmony and/or growing in number (cf. Acts 9:31; 20:32) (NJB's "support" is too weak). Once again the parallel with 1 Cor 8, 10, and 14 should not be taken necessarily to imply that Paul was directing his advice against enthusiasts in Rome. The tensions in Rome were between Jewish and gentile groupings (against Käsemann).

20 μὴ ἕνεκεν βρώματος κατάλυε τὸ ἔργον τοῦ θεοῦ, "do not for the sake of food tear down the work of God." The return to second person singular indicates once again that the plea is addressed to "the strong" (as v 15). καταλύειν is the natural opposite of οἰκοδομεῖν (v 19) (Mark 13:2 par.; 14:58 par; 15:29 par.; 2 Cor 5:1; Gal 2:18). Since the sentence is virtually a variation on v 15b, καταλύω will have the same force as ἀπόλλυμι (see on 14:15). In keeping with the sustained metaphor, ἔργον most obviously refers to the οἰκοδομή of the Christian community (*TDNT* 2:643; so Lietzmann, Barrett, T. W. Manson, Käsemann, Schlier, Wilckens; cf. 1 Cor 3:9; Eph 2:19–21; and 1 Pet 2:5) rather than the weak brother (Lagrange, Gaugler, Cranfield); cf. 1 Cor 3:16–17 and 6:19 where Paul uses the image of God's temple both for the corporate body of believers and for the body of the individual Christian. In other words, v 20a recapitulates not only v 15b but also v 16.

πάντα μὲν καθαρά, "all things are clean." This may be a slogan of "the strong" (cf. 1 Cor 10:23; but also Mark 7:19); but we cannot assume that Paul had that much detailed information about the different viewpoints among the Roman congregations; and it could just as well be an expression of Paul's own view (v 14; cf. 1 Cor 10:26). In this context καθαρός is clearly the opposite of κοινός (v 14; cf. ἅγιος/βέβηλος, καθαρός/ἀκάθαρτος—Lev 10:10; Ezek 22:26; 44:23) and so has primarily the issue of clean and unclean foods in view (a regular usage for καθαρός in the OT, particularly the Torah (Gen 7:2–3, 8; 8:20; Lev 4:12; 6:11; 7:19; etc.; also, e.g., Ezra 6:20; Mal 1:11; more so with ἀκάθαρτος—frequently in Lev-Deut but more consistently in the prophets

[e.g., Isa 52:11; 64:6 (LXX 5); Ezek 4:13; Hos 9:3; Hag 2:14 (LXX 13)]).
The usage thereafter shows the same continuing concern on the issue of
clean/unclean in the "intertestamental" period (Jud 10:5; 12:9; 1 Macc 1:48;
Pss. Sol. 8.12, 22; *Ep. Arist.* 166; *T. Levi* 15.1; 16.4–5; Philo, *Spec. Leg.* 4.106;
Virt. 147; Josephus, *Ap.* 1.307); note also the way in which the clean/unclean
distinction functions as a boundary dividing the elect from the outsiders (Isa
35:8; 52:1; Amos 7:17), with the resulting significance of καθαρίζειν in the
NT in such passages as Mark 7:19, Acts 10:15, 11:9, and 15:9. In distinction
from κοινός (v 14), however, (ἀ)καθαρός had already developed a fuller moral
significance (e.g., Job 4:7; Isa 1:16; Ezek 36:25–26; Hab 1:13; *Ep. Arist.* 2, 234;
T. Reub. 4.8; *T. Ben.* 6.5; 8.2–3; Philo, *Immut.* 132; *Mos.* 2.24; *Legat.* 165)
and in the NT the older, ritual concept of purity falls completely away as
left behind by the new age of the Spirit (e.g., Matt 5:8; John 15:3; 1 Tim
1:5; 3:9; James 1:27; 1 Pet 1:22; cf. *TDNT* 3:417, 423–26). Here of course
it is precisely the tie-up between ritual and moral (or essential) which is the
problem, not that "the weak" thinks "merely" in ritual terms. Hence Paul
here recognizes that for "the weak" brother the opposite of καθαρός is κακός.

ἀλλὰ κακὸν τῷ ἀνθρώπῳ τῷ διὰ προσκόμματος ἐσθίοντι, "but it is wicked for
the person who eats with offense." It is exceedingly difficult to decide whether
"the man/person" refers to "the strong" or to "the weak" (cf. SH). In favor
of the former is the parallel with v 21, and the use of πρόσκομμα with the
same force as in v 13: that is, "a cause of stumbling," causing offense (to
the weak) by so doing (so, e.g., RSV, NEB, NIV, SH, Barrett, Black, Käsemann,
Cranfield)—the διά of attendant circumstances (BDF §223.3; BGD, διά
A.III.1c). In favor of the latter is the parallel with v 14 (on this interpretation
v 20b would be a recapitulation of v 14b), and 1 Cor 8:7, 10–11: that is, the
weak eats with offense = with an offended, bad conscience (e.g., NJB, *TDNT*
6:756–57, Lagrange, Michel, Murray, Schlier, Wilckens). If a choice had to
be made, the proximity of v 21 would seem to tip the balance in favor of
the former (perhaps also the κακός has more the implication of a wicked act
done to someone else?). Paul would then be urging the strong to a course
of action, not only to consider the sensibilities of the weak; and v 20b would
be better taken as a variation on v 14b, with the κακός of v 14 contrasted
with the καλός of v 21. But once again where Paul has written ambiguously
(whether by intention or not [Barrett]), it is best to leave the ambiguity in
translation (as above): both κακός and πρόσκομμα (see on 9:33) are sufficiently
ambiguous to allow his readership to take the clause either or both ways;
the implication either way is that "the weak" stumbles by actually following
the example of the strong (rather than simply by seeing "the strong" eat;
see on 14:15). In which case v 20b forms a parallel to *both* halves of v 21.

21 καλὸν τὸ μὴ φαγεῖν κρέα, "it is fine not to eat meat." For καλός see on
12:17, and for the κακός/καλός contrast cf. also 7:18–19, 21 as well as 12:17.
For the construction, "it is good to," cf. 1 Cor 7:1, 8, 26 and Heb 13:9. The
use of the aorist (φαγεῖν), following immediately on the present (v 20) suggests
that Paul does not envisage the strong abstaining permanently (BDF §338.1—
"it is good not to eat meat *for once* [in a specific instance . . .]"), a restriction
perhaps already foreshadowed in v 2 (but cf. Cranfield). The refusal to eat
flesh could arise from any one or combination of the dietary prohibitions:

meat from which the blood was not properly drained (cf. Gen 9:4; Deut 12:15–16), flesh of unclean animals (as in Lev 11:8; Deut 14:8; 2 Macc 6:18), or meat from animals that had been offered in sacrifice to idols (cf. 1 Cor 8:13, the only other NT occurrence of κρέας). Of course meat eating as such was not forbidden in the Torah (cf., e.g., Exod 12:8; Num 11:18); so we must assume a policy of avoiding all meat in case any of the above taboos had been breached (see further on 14:2).

μηδὲ πιεῖν οἶνον, "nor drink wine." Since drinking wine as such was also *not* forbidden (cf. Deut 7:13, 11:14, and the established Passover practice; not to mention Mark 14:23–25 pars. and John 2:1–11), the possibility that Paul is speaking hypothetically here cannot be ruled out (Cranfield). But it is much more likely that a scrupulousness which avoided *all* meat also avoided wine, not least in case it had been offered in libation to the gods before being sold in the market (cf. particularly Dan 1:3–16; 10:3; Add Esth 14:17; *T. Reub.* 1.10; *T. Jud.* 15.4; *Jos. As.* 8.5; *m. ʿAbod. Zar.* 2.3; 5.2). It is not necessary to think particularly of a Nazirite vow (Num 6:4; Judg 13:4; Amos 2:12; but cf. Acts 18:18 and 21:23), though a Pharisaic extension of the law governing the temple (Lev 10:9; Ezek 44:21) may be in play here, since it coheres so closely with the fundamental distinction between sacred and profane, clean and unclean (Lev 10:9–10; Ezek 44:21–23).

μηδὲ ἐν ᾧ ὁ ἀδελφός σου προσκόπτει, "nor anything by which your brother stumbles." Once again the affective use of ἀδελφός (see on 14:10), as in vv 13 and 15. As in 9:32–33 the metaphor of stumbling over an obstacle is maintained; for προσκόπτω see on 9:32. Here too (as in v 15) what Paul has in mind is not the hurt of the weaker brother seeing "the stronger" eat meat and drink wine, but an actual stumbling by the weaker brother—that is, presumably, by giving in to the pressure from the majority "strong" and doing something which he thinks is wrong (see also 14:15).

22 σὺ πίστιν ἣν ἔχεις κατὰ σεαυτὸν ἔχε ἐνώπιον τοῦ θεοῦ, "the faith which you have keep to yourself before God." As usual the reversion to second person singular address is directed to the strong. For κατὰ σεαυτὸν ἔχε ("keep to oneself") see BGD, κατά II.1c; less satisfactory is NEB, "apply it to yourself." πίστις should *not* be understood "in its special sense of confidence that one's faith allows one to do a particular thing" (Cranfield—which almost amounts to defining πίστις here as faith in one's faith). As always in this letter πίστις denotes trust, reliance directly upon God. There are different measures of faith (12:3), but the faith on each occasion does not have a different character (see further on 12:3). What is in view each time is unconditional trust in God alone which varies in strength from believer to believer. The "stronger" the faith (that is, the more unconditional the trust), the less dependent is it on observance of particular traditions; the "weaker" the faith, the more dependent on such customs (hence the use of πιστεύειν only in the first half of v 2; see on 14:2). Because faith has the character of immediate reliance on God it need not be displayed in public: the relationship of the "strong" can still be without dependence on these traditional rulings even when observing them for the sake of the "weak."

μακάριος ὁ μὴ κρίνων ἑαυτὸν ἐν ᾧ δοκιμάζει, "happy is the one who does not condemn himself by what he approves." For μακάριος see on 4:7–8. The difficulty with the rest of the clause arises from the fact that κρίνω and δοκιμάζειν overlap in their range of meanings (the compounds ἀνακρίνω, διακρίνω, and συνκρίνω can all serve as near synonyms of δοκιμάζω [1 Cor 2:13–15; 14:29; 1 Thess 5:21]); since δοκιμάζειν denotes the process by which a judgment is reached (see on 12:2), the clause is in danger of becoming tautologous. The key is probably to recognize that in rounding off this section of the discussion Paul harks back to the terms of the opening (see *Form and Structure*), so that the use of κρίνω recalls and reflects its use in v 3 (κρίνω = "condemn"; see on 14:3). The happiness of "the strong" need not be disturbed if the weak condemns him, only if he were to condemn himself. It follows that Paul is probably describing the overall state of "the strong," inward as well as outward (Cranfield; the talk is of condemning himself—against Käsemann); though once again the ambiguity allows the fuller sense of "blame himself for causing the weak to stumble (v 21) by what he has approved for his own eating" (so Michel, Wilckens).

23 ὁ δὲ διακρινόμενος ἐὰν φάγῃ κατακέκριται, "but the one who doubts is condemned if he eats." For διακρίνομαι in this sense, see on 4:20 (the only other time Paul uses it in Romans). The usage is established in the NT precisely as a contrast to the unconditional trust in God which comes to expression in prayer (Mark 11:23 // Matt 21:21; James 1:6; Jude 22). With κατακέκριται there seems to be a double sense intended; as in 2:1: "the weak" (who is clearly in view; against Minear, 12, who sees here a third group, "the doubters") regards himself as condemned, because he ate while still held by the conviction that so to eat was to put himself outside the boundary marking off the people of God; and since he continues to think thus in terms of the law, he expects God to judge him by the law (2:12). The terms are partly those which "the doubter" would use for himself, the perfect tense indicating the psychological state of one who thought he had made an irrevocable breach in the covenant (cf. particularly 1 Cor 11:30–31). But they also indicate Paul's own conviction that divine condemnation follows upon any action which does not express one's creaturely dependence on God (1:19–32; and see below).

ὅτι οὐκ ἐκ πίστεως, "because it is not of faith." Once again πίστις denotes the dependent reliance of creature on creator (as in chap. 4, particularly 4:19–20, 12:3, and 14:22), not a secondary conviction (confidence) deduced from his faith (Cranfield; cf. Maillot), or charismatic faith (Zahn), or conscience (Bultmann, *Theology*, 1:220; see Wilckens) or conviction/persuasion (NEB, Käsemann). Michel recognizes that the phrase is a summary of the indictment of 1:19–32 ("a refusal of obedience and an offense against God's glory"; cf. 1:21). But the fact that ἐκ πίστεως is one of Paul's characteristic ways of referring to this thematic word needs also to be recognized (1:17 twice; 3:26, 30; 4:16 twice; 5:1; 9:30, 32; 10:6).

πᾶν δὲ ὃ οὐκ ἐκ πίστεως ἁμαρτία ἐστίν, "everything which is not of faith is sin." In view of the thematic importance of ἐκ πίστεως in the letter (see just above), we might even translate: "everything which is not 'of faith' is sin." Clearly Paul intends this as the statement of a general principle or rule (Michel) and one not limited to the particular issue under discussion ("*everything*"). Cranfield's mistake on this point (following SH) is his continued insistence that πίστις has a special sense here (see on 14:22) and failure to recognize that Paul has in view the basic sense of creaturely dependence which is man's proper attitude and response to God (Lietzmann cites Philo, *Abr.* 18, as an apposite parallel; Dodd and Zeller refer to Luke 6:4 D); for the same reason translation or interpretation in terms of "conscience" (e.g., Aquinas in Denney; Lagrange; Gaugler; Nababan, 106–7; Fitzmyer) also misses and obscures the point. The principle therefore applies not simply to "weak" and "strong" (Schlier) or just to "strong" alone (Wilckens), nor should πίστις here be restricted to "faith in Christ" (Abraham after all was the model of the attitude "of faith" [4:16–17]). Paul would have nothing to do with the view of some rabbis that the good deeds of the Gentiles are inevitably sin because (by definition) not wrought within the covenant (Str-B 3:313), or with the later Christian view that non-Christian works are by definition sinful (see Augustine, in SH); on the contrary, his point is that *whatever* is not an expression of dependence on and trust in God (whether Jewish or Gentile or "Christian" or "non-Christian") is marked by that fatal flaw of human presumption and/ or self-indulgence. At the same time the more general principle applies to the weak and strong in particular: failure to live before God ἐκ πίστεως means a repetition of man's fall into sin (1:19–32). "Christ remains the only measure for all. No one must make his faith a norm for others as they seek to serve Christ. The weak want uniformity by making their law binding for brothers, and the strong seek it too by forcing their insight on the weak. We thus try to make others in our own image and in so doing sin, since faith has to do always and exclusively with the image of Christ" (Käsemann). The use of ἁμαρτία = "sinful act" rather than personified power should not be regarded as surprising (see on 3:9).

Explanation

13 With v 13 Paul turns his attention to the strong. Over against the danger of the more conservative brother's condemnatory attitude toward the more liberal, is the danger that the liberal will despise the conservative for his clinging to the old ways (vv 3, 10). The danger is that the self-consciously "strong" will grow contemptuous of the other's "weakness," of what they regard as too narrowly restrictive practices, and that confident in the rightness of their views they will flaunt their liberty before the traditionalist and ride roughshod over the latter's sensitivities. So with a neat play along the range of meaning of the word "judge," Paul calls on his readers all to avoid passing judgment on one another and to judge their obligation rather in terms of avoiding giving offense to the other.

It is presumably no accident that Paul uses both words, "offense" and "downfall," which are so close to each other in meaning, since he probably wanted to recall his readers to his earlier use of the same two words in the well-known text, Isa 8:14 (9:33). The implication is twofold. On the one hand, a similar sort of "stumbling" is in view: Jews (in this case Jewish believers) stumbling over the challenge to their traditional perspectives—there Christ (9:33), here freedom from the law. And, so Paul clearly thinks, for the same reason: a misunderstanding of the law, of the way in which the law correlates with righteousness (9:31–32)—in both cases a conviction that righteousness is inseparable from "works of the law" (9:32), the characteristic Jewish practices which marked them out as God's (here the food laws and sabbaths and other festivals). On the other hand, there may be a warning implied. It was one thing for *God* to lay the stumbling stone of Christ in the path of his people (9:33). It was quite another for the self-consciously "strong" (mainly Gentile) to do so. That was to usurp the role only God could fulfill, every bit as dangerous as the more conservative's usurping God's role as final judge (vv 10–12).

14 Paul himself was quite clear in his own mind that there was nothing common or unclean in itself: he makes the point with tremendous emphasis ("I know, and am convinced, as standing within the influence of Jesus the Lord") and repeats it later (v 20). In so saying he was consciously shifting his perspective in salvation-history from an internal Jewish one and in effect viewing the whole from a creation standpoint—not just pre-Moses, but even pre-Noah (cf. Gen 9:4–5). The new age should reflect the first age in having no clear boundary between Jew and Gentile, between sacred and profane— a return to the immediacy of dependence on God alone and not on national traditions as well. Almost certainly Paul here echoes a saying of Jesus in the form in which it was cherished in the Hellenistic mission (Mark 7:15, 19). The fact that Paul does not explicitly call on Jesus' authority to back the saying may be significant, as indicating Paul's awareness that the saying was understood in a less radical way elsewhere within the new movement (Matt 15:11). But Paul was quite sure that as related to the question at issue this tradition of Jesus' teaching provided a definitive principle which put the question beyond doubt for him.

Nevertheless, no matter how clear he felt the principle to be and how strongly he felt it, he also recognized that other Christians did not see it so. For them the principle deriving from Jesus' teaching was not so clear-cut; certainly not clear enough to counter the clearer and massive combined force of sacred scripture and national tradition. Paul therefore provides a first check for "the strong" on their liberty to live in the light of their principle: not all accept the principle as thus defined. Paul does not retract from his own conviction that the distinction between clean and unclean has been done away in Christ. But he accepts that the distinction is still operative for some; "if anyone thinks it is unclean, to that person it *is* unclean." That is to say, he genuinely accepts this as a view conscientiously held. He does not attempt to argue the point or to convince the "weaker" brethren. He follows his own advice (v 1). To have stated his own opinion as forcefully as he can is sufficient. The fact that other members of the congregations would still be unable to agree with him then becomes the determinative factor for the conduct of "the strong." That is to say, he recognizes the psychological reality that an individual simply may not be able to throw off a conviction which has been deeply ingrained in that person's character and life. And this must be an important consideration for others.

15 In other words, while the unliberated attitude of the more conservatively minded may be regrettable as displaying a defect in their faith ("weak in faith" [v 1]), nevertheless the fact that it is a conscientiously arrived at attitude (vv 5b–6) means that the more liberally minded must take it into account in determining *their* conduct as it affects their more conservative brothers. The key word here, which links the whole section with the chief motif of the preceding sections (12:9; 13:8–10), is once again love: let your conduct in relation to your brother be determined by love. And clearly implied is that Christ himself is the pattern of that love: the brother is one for whom Christ died! As Christ displayed his love by taking account of the weak and acting on their behalf (5:6; 8:3), so ought they. If Christ was willing to give up his life for the sake of the weak, they surely could not regard food as more important.

Paul clearly wants to inculcate in his readers a genuine sensitivity and sympathy for the more conservative minority. He recognizes that they are in a real and not merely imaginary danger. They may be "deeply upset" by a too cavalier lifestyle of the more liberal. The passive tense here ("is grieved") is probably not accidental. Paul is implying that it is not simply a matter of the strongs' intention in the matter; they might have had no thought, far less purpose, so to upset the weaker brother. What matters, however, is whether the brother actually was upset in any particular event. The conduct of the more liberal toward "the weak" is not to be determined by the "superior" insight of the "strong," or by what they think is best for the "weak" (cf. again v 1), but by the actual effect of their conduct on the "weak."

Paul can even put the danger to the more conservative brother in terms of his destruction: "do not cause his ruin!" Paul takes seriously the fear of the Jewish believer that a deliberate breach of the covenant, a deliberate renunciation of fundamental obligations of the covenant, would result in that person's being excluded from the covenant, cut off from the people of God (cf. Gen 17:14; Josh 7:15; *Jub.* 30.21–22). Whether or not Paul himself fully shared that belief is not the point. Paul here pleads the case of the devout traditionalist in the terms which that person would use (a measure of the degree to which Paul was committed to upholding the right of the weaker brother to be a fully integrated member of the Christian congregation).

16 A second consideration Paul brings before the more liberated Gentile Christians in Rome is the impact of such insensitive conduct upon any onlooking or visiting unbelievers: "do not let your good be brought into contempt." A house church, small in number as it would have to be, which was careless of the anguish of spirit being caused to one of its members, would be a very poor advertisement for the body of Christ. Paul would naturally assume, if only from his experience of the church in Corinth, that uncommitted friends and acquaintances might well visit such a church in Rome (cf. 1 Cor 14:23) or would know enough of the congregation to be aware of such frictions. So "the strong" has to reflect on the fact that not only the individual brother is injured by such abuse of Christian liberty, but also the gospel and the whole cause of Christ. Here again in thinking they were of superior insight and more highly favored by God than the unliberated Jewish brother they might fall into the very error for which they despised their brother (2:23–24; 11:18–20).

17 As an explanation for this advice Paul recalls his Roman audience to a phrase which he must have assumed was familiar to them also from the common stock of Jesus' teaching, which all Christian churches doubtless possessed in one form or other. "For the kingdom of God is not a matter of eating and drinking, but of righteousness, peace, and joy in the Holy Spirit." For his readers would surely recall that characteristic of Jesus' teaching, as indeed of Jesus' own practice, was the same sort of denial that God's rule should be thought to depend on rules about eating and drinking. Much more important were personal relationships: that they should express the mutual acceptance of each by God and mutual responsibility for each before God, the life which each should live out of God's sustaining grace (v 4); that they should contribute to mutual well-being ("peace"), and should give occasion for the joy which they experienced through their shared experience of the Spirit. *This* was the sort of impression they should be making on outsiders. The principle, of course, cut both ways. If "the weak" should not be so insistent on observing strict dietary rules as though they were an essential manifestation of God's kingly rule, neither should "the strong" be so insistent on refusing to have anything to do with such observances and on despising those who did. The ritual moment was just not that important. And genuine liberty in the Spirit would show itself in the freedom not only to ignore such rules but also to observe them if in the event such observance was a manifestation of the relationship of God's rule. Only when liberty is liberty to deny oneself and not just liberty to enjoy all that God the creator has provided is it the liberty of the Spirit of Christ.

18 Paul drives home the point by reminding his readers that the decision in such matters does not lie solely with them. Their conduct should always express their submission to Christ as Lord. The Roman readership would know only too well that the slaves they rubbed shoulders with every day in the streets and forums of Rome were not about their own business and pleasure; not a few of them were slaves themselves. Paul thus recalls them to the point he had made earlier: that this whole exposition on how a congregation should handle its legitimate differences of opinion and practice was predicated on the assumption that each was acting as one of Christ's house slaves, acting "for the Lord" (vv 4, 6). This is the pattern for one who wants to please God and to make a favorable impression on the wider public—not the self-assertion of rights which trampled on the sensibilities of others.

Paul would no doubt also expect his readers to pick up the inference (it is a mark of Paul's own sensitivity to the situation that he does not press it home more explicitly) that Christ himself provides the pattern. The echoes of Jesus' teaching had been a consistent feature of the preceding verses (13–17): on not causing another to fall into temptation, on true cleanliness, on love of neighbor as the single most important guiding principle of conduct, and on the kingdom of God. And implicit too was the thought that Jesus' ministry itself had been characterized by just such concerns, both in the matter of living according to the right priorities (people as more important than consistency of rules or rituals), and in his concern for the "weak," as evidenced not least in his death on behalf of such. To serve the Lord was to follow the pattern he provided (6:17), the pattern contained in the traditions about him (cf. Col 2:6). Consistent with this is the thought of Jesus throughout the chapter as the Lord who directs daily conduct (vv 6, 8, 18) with a view to God as the final arbiter (vv 6, 10, 18).

19 Although Paul has already made his point with sufficient clarity, he obviously feels its importance so strongly that he comes at it once more from a third angle. The more liberal must be conscious of their responsibility not only to the conservative individual, and not only before the wider public, but also to the congregation itself. To press home his point Paul draws on two concepts of rich connotation for him. To be a responsible member of the body of Christ in Rome means actually working for "peace"—that is, once again, not merely an absence or avoidance of friction or antagonism, and not merely an individualistic quietness of mind, but a positive well-being which covers the whole range of spiritual and social relationships. It means also striving to "build up" the mutual relationships of which the church consists (the polar opposite for Paul of a spirituality or worship or fellowship which seeks first and foremost its own benefit and advancement). To belong to God's building means living out one's life as part of that building, mutually dependent on God's grace and mutually interdependent on the interlocking relationships by which the building exists and grows. Despite their greater sense of liberty, the strong are more dependent on the weak than they might at first realize.

20–21 What is at stake therefore is not simply the eternal salvation of the weaker individual (v 15) but the very existence of God's work, the church, which too can be destroyed by irresponsible exercise of liberty. Lest his advocacy of concern for the more conservative be misconstrued, Paul repeats his firm agreement with the more liberated attitude: "All things are clean" (as Jesus' example had shown). But in human relationships absolute rules are dangerous, since any principle governing human conduct must take account of the circumstances in specific instances (as Jesus had also shown). So should the exercise of wholly legitimate liberty result in the downfall of a fellow Christian, that should be enough for anyone who seeks the well-being and upbuilding of the church to which they both belong. Over against the ruling that all is clean, Paul lays out the principle of self-restricted liberty in the most far-reaching terms: what applies to eating meat and drinking wine applies also to *anything* which causes a fellow believer to stumble and fall on his or her own pathway of discipleship.

22–23 Paul has thus expressed with some care his double concern regarding his more conservative readership's continued sense of obligation to the older and clearer boundary markers and rules of conduct for the people of God provided by the traditional Jewish customs: the concern that conservatives should not assume that God's saving righteousness was still dependent on these rules and rituals and so condemn nonobservers as "beyond the pale" (vv 3–12); and the concern that the more liberal majority should not ride roughshod over these sensibilities and should appreciate how firm a hold they had on their more conservative fellows and how vulnerable that left them (vv 13–21). The balance was a difficult one to maintain between Christian liberty and love, and Paul must have been conscious of how easily the full range of liberty can lapse into legalism at one end (cf. 10:3), just as easily as it can lapse into licentiousness at the other (13:13). So he makes one final summarizing attempt to set the proper balance for any congregation where fundamental disagreements exist between members—a kind of charter of Christian liberty.

Basic is the recognition that *liberty* arises out of *faith*. The recall of this motif, so central for Paul's exposition as a whole, is no accident. For Paul's point is precisely that the "strong" have recognized (at least in the matter of foods and sabbaths) that conduct must arise directly out of and as an expression of their unconditional trust in and dependence on God, and not as a claim upon God. This is the danger which the "weak" are ever prey to, the mistake into which Paul's fellow Jews had fallen in their boastful reliance on the distinctive Jewish "works of the law" (2:17–29; 3:27–4:2). But equally, *liberty* must be conditioned by *love,* for a liberty careless of its effects on others is an expression more of self-indulgence than of faith. This is the danger which the "strong" are ever prey to, the mistake characteristic of fallen humanity at large, as indicated in 1:18–32. Here the importance of seeing faith in experiential terms, as a (usually) conscious dependence on God, and not simply as mental assent to a creedal definition, should not be lost sight of.

Basic too is the recognition that liberty means diversity, that Christian liberty is a spectrum embracing a range of options, not all of which can be held by any single person, but all of which may be held within a Christian congregation without destroying its unity. Chapter 14 is therefore the outworking in terms of conduct of Paul's understanding of the congregation as the body of Christ (12:3–8). Unless there is an acceptance along that spectrum of the different possibilities within that spectrum, there can be no real liberty. So even when Paul is addressing his remarks primarily to the "strong," he does so no doubt fully conscious of the presence of the "weak" in the same congregations, and with a view to encouraging them to accept that different practice is possible without transgressing the faith which unites them all.

22 So his summing up starts with a reminder of his opening counsel (v 1). The freedom of faith carries with it the obligation not to force that freedom on others. The more liberal can rejoice in the liberty they have in matters of personal conduct before God without having to parade that liberty before others. The liberty is no less real for not being exercised. Indeed, it only shows itself as true liberty when it restricts its full range for the sake of another.

At the same time liberty, as the individual's right to discern God's will for herself or himself, must be safeguarded. The troubled conscience of the "weak" is not the measure by which the "strong" should judge themselves so far as their own liberty is concerned (even if its outworking is conditioned by love). The freedom to reach a different opinion, even in such important matters as define the character of the faith, and still know oneself to be fully acceptable to God must not be yielded.

23 Equally it is to be accepted that the misgivings of the "weak" will result in their condemnation if they actually go ahead and eat despite such doubts. For they will not be acting "out of faith," out of their relationship with God, and so their actions will push them apart from God. This too is posed simply as a fact that "strong" as well as "weak" should take into consideration. Here however, for the first time, Paul makes it clear that what he has in mind is the act of actually eating by the weak. Thus he confirms what was implicit in his earlier talk of an actual stumble and fall (vv 13, 20, 21), of a real "hurt" (v 15), of final "destruction" (vv 15, 20): that the danger to the conservative arises not merely from seeing the liberal doing something of which the conservative disapproves but from being forced (by example and community pressure) to act against his or her convictions. Paul, in other words, has no intention of encouraging the weak to exercise undue pressure on their own behalf—to blackmail the strong by professing grief or hurt. It is not enough that the weak disapprove of the strong; Paul has in mind situations where the conservatives' trust in God is actually undermined by the action of the more liberated, their trust in God, and not just their scruples. Christian liberty must be defended against the condemnatory attitude of the weak as much as against the disdainful self-indulgence of the strong (v 3). In calling for the more liberal to condition their liberty by sensitive concern for the more conservative, Paul does not mean that they should abandon their liberty altogether. The unconditional character of faith must be allowed to come to expression in liberty; the concern for another which overrestricts liberty is a cheap love which damages faith as well. The balance of faith, liberty, and love must be maintained, however difficult.

For "everything which is not 'of faith' is sin." This is the negatively stated counterpart of love of neighbor. Whatever is not lived out of trust in God, out of the creature's dependence on the creator (which can also be expressed as "justification by faith"), puts one apart from God and within the power of sin. The echo of the indictment of 1:18–3:20 is not accidental. The threat to the believer's relationship is ever present, of once again falling into the primeval trap of acting in disregard of God, of erecting one's own judgments into instruments by which to control others (to "be as God"). The alternative to faith is sin—not as a threat but as a fact—either to live in dependence on God, or to live for something else whose distinctive power does not usually become apparent right away. This alternative lurks at both ends of Christian liberty: the sin of claiming too much freedom in matters of social conduct as well as the sin of claiming too little.

3. Christ as Exemplar (15:1–6)

Bibliography

See 14:1–15:6 *Bibliography*.

Translation

[1] *We the strong ought to support the weaknesses of those without strength, and not to please ourselves.* [2] *Let each of us[a] please his neighbor with a view to what is good, for upbuilding.* [3] *For the Christ too did not please himself; but, as it is written,*
The reproaches of those who reproach you have fallen on me.
[4] *For as much as was written beforehand[b] [c]was written[b] for our instruction, in order that through patience and through[d] the comfort of the scriptures we might*

hold fast hope.^e ⁵*May the God of patience and of comfort give you to live in harmony among yourselves in accordance with Christ Jesus,* ⁶*in order that with one mind and with one voice you might glorify the God and Father of our Lord Jesus Christ.*

Notes

ᵃThe reading ὑμῶν (F G P etc.) presumably was introduced at an early stage on the assumption that Paul was addressing his exhortation only to his readers.

ᵇThe omission of the prefix προ- by B and one or two other witnesses was probably accidental, or the result of confusion with the following ἐγράφη. It is no surprise that A Ψ and others read προεγράφη in the second instance.

ᶜThe insertion of πάντα by B P Ψ and others is a good example of an improving elaboration.

ᵈMany MSS omit the second διά, but the stronger weight lies with its inclusion (א A B C etc.); probably it was omitted by those who thought that Paul wanted both phrases to depend on τῶν γραφῶν: "through the patience and comfort of the scriptures."

ᵉB's insertion of another τῆς παρακλήσεως makes the sequence much too repetitive.

Form and Structure

The chapter break is poorly located in this instance, since 15:1–6 clearly continues the theme of chap. 14. The effect is (1) to summarize the primary responsibility of "the strong," an emphasis which brackets the whole discussion (14:1; 15:1–2), (2) by echoing the guiding principle of love of neighbor (15:2; 13:8–10), (3) by referring at last explicitly to Christ as example (15:3), (4) with the appropriate undergirding of a scripture understood in reference to Christ (15:3), (5) on the assumption that it is precisely the function of scripture to provide such encouragement (15:4). The emphasis on positive consideration for others (15:5) provides the necessary structural contrast to the presumption of both Jew and Gentile attacked both in the opening indictment and subsequently (11:18–20; 12:16). The "prayer wish" of vv 5–6, with its liturgical features, marks the end of a sequence of thought (Zeller). The parallel with Gal 6:2 suggests that Paul is drawing on a familiar line of parenesis:

Gal 6:2	Rom. 15:1, 3, 5
ἀλλήλων τὰ βάρη βαστάζετε	τὰ ἀσθενήματα τῶν ἀδυνάτων βαστάζειν
καὶ οὕτως ἀναπληρώσετε	γὰρ ὁ Χριστὸς οὐχ ἑαυτῷ ἤρεσεν
τὸν νόμον τοῦ Χριστοῦ	· · · κατὰ Χριστὸν Ἰησοῦν

Michel also notes the gradation of titles in vv 3–6: "the Christ," "Christ Jesus," "our Lord Jesus Christ."

Comment

1 ὀφείλομεν δὲ ἡμεῖς οἱ δυνατοὶ τὰ ἀσθενήματα τῶν ἀδυνάτων βαστάζειν, "we, the strong, ought to support the weaknesses of those without strength." For ὀφείλω + infinitive in the sense "be obligated," so "must, ought," much the most common NT usage, see BGD, ὀφείλω 2αβ, TDNT 5:559–64. Such a sense of obligation can arise for Paul from more general considerations (cf. 1 Cor 11:7, 10; 2 Cor 12:14), but here it is clearly tied to the immediate

thought of what Christ has done and the character of it (v 3; cf. 14:15); see also 15:27. The ἡμεῖς is no doubt deliberate, emphasizing (as the previous first person plurals had not [14:7–8, 10, 12, 13, 19]) Paul's stance as one of "the strong." That Paul is referring specifically to those greeted in chap. 16 is possible (Wilckens), but the appeal probably has in view the too confident gentile Christians in general (cf. 11:18; 12:3, 16). On this issue Paul the Jew feels more at one with the gentile (and more liberated Jewish) believers than with the majority(?) of the Jewish Christians.

οἱ δυνατοί = "powerful people" would be a familiar usage in Greek (BGD), including the regular usage in the historical books of the OT/LXX = "the mighty men" (1 Sam 2:10; 17:51; 2 Sam 1:25, 27; 10:7; 16:6; etc.; so also 1 Macc 4:3; Acts 25:5; 1 Cor 1:26). The implication is of a strength or power which gives prominence and the possibility of dominating others. Hence the thought of greater responsibility (cf. Wisd Sol 6:6—a parallel which suggests a certain continuity of thought with 13:1–7). For Paul, of course, the thought is not of physical strength, but the strength of superior knowledge and understanding of how God's grace works (cf. 2 Cor 12:10; 13:9). This does not, however, imply a claim to a particular charismatic endowment (cf. Michel), simply an appreciation of what Paul regards as the basic character of the gospel and of faith.

ἀσθένημα, "weakness" is a little used word, and only here in biblical Greek; "failing" (RSV, NIV) is unnecessarily pejorative. ἀδύνατος, "one who has no ability, capacity or strength," "one who is incapable or incompetent" (*TDNT* 2:285). As almost all agree, βαστάζειν here must be taken in the sense "carry, bear, support." The sense "bear patiently, endure, put up with" is certainly possible (BGD; RSV, NIV, NJB; Kirk, Barrett, Black), and the ambiguity of the word may include this sense. But the meaning here should not be confined to the latter. To reduce this final exhortation merely to a call for tolerance would be too much of an anticlimax following the strong counsel of 14:13–21 (NEB is better, "accept as our own burden"; see particularly Schlatter, Gaugler, and Cranfield). In view of Matt 8:17 an allusion to Isa 53:4 may be present (Michel); βαστάζειν became more prominent in the later translations of the OT and is used by Aquila in Isa 53:11 (see also SH). The parallel with Gal 6:2 suggests further that Paul made the double tie-up between Isa 53:4, Christ's own ministry as the servant of Yahweh, and the obligation on the followers of Jesus to "bear one another's burdens" (cf. Wilckens; see further *Form and Structure*).

καὶ μὴ ἑαυτοῖς ἀρέσκειν, "and not to please ourselves." For ἀρέσκω see on 8:8. It is characteristic of "the mighty" of this world, of course, that they can simply "please themselves" (cf. *T. Mos.* 7.4). The contrast here probably echoes teaching of Jesus such as we find in Mark 8:34–36 pars. and particularly 10:42–45 pars., and is characteristic of Paul (1 Cor 10:24; 10:33–11:1; 13:5; Phil 2:4, 21). See further Kleinknecht, *Gerechtfertigte*, 357–63.

2 ἕκαστος ἡμῶν τῷ πλησίον ἀρεσκέτω εἰς τὸ ἀγαθὸν πρὸς οἰκοδομήν, "let each of us please his neighbor with a view to what is good, for upbuilding." The emphasis on the mutual responsibility of each (ἕκαστος) is typical of Paul and follows from his concept of the congregation as a charismatic community (Käsemann); cf. 12:3–6 and 1 Cor 12, particularly vv 7, 25. The use of πλησίον no doubt deliberately recalls the use of Lev 19:18 in 13:9–10 (these, together with the citation of Lev 19:18 in Gal 5:14, are the only occasions on which Paul uses πλησίον; though also in Eph 4:25). Thus the impression is strengthened that here too Paul is consciously drawing his inspiration from the teaching (as well as example [v 3]) of Jesus. See further on 13:9.

Elsewhere Paul regards mere "man pleasing" as highly undesirable (Gal 1:10; Col 3:22; 1 Thess 2:4; also Eph 6:6; see also on 8:8). Hence the qualification of the double purpose phrases (εἰς . . . πρός . . .); cf. particularly 1 Cor 10:33. As usual in Romans ἀγαθός is chosen for its generality (cf. particularly 2:10; 5:7; 9:11; 12:9, 21; 13:3; 14:16), not just eschatological good (8:28), but what people of good will would widely commend as "good" (εἰς τὸ ἀγαθόν—13:4; 16:19). For οἰκοδομή see on 14:19. The phrase does not have the individual as such in view ("for his edification") but, as the metaphor implies, the growth to maturity of the whole congregation (πρὸς οἰκοδομήν —1 Cor 14:12, 26; Eph 4:29; εἰς οἰκοδομήν—2 Cor 10:8; 13:10; Eph 4:12, 16); or more precisely, the growth to maturity of the weaker brother *as part of* the body of Christ (cf. 1 Cor 14:4); cf. Fitzmyer, NEB, NJB.

3 καὶ γὰρ ὁ Χριστὸς οὐχ ἑαυτῷ ἤρεσεν, "for the Christ too did not please himself." The definite article with Χριστός should be given weight—"the Christ," titular significance, as in v 7 (Michel, Cranfield; see further on 14:18). For ἑαυτῷ ἀρέσκειν see on 15:1. The appeal is not to incarnation (rightly Lietzmann) but primarily to Christ's denying himself by submission to the cross (2 Cor 8:9; Phil 2:5–8; see below on the use of Ps 69:19; cf. 1 Thess 1:6; 2:14; 1 Pet 2:21), but the close parallel with 1 Cor 10:23–11:1 (Cranfield) suggests that the model of Christ's whole ministry (his earlier ministry consistent with and climaxed by his passion; cf. Mark 10:43–45; John 13:1–15) may also be in view (Schulz, *Nachfolgen*, 280, n. 95); hence the echoes of the Jesus tradition in 14:13–18 and 15:1–2.

ἀλλὰ καθὼς γέγραπται, "but as it is written"; see on 1:17. The question of why Paul cites an OT passage rather than an example from the Jesus tradition can certainly not be answered by inferring that such tradition was unknown either to Paul or to the Roman churches: churches which did not cherish at least a substantial portion of the Jesus tradition as an integral part of their founding tradition, which gave them their distinctive identity, are hardly conceivable; and the layering and diverse patterning of the Synoptic tradition points firmly in the same direction. We must deduce rather that the living quality of the Jesus tradition made allusion easier and more effective than formal quotation (see further on 12:14); and/or that at this stage a formal quotation from the (Jewish) scriptures could be expected to carry more weight, particularly if the significance of what Jesus actually did teach on the issue of clean and unclean was not entirely agreed (see on 14:14).

οἱ ὀνειδισμοὶ τῶν ὀνειδιζόντων σε ἐπέπεσαν ἐπ' ἐμέ, "the reproaches of those who reproach you have fallen on me." The quotation is verbatim from the LXX of Ps 69:9 [LXX 68:10]. The psalm is one of the most powerful cries of personal distress in the Psalter, and for that very reason would hardly commend itself to Jewish thought as messianic in character. Just as naturally, however, the earliest Christians scanning the scriptures for prefigurations of what had happened to the Messiah in the event found this psalm to become

luminous with meaning in the light of Jesus' suffering and death. After Pss
2, 22, 110, and 118, it is about the most quoted psalm in the NT (see on
11:9–10)—the most explicit allusions usually with direct reference to Christ's
passion and the events surrounding it (Mark 15:23, 36 pars.; John 2:17; 15:25;
19:28–29; Acts 1:20). Despite Hanson, it is highly unlikely that Paul or his
Roman audiences would intend or understand such usage as words spoken
by the preexistent Christ (*Interpretation*, 115; cf. Harrisville), in reference to
whom the past tense would have been meaningless; a typological interpretation
(the suffering righteous as type of the suffering Jesus [Lagrange]) is much
more natural.

The citation may be more apposite than is generally perceived. In the
psalm, one devoted to the Lord laments his affliction at the hands not only
of his enemies, but also, it would appear, of his own people and kinsfolk
(69:8, 28). Implied therefore is the sort of sharp differences (over what loyalty
to God and to covenant obligations involved) which Paul knew all too well,
which he envisaged among the Roman Christians, and which he saw bound
up with Jesus' own ministry (the echo of Mark 7:15 in 14:14, 20) and in his
death (Gal 3:13). Perhaps implicit therefore is the thought that the reproaches
directed against God (σέ [against SH]) included those which traditionalist
Jews leveled against the thought that God was equally God of the Gentiles
as of the Jews, and that it was just these reproaches which fell on Jesus,
since it was precisely by such teaching (Mark 7:15) and by his death (Gal
3:13) that the way had been opened up to the Gentiles to receive "the blessing
of Abraham" solely by faith in this Christ (Gal 3:14).

4 ὅσα γὰρ προεγράφη, εἰς τὴν ἡμετέραν διδασκαλίαν ἐγράφη, "for as much
as was written beforehand was written for our instruction." The explanation
is not in addition to v 3 but provides the larger principle which justifies the
use just made of scripture; cf. 4:23–24; 1 Cor 9:10; 10:11 (Käsemann). The
ὅσα of course denotes all scripture. In προεγράφη the thought is very similar
to the προεπηγγείλατο of 1:2 (cf. 3:21). διδασκαλία, "teaching, instruction,"
features little in the early Pauline correspondence (elsewhere in the early
Paulines only at 12:7), but becomes a key word in the Pastorals (15 out of
21 occurrences in the NT). Underlying both 2 Tim 3:16 (πρὸς διδασκαλίαν)
and here may be a rabbinic-type expression לְלַמֵּד; cf. *b. Sanh.* 73a (BGD,
διδασκαλία; see further Michel, n.13). The thought is very close to that of
Philo, *Abr.* 4. The sense of scripture as the living word of God is strong
here (cf. Gaugler).

ἵνα διὰ τῆς ὑπομονῆς καὶ διὰ τῆς παρακλήσεως τῶν γραφῶν τὴν ἐλπίδα ἔχωμεν,
"in order that through patience and through the comfort of the scriptures
we might hold fast hope." There is general agreement among the most recent
commentators that the two διά clauses are independent, the first διά of attendant
circumstances, the second causal (see, e.g., Käsemann, Schlier). So we could
translate "with patience and by means of the comfort . . ." It is implicit, of
course, that the patience is modeled on and inspired by that of the suffering
righteous individual (as expressed in Ps 69 and climactically by Christ), but
the comfort which stories of such patience vindicated would provide may be
said to be the more direct or immediate effect of such scriptures. For ὑπομονή
see on 5:3. For παράκλησις see on 12:8 (Barrett's translation, "exhortation,"

has gained no support); Käsemann cites the apposite parallel of 1 Macc 12:9 (other references in Schlier). For ἐλπίς see on 4:18 and 5:4; the thought is clearly similar to that of 5:2–5 and 8:24–25. There should be no need to ask why Paul speaks of hope here (cf. Cranfield): it is fundamental to Paul's argument that the gospel's embrace of Gentile as well as Jew is the beginning of the fulfillment of Israel's eschatological hope; consequently the harmony of Jew and Gentile in the new Christian congregations is an important landmark on the way to the complete fulfillment of that hope; hence also the concluding sequence in vv 7–13 with the same climactic reference to hope. The vision of what should and will be needs to be sustained (ἔχωμεν, "hold fast," not just "hold" [Michel, Cranfield]) in order to maintain the motivation for communal harmony and the self-denial necessary for upbuilding.

5 ὁ δὲ θεὸς τῆς ὑπομονῆς καὶ τῆς παρακλήσεως δῴη ὑμῖν, "may the God of patience and of comfort give you." The form has a liturgical ring and suggests that Paul wrote with a view not only to winding up the section (see *Form and Structure*) but also to the letter's being read within the context of a congregation gathered for worship (Käsemann; cf. SH, Lietzmann). The phrases, "God of . . . ," in themselves carry a note of praise (15:13, 33; 16:20; 2 Cor 1:3; 13:11; Phil 4:9; 1 Thess 5:23; 2 Thess 3:16; Heb 13:20; 1 Pet 5:10); here repeating the words of v 4. The unique use of the optative (δῴη) is also distinctive of the "prayer wish" form (Michel, Cranfield)—2 Thess 3:16; 2 Tim 1:16, 18 (BGD, δίδωμι; BDF, §95.2); see also 15:13.

τὸ αὐτὸ φρονεῖν ἐν ἀλλήλοις, "to live in harmony among yourselves"; see on 12:16.

κατὰ Χριστὸν Ἰησοῦν, "in accordance with Christ Jesus." As the equivalent κατά phrases indicate, the phrase here probably refers primarily to the will of Christ (κατὰ κύριον—2 Cor 11:17; κατὰ πνεῦμα—Rom 8:4–5) (*TDNT* 4:669 n.18, Käsemann, Cranfield). But reference also to the example of Christ should not be dismissed so quickly as those just cited do (contrast, e.g., SH, Lagrange, Knox, T. W. Manson, Murray, Kleinknecht [363], NIV, NJB): Christ has just been evoked as an example (v 3), and the echoes of the Jesus tradition in the preceding exhortation (14:13–15, 18–19; 15:1–2) suggest conduct modeled "after Christ" in a fuller sense (see also on 6:17); Christ functions as κύριος to the believer's slave (14:4–8), but the absence of κύριος here may be significant for that very reason; and in the other similar κατά phrases the double thought of "modeled on and obedient to" seems likewise implicit (Col 2:8 follows 2:6—"as you received the traditions concerning Christ Jesus the Lord, so walk in him"; Eph 4:24—the thought, of course, is of "the new man" modeled in accordance with the image of God = Christ; cf. 13:14 and 2 Cor 3:18, 4:4, 6).

6 ἵνα ὁμοθυμαδὸν ἐν ἑνὶ στόματι δοξάζητε, "in order that with one mind and with one voice you might glorify." ὁμοθυμαδόν probably derives from the political sphere = the unanimous wish of an assembled body (as in Acts 12:20; *TDNT* 5:185; Michel cites *Ep. Arist.* 178; Philo, *Mos.* 1.72; Josephus, *Ant.* 15.277 and notes the frequent use of יחד in the DSS). In the OT it is a favorite word in Job (14 times) and in the NT of Acts (10 times); elsewhere in the NT only here; but in Paul cf. 1 Cor 1:10 and the use of τὸ αὐτὸ φρονεῖν (see on 12:16); cf. also 1 Pet 3:8. The emphasis on "mouth" as well as "mind" is important and reflects the same conviction as 10:8–10 that faith and worship must come to speech and cannot remain interior to heart or mind; cf. also *1 Clem.* 34.7. For δοξάζω see on 1:21. Once again it is not at all accidental that in this winding-up passage Paul recalls one of the key elements in the indictment of humankind and expresses his vision in terms of its complete reversal: when all, Jew and Gentile, will render God the worship which is his by right of creation, and now also of salvation (by narrowing the thought simply to the unanimity of weak and strong Schlier [cf. Leenhardt] misses the wider setting of the whole discussion). Nor is it accidental that Paul expects this unity to come to expression in *worship* rather than in unanimity of *opinion* (14:1–6).

τὸν θεὸν καὶ πατέρα τοῦ κυρίου ἡμῶν Ἰησοῦ Χριστοῦ, "the God and Father of our Lord Jesus Christ." The phrase is quite characteristic of Paul (2 Cor 1:3; 11:31; Col 1:3; also Eph 1:3, 17; 1 Pet 1:3). The clear indication that Paul thought of God as "the God of Christ" should be taken seriously (SH, Cranfield) and not weakened to a formulation like "identify God by reference to Christ [christlich]" (Zeller). Certainly Paul does identify God as the *Father* of Christ (Wilckens—"as such is he the God of patience and comfort'"); the character of the revelation of God through Jesus as Father of the one who so lived, prayed, taught, suffered, died, and rose again is a fundamental distinguishing mark of the God of Christian faith (cf. particularly 1:3–4; 5:10; 8:3, 15–17, 29, 32). But more striking is the fact that Paul speaks of God not only as the God of Christ, but also as "the *God* . . . of our *Lord* Jesus Christ" (cf. also 1 Cor 3:23—God is Christ's lord; Matt 27:46; John 20:17; Heb 1:9). Here it becomes plain that κύριος is not only a way of *identifying* Jesus with God, but also of *distinguishing* Jesus from God (see further on 1:8 and 10:9). In a somewhat dramatic, perhaps even pointed way, therefore, Paul uses the last phrase of the section to confirm the implication of the earlier verses that, at least for the purposes of this discussion, the roles of the one God and of the exalted Christ are kept distinct, with both the immediate authority of Christ and the ultimate authority of God emphasized (see on 14:3).

Explanation

1 Paul sums up the discussion of this very sensitive issue by repeating the main emphasis of the second half of the discussion (14:13–21), and indeed of the whole (14:1): that the primary responsibility is on "the strong" to bear the burden of maintaining the harmony of the community. It is assumed that "those without strength" ("the weak") are at least willing to accept "the strong" as fellow members of the congregation, otherwise the basis for such talk of mutual responsibility would be lacking. If the conservative are thus willing to restrain their condemnation of the more liberal, then it is for "the strong" to make the concessions necessary to maintain the spirit of community.

For the first time Paul gives a label to those who disagree with "the weak": they are "the strong." "The weak" are also identified afresh as "the powerless, those lacking strength." These descriptions and the talk of "the strong supporting the weaknesses of those without strength" is of course, once again, the viewpoint of "the strong." There is something slightly unnerving about the self-confidence and somewhat patronizing attitude expressed in this language, and not a little danger of its falling over into an oppressive intolerance, all the more subtle for its claim to consider others: a view or practice characterized as "weakness" is tolerated, not respected. Paul, however, would probably be aware of these dangers, since the whole thrust of his letter has been directed against the presumption of the human species which boasts of its rights and privileges (strength) over against the less fortunate (weak). His address to "the strong" in their own terms, therefore, as also his identification with them ("we who are strong"), is a way of winning their confidence in the hope of gaining a more effective response.

The thrust of his counsel is actually to commend weakness, or at least the weakness of self-denial and active love of neighbor, as the paradigm and model for Christian conduct. (1) The obligation is for the self-styled "strong" to support the weaknesses of the weak. The wording is odd: to bear up the weaknesses of the weak, not the weak in their weaknesses. In fact the Roman readership would quite likely recognize that the language has been drawn from the picture of the suffering servant in Isa 53:4, 11, as reflected also in Matt 8:17. That is to say, what is in view is not commendation of or approval for these weaknesses, but a lived-out, ready acceptance of the consequences of these weaknesses, a degree of identification with those who are weak, so that the weakness becomes theirs in the day-to-day experience of living for one another. The balance which Paul calls for, between disapproval of the attitudes, and sympathetic identification with those who hold them, is presumably modeled on the identification Christ achieved with sinful flesh with a view to its destruction (8:3).

2 (2) In v 2 Paul recalls the two great principles which, as he had already explained, must condition the liberty of the strong and govern their attitudes and conduct in relation to the weak—love of neighbor (13:8–10; 14:15), and the benefit of the congregation (14:19–21). Such self-limitation, as Christ had shown, involves living within the constraints from which they cannot escape. At the same time, Paul evidently does not expect the strong to please the weak in an undiscriminating way. What counts is not merely what the conservatives say will please them, but what is for the good and benefit of the community as a whole. Once again Paul implies that there is a giving way to the conservative which could be bad and would not benefit the church. Love of neighbor needs to be more discriminating than that.

3 (3) Above all is the example of Christ. What had been implicit in the echo of Jesus' teaching in 14:13–18, in the appeal to Christ's death "on behalf of" those same powerless ones (14:15), in the echo of the picture of the suffering servant in 15:1 and again of the command by which Jesus summed up all the law affecting personal relationships (15:2), is now brought to the fore with climactic force. The model is Christ: if he was willing to suffer misunderstanding and abuse to the extent of giving his own life, how could those who both gloried in their own strength and called Jesus Lord refuse the much less self-limitation of curbing the liberty of their conduct when it was causing their fellow Christians to fall? Greater strength means greater responsibility for others.

(4) In fact Paul here is simply working out the implications of the whole Christian understanding of "strength": God's strength manifested in the weakness of the cross (1 Cor 1:25; 2 Cor 13:4); God's power coming to perfect expression in Paul's weakness (2 Cor 12:9–10); true greatness lived out in the indignity of servitude and powerlessness of slavery (Mark 10:42–45). The message which Paul has been working out all along is implicit here too. Strength is illusory if it means claiming independence of God; only in the weakness of confessed dependence on God is there real strength. And strength as a believer is equally illusory if it means claiming independence of other believers; only in the weakness of mutual interdependence as members of one body in Christ is there the full strength of grace. The message then could be as much for the weak, or more precisely for anyone who thinks he is strong and able to discount or disregard others. Paul has no room for a piety which neglects the neighbor. Strength means not only accepting those who differ as brothers, but also a readiness to take responsibility (as Paul does here) for their right to hold these different views.

3b–4 The scriptures contribute to this strength because they show that God's purpose in salvation-history has frequently worked through weakness and suffering and that God's purpose is of sure fulfillment. So they both provide support and encouragement from the past and direct the vision beyond the immediate limitations and frustrations to the sure hope of what God will accomplish. Paul does not hesitate to describe the reason why the scriptures were written in precisely these terms: not as a source book for all sorts of information, historical or scientific, but "for our instruction," to sustain faith and renew hope. And so again the Roman congregations are reminded that all their thinking and doing must take full account of the eschatological tension between what has already been fulfilled in and through Christ and the not yet of hope.

5–6 Paul rounds off this most lengthy exhortation by praying for the harmony and oneness of mind of his readers, Jews and Gentiles, strong and weak, conservative and liberal, traditionalist and nontraditionalist, in this most divisive issue—as in all issues of great moment for the identity of the new churches and for their understanding of the gospel. By the manner of his formulation he reminds them that the patience and comfort and still more the harmony he wishes for them is not of their own doing or achieving. It is God's, and only as given by him and received from him can it be real and lasting. By adding "in accordance with Christ Jesus" he reminds them also that the mutual responsibility of loving the neighbor has Christ as the exemplar and can only be carried through as service to his lordship. It is also clear that Paul looks not merely for a tacit toleration of differences, but for a mutual acceptance which expresses itself in the common act of worship. Only so is the original failure of humankind to "glorify God" (1:21) reversed, as has now been made possible by "the God and Father of our Lord Jesus Christ," as part of his overall plan for humankind to unite all, Jew first, but also Gentile, in praise of the one God.

H. Concluding Summary: God's Mercy and Faithfulness—Jew First, but Also Gentile (15:7–13)

Bibliography

Frid, B. "Jesaja und Paulus in Röm 15:12." *BZ* 27 (1983) 237–41. **Ljungman, H.** *Pistis.* 48–54. **Nababan, A. E. S.** *Bekenntnis und Mission in Römer 14 und 15.* Ph.D., Heidelberg, 1963. **Schmithals, W.** *Römerbrief.* 95–96, 152–61. **Skehan, P. W.** "Qumran and the Present State of Old Testament Text Studies: The Masoretic Text." *JBL* 78 (1959) 21–25. **Thüsing, W.** *Per Christum.* 42–45. **Williams, S. K.** "Righteousness." 285–89. **Zeller, D.** *Juden.* 218–23.

Translation

[7] *Therefore welcome one another, as Christ also welcomed you,[a] to the glory of God.* [8] *For I declare that Christ has become[b] servant of the circumcised for the sake of God's truth, to confirm the promises of the fathers,* [9] *and the Gentiles to give praise to God for his mercy. As it is written,*

For this reason I will confess you among the Gentiles[c]
and sing praise to your name.

[10] *Furthermore it says,*

Rejoice, Gentiles, with his people.

[11] *And again,[d]*

Praise the Lord, all the Gentiles,
and let all the peoples praise[c] him.

[12] *And again Isaiah says,*

The shoot of Jesse shall come forth,
even the one who arises to rule the Gentiles;
in him the Gentiles shall hope.

[13] *May the God of hope fill[e] you with all joy and peace in believing,[f] that you may overflow[f] in hope, in the power of the Holy Spirit.*

Notes

[a] ἡμᾶς is read by B D* P and other MSS and is favored by Michel and Schlier; however, ὑμᾶς has the stronger and more diversified support, is in greater harmony with the context, and is preferred by most (Metzger). When Paul addresses "the strong" in v 1 he uses ἡμεῖς; here he is addressing the Roman church(es) as a whole (SH).

[b] The aorist γενέσθαι looks like an attempt to conform the tense to what would be the more normal usage.

[c] As might be expected, κύριε was later introduced into v 9 to conform to the complete text of Ps 17:50 LXX, and the verb in v 11b altered to ἐπαινέσατε to conform to Ps 116:1.

[d] Another typical conforming improvement is the insertion of λέγει to match vv 10 and 12.

[e] The reading πληροφορῆσαι . . . ἐν) πάσῃ χαρᾷ καὶ εἰρήνῃ (B F G) probably reflects an instinctive and understandable attempt to heighten the plerophoric language even further (similar tendency in 15:29 and Col 4:12); see also Lietzmann and Cranfield.

[f] Omission of one or other of the two ἐ- . . . -ευ̂ευ phrases (first by D F G, second by B) was presumably due to haplography (see also Cranfield, Wilckens).

Form and Structure

This coda is evidently intended to round off the body of the letter, both the theological treatise and the resulting parenesis, and to link the argument of the letter into the more personal concerns to follow (against Schenke—14:1–15:13 + 16:3–20 to Ephesus; and Schmithals—letter A = 1:1–11:36 + 15:8–13; see already Lietzmann, 119, and Wilckens, 3:104). Thus the opening call for mutual consideration picks up the major theme of 14:1–15:6, with Christ again presented as the pattern to be followed (vv 7–8), and the final triple emphasis on "hope" (vv 12–13) picks up the same emphasis in v 4 (Lietzmann). But Paul's main concern is to underline once more the twin themes of Christ as guaranteeing both the continuity of God's purpose to the circumcised and faithfulness of God to his covenant promises (v 8), and of Christ as the one through whom God has opened these promises to the Gentiles (vv 9–12). The vocabulary of vv 8–9 is particularly carefully chosen to tie together central themes in the whole discussion: ὑπὲρ ἀληθείας θεοῦ—the truth (= faithfulness) of God abused by both Gentile and Jew (1:18, 25; 2:8; 3:7) has thus been vindicated; "the promise to the fathers"—2:25–29; 4:9–22; 9:4, 8–9; God's mercy to Gentiles—9:15–18, 23; 11:30–32; and thus the primal failure to glorify God (1:21) is reversed.

Typical too of Paul the Jew called to be apostle to the Gentiles is the closing catena of scriptures (cf. Fitzmyer, "4QTestimonia," 66), undergirding his controversial claims as apostle by appealing to the sacred writings of his people (1:1–2). It is possible that he is drawing on a string of OT texts already grouped together thematically, which would explain why they do not wholly reflect the double emphasis of vv 8–9a (Wilckens), but just as likely that Paul held over these texts from the collection used so effectively in chaps. 9–11 precisely with a view to bracketing the whole parenetic section (12:1–15:6) with OT material which tied the intervening section more tightly to the overall thrust of the whole letter. Noteworthy is the success in drawing from all three parts of the OT (Law, Prophets, Writings), and the use of so many different "praise" words—ἐξομολογεῖσθαι, ψάλλειν, εὐφραίνεσθαι, αἰνεῖν, and ἐπαινεῖν (Michel). Heil's description of "these stunning scriptural promises," "these electrifying scriptural invitations" is somewhat "over the top."

Comment

7 διὸ προσλαμβάνεσθε ἀλλήλους, "therefore welcome one another." The διό sums up and indicates the conclusion to be drawn from the preceding discussion. The προσλαμβάνεσθε (see on 14:1) indicates that 14:1–15:6 is particularly in view; the ἀλλήλους indicates that Paul enlarges his appeal to one of mutual acceptance (not just of weak by strong [14:1]); and what follows indicates that Paul is in fact broadening out his perspective to take in the main thrust of the whole letter, both the special priority and privilege of the Jews (v 8 [Cranfield]) and the inclusion of the Gentiles within the covenant promise (vv 9–12). This broadening out should occasion no "surprise" (Michel, 442), nor that the tension and debates of 14:1–15:6 disappear (Käsemann). The point is not simply to confirm that the tension between "weak" and "strong" was in large part between Jew and Gentile (as is now generally recognized), but also to confirm that the specific disagreements regarding diet and days were particular expressions of the larger issue of how Gentiles were to be regarded as heirs of the covenant and how this strange new hybrid community was to understand and identify itself (cf. Wilckens; see further on 12:1–15:13 *Introduction* and on 14:2). That Paul has in view *mutual* acceptance among those *continuing* to maintain *different* praxis (14:3–6, 23) tells against Watson's thesis that Paul's objective was "to convert the Jewish Christian congregation [*sic*] to Paulinism" (*Paul*, 97–98; see further *Introduction* §3.3). That mutual welcome to the common meal is particularly in view is possible (Michel, Black).

καθὼς καὶ ὁ Χριστὸς προσελάβετο ὑμᾶς, "as the Christ also welcomed you." Some sort of comparison is indicated, otherwise a different conjunction would have been chosen (against Käsemann, Cranfield). What Paul has in mind is not simply the fact of Christ's acceptance, but the manner of it (διάκονος— v 8): it is precisely the humbling of oneself to a position where one's own opinions do not count and may not be thrust on another (one's master!), which both weak and strong, Gentile and Jew, need to practice. Χριστός is again titular (see on 15:3). The use of "Christ" as the subject of προσελάβετο here, whereas "God" was the subject in 14:3, reflects the ambiguity involved in the κύριος title for Christ (see on 14:3 and 15:6).

εἰς δόξαν τοῦ θεοῦ, "to the glory of God." The phrase has a liturgical ring (Michel—3:7; 1 Cor 10:31; 2 Cor 4:15; Phil 1:11; 2:11); or, perhaps more precisely, it is a more literary and syntactical form of the acclamation, "Praise/glory be to God" (Luke 2:14; 19:38; Rom 11:36; Gal 1:5; Phil 4:20; *1 Clem.* 20.12; 50.7; cf. Rom 4:20; see further BGD, δόξα 3). For δόξα θεοῦ see on 1:21 and 3:23. The phrase can go either with the main clause (Cranfield, Wilckens) or with the καθώς clause (e.g., SH, Schmidt). In terms of the overall argument the latter makes better sense: Christ, the second man (5:12–21), has reversed the damage done by the first (1:23); but the former would underscore the importance of mutual acceptance among believers for that reversal to be complete. Would Paul want to choose between these alternatives (cf. Barrett)?

8 λέγω γάρ, "for I declare"—"maintain, declare, proclaim" (BGD, λέγω II.1e), "a solemn doctrinal declaration" (Cranfield; cf. Michel and Käsemann).

Χριστὸν διάκονον γεγενῆσθαι περιτομῆς ὑπὲρ ἀληθείας θεοῦ, "Christ has become servant of the circumcised for the sake of God's truth." If the definite article with Χριστός is deliberate in v 7, its absence is probably equally so here: it is "Christ" (the proper name), he who has shown himself to be far more than simply the Jewish Messiah, who became "servant of circumcision"; to say that Jesus as "the Messiah" acted for the Jews would seem to be unnecessarily tautologous. The purpose is to focus on the person rather than on the people as the one in and through whom fulfillment of covenant promise and gentile incoming have been made possible (cf. Zeller, *Juden*, 220–21). διάκονος has its usual meaning of "servant"; cf. particularly 2 Cor 3:6. In view of the echoes of the Jesus tradition in the preceding section and the allusion to Christ's self-denial in v 3 (see on 15:3), it is not at all improbable that Paul has in mind the tradition of Mark 10:43–45 (Michel, Cranfield): Christ as the model for service to one's brothers and sisters; the fact that this is the only occasion in which Paul speaks of Christ as διάκονος (apart from the very different Gal 2:17) may also suggest that he is drawing on a particular tradition and not a general line of exhortation. As in 3:30 περιτομή means "the circumcised"—the Jewish people identified by one of their most distinctive features. It would occasion no surprise that after focusing so much on the Jewish distinctives of food laws and holy days Paul reverts once again to the other striking identity marker of the diaspora Jew, circumcision (see on 2:25). The use of the perfect tense (γεγενῆσθαι) must mean that Paul intends to describe Jesus as "servant of the circumcised" not merely during his earthly ministry (cf. particularly Gal 4:4), but as still so (Lietzmann, Barrett, Cranfield, Wilckens), referring not simply to the continuing result of his time on earth (Käsemann). So presumably his ministry (almost exclusively to the Jews; cf. Matt 15:24) and death are in view (as again the echo of Mark 10:43–45 would imply), but also Jesus in his exaltation (Schlier). The priority of the Jews is thus underlined not simply as a temporary factor now no longer operative (as Williams's alternative rendering, "servant *from* the Jews" ["Righteousness," 286–88] could imply), but as a factor which continues to shape the purpose of God—"Jew first and also Gentile" (see on 1:16; cf. SH; Ljungman, 50–52; Wilckens). For ἀλήθεια θεοῦ, here more or less equivalent to "God's covenant faithfulness" (Käsemann, Cranfield, Schlier) see on 3:4 and 3:7. Significantly it is God's faithfulness (ἀλήθεια = πίστις) which, if anything, in this final summary which rounds off the body of the letter, is given more attention than human faith (v 13); this gives added support to the suggestion that ἐκ πίστεως in 1:17 includes the thought of God's faithfulness (see on 1:17), since it reinforces the bracketing effect of 1:16–17 and 15:7–13 (see also on 15:11).

εἰς τὸ βεβαιῶσαι τὰς ἐπαγγελίας τῶν πατέρων, "to confirm the promises of the fathers." βεβαιόω has the basic sense of "make firm" (*TDNT* 1:601) and so can mean "make good one's word" (Lysias 20.32; LSJ), "prove the promises reliable, fulfill them" (BGD, citing Polybius 3.111.10, Diodorus Siculus 1.5.3 and Priene inscription 123.9). The sense "fulfill" is also preferred by Michel and Käsemann. But the regular technical usage common in the papyri, "make firm" = guarantee (MM), should not be ignored in view of 4:16 (εἰς τὸ εἶναι βεβαίαν τὴν ἐπαγγελίαν) and 11:29. The issue is tied up with the question of how v 9 relates syntactically to v 8: does Paul think of the promises as "fulfilled" in the extension of Abraham's promised blessing to the Gentiles (Gal 3:14, 22), or as "guaranteed" for the bulk of the Jews despite their current unbelief? For ἐπαγγελίαι τῶν πατέρων see on 4:3 and 9:4. Thought and language here are close to that of 2 Cor 1:20–21.

9 τὰ δὲ ἔθνη ὑπὲρ ἐλέους δοξάσαι τὸν θεόν, "and the Gentiles to give glory to God for his mercy." The problem of how to relate this clause syntactically to v 8 has not been finally resolved. In terms of grammatical structure the most natural way is to see it as directly dependent on the opening λέγω of v 8 and so parallel but adversative to v 8—

> I declare that Christ became a servant of circumcision for the
> truth of God . . . but that the Gentiles glorify God for his mercy—

also keeping the two ὑπέρ phrases in parallel; see particularly the careful argument of Cranfield; also Lagrange; Zeller, *Juden*, 218–19; and Wilckens. But the resulting thought does not hang together very coherently: Cranfield has to envisage a double ellipsis in both v 8 and v 9, and Wilckens tries to solve the problem by suggesting that v 8 may stem from Jewish-Christian tradition which Paul takes over but completes with a critical twist in the adversative formulation of v 9. The problem in both cases is that reading δέ as a strong adversative here drives a wedge between "the promises of the fathers" and the acceptability of the Gentiles to God, and this seems antithetical to everything Paul has so far argued: 4:16—"to make firm the promise to *all* the seed"; 9:8—the children of the promise as Abraham's seed (see particularly Schmidt—δέ, "and so"; RSV, NEB, NIV, and NJB all take v 9 as a purpose clause conjoint with the last clause of v 8). Relevant also is Michel's observation that ἀλήθεια and ἔλεος correspond to אֱמֶת וְחֶסֶד (a regular OT combination in reference to God; BDB, חֶסֶד II.2) and function more or less as a hendiadys (cf. John 1:14, 17); Paul would be unlikely to set them over against each other (Schlatter; against SH; to describe the reference to these motifs as "merely ornamental" [Lietzmann] betrays a failure to appreciate the chief thrust of the epistle; see also on 15:11). Above all Paul's whole point is that Christ became servant of the circumcised *not* with a view to their salvation alone, but to confirm *both* phases of God's saving purpose: to Jew first but also to Gentile (cf. Nabadan, 115–18). Consequently the translation should not be framed in such a way as to exclude this line of thought. Rather we should allow the translation to express the ambiguity and lack of clear connection. Where Paul has left his Greek somewhat obscure it is sound exegesis to clarify the range of possible meanings he might have had in view, but not to tie the reader down to a firm either-or choice.

ἔθνος appears again for the first time since 11:25, confirming the fundamental role of the mission to the Gentiles, and thus both recalling and summing up the earlier stages of the argument in chaps. 2–4 (2:14, 24; 3:29; 4:17–18) and chaps. 9–11 (9:24, 30; 10:19; 11:11–13, 25) and preparing for the transition back to his travel plans (1:5, 13; 15:16, 18, 27; 16:4); the word is used six times in the following four verses (see also on 1:5). ἔλεος likewise recalls one of the principal motifs in chaps. 9–11 (9:15–16, 18, 23; 11:30–32). And δοξάζω links with both the initial indictment (1:21) and the previous climaxes at 8:30 and 15:6. Harrisville is hardly justified in claiming that Paul here "comes as close to asserting the unity of Christ with God as he ever will"; cf. after all 1:7; 1 Cor 8:6; and 2 Cor 5:19.

καθὼς γέγραπται, "as it is written"; see on 1:17 (introducing a catena of OT quotations, as in 3:10 and 11:8). The following quotations (vv 9–12) elaborate principally the latter theme of vv 8–9a, but that simply underlines the fact that Paul has broadened out the whole discussion from the particular issue of 14:1–15:6 to the overall theme of the letter: the inclusion of the Gentiles within the promises to his people. To that extent Käsemann is correct in stressing that the whole line of thought is an expression of justification by faith, so long as the implication is not obscured that justification by faith here, as throughout the letter, has in view (in Käsemann's own words) "the acceptance of the Gentiles as an eschatological miracle."

διὰ τοῦτο ἐξομολογήσομαί σοι ἐν ἔθνεσιν καὶ τῷ ὀνόματί σου ψαλῶ, "for this reason I will confess you among the Gentiles and sing praise to your name." The quotation is verbatim from the LXX of Ps 18:49 [LXX 17:50] = 2 Sam

22:50, with the exception that κύριε (following ἔθνεσιν) is omitted. Presumably it is significant that the verse does not necessarily envisage the Gentiles themselves joining in the praise. The implication is either that the passage is being read messianically, as words which express the gentile outreach of the mission set in motion by Christ (so most; hence the omission of the κύριε); or that these are the words of the devout Jew (David) foreshadowing the situation of the diaspora Jew, and now particularly of the Jewish Christian. This latter seems to make better sense since it would give the order: David (v 9), Gentiles (vv 10–11), both (v 12) (Michel). Or indeed, if ἐν ἔθνεσιν could be taken to include both Jew and Gentile in the praise, this first quotation would then serve as a heading (*Überschrift*) for the complete catena (Schlier). For ἐξομολογέω see on 14:11. On ψάλλω see BGD.

10 καὶ πάλιν λέγει, "furthermore it says." καὶ πάλιν occurs frequently in a series connecting things which are similar, and, in Christian literature, linking a series of scriptural quotations (BGD, πάλιν 3), reflecting also Jewish usage (Str-B 3:314); in Paul also 1 Cor 3:20. The implied subject of λέγει is probably γραφή (4:3; 9:17; 10:11; 11:2).

εὐφράνθητε, ἔθνη, μετὰ τοῦ λαοῦ αὐτοῦ, "rejoice, Gentiles, with his people." The quotation is verbatim from the LXX of Deut 32:43, the last verse of the song of Moses. But the LXX at this point is markedly different from the MT: in place of the four (half-)lines of the MT we have eight lines in Greek (mainly by addition of lines calling for heavenly rejoicing as well; hence also the quotation in Heb 1:6); more important, however, is the transformation of the equivalent Hebrew line—

Praise his people, O you nations (RSV)—

(though the Greek phrase does raise the question as to whether the עמו is original; see further Lagrange, and Skehan [21–22]). Whatever the facts of the matter on this point, the verse's original Hebrew was clearly intended as a strong promise of God's covenant faithfulness to his people, with more than a hint of the "us/them, God's people/others" attitude ("he avenges the blood of his servants, and takes vengeance on his adversaries, and makes expiation for the land of his people" [RSV]). The expansion of the Greek allows not only a much more universal perspective, but the crucial reading μετὰ τοῦ λαοῦ αὐτοῦ transforms a potentially very hostile meaning into one much more sympathetic to the Gentiles. This is only hinted at in the LXX, which retains all the threatening language of the Hebrew, but would make it less offensive in a diaspora context. But it enables Paul to lift out this single line and to use it as an expression of his own theology, that in accordance with God's original purpose and promise the covenant made to Israel is now open to all who believe.

εὐφραίνω is little used by Paul (two out of the three uses occur in OT quotations—Gal 4:27 and here; the only other reference is 2 Cor 2:2). The note of eschatological rejoicing is present in Deut 32:43 (as in Ps 96 [LXX 95]:11; Isa 44:23; 49:13; as also in Rev 12:12 and 18:20) and reenforces the implication that the final events are being fulfilled in the conversion of the Gentiles (cf. *TDNT* 2:774–75).

11 καὶ πάλιν, "and again"; see on 15:10. The following quotation is only slightly modified from the LXX of Ps 117 [LXX 116]:1:

Romans: αἰνεῖτε, πάντα τὰ ἔθνη, τὸν κύριον καὶ ἐπαινεσάτωσαν αὐτὸν πάντες οἱ λαοί.
Psalms: αἰνεῖτε τὸν κύριον, πάντα τὰ ἔθνη,   ἐπαινέσατε   αὐτόν, πάντες οἱ λαοί.

The Greek is a close rendering of the Hebrew. Although the psalm is very brief (only two verses) it is noticeable that the reason given for the praise is God's steadfast love (חֶסֶד / ἔλεος) "to us" and faithfulness (אֱמֶת / ἀλήθεια) "for ever." Awareness of the OT quotations he was going to use may well have influenced Paul's choice of language in vv 8–9a (see on 15:8). The point once again is that Gentiles can praise God for his "mercy and faithfulness" because it is extended to them, without weakening its enduring validity to Israel.

This is the only time Paul uses these verbs. As usual in such an OT quotation κύριος = God.

12 καὶ πάλιν Ἡσαΐας λέγει, "and again Isaiah says." See on 15:10. The following quotation is highly suitable as the climax to the catena, but Paul would probably have been pleased to be able to conclude with his favorite prophet—explicitly named more often than anyone else (9:27, 29; 10:16, 20; see also on chaps. 9–11 *Introduction*).

ἔσται ἡ ῥίζα τοῦ Ἰεσσαὶ καὶ ὁ ἀνιστάμενος ἄρχειν ἐθνῶν, ἐπ᾽ αὐτῷ ἔθνη ἐλπιοῦσιν, "the shoot of Jesse shall come forth, even the one who arises to rule the Gentiles; in him the Gentiles shall hope" (cf. Frid). The quotation is verbatim from the LXX of Isa 11:10 without the opening phrase ἐν τῇ ἡμέρᾳ ἐκείνῃ, which Paul may have preferred to reserve for the final day of judgment (cf. 2:5, 16; 13:12; 1 Cor 1:8; 3:13; 5:5; etc.). The LXX is different from the Hebrew, but can be regarded as an acceptable paraphrase which does not significantly alter the eschatological prospect of universal peace held out by Isaiah (11:6–10). Michel notes that Isa 11:10 was part of the Passover readings.

The language of the LXX lent itself to Christian interpretation. The "root or shoot (ῥίζα can be taken both ways = the offshoot of an established plant which becomes the root of a new plant) of Jesse" was already established as a title for the royal Messiah (Isa 11:1–5; Sir 47:22; also Rev 5:5; 22:16; cf. Jer 23:5; 33:15; 4QPat 3–4; 4QFlor 1:11; see further *TDNT* 6:986–87, 988). ἀνίστημι can mean simply "arise" (Cranfield; cf. 1 Cor 10:7), but since it occurs so frequently in reference to the resurrection (not least in the passion predictions of the Gospels; also Acts 17:3 and 1 Thess 4:14; cf. the only other references in the Pauline corpus [1 Thess 4:16; Eph 5:14]), it would be surprising if Paul did not have in mind the double reference (cf. particularly Acts 3:22, 26; 7:37) (so Käsemann, Schlier, Wilckens). The final ἐλπίζω enables Paul to turn the slightly more threatening ἄρχειν (cf. Isa 11:4b) to more positive sense. One elaboration of the messianic promise looked for God's vindication of Israel to include the destruction of the Gentiles (Zeller cites appropriately Pss 2:8–9; 72:8–9; 110:1; and *Pss. Sol.* 17.30; see further the references listed by Sanders, *Jesus*, 214; also 11QPs in Hengel, *Judaism*, 1:176–77); likewise the implication of the Hebrew that the Gentiles would come to Jerusalem (the usual Jewish expectation; cf. again Sanders, *Jesus*, 214; see on 9:26) has been reversed in the outreach of the gentile mission. In both cases Israel's typical covenant hope has been transformed.

13 ὁ δὲ θεὸς τῆς ἐλπίδος, "the God of hope." For the genitive construction see on 15:5; for ἐλπίς see on 4:18 and 5:4 (and Knox—"the heart of the epistle and this benediction." As in v 5 the thought is of the God who gives hope (Cranfield, Wilckens); however, the thought of God as the object of hope need hardly be excluded (Murray).

πληρώσαι ὑμᾶς πάσης χαρᾶς καὶ εἰρήνης ἐν τῷ πιστεύειν, "fill you with all joy and peace in believing." πληρώσαι is aorist optative (BDF, §85); see also δῴη in 15:5. For χαρὰ καὶ εἰρήνη ("two sisters" [Michel]) see on 14:17. Käsemann is correct to object to narrowing εἰρήνη here to "peace of soul" (*TDNT* 2:412): the social dimension ("well-being in corporate harmony") cannot be excluded (see on 1:7) and is particularly important here. The final phrase (ἐν τῷ πιστεύειν) is important: not as a scholastic affirmation that joy and peace can follow only from assent to dogma; and not just as underscoring the fact that harmonious unity is possible within mixed churches only when it is firmly recalled that the common ground and only necessary common ground is faith; but also as reminding his readers that openness to God and unreserved reliance on God is the fundamental presupposition of all human good (the double thrust of the whole letter); see also on 15:8.

εἰς τὸ περισσεύειν ὑμᾶς ἐν τῇ ἐλπίδι, "that you may overflow in hope." For περισσεύειν see on 3:7 and 5:15, and for ἐλπίς again on 4:18 and 5:4. "The verbs πληροῦν and περισσεύειν show that Paul with his words about the dispute between the 'strong' and 'weak' does not want a leveling of Christianity, or a balance of opposites, but 'upbuilding,' so a community in which each may take the other along with him *forwards*, to the complete freedom of the children of God, into the new world of hope" (Schmidt).

ἐν δυνάμει πνεύματος ἁγίου, "in the power of the Holy Spirit." As in 14:17 and 15:16, the ἐν is both locative and instrumental. For δύναμις as divine power see on 1:16, and for πνεῦμα ἅγιον see on 5:5. The two concepts are close associates (1:4; 15:19; 1 Cor 2:4; 12:9–10; 15:43–44; 2 Cor 6:6–7; Gal 3:5; Eph 3:16; 1 Thess 1:5; 2 Tim 1:7; cf. Luke 1:17, 35; 4:14; Acts 1:8; 6:5/8; 10:38; Heb 2:4; 6:5–6); cf. 14:17 with 1 Cor 4:20. In fact δύναμις (τοῦ θεοῦ), πνεῦμα, and also χάρις ("grace") all overlap substantially in meaning in Paul's vocabulary and usage (cf. Michel, Schlier).

Explanation

7 As so often, by picking up the language of the adjoining section, Paul succeeds in linking the concerns of the preceding paragraph into what follows, while shifting the focus or theme of the discussion (welcome—14:1, 3, 15:7; glorify/glory—15:6, 7, 9). Here the call to "welcome one another" echoes 14:1, but now as an exhortation to *all*, not just to the "strong" to welcome the "weak." The importance of this seeming slight change should not be lost sight of. For it means that after putting so much stress on the obligation of the "strong" to support the "weak" (14:13–15:4), Paul's final word on the matter is to remind all the parties and individuals involved that acceptance must be two-way, must be mutual if it is to be "in accordance with Christ Jesus." If the more liberal are to express their liberty by restricting it, so the more conservative have genuinely to accept those who profess commitment to Christ as fellow Christians, and neither to use their particular understanding of Christianity to exclude the other in fact or effect.

8 As in 14:4, 6, the yardstick is acceptance by Christ (which only Christ can apply), and Christ's acceptance (of faith) is the model. But it is precisely by evoking once again the example of Christ (as in v 3) that Paul is able to broaden the scope of his concern once again to the overall and more fundamental issue of Jew and Gentile within the purposes of God. The significant fact is that it is not only "Christ," some agent of God so named, but "the Christ," the Jewish messiah, who has accepted them—Gentile as well as Jew. In immediate terms of the preceding discussion, that is a powerful reminder to the gentile "strong": as they were accepted by the Jewish Messiah, so they ought to accept the Jewish "weak." But this is also a climactic feature of the whole sweep of salvation-history, that Christ, the one through whom God is fulfilling his purpose, was a Jew and in his ministry dedicated himself totally to ministering to his fellow Jews (v 8). This proves God's faithfulness to his original choice of Abraham and his offspring through Isaac and Jacob; the overlap in meaning between "the truth of God" and "the faithfulness of God" (3:3–7) allows him thus to pick up both the thematic statement in 1:17 and the reassurance of chap. 11. And since Christ is still a Jew, still the servant of the circumcised, it means that God's promises to the fathers are likewise still in place, still secure, even if complete fulfillment is not yet; the echo of 9:4–5 will be in no way accidental.

9 Equally important, however, is the fact that this mission of Christ had the Gentiles also in view. The precise articulation of the first clause of v 9 with v 8 is unclear, perhaps because Paul did not want to specify it more clearly, simply to state that the outcome of Christ's ministry has in the event been the coming to faith of Gentiles in steadily increasing numbers. This too Paul expresses in a way which chimes in with various notes in his earlier exposition and which broadens the horizon of the discussion once again to the purpose of God as Creator of all. The double reference to the glory of God recalls not only the universal failure of the human species (1:21, 23; 3:23), but the divine countermeasures purposed from the first (9:23), through Abraham (4:20) and Christ (6:4), and now in process of realization in those of faith (5:2; 8:18, 21, 30). Likewise it was precisely the transformation and abuse of "the truth of God," like "the glory of God," which characterized the fall of humankind (1:23, 25) and which is now vindicated and confirmed by Christ's ministry. And the promises of God thus confirmed to Israel were precisely the promises that Abraham would be "heir of the world" and "father of many nations," which could only be fulfilled "through faith" (4:13, 16–17).

The effect of this summary intermeshing of key motifs of the whole preceding argument is very powerful. It holds together the most important strands of that argument in an amazingly comprehensive way which prevents the whole fabric from being pulled apart either in theory or (if maintained) in practice. The truth of God as creator, as one with God's covenant faithfulness to Israel; no dichotomy between creation and salvation. Jesus still a Jew and servant of circumcision, even though now exalted, last Adam and Lord of all; the tension between Jewish priority and universal fulfillment maintained within Christ himself. And not least the unified concept of God's truth-and-mercy expressing that unity in the combination of his faithfulness to circumcised and mercy to Gentile. It is such fundamental theological insights which lie behind Paul's concern to unite Jew and Gentile "in Christ," and on the practical level should provide sufficient impetus for Jew and Gentile to accept each other fully. The Gentiles should never forget that they were called through Jews, and the Jews that their own calling had the Gentiles in view from the first. The Gentiles should remember that Christ was servant of the circumcised, and the Jews that his risen lordship is universal. Clearly implied is Paul's conviction that God's glory can only be complete when there is such united and universal praise.

9–12 Characteristically the point is driven home by Paul citing a catena of scriptures. All of them are united by their references to the nations/Gentiles, with the theme of praise a further strong linking factor. The first evokes the devout diaspora Jew confessing God and singing praise to his name among the Gentiles (v 9—Ps 18:49). The second and third call on the Gentiles and all the peoples to join God's people in a common praise of God (v 10—Deut 32:43; v 11—Ps 117:1). The final scripture, from Paul's favorite prophet (Isa 11:10), fittingly ties together again the thought of the Jewishness of Jesus (the Davidic Messiah) and of the risen Christ, hope of the nations—an effective recall of the themes of the letter's opening paragraph (1:2–5). The effect is similar to that achieved in previous catenae, particularly in the Hosea quotations in 9:25–26 (and conversely in the indictment of 3:10–18): Paul takes OT language, which might more naturally hold out hope of (now dispersed [v 9]) Israel's ultimate dominance over the Gentiles (under the royal Messiah, [v 12]), in fulfillment of God's covenant faithfulness (v 11), and acknowledged (submissively) by the nations (v 10); and by setting it in different sequence and in the different light cast by the Christ event, he transforms it into an expression of the ideal of a humanity (Gentile with Jew) united in worship of the same God and by hope in the same Christ.

13 The final prayer wish echoes that in vv 5–6, but focuses even more on the theme of hope. The language is rich and immoderate, like all uninhibited devotion ("fill," "all," "overflow"). The reminder of the importance of faith ("in believing") is not accidental: it ties the end of this lengthy exposition (1:18–15:13) back into one of the central motifs in the primary theme (1:16–17). The two matching "in" phrases ("in believing," "in the power of the Holy Spirit") neatly hold together the two principal elements in the divine-human encounter—God's powerful outreach to and action in the receptive person. This is the source of two of the great human desirables—joy and peace/well-being. Out of this, despite the still prevailing contradictory and incomplete features, flows and overflows the sure hope that God will yet completely fulfill his original purpose in creation and in the call first of Jew but now also of Gentile.

VII. Conclusion   (15:14–16:27)

Introduction

The final section of the letter contains characteristic elements. The intimation of travel plans (15:14–33) recalls the theme which preceded the body of the letter (1:8–15) and is evidently intended to provide a bracket for the intervening theological and parenetical sections (Michel). This paragraph leads into the closing sequence containing typical Pauline formulae: the request for prayer (15:30–32), the wish for his readers' peace (15:33), a sequence of further greetings (16:1–16, 21–23), with the uniquely Christian call for a "holy kiss" (16:16), and a concluding benediction using Paul's favorite χάρις (16:20b). Unusual is the absence of an autographed greeting, though it is possible that Paul himself penned 16:1–20, with the awkwardly placed final group of greetings added as a kind of postscript by the amanuensis, Tertius (Gamble, *Textual History*, 94).

Travel plans	15:14–33	particularly 1 Cor 16:1–12; 1 Thess 2:17–3:13
Request for prayer	15:30–32	Eph 6:18–20; Col 4:3–4; 1 Thess 5:25; 2 Thess 3:1–2; Philem 22
Wish for peace	15:33	2 Cor 13:11; Gal 6:16; Eph 6:23; Phil 4:9; 1 Thess 5:23; 2 Thess 3:16
Additional greetings	16:1–16 21–23	1 Cor 16:19–20; 2 Cor 13:13; Phil 4:21–22; Col 4:10–15 Philem 23–24
Holy kiss	16:16	1 Cor 16:20; 2 Cor 13:12; 1 Thess 5:26
Concluding grace	16:20b	1 Cor 16:23; 2 Cor 13:13; Gal 6:18; Eph 6:24; Phil 4:23; Col 4:18; 1 Thess 5:28; 2 Thess 3:18; Philem 25

The paragraph 16:17–20a disrupts the more regular pattern of the conclusion, but may simply reflect the depth of Paul's concern about the continuing vulnerability of the Roman house churches. The majority of scholars regard the final paragraph (16:25–27) as a later addition.

A. Paul's Mission and Travel Plans   (15:14–33)

1. Paul's Mission   (15:14–21)

Bibliography

Aus, R. D. "Travel Plans." **Dabelstein, R.** *Beurteilung.* 111–14. **Dahl, N. A.** "Missionary Theology." **Denis, A. M.** "La fonction apostolique et la liturgie nouvelle en esprit."

RSPT 42 (1958) 401–36, 617–56. **Geyer, A. S.** "Un essai d'Explication de Rom 15:19." *NTS* 6 (1959–60) 156–59. **Kettunen, M.** *Abfassungszweck.* 150–54. **Knox, J.** "Rom 15:14–33 and Paul's Conception of His Apostolic Mission." *JBL* 83 (1964) 1–11. **Munck, J.** *Paul.* 49–53. **Newton, M.** *Purity.* 60–75. **Olson, S. N.** "Epistolary Uses of Expressions of Self-Confidence." *JBL* 103 (1984) 585–97. ———. "Pauline Expressions of Confidence in His Addressees." *CBQ* 47 (1985) 282–95. **Pedersen, S.** "Theologische Überlegungen zur Isagogik des Römerbriefes." *ZNW* 76 (1985) 47–67. **Ponthot, J.** "L'expression cultuelle du ministère paulinien selon Rom 15:16." In *L'Apôtre Paul*, ed. A. Vanhoye. Leuven: Leuven UP, 1986. 254–62. **Radl, W.** "Alle Mühe umsonst? Paulus und der Gottsknecht." In *L'Apôtre Paul*, ed. A. Vanhoye. Leuven: Leuven UP, 1986. 144–49. ———. "Kult und Evangelium bei Paulus." *BZ* 31 (1987) 58–75. **Robinson, D. W. B.** "Priesthood." **Roloff, J.** *Apostolat—Verkündigung—Kirche. Ursprung, Inhalt und Funktion des kirchlichen Apostelamtes nach Paulus, Lukas und den Pastoralbriefen.* Gütersloh: Gütersloher, 1965. Esp. 94–96. **Schlier, H.** "Die 'Liturgie' des apostolischen Evangeliums (Röm 15:14–21)." In *Martyria, Leitourgia, Diakonia*, FS H. Volk. Mainz, 1968. 247–59. **Stolz, F.** "Zeichen und Wunder. Die prophetischen Legitimation und ihre Geschichte." *ZTK* 69 (1972) 125–44. **Stuhlmacher, P.** "Erwägungen zum Problem von Gegenwart und Zukunft in der paulinischen Eschatologie." *ZTK* 64 (1967) 423–50. **Wenschkewitz, H.** "Die Spiritualisierung der Kultusbegriffe Tempel, Priester und Opfer im Neuen Testament." *Angelos* 4 (1932) 71–230, esp. 192–93. **Wiener, C.** "Ἱερουργεῖν (Röm 15:16)." *SPCIC* 2:399–404. **Wuellner, W.** "Paul's Rhetoric." 162–68. **Zeller, D.** *Juden.* 64–74, 224–29.

Translation

[14] *My[a] brothers, I myself too am convinced concerning you, that you yourselves too[b] are full of goodness,[c] filled with all[d] knowledge, able also to admonish one another.* [15] *But I wrote to you[f] rather boldly[e] in part as a way of reminding you, by virtue of the grace given me from[g] God,* [16] *so[h] that I might be a minister of Christ Jesus [h]for the Gentiles,[h] serving the gospel of God as a priest, in order that the offering of the Gentiles might be[h] acceptable,[h] sanctified by the Holy Spirit.* [17] *Therefore I have this[i] boasting in Christ Jesus[h] in reference to what concerns God.* [18] *For I will[h] not presume to say[h] anything, except of what Christ has accomplished through me[h] for the obedience[j] of the Gentiles, by word and deed,* [19] *by the power of[k] signs and[h] wonders, by the power of God's[h] Spirit; so that [h]from Jerusalem and in a sweep round to Illyricum[h] I have completed the gospel of Christ,* [20] *thus making it my aim[h] to preach the gospel where Christ has not been named, lest I build on another's foundations.* [21] *But as it is written,*

> *Those who had not been told about him will see;[l]*
> *and those who had not heard shall understand.*

Notes

[a] p[46] D* F G omit μου, presumably in recognition that Paul usually says simply ἀδελφοί.

[b] The same combination omits καὶ αὐτοί, an improving emendation to lighten the sentence.

[c] Some scribes found ἀγαθωσύνης too bland and substituted ἀγάπης, or later, ἁγιωσύνης.

[d] MS evidence is more or less equally divided between the inclusion of τῆς (א B P Ψ) and its omission (p[46] A C D F G); see Cranfield.

[e] A B favor τολμηροτέρως, but the attestation in favor of τολμηρότερον is stronger (p[46] א C etc.).

ᶠThe presence of ἀδελφοί (P⁴⁶ ℵ² etc.) is easier to explain than its omission (an insertion possibly prompted by lectionary use of the epistle [Metzger]).

ᵍThe choice between ὑπό and ἀπό is difficult: ὑπό has the wider range of support, ἀπό is read by ℵ B F; each could be explained as scribal emendation—ὑπό as the more natural sense, ἀπό as assimilation to salutation formulae (as in 1:7). But perhaps ἀπό can be counted as the less obvious and so the more difficult (Cranfield).

ʰVarious omissions and alterations indicate the kind of slips, modifications, and attempted improvements which could easily transform the text little by little—many of them involving B alone. The number of variants in this section is unusually large.

ⁱThe reading with τήν (B C D F G) is probably the more difficult, τήν as a demonstrative adjective referring back (see Cranfield).

ʲB's reading of ἀκοήν is an understandable slip in view of 10:16–17, but loses a key thematic reference.

ᵏThe same combination as in *Notes* a and b insert αὐτοῦ— "in the power of his (Christ's) signs . . ."—unnecessary in view of the δι' ἐμοῦ of v 18.

ˡB here probably retains the correct original, since the strongly attested variant of P⁴⁶ ℵ etc. is easily explained as an assimilation to the word order of the LXX.

Form and Structure

Having completed the main body of argument and instruction Paul returns at once to his travel plans and hopes for a visit to Rome (the plerophoric language of both v 13 and v 14 maintaining the same mood across the transition). The implication is clear that the central treatise section was intended in part at least to forward and facilitate these plans. This is confirmed by v 15 in particular, with its recall of 1:5 and 12:3, and by the tie-in between 11:13–14, 25 and 15:27–28 (Aus): Paul wrote as he did because he had been given the gospel for the Gentiles, and his ministry was crucial to the completion of God's plan of salvation; hence the need both to explain his gospel and to promote it. The emphasis on mission to the Gentiles (v 16) follows from the letter as a whole, both as a personal vocational imperative and as an inevitable theological corollary to his understanding of God's promises and purpose (note again the transition function of vv 9–12). In particular, the use of πεπληρωμένοι and μεστοί in v 14 may recall the equivalent usage in 1:29, with the implication that the gospel provides the appropriate answer to that initial indictment of humankind; the thematic ὑπακοή (v 18) provides a thread which unites missionary impulse, theological rationale, and parenesis (1:5; 5:19; 6:16); and the citation of Isa 52:15 (v 21) links directly back into the argument of chaps. 9–11, where it could easily have been used (cf. 9:30; 10:16, 20). Indicative of both the continuity with and transformation of traditional Jewish categories which Paul saw as integral to the gospel is the use of cultic language to describe his ministry to the Gentiles (vv 15–16), the equivalent for Paul of the daily commitment and social responsibility called for on the part of his readers (12:1; 13:6). Presumably it was this transformation of the older, more restrictively ethnic categories of the typical Jewish understanding of the covenant which made it possible for Paul to speak positively of a boasting πρὸς τὸν θεόν (v 17) which he had disallowed for Abraham (4:2).

Paul clearly saw his work coming to the end of a stage: he had completed the circle of openings in the east (vv 19, 23); the mission to Spain would be a new stage (v 24). But first the eastern phase must be rounded off by taking the collection to Jerusalem (vv 25–28). The linking of Jerusalem, Rome, and

Spain is again indicative of the tension Paul sought to maintain between his Jewish heritage and the more universal openness of the gospel in Paul's understanding; the language of indebtedness recalls 1:14 in particular, and note again the use of cultic terminology in vv 27–28. Paul's own clearly expressed principle of not interfering in churches he had not founded (v 20) is probably sufficient explanation of the diplomatic language which features in this paragraph, including the παρακαλῶ of v 30, whether deliberately chosen as such or a natural expression of Paul's diffidence in view of v 20. The somewhat emotional appeal of vv 30–32 (pathos) is characteristic of the peroration in rhetoric (Wuellner, 163–64), but in fact is less marked here than in 9:1–3; 10:1; and 12:1.

The restatement of themes covered in 1:8–15 is not simply the result of Paul's using a standard mix of sentiments ("apostolic parousia" [Funk]), but is intended to reinforce the bracketing effect of the two sections on the main body of the letter.

15:14	congratulations	1:8
15:15-21	ministry to the Gentiles	1:13b
15:22	hindrance in coming	1:13a
15:23-24, 28-29	desire to see for mutual benefit	1:11-12
15:25-27	indebtedness	1:14
15:30-32	Paul asks them for prayer/prays for them	1:9-10
15:33	commendation of all to God/thanks for all to God	1:8

An imperfect chiastic structure is evident, but the weight given to certain parts of the restatement indicates where Paul's primary concerns lie.

Several echoes of themes used in the Corinthian correspondence may be detected: γνῶσις (v 14; 1 Cor 1:5), τολμᾶν (v 18; 2 Cor 10:12), legitimation (vv 18–19; 2 Cor 13:3; 12:12), character and scope of mission (v 20; 1 Cor 3:10; 2 Cor 10:15–16), προπέμπειν (v 24; 1 Cor 16:6), and of course themes relating to the collection (cf. Zeller, *Juden*, 67–68).

Comment

14 πέπεισμαι δέ, ἀδελφοί μου, καὶ αὐτὸς ἐγὼ περὶ ὑμῶν, "my brothers, I myself too am convinced concerning you." For πέπεισμαι see on 8:38; with περί cf. Heb 6:9 and Ign. *Trall.* 3.2. For ἀδελφοί see on 1:13; here with μου, as in 7:4 and 9:3, but with special warmth as Paul expresses his regard for Christians he has never met. The καὶ αὐτὸς ἐγώ, "even I myself," does not of course express condescension ("I the apostle"), but a deep personal conviction and feeling for his unknown readers: "I am convinced; yes, indeed, I am" (Black). For the diplomatic style see Olson, "Confidence in Addressees," 291–93.

ὅτι καὶ αὐτοὶ μεστοί ἐστε ἀγαθωσύνης, "that you yourselves too are full of goodness." The repetition of the same emphasis, καὶ αὐτοί, matches the καὶ αὐτὸς ἐγώ of the preceding clause (Wilckens), with the implication that their healthy condition (about to be described) is something they have come to without the help of outsiders (or apostles?) like him (Michel, Käsemann, Schlier). μεστός can describe both a positive condition—"full of kindness"

(*P. Oxy.* 130.6), "full of mercy" (James 3:17)—or a negative condition (as in 1:29, the only other Pauline usage; Matt 23:38; 2 Pet 2:14; *2 Clem.* 13.1); see further BGD. ἀγαθωσύνη is exclusively biblical (Spicq, 13–14); the word is general and not specific, though its positive and probably outgoing quality (cf. Judg 8:35 A; 9:16 B; 2 Chron 24:16; Neh 9:25, 35; 2 Thess 1:11; *Barn.* 2.9) is clear; so it strikes the right note, especially when linked with μεστός (cf. the only other two NT references, Gal 5:22 and Eph 5:9).

πεπληρωμένοι πάσης τῆς γνώσεως, "filled with all knowledge." The language, "filled with all," echoes v 13, and the perfect passive contrasts fittingly with 1:29 (see *Form and Structure*). The confidence of v 14 and the prayer wish of v 13 also effectively maintain the eschatological Already/Not yet tension. πᾶς + definite article = all (that is, the whole range of) knowledge; whereas without the definite article it would denote every kind of knowledge (Moule, *Idiom Book*, 93–95; Cranfield; so NEB here). The use of γνῶσις is obviously complimentary, but not just with reference to their knowledge (= experience) of salvation (cf. 2 Cor 2:14; 4:6; 10:5; Phil 3:8); more with reference to their insight into and understanding of God's saving purpose (Michel, Käsemann) (cf. 11:33; 1 Cor 13:2; Col 2:2–3); that is to say, they appreciate what he has been talking about (he did not really need to teach them at such length!), in contrast to the misunderstanding of this covenant purpose typical of his devout fellow Jew (2:20). In view of the preceding discussion and the prominence of the word in 1 Cor 8 (vv 1, 7, 10, 11), a practical note may also be present (cf. Zeller) = "I am sure you know how to handle the situation" (cf. 12:2; Phil 1:9; Col 1:9).

δυνάμενοι καὶ ἀλλήλους νουθετεῖν, "able also to admonish one another." νουθετέω (constructed from νοῦν τίθημι = "put on the mind, instruct") denotes basically the well-intentioned attempt to influence mind and disposition by apposite instruction, exhortation, warning, and correction (*TDNT* 4:1019); so with reference to God's chastening in Jewish wisdom literature (Job 40:4; and in the three Wisd Sol references [11:10; 12:2, 26] chastening as much lighter than divine condemnation; as also *Pss. Sol.* 13.9). Hence the usage in the NT (almost exclusively Pauline)—1 Cor 4:14; Col 1:28; 1 Thess 5:12; also νουθεσία—1 Cor 10:11 and Titus 3:10 (see further *TDNT* 4:1019–22). It was clearly important for Paul that his congregations should be mature enough to exercise this crucial ministry among themselves (Col 3:16; 1 Thess 5:14; 2 Thess 3:15; see also Gaugler); there is no implication that he was thinking of the potential of the Roman church(es) to instruct others (against SH); see also on 15:26.

15 τολμηρότερον δὲ ἔγραψα ὑμῖν ἀπὸ μέρους, ὡς ἐπαναμιμνῄσκων ὑμᾶς, "but I wrote to you rather bluntly in part as a way of reminding you." Both forms τολμηροτέρως and τολμηρότερον (see *Notes*) are adverbs from the comparative τολμηρότερος, and both can be translated "more = rather, or somewhat, boldly" (BGD, Cranfield). The tentativeness arises presumably from the fact that Paul is conscious that this is his first communication with (a) church(es) he had not founded. The ἀπὸ μέρους is a familiar construction (BGD, μέρος 1c) and taken at face value probably refers to part of the letter, that is, presumably 12:1–15:13, where Paul gave instructions not simply on general points of faith (which would apply equally to all Christians) but to specific situations in Rome itself (where the propriety and authority of his so writing was more open to question); so SH, Michel, Cranfield, Wilckens, Zeller; "at times" (NEB); "very boldly on some points" (BGD, RSV—though the "very boldly" seems too strong—see above; NIV, NJB). But since he is linking back in mood and theme to 1:8–15, it may be better to take the ἀπὸ μέρους as a polite self-deprecatory reference to the whole of the letter which came between these two sections (1:16–15:13). On the other hand, to take the ἀπὸ μέρους as qualifying τολμηρότερον (Schlier) is stretching the syntax too far (Lagrange).

ἐπαναμιμνῄσκω occurs only here in biblical Greek but appears occasionally in literary Greek (LSJ, BGD, Cranfield); ἀναμιμνῄσκω in Mark 11:21; 14:72; 1 Cor 4:17; 2 Cor 7:15; 2 Tim 1:6; Heb 10:32. As with the use of γνῶσις in v 14, this is best seen both as a polite but sincere gesture to the quality of their faith (1:8, 12), and as a tactical didactic ploy to indicate that everything he has so far written to them was not (or should not have been) strange to them, or at least that it follows directly from the basic faith and understanding of faith which was the common bond of all who believed in Christ Jesus (cf. Kettunen, 152–54). To see this as a contradiction with v 20 (Klein, "Purpose," 36) is overcritical: the "reminder" is Paul's calling card to ensure that the support he hopes for from Rome (v 24) will know fully who and what they are supporting.

διὰ τὴν χάριν τὴν δοθεῖσάν μοι ἀπὸ τοῦ θεοῦ, "on account of the grace given me from God." The phrase is almost the same as in 12:3, but using διά with accusative rather than with genitive. Where in 12:3 Paul regards his speaking as an expression of grace (see further on 12:3), here he refers to his whole apostolic ministry (1:5) and makes that fuller expression of grace the basis of his speaking so boldly to a church not his own. So "by virtue of ['on the basis of,' BGD, διά B.II.1] the grace given me to be apostle to the Gentiles" (see further on 1:5; also Roloff, 95–96, and Schlier).

16 εἰς τὸ εἶναι με λειτουργὸν Χριστοῦ Ἰησοῦ εἰς τὰ ἔθνη, "in order that I might be a minister of Christ Jesus for the Gentiles." Although λειτουργός can mean merely "servant," as most often in LXX (Josh 1:1; 2 Sam 13:18; 1 Kgs 10:5; etc.; see further on 13:6), almost certainly Paul has in mind here the more specific cultic sense ("priest"), as in Neh 10:39; Isa 61:6; Sir 7:30; and as in Heb 8:2 and *1 Clem.* 41.2; the cultic language of the following clauses puts this almost beyond dispute (so, e.g., *TDNT* 4:230; Spicq, 480; Lietzmann; Barrett; Schlier; and Wilckens; Hultgren, *Gospel*, 134–35, refers particularly to Sir 50:12–13). Barth's suggestion, supported by Cranfield, that Paul has the Levites in mind as assistants to the priest (here Christ) is too strained. It has some support in Philo, *Mos.* 2.276 (where it refers to both ranks of priests—that is, priests and Levites), but otherwise Philo normally uses λειτουργός for priest (*Mos.* 2.94; *Spec. Leg.* 1.249; 4.191; and note the distinctions in *Leg. All.* 3.135, *Post.* 184, *Mos.* 2.149, and *Spec. Leg.* 1.152; as also in *Ep. Arist.* 95; similarly in *T. Levi* λειτουργός = officiating priest [2.10, 4.2, 8.3–10, and 9.3]); apart from the traditional formulation of 8:34, Paul does not have a Christology of Christ as priest; and such a distinction hardly squares anyway with the priestly imagery of v 16b (cf. SH). This is not to say, however, that Paul thought of his own ministry as involving literal cultic activity: the cultic language is transformed (not merely spiritualized) by an eschatological fulfillment (Michel, Schmidt, Käsemann, Schlier); that is to say, the division between cultic and secular (together with that between sacred and profane, clean and unclean—14:14, 20) has been broken down and abolished (see also on 12:1) as part of the breaking down of the (in large part cultically determined) distinction between Jew and Gentile (see also Robinson, "Priesthood," 231). And, as Wenschkewitz, 193, points out, there is certainly no question of Paul acting as a priest in a special way distinct from the ministry of his several communities; he "does not stand as mediator between the community and God," and his priestly ministry neither diminishes nor renders unnecessary the priestly ministry of all believers (see again 12:1).

ἱερουργοῦντα τὸ εὐαγγέλιον τοῦ θεοῦ, "serving the gospel of God as a priest" (BGD, ἱερουργέω). There can be no question of the cultic imagery here. ἱερουργεῖν means basically "perform the work of a priest" (ἱερός + ἐργός). The word does not occur in the LXX (except as v.l. at 4 Macc. 7.8; see below), nor elsewhere in the NT. But in Philo and Josephus it consistently denotes the priestly offering of sacrifice (Philo, Leg. All. 3.130; Plant. 164; Ebr. 138; Conf. 124; Migr. 67; etc.; Josephus, Ant. 5.263; 6.102; 7.333; 9.43; 14.65; 17.166), though it should be noted that for both Philo and Josephus ἱερουργεῖν is something the whole people can do (Philo, Mos. 2.229; Spec. Leg. 2.145; Josephus, War 5.14, 16). Similar usage is also found in non-Jewish Greek writers and with the correlatives formed on the ἱερουργ- root (see LSJ, BGD, TDNT 3:251–52; see further Wiener, 403). Normally the object of the verb would be what was offered, but here that is clearly the Gentiles (see next clause), and a transferred sense is attested in a v.l. of 4 Macc. 7.8 —τοὺς ἱερουργοῦντας τὸν νόμον, "those who serve the law as priests" (the contrast between this reading and 15:16 ["serving the law"/"serving the gospel"] would characterize the contrast between Jew and Christian for Paul [cf. 10:5–8])—as also allegorical applications in Philo, Cher. 96 and Abr. 202 (see also Lagrange). Paul's usage of course is also metaphorical (cf. particularly Odes Sol. 20.1–5): the more clearly cultic is the imagery, the more striking Paul's transformation of it by application to his missionary work (cf. Radl, "Kult," 64–67). For εὐαγγέλιον τοῦ θεοῦ see on 1:1.

ἵνα γένηται ἡ προσφορὰ τῶν ἐθνῶν εὐπρόσδεκτος, ἡγιασμένη ἐν πνεύματι ἁγίῳ, "in order that the offering of the Gentiles might be acceptable, set apart by the Holy Spirit." προσφορά can mean either the act of presenting an offering (as particularly in Heb 10:10, 14, 18; also Acts 24:17 and 1 Clem. 40.4), or, as here, that which is brought, the offering itself (as in Acts 21:26; Eph 5:2; Heb 10:5, 8; 1 Clem. 36.1; Newton, Purity, 72, draws attention particularly to Sir 35:6 and 50:13–15). The offering is probably "the Gentiles" (genitive of apposition)—the idea very likely developed from Isa 66:20, where it is the diaspora Jews who form the eschatological offering (Aus, 241; see further on 15:24 and 25); but it could be the offering made by the Gentiles—that is, the priestly ministry of the Gentiles (cf. 12:1) conjoined to Paul's priestly ministry as evangelist (Robinson, "Priesthood," 231). The (eschatological) transformation of traditional Jewish categories and cultic distinctives is striking. Not only is the priestly ministry of Paul "out in the world," but the offering breaches the fundamental cultic distinction between Jew and Gentile which prevented Gentiles from even getting near the great altar of sacrifice in the

Temple (the law which forbad Gentiles to go beyond the Court of the Gentiles was firmly established and unyielding; cf. SVM 2:284–85; Acts 21:28); the point is the same if the reference is to Gentiles as the sacrifice, since only ritually pure/clean sacrifices were acceptable (Leenhardt).

εὐπρόσδεκτος, "acceptable," can be used more generally (cf. 15:31; 2 Cor 6:2; 8:12), but is particularly apposite for prayers or sacrifices offered to God (as in 1 Pet 2:5; nonbiblical references in LSJ and BGD); see also on 12:1 (εὐάρεστον τῷ θεῷ). "Neither the similarity nor the difference between the formulations in 12:1 and 15:16 can be accidental" (Dahl, "Missionary Theology," 87).

Even more than ἄγιος (see on 1:7), ἁγιάζειν is almost exclusively a biblical word (see BGD, *TDNT* 1:90–91, 97; cf. ἁγιασμός—6:19). It denotes the act of setting apart, dedicating to God, so as to be his alone, or used solely for his purposes. So, as in the case here, of sacrifices (Exod 29:33, 36–37; 30:29; Lev 8:15; Num 18:8–9; 2 Chron 29:33; Matt 23:19; Heb 9:13), priests (Exod 19:22; 29:1, 21, 44; 30:30; 40:13; Lev 8:12, 30; 21:8, 12, 15; 2 Chron 26:18), and temple (1 Kgs 9:3, 7; 2 Chron 2:4; 7:16, 20; 1 Esd 1:49; Tob 1:4; Jud 9:13; *3 Macc.* 2.9, 16). Equally significant, and indicative of the way in which Israel's sense of election came to expression in the cult, is the use of the same language to describe the people (Exod 19:14; Lev 11:44; 20:8; 22:32; Deut 33:3; Ezek 20:41; 28:25; 37:28; 39:27; Jud 6:19; Sir 36:3; *3 Macc.* 6.3; see also on 11:16), the ritual actions also defining the boundaries between Jew and Gentile. In particular the fulfillment and at the same time transformation of the Jewish hope expressed in Ezek 36:22–28 is very striking, especially after the echo of the passage in 2:24. In view of the importance of the sabbath issue in the preceding discussion (see on 14:5) it is also significant that the holiness/set-apartness of the sabbath is one of the most consistent emphases in the OT (Gen 2:3; Exod 20:8, 11; 31:13; Deut 5:12, 15; Neh 13:22; Jer 17:22, 24, 27; Ezek 20:12, 20; 44:24; and feasts, 1 Esd 5:52; Sir 33:9), not least because the sanctity of the people is also dependent on their keeping the sabbath (Exod 31:13). For the thought here, cf. particularly Acts 26:18 (a clear echo of a genuinely Pauline emphasis). For Christians as "those who have been set aside/dedicated" see 1 Cor 1:2; Heb 2:11; 10:10, 14, 29; and 13:12. For the thought of the Spirit as the sanctifying agency, see 1 Cor 6:11 and 2 Thess 2:13 (cf. Heb 10:29; 1 Pet 1:2), but without cultic overtones since the whole has been eschatologically transformed and such specific cultic connections left behind (even in Eph 5:26); see again on 1:7. For ἐν πνεύματι ἁγίῳ see on 5:5 and 15:13.

17 ἔχω οὖν τὴν καύχησιν ἐν Χριστῷ Ἰησοῦ τὰ πρὸς τὸν θεόν, "therefore I have this boasting in Christ Jesus with reference to what concerns God." καύχησις, only here and in 3:27 in Romans, naturally recalls a central point of the original critique of the too presumptuous "Jew" (see on 2:17, 23). τήν (see *Notes*) refers the boasting to the description of Paul's ministry in vv 15–16: Israel's priestly ministry rightly understood in the new age is a ground for boasting (cf. 5:2, 3, 11), but when that ministry is misappropriated and used to exclude others from God's grace, boasting is excluded (3:27; 4:2); it is the blessing he has been instrumental in bringing to others of which Paul characteristically boasts (1 Cor 15:31; 2 Cor 1:12–14; 7:4, 14; 8:24; 1 Thess

2:19; see also on 15:18). For ἐν Χριστῷ Ἰησοῦ see on 3:24; 6:11 is the closest of the other usages of the phrase, but a comparison of its range of usage, and of 5:11 with 15:17, shows just how flexible Paul's thought was:

> 5:11   καυχ· ἐν θεῷ διὰ Χριστοῦ·
> 15:17   καυχ· ἐν Χριστῷ πρὸς θεόν

τὰ πρὸς τὸν θεόν can be taken either as "that which concerns God," or as an adverbial accusative, as above. The phrase is not specific but can denote simply all that God has laid down or required—service of God. So also Heb 2:17 and 5:1. See further BGD, πρός III.5b.

18 οὐ γὰρ τολμήσω τι λαλεῖν, "for I will not presume to say anything." The τολμάω indicates Paul's awareness that any "boasting" or attempt at self-justification is fraught with peril. To that extent the use of τολμάω shows something of the same sensitivity as in 2 Cor 10:2, 12 and 11:21. But the parallel in language provides no support for the view that Paul is here speaking against pneumatics or enthusiasts (as in 2 Cor 10–13) (against Michel), since the language which follows lacks the qualifications of 2 Cor 10–13 ("I have been a fool"—2 Cor 12:11), and since the hubris which threatens Jew and Gentile at Rome is quite different (see particularly 2:17–24; 3:27; 11:18–20; 12:16). The choice of λαλεῖν has no particular significance.

ὧν οὐ κατειργάσατο Χριστὸς δι᾽ ἐμοῦ εἰς ὑπακοὴν ἐθνῶν, "except of what Christ has brought about through me for the obedience of the Gentiles." The structure is rather convoluted: "I will not presume to say anything of those things which Christ has not brought about . . ." Paul probably did not want to say anything which would appear to qualify his distaste for what might too easily appear to be self-glorification, but to take ὧν οὐ as equivalent to "except that" (BGD, κατεργάζομαι 1; rsv, niv, Cranfield) prevents the second οὐ from obscuring the positive force of this last clause, which Paul would certainly not want to have lost.

Here the full sense of κατεργάζομαι is important—"achieve, accomplish, bring about, produce" (BGD). Note the balance of Χριστὸς δι᾽ ἐμοῦ: anything achieved has been done by Christ; but the agency is Paul's. This is the emphasis which Paul wants to retain in any assessment of his work. The use of the thematic ὑπακοή is no accident: it was part of Paul's most basic conviction regarding his mission (see on 1:5). Lietzmann translates "for the conversion of the Gentiles."

λόγῳ καὶ ἔργῳ, "by word and deed." The rhetorical balance of the two concepts was as wide-ranging and unspecific as the same phrase today; see references in BGD, ἔργον 1; in the NT see Luke 24:19; Acts 7:22; Col 3:17; and 2 Thess 2:17. The stereotyped character of the phrase prevents any reading of a "works" theology into the use of ἔργον here.

19 ἐν δυνάμει σημείων καὶ τεράτων, "by the power of signs and wonders." For δύναμις as divine power, see on 1:16. The phrase σημεῖα καὶ τέρατα is undoubtedly intended to recall its regular OT equivalent, where it had become a traditional way of referring to the miracles of the Exodus (Exod 7:3, 9; 11:9–10; Deut 4:34; 6:22; 7:19; 11:3; 26:8; 29:3; 34:11; Neh 9:10; Pss 78:43; 135:9; Jer 32:20–21; Wisd Sol 10:16; Bar 2:11; see also Isa 8:18; 20:3; Dan

4:2–3; 6:27; Wisd Sol 8:8; Philo, *Mos.* 1.95; *Spec. Leg.* 2.218; *TDNT* 7:16–17, 221). This background shows how deeply Paul's thought here is rooted in salvation-history (the eschatological exodus of the gospel out of Palestine into the world as of the same epochal significance as the original Exodus). It also helps explain how Paul can use the phrase so positively and without qualification at this point (cf. also Stolz), whereas in other equally eschatological contexts the phrase has a more negative ring (Mark 13:22 // Matt 24:24; 2 Thess 2:9; cf. Rev 13:13–14; 16:14; 19:20); in 2 Cor 12:12 Paul uses the criterion of "signs and wonders" unwillingly as part of his foolish boasting; though John has a positive theology of "signs," his sole use of the full phrase has the same negative overtone (John 4:48; cf. Mark 8:11–12 pars.; Luke 23:8; 1 Cor 1:22). All this parallels the rather negative attitude of Greek writers when they use the same term; belief in "signs and wonders" as indicative of naive superstition, an attitude which Josephus probably shared (*TDNT* 7:206–7, 224–25). Parallel to the positive (not merely accepting) attitude of 15:19 is Heb 2:4, where the usage reflects an even deeper immersion in the whole Exodus theology, and Acts, whose ninefold use of the phrase indicates a rather uninhibited enthusiasm on the subject of miracle (Dunn, *Jesus,* 167–69; *Unity,* 180–84), reflected also in the late addition of Mark 16:17, 20. Paul's unqualified usage here confirms that he had no fear that Rome was threatened by the sort of overemphasis on spectacular charisms which seems to have been such a feature in the Corinthian church. This is not to say that Paul would question the belief that God's Spirit comes to powerful manifestation in inexplicable events (= miracles, healings, etc.); on the contrary, see 1 Cor 12:10, 28–29 and Gal 3:5. The point is rather that too much weight could be placed on such "signs" and undercut the primary theology of the cross (1 Cor 1:22–23; 2 Cor 12:1–10).

ἐν δυνάμει πνεύματος θεοῦ, "by the power of God's Spirit." See on 15:13; cf. particularly 1 Cor 2:4 and 1 Thess 1:5. There is no real justification for linking this phrase only with the λόγῳ as distinct from the ἔργῳ of v 18 (Lagrange; against Leenhardt).

ὥστε με ἀπὸ Ἰερουσαλὴμ καὶ κύκλῳ μέχρι τοῦ Ἰλλυρικοῦ πεπληρωκέναι τὸ εὐαγγέλιον τοῦ Χριστοῦ, "so that from Jerusalem and in a sweep round to Illyricum I have completed the gospel of Christ." The ὥστε ties vv 18 and 19 together; Christ so working through him had this result (Cranfield, Wilckens). The force of ἀπὸ Ἰερουσαλήμ is disputed. Currently the most popular view is that Paul speaks from a salvation-history perspective, Jerusalem as the starting point of the whole Christian mission (cf. Acts 1:8 and Paul's emphasis on Jewish priority; see on 1:16) (so, e.g., *TDNT* 7:334; Michel, Bruce, Cranfield, Wilckens). In view of the strong salvation-history emphasis of the context, this makes good sense. But weight should also be given to Zeller's observation (*Juden,* 227) that in 15:19 Paul is thinking of his own ministry, not in more general terms of the gospel's expansion (as in Col 1:5–6). A reference to Paul's visit to Jerusalem in Gal 2:1–10 should not be dismissed therefore (but Acts 9:28–29 clashes with Gal 1:17, 18–19, and 2:2), since Paul certainly bore witness to/defended his (understanding of the) gospel there, and it was following that Jerusalem agreement (Gal 2:9), and the Antioch incident (Gal 2:11–14), that Paul became much more independent as a missionary and much more emphatically "apostle to the Gentiles" (see Dunn, "Antioch Incident," and *Introduction* §1.3). There may also be some reference forward to his forthcoming visit to Jerusalem as a legitimate and important part of his work (Schlatter).

κύκλῳ means literally "in a circle," but it is sufficiently clear that what Paul has in mind is the broad arc which can be drawn roughly from Jerusalem through Syrian Antioch, through Asia Minor, "right up to Illyricum" (so most today; see BGD). We should not exclude the possibility that he saw his work not simply as an arc but as the top half of a circle which presupposed that others were engaged in the bottom sweep (through Egypt, Alexandria, and North Africa); cf. Knox, "Rom 15:14–33," 10–11; Hultgren, *Gospel,* 132–33; Maillot.

At this period Ἰλλυρικόν stretched down the northeast coast of the Adriatic (across from Italy), from somewhere near the top of the Adriatic Gulf, to Macedonia (coinciding roughly with modern Yugoslavia and Albania). There is no other evidence that Paul ever pushed so far north in his missionary work (Acts 20:2?), though since the territory did border on Macedonia it is certainly possible (BGD; Dodd; Bruce; Suhl, *Paulus,* 94; Vielhauer, *Geschichte,* 80). But the μέχρι can denote simply "up to" (not "into"), and missionary work in Macedonia might be sufficient for the purposes of the rather self-consciously grandiose style Paul adopts here. Illyricum would then mark the northwestern limit of Paul's missionary work (see SH; also Lagrange, Cranfield, and Wilckens). Since there had been a great Illyrian rebellion in living memory (A.D. 6–9) and Illyricum, now divided into Dalmatia and Pannonia, was linked with the other Danube provinces (see further *OCD*), to a Hellenist like Paul Illyricum could also be said to mark the more dangerous northern fringes of the eastern Empire. See also end of next paragraph.

πεπληρωκέναι has to be filled out—"completed *the preaching of* the gospel." The context indicates clearly enough that Paul was thinking in geographical terms (hence his fierce resistance to those who encroached on his territory; cf. particularly 2 Cor 10:13–16). The perfect ties into v 23: his work in the east is completed. The claim is astonishing and could reflect simply Paul's wanderlust; but much more probably it reflects his conviction of the pressing imminence of the parousia, leaving all too little time to take the gospel to where it had not so far been heard (e.g., Munck, *Paul,* 51–53; Barrett; Black; Käsemann; Schlier; Wilckens; despite Cranfield); the πεπληρωκέναι is theologically linked in Paul's grand design with the πλήρωμα of 11:25 (Stuhlmacher, "Gegenwart," 430–31; cf. the hyperbolic language of 1:8; 1 Cor 1:2; and 1 Thess 1:8). At the same time the phrase should not be read as though Paul was being wildly optimistic or irresponsible. He saw his work very much as the one who laid the foundation (v 20); and his strategy seems also to have included the encouraging of fellow workers to go out from the urban centers where he had established the work to the region around (Col 1:6–8; cf. Acts 19:10; 2 Cor 1:1) (SH, 409; Leenhardt). So the claim to have reached the borders of Illyricum could refer to missionary work done at Paul's behest and with his encouragement and not just to his own personal mission. See also 10:18.

For εὐαγγέλιον Χριστοῦ see on 1:1 and 1:9.

20 οὕτως δὲ φιλοτιμούμενον εὐαγγελίζεσθαι οὐχ ὅπου ὠνομάσθη Χριστός, "and thus making it my aim to preach the gospel where Christ has not been named." The precise force of the οὕτως δέ is disputed. Michel, Cranfield, Schlier, and Wilckens are confident that it refers forward to the εὐαγγελίζεσθαι—"so to preach . . . that . . ." (οὕτως . . . ἵνα . . .) (against Käsemann). But οὕτως thus used can refer both backward and forward (BGD, even in the closest parallel [1 Cor 9:24]), and the implication seems clear that Paul has been able to "complete the gospel of Christ" precisely because he always sought virgin territory. Indeed the sense might best be given by paraphrasing, " . . . complete the gospel of Christ by thus aspiring to preach. . . ."

φιλοτιμέομαι, as the word formation indicates, means basically "love or seek after honor," and so can easily assume a negative tone. But with the infinitive it has the more positive sense, "strive eagerly, endeavor earnestly, aspire" (LSJ), in line with its usage in late Greek, as attested also in papyri and inscriptions (MM). So in its only other two NT uses (2 Cor 5:9; 1 Thess 4:11); elsewhere in biblical Greek only at *4 Macc.* 1.35 A. Here, however, there may just be an overtone of competitive rivalry (see below under οὐχ).

For εὐαγγελίζεσθαι see on 1:15 and 1:1.

The word order gives emphasis to the οὐχ—an indication of the strength of Paul's antagonism to attempts of others to evangelize where he had already preached (2 Cor 10:16; 11:4; Gal 1:6–9). ὀνομάζεσθαι will have its more pregnant sense of "be named in worship, acknowledged, honored" (cf. Josh 23:7; Esth 9:4; Isa 26:13; 1 Macc 3:9; 11:51 S*; 14:10; Eph 1:21; 2 Tim 2:19); so most, against BGD ("be known").

ἵνα μὴ ἐπ᾽ ἀλλότριον θεμέλιον οἰκοδομῶ, "lest I build on another's foundation." NEB and NJB slightly alter the sense by translating ἵνα as "for" here. For ἀλλότριος = "belonging to another, not one's own," see BGD; and for the emphatic character of Paul's conviction here see again 2 Cor 10:15–16 (elsewhere in Paul only 14:4 q.v.; also 1 Tim 5:22). Paul also uses the imagery of laying a foundation for his evangelistic work in 1 Cor 3:10–12; cf. also particularly Heb 6:1; otherwise cf. Eph 2:20 with Rev 21:14. For the imagery of building (οἰκοδομέω) see on 14:19. Despite Klein ("Purpose") it is highly unlikely that Paul saw his projected visit to Rome either as an implementation of this principle or as a contravention of it (Schmidt; see further Pedersen, 51–57). In contrast, Watson, *Paul*, 103–4, argues that the gentile Christians in Rome were (primarily) Paul's converts, which presupposes either a surprisingly small Christian group in Rome or a surprisingly selective list of greetings in chap. 16. See also on 1:15; 15:15; and 15:24; and further *Introduction* §3.1).

21 ἀλλὰ καθὼς γέγραπται, "but as it is written"; see on 1:17. The quotation is verbatim from the LXX of Isa 52:15 (with ὄψονται at the beginning of the first line instead of the end).

> ὄψονται οἷς ἀνηγγέλη περὶ αὐτοῦ,
> καὶ οἳ οὐκ ἀκηκόασιν συνήσουσιν,
>
> "those who had not been told about him will see,
> and those who had not heard shall understand."

The fact that this verse comes near the beginning of the fourth Servant passage (Isa 52:13–53:12) and has reference to the impact of the Servant

on many nations (ἔθνη = Gentiles) and kings makes it particularly fitting for
Paul's use here. The rejection of any thought that Paul saw himself in the
role of the Servant (Gaugler; Knox, "Rom 15:14–33," 5–6; Käsemann; Cranfield; Schlier; Zeller) is understandable; but it ignores the extent to which
Paul *did* evidently see his commission in terms of the commission given to
the Servant (see on 1:1 δοῦλος; cf. further A. Kerrigan, "Echoes of Themes
from the Servant Songs in Pauline Theology," *SPCIC* 2:217–28; Radl, "Mühe").
We should beware of the assumption that the Christological interpretation
of such passages prevented all other reference for them, or that Paul would
think it blasphemous to see his own mission as "completing the gospel of
Christ" (v 19) in this sense too, that is, of completing the Servant's mission
by taking the light of the gospel "to the nations" (Isa 49:6). Particularly if
Paul did see the parousia as imminent, as seems most likely, it would simply
mean that he saw his own climactic mission toward "reconciling the world"
as of a piece with the salvation-history climax spanning the period from
Jesus' resurrection to the Parousia and final resurrection (11:13–15); see also
on 9:3, ὑπὲρ τῶν ἀδελφῶν μου.

Explanation

14 Almost as though the whole sweep of the argument from 1:16 to
15:13 had been one long parenthesis, Paul returns to the theme and mood
of 1:8–15. The warm congratulatory tone of v 14 echoes the similar note of
1:8. He addresses them as "my brothers," although he had never met the
bulk of them; such was the feeling of belonging to a family, with Christ as
eldest brother (8:29), which Paul had enjoyed in so many congregations round
the Great Sea and which transcended the old ties of blood and kinship, that
Paul could take it for granted that the Roman Christians would share a similar
depth of feeling and mutual regard. The fulsome language is of course exaggerated, in the way that courteous compliments in the East tend to be. Paul
would not expect it to be taken literally and phrases the first two items in
deliberately vague and nonspecific terms—"full of goodness, filled with all
knowledge." But the third and climactic phrase has more point—"able to
admonish one another." For this is Paul's way of stressing his confidence in
the maturity of the congregations to which he writes: they are able to engage
in the delicate business of mutual instruction and correction among themselves;
they do not need any help from Paul on that front. Here Paul will have in
mind the mutual interdependence of the members of each church (it is no
mere coincidence that 15:15 echoes 12:3): they have the resources in the
Spirit's engracing through one another to cope with all their problems.

15 As in 1:11–12, Paul is striving to find a satisfactory balance between
his own sense of commission and responsibility toward Gentiles and his desire
that the churches of the gentile mission grow in responsibility for themselves
and maturity among themselves. So here, having laid on the compliments
in no ungenerous spirit, he goes on immediately to stress and elaborate the
other aspect—his own commissioning and enabling by God as minister of
the gospel. The skill and delicacy of Paul's diplomacy ("rather boldly," "as a
way of reminding you") would no doubt be recognized and appreciated.

Likewise his characterization of his commission in terms of "grace given by God," rather than explicitly as authorization or command, would not strike his readers as in any way threatening, but rather remind them that all believers were thus commissioned and responsible for others (12:6)—grace never as something merely received or possessed, but as God's powerful outreach in and through and with a view to its extending to others.

The way in which he thus moves back into what becomes his main subject makes clear that the whole lengthy exposition from 1:16–15:13 had not been an idle self-indulgence, or intended as an independent theological tract. He wrote rather boldly in part as a way of reminding them by virtue of the grace given him. He saw the exposition as, in part at least, a discharge or expression of his apostolic commission. He wanted the Christians in Rome to know what his apostolic commission consisted of, both its theological scope (1:16–15:13) and its geographical scope (1:13–15; 15:16–32). The implication presumably is that Paul saw the two as connected: that he had to explain the theological dimension of his gospel before his particular claims to a particular geographical authorization would be accepted; and that it was the particular understanding of the gospel, to Jew first but also Gentile, summed up at the beginning and end of that lengthy exposition (1:16–17; 15:8–13), which made necessary its proclamation to the Gentiles and to as many Gentiles as possible as soon as possible. With that done he can now expand his overall missionary strategy (15:15–21) and specific plans as they affect Rome in detail (15:22–32).

16 The immediate explanation of what Paul's commissioning means for him ("minister of Christ Jesus for the Gentiles") would inevitably strike Paul's audience very powerfully by virtue of its intense concentration of cultic terminology—"officiating priest," "serving as a priest," "sacrificial offering of the Gentiles," "set apart as a sacrifice"). Such a concentration of imagery can be neither unintentional nor casual. This is Paul's way of underscoring his theological exposition of the gospel (1:16–15:13) in its outworking in his own missionary vocation. For one thing it brings home the continuity between his ministry and the whole revelation of Israel, centered to such a degree as it was on the law and the law of the cult: Paul claims to be wholly in continuity and succession with the main line of salvation-revelation in the OT, *not* excluding the law. But more striking still is the way he transforms and transcends all that had hitherto been bound up in that cultic language. By applying it to his own noncultic ministry of preaching the gospel he confirms that for him the cultic barrier between sacred and secular has been broken through and left behind. And by speaking of the Gentiles as themselves the sacrifice, Gentiles who could not even approach the altar of sacrifice in the Temple, who were instinctively regarded by the typically devout Jew as outside the covenant, unclean, Paul confirms that for him the cultically defined barrier between peoples, between Jew and Gentile, had been broken through and left behind. In view of the tensions within their own congregations on matters of ritual purity (14:1–15:6), the Roman readership would not need reminding that cult and ritual served then (as ever) to express group identity and to mark out group boundaries. Nor would they need reminding that their weekly meetings without priest and without sacrifice or libation were highly unusual

phenomena for their time. Paul's purpose seems to be to underline the eschatologically new fact that within God's redefined people ("set apart by the Holy
Spirit") all ministry on behalf of others is priestly ministry (as in Phil 2:25),
and that cultic sacrifice has been replaced by the sacrifice of committed day-
to-day living in personal relationships (12:1).

17 Paul's ministry thus defined he does regard as a cause of boasting,
because it has been so defined (in a way which breaks out of the narrowing
boasting of "the Jew" [2:17, 23]), and because it is "in Christ Jesus." Where
Abraham had no ground for boasting, so long as that ground was understood
in terms of the ritual acts and Torah practices which reinforced Israel's claim
to be different from others and secure in the matters which concern God
(4:2), Paul could not make that boast. For whereas the law as usually understood
within Judaism divided, Jesus Christ now offered an object of faith and means
of self and communal identity which in no way depended on race or nation
or culture or class.

18 It was this Christ who was the authority behind both Paul's gospel
and Paul's mission (in Paul's eyes the two were one anyway; hence again
the tight cohesion of the central block of the letter with the personal explanations on either side of it). And not only the authority, remote and exalted
in a distant heaven, but the one who was in fact acting through Paul. This
is why Paul could boast, because he could take no credit for what he had
done. And what Christ had done, and not just Paul, was to work "for the
obedience of the Gentiles." The recall of a key motif from 1:5 is no doubt
deliberate since it ties together precisely a key theme of Jewish covenant
self-awareness (obedience) and Paul's outreach to the Gentiles: it is precisely
Paul's claim that the obligations of the covenant were being fulfilled in the
faith response of the Gentiles.

19 For the first and only time Paul gives an overview of his missionary
work. He speaks of the power of signs and wonders, the power of God's
Spirit as characterizing the work through him. Once again the overtones
and allusions would be clear to his readers: Paul's ministry as continuous
with and manifesting the same power/finger of God as every Jew knew to
have characterized the Exodus (e.g., Exod 7:3; 8:19); Christ's ministry through
Paul in the power of the Spirit as the eschatological equivalent of the epochal
ministry of Moses (cf. Matt 12:28 // Luke 11:20). As Moses had established
the first assembly/church of God in the old epoch, so Christ through Paul
was now establishing the redefined people of God for the end time.

19–20 It is more important, however, that his readers should appreciate
the sweep of Paul's work and his missionary strategy. He has already completed
a broad arc from Jerusalem to the northwestern edge of the eastern empire,
in line with his strategy to preach only where Christ is not so far known
and honored. Paul's claim sounds more than a little exaggerated and could
be open to some misunderstanding: he could have visited personally only a
small number of the centers of population within the arc of the circle he
describes ("from Jerusalem up to Illyricum") and so could hardly have "completed" the preaching of the gospel in the east; and his own letters show
that his concerns for his churches went well beyond the laying of foundations.
But all that is beside the point. For what we have here is in no sense a

detailed itinerary, but simply a grand design. It is a sweeping vision of missionary strategy in a single stroke of the brush. And its main function is to prepare the way for his visit to Rome, to explain the reason why he now casts his eyes further westward (vv 23–24).

At the same time the basis of a more detailed strategy is clear, with Paul focusing his work in large cities (in Corinth and Ephesus in particular over a sustained period), and probably using these as centers for a more extended regional outreach through various fellow workers. Paul's vision then could be likened to lighting a series of candles at intervals in a curve round the northeastern quadrant of the Mediterranean; having lit them and ensured that the flame was steady, he left it to others to widen the pool of light while he went on to light more at further discrete centers of influence. This must have been a calculated policy on Paul's part, judged by him to be the most effective way of carrying the message of the gospel as far as he could throughout the gentile world. The corollary of not building on someone else's foundation may then have been motivated by the desire to achieve the greatest missionary expansion with the greatest economy of missionary effort, and not simply by his desire to avoid entanglement of loyalties and confusion of theology, of which he had had some bitter experience, not least with regard to the church from which he was writing (2 Cor 10:13–16; 11:1–6, 12–15; 12:11–13). All this would have been familiar to some of those at Rome who knew Paul's work firsthand and had been fellow workers with him (16:3, 7, 9).

21 As ever, where Paul can find a scripture to round off a line of argument, so here, and from his favorite Isaiah. In addition, however, the passage cited (Isa 52:15) effectively ties together Paul's conviction of his call to fulfill the Servant's commission to the Gentiles (1:1, 5 [Isa 49:6]) with his theological argument about the universal gospel (10:15 [Isa 52:7]; 10:16 [Isa 53:1]). Thus Paul manages to maintain the strong implication that his missionary strategy and plans dovetail into his theology of the gospel in a way which shows the structure of the letter to be ever more compact and integrated.

2. Paul's Travel Plans (15:22–33)

Bibliography

Aus, R. D. "Travel Plans." **Bartsch, H. W.** ". . . wenn ich ihnen diese Frucht versiegelt habe. Röm 15:28. Ein Beitrag zum Verständnis der paulinischen Mission." *ZNW* 63 (1972) 95–107. **Berger, K.** "Almosen für Israel: zum historischen Kontext der paulinischen Kollekte." *NTS* 23 (1976–77) 180–204. **Betz, H. D.** *2 Corinthians 8 and 9.* Hermeneia. Philadelphia: Fortress, 1985. **Bornkamm, G.** "Letter." Here 17–20. **Davies, W. D.** *Land.* 198–208, 214–19. **Georgi, D.** *Geschichte.* 79–87. **Haacker, K.** "Probleme." 3–6. **Holl, K.** "Der Kirchenbegriff des Paulus in seinem Verhältnis zu dem der Urgemeinde." In *Paulusbild,* ed. Rengstorf. 144–78, esp. 164–70. **Keck, L. E.** "The Poor among the Saints in the New Testament." *ZNW* 56 (1965) 100–29. ———. "'The Poor among the Saints' in Jewish Christianity and Qumran." *ZNW* 57 (1966) 54–78.

Kettunen, M. *Abfassungszweck.* 161–75. Knox, J. "Romans 15:14–33 and Paul's Conception of His Apostolic Mission." *JBL* 83 (1964) 1–11. Munck, J. *Paul.* 282–308. Nickle, K. P. *The Collection: A Study in the Strategy of Paul.* London: SCM, 1966. O'Rourke, J. J. "The Participle in Rom 15:25." *CBQ* 29 (1967) 116–18. Pfitzner, V. C. *Paul and the Agon Motif.* NovTSup 16. Leiden: Brill, 1967. 120–25. Radermacher, L. "σφραγίζεσθαι: Rom 15:28." *ZNW* 32 (1933) 87–89. Schmithals, W. *Paul and James.* London: SCM, 1965. 79–84. Stuhlmacher, P. *Evangelium.* 100–105. Zeller, D. *Juden.* 229–36, 279–84.

Translation

22 *For this reason I have also regularly*[a] *been prevented from coming to you.* 23 *But now since I no longer have scope in these regions and have had a longing to come to you for many*[b] *years,* 24 *when I travel to Spain*[c] . . . . *For I hope to see you as I pass through*[d] *and to be sent on my way there by*[e] *you, once I have had the full pleasure of being with you for a time.* 25 *But now I am traveling to Jerusalem in service*[f] *to the saints.* 26 *For Macedonia and Achaia chose to make some contribution for the poor among the saints in Jerusalem.* 27 *For they chose*[f] *to do so and are their debtors. For if the Gentiles have received a share in their spiritual affairs, they ought to minister to them in material affairs.* 28 *When therefore I have completed this and have sealed this fruit to them,*[f] *I will go by way of you to Spain.* 29 *And I know that when I come to you I will come in the fullness*[g] *of*[h] *Christ's blessing.*

30 *I appeal to you, brothers,*[i] *through our Lord Jesus Christ and through the love of the Spirit, to contend with me in your prayers to God on my*[j] *behalf,* 31 *that I might be delivered from the disobedient in Judea and my service*[k] *for Jerusalem might be acceptable to the saints,* 32 *in order that I might come*[f] *to you in joy through the will of God*[l] *and be mutually refreshed*[m] *by your company.* 33 *May the God of peace be with you all. Amen.*[n]

Notes

[a] p46 B D F G read the more expected πολλάκις (cf. 1:13), but the less familiar τὰ πολλά (ℵ A C etc.) is more likely to be original as being the less usual.

[b] Aland26 takes πολλῶν (p46 ℵ A etc.) as original, with ἱκανῶν (B C P etc.) introduced as a more polished substitution (Metzger). But the unusualness of the phrase ἀπὸ ἱκανῶν ἐτῶν gives it more weight as the more difficult reading (Cranfield).

[c] To resolve the incomplete sentence some later witnesses have added ἐλεύσομαι πρὸς ὑμᾶς, clearly modeled on v 29.

[d] p46 A miss the delicate implication of the vocabulary by omitting the prefix δια-.

[e] ἀπό has the support of the quite frequent combination p46 B D F G, an alteration perhaps to decrease the implication that Paul the apostle was dependent on the Roman Christians.

[f] Various minor improving stylistic modifications at these points.

[g] (D*) F G read πληροφορία, "full assurance, certainty."

[h] A late insertion of τοῦ εὐαγγελίου τοῦ gives the clause a more sonorous and stylistically pleasing conclusion—εὐλογίας τοῦ εὐαγγελίου . . . ἐλεύσομαι.

[i] p46 B omit ἀδελφοί; however, its use here is characteristically Pauline, and the much broader attestation in its favor in MS and version may be regarded as sufficient evidence to include it (Lietzmann).

[j] The scribal emendation ὑμῶν ("in your prayers") crept into a number of MSS.

[k] B D* F G have replaced διακονία with what presumably was regarded as the more appropriate δωροφορία, "the bringing of a gift." The same witnesses also replace εἰς with the easier ἐν.

[l] ℵ* B D* F G replace θεοῦ with κυρίου Ἰησοῦ or Χριστοῦ Ἰησοῦ or Ἰησοῦ Χριστοῦ, but Paul always speaks of "the will of God" (otherwise only Eph 5:17).

ᵐThe very unusual συναναπαύσωμαι ὑμῖν has been omitted by P⁴⁶ B, perhaps by accident of transcription (Metzger), and replaced by more familiar alternatives.

ⁿP⁴⁶ omits ἀμήν, presumably because P⁴⁶ added the doxology of 16:25–27 at this point. As an understandable "liturgical reflex," its presence at the instigation of Paul is as likely as its later insertion; in such a case the stronger weight of external evidence for its inclusion (א B C D etc.) should probably decide the matter.

Form and Structure

See 15:14–21 *Form and Structure*.

Comment

22 διὸ καὶ ἐνεκοπτόμην τὰ πολλὰ τοῦ ἐλθεῖν πρὸς ὑμᾶς, "for this reason I have also regularly been prevented from coming to you." Since v 23 coheres with v 19, the implication of the διό is that it has been Paul's busyness in "completing the gospel of Christ" (v 19) which has prevented the visit to Rome, rather than his unwillingness to build on someone else's foundation (v 20) (so Cranfield, Schlier, and Wilckens; against Käsemann, Kettunen, 135–36, et al.). For ἐγκόπτω see BGD, and *TDNT* 3:856 (also BDF, §400.4) and cf. the three other NT epistolary references (Gal 5:7; 1 Thess 2:18; 1 Pet 3:7). The thought is clearly the same as 1:13 and almost as elusive (see on 1:13). πολλά used as an adverb, "greatly, often, frequently, regularly," is common, though usually without the article (LSJ, πολύς IIIa; BGD, πολύς I.2bβ) = πολλάκις (1:13).

23 νυνὶ δὲ μηκέτι τόπον ἔχων ἐν τοῖς κλίμασι τούτοις, "but now no longer having scope in these regions." For τόπος see on 12:19. For κλίμα = "region," see LSJ II.2 and BGD. The claim is a strong one ("this astounding statement" [Dahl, "Missionary Theology," 76]), but the reference is to the strategic vision and policy sketched out in vv 19–20. The words should certainly not be read as a claim to have done all that could be done, even in terms of foundation laying, in the east. Paul limited his mission to the arc "from Jerusalem to Illyricum" (v 19), and his claim to be "apostle to the Gentiles" evidently did not involve, in his perspective, a commission to such important regions as Mesopotamia and Egypt. Others had no doubt been commissioned to cover these regions (cf. 15:19 κύκλῳ). Even so, it is hard to avoid the conclusion that the perspective is informed by the eschatological vision of a pressingly short time in which the gospel can be preached (Käsemann; Cranfield's protest is weakened by confusing the issue of the geographical scope of Paul's vision with that of the near expectation of the Parousia).

ἐπιποθίαν δὲ ἔχων τοῦ ἐλθεῖν πρὸς ὑμᾶς ἀπὸ ἱκανῶν ἐτῶν, "and having had a longing to come to you for many years." ἐπιποθία is a very rare formation from ἐπιποθέω (LSJ lists only this passage; perhaps an echo of 1:11), but its meaning is not in doubt = ἐπιπόθησις (2 Cor 7:7, 11); see BDF, §109.5. The phrase ἀπὸ ἱκανῶν ἐτῶν is also unusual, but with parallels in Luke 8:27 D and 23:8. The reason for his desire to come to Rome is indicated in v 24; see also *Introduction* §3.2 and 1:11–13.

24 ὡς ἂν πορεύωμαι εἰς τὴν Σπανίαν, "when I travel to Spain." As in 5:12ff. (cf. 9:22–23), the sentence is left incomplete—completion coming in effect in v 28, after the sidetracking parenthesis of vv 24–27. For ὡς ἂν + subjunctive indicating the time of an event in the future, "when, as soon as," see BDF, §455.2 ("on my imminent journey to Spain") and BGD, ὡς III.3c; also in 1 Cor 11:34 and Phil 2:23. The reason why Paul was so set on reaching Spain is regrettably much less clear than we might have hoped. (1) It was certainly an obvious step beyond Rome. From the eastern end of the Mediterranean Phoenicians had founded Gades (Cadiz) many centuries before. And in the two and a half centuries since the defeat of the Carthaginians, Rome had been steadily expanding its influence over an increasing extent of the peninsula. It was well regarded by Romans, attracting many businessmen and veterans; Caesar and Augustus had founded a further twenty-one colonies, and several prominent Romans, like Seneca, had been born in Spain (see further *OCD*). For a native of the Mediterranean region and Roman citizen like Paul, Spain would very likely have had much greater appeal than regions further north, including Gaul. (2) It is likely that there were already Jews settled in Spain, but unfortunately there is as yet no reliable evidence to that effect (SVMG 3:84); it would, however, fit best with what we know of earliest Christian expansion, as for the most part growing on and out of earlier Jewish communities with their penumbra of interested, sympathetic, and God-worshiping Gentiles (see *Introduction* §2.2.2). (3) If we follow the image of the arc of a circle used by Paul in v 19, the obvious extension of the arc was a sweep through Italy (Rome) into Spain. This perhaps strengthens the probability that Paul's grand design was to cover the northern half of the Mediterranean while others covered the southern half (thus completing the circle?). Whether Paul ever attained this goal remains an unresolved issue, despite the well-known assertion of *1 Clem.* 5.7 (cf. SH, 413–14). Aus, however, ties together the different threads of Paul's thought (11:25–27; 15:16, 24, 25–27) to maintain the fascinating hypothesis that Paul understood Spain to be the Tarshish of Isa 66:19: only when he has brought Christian representatives from Spain (15:16, 24) as part of his collection enterprise (15:25–27) will the "full number of the Gentiles come in" (11:25) and the grand finale of 11:25–27 unfold.

ἐλπίζω γὰρ διαπορευόμενος θεάσασθαι ὑμᾶς, "for I hope to see you as I pass through." The language is carefully chosen to avoid offense (he is not the church-founding apostle of these churches) and to make it clear that the visit will constitute no infringement of the principle of v 20 (see also on 15:15 and 15:20). For θεάομαι, "see," in the sense "come to see, visit," cf. 2 Chron 22:6, Josephus, *Ant.* 16.6, and Matt 22:11.

καὶ ὑφ' ὑμῶν προπεμφθῆναι ἐκεῖ, "and by you to be sent on my way there." προπέμπω has the specific sense of "help on one's journey," that is, in a variety of possible ways: by providing food, money, letters of introduction, arranging transport, accompanying part of the way, etc.; so 1 Macc 12:4; 1 Esd 4:47; *Ep. Arist.* 172 (BGD). In earliest Christianity it becomes almost a technical term for the provision made by a church for missionary support (Acts 15:3; 20:38; 21:5; 1 Cor 16:6, 11; 2 Cor 1:16; Titus 3:13; 3 John 6; Pol. *Phil.* 1.1) (Dodd, Michel, Cranfield, Schlier); see also *LPGL*. Since Paul drew so many of his assistants/fellow workers from the churches to which he ministered, he may well have hoped that one or more of the Roman Christians who knew Spain would accompany him there.

ἐὰν ὑμῶν πρῶτον ἀπὸ μέρους ἐμπλησθῶ, "once I have had the full pleasure of being with you for a time." ἐὰν πρῶτον most obviously means "when first" (so "once"); however, it could mean "when especially" (cf. BGD, πρῶτος 2a, c). For ἀπὸ μέρους see on 15:15; here used temporally. ἐμπίμπλημι has the sense "fill full" (LSJ), so here "to have one's fill of" (BGD). The sense is positive, of course. Throughout this section Paul shows his skill in expressing his hope in the language of common courtesy (including polite exaggeration) which his audience would no doubt appreciate (cf. Michel, Käsemann).

25 νυνὶ δὲ πορεύομαι εἰς Ἰερουσαλὴμ διακονῶν τοῖς ἁγίοις, "but now I travel to Jerusalem in service to the saints." The repeated νυνὶ δέ (v 23) suggests the momentous juncture which Paul sensed his work to have reached, with something at least of the eschatological overtone which is a regular feature of Paul's usage (see on 3:21). The present tense of πορεύομαι is loosely used with future meaning ("I am going to"), presumably implying imminent departure. Ἰερουσαλήμ is closer to the semitic form of the name than Ἰεροσόλυμα (Michel), but Paul seems to use both forms in Gal (1:17–18; 2:1; 4:25–26); see also BGD. διακονέω, "minister, render a service" is not specifically Christian (LSJ, BGD). Paul uses the verb much less frequently than the correlative nouns, but the range of potential meaning is the same (see on 12:7). Apart from reference to his own ministry (see on 12:7), the word group is most frequently used with reference to the collection (15:31; 2 Cor 8:4, 19–20; 9:1, 12–13; similar use in Acts 11:29 and 12:25); but the variation in Paul's usage hardly supports Betz's suggestion that ἡ διακονία ἡ εἰς τοὺς ἁγίους, "the charitable collection for the saints" is "the official name for the collection" (*2 Corinthians 8–9*, 90). The participle is usually taken as expressing purpose (O'Rourke, Käsemann, Cranfield, Wilckens; against Michel). NEB's "on an errand to God's people" tends to trivialize the thought. For ἅγιοι see on 1:7. In view of the unqualified use here, and the regularity of Paul's reference to the Jerusalem Christians under this title (1 Cor 16:1; 2 Cor 8:4; 9:1, 12), it is certainly quite possible that Paul's usage reflects an early self-designation of the earliest Christian church, parallel to its quite common use elsewhere in Judaism at the time (see on 1:7 and Lietzmann).

As with Paul's desire to reach Spain, so with his desire to take the collection to Jerusalem, the reasons are not so clear as we might have hoped. (1) Clearly Paul regarded it as of first importance: he devoted much energy to it (15:25–26; 1 Cor 16:1–14; 2 Cor 8–9); and he regarded it as a climactic turning point (νυνὶ δέ) in his ministry, so that he could not begin the second large phase of his mission (to the west) until he had completed this task. (2) He regarded it as an obligation on the part of the gentile churches to those through whom the stream of salvation-history blessings had flowed to them (see on 15:27). It was therefore not simply an act of mutual service between fellow Christians (12:7; there were, no doubt, many other poor Christians in other churches), but an attempt to express the continuity of salvation-history, and the mutual interdependence (v 27) of those equally benefiting from it; the unity of the now widespread churches "in Christ" counted heavily with Paul (see particularly Käsemann, Wilckens, Achtemeier).

(3) More open to dispute is the significance of the collection to the Christians in Jerusalem itself. Here the evidence is more ambiguous, an ambiguity which may well reflect the different understandings of the relationship between

Jerusalem and the churches of the diaspora, as between Paul and (some of)
the Jerusalem leadership, and which may indicate Paul's careful nuancing
of his language in the light of these differences (see on 15:26—οἱ πτωχοί τῶν
ἁγίων; 15:27—λειτουργῆσαι). Thus the request (or would Jerusalem have
phrased it more strongly?) that Paul should "remember the poor" (Gal 2:10)
may have been understood (in the light of the importance given to alms
giving within Judaism: Dan 4:27; Sir 29:12; 40:24; Tob 4:10; 12:9; 14:10–
11; Acts 10:35) as the next best thing to circumcision, as the act of righteousness
most important for the loyal covenant member (see further Berger, "Almosen"). Hence, perhaps, Paul's repeated emphasis, by way of contrast, on the
freely willed choice of the Gentiles' giving (vv 26, 27). Whereas food laws
and sacred days were a matter which divided Christians, the responsibility
to care for the poor Paul saw as a strongly consistent and still binding obligation
of biblical revelation, essential for communal harmony and for the unified
identity of the scattered congregations.

(4) Also important would have been the widely held Jewish expectation
that the wealth of the nations would flow into Jerusalem in the end time
(Isa 45:14; 60:5–17; 61:6; Mic 4:13; Tob 13:11; 1QM 12.13–15; see also on
9:26). It would be surprising if this expectation was not a factor somewhere
in the background, since it chimes in so well with Paul's sense of eschatological
urgency (Barrett; despite, once again, Cranfield; also Zeller). Indeed the collection itself may have been a bone of contention for this very reason, with
Paul determined that it should be understood as an act of mutual concern
between Christian equals (hence the repeated εὐδόκησαν in vv 26 and 27),
rather than as an act of submission reinforcing Israel's sense that its priority
in salvation-history must be translated into economic and political dominance,
but fearful of the outcome (so rightly Georgi, *Geschichte*, 85; Stuhlmacher,
Evangelium, 100–103; see on 15:31). Paul would not dispute the prophecies,
but understand them in a transformed sense, equivalent to the transformation
in cultic imagery (and significance) attempted in v 16, though one should
not equate the offering of the Gentiles (v 16) with the collection, as Zeller
rightly notes (*Juden*, 282–84).

(5) Can we go further and say that Paul saw the collection as part of a
climactic strategy to stir the Jews to jealousy (11:13–14) at the success of the
gentile mission, as evidenced by the number of representatives accompanying
the collection (Munck, *Paul*, 303–4)? Did Paul see his own work as the decisive
trigger to initiate the end (cf. 11:13–15, 25–27 with 15:16)? Despite Knox
("Rom 15:14–33," 3–8) and Davies (*Land*, 203), the argument cannot be dismissed on the grounds that Paul contemplated the possibility of his death
(15:31) and further missionary work in Spain (15:24), in view of Aus's more
elaborate thesis (see on 15:24). But in fact Paul does not indicate how he
saw his work fitting into the final sequence of events (the hope of 11:14,
"some of them," is not identical with that of 11:26, "all"), and any reconstruction
inevitably goes beyond the evidence of the text itself.

26   εὐδόκησαν γὰρ Μακεδονία καὶ Ἀχαΐα κοινωνίαν τινὰ ποιήσασθαι, "for Macedonia and Achaia chose to make some contribution." εὐδόκησα as well as
ηὐδόκησα can serve as aorist for εὐδοκέω (BGD). εὐδοκέω + infinitive or accusative
and infinitive indicates choice or preference (as in Sir 25:16; 2 Macc 14:35;

2 Cor 5:8); the repetition of the assertion in v 27 must mean that Paul is stressing that the decision to participate in the collection was wholly theirs, freely made (*TDNT* 2:741). The emphasis is characteristic of the responsibility Paul expected his churches to bear for themselves (see on 15:14); any "legal meaning" here (Betz, *2 Corinthians 8–9*, 123 n.273) is as likely to be coincidental as deliberate. Why Paul mentions only Macedonia and Achaia when others were doubtless involved (Galatia—1 Cor 16:1; Asia—Acts 20:4) remains an unresolved puzzle; but the resolution could be as simple as that he is writing from Achaia and mentions only the regions in closest proximity to Rome (= the near end of the arc so far drawn [v 19]); or it may even be that Paul concentrated his attention most heavily on the churches of these regions (cf. 2 Cor 8:1–7; 9:1–5). The suggestion that Paul was hiding something (Käsemann) would need more support than this. And Luedemann's argument from silence (that the collection in Galatia had been overthrown [*Paul*, 1:86]) depends too much on the overworked assumption that the collection was Paul's all-consuming interest from the Jerusalem conference onwards (see further *Introduction* §1.4).

κοινωνία means basically the act or condition of sharing something in common, and was probably brought into Christian vocabulary by Paul (it occurs only three times in the LXX; thirteen of the nineteen NT occurrences are Pauline, and four of the others are in 1 John 1), though the formulation κοινωνίαν ποιήσασθαι would not seem strange to either Jew (Str-B 3:316) or Greek (LSJ, κοινωνία). For Paul it denotes particularly common participation in or sharing of something (1 Cor 10:16—the blood and body of Christ; 2 Cor 13:13/14 and Phil 2:1—the Holy Spirit; Phil 1:5—the gospel; Phil 3:10—Christ's sufferings; Philem 6—faith). Here and in 2 Cor 8:4 and 9:13, it is used in the extended sense of "expression of what is shared," in reference to the collection; with the implication that in principle Paul wanted his converts to regard their resources as held in common with and for other Christians, or that he saw such financial sharing as the expression of their common life in Christ; so "sign of fellowship, proof of brotherly love," or even more concretely (but with the danger of losing the important sense of "in common") "gift, contribution" (BGD, RSV, NIV, NJB); see also on 12:13. The fact that κοινωνία is something of a favorite word for Paul, not least in this connection, makes it less likely that he has deliberately avoided more "juridical" terms (so justifiably Cranfield; against Holl, 166–68, Georgi, *Geschichte*, 82–84, and Käsemann). If it can be said to have a more administrative sense here (Betz, *2 Corinthians 8–9*, 46), that is almost incidental to its broader Pauline significance.

εἰς τοὺς πτωχοὺς τῶν ἁγίων τῶν ἐν Ἰερουσαλήμ, "for the poor among the saints in Jerusalem." Despite substantial support (including Holl, 167; Lietzmann; *TDNT* 6:909; and Schlier) for the view that the genitive is epexegetic ("the poor who are the saints"), Paul could hardly have expected or intended his readers to take the phrase in other than its most natural sense in the Greek (partitive genitive—so Michel; Munck, *Paul*, 288; Keck, *ZNW* 56 [1965] 119; Käsemann; Cranfield; Wilckens). Nevertheless it is possible that Paul's usage here does reflect in some measure at least the self-understanding of the earliest Christian community in Jerusalem as "the poor." Such a self-designation would be understandable in the light of such passages as Pss 69:32; 72:2; *Pss. Sol.* 5.2, 11; 10.6; 15.1; 18.2; 1QpHab 12.3, 6, 10; 1QM 11.9, 13; 4QpPs37 2.10 (note particularly Ps 72:4—"the poor of the people"; CD 19.9—"the poor of the flock"; see further *TDNT* 6:888–902 and Keck, *ZNW* 57 [1966] 66–77). That the poverty of (many of) the Jerusalem Christians was also, in economic terms, a consequence in large part of the overenthusiastic resourcing of the common fund by means of realizing capital in the earliest days of the new movement (Acts 2:44–45; 4:34–37) is very probable (Dodd). For ἅγιοι see on 1:7 and 15:25. For Ἰερουσαλήμ see on 15:25.

27 εὐδόκησαν γὰρ καὶ ὀφειλέται εἰσὶν αὐτῶν, "for they chose to do so and are their debtors." For εὐδόκησαν see on 15:26. γάρ could be translated "indeed"; cf. BDF, §452.2. For ὀφειλέτης see on 1:14. The debt was moral, but the obligation had been readily accepted by Paul as part of the very important agreement achieved in Gal 2:9–10 (see further on 15:25). The suggestion that Paul was hinting to the Romans that they should also contribute to the collection (Leenhardt) forgets the implication of v 25 that Paul was about to set off for Jerusalem. The αὐτῶν refers of course to the whole church at Jerusalem, not just "the poor" among them; however, that adds nothing to the case for seeing "the poor" and "the saints" as synonymous (v 26), since Paul would naturally regard a gift for the benefit of the poor members of the Jerusalem church as a gift to the church (Althaus).

εἰ γὰρ τοῖς πνευματικοῖς αὐτῶν ἐκοινώνησαν τὰ ἔθνη, "for if the Gentiles have received a share in their spiritual things"; cf. 11:16–18. For πνευματικός see on 1:11 and 7:14. The word is not more fully defined: it refers to all which believers have received from the Spirit (see also below). For κοινωνέω see on 12:13 and 15:26 (κοινωνία).

ὀφείλουσιν καὶ ἐν τοῖς σαρκικοῖς λειτουργῆσαι αὐτοῖς, "they ought also to minister to them in material things." The contrast between πνευματικά and σαρκικά is understandable simply as a contrast between spiritual blessings and material needs. But there may be an overtone here of the πνεῦμα/σάρξ antithesis which has been such a feature of the letter (1:3–4; 2:28–29; 7:5–6, 14; 8:4–13), with the neatly turned implication that the flow of blessing from Jew to Gentile is at the spiritual level and not in terms of ethnic assimilation; on the contrary, at the level of the flesh, the flow of benefit is from Gentile to Jew! With λειτουργέω there will be the same cultic overtone as in 15:16 (against *TDNT* 4:227), with the same implication of the boundary between cultic and profane as broken down in, with and by the breaking down of the boundary between Jew and Gentile, and with once again, probably, the implication of the tables having been turned—Gentiles ministering (as priests) to Jews. That Paul should think of giving practical financial help as a "sacred ministry" (so also 2 Cor 9:12; Phil 2:25, 30) should not surprise us. The principle Paul is applying here is a more general one (1 Cor 9:11; Gal 6:6; Phil 4:15; Philem 19; there are hardly sufficient grounds for saying that he derived it from syncretistic pneumatics [Zeller, *Juden*, 230–31; against Georgi, *Geschichte*, 83]), but it is applied here at a salvation-history level, as an expression of the eschatological coming together of different peoples and of the mutual interdependence of believers across national boundaries.

28 τοῦτο οὖν ἐπιτελέσας καὶ σφραγισάμενος αὐτοῖς τὸν καρπὸν τοῦτον, "when therefore I have completed this and have sealed this fruit to them." ἐπιτελέω can mean simply "end, bring to an end, finish" (as in Gal 3:3; Phil 1:6; and probably also 2 Cor 8:6, 11), or "complete, accomplish, bring about" (as in 2 Cor 7:1). It can also have the more technical sense of "perform a religious service, ritual, or ceremony"—ἐπιτελεῖν τὴν λειτουργίαν/τὰς λειτουργίας/τὰς λατρείας/θυσίας (e.g., Philo, *Som*. 1.214, and papyri; see MM, BGD). And in view of the cultic imagery so prominent in Paul's thought in this passage (vv 16, 27—λειτουργῆσαι) a continuing implication that the significance of the cult has been transformed (see on 15:16) is probable. But it may simply be a standard term for carrying out a piece of official business (Betz, *2 Corinthians 8–9*, 54).

There is some puzzlement over the precise significance of σφραγίζω. Presumably the imagery is drawn from the commercial sphere—the seal as visible mark of ownership (referring to the Spirit in the other Pauline references: 2 Cor 1:22, Eph 1:13, 4:30; probably also John 6:27; cf. John 1:32–34 and 3:33–34), or sealing as denoting secure transfer of responsibility or ownership (Deissmann, *Bible Studies*, 238–39; MM; *NDIEC* 2:191; cf. particularly Tob 9:5). There is no need to agonize over the propriety of the usage or the shades of meaning possible (cf. BGD, Radermacher, Käsemann, Cranfield; see also Lagrange). What we probably have here is an abbreviated mode of expression, reflecting the looser use of the image in popular speech (*TDNT* 7:948)—"sealed it over to"—with the same sort of looseness and implication as the English phrase "signed and sealed," a similar popularization of an older more technical procedure (cf. 1 Cor 16:3); hence NEB, "delivered the proceeds under my own seal" (RSV, NIV, and NJB are less satisfactory). But Fitzmyer may be right in suggesting that in the metaphor "Paul implies that he is still under suspicion in Jerusalem." For καρπός see on 1:13; here it can hardly mean anything other than the collection (Käsemann, Cranfield; though Bartsch argues that it refers to the Macedonians and Achaeans whose contribution to the collection was the seal of the union of the Pauline churches with the founding church in Jerusalem). The talk of transferring (sacks of) fruit confirms the commercial basis of the imagery.

ἀπελεύσομαι δι᾽ ὑμῶν εἰς Σπανίαν, "I will go by way of you to Spain." For ἀπέρχομαι + εἰς see BGD, ἀπέρχομαι 2. Paul confirms that he sees Rome primarily as a staging post on his way to Spain (see on 15:24).

29 οἶδα δὲ ὅτι ἐρχόμενος πρὸς ὑμᾶς ἐν πληρώματι εὐλογίας Χριστοῦ ἐλεύσομαι, "and I know that when I come to you I will come in the fullness of Christ's blessing." For πλήρωμα see on 11:12. For the meaning of εὐλογία = grace bestowed, see on 12:14; cf. Gal 3:14; Eph 1:3; Heb 6:7; 12:17; and 1 Pet 3:9; note the use of it with reference to the collection in 2 Cor 9:5–6. Both thoughts of 1:11–12 are combined (Lietzmann). There is something of the tone of καύχησις, "boasting" (Michel), as in 15:17: Paul was very confident of his commissioning—that it was from Christ and used by Christ (so also 1:11, 13, 15). Käsemann is also probably right to see v 29 "as it were a sigh of relief as Paul can contemplate the approaching end of his task." SH note how strongly these words indicate the authenticity of this chapter: "No one could possibly write in this manner at a later date, knowing the circumstances under which St Paul actually did visit Rome."

30 παρακαλῶ δὲ ὑμᾶς, ἀδελφοί, "I appeal to you, brothers." For παρακαλῶ see on 12:1. There are stronger grounds here for seeing a "diplomatic usage" (Jewett, "Ambassadorial Letter," 18; cf. Bjerkelund, 157–73), since Paul is in effect appealing for support from one section of the Christian churches with a view to potential trouble with another section (the nearest parallels being 1 Cor 1:10; 2 Cor 10:1; and 2 Thess 3:12); note also the solemn weight of the words used in making the appeal. "Ask" (Cranfield) is therefore too weak. For ἀδελφός see on 1:13.

διὰ τοῦ κυρίου ἡμῶν Ἰησοῦ Χριστοῦ, "through our Lord Jesus Christ." For the use of διά see on 12:1, and for the whole phrase see on 5:1. Implied is both Paul's firm conviction that his ministry (including the trip to Jerusalem) is at the behest of his Lord, and the equally strong belief that Christ, including the shared experience of his Lordship ("in Christ"), is a bond between them.

καὶ διὰ τῆς ἀγάπης τοῦ πνεύματος, "and through the love of the Spirit." For διά see again on 12:1. The genitive doubtless means "the love prompted by the Spirit"; see on 5:5, and for ἀγάπη see on 12:9. For the appeal in terms of love, cf. Ign. Trall. 6.1. Barrett notes the "'unintended' Trinitarian formulation" in this verse, as in vv 15–16.

συναγωνίσασθαί μοι ἐν ταῖς προσευχαῖς ὑπὲρ ἐμοῦ πρὸς τὸν θεόν, "to contend along with me in your prayers to God on my behalf." συναγωνίζομαι, only here in biblical Greek, can mean simply "aid, assist, help someone" (LSJ, BGD). But the choice of word, from the ἀγών root ("athletic contest, struggle, fight"), suggests that Paul had something more forceful in mind—"strive, exert oneself" (Barrett, Black, Cranfield); cf. ἀγωνίζομαι (1 Cor 9:25; Col 1:29; 1 Tim 4:10; 6:12; 2 Tim 4:7), particularly the close parallel of Col 4:12. In addition the context (v 31) indicates something of a real or threatened conflict; and the double appeal (συν- μοι, ὑπὲρ ἐμοῦ) strongly suggests that Paul is in effect seeking to draw them into an alliance over against the potential opposition from Judea and the Jerusalem church (v 31). So it is hard to exclude an overtone of danger, requiring the dedicated discipline of the athlete or soldier (Käsemann; against Cranfield). Michel draws attention to the fact that the psalmist often accuses his enemies before God in prayer; however, there is no indication of a particular allusion to Jacob's wrestling (Gen 32:24 ff.); and Pfitzner, 120–25, shows that the thought is more of taking part in Paul's struggle by means of prayer, than of prayer as a kind of contest with God. In which case the discipline required of the pray-er would be no less, but it would be the empathetic identification of the pray-er with the one prayed for which is most to the fore. For προσευχή see on 1:10; cf. 12:12. The several references to the subject, particularly 8:15–16, 26–27 and here, provide the basis for a rich and profound theology of prayer.

31 ἵνα ῥυσθῶ ἀπὸ τῶν ἀπειθούντων ἐν τῇ Ἰουδαίᾳ, "that I might be delivered from the disobedient in Judea." Unlike the other two uses in Romans (7:24 and 11:26), ῥύομαι here does not refer to eschatological deliverance, but means simply "rescue, deliver, preserve" (cf. particularly 2 Cor 1:10; 2 Thess 3:2; 2 Tim 3:11; 4:17–18; see further BGD); Paul fears for his life. "Nothing more fully proves the significance of the fund in Paul's eyes than the fact that he judged its safe delivery to be worth the risk of his life" (Minear, Obedience, 4). In Romans οἱ ἀπειθοῦντες is one of Paul's main descriptions of the bulk of his fellow countrymen who have rejected Christ and the gospel (10:21; 11:30–31; see on 2:8; the word occurs only in Romans within the

Pauline corpus). The mention of "Judea" is not merely geographical, as indicating a wide spread of opposition, but national (it probably denotes the whole national territory of the Jews; cf. particularly 1 Thess 2:14 [*TDNT* 3:382]), as indicating an opposition which is bound up with national identity—the Jews = the people of God (cf. Acts 20:3, 23; 21:11); see further on 2:17 and below.

καὶ ἡ διακονία μου ἡ εἰς Ἰερουσαλὴμ εὐπρόσδεκτος τοῖς ἁγίοις γένηται, "and my service for Jerusalem might be acceptable to the saints." For διακονία see on 11:13 and 12:7; here of the collection, as in 2 Cor 8:4; 9:1, 12–13; see also on 15:25. For Ἰερουσαλήμ see also on 15:25. It is noteworthy that Paul is able to describe the recipients of his "service" simply as "Jerusalem." The implication is not, of course, that Christians have become the majority there, but that Paul saw and acknowledged the salvation-history significance of Jerusalem and therefore of the mother church which belonged there (cf. v 27). For εὐπρόσδεκτος see on 15:16; for ἁγιοι see on 1:7 and 15:25.

The significance of this verse in assessing the relationships between Paul and Jerusalem during his expanding mission through Asia Minor, Macedonia, and Greece, should not be discounted (Cranfield amazingly compares the sensitivities and misunderstandings which often emerge in organizing church collections for charitable purposes; cf. Zeller). The fear which Paul expresses here was that the collection might be refused, with a consequent breach of some magnitude between the mother churches of Judea and those of the Pauline mission in the diaspora (so rightly Käsemann, Schlier, Wilckens; contrast Watson, *Paul*, 105). Schmithals argues from the absence of a second ἱνα that Paul expresses only *one* fear and not *two*. That is, "the menace from the Jews is connected with the possible rejection of the contributions: 'Pray that the Jews do not harm me and (therefore) my contributions are welcome to the Christians' . . . The more sharply the Jews reacted to Paul's arrival the less welcome to the Jewish Christians could the contributions be which Paul brought them" (*Paul*, 82). On this interpretation Paul would not be assuming any or much hostility toward his missionary work on the part of the Jewish-Christian leadership in Jerusalem, but feared that under threat of persecution the Jerusalem church would be forced to reaffirm its solidarity with the ancestral faith in preference to its unity with the diaspora churches. The breach would not be of such magnitude, but would still be serious.

Paul's fears strengthen the probability: (1) That there was strong opposition to Paul's "law-free" mission in the church of Jerusalem (hence the attempts to convert again [= properly!] Paul's converts, so fiercely resisted in Gal, 2 Cor 10–13, and Phil 3). This is confirmed by Acts 21:20–21; the picture in Acts corresponds to a remarkable degree with the picture emerging from Paul's letters at this point (Michel). Brown adds the suggestion that v 31 may in part be explained by Paul's fear that his derogatory comments about the leadership of the Jerusalem church made in his letter to the Galatians (we may think of 2:6) would have been reported back to Jerusalem by his Galatian opponents (*Rome*, 112). (2) That this opposition was probably strongly nationalistic in character. This is implied in Phil 3:3, 5 (the same "boast in the flesh" which Paul contests throughout Romans, particularly 2:28; 4:1; and 9:8), and again in Acts 21:20–21; the Jerusalem Christians would hardly have been uninfluenced by the rising tide of nationalistic feeling which led to the Jewish revolt in A.D. 66; and the faction designated as "sham brothers" in Gal 2:4 probably gained in numbers and influence (Wilckens). In other words the two clauses covered by the one ἵνα in v 31 may be much more closely integrated than at first appears, as Schmithals suggests.

Such nationalistic feeling would tend to view the offering of Gentiles with increased suspicion (according to Josephus the action which made the first Jewish revolt inevitable was the decision that the Temple should accept no further gift or sacrifice from a foreigner [*War* 2.409–10]), and provides the most coherent context and explanation for Paul's fears that his gentile gift (v 27) would be refused (see also Haacker). In view of Luke's silence about the collection (not mentioned in Acts 20:4–5, but cf. 24:17) and silence as to whether it proved acceptable in the event, it is very likely that in the event Paul's fears were realized and that Paul found little support from the bulk of Judean Christians during his imprisonment in Judea (since the first part of his prayer [v 31a] was not answered as Paul had hoped, we cannot assume that the second part [v 31b] was any more "successful"; see Harrisville). The lasting effects of the breach were diminished by the outbreak of the revolt about ten years later and by the defeat of the Jews and destruction of Jerusalem, with consequent reduction in some degree of Jewish-Christian influence.

32 ἵνα ἐν χαρᾷ ἐλθὼν πρὸς ὑμᾶς διὰ θελήματος θεοῦ συναναπαύσωμαι ὑμῖν, "in order that I might come to you in joy through the will of God and be mutually refreshed with you." The ἵνα follows from v 31, not from v 30: only if he was delivered from the disobedient and only if the collection was accepted could he come with joy. χαρά here probably has the overtone of relief (Käsemann); see also 14:17 and 15:13. For διὰ θελήματος θεοῦ see on 1:10, to which the thought is very close (see also Murray). συναναπαύομαι is a highly unusual formulation: elsewhere in biblical Greek only in Isa 11:6; in secular Greek only in the sense "sleep with someone" (LSJ, BGD); the only parallel being in Eusebius, *HE* 4.22.2—συνανεπάημεν τῷ ὀρθῷ λόγῳ, "we were mutually refreshed in the true doctrine" (MM). So probably "find rest with, be mutually refreshed by"; cf. ἀναπαύομαι (1 Cor 16:18; 2 Cor 7:13; and Philem 7, 20). After the traumas of taking the collection to Jerusalem Paul anticipated no serious tension in Rome (SH, Black, Michel, Kettunen, 166; "for a happy time of relaxation in your company" [NJB]).

33 ὁ δὲ θεὸς τῆς εἰρήνης μετὰ πάντων ὑμῶν, ἀμήν, "may the God of peace be with you all. Amen." For εἰρήνη see on 1:7 and 5:1, and for θεός + genitive see on 15:5. Paul uses here a favorite phrase as he winds up to the conclusion of one of his letters (16:20; 2 Cor 13:11; Phil 4:9; 1 Thess 5:23; 2 Thess 3:16; see also Heb 13:20 and *T. Dan.* 5.2; for OT background see further Cranfield). That he chooses this formulation rather than "the God of patience" (v 5) or "the God of hope" (v 13) reflects the depths of the forebodings just expressed (v 31) (Schmidt). μετὰ πάντων ὑμῶν is likewise typical of a final prayer or wish (1 Cor 16:24; 2 Cor 13:13; 2 Thess 3:18). For ἀμήν see on 1:25. The formulation is traditionally and strongly Jewish in character.

Explanation

22 Now at last Paul comes to his most specific request and reason for writing to his Roman fellow Christians. He had prepared the ground in general

terms at the beginning of the letter (1:10–15). And his language here deliberately picks up and repeats the same general concerns: the long sequence of
hindrances which had prevented his coming before (v 22; 1:13); the long-
cherished desire to visit them (v 23b; 1:10–11); the desire for mutual benefit
and refreshment from the visit (vv 24, 29, 32; 1:11–12). But now he can be
more specific: he wants their help on two matters.

23–24 First, he wants to use them as a staging post on the way to his
real goal—Spain. He has already outlined the completion of the first phase
of his grand design as apostle to the Gentiles (v 19). He must have been
conscious of time pressing on; "the fullness of the Gentiles" had to be ingath-
ered (11:25), and he himself was already well into middle age (about 50?).
So in terms of a rapid-sweep ground-breaking strategy *his* work could be
regarded as complete. There was no doubt plenty of scope for building on
the foundation he had laid and for expanding from the centers he had established. But in comparison with the virgin territories in the west, there was
no longer the same need or scope for his particular apostolic calling (v 23).
For one thinking in terms of a broad circular strategy (v 19), the two most
obvious regions were (southern) Gaul and Spain. For whatever reason, no
longer available to us, Paul fixed his sights on Spain (v 24).

The matter is delicately broached. He wants to "visit" them and "have
the full pleasure of their company for a short time," but he is only "passing
through" (v 24, 28). The sensitivities to possible misunderstanding and fear
of some sort of rebuff are even more marked than in 1:11–12. He clearly
wants to avoid giving any impression whatsoever either that he is covertly
seeking a position of leadership and authority among them (he is not *their*
apostle; contrast 1 Cor 9:1–2), or that he intends to abuse their hospitality
(cf. *Did.* 11.4–5). In the midst of these implicit disclaimers comes the actual
request, expressed as a hope: that they will help provision his expedition to
the further west—that is, by offering some financial or personnel assistance,
or as a continuing base from which communication and support would be
maintained during his time in Spain. The matter is delicate, since Paul is in
effect asking the Roman congregations to follow the pattern developed with
the churches he himself had founded in the east—as to the provision both
of financial support and of manpower as assistants and fellow workers. The
manner in which Paul brings in the request probably indicates that the reports
he had had of the Roman churches from those he knew there (chap. 16)
had given him sufficient confidence that such a request would be well received.

25–29 Second, he wants their support in his more immediate task—to
take the collection to Jerusalem—and for this he craves their prayers (v 30).
This was a task on which Paul placed the highest priority: more immediately
important than extending the missionary sweep to the west (v 25); a task to
which he had devoted considerable resources of time and energy for some
years (as we know particularly from his correspondence with Corinth itself).
The way he speaks of it here, using terminology ("service," "fellowship")
which was unspecific in itself, but which had become established in his earlier
correspondence on the subject (2 Cor 8–9), indicates Paul's confidence that
the subject would be well enough known among the Roman Christians. So
he would probably expect them to recognize the same delicacy of touch which

characterized his approach to them. On the one hand, he describes the recipients of the collection in terms which would resonate very positively with the Jerusalem believers themselves—"the saints," "the poor of the saints." Although Paul has already made it clear to his readers that he would have no truck with such a title being used of Jewish believers in a sectarian or exclusive way (1:7), the double use of it here (vv 25, 26) indicates willingness to find common ground and noncontentious language on an issue of great sensitivity. Similarly, the continued use of cultic imagery and talk of gentile obligation toward Jerusalem (vv 27–28), Paul would no doubt be aware, could be taken within a strongly nationalistic Jewish Christian church to give some support to the eschatological expectation of gentile tribute to Jerusalem and gentile acknowledgment of the Jerusalem temple as the focal point of God's final rule (v 16).

26–27 On the other hand, Paul emphasizes twice that this is a free-will offering from the gentile churches (vv 26, 27; for some reason he mentions only those of Macedonia and Greece); it is an act of fellowship (vv 26, 27), not any sort of submission or acknowledgement of supremacy; it is a moral responsibility arising out of recognition of how much Gentile owed to Jew (v 27). This was presumably the way in which Paul understood the obligation he had accepted in Gal 2:10. However the Jerusalem leadership might understand it, for Paul himself it was an act of service, the recognition of a need in one part of the people of Christ which could be met by other parts; it was an act of fellowship arising out of their common experience of grace given in terms of need not merit, the same level of mutual concern and interdependence which characterized the body of Christ at the local level (12:3–8). In this case the salvation-history importance of Jerusalem must have attracted many Jewish Christians, many of them with few resources (largely drained, perhaps, by the trip to Jerusalem itself), and many of them probably cut off from home support by a family unsympathetic with their conversion to the new sect. It would be difficult for such a community, without a strong local economic base, to support itself. If the temple cult depended on the flow of tithes and temple tax and pilgrims from beyond Judea, so too would the Christian community be likely to find itself dependent on support from these diaspora Jews who had established successful business and commercial enterprises in the larger cities of the diaspora. In this situation of continuing need Paul saw an ideal opportunity to maintain the salvation-history continuity between the churches of his mission and Jerusalem, and the unity of the eschatological people of God despite the diversity of understanding of how Gentile should be related to Jew within the whole.

The delicacy of the balancing act Paul strives for is indicated in v 27: the flow of benefit from Jew to Gentile has been at the level of the Spirit, in spiritual matters—this is the common ground between gentile believer and true Jew (2:29) and law (7:14; 8:4); whereas the flow of benefit on the level of the flesh is from Gentile to Jew. That is an example of the reciprocity of the eschatological congregation, unlike the alternative claim that life in accordance with the Spirit is tied to a community defined in accordance with the flesh, where Gentile can never be other than indebted to Jew. Moreover, it is noticeable that Paul uses language of cultic imagery for the gentile ministry to Jews, not the other way around. It is not that Jewish believers act as priests on behalf of the Gentiles; once again, in the eschatological congregation of God's will, both cultic and ethnic boundaries have been removed and completely transformed.

30 The reason why Paul explains his objective in going to Jerusalem only becomes clear in the final paragraph. He appeals to them, once again as "brothers," appealing for their prayers in terms both of their commitment to the same Lord (10:9) and of their common experience of the love of God and neighbor given by the Spirit (5:5). Whether he thought Roman contacts with Jerusalem would be able to influence the outcome at Jerusalem or not, or would be in time to do so in the event, is unclear and unlikely. What he asks for is their prayers. No light request, for he believes in the effectiveness of prayer. And no light request either, for what he calls for is a hard discipline of prayer, an earnest striving, an agonizing. The language should not be treated lightly: Paul envisaged his time in Jerusalem as his severest challenge yet, a fierce contest in which he might well be the loser.

31 The fear becomes explicit in v 31. It was twofold. First, that the main body of his fellow Jews, who had not (yet) recognized what the obedience was which God now required (the obedience of faith [1:5]), would regard Paul's breach of traditional ethnic and cultically marked boundaries as traitorous and heretical. Paul would have no illusions on this score: he himself had once shared the very same attitude (10:2; Gal 1:13; Phil 3:6); and the mounting nationalistic and religious fervor in Judea in the interval would have increased the likelihood that some group of zealots would see it as a religious duty to put Paul out of the way (cf. Acts 23:12–15). So he asks their prayers that he might be kept safe and delivered from such threats and peril to life. His second fear was that the collection might not be accepted by the Jerusalem church. The two were no doubt as closely linked in Paul's mind as his syntax makes them: a church composed of large numbers of Jewish Christians who shared much of that nationalist and religious fervor would not take kindly (to say the least) to one who had threatened and abandoned some of the most basic beliefs and practices in terms of which Israel understood its divine calling as the people of God. And even if some of the leaders were more open to or even sympathetic to the gentile mission so much identified with Paul, the political and social pressures of a Judea beginning to gear itself for rebellion might have made it impossible to accept anything from the apostate Paul.

In view of all this the strength of Paul's determination to deliver the collection becomes all the more impressive, and his determination to maintain the continuity and unity between the diaspora churches and Jerusalem, even at the risk of his life, can be seen in its full significance. The sharpness of the differences and the breadth of the diversity gave him no desire to break Christianity up into discontinuous entities.

31–33 The strain which Paul was under as he contemplated the possible outcome of his trip to Jerusalem continues to be reflected in his closing remarks. To complete their prayers they should ask that he be able to come to them, so that in their company he could relax and find rest and refreshment after the tensions of even a successful visit to Jerusalem. And his concluding wish appropriately is addressed to "the God of peace." Paul the Jew, who is also apostle to the Gentiles, says the Jewish benediction over his gentile readers.

The reason why Paul has inserted his lengthy exposition between the two sets of personal explanations (1:8–15 and 15:14–33), and why he delayed going into detail regarding his reasons for writing, has now become clearer. The long discussion from 1:16–15:13 was preparing the way for these more detailed requests in two ways: on the one hand, it served as an indication of what Paul could contribute to them in the mutual sharing of their faith— the teaching embodied in the letter is in part exchange for the help he asks from them; and, on the other, it indicated the argument he would use to defend himself in Jerusalem, if called upon to do so, as he no doubt fully expected to be. This recognition of the significance of the structure thus helps to explain the character and unified but several purposes of the whole letter.

B. Final Greetings (16:1–23)

Introduction

Despite the championship of T. W. Manson and many others ("the Ephesian destination of 16:1–20 can hardly be disputed"!—Klein, *IDBS*, 752), the view that chap. 16 did not originally belong to Romans can readily be rejected. (1) 15:33 is not a concluding formula elsewhere in Paul (not even 2 Cor 13:11; Gal 6:16; Eph 6:23; 1 Thess 5:23) (Gamble 84, 90). (2) The δέ of 16:1 implies a continuation from what has gone before (to argue for a lost prescript would only be necessary if there were compelling grounds for chap. 16's existence as an independent letter). (3) Paul invariably ends his letters with a χάρις benediction, which here comes in 16:20b. (4) The absence of additional greetings would be very surprising in such a substantial letter: the list is unusually long (26 names), but that Paul should know personally or by name so many in the capital city of the Empire ("all roads lead to Rome") is not surprising (see, e.g., W. L. Knox, *Jerusalem*, 354–56 n.24; Dodd, xix–xxiii; Bruce; Donfried, "Romans 16"; Kümmel, *Introduction*, 318–19; Gamble, 91–92; Cranfield, 9–11; Brown, *Rome*, 106–9; Achtemeier, 235; Lampe, 126–30); nor that he should attempt to establish personal relationships with congregations he had not himself established (Kennedy, 154); compare Col 4.10–17 and 2 Tim 4:19–22 with the letters to his own churches which refrain from singling out individual members in just such a fashion (Zahn, Lietzmann). (5) The wholly exceptional character of 16:1–23 as a separate letter in comparison with all other Pauline letters, even when themselves (some of them) broken down to separate letters, tells strongly against the whole hypothesis. In contrast, "ch 16 has all the earmarks of an epistolary conclusion" (Gamble, 91). (6) The greeting from "all the churches of Christ" (v 16) would be most appropriate to the Christians living in the capital city (Dodd, xx; Bruce; Zeller;

Wilckens, 1:25–27; against Schmithals, *Römerbrief*, 146–47—to the house church of Onesiphorus!). For the mutual relationship of the constituent parts of the chapter see particularly 16:21–23 *Form and Structure*.

1. Commendation of Phoebe (16:1–2)

Bibliography

This bibliography serves for Romans 16:1–16

Benko, S. "The Kiss." *Pagan Rome and the Early Christians.* Bloomington: Indiana University, 1984. 79–102. **Brooten, B. J.** " 'Junia . . . Outstanding among the Apostles' (Romans 16:7)." In *Women Priests*, ed. L. and A. Swidler. New York: Paulist, 1977. 141–44. ———. *Women Leaders in the Ancient Synagogues.* Brown Judaic Studies 36. Chico: Scholars, 1982. **Bruce, F. F.** *Paul.* 385–89. **Donfried, K. P.** "A Short Note on Romans 16." *JBL* 89 (1970). Repr. in Donfried, *Romans Debate.* 50–60. **Doty, W. G.** *Letters.* 39–42. **Filson, F. V.** "The Significance of the Early House Churches." *JBL* 58 (1939) 105–112. **Fiorenza, E. S.** *In Memory of Her: A Feminist Theological Reconstruction of Christian Origins.* London: SCM, 1983. **Gamble, H.** *The Textual History of the Letter to the Romans.* Grand Rapids: Eerdmans, 1877. **Gielen, M.** "Zur Interpretation der Formel ἡ κατ᾽ οἶ/κον ἐκκλησία." *ZNW* 77 (1986) 109–25. **Goodspeed, E. J.** "Phoebe's Letter of Introduction." *HTR* 44 (1951) 55–57. **Hainz, J.** *Ekklesia.* 193–98. **Harnack, A. von.** "Κόπος (κοπιᾶν, οἱ κοπιῶντες) im frühchristlichen Sprachgebrauch." *ZNW* 27 (1928) 1–10. **Kaye, B. N.** " 'To the Romans and Others' Revisited." *NovT* 18 (1976) 37–77. **Kim, C.-H.** *The Familiar Letter of Recommendation.* SBLDS 4. Missoula: Scholars, 1972. **Klauck, H. J.** *Hausgemeinde und Hauskirche im frühen Christentum.* SBS 103. Stuttgart: KBW, 1981. **Kraemer, R. S.** "Women in the Religions of the Greco-Roman World." *RelSRev* 9 (1983) 127–39. **Lampe, P.** "Iunia/Iunias: Sklavenherkunft im Kreise der vorpaulinischen Apostel (Röm 16:7)." *ZNW* 76 (1985) 132–34. ———. *Stadtrömischen Christen.* 124–53, 156–64. **Lightfoot, J. B.** *Saint Paul's Epistle to the Philippians.* London: Macmillan, [4]1878. 173–77. **McDonald, J. I. H.** "Was Romans 16 a Separate Letter?" *NTS* 16 (1969–70) 369–72. **Manson, T. W.** "St Paul's Letter to the Romans— and Others." *Studies in the Gospels and Epistles.* Manchester University, 1962. Repr. in Donfried, *Romans Debate.* 1–16. **Meeks, W.** *Urban Christians.* 23–25. **Montevecchi, O.** "Una donna 'prostatis' del figlio minorenne in un papiro del II[a]." *Aegyptus* 61 (1981) 103–15. **Mullins, T. Y.** "Greeting as a New Testament Form." *JBL* 87 (1968) 418–26. **Ollrog, W.-H.** *Paulus und seine Mitarbeiter.* WMANT 50. Neukirchen: Neukirchener, 1979. **Pomeroy, S. B.** *Goddesses, Whores, Wives and Slaves.* New York: Schocken, 1975. **Richardson, P.** "From Apostles to Virgins: Romans 16 and the Roles of Women in the Early Church." *TJT* 2 (1986) 232–61. **Schmithals, W.** *Römerbrief.* 125–51. **Schnackenburg, R.** "Apostles Before and During Paul's Time." *Apostolic History and the Gospel,* FS F. F. Bruce, ed. W. W. Gasque and R. P. Martin. Exeter: Paternoster, 1970. 287–303. **Swidler, L.** *Biblical Affirmations of Woman.* Philadelphia: Westminster, 1979. **Trebilco, P.** *Studies.* Chap. 5. **Watson, F.** *Paul.* 98–102.

Translation

[1] *I recommend to you Phoebe our* [a] *sister, who is also deacon of the church in Cenchreae,* [2] *that you welcome her in the Lord in a manner worthy of the saints*

*and assist her in whatever matter she may have need of you. For she herself has
also been patron of many* [b] *and of me myself.*

Notes

[a] The ὑμῶν of P[46] A F G etc. is probably a transcriptional error.

[b] There are a number of textual variations which look like attempts to improve the somewhat
stilted style.

Form and Structure

Vv 1–2 clearly constitute a letter of recommendation on behalf of Phoebe
(McDonald; Kim, 132–34), however their relation to the rest of the letter
may be envisaged. Gamble (84–87) shows that commendations of a third
party are not foreign to epistolary conclusions of the period, including cases
of lengthy letters.

Comment

16:1   συνίστημι δὲ ὑμῖν Φοίβην τὴν ἀδελφὴν ἡμῶν, "I recommend to you Phoebe
our sister." συνίστημι in the sense "recommend" someone to another is well
attested in the papyri and elsewhere (LSJ IV, MM, BGD, *TDNT* 7:897); so
in our literature—1 Macc 12:43 and 2 Macc 9:25, with 2 Cor 3:1 indicating
the practice of providing letters of recommendation elsewhere in Christianity.
Phoebe is often taken to be the bearer of the letter to Rome (see, e.g., those
cited by Schlier), and it is a natural deduction from the fact that she is named
first (cf. 2 Cor 8:16–24; Phil 2:25–30; Philem 8–20; Pol. *Phil.* 13.1). Since
the name Φοίβη was frequently used in Greek mythology (BGD, *OCD*,
"Phoebe"), it is certainly most probable that she was a Gentile (Michel, Cranfield).

In contrast to the masculine ἀδελφός used for members of religious associations (see on 1:13) the relative lack of attribution for a similar use of the
feminine ἀδελφή is striking (BGD). Yet women were active in religious cults
of the time, particularly that of Isis (Pomeroy, 217–26—"nearly one-third of
the devotees [of Isis] named in inscriptions in Italy are female"; MacMullen,
Paganism, 116–17; Meeks, *Urban Christians*, 24–25). However, the designation
of a woman fellow-Christian as "sister" seems to have been particularly characteristic of Christianity (1 Cor 7:15; 9:5; Philem 2; James 2:15; Ign. *Pol.* 5.1;
2 *Clem.* 12.5; 19.1; 20.2; Herm. *Vis.* 2.2.3; 2.3.1). The ἡμῶν must denote
Christians as a whole (Cranfield): the concept of a universal, or at least fully
international brotherhood and sisterhood is already well established.

οὖσαν καὶ διάκονον τῆς ἐκκλησίας τῆς ἐν Κεγχρεαῖς, "who is also deacon of
the church in Cenchreae." διάκονος (which can serve either as masculine or
feminine—BGD) could be understood simply in terms of a regular pattern
of service undertaken by Phoebe on behalf of her local church (cf. on 13:4;
15:8; and 12:7); but this would probably have been expressed by use of
διακονέω (cf. 15:25) or διακονία (cf. 1 Cor 16:15); so NIV's "servant" is inadequate.
διάκονος together with οὖσα points more to a recognized ministry ("minister"—

Maillot) or position of responsibility within the congregation (so most; see again, e.g., those cited by Schlier); though Fiorenza (47) notes a tendency to reduce the status implied in the title in comparison with Phil 1:1, the fact nevertheless remains that Phoebe is the first recorded "deacon" in the history of Christianity. At the same time it would be premature to speak of an established office of diaconate, as though a role of responsibility and authority, with properly appointed succession, had already been agreed upon in the Pauline churches. We are still at the stage of ministry beginning to take regular and formal shape (Barrett, Käsemann), and the form in each case would depend very much on the context and needs of particular congregations (the same is true of Phil 1:1, where responsibilities are not even hinted at; but in 1 Tim 3:8–13 the reality of church office has taken clear form; Pliny, *Ep.* 10.96.8, speaks of two female slaves who were called *ministrae* in Bithynia— text in SH). In this case, with Cenchreae a port city (the eastern port of Corinth—Strabo, 8.6.22; Philo, *Flacc.* 155), a ministry of hospitality would be very likely (see also 16:2—προστάτις). It is significant that one of the earliest of the diverse roles within the Christian churches (cf. 12:3–8) to begin to gain a more formal status was that of "servant." Lagrange notes a sixth century inscription found on the Mount of Olives which describes a deaconess called Sophie as "the second Phoebe; now in *NDIEC* 4:239–41, with further data. See also *NDIEC* 2:193–94."

The fact that ἐκκλησία appears for the first time in the letter is striking, since its casual use in reference to Cenchreae makes its absence hitherto all the more noticeable (see further *Introduction* §2.4.3). It was a peculiarly suitable title for the Christian congregations, because it drew heavily on the LXX use of ἐκκλησία to denote the assembly of Yahweh (e.g., Deut 23:1–2; 1 Chron 28:8; Neh 13:1; Mic 2:5; BGD, 3; *TDNT* 3:527), while using a concept which was sufficiently widespread and noncontentious to avoid comment ("assembly" = regularly summoned political body—LSJ; occasionally for business meetings of clubs—Meeks, *Urban Christians,* 222 n.24). It is noteworthy that Paul uses the word consistently for the local assembly of Christians and never for "the church universal" (for the first time in Eph): hence the plurals (16:16; 1 Cor 7:17; 16:1, 19; 2 Cor 8:18–19, 23–24; etc.; see, e.g., those cited in Dunn, *Jesus,* 429 n.17; also Beker, *Paul,* 314–16). But since he also uses it for groups of Christians meeting in homes, "home churches" (see further on 16:5 and 23), the meaning is more precisely Christians in one place gathered to share their common life of worship and discipleship (Dunn, *Jesus,* 262–63; Banks, *Community,* 35–37; Beker, *Paul,* 317).

2 ἵνα αὐτὴν προσδέξησθε ἐν κυρίῳ ἀξίως τῶν ἁγίων, "that you welcome her in the Lord in a manner worthy of the saints." For προσδέχομαι = "receive favorably, accept, welcome," see LSJ, BGD, and cf. particularly Phil 2:29. ἐν κυρίῳ is a variant of the more common ἐν Χριστῷ Ἰησοῦ (see on 6:11) or an abbreviated form of the liturgically fuller ἐν Χριστῷ Ἰησοῦ τῷ κυρίῳ ἡμῶν (6:23; 8:39). The brief form using ἐν κυρίῳ alone is used repeatedly here (vv 2, 8, 11, 12, 13, 22), perhaps as a way of expressing a degree of intimacy (cf. 1 Cor 4:17; 9:1–2; 15:31; 16:19; 1 Thess 3:8; Philem 20; here particularly Phil 2:29); elsewhere apparently to bring out the more authoritative force of κύριος (14:14; 1 Cor 7:22, 39; 11:11; 2 Cor 2:12; Gal 5:10; Phil 1:14;

2:19, 24; 1 Thess 5:12) or in exhortation (1 Cor 15:58; Phil 3:1; 4:2, 4; Col 3:18, 20). ἀξίως, "worthily, suitably"—more often "of God/the Lord" (Col 1:10; 1 Thess 2:12; 3 John 6; equivalents popular in inscriptions—Deissmann, *Bible Studies*, 248); but quite appropriate here (cf. Eph 4:1—ἀξίως . . . τῆς κλήσεως; Phil 1:27—ἀξίως τοῦ εὐαγγελίου). The allusion is no doubt to the strong tradition of hospitality and concern for strangers within Judaism (see on 12:13)—hence again "the saints" (see on 1:7 and 15:25).

καὶ παραστῆτε αὐτῇ ἐν ᾧ ἂν ὑμῶν χρῄζῃ πράγματι, "and assist her in whatever matter she may have need of you." παρίστημι probably means "stand by, help, come to the aid of, assist" (BGD, 2aγ; *TDNT* 5:837, 839); cf. 2 Tim 4:17. χρῄζειν τινός, "to have need of someone/something" is both classical and popular (LSJ, MM, BGD); so Matt 6:32 // Luke 12:30; Luke 11:8; and 2 Cor 3:1. πρᾶγμα is unspecific—"undertaking, task, matter, affair." But the more specific sense of "lawsuit, dispute," frequent in the papyri and also in 1 Cor 6:1, should not be ruled out here (cf. Michel); there is sufficient testimony of women acting as independent litigants (MacMullen, cited by Meeks, *Urban Christians*, 24). If Phoebe was a person of some prestige and influence (see below) it would be all the more likely.

καὶ γὰρ αὐτὴ προστάτις πολλῶν ἐγενήθη καὶ ἐμοῦ αὐτοῦ, "for she herself has also been patron of many and of me myself." The unwillingness of commentators to give προστάτις its most natural and obvious sense of "patron" is most striking (*TDNT* 6:703 and Maillot are unusual in translating "protectress, patroness"; contrast, e.g., Kühl, comparing προϊστάμενος in 12:8; Lietzmann; Leenhardt; Gaugler; Murray; BGD, "she has been of great assistance to many"; so also RSV, "a helper of"; NEB, "a good friend to"; NIV, "a great help to"; NJB, "come to the help of"). That the word should be given full weight = "patron, protector" (or alternatively, "leader, ruler," as Swidler, 310–11) is very probable, however. (1) The masculine equivalent, προστάτης, is well known and was well established in this sense, not least for the role of some wealthy or influential individual as patron (and so protector) of Hellenistic religious societies (Poland, 346; BGD, προστάτις; in Philo, e.g., *Virt.* 155, and Josephus, e.g., *Ant.* 14.157, 444—Trebilco, 116); there are two occurrences of it in the Jewish inscriptions from Rome (*CIJ* 100, 365), probably in this sense (Leon, 191–92). The Latin equivalent, *patronus*, was equally significant, and would be familiar to Paul's readers in reference to patronage of *collegia* or clubs (*OCD*, "Patronus"; MacMullen, *Social Relations*, 74–76). (2) The use of the feminine προστάτις in this role was long unattested in epigraphical and papyrological evidence (MM), but now appears with similar force in a second-century papyrus (Montevecchi; further data and discussion in *NDIEC* 4:242–44). In the long Jewish synagogue inscription from Aphrodisias (third century), line 9 on face *a* reads Ἰαηλ προστάτης; despite the masculine form of the title, Ἰαηλ could be taken as feminine, since it was most likely given (or taken) in honor of the only Jael of significance in Jewish history (Judg 4:18–22; 5:24–57) (Trebilco, 114–15; otherwise, Reynolds and Tannenbaum, 101). (3) There was a stronger tradition of women filling roles of prominence in this period than has previously been realized—women with titles, for example, of ἀρχισυνάγωγος or γυμνασίαρχος (LSJ cite *IGRom* 3:802; see further Brooten, *Women Leaders*, particularly chap. 1; Trebilco, chap. 5), and acting precisely as protectors and benefactors ("perhaps a tenth of the protectors and donors that *collegia* sought out were women"—MacMullen, cited by Meeks, 24; on Phoebe, 60). Women also have a higher profile in the Judaism of the period than has previously been realized, if Judith, *T. Job* (the prominence given to Job's wife—21–26, 39–40) and Pseudo-Philo (the prominence given to Deborah—Ps. Philo 30–33) are anything to go by. In Rome they would be familiar with the prominent role played by such women as Fulvia (see *OCD*). Nor is it without significance that of the following list of 28 greeted in vv 3–16 no less than nine are women (seven by name, three of them among the first five, and four of them noted for their hard work = leading roles); though Richardson (237) notes the absence of women in the list of vv 21–23 (see further 16:21–23 *Form and Structure*). For the subsequent tendency to "domesticate" women within the churches, see Richardson; and for review of related literature see Kraemer.

In short, Paul's readers were unlikely to think of Phoebe as other than a figure of significance, whose wealth or influence had been put at the disposal of the church in Cenchreae. In the Greek cities there were patrons who looked after the interests of foreign residents (LSJ, προστάτης III.2); in view of Cenchreae's role as a port and the description of Phoebe already as διάκονος (v 1), it may be that we should see the two roles as linked—"deacon" of the church because of her well-known patronage of "many" foreign visitors, including resident Jews and visiting Christians. There is no difficulty in reading the καὶ ἐμοῦ αὐτοῦ as Paul's recollection of a particular occasion (or more than one) when he had been the beneficiary of Phoebe's patronage and protection (cf. Acts 18:18). The chapter is dotted with such reminiscences (vv 4, 5, 7, 13). Lydia is another example of a wealthy patron, though probably not so influential (Acts 16:14–15), and note Acts 17:12: Paul was not the first leader of the new movement to benefit from the patronage of influential or wealthy women (cf. Luke 8:3!), and he certainly was not the last.

Explanation

Paul begins his final section by commending Phoebe to the Roman churches. She was a lady of some stature who had acted as patron or protector for many, that is presumably mostly, but not necessarily exclusively Christians, including Paul himself. She was also deacon of the nearby church at Cenchreae and must have used some of her means and influence in the service of the Christians there. She had business in Rome, quite probably a lawsuit. Paul probably had known ahead of her intention to travel to Rome and took the opportunity to write the whole letter, with the commendation of Phoebe attached, so that on passing through to Corinth's western port, she could pick up the letter and carry it forward. Whatever the business Phoebe was to be engaged in at Rome, people like Prisca and Aquila, themselves of some means and influence, and others, probably freedmen in the great households of Rome, including the emperor's, could provide a variety of help—hospitality, advice on the current state of Roman politics and law, friendship, and Christian company. The verses therefore contain an intriguing glimpse of the combination of business affairs and social influence on which contacts between the early churches in significant part depended (in which women evidently played leading parts)—a not unimportant reminder of the historical and social realities within which Christianity first made its mark.

2. Greetings   (16:3–16)

Bibliography

See 16:1–2 Bibliography.

Translation

   [3] *Greet Prisca and Aquila my fellow workers in Christ Jesus,* [4] *who risked their necks for my sake, and for whom not only I give thanks, but also all the churches of the Gentiles;* [5] *also the church in their house. Greet my beloved Epaenetus, who is the firstfruits* [a] *of Asia* [b] *for* [c] *Christ.* [6] *Greet Mary,* [d] *who has labored much for you.* [7] *Greet Andronicus and Junia,* [e] *my kinsfolk and my fellow prisoners, who are outstanding among the apostles, and* [f] *also were in Christ before me.* [8] *Greet Ampliatus, my* [g] *beloved in the Lord.* [9] *Greet Urbanus, our fellow worker in Christ,* [h] *and my beloved Stachys.* [10] *Greet Apelles, approved in Christ. Greet those from the household of Aristobulus.* [11] *Greet Herodion, my kinsman. Greet those of the household of Narcissus who are in the Lord.* [12] *Greet Tryphaena and Tryphosa, who have worked hard in the Lord. Greet the beloved Persis, who has labored much in the Lord.* [13] *Greet Rufus, the chosen one in the Lord; also his mother and mine.* [14] *Greet Asyncritus, Phlegon, Hermes, Patrobas, Hermas, and the brothers with them.* [15] *Greet Philologus and Julia,* [e] *Nereus and his sister; also Olympas and all the saints with them.* [16] *Greet one another with a holy kiss. All the churches of Christ greet you.* [i]

Notes

   [a] p[46] D read ἀπ' ἀρχῆς in an understandable error through mishearing in transcription.
   [b] The reading Ἀχαῖας may be the result of unconscious assimilation to 1 Cor 16:15.
   [c] The reading ἐν Χριστῷ is an obvious attempt to improve the more awkward εἰς Χριστόν, especially since ἐν Χριστῷ is such a regular phrase in the chapter.
   [d] There is not much to choose between Μαριάμ (p[46] ℵ D F G) and Μαρίαν (A B C P Ψ).
   [e] p[46] reads Ἰουλίαν, probably just a slip (in view of v 15); some MSS make the alteration the other way round in v 15.
   [f] D F G make the relative clause agree with "apostles"—τοῖς πρὸ ἐμοῦ; but the weight of attestation in favor of the text used is too strong (Metzger).
   [g] p[46] D F omit μοῦ.
   [h] C D F G etc. read κυρίῳ—an understandable variation in view of Paul's own variation between the two phrases in this chapter.
   [i] D F G have transferred this clause to the end of v 21.

Form and Structure

The list of greetings functions to ensure a warm welcome not only for Phoebe, but also for the letter (she carries), and in due course for Paul himself. Prisc(ill)a and Aquila are given special prominence for understandable reasons (Acts 18:2–3, 18; 1 Cor 16:19; 2 Tim 4:19), and the earlier names with laudatory modifiers probably reflect personal acquaintance as against those merely mentioned in the second half of the list (Michel). The suggestion is attractive that the groupings indicate at least five different house churches in Rome (vv 5, 10, 11, 14, 15; e.g., Minear, *Obedience*, 7), and is more likely than Zahn's suggestion that those mentioned in vv 5–13 were all members of the home church of Prisca and Aquila, which would imply a double greeting on Paul's part (v 5a, vv 5–13). The extensive use of second-person greetings (Mullins, 425) may simply reflect Paul's awareness that the letter would have to be read several times within the different home churches; 1:7 is hardly sufficient evidence that Paul envisaged a single reading to the whole community gathered in one place (against Hainz, 195; see further *Introduction* §2.4 and on 16:1 and 16:23).

Comment

3 ἀσπάσασθε Πρίσκαν καὶ Ἀκύλαν τοὺς συνεργούς μου ἐν Χριστῷ Ἰησοῦ, "greet Prisca and Aquila, my fellow workers in Christ Jesus." ἀσπάζομαι is frequently used thus in written greetings of the time as the established form for conveying greetings at the end of a letter (MM, BGD; see also chap. 16 *Introduction*); so here—sixteen times in the imperative form in vv 3–16 plus a further five times in vv 16, 21–23. "The imperative form of the greeting verb functions here as a surrogate for the first person indicative form, and so represents a direct personal greeting of the writer himself to the addressees" (Gamble 93). We could translate "Greetings to. . . ." This standard formulaic use of the imperative is ignored by Watson when he argues that Paul was in effect requesting the separate Jewish Christian and gentile Christian groups in Rome "to introduce themselves to one another" (*Paul*, 101–2).

Prisca and Aquila were two of the most important people in Paul's missionary enterprise, hence their place at the head of the list of greetings. Aquila is specifically described as a Jew from Pontus (Acts 18:2), and his wife was also probably Jewish, but not necessarily so. According to Acts 18:2 they came from Italy to Corinth following the expulsion of the Jews from Rome by Claudius in A.D. 49 (see further *Introduction* §2.2.3). Since their conversion by Paul is not noted by Luke, we may assume they were already Christians before he met them; as W. L. Knox also notes, their departure from Rome probably indicates some involvement in the disturbances over "Chrestus" which resulted in Claudius' expulsion, and if they had been opponents of the "Chrestus" faction they would hardly have associated with Paul (*Jerusalem*, 260 n.24). On the contrary, they may have been expelled precisely because they were "key figures" on the Christian side of the disputes in Rome (Lampe, 5, 7). According to Luke (Acts 18:3) Paul stayed with them during his time in Corinth, and they worked together because they shared the same trade—tentmaker (σκηνοποιοί; see BGD; Lampe, 156–58); the plural seems to include both husband and wife—a family business. Thereafter they traveled with Paul from Corinth to Ephesus (Acts 18:18–19) and seem to have established themselves there for some time (1 Cor 16:19). Evidently they were now back at Rome, following the relaxation of the Claudian decree (Claudius having died in A.D. 54). 2 Tim 4:19 subsequently places them back in Ephesus. For other possible information on the couple see particularly SH and Cranfield.

The most obvious inference to draw from the evidence is that Prisca and Aquila were well-to-do business people (though the claim should not be exaggerated in terms of high social status [Lampe, 159–64]). (1) They seem to have been able to travel quite extensively. (2) Their return to Rome may suggest that they had been able to leave their business in Rome in safe hands (trusted slaves) while they used the opportunity provided by Claudius' edict to establish branches of their business, first in Corinth (unsuccessful?—Theissen, *Social Setting*, 90), then in Ephesus; at any rate they were able to reestablish themselves in Rome and to assume a position of prominence within the Christian community (first in the list of greetings, and hosts to a house church) very quickly. This information tells against Watson's suggestion (*Paul*, 105) that Prisca and Aquila had gone to Rome to prepare the way for Paul. (3) They provided regular and extensive hospitality to Paul (Acts 18:2–3) and then probably Apollos (Acts 18:26). (4) Wherever they established themselves they seem to have used their home as a meeting place for believers (16:5; 1 Cor 16:19)—implying they had the means to purchase a house in different centers, large enough for a (small?) congregation to meet regularly (see on 16:23). (5) They "risked their necks" for Paul (v 4), which may well imply the attempt to exercise some of the influence which their wealth and social position gave them. (6) "All the churches of the Gentiles" were grateful to them, which may suggest generous sponsorship and support for many small groups of Christians, though other missionary leadership, or teaching roles (16:3—συνεργοί; Acts 18:26) could also be the cause for such gratitude.

Equally notable is the fact that Prisca, or as diminutive, Priscilla, is more often named first of the two: Prisc(ill)a and Aquila—Acts 18:18, 26; Rom 16:3; and 2 Tim 4:19; Aquila and Prisc(ill)a—Acts 18:2 (because first time mentioned?) and 1 Cor 16:19 (because of the situation in Corinth?—14:33–36). The most obvious deduction is that Prisca was the more dominant of the two or of higher social status (see BGD, Πρίσκα), and she may either have provided the financial resources for the business or have been the brains behind it.

συνεργός is regularly used by Paul to describe associates (16:9, 21; 1 Cor 3:9; 2 Cor 1:24; 8:23; Phil 2:25; 4:3; Col 4:11; 1 Thess 3:2; Philem 1, 24; elsewhere in the NT it appears only in 3 John 8). The work here is unspecified, but on the basis of the other references Ollrog defines a συνεργός as "one who labors together with Paul as commissioned by God at the shared 'work' of mission preaching" (*Paulus*, 67; see further 63–72). That such evangelism took place through the opportunities for social contact provided by their business is quite possible (Hock, 37–42). For ἐν Χριστῷ see on 6:11; the phrase is used in this list (vv 3, 7, 9, 10) as a variant for ἐν κυρίῳ (see on 16:2).

4 οἵτινες ὑπὲρ τῆς ψυχῆς μου τὸν ἑαυτῶν τράχηλον ὑπέθηκαν, "who risked their neck for my sake." The second part of the phrase is almost certainly symbolic, as the parallel cited by Deissmann (*Light*, 117–18) indicates. "For the sake of my soul" is semitic (Michel; see further *TDNT* 9:648). The occasion referred to is unspecified, but there is no lack of situations where the influence of Prisca and Aquila at considerable risk to themselves may have been decisive (cf. Acts 18:12–17; 19:23–41; 1 Cor 15:32; 2 Cor 1:8–10; 6:5; 8:2; 11:23).

οἷς οὐκ ἐγὼ μόνος εὐχαριστῶ ἀλλὰ καὶ πᾶσαι αἱ ἐκκλησίαι τῶν ἐθνῶν, "for whom not only I give thanks, but also all the churches of the Gentiles." For εὐχαριστέω see on 1:8. The language is hyperbolic, but it attests not only the esteem and regard in which Paul held Prisca and Aquila, but also the very widespread nature of their influence, of whatever kind it was (see also on 16:3). For ἐκκλησία see on 16:1; and for the fuller title see 16:16.

5 καὶ τὴν κατ' οἶκον αὐτῶν ἐκκλησίαν, "also the church in their house." House churches are mentioned by Paul in 1 Cor 16:19 (Aquila and Priscilla again); Col 4:15; and Philem 2 (cf. also Acts 12:12, and the conversion of households—Acts 10:44–48; 16:15, 30–34; 18:8; and 1 Cor 1:16 [Dodd]). Such churches may have been quite small and presumably functioned on a regular basis (weekly?—cf. Acts 20:6–7 and 1 Cor 16:2), quite possibly with a number of such churches in a single city (the earliest Roman churches may have been built on the sites of such houses [SH]) and only coming together as "the whole church" (16:23) less frequently (once a month?—as did many voluntary and cult associations). As Meeks notes: "the local structure of the early Christian groups was thus linked with what was commonly regarded as the basic unit of society" (*Urban Christians,* 75). On the whole subject see Banks and Klauck; also P. Stuhlmacher, *Philemon* (EKK [1975] 70–75), and Gielen; see further on 16:23.

ἀσπάσασθε Ἐπαίνετον τὸν ἀγαπητόν μου, ὅς ἐστιν ἀπαρχὴ τῆς Ἀσίας εἰς Χριστόν, "greet my beloved Epaenetus, who is the first fruits of Asia for Christ." Epaenetus as a name occurs in Diodorus Siculus 19.79.2 and inscriptions (SH, MM, BGD), but nowhere else in biblical Greek. Almost certainly he was a Gentile. The fact that he is given such prominence and mentioned immediately after Prisca and Aquila is presumably explained by the following phrases, but it could be that he belonged to the house church of Prisca and Aquila, or had been converted by them, or, indeed, had joined the business of Aquila and Priscilla and had returned with them from Asia to Rome. ἀγαπητός, as also in vv 8, 9, 12, simply denotes a warm personal relationship, but not necessarily anything more specific (cf. 12:19; 1 Cor 4:14, 17; 10:14; 15:58; 2 Cor 7:1; 12:19; etc.); "my dear friend" is the translation of NEB, NIV, NJB. Paul is obviously trying to add a personal note to each of his greetings, but since he can say something specific about Epaenetus (the following phrase), the additional τὸν ἀγαπητόν μου should not be regarded as merely formal. Here, as in 1 Thess 2:8 and Philem 16 (and cf. 1 Cor 10:1 with 10:14), ἀγαπητός is more or less interchangeable with ἀδελφός (*TDNT* 1:51; Käsemann). For ἀπαρχή see on 8:23; as "first convert in Asia" Epaenetus ranks in significance and special affection with Stephanas, "first convert in Achaia" (1 Cor 16:15; see also 2 Thess 2:13). It was natural that those who had taken the bold step of allying with this new sect should emerge as leading figures within it—though *1 Clem.* 42.4 assumes a much more formal structure than the rest of the evidence indicates. εἰς Χριστόν presumably has overtones of conversion-initiation (see on 6:3).

6 ἀσπάσασθε Μαρίαν, ἥτις πολλὰ ἐκοπίασεν εἰς ὑμᾶς, "greet Mary, who has labored much for you." Mary is such a common Jewish name (5 or 6 other Marys in the NT) that the most natural assumption is that she was Jewish; but it is also attested as the feminine form of the Roman name Marius (BGD; SH; Lagrange; Lampe, 146–47). κοπιάω denotes hard work, "toil, strive, struggle" (BGD), without being more specific. Paul refers to his own apostolic labors in these terms (1 Cor 15:10; Gal 4:11; Phil 2:16; Col 1:29; see also 1 Tim 4:10; and cf. 1 Cor 4:12 and Eph 4:28). But he also uses the word as a special commendation of others, as here (16:12; 1 Cor 16:16; 1 Thess 5:12). In these cases it still does not denote specific tasks or tasks formally given, but rather tasks voluntarily undertaken at their own initiative—that is, denoting a sensitivity to needs within a new congregation and willingness to expend energy and time in meeting them (cf. the Roman inscription *CIG* 9592, cited by Deissmann, *Light*, 313). Thus it does not denote a leadership function as such (cf. 1 Thess 5:17); Paul's point elsewhere is rather that those who do so devote themselves to working for the good of the church ought to be given recognition (1 Cor 16:16; 1 Thess 5:12; for προϊσταμένους there, see on 12:8). Nevertheless, it is noticeable here that Mary is picked out first for such commendation, confirming that women played a not insignificant part in the emerging roles of leadership within the infant Christian communities— the weightier the significance of κοπιάω (Harnack), the more significant their role.

7   ἀσπάσασθε Ἀνδρόνικον καὶ Ἰουνίαν τοὺς συγγενεῖς μου καὶ συναιχμαλώτους μου, "greet Andronicus and Junia my kinsfolk and my fellow prisoners." Andronicus is a Greek name found frequently, but here obviously of a presumably Hellenized Jew (cf. Josephus, *Ant.* 13.75, 78) (BGD, SH). Ἰουνίαν has usually been taken in the modern period as Ἰουνιᾶν = Junias, a contraction of Junianus (so RSV, NEB, NIV, NJB). But the simple fact is that the masculine form has been found nowhere else, and the name is more naturally taken as Ἰουνίαν = Junia (Lampe 139–40, 147 indicates over 250 examples of "Junia," none of Junias), as was taken for granted by the patristic commentators, and indeed up to the Middle Ages. The assumption that it must be male is a striking indictment of male presumption regarding the character and structure of earliest Christianity (see, e.g., Schlatter, Lietzmann, Althaus, Gaugler, Michel, Murray, Schlier). But see Lagrange, Barrett, Cranfield, Wilckens, and Brooten, "Junia." The most natural way to read the two names within the phrase is as husband and wife (cf. v 3). The name probably indicates a slave origin (Lampe, "Sklavenherkunft"). συγγενεῖς = "fellow countrymen," that is, Jews (see on 9:3); that συγγενής is simply a variation on ἀγαπητός = φίλος (*TDNT* 7:741–42) is unlikely (see further on 16:11). In view of the tensions within Rome, the prominence given to these Jewish Christians would not be without significance (cf. Michel). συναιχμάλωτος means "fellow prisoner," as in Col 4:10 (Aristarchus) and Philem 23 (Epaphras). The reference will hardly be metaphorical (despite *TDNT* 1:196–97); but which of Paul's several imprisonments is in view is left unclear (2 Cor 6:5; 11:23; *1 Clem.* 5.6).

οἵτινές εἰσιν ἐπίσημοι ἐν τοῖς ἀποστόλοις, οἳ καὶ πρὸ ἐμοῦ γέγοναν ἐν Χριστῷ, "who are outstanding among the apostles, who also were in Christ before me." ἐπίσημος, "splendid, outstanding, prominent" (BGD). The full phrase almost certainly means "prominent among the apostles," rather than "outstanding in the eyes of the apostles" (see, e.g., RSV, NEB, NIV, NJB, Cranfield, Käsemann and those cited by him). The straightforward description "the apostles" (contrast 2 Cor 8:23 and Phil 2:25), and the following clause, together strongly suggest that Andronicus and Junia belonged to the large group (larger than the twelve) of those appointed apostles by the risen Christ in

1 Cor 15:7 (Schnackenburg, "Apostles," 293–94, surprisingly ignores 1 Cor 15:7 when he argues that Andronicus and Junias [*sic*] had never "seen the risen Lord"). That is, they belonged most probably to the closed group of apostles appointed directly by the risen Christ in a limited period following his resurrection (Paul himself being aborted = born early, in order to enter this circle of uniquely appointed apostles before it closed—"last of all as to the abortion" [1 Cor 15:8]). This would give Andronicus and Junia a higher status in the eyes of Paul and of others—higher than the "(false) apostles" of 2 Cor 11:13 or the later wandering apostles = missionaries of *Did.* 11.4– 6 (the implication of Acts 14:4, 14 is that Barnabas and Paul were "apostles" of a lower significance = "missionaries of Antioch," than "the apostles" = the twelve [Acts 1:21–26; 2:37, 42; 6:2, 6]), and would include Andronicus and Junia within the select group of "premier" apostles (Eph 2:20), along with Barnabas (Gal 2:9; 1 Cor 9:5–6) and probably Silvanus (1 Thess 2:6– 7). Whether they had played any role in founding one or more of the Roman (house) churches (cf. 1 Cor 9:1–2) and thus were apostles of (the body of Christ in) Rome (cf. 1 Cor 12:27–28) is left unclear by the text (*pace* Hainz, 197). We may firmly conclude, however, that one of the foundation apostles of Christianity was a woman and wife.

That they had been converted before Paul puts them among the earliest Palestinian Christians, probably the Hellenists in Jerusalem (Acts 6–8); see particularly Wilckens, who also notes an element of "church politics" in the reference: these were Jewish Christians, but also apostles, and indeed apostles "prominent" among the earliest leadership of the first church(es), who were wholly at one with Paul in his mission (against Watson, *Paul*, 101, who assumes "that Andronicus and Junias [*sic*] shared the Jerusalem church's deep suspicion of Pauline "freedom from the law' "; but "fellow prisoners" indicates other- wise). The fact that we know nothing more of such significant figures shows how fragmentary is our knowledge of this whole period (Zeller). For ἐν Χριστῷ see on 16:3.

8 ἀσπάσασθε ᾿Αμπλιᾶτον τὸν ἀγαπητόν μου ἐν κυρίῳ, "greet Ampliatus my beloved in the Lord." Ampliatus is a common slave name, attested in Rome but also elsewhere (Pompeii, Spain, Athens, Ephesus) (MM, BGD); but also, perhaps significantly, in the catacomb of Domitilla (see further SH; Lietzmann; Lagrange; Cranfield; Lampe, 144). Its frequency weakens the case for linking Ampliatus to the imperial household (as suggested by Lightfoot). For ἀγαπητός see on 16:5; and for ἐν κυρίῳ see on 16:2.

9 ἀσπάσασθε Οὐρβανὸν τὸν συνεργὸν ἡμῶν ἐν Χριστῷ, "greet Urbanus our fellow worker in Christ." Urbanus was a common Roman slave name. Given the arbitrary historical character of the inscriptional evidence, all we can say is that there is a fair possibility that he belonged to the imperial household (Lightfoot; SH; Cranfield; Lampe, 150–51). For συνεργός and ἐν Χριστῷ see on 16:3.

καὶ Στάχυν τὸν ἀγαπητόν μου, "and my beloved Stachys." For inscriptional evidence see BGD; it includes a reference to a slave of the imperial household by that name (Lightfoot; SH; Lietzmann; Cranfield; Lampe, 150). For ἀγαπητός see on 16:2.

10 ἀσπάσασθε ᾿Απελλῆν τὸν δόκιμον ἐν Χριστῷ, "greet Apelles, approved in

Christ." Apelles is quite a common name. Horace, *Sat.* 1.5.100, speaks of "Apella [Latin form] the Jew"; so it was in use among the Jewish community in Rome (on the basis of this reference BGD claims it was "common among Jews"). An Apelles was mentioned as a member of the imperial household (Lightfoot; Lampe, 149). For δόκιμος see on 14:18 (also 1:28): in such a list, where Paul attempts to say something friendly or complimentary about each, δόκιμος may simply refer to Apelles' maturity—"respected, esteemed" ("that genuine Christian" [Barrett]); but Paul could have in mind some particular trial or test through which Apelles had come strongly—"the tried and true Christian" (BGD), "tested and approved" (NIV). For ἐν Χριστῷ see on 16:3.

ἀσπάσασθε τοὺς ἐκ τῶν Ἀριστοβούλου, "greet those from the household of Aristobulus." Although Aristobulus was a common name (MM, BGD), there is certainly a strong plausibility in the suggestion that the Aristobulus here mentioned was the grandson of Herod the Great and brother of Agrippa I. According to Josephus (*War* 2.221) he died ἰδιώτης, as "a private person," that is, as opposed to one who held a public office or took part in public affairs (LSJ). Since his brother Agrippa had lived long in Rome and had been on friendly terms with Claudius (e.g., *Ant.* 20.12), it is quite probable that he was kept out of the way (and under surveillance) in Rome till his death (in the second half of the 40s? [Agrippa died in A.D. 44]). Even if he had died some years before the occasion of this letter, his household staff could well have retained their identity when merged with another (the imperial?) household (Lightfoot, SH, Cranfield). His household slaves and freemen would then still be known as οἱ Ἀριστοβούλου, and the Christians among them therefore as οἱ ἐκ τῶν Ἀριστοβούλου. Presumably some at least of them would have been Jews.

11 ἀσπάσασθε Ἡρῳδίωνα τὸν συγγενῆ μου, "greet my kinsman Herodion." Herodion is clearly a Jew (on συγγενής see 16:7). The name strongly suggests a freedman of one of the Herod family (freedmen and enfranchised foreigners took their patron's name [*OCD* 721a]). The fact that Paul mentions Herodion immediately after the members of the household of Aristobulus can certainly be regarded as support for the above suggestion (see on 16:10) regarding Aristobulus (Lightfoot, SH, Michel, Cranfield; against Käsemann). Whether the use of συγγενής means that only those so designated were Jews (Andronicus, Junia, Herodion; but what then of Aquila, Mary, and Rufus?), or that the only thing Paul knew of Herodion was the fact of his being a Jew (whereas in other cases he had other descriptive phrases at hand and did not need to mention this) remains unclear.

ἀσπάσασθε τοὺς ἐκ τῶν Ναρκίσσου τοὺς ὄντας ἐν κυρίῳ, "greet those from the household of Narcissus who are in the Lord." Narcissus is a name which also seems to have been common among slaves and freedmen (BGD, SH, Lietzmann). If a prominent Narcissus, a freedman who maintained a substantial household in the early 50s, is sought, the most obvious candidate would be the freedman of that name who served as one of Claudius' closest aides (Juvenal, *Sat.* 14.329–31); cf. *CIL* 3.3973 and 6.15640—"Narcissiani." After the accession of Nero (A.D. 54) he himself became a victim of Agrippina's vengeance (Tacitus, *Ann.* 13:1) and his household would probably have been absorbed by the emperor's (Lightfoot, SH, Cranfield). τοὺς ὄντας ἐν κυρίῳ could be translated "who are Christians"; for ἐν κυρίῳ see on 16:2.

12 ἀσπάσασθε Τρύφαιναν καὶ Τρυφῶσαν τὰς κοπιώσας ἐν κυρίῳ, "greet Try-phaena and Tryphosa, those hard workers in the Lord." Tryphaena is well attested as a name in inscriptions, including the name of a Jewess; and Try-phosa is also found in both Greek and Latin inscriptions (BGD; Lietzmann; Lampe, 150). Since it was quite common, then as now, to give members of the same family names derived from the same root or similar in sound, it is certainly quite possible that the two were sisters (Lightfoot; despite Käsemann). The fact that they had opportunity to work hard (for κοπιάω see on 16:6) suggests they were freedwomen, probably with a fair degree of independence. "One cannot fail to be slightly amused by the allusion to these 'workers in the Lord,' 'Dainty' and 'Delicate' " (Knox). For ἐν κυρίῳ see on 16:2.

ἀσπάσασθε Περσίδα τὴν ἀγαπητήν, ἥτις πολλὰ ἐκοπίασεν ἐν κυρίῳ, "greet the beloved Persis, who has labored much in the Lord." Persis seems to have been a popular name for female slaves (BGD; Lietzmann; Lampe, 145–46). At a point in the list of greetings where the descriptive notes have tended to become briefer and more stereotyped, the double description here is notice-able. Persis is "the beloved," not "my beloved" (as in vv 5, 8, 9)—perhaps a note of coyness on Paul's part, but perhaps also an indication of how widely and well regarded Persis was by all who knew her (for ἀγαπητός see on 16:5). The further description, echoing that given to Mary, indicates also someone whose devotion and hard work gave her a particular prominence within the Roman congregations (see on 16:6). As with Tryphaena and Tryphosa, we should probably presume she was a freedwoman. For ἐν κυρίῳ see on 16:2.

13 ἀσπάσασθε Ῥοῦφον τὸν ἐκλεκτὸν ἐν κυρίῳ καὶ τὴν μητέρα αὐτοῦ καὶ ἐμοῦ, "greet Rufus the chosen one in the Lord, also his mother and mine." Rufus is a Latin name found frequently even in its Greek spelling (MM, BGD), again often of slaves and freedmen (SH; Michel; Lampe, 151). If Mark was written from Rome (most recently see M. Hengel, *Studies in the Gospel of Mark* [London: SCM, 1985] 28–30), the reference in Mark 15:21 certainly indicates that there was a Christian Rufus well known to the Roman Christian community. Since the Christians in Rome cannot (yet) have been all that large in number, and since Paul evidently knows of no other Christian Rufus in Rome, it is certainly very plausible to identify this Rufus with the son of Simon of Cyrene (Mark 15:21; so Lightfoot, Cranfield; despite Fitzmyer and Käsemann). Since ἐκλεκτός is an epithet which we would normally think of as being applied to all Christians (see on 8:33), it may be that Paul in looking for something to say about each of those greeted has used it of Rufus simply as a stronger equivalent to ἀγαπητός (see on 16:5), equally applicable to all believers (so particularly Käsemann and Cranfield). But ἐκλεκτός is used also of individuals chosen for a particular task (as within the Jewish tradition in *Ep. Arist.* 13; *Sib. Or.* 3.521; cf. Ps 18:26 [LXX 17:27]; Wisd Sol 3:14); and within the early Christian tradition application to a particular individual is also attested (2 John 1; Ign. *Philad.* 11.1). So the designation here may indicate that Rufus was known as one specially chosen for some role or to bear some significance (possibly even related to Simon of Cyrene's carrying of the cross) (cf. Ambrosiaster in Cranfield; SH, Lagrange, Barrett, Black); presumably the recipients of the letter would know what Paul meant (Michel). For ἐν κυρίῳ see on 16:2.

That Rufus's mother was also present may well mean that Rufus had been born in Rome. But if she was "mother" to Paul as well, she must have traveled to some extent, perhaps as a member of some important household or business.

14 ἀσπάσασθε Ἀσύγκριτον, Φλέγοντα, Ἑρμῆν, Πατροβᾶν, Ἑρμᾶν, καὶ τοὺς σὺν αὐτοῖς ἀδελφούς, "greet Asyncritus, Phlegon, Hermes, Patrobas, Hermas, and the brothers with them." Asyncritus, which means "incomparable," is attested in a number of inscriptions, including that of an imperial freedman (*CIL* 6:12565—BGD, SH, Lietzmann). Phlegon too is quite well known as a name for slaves and freedmen, including one freed by Claudius (*CIL* 6:15202; see Lietzmann and Lampe, 150). Since slaves were often named after gods, Hermes is probably a slave, as in other occurrences of the name (Lightfoot; Lietzmann; Lampe, 144–45). Patrobas, an abbreviated form of Patrobius, was the name of a well-known freedman of Nero (Tacitus, *Hist.* 1:49), who gained an ill reputation for greed and self-indulgence (Tacitus, *Hist.* 2.95). The name was not common, but the reports of Tacitus make an identification hardly likely. Lightfoot, however, suggests that the individual named here could have been a member of the powerful Patrobius' household (see also Lietzmann). Hermas could be a dialectic variation on Hermes, or a briefer form of a name beginning Ἑρμ-; so in inscriptions (Lietzmann). The name was quite common among slaves (*CIL* 6:8121—Michel), but not as common as Hermes (SH). "The brothers with them" is best understood as a reference to a house church among whom Paul knew only five members by name, not including the host(ess).

15 ἀσπάσασθε Φιλόλογον καὶ Ἰουλίαν, Νηρέα καὶ τὴν ἀδελφὴν αὐτοῦ, καὶ Ὀλυμπᾶν καὶ τοὺς σὺν αὐτοῖς πάντας ἁγίους, "greet Philologus and Julia, Nereus and his sister; also Olympas and all the saints with them." Philologus occurs in Greek and Latin inscriptions especially of slaves and freedmen (Lietzmann), including members of the imperial household (Lightfoot; SH; BGD; Lampe, 149). Julia was one of the most common of Roman female names, and very common among slaves of the imperial household (SH; MM; Lampe, 146). Very probably therefore Philologus and Julia, husband and wife, or brother and sister, were slaves in the emperor's household. Nereus, a name drawn from mythology, is found quite widely (MM), again as a slave name and again in imperial service (*CIL* 6:4344, 5248; SH; Lietzmann; Lampe, 145). The possibility that Nereus and his sister were son and daughter of Philologus and Julia is simply that—a possibility. For possible link with the *Acts of Nereus and Achilleus* (fifth or sixth century [Hennecke, 2:572]), see SH. Olympas, another abbreviated form for a name beginning Ὀλυμπιο-, was also as a name common throughout the empire (MM), including an imperial freedman (*CIL* 6:536—Lietzmann). "All the saints with them" presumably refers to another house church, of whom Paul knew only these five. Perhaps the whole group consisted of members of the imperial household, who met in "off-hours."

16 ἀσπάσασθε ἀλλήλους ἐν φιλήματι ἁγίῳ, "greet one another with a holy kiss." Paul uses the same formula regularly with only minor variations (1 Cor 16:20; 2 Cor 13:12; 1 Thess 5:26); also 1 Pet 5:14 (ἐν φιλήματι ἀγάπης) and Justin, *Apol.* 1.65 (without ἁγίῳ; text in Cranfield). Kissing as a form of social respect and regard, at greeting or parting, was widespread throughout the Orient (*TDNT* 9:121; see further 9:119–24); similarly within Jewish tradition (*TDNT* 9:125–27). Mark 14:45 par.; Luke 7:45; 15:20; and 22:48 indicate that it was customary among Jesus' contemporaries and disciples, and Acts

20:37, for Paul too. The addition of ἁγίῳ suggests a degree of solemnity, or a kiss reserved for fellow Christians or for particular occasions (liturgical = when they came together for worship, as part of their worship—an act which marked the family bond of those who believed in Christ; but NEB's rendering, "kiss of peace," is too free). So it is quite likely that Paul intended this counsel to be enacted at the conclusion of his letter, and though it goes beyond the evidence to assume (on the basis of 1 Cor 16:20–22, compared with *Did.* 10.6, Justin, *Apol.* 1.65, and the later liturgies, cited, e.g., in SH) that the "holy kiss" would form part of the introduction to the common meal/Lord's Supper, we can properly conclude that Paul did expect his letter to be read out in the regular gathering for worship (cf. *TDNT* 9:139, and most commentators). See further Benko.

ἀσπάζονται ὑμᾶς αἱ ἐκκλησίαι πᾶσαι τοῦ Χριστοῦ, "all the churches of Christ greet you." For ἐκκλησία see on 16:1. The form ("of Christ") and the breadth ("all the churches") makes the greeting unique in Paul. He speaks usually of "the church of God" (1 Cor 1:2; 10:32; 11:22; 15:9; 2 Cor 1:1; Gal 1:13; 1 Thess 2:14; 2 Thess 1:4; also 1 Tim 3:5, 15; "in God"—1 Thess 1:1 and 2 Thess 1:1; "in Christ"—Gal 1:22). Since synagogues could also describe themselves as "churches = assemblies of (the people of) God," Paul may have chosen here to demarcate the use of ἐκκλησία more strictly in Christian terms. Paul appeals to "all the churches" on several occasions (16:4; 1 Cor 4:17; 7:17; 14:33; 2 Cor 8:18; 11:28), but nowhere else in a greeting (cf. 1 Cor 16:19–20; 2 Cor 13:12–13; Phil 4:22). The claim is not so hyperbolic or exaggerated as might at first appear. As the same references ("all the churches") clearly indicate, Paul has the churches of his own mission in mind ("all the churches" is not an unfair abbreviation for "all the churches with which I am associated" = "all the churches of the Gentiles"—v 4). And it is fairly clear, not least from the fact of his letters themselves, that he was in regular contact with his churches in Galatia, Asia, Macedonia, and Achaia (Michel, Cranfield). The greeting thus has a "political" overtone: Paul speaks for all these churches, and they are behind him in his mission as articulated both in theological and political terms in the preceding chapters (cf. Dodd). Paul will also have been anxious that the potentially influential Roman churches should be fully at one with his churches, so that we can properly speak of "the ecumenical aim of the letter" on the basis of this claim (Wilckens; similarly Gaugler). But it is hardly justified on the basis of this clause to speak of "a quite special veneration" for "the church [*sic*] of Rome" (as Lagrange).

Explanation

The greetings which follow the commendation of Phoebe obviously serve a number of functions: in particular, they give Phoebe herself a list of people to call on when she first arrives, to whom she could look for hospitality and subsequent support; and they ensure that the letter she presumably took with her would be well received, since Paul already knew so many of the Roman congregations, including a number of leading figures.

The list itself has several interesting features. (1) Paul obviously has strong personal links with a number of those named. Prisca and Aquila are preeminent in this regard: they had worked with him, they had risked their lives for him, and they often provided him a home (vv 3–4). Another of Paul's coworkers in early missionary work was Urbanus (v 9). In other cases Paul makes a point of calling the one greeted "my beloved"—Epaenetus, the first of his converts in Asia, Ampliatus and Stachys (vv 5, 8, 9). Andronicus and Junia were outstanding among the apostles, having become Christians before Paul (v 7). And particularly touching is the note in v 13—Rufus's mother "and mine"—Paul no doubt recalling occasions of warm and comforting hospitality from Rufus's mother in previous travels. Even though Paul obviously attempts to add a special note to those he knew best in the list, these particular greetings stand out.

(2) The social composition of those listed is also noteworthy. There is an absence of specifically Roman names (though note Julia), and Paul indicates that three of those listed are Jews (Andronicus, Junia, and Herodion—vv 7, 11), though it is likely that Aquila and Prisca, Mary, Rufus and his mother (vv 3, 6, 13) were also Jews. Even so, the list is predominantly gentile, and may well reflect the relative balance between Jews and Gentiles in the Roman congregations. Equally notable is the fact that most of the names were common among slaves, freedmen, and freedwomen—Junia, Ampliatus, Urbanus, Stachys, Persis, Rufus, Asyncritus, Phlegon, Hermes, Patrobas, Hermas, Philologus and Julia, Nereus and Olympas, as well, of course, as the households of Aristobulus and Narcissus. This gives a fairly clear picture of the extent to which the first Christian groups in Rome drew their strength from the lower strata of Roman society. At the same time Prisca and Aquila would be not without contacts and influence. The hard workers Mary, Tryphaena and Tryphosa, and Persis (vv 6, 12) may have had some means of their own. And several of those listed must have traveled a fair amount—all those indeed listed under (1), since they had all obviously been personally in contact with Paul earlier in his mission work and were now in Rome.

(3) Not least in significance is the number of women who evidently assumed roles of some prominence in the Roman churches: Prisca, a coworker; Junia, one of the earliest and leading members of the larger group of apostles (1 Cor 15:7); Mary, Tryphaena and Tryphosa, and Persis, the only ones in the list (all four, and only these four) whom Paul commends for their hard work—activity elsewhere (1 Cor 16:16 and 1 Thess 5:12) deserving respect and submission. So far as this list is concerned, at any rate, Paul attributes leading roles to more women than men in the churches addressed. We cannot rule out the possibility that the more restrictive rulings on women's participation in leadership probably reflected in *1 Clement* (cf., e.g.*1 Clem.* 20.7 with the Pastorals) constituted a second or third generation reaction against the greater charismatic liberty of the earlier years.

3. A Final Personal Note   (16:17–20)

Bibliography

Baumgarten, J. *Paulus.* 213–16. **Jewett, R.** *Tolerance.* 17–22. **Müller, K.** *Anstoss.* 46–67. **Müller, U. B.** *Prophetie.* 185–90. **Ollrog, W.-H.** "Die Abfassungsverhältnisse von

Röm 16." In *Kirche*, FS G. Bornkamm. Tübingen: Mohr, 1980. 221–44. **Schmithals, W.** "The False Teachers of Romans 16:17–20." *Paul and the Gnostics*. Nashville: Abingdon, 1972. 219–38.

Translation

[17] *I appeal to you, brothers, to look out[a] for those who[a] cause divisions and temptations contrary to the teaching which you learned, and keep away[b] from them.* [18] *For such people do not serve our Lord Christ but their own appetites, and through smooth speech and fine-sounding words they deceive the hearts of the unsuspecting.* [19] *For your obedience has become known to all.* [c]*So I rejoice over you, but want you to be wise*[c] *regarding what is good and innocent regarding what is bad.* [20] *And the God of peace will crush the Satan under your feet speedily. The grace of our Lord Jesus*[d] *be with you.*[e]

Notes

[a] D F G in particular show a tradition in which the text has been slightly expanded at these points.

[b] The aorist is read by $\mathfrak{P}^{46}$ $\aleph^2$ A D F G, but presumes an already pressing threat with which relations have to be broken; the change from present to aorist is easier to explain than vice-versa (Cranfield).

[c-c] The textual tradition is quite disturbed between these points, but the variations are insignificant.

[d] As might be expected, Χριστοῦ is inserted by a number of witnesses—the result of liturgical polishing.

[e] Several Western witnesses transfer "the grace" to follow v 23 (so = v 24, including D F G) as being more appropriate following the additional greetings (vv 21–23); but since no scribe would have inserted the grace here had it not already been so, the text is almost certainly correct (SH, Metzger). Gamble 88, 94, 129–32, however, favors the view that Paul repeated the benediction at v 24 following the postscript of vv 21–23.

Form and Structure

The fierceness of the sudden interjected warning in vv 17–20 is surprising, and in this regard is most closely paralleled by Phil 3:2–21 and Gal 6:11–15. There are too few grounds for regarding it as an interpolation (see Wilckens, against Ollrog, "Abfassungsverhältnisse," 226–34); though stylistically it could best be regarded as a postscript (and so with little immediate connection with what preceded); and structurally it is most closely parallel to Paul's practice of appending a final paragraph in his own hand (1 Cor 16:21–24; Gal 6:11–18; Col 4:18; 2 Thess 3:17), in which he was by no means averse to a final polemical thrust (1 Cor 16:22; Gal 6:12–13); so, e.g., Dodd and Lietzmann. Conceivably the references to the house churches reminded Paul of the strains and tensions he knew or guessed were being experienced within the Roman congregations (Minear, *Obedience*, 27–29). But the dangers addressed are not those of 14:1–15:6, despite the use of σκάνδαλον (14:13; 16:17) (Donfried, "Romans 16," 59), and it is more likely that the paragraph results from Paul's realization that his preoccupation with the issue of Jew/Gentile relationships within the Roman churches had almost completely by-passed other dangers from other quarters—more libertinist teaching (cf. the similar turns in Gal 5:13 ff. and Phil 3:17–19) or seductive word spinners (cf. 1 Cor 1:18–2:5) (also cf. Wilckens). A few final aphorisms of general import at this point (in Paul's own hand?) should therefore occasion less surprise than they do; talk of "a confused jumble of ideas" (Käsemann) is inappropriate, particularly if the paragraph functions as a postscript.

Comment

17 παρακαλῶ δὲ ὑμᾶς, ἀδελφοί, "I appeal to you, brothers." The lack of continuity with what has preceded should cause no surprise at this point in the letter (see *Form and Structure*), though the discontinuity should not be exaggerated (see particularly Cranfield), so that the force of the δέ remains unclear (cf. Michel with Schlier). For παρακαλέω see on 12:1 and 15:33; depending on the seriousness of the danger Paul warns against we could translate, "I implore you," or even "I adjure" (Käsemann); but the verb itself does not tell us how weighty a warning Paul is going to give. For ἀδελφοί see on 1:13. When so many of those greeted are women, the use of the masculine form alone is surprising to modern ears, but presumably it simply indicates that powerful characters like Prisca read it as inclusive language, since the feminine form was so little used in this connection (see on 16:1).

σκοπεῖν τοὺς τὰς διχοστασίας καὶ τὰ σκάνδαλα παρὰ τὴν διδαχὴν ἣν ὑμεῖς ἐμάθετε ποιοῦντας, "to look out for those who cause divisions and temptations which are contrary to the teaching which you learned." σκοπέω has the force of "look at carefully, consider, examine" (cf. LSJ), "look at critically" (*TDNT* 7:414–15). Apart from Luke 11:35 it occurs only in Paul in the NT (and only twice in the LXX)—2 Cor 4:18; Gal 6:1; Phil 2:4; and 3:17—and is characteristic of Paul in that it calls his readers to circumspect and responsible judgment. διχοστασία, "dissension," occurs elsewhere in biblical Greek only in 1 Macc 3:29; 1 Cor 3:3 *v.l.;* and Gal 5:20 (with ἐριθεῖαι and αἱρέσεις); also in *1 Clem.* 46.5 and 51.1, and several times in Hermas (BGD, Schlier); these can hardly be described as divisions "always caused by the Gnostics" (against Schmithals, "False Teachers," 225). For σκάνδαλον see on 9:33 and 14:13. διδαχή is not a regular Pauline word (but see 6:17 and 12:7), but, as the full phrase indicates, it must refer to the traditions the Roman Christians received when they were converted and baptized (ἐμάθετε, aorist), to which Paul more often refers by use of παραδίδωμι and παραλαμβάνω (1 Cor 11:2, 23; 15:1–3; Gal 1:9; Phil 4:9; Col 2:6–7 [ἐδιδάχθητε]; 1 Thess 4:1; 2 Thess 2:15 [ἐδιδάχθητε]; 3:6); Müller, *Anstoss,* 49–50 compares particularly 1QH 16.15). It is to be noted that Paul can take it for granted that such basic teaching, no doubt including a fair amount of Jesus tradition (see on 12:14), had been given to (a) church(es) which others than he had founded—so much must it have been typical throughout the Christian mission (cf. Michel). Regarding the identity of those warned against, see on 16:18.

καὶ ἐκκλίνετε ἀπ' αὐτῶν, "and keep away from them." The language is characteristic of wisdom exhortation; cf. particularly Pss 34:14 [LXX 33:15]; 37 [LXX 36]:27; Prov 1:15; 3:7; 4:15; 14:16; 16:6 [LXX 15:27]; Sir 2:7; 22:13; elsewhere in the NT only 3:12 (citing Ps 14:3) and 1 Pet 3:11 (citing Ps 34:14). It therefore has something of a stereotyped character (not "stereotyped anti-Gnostic," as Schmithals, "False Teachers," 229) and consequently may be unable to yield any clear picture of the dangers Paul envisaged or of the policy he was advocating (Cranfield probably presses the language and tenses too strongly). It suggests rather that Paul is envisaging possible rather than imminently threatening events. Cf. the exhortations of 1 Cor 5:9, 11; 2 Thess 3:6, 14; 2 Tim 2:22; 3:5; Titus 3:10; and 2 John 10 (Zeller).

18 οἱ γὰρ τοιοῦτοι τῷ κυρίῳ ἡμῶν Χριστῷ οὐ δουλεύουσιν ἀλλὰ τῇ ἑαυτῶν κοιλίᾳ, "for such people do not serve our Lord Christ but only their belly." δουλεύειν κυρίῳ/Χριστῷ echoes the same language used in 12:11 and 14:18. It is unclear whether οἱ τοιοῦτοι . . . is intended as a description of non-Christians (those to be avoided are conceived of as outside the Christian community, not baptized or committed to Christ as Lord) or as a rebuke to Christians (they should be "serving Christ," and may indeed think or claim they are doing so, but are not). The use of κοιλία, "stomach," to denote gluttony, or at least domination by the merely animal appetites (so = κατὰ σάρκα [8:12–13]), seems to be particularly Pauline in character (cf. especially Phil 3:19—"whose god is their belly"). But though it has not been much evident in earlier Jewish writing (cf. Sir 23:6), the line of attack seems to have become well established around this period in Jewish polemic against what was perceived as apostasy (Philo, *Virt.* 182; *3 Macc.* 7.11; *T. Mos.* 7.4). Here too the language is not sufficiently targeted and smacks too much of an already conventional polemic to enable us to identify particular viewpoints. The fact that *T. Mos.* 7 can use such language in what was probably an attack on Pharisees (so Lagrange; Michel; Jeremias, *Jerusalem*, 250; see particularly *T. Mos.* 7.9) may be sufficient indication that the language belongs to the category of disinformation propaganda or the imaginative caricature of a polemic of suspicion such as both Christianity and Judaism suffered from in subsequent centuries (perpetuated in Leenhardt's talk of the "stupid food laws" of the "judaizers").

καὶ διὰ τῆς χρηστολογίας καὶ εὐλογίας ἐξαπατῶσιν τὰς καρδίας τῶν ἀκάκων, "and through smooth speech and fine-sounding words they deceive the hearts of the unsuspecting." χρηστολογία is a rare word and occurs only here in biblical Greek. Taken by itself it means "fair speaking"; but here obviously it carries a note of warning, so "smooth, plausible speech" (BGD). A play on Χριστός is unlikely but possible (see particularly Black). Likewise εὐλογία means "fine speaking," but use in a negative sense is attested elsewhere (SH, BGD): so here again "fine words," warning of an eloquence which could deceive and mislead, since style could distract from content. This is the only (and somewhat surprisingly) negative use in the NT of a word which elsewhere has very positive content (cf. 15:29!). The two words could be taken as a hendiadys (Wilckens). For ἐξαπατάω see on 7:11; cf. here Eph 5:6 and Titus 1:10. ἄκακος (elsewhere in the NT only Heb 7:26) is again clearly drawn from Jewish wisdom exhortation such as we find quite often in Proverbs, where the dominant reference is to the "simple" (Prov 1:4, 22; 8:5; 14:15 —"the simple believes everything"; 21:11—"when a scoffer is punished, the simple becomes wise"; Wisd Sol 4:12—"roving desire perverts the innocent mind," RSV); hence "innocent, guileless, unsuspecting" (BGD, who note that Diodorus Siculus 13.76 correlates it with ἁπλοῦς, "single, simple"); NIV's "naive" sounds too critical, and NJB's "unwary" catches a congruent implication.

Against whom is Paul warning? There is a fair consensus that he can hardly have "the strong" in view, since the tone is quite different from 14:1–15:6; and besides, Paul counted himself as one of the strong (cf. e.g., Michel, Käsemann, Wilckens). Beyond that, options remain open, without any clear indicator in favor of one against another. In view of the parallel of *T. Mos.* 7.4–7 (see above) an attack on Paul's Jewish(-Christian) opponents is possible (*TDNT* 3:788, Barrett, Wilckens); cf. after all the fierceness of Paul's other polemic on this front (2 Cor 11:12–15; Gal 1:7–9; Phil 3:2). More plausible is the suggestion that the language is directed against antinomians or gnosticizing (Jewish?) Christians (Dodd, Käsemann; but see on 16:19; and Schmithals' description of them as "Gnostic" is both tendentious and anachronistic). But it is not even clear whether Christians as such are in view, since "serving Christ" may mark out the *contrast* to the servility to animal appetites which they manifest, rather than any claim they make (see on 16:17; here the parallel with 2 Cor 11:13 and Phil 3:18–19 may not be as close as some of the language at first suggests); division can be caused by pressures from without as much as by pressures from within. Moreover, the use of the definite article before διχοστασίας and σκάνδαλα (v 17) does not necessarily mean that Paul is referring to specific divisions and temptations known to Paul (against Schmidt), but may simply be part of the style of such exhortations (Michel); divisions and cause of stumbling are not necessarily wrong in themselves (cf. 9:33!), only those which are "contrary to the teaching which you learned" (Cranfield). More likely Paul in fact intends a broad and nonspecific warning (cf. Cranfield) to cover a number of possible eventualities, drawing on (1) some traditional advice from Jewish wisdom (see also on 16:19), (2) his experience of what can happen to congregations, as gained elsewhere and not least with regard to the church in Corinth (cf. v 17b with 1 Cor 1:10–17; v 17c with 2 Thess 3:6; v 18a with Phil 3:19; v 18b with 1 Cor 2:1–5; 2 Cor 11:5; and Col 2:4), and (3) his knowledge of the morally dangerous social conditions in Rome (cf. 13:12–14). In other words, he writes in the manner of a parting exhortation in which the accumulated resources of both his ancestral wisdom and his own hard-won experience serve as guidelines and warning posts for potential hazards for the servants of Christ in Rome.

19 ἡ γὰρ ὑμῶν ὑπακοὴ εἰς πάντας ἀφίκετο, "for your obedience has become known to all." After the (over-)dramatic warning, here is a compensating word of lavish praise (cf. 1:8; 15:14). For ὑπακοή, a key thematic word, see on 1:5; here cf. particularly 6:17. For ἀφικνέομαι, "reach" (of a report), see BGD. The change of tone confirms that Paul sees the preceding threats as possibilities, not as the actual situation within the Roman congregations themselves.

ἐφ᾽ ὑμῖν οὖν χαίρω, θέλω δὲ ὑμᾶς σοφοὺς εἶναι εἰς τὸ ἀγαθόν, ἀκεραίους δὲ εἰς τὸ κακόν, "so I rejoice over you, but I want you to be wise in regard to what is good and innocent in regard to what is bad." For χαίρω see on 12:12. The use of σοφός, elsewhere little used by Paul outside 1 Corinthians, confirms Paul's dependence on the heritage of Jewish wisdom (the wisdom literature heavily dominates the use of σοφός in the LXX; see also on 1:22) and makes less likely that Paul is directing his fire specifically at an identifiably gnosticizing danger in Rome. Likewise the contrast between "the good" and "the bad" is characteristic of (though by no means exclusive to) Jewish wisdom (see on

2:10). On the other hand, ἀκέραιος, "pure, innocent," "guileless" (RSV), "unsophisticated" (NJB), does not occur in Jewish wisdom (instances like Esth 8:12 f. and *Ep. Arist.* 31, 264 show no particular wisdom influence). However, the only other occurrence of the word in the biblical tradition, other than Phil 2:15, is Matt 10:16, where the twofold emphasis, "wise" (φρόνιμος) and "innocent" (ἀκέραιος) is very close to Paul's emphasis here. The best explanation therefore is that Paul has drawn here on the combined heritage of Jewish wisdom as added to by Jesus (cf. Black; most leave the question of specific influence open, but see on 12:14).

20 ὁ δὲ θεὸς τῆς εἰρήνης συντρίψει τὸν σατανᾶν ὑπὸ τοὺς πόδας ὑμῶν ἐν τάχει, "and the God of peace will crush the Satan under your feet speedily." For ὁ θεὸς τῆς εἰρήνης see 15:33; but here the prayer wish is expressed as a confident hope. σατανᾶς is a Greek transliteration from שָׂטָן, used originally to denote a role of accuser within the counsel of God (Job 1–2; Zech 3:1–2; so also 1 Chron 21:1, an interpretation of 2 Sam 24:1). But in the postbiblical period the role crystallized into that of outright adversary to God, leader of the angelic armies opposed to God (so the "opposite number" of Michael), with "Satan" only one of a number of names used for the archdemon, including Beliar/Belial, the devil, Mastema, Azazel, and the angel of darkness (see, e.g., *1 Enoch* 53.3; 54.6; *Adam and Eve* 12.1; 17.1—"this adversary"; *Jub.* 10.8, 11; 11.5, 11; *T. Reub.* 2.2; *T. Sim.* 2.7; etc.; 1QM 13.2, 4, 10–11; 17.5–6; 1QS 3.20–21; see also Müller, *Anstoss*, 61–64). The definite article with σατανᾶς, as almost always in the NT, should be translated since it probably reflects the functional significance which still attached to the name. Paul works with this conception of a personal focus for evil (1 Cor 5:5; 7:5; 2 Cor 2:11; 11:14; 12:7; 1 Thess 2:18; 2 Thess 2:9), although in this letter the more important threats to humankind and to God's purposes of salvation are what might fairly be called the demythologized or existentially oppressive powers of sin and death (chaps. 6–8).

The hope of Satan being "crushed under foot" is part of a larger eschatological hope for the final binding or defeat of the angelic power hostile to God (see e.g., *Jub.* 5.6; 10:7, 11; 23.29; *1 Enoch* 10.4, 11–12; 13.1–2; etc.; *2 Enoch* 7.1; *T. Mos.* 10.1; 1QS 3.18; 4.18–23; 1QM 17.5–6; 18.1; Rev 20:10). That there is an influence from Gen 3:15 is probable, but not necessarily direct (LXX uses different language) and quite likely through the influence of Gen 3:15 on the whole strand of Jewish hope (cf. Ps 91:13; *T. Sim.* 6.6; *T. Levi* 18.12; Luke 10:18–19); so e.g., *TDNT* 5:81, Michel, Käsemann, Cranfield. It is hard to diminish the strong eschatological note here, and the note of imminence implied in the ἐν τάχει (cf. Luke 18:8; Rev 1:1; 22:6/7); cf. particularly 13:11–12 (so Michel, Schmidt, Käsemann; despite Cranfield and Baumgarten [215–16] who regards Paul's replacement of αὐτοῦ by ὑμῶν as an implied de-eschatologizing of the apocalyptic tradition). An allusion to victory over opponents indicated in vv 17–18 is by no means called for (Baumgarten and Cranfield; against *TDNT* 7:924, Schmidt, Wilckens): both there and here Paul is using traditional motifs (there from wisdom, here from apocalyptic) to provide a rousing hortatory and faith-confident conclusion.

ἡ χάρις τοῦ κυρίου ἡμῶν Ἰησοῦ μεθ' ὑμῶν, "the grace of our Lord Jesus be with you." Paul concludes with his usual grace (see 15:14–16:27 *Introduction*),

though here in its briefer form (without even Χριστοῦ: see *Notes*), as in 1
Cor 16:23 (only Col 4:18 is briefer). For χάρις see on 1:5. As in the greeting
(1:7), the normal epistolary conclusion (ἔρρωσο, ἔρρωσθε, εὐτύχει, ὑγίαινε [Mi-
chel; Roller 72 ff.]) has been replaced by the more characteristically Christian
form. Schmidt follows Schlatter in reading the verb (understood) as indicative:
"the grace of our Lord is with you."

Explanation

17 Paul at this point probably took the pen from his amanuensis (Tertius)
and added a final personal note. This was certainly his regular style, and
though he does not draw attention to the fact as he did when writing to the
churches of his own mission, it would be evident enough from the change
of writing style on the papyrus. He followed no regular pattern in these
personal notes, and they probably varied as the mood took him. But he
clearly felt no obligation to confine himself to pleasantries (as Gal 6:11–18
shows), and he evidently thought warnings as well as words of encouragement
quite appropriate (as in 1 Cor 16:21–24). In this case it would seem that he
felt no need to underline or reemphasize any of the extensive line of argument
or of the following exhortation; perhaps he realized enough was enough
and that to reopen any of the earlier topics could too easily lead into a more
extensive recapitulation.

Instead he draws on the extensive strands of Jewish wisdom and apocalyptic
to utter appropriate words of caution and encouragement which his experience
as a church founder and nurturer showed to be appropriate to any church.
They must be circumspect and vigilant: they live as aliens within a hostile
world. Pressures can easily build up, whether from within or from without,
which can cause dissension and individual failure. They need not doubt their
ability to recognize these dangers and pressures, for in the teaching they
assuredly received as part of their initiation, including key material from
the Jesus tradition, such as Paul had alluded to earlier, they had a pattern
on which they could model most of their personal obedience and relationships
(cf. 6:17). But they must appreciate that there are people who should be
avoided.

18 Who such people were is not made explicit, for Paul does not have
any particular people in mind. He is dealing in the types of wisdom exhortation—the types of evil to be avoided. People who can be characterized by
the fact that they put the satisfaction of their own appetites in the place
which, for a Christian, can only be filled by Christ. People who can be characterized by their persuasive speech and the attractive packaging they give to
their values and lifestyle, such as will always be appealing and seductive to
the unsuspecting and guileless. In a city like Rome there would be no end
of such attractive options for those seeking truth or liberty—in the range of
different sects with their different offers to entice converts, or indeed in the
lifestyle which aped the wealthy and self-indulgent (13:11–12). The new movement of Christians was still very new, and there would no doubt be a good
deal of coming and going of interested seekers (and others too) into the

meetings, even of the house churches, as one slave might invite a fellow slave, or someone in business might invite a business associate (cf. 1 Cor 14:23–24). The traffic would be two-way, as some decided they did not like what they heard and others moved to committed membership. So clear lines of distinction between "insiders" and "outsiders" could not always be drawn, and the policy of avoiding potential danger would not always be easy to follow.

19 Not unmindful of this, Paul hastens to reassure those still largely unfamiliar congregations that he is not "getting at" them or particularly fearful in their case. In the acceptable exaggeration of a lavish compliment he rejoices at their obedience so widely known. This closing echo of Paul's introductory remarks right back at the beginning of the letter (1:5, 8) is no accident. It shows how readily Paul can sum up the meaning and force of the gospel in terms of "obedience" and so confirms for the last time the importance Paul places on a faith which works out in a daily discipline under Christ's lordship ("obedience," v 19 = "serving Christ," v 18)—as a faith, that is, in full continuity with the obedience of faith which characterized the witness of the scriptures.

But the dangers just referred to (vv 17–18) are real and are likely to afflict any congregation of God's people. So Paul winds up his final personal exhortation by calling once again on the counsel of the sages which had proved its value over generations of the people of faith and obedience: be wise as to what is good, innocent of evil. The vagueness and impreciseness of the language matters little: it reflects a general rather than a specific concern of Paul. And its importance lies in reminding his readers that evil can take many deceptive forms and that a combination of worldly wisdom and sensitive innocence is their best defense. Just as important here is that Paul draws his terms both from Israel's centuries-old wisdom and from the wisdom of Messiah Jesus (Matt 10:16)—reinforcing once again the claim made throughout the letter that the revelation of Christ and its meaning for daily living is simply an extension of the revelation given and wisdom accumulated earlier in Israel's pilgrimage.

20 With a final flourish Paul pens a slogan of victorious hope: "the God of peace will crush the Satan under your feet speedily." Here too the continuity with earlier and contemporary Jewish apocalyptic hope is strong: Christians share with their fellow members of God's election the confidence of a final triumph of good over evil, of God over the most powerful force of evil that afflicts this world. Not only does the slogan reflect this continuity of hope, but it reflects the eschatological expectation which seems to have been characteristic of the Christian movement from the beginning—of the final power of God already pushing back the frontiers of evil (cf. Mark 3:23–27; Luke 10:17–18), of a victory already being won and soon ("speedily") to be completed. Above all, the slogan, with its echo of Gen 3:15, effectively ties together the whole sweep of salvation-history: God's purpose is nothing less than the complete destruction of all the evil which has grown like a large malignant cancer within the body of humankind and the restoration of his creation to the peace and well-being he originally designed for it.

After a last greeting in his characteristic Christian terms, "the grace of our Lord Jesus Christ be with you," Paul restores the pen to Tertius.

4. Additional Greetings   (16:21–23)

Bibliography

Bahr, G. J. "The Subscriptions in the Pauline Letters." *JBL* 87 (1968) 27–41. **Cadbury, H. J.** "Erastus of Corinth." *JBL* 50 (1931) 42–58. **Deissmann, A.** *Light.* 435–38. **Ellis, E. E.** "Paul and His Co-Workers." *NTS* 17 (1970–71) 437–52. **Fitzmyer, J.** "Aramaic Epistolography." In White, ed. *Studies.* 25–57. **Goodspeed, E. J.** "Gaius Titius Justus." *JBL* 69 (1950) 382–83. **Longenecker, R. N.** "Ancient Amanuenses and the Pauline Epistles." In *New Dimensions in New Testament Study,* ed. R. N. Longenecker and M. C. Tenney. Grand Rapids: Zondervan, 1974. 281–97. **Murphy-O'Connor, J.** *St Paul's Corinth: Texts and Archeology.* Wilmington: Glazier, 1983. 153–59. **Theissen, G.** *Social Setting.* 75–83.

Translation

²¹ *Timothy my fellow worker greets you, also Lucius, Jason, and Sosipater, my kinsmen.*ᵃ ²² *I, Tertius, who have written the letter, greet you in the Lord.* ²³ *Gaius, who is host to me and to the whole church,*ᵇ *greets you. Erastus, the city treasurer, greets you, also brother Quartus.*ᶜ

Notes

ᵃD F G insert v 16b at this point.
ᵇF G have ὅλαι αἱ ἐκκλησίαι, an inelegant form, presumably, for "all the churches" (ὅλος elsewhere in the NT is used only in the singular, except Titus 1:11).
ᶜSee *Notes* on 16:20.

Form and Structure

Käsemann is clearly irritated that such a powerful letter should tail off in such a lame fashion. The difficulty is eased by a number of considerations. It should not be assumed that vv 21–23 would more naturally follow immediately upon vv 3–16. In fact, vv 3–16, as well as being a list of greetings, have a more important function to fulfill, namely, the aim of securing a warm welcome for Phoebe and subsequently for Paul himself. Only vv 21–23 fulfill the role of final greetings as such, and they come where we would expect, at the very end. If vv 17–20 are a final rousing call written in Paul's own hand, as seems quite probable, vv 21–23 are a final postscript, very likely penned by Tertius himself, before the letter was sealed and passed to the messenger.

The absence of women in this list, in contrast to vv 1–16, noted by Richardson (see on 16:2), is perhaps to be explained by the "domestic" context of Paul's actual letter writing, as distinct from the contexts of community life/worship and work/evangelism implied in vv 1–16.

Comment

21 ἀσπάζεται ὑμᾶς Τιμόθεος ὁ συνεργός μου, "Timothy my fellow worker greets you." Timothy is the person who is most frequently mentioned elsewhere in Paul's letters (1 Cor 4:17; 16:10; 2 Cor 1:19; Phil 2:19; 1 Thess 3:2, 6; see also below, and Acts 16:1; 17:14–15; 18:5; 19:22; 20:4; 1 and 2 Tim; for an outline biography see BGD). As these same references indicate, he was one of Paul's closest lieutenants, having "a matchless claim to the predicate ὁ συνεργός μου" (Käsemann). For συνεργός see on 16:3. Timothy is regularly named at the beginning of Paul's letters (in no less than six of them; see on 1:1). Conceivably he could have been absent when Paul began to write the letter to Rome (it would probably take some time to compose such a lengthy and closely argued letter). But the difference from his usual practice is probably sufficiently explained by the fact that Timothy was well enough known as Paul's aide-de-camp in the other cases but less known in Rome (Schmidt); in writing to introduce himself, Paul presumably thought it more appropriate to do so only in his own name (see also on 1:1).

καὶ Λούκιος καὶ Ἰάσων καὶ Σωσίπατρος οἱ συγγενεῖς μου, "also Lucius, Jason, and Sosipater, my kinsmen." Lucius is unlikely to be the man of the same name in Acts 13:1, since someone associated with Paul so long ago in the leadership of the church at Antioch would probably have been given a fuller description. But identification with Luke (Λουκᾶς), mentioned in Col 4:14; Philem 24; and 2 Tim 4:11, and regularly taken to be the author of Luke-Acts, is by no means impossible, since Λουκᾶς is known to be an alternative form for Λούκιος (Deissmann, *Light*, 435–38; BGD, Λουκᾶς); the equation has been made regularly from Origen onwards. Jason could be Paul's host from Thessalonica (Acts 17:5–7, 9); the implication of the distinction between Timothy on the one hand (a coworker = one of Paul's "team") and the group in v 23 (residents in Corinth) may be that the three mentioned here were delegates from other churches traveling with Paul to deliver the collection (Schmidt; Georgi, *Geschichte*, 80; Ollrog, *Paulus*, 58). This probability is strengthened since Sosipater could be a longer form of Sopater (BGD; the name is common under both forms [MM]), who is mentioned in Acts 20:4 as one of the delegates of the Pauline churches traveling with him (so e.g., Lietzmann, Cranfield). For συγγενεῖς see on 9:3. Like Andronicus, Junia, and Herodion (vv 7, 11), all three are Jewish Christians; or, at least, both Jason and Sosipater are Jews, since the συγγενεῖς may refer only to these last two (Deissmann, *Light*, 438; Cranfield); why this fact would prevent them representing gentile (or better, mixed) churches is a mystery (rightly Wilckens; against Dodd and Käsemann), since Paul would no doubt have regarded himself as a representative of the churches of his mission (that other representatives are not mentioned may indicate simply that all the delegates had not yet arrived, or that only these three were known in Rome). We should note the readiness of diaspora Jews to substitute purely Greek names for their more Jewish forms (Jason for Joseph or Jesus [BGD, Ἰάσων]).

22 ἀσπάζομαι ὑμᾶς ἐγὼ Τέρτιος ὁ γράψας τὴν ἐπιστολὴν ἐν κυρίῳ, "I, Tertius, who have written the letter greet you in the Lord." Tertius, a Roman name quite common among slaves and freedmen (Michel), is not otherwise known; but he may have been known in Rome. On the other hand, having been so much part of such an important letter he may have felt it appropriate to add his personal greetings, even though greetings in the first person were unusual (*TDNT* 1:501; we do not know the names of the other secretaries/

scribes used by Paul); he was after all a fellow Christian and not merely a scribe (cf. *Mart. Pol.* 20.2). The extent of his involvement in the letter has been helpfully discussed by Cranfield (2–5): Cranfield justifiably rejects Roller's argument that Tertius had a much more free hand in composing the letter ("the inherent improbability that someone capable of the highly original, closely articulated and also extremely difficult thought which has gone into the Epistle to the Romans would ever have voluntarily entrusted the expression of it to another person" [4]); he favors either of the alternatives, that Tertius wrote to Paul's longhand dictation, or that he used some form of shorthand ("we might perhaps think of him taking down a few sentences at a time in this way and then writing them out in longhand while Paul thought out his next few sentences" [4]); for use of shorthand at the time of Paul, cf. particularly Seneca, *Ep.* 90.25—"the shorthand symbols by means of which even a rapidly delivered speech is taken down and the hand is able to keep up with the quickness of the tongue"; for evidence of use of a scribe or secretary in Greek letters, see, e.g., Longenecker, "Amanuenses," and in Aramaic letters see Fitzmyer, "Epistolography," 36–37. The ἐν κυρίῳ should almost certainly be taken with ἀσπάζομαι (Cranfield)—Tertius following the pattern set by Paul in the earlier greetings (vv 8, 11, 12, 13).

23 ἀσπάζεται ὑμᾶς Γάϊος ὁ ξένος μου καὶ ὅλης τῆς ἐκκλησίας, "Gaius, who is host to me and to the whole church, greets you." Gaius is almost certainly to be identified with the man mentioned in 1 Cor 1:14, one of only a handful personally baptized by Paul, and, as one of his first converts, quite likely a leading figure in the church at Corinth. That he could also be the Titius Justus mentioned in Acts 18:7 (full name = Gaius Titius Justus) fits with the little information we have (one of Paul's earliest converts in Corinth, who acted as host to Paul and the earliest meetings of the church in Corinth; see, e.g., Goodspeed), but we can say no more than that. ξένος usually means "guest," or "stranger," but it does appear less frequently in the sense of "host" (LSJ, BGD). The phrase ὅλης τῆς ἐκκλησίας is usually taken to mean that Gaius offered hospitality to traveling Christians (e.g., Lagrange, Lietzmann, Leenhardt, Schmidt, Black, Käsemann, Schlier, Wilckens; and see on 12:13). But (1) nowhere else in the undisputed letters does Paul use ἐκκλησία of the universal church, only of the church in a particular area or region, and usually of Christians from a particular locality gathered for worship (see on 16:1); (2) the phrase "the whole church" is a clear echo of the phrase πᾶσα ἡ ἐκκλησία which occurs regularly in the historical books of the OT for actual meetings of Israel's representatives gathered together for consultation or worship (Deut 31:30; Josh 8:35 [LXX 9:2f.]; 1 Sam 17:47; 1 Kgs 8:14, 22, 55; 12:3 A; etc.); (3) to speak of Gaius as host to the universal church, even allowing for hyperbole, would set Gaius' hospitality far beyond the hospitality of such as Phoebe and Prisca and Aquila, in a wholly invidious (and indeed unpauline) manner; (4) besides, where the universal application of Paul's understanding of the gospel was itself in dispute, to speak of the universal church would either be unrealistic (would Gaius have offered hospitality to out-and-out opponents of Paul?) or factional (the whole church = the churches of the Pauline mission).

The most obvious way to take the phrase therefore is as a reference to "the whole church in Corinth" (BGD, ξένος 2c). The objection that Gaius' house could hardly have accommodated all the Christians in Corinth (Michel) makes unsubstantiated assumptions about the size of the church in Corinth. A typical well-to-do home of the time could accommodate meetings of 30–40, at best 50 (Banks, *Community,* 41–42, 120–21; J. D. G. Dunn, "The Responsible Congregation (1 Cor 14:26–40)," in *Charisma und Agape (1 Kor 12–14),* ed. L. de Lorenzi [Rome: Abtei von St Paul, 1983] 204–5; Murphy-O'Connor, 156–58), and there is no good reason to suppose that "the whole church" in Corinth was by this time any larger. As Banks (38) points out, the adjective "whole" must mean that there were other meetings of the church in Corinth, that is, in smaller house churches (if the Corinthian Christians met only as a single group the adjective would be superfluous), and it probably means that "the whole church" was able to meet only at less frequent intervals (since the atrium of Gaius's house would probably be very crowded and uncomfortable with a number much in excess of about 40 [Murphy-O'Connor]), presumably for special celebrations and meetings. Whatever the precise facts, Gaius must have been a man of considerable means.

ἀσπάζεται ὑμᾶς Ἔραστος ὁ οἰκονόμος τῆς πόλεως καὶ Κούαρτος ὁ ἀδελφός, "Erastus the city treasurer greets you, also brother Quartus." Erastus was probably different from the man of the same name who is mentioned as one of Paul's helpers (Acts 19:22; 2 Tim 4:20), though not necessarily so (Theissen, 76). Though οἰκονόμος denotes a financial officer within the local government of Corinth, it is not clear how high the rank was within the administrative hierarchy. οἰκονόμος could denote a high financial officer, but also a role fulfilled by slaves and freedmen (see LSJ 2b; MM; Cadbury, 47–52; Theissen, 77–78; inscriptional data in *NDIEC* 4.160–61; contrast the overconfident rendering of NIV, "the city's director of public works," with Cadbury's skepticism—"improbable if not impossible" [58]). The definite article does not necessarily indicate that there was only one οἰκονόμος in Corinth; it could just mean the οἰκονόμος who was a Christian. Still, it is possible that Erastus was quite a high official in local government, even as a freedman; see particularly Theissen, who argues that the rank may have been equivalent to that of quaestor and that Erastus may have gone on to the office of aedile (ἀγορανόμος) and be identical with the Erastus who is commemorated in an inscription from Corinth dated to about this period. Be that as it may, the possibility remains (we can put it no more strongly) that Erastus was a Roman citizen (Corinth was a Roman colony) of some wealth and notable social status.

Like Tertius, Quartus is a common name among slaves and freedmen (Michel). He is not Erastus' brother (Paul would have added αὐτοῦ). Nor should ἀδελφός be taken as an honorific title = "colleague" (see Dunn, *Jesus,* 288; against Ellis, "Co-Workers"). ἀδελφός designates him simply as a fellow believer. His name is stuck on at the end since, presumably, of those closest to Tertius at the time of writing, he was known to some of the Christians at Rome.

24 See *Notes* on 16:20.

Explanation

Paul's task is now complete. After such a lengthy business, involving considerable concentration and staying power, and presumably also after reading over what Tertius had written (it is not unlikely that some of the earliest textual variations go back to Paul himself!), Paul must have been very relieved. All that remained was to add greetings from his immediate companions, two of the (probably) leading Christians at Corinth, his host, Gaius, and the city treasurer, Erastus, and a couple of Christians who presumably had some personal connections with one or other of the churches in Rome, Quartus and Tertius himself. With no one else asking to add his or her greetings, the scroll could be sealed, addressed, and ready for Phoebe to take with her to Rome, to start its journey into the Christian canon and to begin exercising its incalculable influence on nineteen centuries of Christian faith and theology.

C. Concluding Doxology (16:25–27)

Bibliography

Aland, K. "Der Schluss und die ursprüngliche Gestalt des Römerbriefes." *Neutestamentliche Entwürfe.* Munich, 1979. 284–301. **Deichgräber, R.** *Gotteshymnus.* 25–40. **Delling, G.** "ΜΟΝΟΣ ΘΕΟΣ." *TLZ* 77 (1952) 469–76. **Dewailly, L. M.** "Mystère et silence dans Rom 16:25." *NTS* 14 (1967–68) 111–18. **Dupont, J.** "ΜΟΝΩΙ ΣΟΦΩΙ ΘΕΩΙ (Rom 16:27)." *ETL* 22 (1946) 362–75. ———. "Pour l'histoire de la doxologie finale de l'épître aux Romains." *RBen* 58 (1948) 3–22. **Elliott, J. K.** "The Language and Style of the Concluding Doxology to the Epistle to the Romans." *ZNW* 72 (1981) 124–30. **Hurtado, L. W.** "The Doxology at the End of Romans." In *New Testament Textual Criticism,* FS B. M. Metzger, ed. E. J. Epp and G. D. Fee. Oxford: Clarendon, 1981. 185–99. **Lampe, P.** "Zur Textgeschichte des Römerbriefes." *NovT* 27 (1985) 273–77. **Lührmann, D.** *Offenbarungsverständnis.* 122–24. **Mowry, L.** "The Early Circulation of Paul's Letters." *JBL* 63 (1944) 73–86. **Schmithals, W.** "On the Composition and Earliest Collection of the Major Epistles of Paul." *Paul and the Gnostics.* Nashville: Abingdon, 1972. 239–74. ———. *Römerbrief.* 108–24.

Translation

[25] [a] *To him who is able to strengthen you, in accordance with my gospel and the preaching of Jesus Christ, in accordance with the revelation of the mystery concealed for long ages,* [26] *but now made manifest and through the prophetic scriptures,* [b] *in accordance with the command of the eternal God, made known for the obedience of faith for all the nations,* [27] *to the only wise God, through Jesus Christ, to him* [c] *be glory for ever.* [d] *Amen.* [e]

Notes

[a] Vv 25–27 appear after 14:23 in some witnesses (including Ψ and some Origen MSS), after 15:33 in P[46], at both places in one minuscule, after 14:23 and here in A P etc., and here alone in P[61] ℵ B C D etc. (including other Origen MSS) (MS evidence fully laid out in Aland, "Schluss," 287–90). The textual history has been repeatedly reviewed and a fair consensus achieved for the conclusion that vv 25–27 were first added to an abbreviated (Marcionite) version of the letter (= 1:1–14:23), then incorporated into the longer original (see particularly Lietzmann;

Barrett, 10–13; Kümmel, *Introduction,* 314–17; Gamble; Cranfield, 6–9; Wilckens 1:22–24; Lampe). SH, Schmidt, Bruce, and Hurtado still wish to defend the authenticity of vv 25–27 as Paul's original conclusion to the letter. But though the matter is hardly cut and dried, the greater probability lies in favor of a post-Pauline addition: (1) Paul nowhere else formulates such a long doxology, and its use to conclude a letter would be a departure from his usual style; (2) the tone of the whole fits better with a later perspective, more influenced by the more developed "mystery/revelation" theology of Colossians and Ephesians and the Pastorals (see particularly on 16:25b and 16:26 γνωρισθέντος; and the fuller vocabulary analysis of Elliott), so that the echoes of Romans itself (see *Form and Structure*) are probably best seen as something of a pastiche culled from the letter itself but going a little beyond it; (3) the history of the textual tradition is better explained on the above hypothesis.

ᵇThe addition of καὶ τῆς ἐπιφανείας τοῦ κυρίου ἡμῶν Ἰησοῦ Χριστοῦ is attested in Origen, but looks very much like a further liturgical expansion modeled on 1 Tim 6:14.

ᶜThe clearly original ᾧ (P⁴⁶ ℵ A C D Ψ etc.) has been modified (αὐτῷ —P; omitted—B) to eliminate the anacoluthon and complete the sentence (Metzger).

ᵈThe addition of τῶν αἰώνων by P⁶¹ ℵ D P etc. looks like a natural liturgical expansion since the single αἰῶνας seems rather abrupt; the shorter version also accords with 1:25; 9:5; 11:36; and 2 Cor 11:31—the longer with Gal 1:5; Eph 3:21; Phil 4:20; 1 Tim 1:17; and 2 Tim 4:18.

ᵉIt was natural that some MSS which belong to the textual tradition with the grace after v 23 (see 16:20 *Notes*) should reflect also the insertion of vv 25–27 and add the grace at this point.

Form and Structure

Even if the idiom is not quite Paul's (see *Note* a), the doxology succeeds quite well in summing up the central themes of the letter—God's power (1:16), Paul's gospel (2:16), the message of Christ (cf. 1:9), the mystery revealed (11:25), the "now" revelation (3:21), the prophetic scriptures (1:2; 3:21), and not least "the obedience of faith" "to all the nations" (1:5).

The structure is clearly liturgical in character:

1. τῷ δὲ δυναμένῳ ὑμᾶς στηρίξαι
2.   κατὰ τὸ εὐαγγέλιόν μου
3.   καὶ τὸ κήρυγμα Ἰησοῦ Χριστοῦ,
4.   κατὰ ἀποκάλυψιν μυστηρίου
5.   χρόνοις αἰωνίοις σεσιγημένου,
6.   φανερωθέντος δὲ νῦν
7.   διά τε γραφῶν προφητικῶν
8.   κατ᾽ ἐπιταγὴν τοῦ αἰωνίου θεοῦ
9.   εἰς ὑπακοὴν πίστεως
10.   εἰς πάντα τὰ ἔθνη
11.   γνωρισθέντος,
12. μόνῳ σοφῷ θεῷ
13.   διὰ Ἰησοῦ Χριστοῦ,
14. ᾧ ἡ δόξα εἰς τοὺς αἰῶνας, ἀμήν.

(1) The one acclaimed is put in the dative (as in 11:36b; Gal 1:5; Eph 3:20–21; Phil 4:20; 1 Tim 1:17; and 2 Tim 4:18).

(2) The series of short rhythmical phrases which follow (lines 2–11) are evidently structured for easy liturgical repetition by the worship leader or a group speaking in unison.

(3) Lines 2–5 form a balanced unit structured round the two κατά clauses, with each line ending with the open diphthong -ου; note also the development in lines 2–4: my gospel, Christ's preaching, (God's) mystery (Schmidt).

(4) Lines 6–11 are bracketed by the two aorist passive participles ending in -θεντος. (Since the three participles, lines 5, 6, 11, all depend on μυστηρίου, the liturgical form pulls somewhat against the syntactical structure.)

(5) The stark simplicity of the three two-syllable words ending in -ῳ (line 12) is very impressive.

(6) The addition of διὰ Ἰησοῦ Χριστοῦ (line 13) provides the necessary Christian qualification, linking Jesus Christ with the one God.

(7) The final line is probably intended for congregational response, with the ᾧ taken demonstratively ("to him") resolving the anacoluthon (Käsemann, Cranfield, Schlier, Wilckens).

Comment

25 τῷ δὲ δυναμένῳ ὑμᾶς στηρίξαι, "to him who is able to strengthen you," "to him who has the power to make your standing sure" (NEB). We find the same opening formulation, τῷ δὲ δυναμένῳ in Eph 3:20, Jude 24, and *Mart. Pol.* 20.2 (cf. James 4:12). The theme of God's power emerged at crucial points within the preceding exposition—1:16, 20; 4:21; 9:17, 22; 11:23; 14:4 (see on 1:16 and 1:20); so the opening of the acclamation makes a fitting conclusion. For στηρίζω see on 1:11; the thought of the eschatological tribulation is close at hand (Michel; cf. 1 Thess 3:2–4, 13; 2 Thess 3:3; James 5:7–8; 1 Pet 5:10; Rev 3:2).

κατὰ τὸ εὐαγγέλιόν μου καὶ τὸ κήρυγμα Ἰησοῦ Χριστοῦ, "in accordance with my gospel and the preaching of Jesus Christ." It is unnecessary to press for a decision between κατά denoting means and κατά denoting norm; since κατά can have both senses (BGD, κατά II.5aδ—"because of, as a result of, on the basis of"), there is no reason the writer should not have had both senses in mind (so Schmidt, Schlier; against Käsemann). For εὐαγγέλιον see on 1:1, and for τὸ εὐαγγέλιόν μου see on 2:16. The καί is probably epexegetic = "that is to say" (BDF §442.9): Paul's gospel is the proclamation of Jesus Christ common to all Christian missionaries (cf. 1 Cor 15:1, 3, 11). κήρυγμα can mean either what is preached or the act of preaching (cf. the other uses in the Pauline literature—six out of the eight NT occurrences: 1 Cor 1:21; 2:4; 15:14; 2 Tim 4:17; Titus 1:3). Ἰησοῦ Χριστοῦ could grammatically denote the preaching of which Jesus was author, the message he preached during his own ministry (*TDNT* 2:731; 3:716; Schmidt); and to take the genitive as objective (Jesus Christ as the content of the message) would make this use of κήρυγμα unusual in the NT. But while the continuity with Jesus' message (echoed in chaps. 14–16; see on 12:14) is a possible implication, the weight of emphasis must be expected to fall on the Christian proclamation focusing on Christ's death and resurrection (1 Cor 1:21; 2:4; 15:14) (so most, e.g., SH, Käsemann, Cranfield, Schlier; the other genitive forms in the Pauline corpus are three of the five references with (ἐ)μου or ἡμῶν [1 Cor 2:4; 15:14; 2 Tim 4:17]).

κατὰ ἀποκάλυψιν μυστηρίου, "in accordance with the revelation of the mystery." As with 2:5 and 8:19, ἀποκάλυψις has its full force of the unveiling of a heavenly secret in the end time (see on 1:17). For μυστήριον see on 11:25; here cf. particularly Col 1:26–27 and Eph 3:3–6. In parallel with or explication of εὐαγγέλιον and κήρυγμα, the phrase will include God's salvation purpose revealed and the unveiling of it through Paul's preaching (cf. particularly Eph 3:3–6, 7–9 and Col 1:25–27).

χρόνοις αἰωνίοις σεσιγημένου, "concealed for long ages." χρόνος used in the plural denotes a long period of time composed of several shorter ones (among texts cited by BGD, see Diodorus Siculus 1.5.1, 5.9.4 and *Sib. Or.* 3:649). The concept of limited periods of time jars with αἰώνιος, "eternal" (*TDNT* 1:199), but reflects the semitic conception of eternity (Käsemann). The force is "from the beginning of time" (cf. 2 Tim 1:9; Titus 1:2). The passive form of σιγάω, "be silent," so "kept secret, concealed," clearly a divine passive, is a variation on the same μυστήριον theme: that the salvation purpose determined by God from the beginning was only revealed by him in this final climactic age (see 3:21; 11:25; Eph 3:5, 9—τοῦ μυστηρίου τοῦ ἀποκεκρυμμένου ἀπὸ τῶν αἰώνων; Col 1:26—ditto; 2 Tim 1:9–10; Titus 1:2–3; 1 Pet 1:20). The thought of the primeval silence (as in *4 Ezra* 6.39; 7.30; and *2 Apoc. Bar.* 3.7) is different, as is the use of the image of silence in Wisd Sol 18:14. The image is obviously evocative and lends itself to varied usage. Further variations occur in Ign. *Eph.* 19.1 and *Magn.* 8.2. The Gnostic σιγή speculation (as in Irenaeus, *Adv. Haer.* 1.1 and 2.1; further references in Foerster, *Gnosis* 2, Index "Sige") is much more developed and is hardly relevant to the exegesis here, even though the varied usages of the motif, including the language here, may well have contributed to the later Gnostic thought (cf. Michel, Käsemann, Cranfield, Wilckens).

26 φανερωθέντος δὲ νῦν, "but now revealed." The phrase has the same eschatological force as in 3:21; and cf. again Col 1:26 and 2 Tim 1:10. It clearly denotes the ending (aorist) of the divine silence by God (passive) and so further describes the ἀποκάλυψις μυστηρίου (see on 16:25).

διά τε γραφῶν προφητικῶν, "and through the prophetic scriptures." The force of the τέ should certainly not be ignored (so rightly SH, Lagrange, Cranfield, Wilckens; against Barrett, Käsemann), since it links the phrase to what follows rather than to what precedes; thus, it is not "and now revealed through the prophetic scriptures," but " . . . and through the prophetic scriptures . . . made known" (so RSV, NEB, NIV; against NJB). The force is not so very different, since the γνωρισθέντος clause is simply an elaboration of φανερωθέντος, and everything caught between them (see *Form and Structure*) is the explication of a single basic idea—the revealing of the mystery. The "prophetic writings" clearly refer to the OT prophets (cf. particularly 1:2). Assuming the doxology to be a later addition (see *Notes*), it is certainly possible that the prophetic writings here include Paul's own letters; cf. after all 2 Pet 3:16 (so Schmithals, *Römerbrief,* 117–22; Lührmann 123–24; Käsemann; Wilckens). But on the whole it is unlikely. (1) The doxology is penned in the name of Paul and drawn from Pauline language; within that perspective the "scriptures" would certainly be the Jewish scriptures; whereas Paul never describes his writing in terms of prophecy. (2) The schema is quite a familiar one: of a mystery previously hidden now unveiled and made known by the correct hermeneutical key to explain the scriptures (so especially at Qumran— see particularly 1QH 2.13–19; and the commentaries, 1QpHab, 4QpPs 37, etc.; also 1 Pet 1:10–12, and particularly 2 Pet 1:19–21) (Lietzmann, Schmidt, Michel, Cranfield, Zeller).

κατ᾽ ἐπιταγὴν τοῦ αἰωνίου θεοῦ, "in accordance with the command of the eternal God." ἐπιταγή is not used elsewhere in Romans, but in the NT is confined to the Pauline corpus (1 Tim 1:1; Titus 1:3; 2:15; used differently in 1 Cor 7:6, 25 and 2 Cor 8:8). αἰώνιος θεός occurs nowhere else in Paul (though cf. 1:20—ἀίδιος αὐτοῦ δύναμις καὶ θειότης; 1:23—ὁ ἄφθαρτος θεός; also 1 Tim 1:17—see on 16:27; Heb 9:14); but it is a familiar phrase across the spectrum of Jewish literature (Gen 21:33; Isa 26:4; 40:28; Bar 4:8, 10, 14, 20, 22, 35; 5:2; Dan LXX Sus 35 = Theod. Sus 42: ὁ θεὸς ὁ αἰώνιος ὁ τῶν κρυπτῶν γνώστης ὁ εἰδὼς τὰ πάντα πρὶν γενέσεως αὐτῶν; 2 Macc 1:25—see on 16:27; 3 Macc. 6.12; 1 Enoch 1.4; Jub. 12.29; 13.8; 25.15; Sib. Or. 3.698; T. Mos. 10.7; Philo, Plant. 8, 74, 89) (BGD; TDNT 1:200–201; Michel).

εἰς ὑπακοὴν πίστεως εἰς πάντα τὰ ἔθνη, "for the obedience of faith for all the nations." The echo of 1:5 is strong and deliberate—εἰς ὑπακοὴν πίστεως ἐν πᾶσιν τοῖς ἔθνεσιν (see on 1:5). The second εἰς may be used here to increase the rhythmic parallel, but the meaning is little different whether the second εἰς depends on ὑπακοή or directly on the verb in parallel with the first εἰς.

γνωρισθέντος, "made known." This is the third participle dependent on μυστηρίου (v 25). The motif of "making known" the mystery is part of the "revelation schema" used here (cf. Eph 1:9; 3:3–5, 10; 6:19; Col 1:27; in the DSS particularly 1QpHab 7.4–5 and 1 QH 4.27–28; 7:27).

27 μόνῳ σοφῷ θεῷ, "to God only wise." We need not decide whether the alternative translation, "only and wise God," is better, since in both cases a monotheistic confession is clearly intended (cf. John 5:44; 17:3—τὸν μόνον ἀληθινὸν θεόν; 1 Tim 1:17—τῷ βασιλεῖ τῶν αἰώνων, ἀφθάρτῳ ἀοράτῳ μόνῳ θεῷ; 6:15–16; Jude 25; Rev 15:4; 2 Clem. 20.5; in earlier Jewish thought cf. particularly 2 Macc 1:24–25: ὁ μόνος βασιλεὺς καὶ χρηστός, ὁ μόνος χορηγός, ὁ μόνος δίκαιος καὶ παντοκράτωρ καὶ αἰώνιος; Ep. Arist. 132; and for the full phrase Sir 1:8—εἷς ἐστιν σοφός; Philo, Fuga 47; Ps. Phoc. 54); see further Dupont, "ΜΟΝΩΙ ΣΟΦΩΙ ΘΕΩΙ," and Delling, "ΜΟΝΟΣ ΘΕΟΣ." On God as one, see also 3:30; and for the wisdom of God, see also 4 Macc. 1.12; 1 Enoch 48.7; Sib. Or. 5.360; 1 Cor 1:25; 1 Tim 1:17 v.l.; Jude 25 v.l.; 1 Clem. 60.1.

διὰ Ἰησοῦ Χριστοῦ, "through Jesus Christ"; see on 1:8. Here cf. particularly 1 Pet 4:11; Jude 25; Did. 9.4; 1 Clem. 58.2; 61.3; 64; 65.2; Mart. Pol. 14.3; 20.2. As these parallels make clear, the διά clause would not be regarded as awkward or "very difficult" (SH); on the contrary, given the phrasing of the liturgical form (see Form and Structure), it reads quite fittingly.

ᾧ ἡ δόξα εἰς τοὺς αἰῶνας, ἀμήν, "to him be glory for ever, amen." The ᾧ should almost certainly be taken in reference to God, that is, the same referent as the preceding datives, as would be appropriate if indeed the phrase is intended to function as a liturgical response (see Form and Structure); though grammatically it could be taken to refer to Christ (so Barrett; cf. Heb 13:21 and 1 Pet 4:11). For the whole phrase, see on 11:36; and for ἀμήν, see on 1:25.

Explanation

At some stage within the first 150 years of its existence the doxology was added to the letter (probably initially to a form abbreviated to end at 14:23).

The reason is obvious: the letter would continue to be read out in congregations, with the continuing force of apostolic authority and with the increasing weight of sacred tradition; but the ending was unsatisfactory. What better than to append a doxology which drew together key themes and language from the letter and thus brought any reading of the letter to a resounding conclusion? This was evidently done, and the reading became established at this point in most of the major versions of the letter in circulation. The doxology, therefore, probably can be taken as good evidence for the regular use of the letter in the context of the local church gathered for worship (cf. Justin, *Apol.* 1.67), presumably also for the widening circulation of the letter, and therefore possibly also for the collection of (some of) Paul's letters into a corpus of broader usefulness.

If indeed, then, the doxology was added at some later stage, it makes exegesis a good deal more difficult. For it has then to be attributed to an unknown individual (or group or tradition process), for whom we have no other firm evidence with which to compare this paragraph. Without such material from the same hand(s) we lack parameters for an informed interpretation of the intention behind this one sentence. Of course, the doxology is presented as Paul's ("my gospel"; no impropriety was evidently perceived in making such an addition in Paul's own name), and in view of the number of echoes from earlier in the letter it is clearly intended as a fitting liturgical summary of Paul's teaching in Romans. But even so, without fuller information as to the date and context within which the doxology emerged and took its present shape, it is impossible to gain a clear grasp of the perspective from which it was written.

All we can say is that the doxology has summarized well some of the basic concerns of the letter. All begins and ends with God. His power alone is sufficient to sustain those who rely on him in faith. The gospel, which made this clear and with which Paul was entrusted, focused on Jesus Christ and contained the revelation of the mystery of the divine purpose for the salvation of humankind. That purpose was in full continuity with God's earlier revelation through prophet and scripture. But what had now been made clear, as God had always intended it should, was that God's saving purpose reached out to all nations and that it was entered into through faith—a faith which was not different from nor opposed to the obedience God had always looked for in his people, but which in fact came to expression in the dependent submissiveness of the creature to its Creator. It is to this God, the one God, the God who is the source and measure of all real wisdom, now most fully understood and approached through Jesus Christ, that all the glory of the ages belongs. Amen and amen.

Index of Modern Authors

Index of Principal Topics

Index of Biblical and Other Ancient Sources

A. The Old Testament

* Parenthetical numbers signify number of Scripture references on the page cited.

B. The New Testament

Old Testament Apocrypha

Jewish Pseudepigrapha

Dead Sea Scrolls, Philo, Josephus, and Rabbinic Texts

Apostolic Fathers

Other Early Christian and Gnostic Writings

Other Ancient and Classical Texts

Papyri and Inscriptions